An Engineer's Guide
to MATLAB®

An Engineer's Guide to MATLAB®

with Applications from Mechanical, Aerospace, Electrical, and Civil Engineering

Second Edition

Edward B. Magrab
Department of Mechanical Engineering, University of Maryland, College Park, MD

Shapour Azarm
Department of Mechanical Engineering, University of Maryland, College Park, MD

Balakumar Balachandran
Department of Mechanical Engineering, University of Maryland, College Park, MD

James H. Duncan
Department of Mechanical Engineering, University of Maryland, College Park, MD

Keith E. Herold
Department of Mechanical Engineering, University of Maryland, College Park, MD

Gregory C. Walsh
Leica Geosystems, Inc., San Ramon, CA

PEARSON

Prentice
Hall

Upper Saddle River, NJ 07458

Library of Congress Cataloging-in-Publication Data

An engineer's guide to MATLAB : with applications from mechanical, aerospace,
electrical, and civil engineering / Edward B. Magrab ... [et al.].-- 2nd ed.
    p. cm.
  Includes bibliographical references and index.
  ISBN 0-13-145499-4
   1. Engineering mathematics--Data processing. 2. MATLAB. I. Magrab, Edward B.

TA345.A52 2005
620'.001'51--dc22

                                                           2004060007

Vice President and Editorial Director, ECS: *Marcia J. Horton*
Vice President and Director of Production and Manufacturing, ESM: *David W. Riccardi*
Acquisitions Editor: *Dorothy Marrero*
Editorial Assistant: *Richard Virginia*
Executive Managing Editor: *Vince O'Brien*
Managing Editor: *David A. George*
Production Editor: *Kevin Bradley*
Director of Creative Services: *Paul Belfanti*
Art Director: *Jayne Conte*
Cover Designer: *Bruce Kenselaar*
Art Editor: *Greg Dulles*
Manufacturing Manager: *Trudy Pisciotti*
Manufacturing Buyer: *Lynda Castillo*
Senior Marketing Manager: *Holly Stark*
Cover images: *Courtesy of Getty Images, Inc.*

© 2005, 2000 by Pearson Education, Inc.
Pearson Prentice Hall
Pearson Education, Inc.
Upper Saddle River, NJ 07458

Pearson Prentice Hall® is a trademark of Pearson Education, Inc.

MATLAB and Simulink are registered trademarks of The MathWorks, Inc., 3 Apple Hill, Natick, MA 01760-2098.

The author and publisher of this book have used their best efforts in preparing this book. These efforts include the
development, research, and testing of the theories and programs to determine their effectiveness. The author and
publisher make no warranty of any kind, expressed or implied with regard to these programs or the documentation
contained in this book. The author and publisher shall not be liable in any event for incidental or consequential
damages in connection with or arising out of the furnishing, performance or use of these programs.

Printed in the United States of America

10 9 8 7 6 5 4 3 2

ISBN 0-13-145499-4

Pearson Education Ltd., *London*
Pearson Education Australia Pty. Ltd., *Sydney*
Pearson Education Singapore, Pte. Ltd.
Pearson Education North Asia Ltd., *Hong Kong*
Pearson Education Canada, Inc., *Toronto*
Pearson Educación de Mexico, S.A. de C.V.
Pearson Education—Japan, *Tokyo*
Pearson Education Malaysia, Pte. Ltd.
Pearson Education, Inc., *Upper Saddle River, New Jersey*

For June Coleman Magrab

Contents

6   2D Graphics   194
Edward B. Magrab

7   3D Graphics   244
Edward B. Magrab

12   Heat Transfer   554
Keith E. Herold

13   Optimization   603
Shapour Azarm

List of Examples

Chapter 5

Chapter 6

Chapter 7

Chapter 8

Chapter 9

Chapter 13

Chapter 14

Preface to Second Edition

The primary goal of the second edition remains the same as that for the original edition—that is, to guide the reader in developing a strong working knowledge of MATLAB® to solve engineering problems. Since the book's introduction, however, MATLAB has continued to evolve. Consequently, for this edition, numerous changes have been made to reflect MATLAB Version 7, Release 14. This should be especially apparent in the examples presented in each chapter, where simplifications to different portions of many of the computer programs have been made.

Chapter 1 has been completely revised, with considerable emphasis on how to set up and then navigate the MATLAB environment and the various ways in which MATLAB can be used. Material in the introductory chapters has been reorganized to improve its clarity. In addition, we have created the following aids for the reader: a summary table of the MATLAB commands introduced in each chapter; a List of Examples, so the reader can find a representative example in an area of interest; tables in the introductory chapters to concisely illustrate the different results that families of commands produce; and a consistent set of fonts and font styles to make the computer code more readable.

We have expanded the material to include the following major new topics: symbolic mathematics using the Symbolic Toolbox; system identification using the System Identification Toolbox; and aerodynamics, open channel flow, and the solutions of two-point boundary value problems. We have also increased the number of examples and topics in the chapters on Vibrations, Fluid Mechanics, Optimization, and Control Systems.

Our colleagues Dr. George E. Dieter, Professor Emeritus, and Prof. Donald Barker provided important feedback. Dr. Dieter carefully read Chapters 1 to 8 and Chapter 14 and gave us numerous suggestions for their improvement. Based on his many years of teaching the sophomore-level MATLAB course in the department, Dr. Barker shared with us his experiences and materials. Finally, we appreciate the comments and suggestions that we have received from our readers.

E. B. MAGRAB
S. AZARM
B. BALACHANDRAN
J. H. DUNCAN
K. E. HEROLD
G. C. WALSH
College Park, MD

Preface to First Edition

The primary goal of this book is to guide the reader in developing a strong working knowledge of MATLAB to solve engineering problems. Typically, solving these problems involves writing relatively short, one-time-use programs. Therefore, in this book, we attempt to teach how to effectively develop such programs in MATLAB—ones that are compact yet readable, are easy to debug, and execute fast.

The first seven chapters are intended for use in a sophomore/junior-level class that introduces programming and the use of computer languages in engineering. In the remaining seven chapters, we present applications of MATLAB to a wide range of engineering topics. The emphasis of the book is on using MATLAB to obtain solutions to several classes of engineering problems, not the technical subject matter *per se*. Therefore, the technical material is presented in summary form only, and no attempt has been made to present the basic material in each of these topic areas. The book also can be used as a companion book to junior-, senior-, and graduate-level textbooks in engineering; as a reference book for obtaining numerical solutions to a wide range of engineering problems, and; as a source of applications of a wide variety of MATLAB solution techniques.

Engineering programming applications are typically used to do the following: analyze a predictive model, such as an algebraic equation, an ordinary or partial differential equation, or an approximation to these; obtain statistical inferences from data; visualize a model or data to enhance one's understanding; either verify or obtain an empirical model from experimental results; and monitor/control/analyze external events. In this book, all but the last application are addressed.

The presentation of the material in this book is made with the assumption that the reader can employ the engineering approach to problem solving—that is, one that uses approximate mathematical models to predict the response of elements, devices, and systems. This approach also requires that one have a good comprehension of the physical problem so that he or she can tell when the model's results are correct (or at least reasonable). These qualities are an important prerequisite to creating programs that function correctly. The book also assumes that the reader is moderately fluent in calculus and engineering mathematics.

The first seven chapters are devoted to the introduction of MATLAB, where vector and matrix notation and definitions are introduced immediately and their fundamental importance to using MATLAB effectively is demonstrated. Numerous examples and detailed explanations are used to proceed through the material. The scripts and functions used to solve the example problems emphasize the employment of a relatively small number of readable MATLAB expressions to generate primarily graphical presentations of the results. This approach reinforces the importance of the vector/matrix formulations and the advantages of the resulting compactness of the code. Many of the example problems have been selected to illustrate the graphical presentation of data.

The approach used in the first seven chapters is then applied in the remaining seven chapters, each of which presents the application of MATLAB solution methods and toolboxes to classes of problems in the following areas: design of machine elements, dynamics and vibrations, controls, fluid mechanics, heat transfer, optimization, and engineering statistics. The material in these chapters is illustrated by numerous MATLAB solutions to classes of problems, and it includes brief discussions of the program listings and their results. Each chapter provides exercises for which many of the solutions require annotated two- or three-dimensional figures.

The MATLAB scripts and functions developed throughout the book use the most appropriate MATLAB function to obtain the numerical results, and they have been verified to work correctly through Version 5.3, Release 11. We assume that the reader has access to all functions demonstrated. Furthermore, we have tried to keep to a minimum much of the detailed information that is readily available from the online *Help* files. However, for a number of frequently used functions and for many functions in the toolboxes, we have included a sufficient amount of information so that the reader can clearly determine what equations the functions solve and how the numerical method represented by the function can be used. In addition, several of the chapters use MATLAB's controls, statistics, optimization, and partial differential equation toolboxes, thereby extending the traditional range of the types of problems usually examined. Furthermore, we present solution techniques that take advantage of MATLAB's numerical procedures where practical, as opposed to first obtaining algebraic solutions and then programming them.

Several preliminary versions of the book have been used over the last five semesters in the Mechanical Engineering department at the University of Maryland, both in an introductory MATLAB course and as companion material in junior- and senior-level courses in vibrations, controls, heat transfer, fluid mechanics, optimization, solid mechanics, and engineering statistics. The authors have found that with a good working knowledge of MATLAB, they could expand the type of realistic engineering problems that could be examined in these classes, and they have frequently marveled at the relative ease with which these solutions could be obtained. We hope that the reader will also reap the rewards of applying MATLAB to determine the solutions to his or her engineering problems.

E. B. MAGRAB
S. AZARM
B. BALACHANDRAN
J. H. DUNCAN
K. E. HEROLD
G. C. WALSH

College Park, MD
March 2000

1

Introduction

Edward B. Magrab

The characteristics of the MATLAB environment and the language's basic syntax are introduced.

1.1 INTRODUCTION

MATLAB®, which derives its name from *Matrix Lab*oratory, is a computing language devoted to processing data in the form of matrices of numbers. MATLAB integrates computation and visualization into a flexible computer environment, and it provides a diverse family of built-in functions that can be used in a straightforward manner to obtain numerical solutions to a wide range of engineering problems.

1

1.2 THE MATLAB ENVIRONMENT

When the MATLAB program is launched, three windows appear, as shown in Figure 1.1. The upper left-hand window is the *Workspace* window, which displays a list of the variables that the user has currently defined and their properties: type of variable and their size. This window can be alternated with the *Current Directory* window, which displays the current directory being used by MATLAB and the names of the files in that directory. The right-hand window is the MATLAB *Command* window. The lower left-hand window is the *Command History* window, which gives a display of all entries made in the command window during each session. A session is the interval between the start of MATLAB and its termination. A time and date appear before each list in this window to indicate when these entries began being recorded. It is a convenient way to review past sessions and to recapture previously used commands if they weren't recorded elsewhere. The command histories are maintained until they are cleared using the *Clear Command History* selection from the *Edit* menu. Similar choices exist for the *Workspace* and the *Command* windows. These latter two clearing operations will be discussed subsequently.

To bring up the MATLAB Editor/Debugger, which provides a convenient means to create and run programs, one clicks on the white rectangular icon that appears under *File* in the left uppermost corner of the window. This results in the configuration shown in Figure 1.2. Other windows can be employed and can be accessed from the *View* menu. To eliminate any of the windows, simply close it. One way to configure these windows is to use only the command window and the editor window and to call up the other windows when needed. One such configuration of these two windows is shown in Figure 1.3. Upon restarting MATLAB, the system will remember this configuration, and this arrangement of the windows will appear.

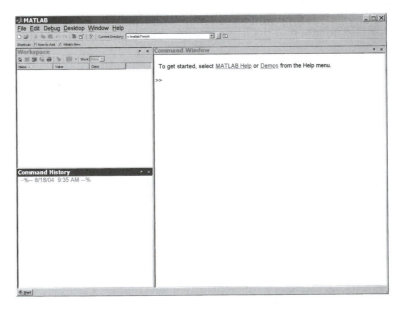

Figure 1.1 MATLAB default windows.

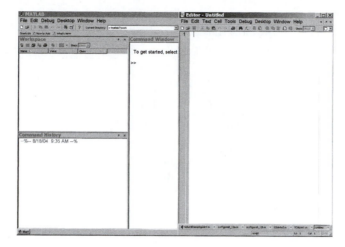

Figure 1.2   MATLAB default windows and the Editor.

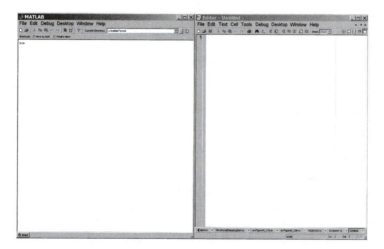

Figure 1.3   MATLAB default windows and Editor window rearranged after closing the command history and workspace windows.

1.3 WAYS TO USE MATLAB

1.3.1 Preliminaries—Command Window Management

During any MATLAB session—that is, during any time until the program is exited—MATLAB retains in its memory the most recently obtained values of all variables defined by each expression that has been either typed in the command window or evaluated from a script file, unless the clear function is invoked. This clearing of the variables in the workspace can also be obtained by selecting *Clear Workspace* from the *Edit* pull-down menu (see Figure 1.4). The clear function deletes all the

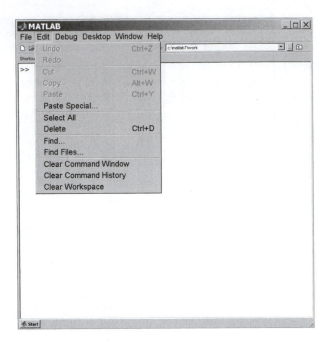

Figure 1.4 *Edit* pull-down menu selections.

variables from memory. The numerical values assigned most recently to these variables are accessible anytime during the session (provided that `clear` hasn't been used) by simply typing the variable's name or using it in an expression. These variables are referred to as global variables.

Typing performed in the MATLAB command window remains in the window and can be accessed by scrolling back until the scrolling memory has been exceeded, at which point the earliest-entered information has been lost. However, the expressions evaluated from a script file are not available in the command window, although the variable names and their numerical values are available, as indicated in the preceding paragraph. This record of previously typed expressions in the command window can be removed by going to the *Edit* pull-down menu at the top of the MATLAB command window and selecting *Clear Command Window*, which clears the MATLAB command window but does not delete the variables, which have to be removed by using `clear` (see Figure 1.4). One could also clear the command window by typing `clc` in the command window. In addition, the copy and paste icons can be used either to reproduce previously typed expressions in the current (active) line in the MATLAB command window or to paste MATLAB expressions from the MATLAB command window into the editor, or vice versa.

For a listing of what variables have been created since the use of the last application of `clear`, one either types `whos` in the MATLAB command window or goes to the pull-down *View* menu and selects *Workspace*, which opens a window with this information. Either method reveals the names of the variables, their sizes, the number of bytes of storage that each variable uses, and their type: numerical (see Chapter 2), string (see Section 3.1), symbolic (see Section 5.6), cell (see Section 3.4) or an `inline` object (see Section 5.2.3). The *Workspace* window can be unlocked from its default location by clicking on the icon next to the × in its upper right-hand corner. When one is done with the window, it can be minimized so that this information is readily available for the next time.

To make the letters and numbers that appear in the command window more readable, MATLAB offers several options with the `format` function. Two that are particularly useful are the functions

```
format compact
```

and

```
format long e
```

The former removes most empty (blank) lines, and the latter provides a toggle from the default format of 5 digits to a format with 16 digits plus a 3-digit exponent. The `format long` e option is useful when debugging scripts that produce numbers that either change by very small amounts or vary over a wide range. To toggle back to the default settings, type the command

```
format short
```

These attributes can also be changed by selecting *Preferences* from the *File* pull-down menu and selecting *Command Window*, as shown in Figure 1.5. The changes are then made by selecting the desired format from the list of available formats.

Two keyboard entries that are very useful are ^c (Ctrl and c simultaneously) and ^p (Ctrl and p simultaneously). Application of ^p places in the MATLAB command window the last entry typed from the keyboard, which can then be implemented by pressing *Enter*. In addition, before pressing *Enter*, one can modify the expression. If *Enter* is not pressed and, instead, ^p is entered again, then the next most recently typed entry replaces the most recent entry, and so on. This same result can be obtained using the up-arrow (↑) and down-arrow (↓) keys. The application of ^c is used either to abort a running program or to exit a paused program.

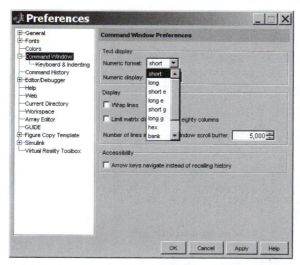

Figure 1.5   *Preferences* menu selections.

1.3.2 Executing Expressions from the MATLAB Command Window—Basic MATLAB Syntax

MATLAB permits the user to create variable names with a length of up to 63 alphanumerical characters, with the characters after the sixty-third being ignored. Each variable name must start with either an uppercase or lowercase letter, which can then be followed by any combination of uppercase and lowercase letters, numbers, and the underscore character (_). No blank spaces may appear between these characters. Variable names are case sensitive, so a variable named *junk* is different from a variable named *junK*. There are two commonly used conventions: one that uses the underscore and one that uses capital letters. For example, if the exit pressure is a quantity that is being evaluated, then it could be defined in a MATLAB command line, script, or function as either *exit_pressure* or *ExitPressure*.

Creating suitable variable names is a trade-off between easily recognizable identifiers and readability of the resulting expressions. If the expression is very long, then short variable names are preferable. This becomes increasingly important as the grouping of the symbols becomes more complex. Shorter names tend to decrease errors caused by the improper grouping of terms and the placement of arithmetic operators. In addition, one can't use Greek letters literally as variable names, nor can one use subscripts and superscripts. However, one can spell the Greek letter or simply precede the subscript by the underscore character. For example, one could represent σ_r as sigma_r and c_3 as c3 or c_3.

One typically begins in the command window by defining one or more variables at the prompt ($>>$). MATLAB requires that all variables, except those used by the Symbolic Toolbox, be assigned numerical values before being used in an expression. The assignment operator is the equal sign ($=$). Typing the variable name, an equal sign, the numerical value(s), and then pressing *Enter* performs the assignment. Thus, if we wish to assign $p = 7.1$, $x = 4.92$, and $k = -1.7$, then the following interaction in the MATLAB command window is obtained:

```
» p = 7.1       ◄——— User types and hits Enter
p =
    7.1000      ◄——— System response
» x = 4.92      ◄——— User types and hits Enter
x =
    4.9200      ◄——— System response
» k = -1.7      ◄——— User types and hits Enter
k =
    -1.7000     ◄——— System response
```

If one wants to suppress the system's response, then a semicolon (;) is placed as the last character of the expression. Thus, typing each of the following three expressions on their respective lines followed by *Enter* gives

```
»  p = 7.1;
»  x = 4.92;
»  k = -1.7;
»
```

MATLAB also lets one place several expressions on one line, a line being terminated by *Enter*. In this case, each expression is separated by either a comma (,) or a semicolon (;). When a comma is used, the system echoes the input. Thus, if the following is typed,

p = 7.1, x = 4.92, k = –1.7

then the system responds with

p =
   7.1000
x =
   4.9200
k =
   –1.7000
»

The use of semicolons instead of the commas would have suppressed this output.

The five arithmetic operators to perform addition, subtraction, multiplication, division, and exponentiation are +, −, *, / and ^, respectively. For example, the mathematical expression

$$t = \left(\frac{1}{1 + px}\right)^k$$

is written in MATLAB as

t = (1/(1+p*x))^k

The quantities p, x, and k must be assigned numerical values by the user before the execution of this statement. If this has not been done, then an error message to that effect will appear. Assuming that the quantities p, x, and k were those entered previously and not cleared, the system returns

t =
   440.8779

The parentheses in the MATLAB expression for t have to be used so that the mathematical operations are performed on the proper collections of quantities in their proper order within each set of parentheses. There is a hierarchy and a specific order that MATLAB uses to compute arithmetic statements. One can take advantage of this to minimize the number of parentheses. However, parentheses that are unnecessary from MATLAB's point of view can still be used to remove visual ambiguity and to make the expression easier to understand. The highest level in the hierarchy is exponentiation, followed by multiplication and division and then by addition and subtraction. Within each set of parentheses and all levels of the hierarchy, MATLAB performs its operations from left to right.

TABLE 1.1   Examples of MATLAB Syntax

Mathematical expression	MATLAB expression
$1 - dc^{x+2}$	1−d*c^(x+2)
$dc^x + 2$	d*c^x+2 or 2+d*c^x
$(2/d)c^{x+2}$	(2/d)*c^(x+2) or 2/d*c^(x+2) or 2*c^(x+2)/d
$(dc^x + 2)/g^{2.7}$	(d*c^x+2)/g^2.7
$\sqrt{dc^x + 2}$	sqrt(d*c^x+2) or (d*c^x+2)^0.5

Consider the examples shown in Table 1.1 involving the scalar quantities c, d, g, and x. The MATLAB function

    sqrt

takes the square root of its argument. Notice that in the first row of Table 1.1, the parentheses around the quantity $x + 2$ are required. If they weren't used and the relation was written as

    1-d*c^x+2

then we would have coded the expression $1 - dc^x + 2$. The same reasoning is true for the exponent in the third row of the table. In the third row, notice that the form

    2*c^(x+2)/d

is correct because of the rules of the hierarchy. The innermost set of parenthesis is $(x + 2)$, which is computed first. Then, exponentiation is performed, because this is the highest level of the computational order. Next, the multiplications and divisions are performed from left to right, because the three quantities, 2, the result of c^{x+2}, and d are all on the same hierarchical level: multiplication and division.

Clarification and Exceptions to MATLAB's Syntax

Blanks   In an arithmetic expression, the use of blanks can be employed with no consequence, except when this expression appears in an array specification—that is, between two brackets ([ ]). This is discussed in Section 2.3. Excluding blanks in assignment statements, variable names on the right-hand side of the equal sign must be separated by one of the five arithmetic operators, a comma (,), or a semicolon (;). There are **two exceptions** to this. The first is when one represents a complex number $z = a + jb$ or $z = a + ib$, where $i = j = \sqrt{-1}$. Consider the following script:

    a = 2; b = 3;
    z = a+j*b % or a+b*j

which upon execution gives

    z =
       2.0000 + 3.0000i

Notice that the programmer used j, but the system responded with an i, showing the system's equivalent treatment of these two quantities. Also, note that j was not defined previously; therefore, MATLAB assumes that it is equal to $\sqrt{-1}$. However, when a and b are replaced with numerical values directly in the expression, then no arithmetic operator is required. Thus, the script

```
a = 2; b = 3;
z = (a+j*b)*(4-7j)
```

upon execution gives

```
z =
  29.0000 - 2.0000i
```

In this usage, the j (or i) must follow the number without a space.

The second exception is when we express a number in exponential form, such as $x = 4.56 \times 10^{-2}$. This number can be expressed as

```
x = 0.0456
```

or

```
x = 4.56*10^-2
```

or

```
x = 4.56e-2
```

The last expression is the exponential form. Notice that no arithmetic operator is placed between the last digit of the magnitude and the 'e'. The maximum number of digits that can follow the 'e' is 3. Thus, if we desired the quantity x^2 and we used the exponential form, the script would be

```
x2 = 4.56e-2^2
```

which upon execution displays to the command window

```
x2 =
  0.0021
```

If the value of x were 4.56×10^2, the implied '+' sign may be omitted; that is, the square of x can be written as

```
x = 4.56e2^2
```

or

```
x = 4.56e+2^2
```

System Assignment of Variable Names   When the command window is used as a calculator and no assignment of the expression has been made, MATLAB will always assign the answer to the variable named *ans*. For example, let us assume that one wants to know what the cosine of $\pi/3$ is. We simply type in the command window[1]

```
cos(pi/3)
```

---

[1] In the command window, the alphanumerical characters will appear in the same font. We are using different fonts to enhance the understanding of the expression as discussed at the end of this section.

and the system will respond with

```
ans =
   0.5000
```

The variable *ans* can now be used as any other variable. If we now wanted to add 2 to the previous result, then we would type in the command window

```
ans+2
```

and the system would respond with

```
ans =
   2.5000
```

Thus, *ans* has been assigned the new value of 2.5. The previous value of *ans* (0.5) is no longer available.

Scalars Versus Arrays   MATLAB considers all variables as arrays of numbers; therefore, when using the five arithmetic operators $(+, -, *, /, \text{ and } \wedge)$, these operations have to obey the rules of linear algebra. The rules are discussed in Section 2.6. When the variables are scalar quantities—that is, when they are arrays of one element (one row and one column)—the usual rules of algebra apply. However, one can operate on arrays of numbers and suspend the rules of linear algebra by using dot operations, which are discussed in Section 2.5.

Complex Quantities   MATLAB permits one to mix real and complex numbers without any special operations on the part of the user. Thus, if one types in the command window

```
z = 4 + sqrt(-4)
```

then the system would display

```
z =
   4.0000 + 2.0000i
```

MATLAB also includes a large set of elementary—and not so elementary—functions. Some of the elementary ones and some built-in constants are listed in Tables 1.2, 1.3, and 1.4. The arguments to these functions can be scalars, vectors, or

---

TABLE 1.2   Some Elementary MATLAB Functions

Mathematical function	MATLAB expression
e^x	exp(x)
$\sqrt{x}$	sqrt(x)
$\ln(x)$ or $\log_e(x)$	log(x)
$\log_{10}(x)$	log10(x)
$|x|$	abs(x)
$\text{signum}(x)$	sign(x)

TABLE 1.3   MATLAB Trigonometric and Hyperbolic Functions

	Trigonometric		Hyperbolic	
Function	Function	Inverse function	Function	Inverse function
sine	`sin(x)`	`asin(x)`	`sinh(x)`	`asinh(x)`
cosine	`cos(x)`	`acos(x)`	`cosh(x)`	`acosh(x)`
tangent	`tan(x)`	`atan(x)` †	`tanh(x)`	`atanh(x)`
secant	`sec(x)`	`asec(x)`	`sech(x)`	`asech(x)`
cosecant	`csc(x)`	`acsc(x)`	`csch(x)`	`acsch(x)`
cotangent	`cot(x)`	`acot(x)`	`coth(x)`	`acoth(x)`

† `atan2(y,x)` is the four-quadrant version.

TABLE 1.4   Some MATLAB Constants

Mathematical constant	MATLAB expression
π	`pi`
$\sqrt{-1}$	`i` or `j` (used to indicate a complex quantity as $a + jb$, where a and b are real)
Floating-point relative accuracy	`eps`—The distance from 1.0 to the next largest floating-point number ($\approx 2.22 \times 10^{-16}$)
∞	`inf`

matrices. The definitions of vectors and matrices and details of their creation in MATLAB are given in Sections 2.3 and 2.4.

For an example of the use of the built-in functions, consider the following expression to be evaluated at $x = 0.1$ and $a = 0.5$:

$$y = \sqrt{|e^{(-\pi x)} - \sin(x)/\cosh(a) - \ln_e(x + a)|}$$

This expression is evaluated with the following script:

```
x = 0.1; a = 0.5;
y = sqrt(abs(exp(-pi*x)-sin(x)/cosh(a)-log(x+a)))
```

where the MATLAB function `pi` $= \pi$. Upon execution, the following result is displayed in the command window:

```
y =
    1.0736
```

Although the choice of variable names is virtually unlimited, one should avoid choosing names that are the same as those used for MATLAB's built-in functions or user-created functions. MATLAB permits one to overload a built-in function name. For example, the following expression is a valid MATLAB expression:

```
cos = a+b*x^2;
```

However, since 'cos' is also the name used for the cosine function, $\cos(x)$, this is a poor choice for a variable name, and it is strongly recommended that such redefinitions

TABLE 1.5   MATLAB Decimal-to-Integer Conversion Functions

MATLAB function	x	y	Description
y = fix(x)	2.7 -1.9 2.49-2.51j	2.0000 -1.0000 2.0000-2.0000i	Round toward zero
y = round(x)	2.7 -1.9 2.49-2.51j	3.0000 -2.0000 2.0000-3.0000i	Round to nearest integer
y = ceil(x)	2.7 -1.9 2.49-2.51j	3.0000 -1.0000 3.0000-2.0000i	Round toward infinity
y = floor(x)	2.7 -1.9 2.49-2.51j	2.0000 -2.0000 2.0000-3.0000i	Round toward minus infinity

be avoided. A reasonable exception to this recommendation is when i and j are redefined as real quantities, usually representing integers.

Several MATLAB functions are available to round decimal numbers to the nearest integer value using different rounding criteria. These are fix, round, ceil, and floor. The operations of these four functions are summarized in Table 1.5.

There are also several MATLAB functions available to create and manipulate complex numbers. These are complex, abs, conj, real, and imag. The operations of these five functions are summarized in Table 1.6.

In addition to the five arithmetic operators $(+, -, *, /,$ and $^\wedge)$, there are several other symbols that are reserved by MATLAB to have special meaning. These are listed in Table 1.7 and are discussed in Chapters 2 to 5.

Script Notation Conventions

To facilitate the recognition of the significance of variable names and the origin of numerical values—that is, whether they are input or output—we shall employ the following conventions:

Variable Name	Font	Example
User created	Times Roman	ExitPressure, a2, sig
MATLAB function	Courier	cosh(x), pi
User-created function	Times Roman Bold	**BeamRoots**(a, x, k)

Numerical Value	Font	Example
Provided in script	Times Roman	5.672
Output to command window or to graphic	Helvetica	5.672

TABLE 1.6   MATLAB Complex Number Manipulation Functions

MATLAB function	z	y	Description
z = complex(a, b)	a+b*j	-	Form complex number; a and b real
y = abs(z)	3+4j	5	Absolute value
y = conj(z)	3+4j	3-4j	Complex conjugate
y = real(z)	3+4j	3	Real part
y = imag(z)	3+4j	4	Imaginary part

TABLE 1.7   Additional Special Characters and a Summary of Their Usage[†]

Character	Name	Usage
.	Period	(a) Decimal point. (b) Part of arithmetic operators to indicate a special type of vector or matrix operation, called the dot operation, such as $c = a.*b$.
,	Comma	(a) Separator within parentheses of matrix elements, such as $b(2,7)$, and functions, such as besselj$(1, x)$, or brackets creating vectors, such as v = [1, x], or the output of function arguments, such as [x, s] = max(a). (b) Placed at the end of an expression when several expressions appear on one line.
;	Semicolon	(a) Suppresses display of the results when placed at end of an expression. (b) Indicates the end of a row in matrix creation statement, such as $m = [x\ y\ z; a\ b\ c]$.
:	Colon	(a) Separator in the vector creation expression x = a:b:c. (b) For a matrix z, it indicates "all rows" when written as $z(:,k)$ or "all columns" when written as $z(k,:)$.
( )	Parentheses	(a) Denotes subscript of an element of matrix z, where $z(j, k)$ is the element in row j and column k. (b) Delimiters in mathematical expressions, such as $a^\wedge(b + c)$. (c) Delimiters for the arguments of functions, such as sin(x).
[ ]	Brackets	Creates an array of numbers, either a vector or a matrix, or a string (literal).
{ }	Braces	Creates a cell matrix or structure.
%	Percentage	Comment delimiter; used to indicate the beginning of a comment wherein the MATLAB compiler ignores everything to its right. The exception is when it is used inside a pair of quotes to define a string, such as a = 'p1 = 14 % of the total'.
'	Quote or apostrophe	(a) '*Expression*' indicates that *Expression* is a string (literal) (b) Indicates the transpose of a vector or matrix.
. . .	Ellipsis	Continuation of a MATLAB expression to the next line. Used to create code that is more readable.
	Blank	Context dependent: either ignored; indicates a delimiter in a data creation statement, such as c = [a b]; or is a character in a string statement.
@	At sign	Construct a function handle by placing @ before a function name, such as **@FunctionName**.
\	Backslash	A mathematical operator to perform certain matrix operations.

[†] See also Table 4.1.

1.3.3 Creating Scripts and Executing Them from the MATLAB Editor

When the user is required to enter many expressions or to repeatedly retype a series of expressions at the command window, the task can become tedious. To alleviate this potential problem, MATLAB has introduced script files—files that contain a list of commands, each of which will be operated on by MATLAB as if they were typed at the command line in the command window. A script file is created in either a word processor, a text editor, or the MATLAB-supplied text editor and debugger, and saved as a text file with the suffix ".m". Such files are commonly called M-files. If a word processor or text editor is used, then the file is executed by typing the file name without the suffix ".m" in the MATLAB command window. If the MATLAB editor is used, then one can use the previous method or can click on the *Save and Run* icon on the top of the Editor's window, as shown in Figure 1.6. However, before one can use this icon, the file must be saved the first time using the *Save As* option from the *File* pull-down menu. The file-naming convention is the same as that for variable names: It must start with an uppercase or lowercase letter, followed by up to 62 contiguous alphanumerical characters and the underscore character. No blank spaces are allowed in file names. (This is different from what is allowed by the Windows operating system.) If the MATLAB text editor/debugger is used, an ".m" suffix will be affixed to the file name; otherwise, it must be added when the file name is created.

Another form of a file created in the Editor is the function file, which cannot be created in the command window. These functions are created either because one of MATLAB's built-in functions requires it or because one wants to use them to better manage the programming task. Functions differ from scripts in that they allow a structured approach to managing the programming task. They differ from expressions entered at the command line in that MATLAB allots them their own private workspace and they have formally defined input–output relationships with the MATLAB environment. Functions are discussed in Chapter 5.

The MATLAB Editor has several features that make it especially suitable for creating scripts and functions files. During program development, one can convert one or more lines of code to comment statements and then convert them back to executable statements. With the cursor, one highlights the lines to be converted, goes to the *Text* pull-down menu on top of the window and selects the appropriate action (see Figure 1.7). When creating program flow control structures as described in Chapter 4, one can indent lines of code to improve readability. Again, one uses the cursor to highlight the lines of code of interest and presses ^i (ctrl and i simultaneously). An equivalent method is to go to the *Text* pull-down menu and select *Smart Indent* (see Figure 1.7).

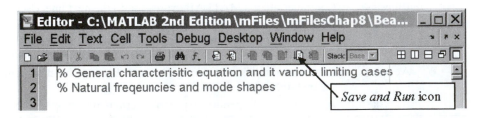

Figure 1.6 The *Save and Run* (execute) icon in the *Editor*.

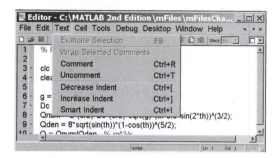

Figure 1.7   The *Text* pull-down menu in the Editor.

The Editor also employs a color scheme. Certain key words appear in blue, letters and numbers between a pair of apostrophes in red, and comments in green. Finally, the Editor keeps track of open and closed parentheses when typing a line of code. Each time a closed parenthesis is typed, the appropriate open parenthesis to the left is momentarily highlighted. This can be of great aid in verifying the grouping of terms.

We will emphasize the interactive use of the command window and the Editor throughout the book. We encourage the reader to create all programs, no matter how small, in the Editor and to run them directly from the Editor.

Script files are usually employed in those cases where:

1. The program will contain more than a few lines of code.
2. The program will be used again.
3. A permanent record is desired.
4. It is expected that occasional upgrading will be required.
5. Substantial debugging is required.
6. One wants to transfer the listing to another person or organization.

In addition, a script or a function typically has the following attributes:

1. *Documentation*, which at a minimum indicates:

   Purpose and operations performed
   Programmer's name
   Date originated
   Date(s) revised
   Description of the input(s): number, meaning, and type
   Description of the output(s): number, meaning, and type

2. *Input*, which includes numerous checks to ensure that all input values have the qualities required for the script/function to work properly.
3. *Initialization*, where the appropriate variables are assigned their numerical values.
4. *Computation*, where the numerical evaluations are performed.
5. *Output*, where the results are presented as graphical and/or annotated numerical quantities.

To execute a script file, MATLAB must be provided with the path to the directory in which the file resides. The path information is entered by going to the *File* pull-down menu and selecting *Set Path*. This opens the *Set Path* window shown in Figure 1.8. Click on the *Add Folder* text box, and choose the folder in which the file will reside (see Figure 1.9). Before leaving the *Path Browser*, it is suggested that you

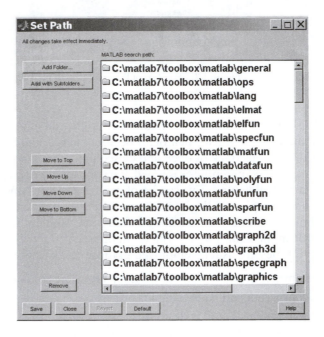

Figure 1.8   *Set Path* window.

Figure 1.9   Pop-up window to locate a directory.

select *Save*, which saves the path for the next time MATLAB is used. If you attempt to execute a script from the Editor that is not in the current path, MATLAB will ask you, via the pop-up window shown in Figure 1.10, if you would like to change the current path to the one in which the file resides. If the answer is yes, click on the *OK* text box. One can also set the current path name by clicking the icon in the command window shown in Figure 1.11. This brings up a browser that permits one to select a directory as the current directory. After a selection is made, the system also

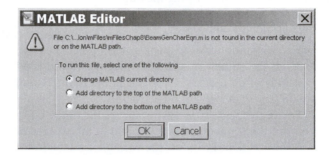

Figure 1.10   Pop-up window to change the current path to the path of the file being executed.

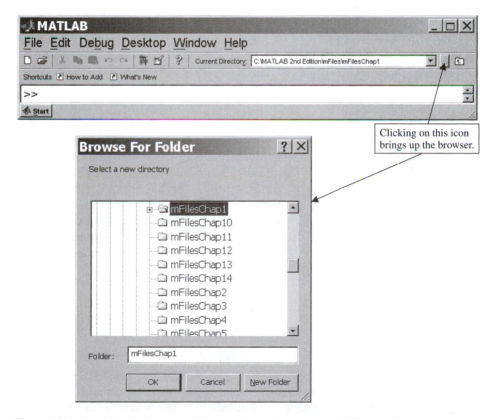

Figure 1.11   Accessing the *Browser* window to change the current path (directory).

changes the directories that will appear in the Editor when either *Open*, *Save*, or *Save As* is selected in the *File* pull-down menu.

If either a script or a function requires the user to enter a numerical value (or a series of numerical values if the quantity is either a vector or a matrix—see Sections 2.3 and 2.4) from the MATLAB command window, then the script (or function) contains the statement

VariableName = input('Any message')

where input is a MATLAB function and *Any message* is displayed in the MAT-LAB command window. After this expression is executed, the response typed, and *Enter* pressed, the value (or series of values) entered is assigned to *VariableName*. Other methods of data entry are given in Section 3.3, and further clarifications of the usage of input are given in Section 3.2.

There are two ways to get program results to the command window. The first is simply to omit the semicolon (;) at the end of an expression. In this case, MATLAB displays in the command window the variable's name, followed by an equal sign, and then skips to the next line and displays the value(s) of the variable. This method is useful during debugging. When output values are to be annotated for clarity, one uses either

disp

or

fprintf

which are discussed in Section 3.1.

It is good practice when creating scripts to start each script with the functions clc and clear. This clears all variables created previously and also clears the command window. In addition, when one has created graphics, which appear in separate windows, as discussed in Chapters 6 and 7, one should close them using close all. Lastly, when global variables have been created, as discussed in Section 5.2.2, one should use clear global. The more inclusive function clear all also clears global variables. Thus, in general, each program should start with the following functions:

```
clear % or clear all
clc
clear global % not required if clear all is used
close all
```

We shall now summarize this material with an example, and we shall show what the windows discussed previously look like when the commands are entered.

Example 1.1   Flow in a circular channel

The flow rate Q in m³/s in the open channel of circular cross-section shown in Figure 1.12 is given by[2]

$$Q = \frac{2^{3/2} D_c^{5/2} \sqrt{g} (\theta - 0.5 \sin(2\theta))^{3/2}}{8 \sqrt{\sin\theta}(1 - \cos\theta)^{5/2}}$$

where $g = 9.8$ m/s² is the gravitational constant and D_c is given by

$$D_c = \frac{d}{2}(1 - \cos\theta)$$

If we assume that $d = 2$ m and $\theta = 60° = \pi/3$, then the MATLAB script is that shown in Figure 1.13a and repeated below for clarity:

```
g = 9.8;  d = 2;  th = pi/3;  % Input
Dc = d/2*(1-cos(th));
Qnum = 2^(3/2)*Dc^(5/2)*sqrt(g)*(th-0.5*sin(2*th))^(3/2);
Qden = 8*sqrt(sin(th))*(1-cos(th))^(5/2);
Q = Qnum/Qden   % m^3/s
```

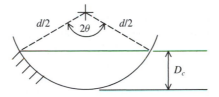

Figure 1.12   Circular channel.

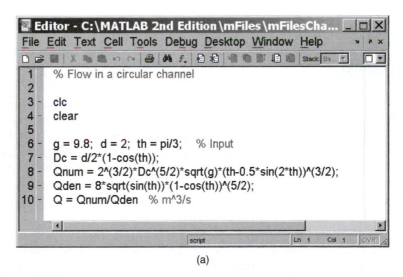

(a)

Figure 1.13   (a) Script for Example 1.1 in the Editor, and (b) workspace and command windows.

---

[2]T. G. Hicks, *Mechanical Engineering Formulas: Pocket Guide*, McGraw-Hill, New York, 2003, p. 254.

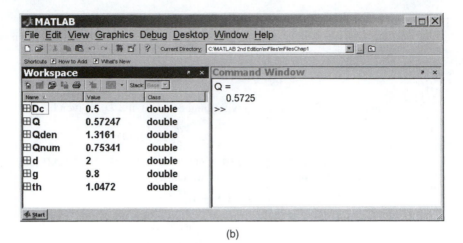

(b)

Figure 1.13   (*Continued*)

After clicking on the *Save and Run* icon in the Editor, the answer, $Q = 0.5725$, is displayed in the command window. Upon execution of the script file, the workspace window is populated as shown in Figure 1.13b. It displays a record of the seven variables that have been created: *Dc, Q, Qnum, Qden, g, d*, and *th*. Since all the commands have been issued from the Editor, the *Command History* window is empty and has not been displayed.

As a final comment, the form of the definitions of the various quantities appearing in the script were chosen to make the independent calculations used to verify the script both easier to perform and to compare with what the script gives. During the debugging stage, each quantity can be calculated independently and compared to those computed by the script by temporarily omitting the semicolon at the end of each expression.

1.4 ONLINE HELP

MATLAB has a complete online help capability, which can be accessed several ways. One way is to click on the question mark (?) icon on the toolbar of the command window. This opens the *Help* windows shown in Figure 1.14. It should be minimized after each use so that it is readily available. Going to the *Help* pull-down menu also brings up the window shown in Figure 1.14, except that it opens at specific locations depending on what has been selected. If *MATLAB Help* is selected, this gives the same starting point as (?). If *Using the Desktop* is selected, it opens the right-hand window to the section titled *Desktop*.

If *Using the Command Window* is selected, then it opens the right-hand window to the section titled Running Functions—Command Window and History. If one wants specific information about a particular MATLAB function, then the *Index* tab in the left-hand window is activated, and the command is typed in the blank area. Another way to obtain access to information about a specific function is to type in the MATLAB command window

```
help FunctionName
```

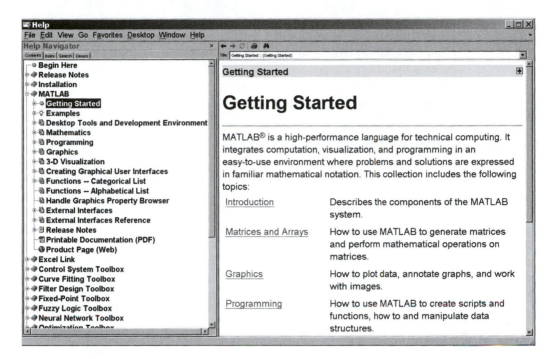

Figure 1.14 *Help* windows.

where *FunctionName* is the name of the function about which information is sought. Almost the same information that appears from using the *Index* search in the *Help* window is obtained, only in a less elegant format. Usually, the command window version of *Help* does not include equations.

1.5 SOME SUGGESTIONS ON HOW TO USE MATLAB

Listed below are some suggestions on how to use the MATLAB environment to efficiently create MATLAB scripts and functions:

- *Use the Help files extensively.* This will minimize errors caused by incorrect syntax and by incorrect or inappropriate application of a MATLAB function.
- *Write scripts and functions in a text editor, and save them as M-files.* This will save time, save the code, and greatly facilitate the debugging process, especially if the MATLAB editor/debugger is used.
- *Attempt to minimize the number of expressions comprising scripts and functions.* This usually leads to a trade-off between readability and compactness, but it can encourage the search for MATLAB functions and procedures that can perform some of the steps faster and more directly.

- *When practical, use graphical output as the script or function is being developed*. This usually shortens the code development process by identifying potential coding errors, and it can facilitate the understanding of the physical process being modeled or analyzed.

- *Most importantly, verify by* independent *means that the outputs from the scripts and functions are correct.*

1.6 ORGANIZATION OF THE BOOK AND ITS GOALS

The primary goal of this book is for the reader to be able to generate readable, compact, and verifiably correct MATLAB programs that obtain numerical solutions to a wide range of physical and empirical models and to display the results with fully annotated graphics.

The book can be used in several ways:

- To learn MATLAB
- As a companion to engineering texts
- As a reference for obtaining numerical solutions to a wide range of engineering problems
- As a source of applications of a wide variety of MATLAB solution techniques

The level of the book assumes that one has some fluency in calculus, linear algebra, and engineering mathematics; can employ the engineering approach to problem solving; and has some experience in using mathematical models to predict the response of elements, devices, and systems. These qualities play an important role in creating programs that function correctly. The book has two interrelated parts. The first part consists of Chapters 1 to 7, which introduce the fundamentals of MATLAB syntax and commands and structured programming techniques. The second part, consisting of Chapters 8 to 14, makes extensive use of the first seven chapters to obtain numerical solutions to engineering problems for a wide range of topics. In several of these topical areas, MATLAB toolboxes are used extensively to minimize programming complexity so that we can obtain numerical solutions to engineering problems of varying degrees of difficulty. In particular, we illustrate the use of the Controls toolbox and Simulink in Chapter 10; the Optimization toolbox in Chapter 13; the Statistics toolbox in Chapter 14; the PDE (Partial Differential Equation) toolbox in Chapters 8, 11, and 12; and the Symbolic toolbox in Chapters 5 and 9.

1.7 SUMMARY OF FUNCTIONS INTRODUCED

Some elementary mathematical functions are given in Table 1.2, trigonometric and hyperbolic functions in Table 1.3, some special constants in Table 1.4, and the language's use of special characters in Table 1.7. In Tables 1.5 and 1.6, we have summarized decimal-to-integer conversion and manipulation of complex numbers, respectively. A summary of the additional functions introduced in the chapter is presented in Table 1.8.

TABLE 1.8   MATLAB Functions Introduced in Chapter 1

MATLAB function	Description
clc	Clear the command window
clear	Removes variables from the workspace (computer memory)
close all	Closes (deletes) all graphic windows
format	Formats the display of output to the command window

EXERCISES

1.1 The moment of inertia of a sector of a circle is[3]

$$I = \left(\frac{\pi}{8} - \frac{8}{9\pi}\right)r^4$$

where r is the radius of the circle. Determine I when $r = 2.5$ cm.

1.2 The correction for curvature of a helical compression spring is[4]

$$K = \frac{4c - 1}{4c - 4} + \frac{0.615}{c}$$

where $c = D/d$, D is the diameter of the spring coil, and d is the diameter of the wire forming the coil. Determine K when $c = 5$.

1.3 The shape factor for the deflection of a flat trapezoidal leaf spring is[5]

$$K = \frac{3}{(1 - B)^3}[0.5 - 2B + B(1.5 - \ln B)]$$

where $B < 1$ is the ratio of the ends of the trapezoid. Determine K when $B = 0.6$.

1.4 The length L of a belt that traverses two pulley wheels, one of radius R and one of radius r, whose centers are a distance S apart, is given by[6]

$$L = 2S \cos\theta + \pi(R + r) + 2\theta(R - r)$$

where

$$\theta = \sin^{-1}\left(\frac{R - r}{S}\right)$$

Determine L when $R = 30$ cm, $r = 12$ cm, and $S = 50$ cm.

1.5 The torque T on a block brake is given by[7]

$$T = \frac{4f F_n r \sin(\theta/2)}{\theta + \sin\theta}$$

---

[3]T. G. Hicks, *ibid.*, p. 8.

[4]T. G. Hicks, *ibid.*, p. 78.

[5]T. G. Hicks, *ibid.*, p. 95.

[6]T. G. Hicks, *ibid.*, pp. 105–106.

[7]T. G. Hicks, *ibid.*, p. 109.

where θ is the contact angle in radians, f is the coefficient of friction, r is the radius of the drum, and F_n is the normal force acting on the drum. Determine T when $F = 250$ N, $f = 0.35$, $r = 0.4$ m, and $\theta = 60°$.

1.6 Air flow in a rectangular duct with sides of length A and B has an equivalent flow resistance to that of a circular duct of diameter D, which is given by the following equation:[8]

$$D = 1.265\left[\frac{(AB)^3}{A + B}\right]^{1/5}$$

Determine D when $A = 1.7$ m and $B = 1.2$ m.

1.7 The maximum angular acceleration of a Geneva wheel containing n slots is[9]

$$a_G = \omega^2 \frac{M(1 - M^2)\sin\alpha}{(1 + M^2 - 2M\cos\alpha)^2}$$

where

$$\cos\alpha = \sqrt{\left(\frac{1 + M^2}{4M}\right)^2 + 2} - \left(\frac{1 + M^2}{4M}\right)$$

$$M = \frac{1}{\sin(\pi/n)}$$

Determine a_G/ω^2 when $n = 6$.

1.8 The pressure drop of air at standard condition flowing through a steel pipe is[10]

$$\Delta p = \frac{0.03L}{d^{1.24}}\left(\frac{V}{1000}\right)^{1.84}$$

where L is the length of the pipe in meters, V is the velocity of air in meters per minute and d is the diameter of the pipe in millimeters. Determine Δp when $L = 3000$ m, $d = 45$ mm, and $V = 1600$ m/min.

1.9 The following expressions[11] describe the principal contact stresses in the x-, y-, and z-directions, respectively, when two spheres are pressed together with a force F:

$$\sigma_x = \sigma_y = -p_{max}\left[\left(1 - \frac{z}{a}\tan^{-1}\left(\frac{a}{z}\right)\right)(1 - \nu_1) - 0.5\left(1 + \frac{z^2}{a^2}\right)^{-1}\right]$$

$$\sigma_z = \frac{-p_{max}}{1 + z^2/a^2}$$

where

$$a = \sqrt[3]{\frac{3F}{8}\frac{(1 - \nu_1^2)/E_1 + (1 - \nu_2^2)/E_2}{1/d_1 + 1/d_2}}$$

$$p_{max} = \frac{3F}{2\pi a^2}$$

[8]T. G. Hicks, *ibid.*, p. 165.
[9]T. G. Hicks, *ibid.*, p. 125.
[10]T. G. Hicks, *ibid.*, p. 223.
[11]J. E. Shigley and C. R. Mischke, *Mechanical Engineering Design*, 5th ed., McGraw-Hill, New York, 1989.

and v_j, E_j, and d_j (where $j = 1, 2$) are the Poisson's ratio, Young's modulus, and diameter, respectively, of the two spheres.

Determine the principal stresses when $v_1 = v_2 = 0.3$, $E_1 = E_2 = 3 \times 10^7$ psi, $d_1 = 1.5$ in., $d_2 = 2.75$ in., $F = 100$ lb., and $z = 0.01$ in. [Answer: $\sigma_x = -20{,}002$ psi, and $\sigma_z = -177{,}120$ psi.]

1.10 The following expressions[12] describe the principal contact stresses in the x-, y-, and z-directions, respectively, when two cylinders, whose axes are parallel, are pressed together with a force F:

$$\sigma_x = -2v_2 p_{max}\left(\sqrt{1 + \frac{z^2}{b^2}} - \frac{z}{b}\right)$$

$$\sigma_y = -p_{max}\left(\left(2 - \left(1 + \frac{z^2}{b^2}\right)^{-1}\right)\sqrt{1 + \frac{z^2}{b^2}} - 2\frac{z}{b}\right)$$

$$\sigma_z = \frac{-p_{max}}{\sqrt{1 + z^2/b^2}}$$

$$\tau_{yz} = 0.5(\sigma_y - \sigma_z)$$

where

$$p_{max} = \frac{2F}{\pi b L}$$

$$b = \sqrt{\frac{2F}{\pi L} \frac{(1 - v_1^2)/E_1 - (1 - v_2^2)/E_2}{1/d_1 + 1/d_2}}$$

and v_j, E_j, and d_j (where $j = 1, 2$) are the Poisson's ratio, Young's modulus, and diameter, respectively, of the two cylinders.

Determine the principal stresses when $v_1 = v_2 = 0.3$, $E_1 = E_2 = 3 \times 10^7$ psi, $d_1 = 1.5$ in., $d_2 = 2.75$ in., $F = 100$ lb., $L = 2$ in., and $z = 0.001$ in. [Answer: $b = 0.0014$ in., $p_{max} = 23{,}251$ psi, $\sigma_x = -7085.7$ psi, $\sigma_y = -4843.8$ psi, and $\sigma_z = -18{,}775$ psi.]

1.11 The load number of a hydrodynamic bearing is given by[13]

$$N_L = \frac{\pi \varepsilon \sqrt{\pi^2(1 - \varepsilon^2) + 16\varepsilon^2}}{(1 - \varepsilon^2)^2}$$

where ε is the eccentricity ratio. Determine the value of N_L when $\varepsilon = 0.8$. [Answer: $N_L = 72.022$.]

1.12 Consider a threaded bolt of height h and whose material has a Young's modulus E. The stiffness k of the bolt when it is passed through a hole of diameter d_0 can be estimated from[14]

$$k = \frac{\pi E d_0 \tan 30°}{\ln\left(\dfrac{(d_2 - d_0)(d_1 + d_0)}{(d_2 + d_0)(d_1 - d_0)}\right)}$$

[12]J. E. Shigley and C. R. Mischke, *ibid.*

[13]R. L. Norton, *Machine Design: An Integrated Approach*, Prentice Hall, Upper Saddle River, NJ, 1996.

[14]A. H. Burr and J. B. Cheatham, *Mechanical Analysis and Design*, 2nd ed., Prentice Hall, Upper Saddle River, NJ, 1995, p. 423.

where d_1 is the diameter of the washer under the bolt and

$$d_2 = d_1 + h \tan 30°$$

Determine the value of k when $h = 1.25$ in., $d_0 = 0.25$ in., $d_1 = 0.625$ in., and $E = 3 \times 10^7$ psi. Remember that the arguments of trigonometric functions must be in radians. [Answer: $d_2 = 1.3467$ in., and $k = 2.8842 \times 10^7$ lb/in.]

1.13 The radial and tangential stresses in long tubes due to a temperature T_a at its inner surface of radius a and a temperature T_b at its outer surface of radius b are, respectively,[15]

$$\sigma_r = \frac{\alpha E(T_a - T_b)}{2(1 - v)\ln(b/a)}\left[\frac{a^2}{b^2 - a^2}\left(\frac{b^2}{r^2} - 1\right)\ln\left(\frac{b}{a}\right) - \ln\left(\frac{b}{r}\right)\right]$$

$$\sigma_t = \frac{\alpha E(T_a - T_b)}{2(1 - v)\ln(b/a)}\left[1 - \frac{a^2}{b^2 - a^2}\left(\frac{b^2}{r^2} + 1\right)\ln\left(\frac{b}{a}\right) - \ln\left(\frac{b}{r}\right)\right]$$

where r is the radial coordinate of the tube, E is the Young's modulus of the tube material, and α is the coefficient of thermal expansion. The temperature distribution through the wall of the tube in the radial direction is

$$T = T_b + \frac{(T_a - T_b)\ln(b/r)}{\ln(b/a)}$$

Determine the stresses and the temperature T when $\alpha = 1.2 \times 10^{-5}$ in./in./°F, $E = 3 \times 10^7$ psi, $v = 0.3$, $T_a = 500$°F, $T_b = 300$°F, $a = 0.25$ in., $b = 0.5$ in, $r = 0.375$ in. [Answer: $\sigma_r = -8011.5$ psi, $\sigma_t = 5231.9$ psi, and $T = 383.0075$.]

1.14 The mass flow rate of a gas escaping from a tank at pressure p_0 and under reversible adiabatic conditions is proportional to[16]

$$\psi = \sqrt{\frac{k}{k - 1}}\sqrt{\left(\frac{p_e}{p_0}\right)^{2/k} - \left(\frac{p_e}{p_0}\right)^{(k+1)/k}}$$

where p_e is the pressure exterior to the tank's exit and k is the adiabatic reversible gas constant.

Determine ψ when $k = 1.4$ and $p_e/p_0 = 0.3$. [Answer: $\psi = 0.4271$.]

1.15 The discharge factor for flow through an open channel of parabolic cross-section is[17]

$$K = \frac{1.2}{x}\left[\sqrt{16x^2 + 1} + \frac{1}{4x}\ln\left(\sqrt{16x^2 + 1} + 4x\right)\right]^{-2/3}$$

where x is the ratio of the maximum water depth to the breadth of the channel at the top of the water.

Determine K when $x = 0.45$. [Answer: $K = 1.3394$.]

---

[15]A. H. Burr and J. B. Cheatham, *ibid.*, p. 496.
[16]W. Beitz and K. H. Kuttner, Eds., *Handbook of Mechanical Engineering*, Springer-Verlag, New York, 1994, p. C15.
[17]H. W. King, *Handbook of Hydraulics*, 4th ed., McGraw-Hill, New York, 1954, pp. 7–24.

1.16 Show that with the following formula[18] one can approximate π to within less than 10^{-7} with one term ($n = 0$) and to within less than 10^{-15} with two terms ($n = 0, 1$). In fact, for each term used, the approximation of π improves by almost a factor of 10^{-8}. Thus, after summing the first four terms ($n = 0, 1, 2, 3$), one would correctly obtain the first 31 digits of π, which can be verified using the Symbolic toolbox:

$$\frac{1}{\pi} = \frac{\sqrt{8}}{9801} \sum_{n=0}^{\infty} \frac{(4n)!(1103 + 26{,}390n)}{(n!)^4 396^{4n}}$$

Note: The factorial is evaluated using gamma as follows: $\text{gamma}(n + 1) = n!$; $\text{gamma}(4n + 1) = (4n)!$, $n = 0, 1, \ldots$.

1.17 The thermal efficiency of a Diesel cycle on a cold air standard basis is expressed as[19]

$$\eta = 1 - \frac{1}{r^{k-1}} \left[\frac{r_c^k - 1}{k(r_c - 1)} \right]$$

where r is the compression ratio, r_c is the cutoff ratio, and $k = 1.4$ for air.
Determine η for air when $r = 10$ and $r_c = 3$.

1.18 In a converging–diverging nozzle, the expression for the ratio of the area A of any section to the area $A*$ that would be required for sonic flow—that is, when the Mach number $M = 1$—is given by[20]

$$\frac{A}{A*} = \frac{1}{M} \left[\left(\frac{2}{k + 1} \right) \left(1 + \frac{k - 1}{2} M^2 \right) \right]^{(k+1)/[2(k-1)]}$$

where, for air, $k = 1.4$.
Determine $A/A*$ for air when $M = 2$.

---

[18]S. Ramanujan, "Modular equations and approximations to π," *Quart. J. Math*, **45**, pp. 350–372.
[19]M. J. Moran and H. N. Shapiro, *Fundamentals of Engineering Thermodynamics*, John Wiley and Sons, New York, 1992, p. 367.
[20]M. J. Moran and H. N. Shapiro, *ibid.*, p. 418.

2

Matrices and MATLAB

Edward B. Magrab

MATLAB syntax is introduced in the context of vectors and matrices and their manipulation.

2.1 INTRODUCTION

MATLAB is a language whose operating instructions and syntax are based on a set of fundamental matrix operations and their extensions. Therefore, to fully utilize the advantages and compactness of the MATLAB language, we summarize some basic matrix definitions and symbolism and present several examples of their usage. The material presented in Sections 2.2, 2.3, and 2.4 is used extensively in the code developed throughout this and subsequent chapters.

2.2 DEFINITIONS OF MATRICES AND VECTORS

An array A of m rows and n columns is called a matrix of order $(m \times n)$, which consists of a total of mn elements arranged in the following rectangular array:

$$A = \begin{bmatrix} a_{11} & a_{12} & \cdots & a_{1n} \\ a_{21} & a_{22} & & \\ \vdots & & \ddots & \\ a_{m1} & & & a_{mn} \end{bmatrix} \rightarrow (m \times n)$$

The elements of the matrix are denoted a_{ij}, where i indicates the row number and j the column number.

Several special cases of this general matrix are as follows.

Square Matrix

When $m = n$, we have a square matrix.

Diagonal Matrix

When $a_{ij} = 0, i \neq j$, and $m = n$, we have the diagonal matrix

$$A = \begin{bmatrix} a_{11} & 0 & \cdots & 0 \\ 0 & a_{22} & & \\ \vdots & & \ddots & \\ 0 & & & a_{nn} \end{bmatrix} \rightarrow (n \times n)$$

When $a_{ii} = 1$ and $m = n$ we have the identity matrix I—that is,

$$I = \begin{bmatrix} 1 & 0 & \cdots & 0 \\ 0 & 1 & & \\ \vdots & & \ddots & \\ 0 & & & 1 \end{bmatrix}$$

Column and Row Matrices (Vectors)

When $a_{ij} = a_{i1}$ (i.e., there is only one column), then $a = A$ is called a column matrix or, more commonly, a vector—that is,

$$a = \begin{bmatrix} a_{11} \\ a_{21} \\ \vdots \\ a_{m1} \end{bmatrix} = \begin{bmatrix} a_1 \\ a_2 \\ \vdots \\ a_m \end{bmatrix} \rightarrow (m \times 1)$$

The quantity m is called the length of the vector.

When $a_{ij} = a_{1j}$—that is, we have only one row—then a is called a row matrix or a vector—that is,

$$a = [a_{11} \quad a_{12} \quad \cdots \quad a_{1n}] = [a_1 \quad a_2 \quad \cdots \quad a_n] \rightarrow (1 \times n)$$

This is the default definition of a vector in MATLAB. In this case, n is called the length of the vector. Thus, a vector can be represented by a row or a column matrix.

Transpose of a Matrix and a Vector

The transpose of a matrix is denoted by an apostrophe (') and is defined as follows:
When A is the $(m \times n)$ matrix

$$A = \begin{bmatrix} a_{11} & a_{12} & \cdots & a_{1n} \\ a_{21} & a_{22} & & \\ \vdots & & \ddots & \\ a_{m1} & & & a_{mn} \end{bmatrix} \rightarrow (m \times n)$$

then its transpose $W = A'$ is the following $(n \times m)$ matrix:

$$W = A' = \begin{bmatrix} w_{11} = a_{11} & w_{12} = a_{21} & \cdots & w_{1m} = a_{m1} \\ w_{21} = a_{12} & w_{22} = a_{22} & & \\ \vdots & & \ddots & \\ w_{n1} = a_{1n} & & & w_{nm} = a_{mn} \end{bmatrix} \rightarrow (n \times m)$$

that is, the rows and columns are interchanged.

For column and row vectors, we have the following: If

$$a = \begin{bmatrix} a_1 \\ a_2 \\ \vdots \\ a_m \end{bmatrix} \rightarrow (m \times 1) \quad \text{then} \quad a' = [a_1 a_2 \cdots a_m] \rightarrow (1 \times m)$$

and if

$$a = [a_1 a_2 \cdots a_m] \rightarrow (1 \times m) \quad \text{then} \quad a' = \begin{bmatrix} a_1 \\ a_2 \\ \vdots \\ a_m \end{bmatrix} \rightarrow (m \times 1)$$

2.3 CREATION OF VECTORS

Vectors in MATLAB are expressed as either

$$f = [a \; x \; b \ldots]$$

or

$$f = [a, x, b, \ldots]$$

where a, x, b, ... are either variable names, numbers, expressions, or strings (see
Section 3.1). If they are variable names or expressions, then all variable names and
the variable names composing the expressions must be defined such that a numerical value has been obtained for each of these variable names before the execution of
this statement. Variable names, expressions, and numbers can appear in any combination and in any order. In the form

$$f = [a \; x \; b \ldots]$$

the space (blank) between symbols is required, whereas in the form

$$f = [a, x, b, \ldots]$$

it is optional.[1]

It is important to note, however, that if a, say, is an expression that is explicitly written in the location where a is, then there may be no spaces between any of the alphanumerical characters and the mathematical operator symbols. For example, if $a = h + d^s$, then f is written as either

$$f = [h+d^\wedge s \, x \, b \ldots]$$

or

$$f = [h+d^\wedge s, x, b, \ldots]$$

Colon Notation

MATLAB gives several other ways to assign numerical values to the elements of a vector. The techniques for the creation of matrices are given in Section 2.4. The first means, described below, uses the *colon notation* to specify the range of the values and the increment between adjacent values. The second method specifies the range of the values and the number of values desired. In the former method, the increment either is important or has been specified, whereas in the latter method, the number of values is important.

The colon notation to create a vector is

x = s:d:f

or

x = (s:d:f)

or

x = [s:d:f]

where

s = start or initial value
d = increment or decrement
f = end or final value

Thus, the following row vector x is created:

$$x = [s, s + d, s + 2d, \ldots, s + nd]$$

where $s + nd \leq f$. Note that the number of values n created for x is not specified directly. The quantities s, d, and f can be any combination of numerical values, variable

---

[1]MATLAB occasionally has two or more equivalent ways in which to represent quantities. We will present, when appropriate, these equivalent representations. There is often no preferred form; however, readability can be a deciding factor.

names, and expressions. The number of terms (i.e., the length of the vector) that this expression has created is determined from the MATLAB function

   length(x)

When d is omitted, MATLAB assumes that $d = 1$. Then,

  x = s:f

creates the vector

$$x = [s, s + 1, s + 2, \ldots, s + n]$$

where $s + n \le f$. Again, s and f can be any combination of numerical values, variable names, and expressions.

    We now illustrate these functions with several examples. We first create a row vector that goes for 0.2 to 1.0 in increments of 0.1. The script is

  x = 0.2:0.1:1
  n = length(x)

which, when executed, gives

  x =
    0.2000 0.3000 0.4000 0.5000 0.6000 0.7000 0.8000 0.9000 1.0000
  n =
    9

    We can create a column vector by taking the transpose of a row vector. Thus, the above script is modified to

  x = (0.2:0.1:1)'
  n = length(x)

where we have to use the form that employs the parentheses. If we did not use the parentheses (or, equivalently, the brackets), MATLAB would have only taken the transpose of the number 1, which is equal to 1. Upon execution of this script, we obtain

  x =
    0.2000
    0.3000
    0.4000
    0.5000
    0.6000
    0.7000
    0.8000
    0.9000
    1.0000
  n =
    9

   If we now wish to create a row vector that goes for 0.2 to 1.0 in increments of 0.12, the script is

    x = 0.2:0.12:1
    n = length(x)

which, when executed, gives

    X =
      0.2000 0.3200 0.4400 0.5600 0.6800 0.8000 0.9200
    n =
      7

We notice that in this case, the highest value is 0.92, since $0.92 + 0.12 = 1.04 > 1$.
   Now, let us generate a row vector that goes from 1 to 7 in increments of 1. The script is

    x = 1:7
    n = length(x)

since, upon omitting the increment, MATLAB assumes an increment of 1. Upon execution, we obtain

    X =
      1 2 3 4 5 6 7
    n =
      7

   However, when we create a row vector from 0.5 to 7 in increments of 1, the script becomes

    x = 0.5:7
    n = length(x)

which upon execution gives

    X =
      0.5000 1.5000 2.5000 3.5000 4.5000 5.5000 6.5000
    n =
      7

Generation of n *Equally Spaced Values*

In the second method, one specifies n equally spaced values starting at s and ending at f as follows:

    x = linspace(s, f, n)

where the increment (decrement) is computed by MATLAB from

$$d = \frac{f - s}{n - 1}$$

The values of s and f can be either positive or negative, and either $s > f$ or $s < f$. When n is not specified, it is assigned a value of 100. Thus, linspace creates the vector

$$x = [s, s + d, s + 2d, \ldots, f = s + (n - 1)d]$$

Thus, if we wish to create eight equally spaced values from -2 to 6.5, the script is

```
x = linspace(-2, 6.5, 8)
```

which upon execution gives

```
x =
   -2.0000  -0.7857  0.4286  1.6429  2.8571  4.0714  5.2857  6.5000
```

If equal spacing on a logarithmic scale is desired, then

```
x = logspace(s, f, n)
```

where the initial value is 10^s, the final value is 10^f, and d is defined above. Thus, this expression creates the row vector

$$x = [10^s \ 10^{s+d} \ 10^{s+2d}, \ldots, 10^f]$$

When n is not specified, MATLAB assigns it a value of 50. Thus, if we wish to create five equally spaced values on a logarithmic scale from 1 to 100, the script is

```
x = logspace(0, 2, 5)
```

which upon execution gives

```
x =
   1.0000  3.1623  10.0000  31.6228  100.0000
```

Accessing Elements of Vectors

We now show how to access individual elements of vector arrays and perform arithmetic operations on them. Let

$$b = [b_1 \ b_2 \ b_3 \ldots b_n]$$

This means that we have created a vector b that has one row and n columns. To access individual elements of this array, we use MATLAB's subscript notation. This notation has the form $b(j)$; that is, $b(j)$ corresponds to b_j, where $j = 1, 2, , \ldots, n$ is the jth location in the array b. Thus, if we write $b(3)$, MATLAB will return the numerical value assigned to b_3, the third element of the vector. However, MATLAB's interpreter is smart enough to know that the matrix b is a $(1 \times n)$ matrix, and in some sense, it ignores the double subscript requirement. That is, writing $b(3)$, where b is a vector defined above, is the same as writing it as $b(1,3)$. However, if one were to either directly or implicitly require $b(3,1)$, then an error message would appear, because this row (the third row) hasn't been defined (created).

Conversely, if we let

$$b = [b_1 \ b_2 \ b_3 \ldots b_n]'$$

we have created a column vector—that is, an $(n \times 1)$ matrix. If we want to locate the third element of this vector, then we again write $b(3)$, and MATLAB returns the numerical value corresponding to b_3. This is the same as having written $b(3,1)$. If one were to either directly or implicitly require $b(1,3)$, then an error message would appear, because this column (the third column) hasn't been defined (created).

Manipulations of Vector Elements

Suppose that we want to create a vector x that is to have the seven values $[-2, 1, 3, 5, 7, 9, 10]$. This can be created with either the statement

  x = [-2, 1:2:9, 10]

or

  x = [-2, 1, 3, 5, 7, 9, 10]

which means that the elements of this vector are $x_1 = -2$, $x_2 = 1$, $x_3 = 3$, $x_4 = 5$, $x_5 = 7$, $x_6 = 9$, and $x_7 = 10$ and its length is 7. We access the elements of x with the MATLAB expression $x(j)$, where $j = 1, 2, \ldots, 7$. For example, the expression $x(5)$ returns the value 7. To access the last element in a vector, one can use the reserved word end as follows:

  x = [-2, 1:2:9, 10];
  xlast = x(end)

Upon execution, the following is displayed on the command window:

  xlast =
     10

    When we add or subtract a scalar from a vector, the scalar is added or subtracted from each element of the vector. Thus, the execution of

  x = [-2, 1, 3, 5, 7, 9, 10];
  z = x−1

results in

  z =
    -3   0   2   4   6   8   9

However, the rules for multiplication, division, and exponentiation have some restrictions, as discussed in Section 2.6.2.

    On the other hand, we may want to modify only some of the elements of a vector. For example, let $z = [-2\ 1\ 3\ 5\ 7\ 9\ 10]$. Then, to divide the second element by 2, we have

  z = [-2, 1, 3, 5, 7, 9, 10];
  z(2) = z(2)/2;
  z

which upon execution gives

```
z =
   -2.0000  0.5000  3.0000  5.0000  7.0000  9.0000  10.0000
```

If, further, we multiply the third and fourth elements by 3 and subtract 1 from each of them, the script is

```
z = [-2, 1, 3, 5, 7, 9, 10];
z(2) = z(2)/2;
z(3:4) = z(3:4)*3−1;
z
```

The execution of this script gives

```
z =
   -2.0000  0.5000  8.0000  14.0000  7.0000  9.0000  10.0000
```

Notice that the rest of the elements remain unaltered. The assignment statement $z(3:4) = z(3:4)*3−1$ is interpreted by MATLAB as follows: The existing values of the elements $z(3)$ and $z(4)$ are each multiplied by 3, and then 1 is subtracted from their respective results. These new results are then used to replace the original values of $z(3)$ and $z(4)$. This syntax is a very effective in writing compact code and is a frequently used programming construction.

One can access the elements of a vector several other ways. Consider the eight-element vector

```
y = [-1, 6, 15, -7, 31, 2, -4, -5];
```

If one wanted to create a new vector x composed of the third through fifth elements of y, then the execution of the script

```
y = [-1, 6, 15, -7, 31, 2, -4, -5];
x = y(3:5)
```

creates the three-element vector

```
x =
   15  -7   31
```

Suppose, instead, we wanted to create a vector x composed of the first two and the last two elements of y. This can be done either by

```
y = [-1, 6, 15, -7, 31, 2, -4, -5];
x = [y(1), y(2), y(7), y(8)]
```

or by first defining the locations in the vector array as a variable called *index* and then employing it as follows:

```
y = [-1, 6, 15, -7, 31, 2, -4, -5];
index = [1, 2, 7, 8];
x = y(index)
```

or, more compactly, as

    y = [-1, 6, 15, -7, 31, 2, -4, -5];
    x = y([1, 2, 7, 8])

    The last two representations have many useful applications. Let us assume that corresponding to the vector y is a vector z, which is also a vector with eight elements. The vectors are assumed to have the values

    y = [-1, 6, 15, -7, 31, 2, -4, -5];
    z = [10, 20, 30, 40, 50, 60, 70, 80];

One can think of this set of vectors as being correlated or linked such that $y(j)$ corresponds to $z(j)$. Suppose that we would like to sort the vector y in ascending order (most negative to most positive) using the sort function and then rearrange the order of the elements of z to correspond to the new order of the elements of y. Thus, from the *Help* file, we find that one form of the sort function is

    [ynew, indx] = sort(y)

where *ynew* is the vector with the rearranged (sorted) elements of y and *indx* is a vector containing the *original* locations of the elements in y. Thus, the script

    y = [-1, 6, 15, -7, 31, 2, -4, -5];
    z = [10, 20, 30, 40, 50, 60, 70, 80];
    [ynew, indx] = sort(y)
    znew = z(indx)

when executed gives

    ynew =
       -7 -5 -4 -1   2   6 15 31
    indx =
        4   8   7   1   6   2   3   5
    znew =
       40 80 70 10 60 20 30 50

Therefore, we see that $indx(1) = 4$ means that $ynew(1)$ used to be $y(4)$. Thus, to obtain the corresponding z, we defined *znew* as the vector z whose indices (order) are now given by *indx*.

    We can extend this capability further by introducing find, which determines the locations (not the values) of all the elements in a vector (or matrix) that satisfy a user-specified condition or expression. We illustrate its usage by creating a new vector s that contains only those elements of y that are either negative or zero. The MATLAB relational operator <= stands for $\leq$ (see Table 4.1). Then,

    y = [-1, 6, 15, -7, 31, 2, -4, -5];
    indxx = find(y<=0)
    s = y(indxx)

which, when executed, results in

```
indxx =
   1  4  7  8
s =
  -1  -7  -4  -5
```

The script could be written compactly as

```
y = [-1, 6, 15, -7, 31, 2, -4, -5];
s = y(find(y<=0))
```

One of the great advantages of MATLAB's implicit vector and matrix notation is that it provides the user with a compact way of performing a series of operations on an array of values. For example, suppose that we would like to determine $\sin(x)$ at 10 equally spaced values of x from $-\pi \leq x \leq \pi$. Then, the MATLAB statements

```
x = linspace(-pi, pi, 10);
y = sin(x)
```

yield the following vector

```
y =
  -0.0000 -0.6428 -0.9848 -0.8660 -0.3420 0.3420 0.8660 0.9848 0.6428
   0.0000
```

Minimum and Maximum Values in a Vector

MATLAB provides a means to find the extreme values in a vector (or a matrix). To find the magnitude of the smallest element and its location in a vector, we use `min`, and to find the magnitude of the largest element and its location in a vector, we use `max`. Thus, to determine the minimum and maximum values created by the previous script, we have

```
x = linspace(-pi, pi, 10);
y = sin(x);
[ymax, kmax] = max(y)
[ymin, kmin] = min(y)
```

Upon execution, we find that

```
ymax =
   0.9848
kmax =
   8
ymin =
  -0.9848
kmin =
   3
```

Thus, the maximum value is 0.9848, and it is the eighth element in the vector. The minimum value is -0.9848, and it is the third element in the vector.

2.4 CREATION OF MATRICES

Consider the following (4×3) matrix A:

$$A = \begin{bmatrix} a_{11} & a_{12} & a_{13} \\ a_{21} & a_{22} & a_{23} \\ a_{31} & a_{32} & a_{33} \\ a_{41} & a_{42} & a_{43} \end{bmatrix} \rightarrow (4 \times 3)$$

This matrix can be created several ways. The basic syntax to create a matrix is

$$A = [a_{11}\ a_{12}\ a_{13};\ a_{21}\ a_{22}\ a_{23};\ a_{31}\ a_{32}\ a_{33};\ a_{41}\ a_{42}\ a_{43}]$$

where the semicolons are used to indicate the end of a row. Each row must have the *same* number of columns. If a more readable presentation is desired, then one can use the form

$$A = [a_{11}\ a_{12}\ a_{13};\ \dots$$
$$a_{21}\ a_{22}\ a_{23};\ \dots$$
$$a_{31}\ a_{32}\ a_{33};\ \dots$$
$$a_{41}\ a_{42}\ a_{43}]$$

where the ellipses (...) are required to indicate that the expression continues on the next line. One can omit the ellipsis (...) and, instead, use the *Enter* key to indicate the end of a row. In this case, the expression will look like

$$A = [a_{11}\ a_{12}\ a_{13}$$
$$a_{21}\ a_{22}\ a_{23}$$
$$a_{31}\ a_{32}\ a_{33}$$
$$a_{41}\ a_{42}\ a_{43}]$$

A fourth way is create four separate row vectors, each with the same number of columns, and then to combine these vectors to form the matrix. In this case, we have

$$v_1 = [a_{11}\ a_{12}\ a_{13}];$$
$$v_2 = [a_{21}\ a_{22}\ a_{23}];$$
$$v_3 = [a_{31}\ a_{32}\ a_{33}];$$
$$v_4 = [a_{41}\ a_{42}\ a_{43}];$$
$$A = [v_1;\ v_2;\ v_3;\ v_4]$$

where the semicolons in the first four lines are used to suppress display to the command window.

In all the forms above, the a_{ij} are numbers, variable names, expressions, or strings. If they are either variable names or expressions, then the variable names or the variable names comprising the expressions must have been assigned numerical values, either by the user or from previously executed expressions, before the execution of this statement. Expressions and numbers can appear in any combination. If they are strings, then the number of characters in each row must be the same (see Section 3.1).

Let us represent the following matrix in MATLAB:

$$A = \begin{bmatrix} 11 & 12 & 13 & 14 \\ 21 & 22 & 23 & 24 \\ 31 & 32 & 33 & 34 \\ 41 & 42 & 43 & 44 \end{bmatrix}$$

Then, the script is

A = [11, 12, 13, 14; 21, 22, 23, 24; 31, 32, 33, 34; 41, 42, 43, 44]

which upon execution displays in the command window

```
A =
   11   12   13   14
   21   22   23   24
   31   32   33   34
   41   42   43   44
```

The script could also have been written as is

```
A = [11, 12, 13, 14; ...
     21, 22, 23, 24; ...
     31, 32, 33, 34; ...
     41, 42, 43, 44]
```

or

```
A = [11, 12, 13, 14
     21, 22, 23, 24
     31, 32, 33, 34
     41, 42, 43, 44]
```

or

```
v1 = [11, 12, 13, 14];
v2 = [21, 22, 23, 24];
v3 = [31, 32, 33, 34];
v4 = [41, 42, 43, 44];
A = [v1; v2; v3; v4]
```

which upon execution would produce the same result as that obtained by the initial script.

The order of the matrix is determined by

[m, n] = size(A)

where m is the number of rows and n is the number of columns. Thus, to confirm that the order of A is a (4×4) matrix, the script is

```
A = [11, 12, 13, 14; 21, 22, 23, 24; 31, 32, 33, 34; 41, 42, 43, 44];
[m, n] = size(A)
```

which upon execution gives

```
m =
   4
n =
   4
```

If one were to use the `length` function on a matrix, `length` would return the number of *columns* in the array. For example, if A is a (2×4) array, then the script

```
A = [1 2 3 4; 5 6 7 8];
L = length(A)
```

when executed gives

```
L =
   4
```

We take the transpose of a matrix using the apostrophe (`'`). Thus, the transpose of A is

$$A = [11, 12, 13, 14; 21, 22, 23, 24; 31, 32, 33, 34; 41, 42, 43, 44]'$$

which upon execution gives

```
A =
   11   21   31   41
   12   22   32   42
   13   23   33   43
   14   24   34   44
```

Generation of Special Matrices

We shall introduce four functions that can be used to create matrices with specific values for its elements.

An $(r \times c)$ matrix in which each element has the value 1 is created with

```
ones(r, c)
```

The function `ones` is a convenient replacement for the equivalent expression

$$ones(r, c) \rightarrow one(1{:}r, 1{:}c) = 1$$

An $(r \times c)$ matrix in which each element has the value 0, which is called a null matrix, is created with

```
zeros(r, c)
```

The function `zeros` is a convenient replacement for the equivalent expression

$$zeros(r, c) \rightarrow zero(1{:}r, 1{:}c) = 0$$

To create an $(n \times n)$ diagonal matrix whose diagonal elements are given by a vector a of length n, we use

```
diag(a)
```

This function can also be used to extract the diagonal elements of an $(n \times n)$ matrix A. Thus,

    b = diag(A)

where b is a vector of length n containing the diagonal elements of the matrix A.

To create an $(n \times n)$ identity matrix I, we use

    eye(n)

We shall now illustrate the use of these four functions. To create a (2×5) matrix with all of its elements equal to 1, the script is

    on = ones(2, 5)

which upon execution produces

    on =
       1 1 1 1 1
       1 1 1 1 1

To create a (3×2) matrix with all of its elements equal to zero, the script is

    zer = zeros(3, 2)

which upon execution produces

    zer =
       0 0
       0 0
       0 0

To create a (3×3) diagonal matrix A with elements $a_{11} = 4$, $a_{22} = 9$, and $a_{33} = 1$, the script is

    a = [4, 9, 1];
    A = diag(a)

or, more compactly,

    A = diag([4, 9, 1])

Either script, when executed, produces

    A =
       4 0 0
       0 9 0
       0 0 1

On the other hand, if we are given a $(n \times n)$ matrix, then diag can be used to extract its diagonal elements. If the matrix is the (4×4) matrix A defined previously, then the script to extract its diagonal elements is

    A = diag([11, 12, 13, 14; 21, 22, 23, 24; 31, 32, 33, 34; 41, 42, 43, 44])

Upon execution, we obtain

```
A =
   11
   22
   33
   44
```

Furthermore, we can create a diagonal matrix composed of the diagonal elements of *A* as follows.

A = [11, 12, 13, 14; 21, 22, 23, 24; 31, 32, 33, 34; 41, 42, 43, 44];
Adiag = diag(diag(A))

Upon execution, we obtain

```
Adiag =
   11   0   0   0
    0  22   0   0
    0   0  33   0
    0   0   0  44
```

To create a (3×3) identity matrix, the script is

A = eye(3)

Upon execution, we obtain

```
A =
   1  0  0
   0  1  0
   0  0  1
```

Manipulation of Matrix Elements

Consider the construction of the (3×5) matrix

$$A = \begin{bmatrix} 3 & 5 & 7 & 9 & 11 \\ 20.0 & 20.25 & 20.5 & 20.75 & 21.0 \\ 1 & 1 & 1 & 1 & 1 \end{bmatrix} \rightarrow (3 \times 5)$$

This matrix is created with the statement

A = [3:2:11; linspace(20,21,5); ones(1,5)]

which yields

```
A=
    3.0000   5.0000   7.0000   9.0000  11.0000
   20.0000  20.2500  20.5000  20.7500  21.0000
    1.0000   1.0000   1.0000   1.0000   1.0000
```

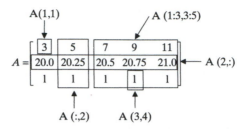

Figure 2.1   Accessing elements of a matrix.

Referring to Figure 2.1, we access the elements a_{ij}, $(i = 1, 2, 3,$ and $j = 1,$ $2, \ldots, 5)$ of this matrix as follows: The element is the first row and first column, a_{11}, is

$A(1, 1) \rightarrow 3$

and the element in the third row and fourth column, a_{34}, is

$A(3, 4) \rightarrow 1$

All the elements in the second column—a_{12}, a_{22}, and a_{32}—are accessed by

$A(:,2) \rightarrow [5, 20.25, 1]'$

where we have used the transpose symbol to indicate that it is a column vector. The notation

$A(:,2)$

means "all the rows of column 2." All the elements of row 2—a_{21}, a_{22}, a_{23}, a_{24}, and a_{25}—can be accessed by

$A(2,:) \rightarrow [20, 20.25, 20.5, 20.75, 21]$

where the notation

$A(2,:)$

means "all the columns of row 2."

To access the submatrix composed of the elements in columns 3 to 5 and rows 1 to 3, we use the colon notation as follows:

$A(1:3,3:5) \rightarrow [7, 9, 11; 20.5, 20.75, 21; 1, 1, 1]$

which is a (3×3) matrix. We see that in writing the indices of A, we used the default form that sets the increment to $+1$. Thus, if we construct the script

```
A = [3:2:11; linspace(20, 1, 5); ones(1, 5)];
B = A(1:3,3:5)
```

then its execution gives the (3×3) matrix

```
B =
   7.0000   9.0000   11.0000
  20.5000  20.7500   21.0000
   1.0000   1.0000    1.0000
```

Let us now create a matrix that is the same size as A but with all of its elements equal to 4. This is done with the script

$A = [3{:}2{:}11; \texttt{linspace}(20, 21, 5); \texttt{ones}(1, 5)];$
$[\texttt{r}, \texttt{c}] = \texttt{size}(A);$
$Z = 4{*}\texttt{ones}(\texttt{r}, \texttt{c})$

which creates

```
Z =
   4  4  4  4  4
   4  4  4  4  4
   4  4  4  4  4
```

This can be written more compactly as

$A = [3{:}2{:}11; \texttt{linspace}(20, 21, 5); \texttt{ones}(1, 5)];$
$Z = 4{*}\texttt{ones}(\texttt{size}(A))$

One can alter elements of a matrix in a manner similar to that used for vectors. Let us use the `magic` function[2] to create a matrix. The `magic` function creates a matrix in which the sum of the elements in each column and the sum of the elements of each row and the sum of the elements in each diagonal are equal. For a (4×4) matrix, the value is 34. Then, executing

$Z = \texttt{magic}(4)$

we obtain

```
Z =
  16   2   3  13
   5  11  10   8
   9   7   6  12
   4  14  15   1
```

Let us divide all the elements in row 2 of this matrix by 2 and then add all the elements in column 2 to those in column 4 and place the result in column 4. The script is

$Z = \texttt{magic}(4);$
$Z(2,:) = Z(2,:)/2;$
$Z(:,4) = Z(:,4)+Z(:,2);$
Z

---

[2]There are more than 50 special matrices available (see `gallery` in *Help*).

which results in

```
Z =
  16.0000    2.0000    3.0000   15.0000
   2.5000    5.5000    5.0000    9.5000
   9.0000    7.0000    6.0000   19.0000
   4.0000   14.0000   15.0000   15.0000
```

To set all the diagonal elements of the original matrix Z to zero, we use the previously discussed technique to obtain

```
Z = magic(4);
Z = Z-diag(diag(Z))
```

which results in

```
Z =
   0    2    3   13
   5    0   10    8
   9    7    0   12
   4   14   15    0
```

To replace all the diagonal elements with the value 5, we use the script

```
Z = magic(4);
Z = Z-diag(diag(Z))+5*eye(4)
```

which results in

```
Z =
   5    2    3   13
   5    5   10    8
   9    7    5   12
   4   14   15    5
```

To place the values $11, 23, 54,$ and 61 in the diagonal elements of Z, we use the script

```
Z = magic(4);
Z = Z-diag(diag(Z))+diag([11,23,54,61])
```

which results in

```
Z =
  11    2    3   13
   5   23   10    8
   9    7   54   12
   4   14   15   61
```

Minimum and Maximum Values in a Matrix

The minimum and maximum values of a matrix are also determined using `min` and `max`, except that for a matrix, the functions determine the minimum/maximum on a column-by-column basis. Thus, if the order of the matrix is $(m \times n)$, the output of `min` and `max` are vectors of length n, where each element of the vector is the minimum/maximum value of each column. For example, let us determine the minimum and maximum values of the `magic(4)`. The script is

```
M = magic(4)
minM = min(M)
maxM = max(M)
```

The execution of the script gives

```
M =
   16   2   3   13
    5  11  10    8
    9   7   6   12
    4  14  15    1
minM =
    4   2   3   1
maxM =
   16  14  15   13
```

To find the maximum value of all the elements, we have to use `max` twice. Thus,

```
M = magic(4);
maxM = max(max(M))
```

which upon execution gives

```
maxM =
   16
```

Manipulation of Arrays

MATLAB provides two functions that can be used to create matrices by replicating a scalar, a column or row vector, or a matrix a specified number of times. These two functions are

```
repmat
```

and

```
meshgrid
```

which uses `repmat`. The general form of `repmat` is

```
repmat(x, r, c)
```

where x is either a scalar, vector, or matrix; r is the number times that the rows of x will be replicated; and c is the number of times that the columns of x will be replicated. The repmat function is very useful in generating annotated output, as illustrated in Chapter 3. The meshgrid function has numerous applications in evaluating series, as shown in Section 2.6, and in displaying three-dimensional surfaces, as shown in Chapter 7 and subsequent chapters.

We shall now illustrate how repmat can be used to create different matrices and vectors from an original vector or matrix. We shall first create a column or a row vector of arbitrary length in which each element of the vector has the same numerical value. Thus, if we wish to create a row vector w composed of six values of the number 45.72, then the script is

w = repmat(45.72, 1, 6)

This expression is equivalent to a vector created from the fundamental form

w = [45.72, 45.72, 45.72, 45.72, 45.72, 45.72]

or created using colon notation

w(1,1:6) = 45.72

If, instead, we want to create a (3×3) matrix of these values, then we have the script

W = repmat(45.72, 3, 3)

which could also have been created using the fundamental form

W = [45.72, 45.72, 45.72; 45.72, 45.72, 45.72; 45.72, 45.72, 45.72]

or by using colon notation

W(1:3,1:3) = 45.72

All of these expressions will produce in the command window

```
W =
   45.7200   45.7200   45.7200
   45.7200   45.7200   45.7200
   45.7200   45.7200   45.7200
```

Now, consider the vector

$$s = [a_1\ a_2\ a_3\ a_4]$$

The expression

V = repmat(s, 3, 1)

creates the numerical equivalent[3] of the matrix

$$V = \begin{bmatrix} a_1 & a_2 & a_3 & a_4 \\ a_1 & a_2 & a_3 & a_4 \\ a_1 & a_2 & a_3 & a_4 \end{bmatrix}$$

That is, it creates three rows of the vector s, with each row in this case having four columns. The expression

```
repmat(s, 3, 2)
```

creates the numerical equivalent of the matrix

$$V = \begin{bmatrix} a_1 & a_2 & a_3 & a_4 & a_1 & a_2 & a_3 & a_4 \\ a_1 & a_2 & a_3 & a_4 & a_1 & a_2 & a_3 & a_4 \\ a_1 & a_2 & a_3 & a_4 & a_1 & a_2 & a_3 & a_4 \end{bmatrix}$$

On the other hand, the command

$$V = \text{repmat}(s', 1, 3)$$

yields a matrix of three columns of the numerical equivalent of the column vector s', with each column in this case having four rows:

$$V = \begin{bmatrix} a_1 & a_1 & a_1 \\ a_2 & a_2 & a_2 \\ a_3 & a_3 & a_3 \\ a_4 & a_4 & a_4 \end{bmatrix}$$

The expression

$$V = \text{repmat}(s', 2, 3)$$

gives the numerical equivalent of the matrix

$$V = \begin{bmatrix} a_1 & a_1 & a_1 \\ a_2 & a_2 & a_2 \\ a_3 & a_3 & a_3 \\ a_4 & a_4 & a_4 \\ a_1 & a_1 & a_1 \\ a_2 & a_2 & a_2 \\ a_3 & a_3 & a_3 \\ a_4 & a_4 & a_4 \end{bmatrix}$$

If we have two row vectors s and t, then the MATLAB expression

$$[U, V] = \text{meshgrid}(s, t)$$

---

[3]By numerical equivalent, we mean that in MATLAB, the v_{ij} have had numerical values assigned to them. The notation here is used to better illustrate what repmat does by symbolically showing the arrangement of the elements of the resulting array.

gives the same result as that produced by the two commands:

$U = \text{repmat}(s, \text{length}(t), 1)$
$V = \text{repmat}(t', 1, \text{length}(s))$

In either case, U and V are each matrices of order $(\text{length}(t) \times \text{length}(s))$. Thus, if

$$s = [s_1 \; s_2 \; s_3 \; s_4]$$
$$t = [t_1 \; t_2 \; t_3]$$

then

$[U, V] = \text{meshgrid}\,(s, t)$

produces the numerical equivalent of the two (3×4) matrices

$$U = \begin{bmatrix} s_1 & s_2 & s_3 & s_4 \\ s_1 & s_2 & s_3 & s_4 \\ s_1 & s_2 & s_3 & s_4 \end{bmatrix} \tag{2.1a}$$

$$V = \begin{bmatrix} t_1 & t_1 & t_1 & t_1 \\ t_2 & t_2 & t_2 & t_2 \\ t_3 & t_3 & t_3 & t_3 \end{bmatrix} \tag{2.1b}$$

The meshgrid function can also be used to return only one matrix as follows:

$W = \text{meshgrid}(s, t)$

which creates $W = U$, where U is given by Eq. 2.1a. The use of this form is illustrated in Example 2.5.

There are two matrix manipulation functions that are useful in certain applications: $\text{fliplr}(A)$ and $\text{flipud}(A)$, which flip the rows and columns, respectively. Consider the (2×5) matrix

$$A = \begin{bmatrix} a_{11} & a_{12} & a_{13} & a_{14} & a_{15} \\ a_{21} & a_{22} & a_{23} & a_{24} & a_{25} \end{bmatrix} \rightarrow (2 \times 5)$$

which is created with the statement

$$A = [a_{11} \, a_{12} \, a_{13} \, a_{14} \, a_{15}; a_{21} \, a_{22} \, a_{23} \, a_{24} \, a_{25}]$$

Then,

$$\text{fliplr}(A) \rightarrow \begin{bmatrix} a_{15} & a_{14} & a_{13} & a_{12} & a_{11} \\ a_{25} & a_{24} & a_{23} & a_{22} & a_{21} \end{bmatrix} \rightarrow (2 \times 5)$$

$$\text{flipud}(A) \rightarrow \begin{bmatrix} a_{21} & a_{22} & a_{23} & a_{24} & a_{25} \\ a_{11} & a_{12} & a_{13} & a_{14} & a_{15} \end{bmatrix} \rightarrow (2 \times 5)$$

and

$$\text{flipud}(\text{fliplr}(A)) \rightarrow \begin{bmatrix} a_{25} & a_{24} & a_{23} & a_{22} & a_{21} \\ a_{15} & a_{14} & a_{13} & a_{12} & a_{11} \end{bmatrix} \rightarrow (2 \times 5)$$

The results of the $\texttt{fliplr}(A)$ and $\texttt{flipud}(A)$ functions can also be obtained with the colon notation. For example,

$C = \texttt{fliplr(A)}$

produces the same results as

$C = \texttt{A(:,length(A):-1:1)}$

Now, consider the vector

$$C = [A \ \texttt{fliplr}(A)]' \rightarrow \begin{bmatrix} a_{11} & a_{21} \\ a_{12} & a_{22} \\ a_{13} & a_{21} \\ a_{14} & a_{24} \\ a_{15} & a_{25} \\ a_{15} & a_{25} \\ a_{14} & a_{24} \\ a_{13} & a_{23} \\ a_{12} & a_{22} \\ a_{11} & a_{21} \end{bmatrix} \rightarrow (10 \times 2)$$

which has created two identical rows: 5 and 6. Suppose that we wish to remove one of these repeating rows. This is done by setting one of the rows to a null value using the expression [], where there is no space (blank) between the brackets. Then, either the expression

$C(\texttt{length(A)},:) = []$

or

$C(\texttt{length(A)+1},:) = []$

reduces C to

$$C = \begin{bmatrix} a_{11} & a_{21} \\ a_{12} & a_{22} \\ a_{13} & a_{23} \\ a_{14} & a_{24} \\ a_{15} & a_{25} \\ a_{14} & a_{24} \\ a_{13} & a_{23} \\ a_{12} & a_{22} \\ a_{11} & a_{21} \end{bmatrix} \rightarrow (9 \times 2)$$

where the order of C is now (9×2). The expression $C(\texttt{length}(A),:) = []$ means that all the columns of row number $\texttt{length}(A)$ in C are to be assigned the value [] (removed, in this case). Although we know that the length of A is 5, it is good practice to let MATLAB do the counting; hence, the use of the function $\texttt{length}(A)$.

We further clarify the above notations by presenting the results of three different MATLAB operations. First we create the following two (2×5) matrices A and B:

$$A = \begin{bmatrix} a_{11} & a_{12} & a_{13} & a_{14} & a_{15} \\ a_{21} & a_{22} & a_{23} & a_{24} & a_{25} \end{bmatrix}$$

$$B = \begin{bmatrix} b_{11} & b_{12} & b_{13} & b_{14} & b_{15} \\ b_{21} & b_{22} & b_{23} & b_{24} & b_{25} \end{bmatrix}$$

Now, consider their use in the following three MATLAB operations:

Addition/subtraction: $C = A \pm B$

$$C = \begin{bmatrix} a_{11} \pm b_{11} & a_{12} \pm b_{12} & a_{13} \pm b_{13} & a_{14} \pm b_{14} & a_{15} \pm b_{15} \\ a_{21} \pm b_{21} & a_{22} \pm b_{22} & a_{23} \pm b_{23} & a_{24} \pm b_{24} & a_{25} \pm b_{25} \end{bmatrix} \rightarrow (2 \times 5)$$

Thus, C is a (2×5) matrix.

Column augmentation: $C = [A, B]$

$$C = \begin{bmatrix} a_{11} & a_{12} & a_{13} & a_{14} & a_{15} & b_{11} & b_{12} & b_{13} & b_{14} & b_{15} \\ a_{21} & a_{22} & a_{23} & a_{24} & a_{25} & b_{21} & b_{22} & b_{23} & b_{24} & b_{25} \end{bmatrix} \rightarrow (2 \times 10)$$

Thus, C is (2×10) matrix.

Row augmentation: $C = [A; B]$

$$C = \begin{bmatrix} a_{11} & a_{12} & a_{13} & a_{14} & a_{15} \\ a_{21} & a_{22} & a_{23} & a_{24} & a_{25} \\ b_{11} & b_{12} & b_{13} & b_{14} & b_{15} \\ b_{21} & b_{22} & b_{23} & b_{24} & b_{25} \end{bmatrix} \rightarrow (4 \times 5)$$

Thus, C is (4×5) matrix.

Furthermore, if

$$x = [x_1 \ x_2 \ x_3]$$
$$y = [y_1 \ y_2 \ y_3]$$

then either

$$Z = [x', y']$$

or

$$Z = [x; y]'$$

produces

$$Z = \begin{bmatrix} x_1 & y_1 \\ x_2 & y_2 \\ x_3 & y_3 \end{bmatrix} \rightarrow (2 \times 3)$$

whereas

$$Z = [x'; y']$$

yields

$$Z = \begin{bmatrix} x_1 \\ x_2 \\ x_3 \\ y_1 \\ y_2 \\ y_3 \end{bmatrix} \rightarrow (6 \times 1)$$

These relationships are very useful when placing data in a specific order.

Let us illustrate these results with the following two vectors: $a = [1, 2, 3]$ and $b = [4, 5, 6]$. Then, the script is

```
x = [1, 2, 3];
y = [4, 5, 6];
Z1 = [x,' y']
Z2 = [x; y]'
Z3 = [x'; y']
```

The execution of this script gives

```
Z1 =
     1    4
     2    5
     3    6
Z2 =
     1    4
     2    5
     3    6
Z3 =
     1
     2
     3
     4
     5
     6
```

2.5 DOT OPERATIONS

We now introduce MATLAB's dot (.) notation, which is MATLAB's syntax for performing, on matrices of the *same* order, arithmetic operations on an element-by-element basis. Consider the following (3×4) matrices:

$$X = \begin{bmatrix} x_{11} & x_{12} & x_{13} & x_{14} \\ x_{21} & x_{22} & x_{23} & x_{24} \\ x_{31} & x_{32} & x_{33} & x_{34} \end{bmatrix}$$

and

$$M = \begin{bmatrix} m_{11} & m_{12} & m_{13} & m_{14} \\ m_{21} & m_{22} & m_{23} & m_{24} \\ m_{31} & m_{32} & m_{33} & m_{34} \end{bmatrix}$$

We now write out explicitly the numerical equivalent form of the following MATLAB dot (.) operations:

$$Z_m = X.*M = \begin{bmatrix} x_{11}*m_{11} & x_{12}*m_{12} & x_{13}*m_{13} & x_{14}*m_{14} \\ x_{21}*m_{21} & x_{22}*m_{22} & x_{23}*m_{23} & x_{24}*m_{24} \\ x_{31}*m_{31} & x_{32}*m_{32} & x_{33}*m_{33} & x_{34}*m_{34} \end{bmatrix} \qquad (2.2a)$$

$$Z_d = X./M = \begin{bmatrix} x_{11}/m_{11} & x_{12}/m_{12} & x_{13}/m_{13} & x_{14}/m_{14} \\ x_{21}/m_{21} & x_{22}/m_{22} & x_{23}/m_{23} & x_{24}/m_{24} \\ x_{31}/m_{31} & x_{32}/m_{32} & x_{33}/m_{33} & x_{34}/m_{34} \end{bmatrix} \qquad (2.2b)$$

$$Z_e = X.^\wedge M = \begin{bmatrix} x_{11}{}^\wedge m_{11} & x_{12}{}^\wedge m_{12} & x_{13}{}^\wedge m_{13} & x_{14}{}^\wedge m_{14} \\ x_{21}{}^\wedge m_{21} & x_{22}{}^\wedge m_{22} & x_{23}{}^\wedge m_{23} & x_{24}{}^\wedge m_{24} \\ x_{31}{}^\wedge m_{31} & x_{32}{}^\wedge m_{32} & x_{33}{}^\wedge m_{33} & x_{34}{}^\wedge m_{34} \end{bmatrix} \qquad (2.2c)$$

Note that the dot (.) must be placed before the symbol for multiplication, division, and exponentiation; that is, $* \rightarrow .*;\ / \rightarrow ./;$ and $^\wedge \rightarrow .^\wedge$. The dot operation for either addition or subtraction is not required, since the matrix notation causes the same operation—that is, an element-by-element addition or subtraction. Recall the results at the end of the previous section, and see Eq. 2.6.

We now examine several special cases of these three operations. For dot multiplication, if $X = x_0$, a scalar constant, then the dot operation is not needed and the multiplication can be written as

$$Z_m = x_0*M$$

Similarly, when $M = m_0$, a scalar constant, we can write the multiplication as

$$Z_m = X*m_0$$

In both cases, the dot operations are not required.

For dot division, when $M = m_0$, a scalar constant, we have

$$Z_d = X/m_0$$

and the dot operation is not required. However, when $X = x_0$, a scalar constant, we must use dot division; that is,

$$Z_d = x_0./M$$

For exponentiation, we must always use dot operations whether $M = m_0$, a scalar constant, or $X = x_0$, a scalar constant; that is,

$$Z_e = x_0.^\wedge M$$

and

$$Z_e = X.^\wedge m_0$$

Example 2.1   Generation of a vector of exponents

We shall illustrate the dot operation for exponentiation. Consider the computation of 2^j for $j = 1, 2, \ldots, 8$. The script is

```
x = 1:8;
y = 2.^x
```

which yields

```
y =
    2   4   8   16   32   64   128   256
```

Thus, the placement of a decimal point before the exponentiation operator ($^$) signifies to MATLAB that it is to take the scalar 2, compute its power at each of the values of x, and then place the results in the corresponding elements of a vector y of the same length. The previous script can be written more compactly as

```
y = 2.^(1:8)
```

where the parenthesis are required, or as

```
y = 2.^[1:8]
```

where the brackets are required.

If the problem is reversed and we want to determine j^2, then the script is

```
y = (1:8).^2      % or y = [1:8].^2
```

which yields

```
y =
    1   4   9   16   25   36   49   64
```

If we let $f(Y)$ stand for the operation of any function, such as $f(Y) = \sin(Y)$, $f(Y) = \cosh(Y)$, etc., on the matrix Y, then if Y, for example, is a (3×4) matrix

$$Z = f(Y) = \begin{bmatrix} f(y_{11}) & f(y_{12}) & f(y_{13}) & f(y_{14}) \\ f(y_{21}) & f(y_{22}) & f(y_{23}) & f(y_{24}) \\ f(y_{31}) & f(y_{32}) & f(y_{33}) & f(y_{34}) \end{bmatrix}$$

we can perform dot operations only if the order of each quantity is the same. For example, if a, b, c, d, and g are each a (3×2) matrix, then the expression

$$Z = \left[\tan a - g \left(\frac{b}{c} \right)^d \right]^2$$

is written as (assuming that a, b, c, d, and g are each assigned numerical values before this expression)

```
Z = (tan(a)-g.*(b./c).^d).^2;
```

which results in the elements of Z having the numerical values computed from the following expressions:

$$Z = \begin{bmatrix} (\tan(a_{11}) - g_{11}*(b_{11}/c_{11})^{\wedge}d_{11})^{\wedge}2 & (\tan(a_{12}) - g_{12}*(b_{12}/c_{12})^{\wedge}d_{12})^{\wedge}2 \\ (\tan(a_{21}) - g_{21}*(b_{21}/c_{21})^{\wedge}d_{21})^{\wedge}2 & (\tan(a_{22}) - g_{22}*(b_{22}/c_{22})^{\wedge}d_{22})^{\wedge}2 \\ (\tan(a_{31}) - g_{31}*(b_{31}/c_{31})^{\wedge}d_{31})^{\wedge}2 & (\tan(a_{32}) - g_{32}*(b_{32}/c_{32})^{\wedge}d_{32})^{\wedge}2 \end{bmatrix}$$

Example 2.2   Dot operations for expressions

To illustrate the dot operations for expressions, let us evaluate

$$v = e^{-a_1 t}\frac{\sin(b_1 t + c_1)}{t + c_1}$$

for the six equally spaced values of t in the interval $0 \le t \le 1$. We assume that $a_1 = 0.2$, $b_1 = 0.9$, and $c_1 = \pi/6$. Then, the script is

```
a1 = 0.2; b1 = 0.9; c1 = pi/6;
t = linspace(0, 1, 6);
v = exp(-a1*t).*sin(b1*t+c1)./(t+c1)
```

Upon executing this script, we obtain

```
v =
    0.9549   0.8590   0.7726   0.6900   0.6097   0.5316
```

Notice that since a_1, b_1, and c_1 are scalar quantities and only involve multiplication and addition, we do not have to use the dot operators.

To show another application of the dot operations, let us return to the `meshgrid` example where the two vectors $s = [s_1 \, s_2 \, s_3 \, s_4]$ and $t = [t_1 \, t_2 \, t_3]$ were used in the statement

$$[U, V] = \texttt{meshgrid}(s, t)$$

to produce the two (3×4) matrices

$$U = \begin{bmatrix} s_1 & s_2 & s_3 & s_4 \\ s_1 & s_2 & s_3 & s_4 \\ s_1 & s_2 & s_3 & s_4 \end{bmatrix} \quad \text{and} \quad V = \begin{bmatrix} t_1 & t_1 & t_1 & t_1 \\ t_2 & t_2 & t_2 & t_2 \\ t_3 & t_3 & t_3 & t_3 \end{bmatrix} \tag{2.3}$$

Suppose that we wish to multiply the corresponding elements of U and V. Then, the dot multiplication

$$Z = U.*V$$

results in numerical equivalent (recall Eq. 2.2a)

$$Z = \begin{bmatrix} s_1*t_1 & s_2*t_1 & s_3*t_1 & s_4*t_1 \\ s_1*t_2 & s_2*t_2 & s_3*t_2 & s_4*t_2 \\ s_1*t_3 & s_2*t_3 & s_3*t_3 & s_4*t_3 \end{bmatrix} \tag{2.4}$$

The elements of Z can be interpreted as corresponding to the product of all combinations of the elements of vectors s and t. A similar interpretation is obtained when addition, subtraction, division, and exponentiation are performed, since the multiplication symbol (*) can be replaced by the respective operator.

Example 2.3   Polar to Cartesian coordinates

We illustrate the use of meshgrid by mapping an array of polar coordinates to Cartesian coordinates through the relationships

$$x = r \cos \theta$$
$$y = r \sin \theta$$

as shown in Figure 2.2. We shall select three values of r in the range $0.5 \leq r \leq 1$ and four values of θ in the range $0 \leq \theta \leq \pi/2$. The script is

```
rr = linspace(0.5, 1, 3);
thet = linspace(0, pi/2, 4);
[r, theta] = meshgrid(rr, thet);
x = r.*cos(theta)
y = r.*sin(theta)
```

Upon execution, we find that

```
x =
    0.5000   0.7500   1.0000
    0.4330   0.6495   0.8660
    0.2500   0.3750   0.5000
    0.0000   0.0000   0.0000
y =
       0        0        0
    0.2500   0.3750   0.5000
    0.4330   0.6495   0.8660
    0.5000   0.7500   1.0000
```

As a quick check, we note that at $\theta = 0$, $y = 0$, which comprise the first row of the y array; the corresponding values of x are $x = 0.5, 0.75$, and 1, which are values shown in the first row of the x array. Another way to get these results is shown in Example 2.8.

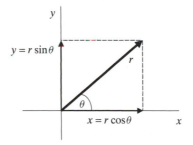

Figure 2.2   Transformation from polar to Cartesian coordinates.

We now introduce the summation function

```
sum
```

and the cumulative summation function

```
cumsum
```

which are often used in conjunction with dot operations.

Let us examine `sum` first. When $v = [v_1, v_2, \ldots, v_n]$, then

$$S = \text{sum}(v) \rightarrow \sum_{k=1}^{\text{length}(v)} v_k$$

where S is a scalar. When the argument is a matrix, the function sums the columns of the matrix and returns a row vector whose length is equal to the number of columns of the original matrix. Thus, if Z is a (3×4) matrix with elements z_{ij}, then

$$S = \text{sum}(Z) \rightarrow \left[\sum_{n=1}^{3} z_{n1} \quad \sum_{n=1}^{3} z_{n2} \quad \sum_{n=1}^{3} z_{n3} \quad \sum_{n=1}^{3} z_{n4} \right] \rightarrow (1 \times 4) \qquad (2.5)$$

is a three-element vector. To sum all the elements in an array, we use

$$S = \text{sum}(\text{sum}(Z)) \rightarrow \sum_{n=1}^{3} z_{n1} + \sum_{n=1}^{3} z_{n2} + \sum_{n=1}^{3} z_{n3} + \sum_{n=1}^{3} z_{n4} \rightarrow \sum_{i=1}^{4} \sum_{n=1}^{3} z_{ni} \rightarrow (1 \times 1)$$

Example 2.4   Summing a series

To illustrate the use of `sum`, consider the evaluation of the following equation:

$$z = \sum_{m=1}^{4} m^m$$

The script to evaluate this expression is

```
m = 1:4;
z = sum(m.^m)
```

which, when executed, gives

```
z =
   288
```

This can be written more compactly as

```
z = sum((1:4).^(1:4))
```

Example 2.5   Normal cumulative distribution function

An approximation to the normal cumulative probability distribution function, which estimates the probability P that $0 \leq X \leq x$ is given as[4]

$$P(x) = P(X \leq x) \cong 1 - \frac{1}{\sqrt{2\pi}}e^{-x^2/2}\sum_{m=1}^{5}b_m(1 + 0.2316419x)^{-m} \quad 0 \leq x \leq \infty$$

where $0.5 \leq P(x) \leq 1$ and

$b_1 = 0.319381530$
$b_2 = -0.356563782$
$b_3 = 1.781477937$
$b_4 = -1.821255978$
$b_5 = 1.330274429$

The region for $-\infty \leq x \leq 0$ is obtained from $1 - P(|x|)$, where $0 \leq 1 - P(|x|) \leq 0.5$.

The objective is to compute and plot the cumulative distribution for $-3 \leq x \leq 3$ every $\Delta x = 0.2$. From the problem statement, we find that the order of m is (1×5) and that of x is (1×16) for $0 \leq x \leq 3$. The size of the vectors and the subsequent matrices can be obtained from the workspace window discussed in Chapter 1. The first step is to convert the vector variables into matrices of the order (16×5) so that we will be able to perform dot operations and the summation. The conversion of the various vectors is done with meshgrid. However, in the sum function, we must take the transpose of the results from meshgrid, because the sum function sums a matrix on a column-by-column basis. In our case, we want to sum over five terms. Once we have the function for the region $0 \leq x \leq 3$, we can compute it for the region $-3 \leq x \leq 0$.

The script is

```
b = [0.319381530, −0.356563782, 1.781477937, ...
       −1.821255978, 1.330274429];                          % (1×5)
m = 1:length(b);                                            % (1×5)
x = 0:0.2:3;                                                % (1×16)
[mm, Xm] = meshgrid(m, (1./(1+0.231641*x)));               % (16×5)
bmx = meshgrid(b, x);                                       % (16×5)
Px = 1-exp(-0.5*x.^2).*sum((bmx.*(Xm.^mm))')/sqrt(pi*2);    % (1×16)
plot(x, Px, -fliplr(x), fliplr(1-Px) )
```

The plot function, which is discussed in Section 6.2, uses two pairs of coordinates for its arguments. The first pair gives the values of $P(x)$ from 0 to 3. The second pair plots $1 - P(x)$ from 0 to -3, but without actually having to compute the value of $P(x)$ at these negative values. We do this by flipping the data with the aid of fliplr. The expression $-$fliplr(x) is the same as creating a new vector $x = -3{:}0.2{:}0$. The expression fliplr(1-Px) reverses the order of the elements of the vector $1 - P(x)$ and creates a vector whose elements correspond to the negative x-values given by $-$fliplr(x). The execution of this script produces Figure 2.3.

---

[4]M. Abramowitz and I. A. Stegun, *Handbook of Mathematical Functions*, National Bureau of Standards, Applied Mathematics Series 55, U.S. Government Printing Office, Washingtom D.C., 1964, p. 932.

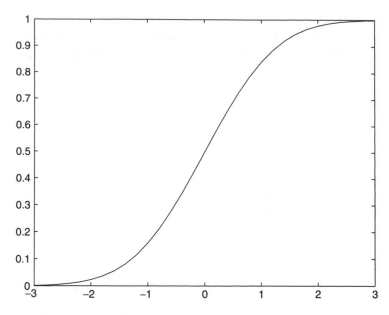

Figure 2.3   Normal cumulative probability distribution.

The cumsum function for a vector v composed of n elements v_j is another vector of length n whose elements are

$$y = \text{cumsum}(v) \rightarrow \left[\sum_{k=1}^{1} v_k \quad \sum_{k=1}^{2} v_k \quad \cdots \quad \sum_{k=1}^{n} v_k \right] \rightarrow (1 \times n)$$

On the other hand, if W is $(m \times n)$ matrix composed of elements w_{jk}, then cumsum(W) is the following matrix:

$$Y = \text{cumsum}(W) \rightarrow \begin{bmatrix} \sum_{k=1}^{1} w_{k1} & \sum_{k=1}^{1} w_{k2} & \cdots & \sum_{k=1}^{1} w_{kn} \\ \sum_{k=1}^{2} w_{k1} & \sum_{k=1}^{2} w_{k2} & & \\ \vdots & & \ddots & \\ \sum_{k=1}^{m} w_{k1} & & & \sum_{k=1}^{m} w_{kn} \end{bmatrix} \rightarrow (m \times n)$$

Example 2.6   Convergence of a series

We consider the series

$$S = \sum_{n=1}^{10} \frac{1}{n^2}$$

and explore its rate of convergence for its first 10 terms. The script is

```
S = cumsum(1./(1:10).^2)
```

which upon execution gives

S =
   1.0000 1.2500 1.3611 1.4236 1.4636 1.4914 1.5118 1.5274 1.5398
   1.5498

Each element of S is a partial sum of n terms of the series; that is, $S(1)$ is the first term, $S(2)$ is the sum of the first two terms, and so on.

Example 2.7   Evaluation of the hyperbolic secant

Let us evaluate the following series expression[5] for the hyperbolic secant for $N = 305$ and for five equally spaced values of x from $0 \le x \le 2$.

$$\text{sech } x = 4\pi \sum_{n=1,3,5}^{N \to \infty} \frac{n(-1)^{(n-1)/2}}{(n\pi)^2 + 4x^2}$$

We shall also compare the summed values to the exact values. To perform dot operations, we first have to convert two vectors, one for the summation index n and the other for the argument x, into matrices of the same order using meshgrid.
    The script is

```
nn = 1:2:305;                                      % (1×153)
xx = linspace(0, 2, 5);                            % (1×5)
[x, n] = meshgrid(xx, nn);                         % (153×5)
s = 4*pi*sum(n.*(−1).^((n−1)/2)./((pi*n).^2+4*x.^2));   % (1×5)
se = sech(xx);                                     % (1×5)
compare = [s' se']                                 % (5×2)
```

which upon execution displays in the command window

```
compare =
    1.0021   1.0000
    0.8889   0.8868
    0.6501   0.6481
    0.4272   0.4251
    0.2679   0.2658
```

where the right-hand column is the exact solution. We have selected the order of the arguments of meshgrid to produce matrices of order (153×5), because sum performs the summation on a column-by-column basis.

2.6 MATHEMATICAL OPERATIONS WITH MATRICES

We now define several fundamental matrix operations: addition, subtraction, multiplication, inversion, determinants, solutions of systems of equations, and roots (eigenvalues). These results are then used to obtain numerical solutions to classes of engineering problems.

---

[5]L. B. W. Jolley, *Summation of Series*, 2nd ed., Dover Publications, New York, 1961.

2.6.1 Addition and Subtraction

If we have two matrices A and B, each of the order $(m \times n)$, then

$$A \pm B = \begin{bmatrix} a_{11} \pm b_{11} & a_{12} \pm b_{12} & \cdots & a_{1n} \pm b_{1n} \\ a_{21} \pm b_{21} & a_{22} \pm b_{22} & & \\ \vdots & & \ddots & \\ a_{m1} \pm b_{m1} & & & a_{mn} \pm b_{mn} \end{bmatrix} \rightarrow (m \times n) \quad (2.6)$$

2.6.2 Multiplication

If we have an $(m \times k)$ matrix A and a $(k \times n)$ matrix B, then

$$C = AB = \begin{bmatrix} \sum_{j=1}^{k} a_{1j}b_{j1} & \sum_{j=1}^{k} a_{1j}b_{j2} & \cdots & \sum_{j=1}^{k} a_{1j}b_{jn} \\ \sum_{j=1}^{k} a_{2j}b_{j1} & \sum_{j=1}^{k} a_{2j}b_{j2} & & \vdots \\ \vdots & & \ddots & \\ \sum_{j=1}^{k} a_{mj}b_{j1} & \cdots & & \sum_{j=1}^{k} a_{mj}b_{jn} \end{bmatrix} \rightarrow (m \times n) \quad (2.7)$$

where C is of order $(m \times n)$. Notice that the product of two matrices is defined only when the adjacent integers of their respective orders are equal, or k in this case. In other words, $(m \times k)(k \times n) \rightarrow (m \times n)$, where the notation indicates that we have summed k terms as indicated in Eq. 2.7. The MATLAB expression for matrix multiplication is

    C = A*B

When $m = n$, it should be noted that in general, $AB \neq BA$. It can be shown that if $C = AB$, then its transpose is

$$C' = (AB)' = B'A'$$

If A is an identity matrix $(A = I)$ and $m = n$, then

$$C = IB = BI = B$$

For example, let us multiply the following two matrices and then show numerically that the transpose can be obtained either of the two ways given above:

$$A = \begin{bmatrix} 11 & 12 & 13 \\ 21 & 22 & 23 \end{bmatrix}$$

$$B = \begin{bmatrix} 11 & 12 \\ 21 & 22 \\ 31 & 32 \end{bmatrix}$$

The script is

```
A = [11, 12, 13; 21, 22, 23];
B = [11, 12; 21, 22; 31, 32];
C = A*B
Ctran1 = C'
Ctran2 = B'*A'
```

Upon execution, we obtain

C =
776	812
1406	1472

Ctran1 =
776	1406
812	1472

Ctran2 =
776	1406
812	1472

Let us examine the results of the matrix multiplication further and give one interpretation of the result. Consider the following series[6]

$$w(x, y) = \sum_{j=1}^{k} f_j(x)g_j(y)$$

Suppose that we are interested in the value of $w(x, y)$ over a range of values for x and y: $x = x_1, x_2, \ldots, x_m$ and $y = y_1, y_2, \ldots, y_n$. Then, one can consider

$$w(x_i, y_j) = \sum_{l=1}^{k} f_l(x_i)g_l(y_j) \quad i = 1, 2, \ldots, m \quad j = 1, 2, \ldots, n$$

as one element of a matrix W of order $(m \times n)$ as follows: Let F be a matrix of order $(m \times k)$

$$F = \begin{bmatrix} f_1(x_1) & f_2(x_1) & \cdots & f_k(x_1) \\ f_1(x_2) & f_2(x_2) & & \\ \vdots & & \ddots & \\ f_1(x_m) & \cdots & & f_k(x_m) \end{bmatrix} \rightarrow (m \times k)$$

and G be a matrix of order $(k \times n)$

$$G = \begin{bmatrix} g_1(y_1) & g_1(y_2) & \cdots & g_1(y_n) \\ g_2(y_1) & g_2(y_2) & & \\ \vdots & & \ddots & \\ g_k(y_1) & \cdots & & g_k(y_n) \end{bmatrix} \rightarrow (k \times n)$$

---

[6]This form of a series results from a family of solutions to differential equations with certain boundary conditions.

Then, from Eq. 2.7,

$$
W = FG = \begin{bmatrix}
\sum_{j=1}^{k} f_j(x_1)g_j(y_1) & \sum_{j=1}^{k} f_j(x_1)g_j(y_2) & \cdots & \sum_{j=1}^{k} f_j(x_1)g_j(y_n) \\
\sum_{j=1}^{k} f_j(x_2)g_j(y_1) & \sum_{k=1}^{k} f_j(x_2)g_j(y_2) & & \vdots \\
\vdots & & \ddots & \\
\sum_{j=1}^{k} f_j(x_m)g_j(y_1) & \cdots & & \sum_{j=1}^{k} f_j(x_m)g_j(y_n)
\end{bmatrix} \rightarrow (m \times n)
$$

$$(2.8)$$

In other words, matrix multiplication performs the summation of the series at each combination of values for x and y. As we shall see subsequently, this observation provides a very compact means of summing a series at each point in a grid that is defined by all combinations of the elements of the vectors x and y.

We now consider three special cases of this general matrix multiplication:

1. The product of a row and a column vector
2. The product of a column and a row vector
3. The product of a row vector and a matrix

These three cases provide one means by which we can take advantage of MATLAB's compact notation and matrix solution methods for a class of engineering problems.

Case 1—Product of a row and column vector

Let a be the row vector

$$a = [a_1 \, a_2 \dots a_k] \rightarrow (1 \times k)$$

which is of order $(1 \times k)$, and b be the column vector

$$b = [b_1 \, b_2 \dots b_k]' \rightarrow (k \times 1)$$

which is of order $(k \times 1)$. Then, the product $d = ab$ is the scalar

$$
d = ab = [a_1 \quad a_2 \quad \cdots \quad a_k] \begin{bmatrix} b_1 \\ b_2 \\ \vdots \\ b_k \end{bmatrix} = \left[\sum_{j=1}^{k} a_j b_j \right] = \sum_{j=1}^{k} a_j b_j \rightarrow (1 \times 1) \quad (2.9)
$$

since the product of the orders gives $(1 \times k)(k \times 1) \rightarrow (1 \times 1)$. This is called the dot product of two vectors. The MATLAB expression for matrix multiplication of the two vectors as defined above is either

d = a*b

or

d = dot(a, b)

Case 2—Product of a column and row vector

Let b be an $(m \times 1)$ column vector and a a $(1 \times n)$ row vector. Then, the product $H = ba$ is

$$H = ba = \begin{bmatrix} b_1 \\ b_2 \\ \vdots \\ b_m \end{bmatrix} \begin{bmatrix} a_1 & a_2 & \cdots & a_n \end{bmatrix} = \begin{bmatrix} b_1 a_1 & b_1 a_2 & \cdots & b_1 a_n \\ b_2 a_1 & b_2 a_2 & & \\ \vdots & & \ddots & \\ b_m a_1 & & \cdots & b_m a_n \end{bmatrix} \rightarrow (m \times n) \quad (2.10)$$

which is a matrix of order $(m \times n)$, since the product of their orders gives $(m \times 1)$ $(1 \times n) \rightarrow (m \times n)$. Thus, the elements of H, which are $h_{ij} = b_i a_j$, are the individual products of all the combinations of the elements of b and a.

Example 2.8   Polar to Cartesian coordinates revisited

Let us again examine the transformation from polar coordinates to Cartesian coordinates as shown in Figure 2.2; that is,

$$x = r \cos \theta$$
$$y = r \sin \theta$$

If we have a vector of radial values $r = [r_1 \, r_2 \ldots r_m]$ and a vector of angular values $\theta = [\theta_1 \, \theta_2 \ldots \theta_n]$, then the corresponding Cartesian coordinates are[7]

$$X = r'*\cos(\theta) = \begin{bmatrix} r_1 \\ r_2 \\ \vdots \\ r_m \end{bmatrix} \begin{bmatrix} \cos \theta_1 & \cos \theta_2 & \cdots & \cos \theta_n \end{bmatrix}$$

$$= \begin{bmatrix} r_1 \cos \theta_1 & r_1 \cos \theta_2 & \cdots & r_1 \cos \theta_n \\ r_2 \cos \theta_1 & r_2 \cos \theta_2 & & \\ \vdots & & \ddots & \\ r_m \cos \theta_1 & & \cdots & r_m \cos \theta_n \end{bmatrix} \quad (2.11a)$$

and

$$Y = r'*\sin(\theta) = \begin{bmatrix} r_1 \\ r_2 \\ \vdots \\ r_m \end{bmatrix} \begin{bmatrix} \sin \theta_1 & \sin \theta_2 & \cdots & \sin \theta_n \end{bmatrix}$$

$$= \begin{bmatrix} r_1 \sin \theta_1 & r_1 \sin \theta_2 & \cdots & r_1 \sin \theta_n \\ r_2 \sin \theta_1 & r_2 \sin \theta_2 & & \\ \vdots & & \ddots & \\ r_m \sin \theta_1 & & \cdots & r_m \sin \theta_n \end{bmatrix} \quad (2.11b)$$

Thus, we have mapped the polar coordinates into their Cartesian counterparts. This procedure is very useful in the plotting of results, as illustrated in Example 2.9.

---

[7]This conversion can also be performed with `pol2cart`; however, this function is restricted to the case when $m = n$.

Example 2.9   Mode shape of a circular membrane

Consider the following mode shape for a solid circular membrane clamped along its outer boundary $r = 1$:

$$z(r, \phi) = J_1(3.8316r)\cos(\phi)$$

where $J_1(x)$ is the Bessel function[8] of the first kind of order 1 and (r, ϕ) are the polar coordinates of any point on the membrane. The Bessel function is determined by the function

```
besselj(n, x)
```

where n is the order and x is its argument. The origin of the coordinate system is at the center of the membrane, which is at $r = 0$. The value 3.8316 is one of the natural frequency coefficients for the membrane. This mode shape can be plotted using the surface plotting function

```
mesh(x, y, z)
```

where (x, y) are the Cartesian coordinates of a point on the surface $z(x, y)$. The mesh function is discussed in Section 7.2. We will plot the surface over the range $0 \le r \le 1$ in increments of 0.05 and over the range $0 \le \theta \le 2\pi$ in increments of $\pi/20$. Using Eq. 2.11, the script is

```
r = [0:0.05:1]';                        % (21×1)
phi = 0:pi/20:2*pi;                     % (1×41)
x = r*cos(phi);                         % (21×41)
y = r*sin(phi);                         % (21×41)
z = besselj(1, 3.8316*r)*cos(phi);      % (21×41)
mesh(x, y, z)
```

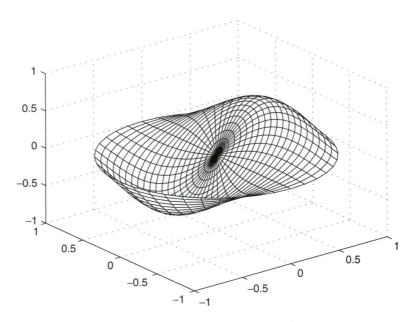

Figure 2.4   A mode shape of a clamped solid circular membrane.

[8]See, for example, F. B. Hildebrand, *Advanced Calculus for Applications*, Prentice Hall, Upper Saddle River, NJ, 1976.

The coordinate transformations are required because the surface as defined by the mesh function has to be plotted in the Cartesian coordinate system. It should also be realized that this technique works because the functions cos, sin, and besselj accept matrices for their arguments and return matrices of the same order. The execution of this script results in Figure 2.4.

Example 2.10   A solution to the Laplace equation

The solution of the Laplace equation in terms of the variable u and subject to the boundary conditions $u(0, \xi) = u(1, \xi) = u(\eta, \infty) = 0$ and $u(\eta, 0) = \eta(1 - \eta)$ is

$$u(\eta, \xi) = 4 \sum_{n=1}^{N \to \infty} \frac{1 - \cos(n\pi)}{(n\pi)^3} e^{-n\pi\xi} \sin(n\pi\eta)$$

where $0 \leq \eta \leq 1$ and $\xi \geq 0$. We shall plot the surface $u(\xi, \eta)$ using mesh $(\eta, \xi, u(\xi, \eta))$ for $N = 25$ and for increments $\Delta\eta = 0.025$ and $\Delta\xi = 0.05$ up to $\xi_{max} = 0.7$.

The approach to coding this series expression is to manipulate the multiplicative terms comprising the summation so that the summation is a natural outcome of array multiplication. That is, we would like to manipulate the expressions appearing in the summation so that Eqs. 2.8 and 2.10 apply. The manipulation is performed in several stages as follows: First, we assume that the sizes of the vectors are $n \to (1 \times N)$, $\eta \to (1 \times N_e)$, and $\xi \to (1 \times N_x)$. Next, we place these orders beneath the appropriate terms in the summation; that is,

$$\underbrace{\left(\frac{1 - \cos n\pi}{(n\pi)^3}\right)}_{(1 \times N)} \times \underbrace{(e^{-n\pi\xi})}_{(1 \times N)\,(1 \times N_x)} \times \underbrace{(\sin n\pi\eta)}_{(1 \times N)\,(1 \times N_e)}$$

We see that the sizes of the various vectors in the three expressions are not yet correctly sized so that we can perform array and dot multiplications. In the second and third terms, the inner products are incorrect; therefore, we first have to take the transpose of the $(1 \times N)$ arrays. When this is done, the second term will become $(1 \times N)'(1 \times N_x) \to (N \times N_x)$, and the third term becomes $(1 \times N)'(1 \times N_e) \to (N \times N_e)$. The first expression does not require any multiplication of vectors; it only requires dot exponentiation and division. However, if we make it the same size (order) as the second term, we can perform a dot multiplication with the second term, because MATLAB performs its operations on each level in the hierarchy from left to right. Thus, we want to convert the first term, which is a $(1 \times N)$ vector, into an array that is the size of the adjacent expression, which is $(N \times N_x)$. This is accomplished by using meshgrid. After this conversion, we can use dot multiplication to multiply the modified first and second expressions. The result, which we denote R_{nx}, is a matrix of order $(N \times N_x)$. Next, R_{nx} has to be multiplied with the third term, whose modified order is $(N \times N_e)$. Before this multiplication can be performed, however, we must take the transpose of R_{nx} so that the dimensions of the inner product are equal. This results in the matrix product $(R_{nx})'(N \times N_e) \to (N \times N_x)'(N \times N_e) \to (N_x \times N)(N \times N_e) \to (N_x \times N_e)$. Thus, we have summed over n for each combination of ξ and η, which is what we set out to do.

The script is

```
n = (1:25)*pi;                                    % (1×25)
eta = 0:0.025:1;                                  % (1×41)
xi = 0:0.05:0.7;                                  % (1×15)
[X1, temp1] = meshgrid(xi, (1-cos(n))./n.^3);     % (25×15)
temp2 = exp(-n'*xi);                              % (25×15)
```

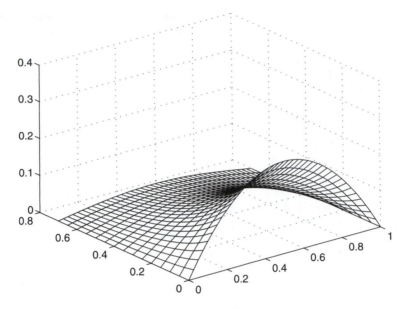

Figure 2.5   Display of a series solution to the Laplace equation.

```
Rnx = temp1.*temp2;                          % (25×15)
temp3 = sin(n'*eta);                         % (25×41)
u = 4*Rnx'*temp3;                            % (15×41)
mesh(eta, xi, u)
```

The result is shown in Figure 2.5. In the mesh command, MATLAB allows one to have the first two arguments, *eta* and *xi*, be vectors whose lengths agree with the respective values of the order of *u*. See the Help file for mesh.

Case 3—Product of a row vector and a matrix

Let B be an $(m \times n)$ matrix and a a $(1 \times m)$ row vector. Then, the product $g = aB$ is

$$g = aB = \begin{bmatrix} a_1 & a_2 & \cdots & a_m \end{bmatrix} \begin{bmatrix} b_{11} & b_{12} & \cdots & b_{1n} \\ b_{21} & b_{22} & & \\ \vdots & & & \ddots \\ b_{m1} & & \cdots & b_{mn} \end{bmatrix}$$

$$= \begin{bmatrix} \sum_{k=1}^{m} a_k b_{k1} & \sum_{k=1}^{m} a_k b_{k2} & \cdots & \sum_{k=1}^{m} a_k b_{kn} \end{bmatrix} \rightarrow (1 \times n) \qquad (2.12)$$

which is a row vector of order $(1 \times n)$, since the product of their orders gives $(1 \times m)(m \times n) \rightarrow (1 \times n)$.

This result can be interpreted as follows. Consider the series[9]

$$r(x) = \sum_{k=1}^{m} p_k h_k(x) \qquad (2.13)$$

---

[9]Series of this form result from the solution of differential equations with certain boundary conditions and from Fourier series expansions of periodic functions.

Suppose that we are interested in the value of $r(x)$ over a range of values $x_1, x_2, \ldots, x_n$. Then, one can consider

$$r(x_i) = \sum_{k=1}^{m} p_k h_k(x_i) \quad i = 1, 2, \ldots, n$$

one element of a vector r of order $(1 \times n)$ as follows: Let p be a vector of order $(1 \times m)$ with elements p_k and V be the $(m \times n)$ matrix:

$$V = \begin{bmatrix} h_1(x_1) & h_1(x_2) & \cdots & h_1(x_n) \\ h_2(x_1) & h_2(x_2) & & \\ \vdots & & \ddots & \\ h_m(x_1) & & & h_m(x_n) \end{bmatrix} \rightarrow (m \times n)$$

Then, $r = pV$ gives

$$r = pV = \begin{bmatrix} \sum_{k=1}^{m} p_k h_k(x_1) & \sum_{k=1}^{m} p_k h_k(x_2) & \cdots & \sum_{k=1}^{m} p_k h_k(x_n) \end{bmatrix} \rightarrow (1 \times n)$$

Example 2.11   Summation of a Fourier series

The Fourier series representation of a rectangular pulse of duration d and period T is given by[10]

$$f(\tau) = \frac{d}{T} \left[1 + 2 \sum_{k=1}^{K \to \infty} \frac{\sin(k\pi d/T)}{(k\pi d/T)} \cos(2\pi k\tau) \right]$$

where $\tau = t/T$. We see that this equation is of the form given by Eq. 2.14. Let us sum 150 terms of $f(\tau)(K = 150)$ and plot it from $-1/2 < \tau < 1/2$ when $d/T = 0.25$. To do this, we use $\texttt{plot(x, y)}$, where $x = \tau$ and $y = f(\tau)$. (See Section 6.2 for a discussion of $\texttt{plot}$.)

Upon comparing the series expression for $f(\tau)$ with that given in Eq. 2.14, we find that

$$r(x_i) \rightarrow f(\tau_i)$$
$$p_k \rightarrow \frac{\sin(k\pi d/T)}{(k\pi d/T)}$$
$$h_k(x_i) \rightarrow h_k(\tau_i) \rightarrow \cos(2\pi k\tau_i)$$

If the order of k is $(1 \times K)$ and that of τ is $(1 \times N_\tau)$, then the order p_k is $(1 \times K)$. We see that as written, the vector product of $k\tau \rightarrow (1 \times K)(1 \times N_\tau)$ cannot be performed, because the dimensions of the inner product do not agree. To obtain a valid multiplication, we first take the transpose of k, which results in $k'\tau \rightarrow (1 \times K)'(1 \times N_\tau) \rightarrow (K \times N_\tau)$. Then, the matrix product $ph \rightarrow (1 \times K)(K \times N_\tau) \rightarrow (1 \times N_\tau)$, with the summation being taken over all k, where $k = 1, \ldots, K$.

The script is

```
k = 1:150;                          % (1×150)
tau = linspace(-0.5, 0.5, 100);     % (1×100)
sk = sin(pi*k/4)./(pi*k/4);         % (1×150)
cntau = cos(2*pi*k'*tau);           % (150×100)
f = 0.25*(1+2*sk*cntau);            % (1×150)(150×100) → (1×100)
plot(tau, f)
```

The execution of this script produces Figure 2.6.

---

[10]See, for example, H. P. Hsu, *Applied Fourier Analysis*, Harcourt Brace Jovanovich, San Diego, CA, 1984.

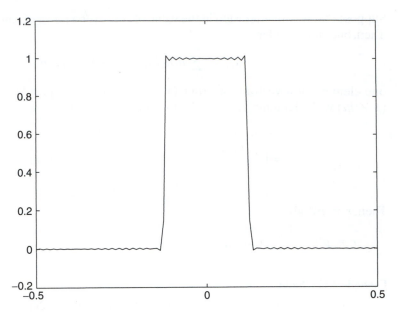

Figure 2.6   Summation of 150 terms of a Fourier series representation of a periodic pulse.

2.6.3 Determinants

A determinant of an array A of order $(n \times n)$ is represented symbolically as

$$|A| = \begin{vmatrix} a_{11} & a_{12} & \cdots & a_{1n} \\ a_{21} & a_{22} & & \vdots \\ \vdots & & \cdots & \\ a_{n1} & \cdots & & a_{nn} \end{vmatrix}$$

For $n = 2$,

$$|A| = a_{11}a_{22} - a_{12}a_{21}$$

For $n = 3$,

$$|A| = a_{11}a_{22}a_{33} + a_{12}a_{23}a_{31} + a_{13}a_{21}a_{32} - a_{13}a_{22}a_{31} - a_{11}a_{23}a_{32} - a_{12}a_{21}a_{33}$$

The MATLAB expression for the determinant is

```
det(a)
```

For example, if A is defined as

$$A = \begin{bmatrix} 1 & 3 \\ 4 & 2 \end{bmatrix}$$

then the determinant of A is obtained from

```
A = [1, 3; 4, 2];
d = det(A)
```

which upon execution gives

d =
   -10

A class of problems, called the eigenvalue problems, results in a determinant of the form

$$|A - \lambda B| = 0$$

where A and B are $(n \times n)$ matrices and λ_j, where $j = 1, 2, , \ldots, n$ are the roots (called eigenvalues) of this equation. See Chapter 9 for several applications of this equation in the area of vibrations. The solution of this polynomial equation is obtained from the eig function, which has several forms, one of which is

lambda = eig(A, B)

Example 2.12   Eigenvalues of a spring–mass system

We shall determine the eigenvalues of a three-degree-of-freedom spring–mass system whose characteristic equation is

$$|K - \omega^2 M| = 0$$

where the stiffness matrix K is given by

$$K = \begin{bmatrix} 50 & -30 & 0 \\ -30 & 70 & -40 \\ 0 & -40 & 50 \end{bmatrix}$$

the mass matrix is given by

$$M = \begin{bmatrix} 3 & 0 & 0 \\ 0 & 1.4 & 0 \\ 0 & 0 & 5 \end{bmatrix}$$

and the eigenvalue $\lambda = \omega^2$ is related to the natural frequency of the system by $\omega_j = \sqrt{\lambda_j}$, where $j = 1, 2, 3$.

The natural frequencies are obtained from the following script:

```
K = [50, -30, 0; -30, 70, -40; 0, -40, 50];
M = diag([3, 1.4, 5]);
w = sqrt(eig(K, M))
```

which upon execution gives

w =
   1.6734
   3.7772
   7.7201

Example 2.13   Transformation of a polynomial

A polynomial of the form

$$ax^2 + by^2 + cz^2 + 2dxy + 2exz + 2gyz$$

where a, b, c, d, e, and g are real numbers, can be transformed into the real diagonal form

$$r_1 x'^2 + r_2 y'^2 + r_3 z'^2$$

where x', y', and z' is another coordinate system whose origin is also at $(0, 0, 0)$, and $r_1 \geq r_2 \geq r_3$ are the roots of

$$|A - rI| = 0$$

The matrix I is the identity matrix, and A is the real symmetric matrix

$$A = \begin{bmatrix} a & d & e \\ d & b & g \\ e & g & c \end{bmatrix}$$

Consider the polynomial

$$4x^2 + 3y^2 - z^2 - 12xy + 4exz - 8gyz$$

Thus,

$$A = \begin{bmatrix} 4 & -6 & 2 \\ -6 & 3 & -4 \\ 2 & -4 & -1 \end{bmatrix}$$

To determine the roots r_j, we use the following script:

```
r = eig([4, -6, 2;-6, 3, -4; 2, -4, -1], eye(3))
```

which upon execution gives

```
r =
  -4.0000
  -1.0000
  11.0000
```

The roots from `eig` do not come out any particular order. To place them in the desired order, we use `sort`. However, `sort` arranges the values in ascending order (most negative to most positive). Therefore, we use either of the following expressions, which will work for any combination of positive and negative real values, to obtain the values in descending order:

Form 1

```
r = eig([4, -6, 2; -6, 3, -4; 2, -4, -1], eye(3));
r = −sort(-r)
```

which upon execution gives

```
r =
  11.0000
  -1.0000
  -4.0000
```

Form 2

```
r = eig([4, -6, 2; -6, 3, -4; 2, -4, -1], eye(3));
r = flipud(sort(r))
```

which upon execution also gives the above order. If *r* were a row vector, then we would replace flipud with fliplr.

We could also have written the first form more compactly as

```
r = -sort(−eig([4, -6, 2; -6, 3, -4; 2, -4, -1]))
```

The real diagonal form, therefore, is

$$11x'^2 - y'^2 - 4z'^2$$

2.6.4 Matrix Inverse

The inverse of a square matrix A is a matrix such that

$$A^{-1}A = AA^{-1} = I$$

provided that A is not singular—that is, its determinant is not equal to zero ($|A| \neq 0$). The quantity I is the identity matrix. The superscript "-1" denotes the inverse. The expression for obtaining the inverse of matrix A is either

inv(A)

or

A^−1

It is important to note that $1/A \neq A^{\wedge}(-1)$; $1/A$ will cause the system to respond with an error message. The inverse can also be obtained using the backslash operator, which is discussed in Section 2.6.5.

Example 2.14   Inverse of a matrix

Consider the (3×3) matrix M created by the magic function. Its inverse is obtained from the script

```
invM = inv(magic(3))
```

Upon executing this script, we obtain

```
invM =
    0.1472  -0.1444   0.0639
   -0.0611   0.0222   0.1056
   -0.0194   0.1889  -0.1028
```

We can verify that the product of a square matrix and its inverse is the identity matrix by modifying the above script as follows:

```
invM = inv(magic(3));
IdentMat = invM*magic(3)
```

Its execution gives

IdentMat =
    1.0000   0 -0.0000
         0   1.0000   0
         0   0.0000   1.0000

Now, consider the matrix

$$C = \begin{bmatrix} 1 & 2 & 3 \\ 6 & 9 & 13 \\ 6 & 12 & 18 \end{bmatrix}$$

The script to determine the inverse of C is

C = [1, 2, 3; 6, 9, 13; 6, 12, 18];
Iv = inv(C)

The execution of this script gives

Warning: Matrix is close to singular or badly scaled.
        Results may be inaccurate. RCOND = 2.176908e-018.
Iv =
  1.0e+015 *
    0.0000 -0.2502   1.5012
   -0.0000   1.2510 -7.5060
         0 -0.7506   4.5036

which contains an error message and an inverse with a column of zeros. The number and operator in the second line, $1.0e + 015\,*$, indicates that each number that follows is to be multiplied by 10^{15}. The quantity RCOND is the condition number of the matrix; a well-conditioned matrix has a condition number close to 1 and an ill-conditioned matrix a value close to zero. If det had been used, we would have found that $|C| = 0$ and, therefore, that the matrix does not have an inverse.
    Another way to determine if the matrix has an inverse is to use

rank

which provides an estimate of the number of linearly independent rows or columns of a full matrix. Thus, for an $(n \times n)$ matrix, the number of linearly independent rows or columns is n minus its rank. In this case, rank(C) brings back a 2, indicating that $3 - 2 = 1$ row or column is linearly proportional to another one. In this case, we see that row 3 is six times that of row 1.

2.6.5 Solution of a System of Equations

Consider the following system of n equations and n unknowns x_k, where $k = 1, 2, \ldots, n$:

$$a_{11}x_1 + a_{12}x_2 + \cdots + a_{1n}x_n = b_1$$
$$a_{21}x_1 + a_{22}x_2 + \cdots + a_{2n}x_n = b_2$$
$$\vdots$$
$$a_{n1}x_1 + a_{n2}x_2 + \cdots + a_{nn}x_n = b_n$$

We can rewrite this system of equations in matrix notation as follows:

$$Ax = b$$

where A is the $(n \times n)$ matrix

$$A = \begin{bmatrix} a_{11} & a_{12} & \cdots & a_{1n} \\ a_{21} & a_{22} & & \vdots \\ \vdots & & \ddots & \\ a_{n1} & \cdots & & a_{nn} \end{bmatrix} \rightarrow (n \times n)$$

and x and b are, respectively, the $(n \times 1)$ column vectors

$$x = \begin{bmatrix} x_1 \\ x_2 \\ \vdots \\ x_n \end{bmatrix} \rightarrow (n \times 1) \quad \text{and} \quad b = \begin{bmatrix} b_1 \\ b_2 \\ \vdots \\ b_n \end{bmatrix} \rightarrow (n \times 1)$$

The symbolic solution is obtained by premultiplying both sides of the matrix equation by A^{-1}. Thus,

$$A^{-1}Ax = A^{-1}b$$
$$x = A^{-1}b$$

since $A^{-1}A = I$, the identity matrix, and $Ix = x$. The preferred expression for solving this system of equations is[11]

    x = A\b

where the backslash operator indicates matrix division and is referred to by MAT-LAB as left matrix divide. Left division uses a procedure that is more numerically stable compared to the methods used for either of the following alternative notations:

    x = A^−1*b

or

    x = inv(A)*b

These latter two alternatives also execute considerably slower than when the backslash operator is used.

Example 2.15   Solution of a system of equations

Consider the following system of equations:

$$8x_1 + x_2 + 6x_3 = 7.5$$
$$3x_1 + 5x_2 + 7x_3 = 4$$
$$4x_1 + 9x_2 + 2x_3 = 12$$

---

[11]The notation $A\backslash b$ can be applied even when A is not a square matrix, whereas $\text{inv}(A)$ is only applicable when A is square. That is, if A is an $(m \times n)$ matrix, x an $(n \times 1)$ vector, and b an $(m \times 1)$ vector, then if $Ax = b$, left division $A\backslash b$ finds $x = cb$, where $c = (A'A)^{-1}A'$ is the pseudo-inverse of A.

which in matrix notation is

$$\begin{bmatrix} 8 & 1 & 6 \\ 3 & 5 & 7 \\ 4 & 9 & 2 \end{bmatrix} \begin{bmatrix} x_1 \\ x_2 \\ x_3 \end{bmatrix} = \begin{bmatrix} 7.5 \\ 4 \\ 12 \end{bmatrix}$$

The solution is obtained with the following script:

```
A = [8, 1, 6; 3, 5, 7; 4, 9, 2];
b = [7.5, 4, 12]';
x = A\b
```

which upon execution gives

```
x =
   1.2931
   0.8972
  -0.6236
```

This script could also have been written compactly as

```
x = [8, 1, 6; 3, 5, 7; 4, 9, 2]\[7.5, 4, 12]'
```

Since $b = Ax$, we can verify that the above solution is correct by modifying the above script as follows:

```
A = [8, 1, 6; 3, 5, 7; 4, 9, 2];
b = [7.5, 4, 12]';
x = A\b;
z = A*x
```

Upon execution, we find that

```
z =
    7.5000
    4.0000
   12.0000
```

Example 2.16 Static deflection of a clamped square plate

In the determination of the solution to the static deflection of a square plate clamped on all four of its edges and subjected to a uniform loading over its surface, one must first obtain the constants E_m from the truncation of the following infinite set of equations:[12]

$$a_i E_i + \sum_{m=1,3,\ldots} b_{im} E_m = c_i \quad i = 1, 3, 5, \ldots$$

---

[12]S. Timoshenko and S. Woinowsky-Krieger, *Theory of Plates and Shells*, McGraw-Hill, New York, 1959, pp. 197–202.

where

$$a_i = \frac{1}{i}\left(\tanh \alpha_i + \frac{\alpha_i}{\cosh^2 \alpha_i}\right)$$

$$b_{im} = 8i\left(\pi m^3\left(1 + \frac{i^2}{m^2}\right)^2\right)^{-1}$$

$$c_i = \frac{4}{\pi^3 i^4}\left(\frac{\alpha_i}{\cosh^2 \alpha_i} - \tanh \alpha_i\right)$$

and $\alpha_i = i\pi/2$. If we take only the first four terms of this system of equations, then we have the following set of equations in matrix notation:

$$\begin{bmatrix} a_1 + b_{11} & b_{13} & b_{15} & b_{17} \\ b_{31} & a_3 + b_{33} & b_{35} & b_{37} \\ b_{51} & b_{53} & a_5 + b_{55} & b_{57} \\ b_{71} & b_{73} & b_{75} & a_7 + b_{77} \end{bmatrix} \begin{bmatrix} E_1 \\ E_3 \\ E_5 \\ E_7 \end{bmatrix} = \begin{bmatrix} c_1 \\ c_3 \\ c_5 \\ c_7 \end{bmatrix}$$

We see that the coefficients b_{im} are a function of the indices i and m, which are each vectors of length 4. Thus, we convert these vectors into two (4×4) matrices using meshgrid so that we can use dot operations.

The solution of these four equations is obtained with the following script:

```
m = 1:2:7;  i = m;                                 % (1×4)
alp = m*pi/2;                                       % (1×4)
ai = (tanh(alp)+alp./cosh(alp).^2)./i;             % (1×4)
ci = 4.*(alp./(cosh(alp).^2)-tanh(alp))./((pi^3)*i.^4); % (1×4)
[ii, mm] = meshgrid(i, m);                          % (4×4)
bim = (8/pi)*ii./(((1+(ii.^2)./(mm.^2)).^2).*mm.^3); % (4×4)
ee = (diag(ai)+bim)\ci'
```

The execution of the script yields

```
ee =
  -0.0480
   0.0049
   0.0023
   0.0011
```

Thus, $E_1 = ee(1, 1) = -0.0480$, $E_3 = ee(2, 1) = 0.0049$, $E_5 = ee(3, 1) = 0.0023$, and $E_7 = ee(4,1) = 0.0011$.

2.7 SUMMARY OF FUNCTIONS INTRODUCED

A summary of the functions introduced in the chapter is presented in Table 2.1. See also Table 1.7 for a summary of the special symbols used in this chapter: colon, backslash, apostrophe, semicolon, period (dot), parentheses, brackets, and comma.

TABLE 2.1   MATLAB Functions Introduced in Chapter 2

MATLAB function	Description
besselj	Bessel function of the first kind
cumsum	Cumulative sum of an array
det	Determinant of a square matrix
diag	Diagonal of a square matrix; create a diagonal matrix
dot	Dot product of two vectors
eig	Eigenvalues and eigenvectors of a special matrix equations
end	Last index in an array (see also Table 4.2)
eye	Create the identity matrix
find	Find indices and values of an array satisfying a logical expression
fliplr	Flip elements of an array from left to right
flipud	Flip elements of an array from bottom to top
inv	Inverse of a square matrix
length	Length of a vector
linspace	Create equally spaced elements of a vector
logspace	Create equally spaced elements of a vector on a $\log_{10}$ scale
magic	Create a square matrix whose sum of each row and column is equal
max	Determine the maximum value in an array
mesh	Create wire-frame geometric surfaces
meshgrid	Transform two different vectors into arrays of the same size
min	Determine the minimum value in an array
ones	Create an array whose elements equal 1
plot	Plot curves in a plane using linear axes
rank	Estimates number of linearly independent rows or columns of a matrix
repmat	Replicate arrays
size	Order (size) of an array
sort	Sort elements of an array in ascending order
sum	Sum elements of an array
zeros	Create an array whose elements equal zero

EXERCISES

Section 2.3

2.1 Create two vectors, one whose elements are $2n - 1$ and the other whose elements are $2n + 1$, where $n = 0, 1, \ldots, 7$. Call the former a and the latter b.

  a. What is the sum of a and b?

  b. What is the difference of a and b?

  c. What are the product of $a'b$ and the value of its determinant?

  d. What is the product ab'?

2.2 Given the vector $x = [17\ -3\ -47\ 5\ 29\ -37\ 51\ -7\ 19]$, create a script that rearranges them into the following vector: $y = [-3\ -7\ -37\ -47\ 51\ 29\ 19\ 17\ 5]$. The script should be written to work on a vector of arbitrary length. Place the value 0 (for the general vector) with the negative quantities; that is, when a 0 is an element of the vector, it will be the first element of y.

2.3 Given the vector $y = [0, -0.2, 0.4, -0.6, 0.8, -1.0, -1.2, -1.4, 1.6]$. If $z = \sin(y)$, then:

a. Determine the minimum and maximum of only the negative values of z.

b. Determine the square root of only the positive values of z.

2.4 a. Create a vector of eight values that are equally spaced on a logarithmic scale. The first value of the vector is 6, and the last value is 106.

b. Display the value of the fifth element of the vector created in a.

c. Create a new vector whose elements are the first, third, fifth, and seventh elements of the vector created in a.

Section 2.4

2.5 Let $z = $ magic(5).

a. Perform the following operations to z in the order given:

i. Divide column 2 by $\sqrt{3}$.

ii. Add the elements of the elements of the third row to the elements in the fifth row (the third row remains unchanged).

iii. Multiply the elements of the first column by the corresponding elements of the fourth column, and place the result in the first column.

iv. Set the diagonal elements to 2.

b. If the result obtained in a is denoted q, then display the diagonal of qq'. [Answer: $[486\ 104189\ 7300\ 44522\ 111024]'$.]

c. Display the square of each element of q.

d. Display the maximum and minimum values of the elements in c.

2.6 Let $w = $ magic(2) and w' be the transpose of w.

a. Using repmat, create the following (4 × 4) matrix:

$$\begin{bmatrix} w & w \\ w & w \end{bmatrix}$$

b. Using repmat, create the following (6 × 2) matrix:

$$\begin{bmatrix} w \\ w \\ w \end{bmatrix}$$

c. Using `repmat` and the column augmentation procedure, create the following (6×4) matrix:

$$\begin{bmatrix} w & w' \\ w & w' \\ w & w' \end{bmatrix}$$

d. Repeat a, b, and c without using `repmat`—that is, using only column and row augmentation procedures.

2.7 Let $x = $ `magic(3)`.

    a. Create a new matrix in which each row of x has been moved up one row and the first row becomes the last row.

    b. Create a new matrix in which each column of x has been moved to the right and the last column becomes the first column.

Section 2.5

2.8 The displacement of the slider of the slider crank mechanism shown in Figure 2.7 is given by

$$s = a \cos(\varphi) + \sqrt{b^2 - (a \sin(\varphi) - e)^2}$$

Plot the displacement s as a function of the angle φ (in degrees) when $a = 1, b = 1.5$, $e = 0.3$, and $0 \le \varphi \le 360°$—that is, use `plot(`φ, s`)`. Reminder: The argument of the trigonometric functions must be in radians.

2.9 The percentage of the total power P in a periodic series of rectangular-shaped pulses as a function of the number of terms N_H in its series expansion is

$$P = 100 P_o / P_T \%$$

where P_T is the total nondimensional power in the signal

$$P_o = 1 + 2 \sum_{n=1}^{N_H} \frac{\sin^2(n\pi\tau_o/T)}{(n\pi\tau_o/T)^2}$$

and τ_o/T is the ratio of the pulse duration to its period. If we let $\tau_o/T = 1/\sqrt{19}$, then $P_T \cong 4.3589$. For this case, plot the percentage total power as a function of N_H for $2 \le N_H \le 25$; that is, use `plot(`N_H, P_o`)`.

2.10 Consider the following product:[13]

$$S_N = \prod_{n=1}^{N} \left(1 - \frac{x^2}{n^2 - a^2} \right)$$

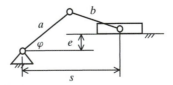

Figure 2.7   Slider crank mechanism.

---

[13]L. B. W. Jolley, *ibid.*

where, when $N \to \infty$,

$$S_\infty = \frac{a}{\sin \pi a \sqrt{a^2 + x^2}} \sin\left(\pi \sqrt{a^2 + x^2}\right)$$

The percentage error between S_N and S_∞ is defined as

$$e_N = 100 \frac{S_N - S_\infty}{S_\infty}\%$$

If x varies from 1 to 5 in increments of 0.5 and $a = \sqrt{2.8}$, what is the percentage error at these nine values of x when $N = 100$. Use the function prod to obtain S_N. [Answer: $e_{100} = [1.0001 \ 2.2643 \ 4.0610 \ 6.4176 \ 9.3707 \ 12.9670 \ 17.2642 \ 22.3330 \ 28.2588]$.]

2.11 One means of obtaining an estimate of a parameter δ appearing in the Weibull probability density function (see Section 14.2.2) is obtained from

$$\delta = \left[\frac{1}{n} \sum_{i=1}^{n} x_i^\beta\right]^{1/\beta}$$

where x_i are obtained from a random sample of size n and β is a known parameter. If $x = [72, 82, 97, 103, 113, 117, 126, 127, 127, 139, 154, 159, 199, 207]$ and $\beta = 3.644$, determine the value of δ.

2.12 The transformation from spherical to Cartesian coordinates is given by

$$x = b \sin \phi \cos \theta$$
$$y = b \sin \phi \sin \theta$$
$$z = b \cos \phi$$

Take 10 equally spaced values of ϕ in the range $0 \le \phi \le 90°$ and 24 equally spaced values of θ in the range $0 \le \theta \le 360°$, and plot the hemisphere using mesh(x, y, z) when $b = 2$.

2.13 Evaluate the following series for $N = 25$ and for five equally spaced values of x from $0.1 \le x \le 1$. Compare these values with exact values $(N \to \infty)$.

$$\sum_{N \to -\infty}^{N \to \infty} \frac{1}{n^4 + x^4} = \frac{2\pi^4}{y^3} \frac{\sinh y + \sin y}{\cosh y - \cos y}, \quad y = \pi x \sqrt{2}$$

2.14 The series representation for the Bessel function of the first kind of order n is given by

$$J_n(x) = \sum_{k=0}^{K \to \infty} \frac{(-1)^k (x/2)^{2k+n}}{k! \Gamma(k + 1 + n)}$$

For $K = 25$, determine a vector of values of $J_n(x)$ for $n = 2$ and for six equally spaced values of x in the range $1 \le x \le 6$. Both the gamma function Γ and the factorial are obtained with gamma. Compare your answers with those obtained from MATLAB's built-in function besselj.

2.15 Show numerically that the following series[14] sums to the value indicated when $n = 7$:

$$\sum_{k=1}^{2n-1} \cos(k\pi/n) = -1$$

---

[14]L. B. W. Jolley, *ibid.*, pp. 86–87.

Section 2.6.2

2.16 A matrix is said to be an orthogonal matrix if

$$X'X = I$$

and, therefore, $(X'X)^{-1} = I$. Show that each of the following matrices is orthogonal:

$$w = \frac{1}{2}\begin{bmatrix} -1 & -1 \\ 1 & -1 \\ -1 & 1 \\ 1 & 1 \end{bmatrix} \qquad q = \frac{1}{2}\begin{bmatrix} 1 & -1 & -1 & 1 \\ 1 & 1 & -1 & -1 \\ 1 & -1 & 1 & -1 \\ 1 & 1 & 1 & 1 \end{bmatrix}$$

2.17 Consider the planar three-degree-of-freedom linkages shown in Figure 2.8. The location and orientation of point O_3 with respect to the fixed coordinate system O_0 is

$$T_3 = A_1 A_2 A_3$$

where

$$A_j = \begin{bmatrix} \cos\theta_j & -\sin\theta_j & 0 & a_j\cos\theta_j \\ \sin\theta_j & \cos\theta_j & 0 & a_j\sin\theta_j \\ 0 & 0 & 1 & 0 \\ 0 & 0 & 0 & 1 \end{bmatrix} \qquad j = 1, 2, 3$$

and

$$T_3 = \begin{bmatrix} u_x & v_x & 0 & q_x \\ u_y & v_y & 0 & q_y \\ 0 & 0 & 1 & 0 \\ 0 & 0 & 0 & 1 \end{bmatrix}$$

The components q_x and q_y are the (x, y)-coordinates of the point O_3 with respect to the coordinate system centered at O_0. If $\theta_j = 30°$, $j = 1, 2, 3$, and $a_1 = 1$, $a_2 = 2$, and $a_3 = 3$, what is the location of point O_3 with respect to the coordinate system centered at O_0 and the orientation of the (x_3, y_3) axes system. [Answer: $q_x = 1.8660$, $q_y = 5.2321$, x_3 is parallel to y_0, and y_3 is parallel to x_0 but in the opposite direction.]

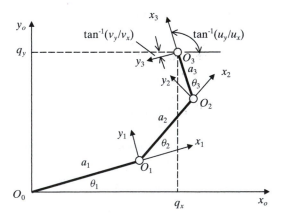

Figure 2.8 Planar three-degree-of-freedom linkages.

2.18 In multiple linear regression analysis, the following matrix quantity has some utility (see Exercise 14.13):

$$H = X(X'X)^{-1}X'$$

If

$$X = \begin{bmatrix} 17 & 31 & 5 \\ 6 & 5 & 4 \\ 19 & 28 & 9 \\ 12 & 11 & 10 \end{bmatrix}$$

determine the diagonal of H. [Answer: diagonal H = [0.7294 0.9041 0.4477 0.9188]'.]

2.19 Plot the Fourier series[15] given below for 200 values of τ over its indicated range using $\text{plot}(\tau, f(\tau))$. Unless otherwise stated, use 200 terms to sum each series. Obtain the solutions by using the vector multiplication procedures given for Case 3 in Section 2.6.2.

a. Square wave:

$$f(\tau) = \frac{4}{\pi} \sum_{n=1,3,5\ldots} \frac{1}{n}\sin(2n\pi\tau) \quad -\frac{1}{2} \le \tau \le \frac{1}{2}$$

b. Sawtooth:

$$f(\tau) = \frac{1}{2} + \frac{1}{\pi}\sum_{n=1}\frac{1}{n}\sin(2n\pi\tau) \quad -1 \le \tau \le 1$$

c. Sawtooth:

$$f(\tau) = \frac{1}{2} - \frac{1}{\pi}\sum_{n=1}\frac{1}{n}\sin(2n\pi\tau) \quad -1 \le \tau \le 1$$

d. Triangular wave:

$$f(\tau) = \frac{\pi}{2} - \frac{4}{\pi}\sum_{n=1}\frac{1}{(2n-1)^2}\cos((2n-1)\pi\tau) \quad -1 \le \tau \le 1$$

e. Rectified sine wave:

$$f(\tau) = \frac{2}{\pi} + \frac{4}{\pi}\sum_{n=1}\frac{1}{1-4n^2}\cos(2n\pi\tau) \quad -1 \le \tau \le 1$$

f. Half sine wave:

$$f(\tau) = \frac{1}{\pi} + \frac{1}{2}\sin \pi\tau - \frac{2}{\pi}\sum_{n=2,4,6,\ldots}^{106}\frac{\cos n\pi\tau}{n^2-1} \quad -2 \le \tau \le 2$$

g. Exponential:

$$f(\tau) = \frac{e^{2\pi}-1}{\pi}\left[\frac{1}{2} + \sum_{n=1}^{250}\frac{1}{1+n^2}(\cos n\tau - n\sin n\tau)\right] \quad 0 \le \tau \le 4\pi$$

Use 350 values of τ to display the results.

---

[15]H. P. Hsu, *ibid.*

h. Trapezoidal:

$$f(\tau) = \frac{4}{\alpha^2} \sum_{n=1,3,5,\dots}^{105} \frac{\sin n\pi\alpha}{(\pi n)^2} \sin n\pi\tau \quad -2 \leq \tau \leq 2$$

Let $\alpha = 0.25$.

2.20 Consider the following two series:[16]

$$S_{1N} = \sum_{n=1}^{N} \frac{\cos(n\theta)}{n^2 + a^2} \quad 0 < \theta < \pi$$

$$S_{2N} = \sum_{n=1}^{N} \frac{n\sin(n\theta)}{n^2 + a^2} \quad 0 < \theta < 2\pi$$

where, when $N \to \infty$,

$$S_{1\infty} = \frac{\pi\cosh[a(\pi - \theta)]}{2a\sinh \pi a} - \frac{1}{2a^2} \quad 0 < \theta < \pi$$

$$S_{2\infty} = \frac{\pi\sinh[a(\pi - \theta)]}{2\sinh \pi a} \quad 0 < \theta < 2\pi$$

The percentage error between S_{jN} and $S_{j\infty}$ is defined as

$$e_{jN} = 100\frac{S_{jN} - S_{j\infty}}{S_{j\infty}}\% \quad j = 1, 2$$

If θ varies from $10°$ to $80°$ every $10°$ and $a = \sqrt{3}$, determine the percentage error for the two series at the eight values of θ when $N = 25$. Obtain the solutions by using the vector multiplication procedures given for Case 3 in Section 2.6.2. [Answer: $e_1 = [-1.2435\ 0.8565\ 0.8728\ -1.9417\ -0.9579\ -8.1206\ 0.7239\ 1.1661]$ and $e_2 = [8.0538\ 10.4192\ -8.9135\ -5.4994\ 12.9734\ -0.5090\ -17.2259\ 11.2961]$.]

2.21 The nondimensional steady-state temperature distribution in a rectangular plate that is subjected to a constant temperature along the edge $\eta = 1$ is given by[17]

$$T(\eta, \xi) = \frac{4}{\pi} \sum_{n=1,3,5}^{\infty} \frac{\sinh(n\pi\alpha\eta)}{n\sinh(n\pi\alpha)}\sin(n\pi\xi)$$

where $\eta = x/d$; $\xi = y/b$; d and b are the lengths of the plate in the x and y directions, respectively; $\alpha = d/b$; $0 \leq \eta \leq 1$; and $0 \leq \xi \leq 1$. Display the temperature distribution throughout the plate when $\alpha = 2$ using mesh(ξ, η, T) Let $\Delta\eta = \Delta\xi = 1/14$. Obtain the solutions by using the vector multiplication procedures given for Case 2 in Section 2.6.2.

2.22 The displacement of a wave propagating in a string subject to an initial velocity of zero and an initial displacement of

$$u(\eta, 0) = \frac{\eta}{a} \quad 0 \leq \eta \leq a$$

$$u(\eta, 0) = \frac{1 - \eta}{1 - a} \quad a \leq \eta \leq 1$$

[16]L. B. W. Jolley, *ibid.*:
[17]H. P. Hsu, *ibid.*

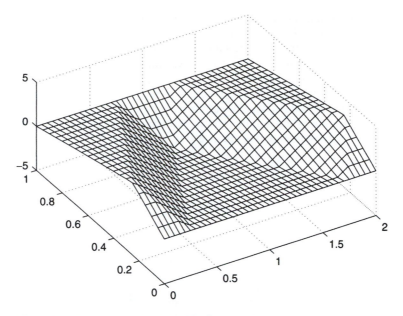

Figure 2.9 Propagation of an initial displacement in a string.

is given by

$$u(\eta, \tau) = \frac{2}{a\pi(1 - a)} \sum_{n=1}^{N \to \infty} \frac{\sin n\pi a}{n^2} \sin(n\pi\eta)\cos(n\pi\tau)$$

Using mesh(τ, η, u), display $u(\eta, \tau)$ over the range $0 \le \tau \le 2$ when $N = 50$ and $a = 0.25$. Let $\Delta\eta = 0.05$ and $\Delta\tau = 0.05$. Obtain the solutions by using the vector multiplication procedures given for Case 2 in Section 2.6.2. The result is shown in Figure 2.9, which was obtained after using the rotate icon in the figure window.

Section 2.6.3

2.23 Given the two matrices

$$A = \begin{bmatrix} 1 & 3 & 4 \\ 31 & 67 & 9 \\ 7 & 5 & 9 \end{bmatrix} \quad \text{and} \quad B = \begin{bmatrix} 11 & 34 & 6 \\ 7 & 13 & 8 \\ 43 & 10 & 53 \end{bmatrix}$$

Show numerically that $|AB| = |A||B|$.

Section 2.6.5

2.24 Given the following system of equations:

$$16s + 32u + 33p + 13w = 91$$
$$5s + 11u + 10p + 8w = 16$$
$$9s + 7u + 6p + 12w = 5$$
$$34s + 14u + 15p + w = 43$$

determine the values of s, u, p, and w and the values of the determinant and the inverse of the coefficients of s, u, p, and w. [Answer: $s = -0.1258, u = -8.7133, p = 11.2875$ and $w = -0.0500$. Determinant $= 7680$.]

2.25 Consider two long cylinders of two different materials where one cylinder fits just inside the other cylinder. The inner radius of the inner cylinder is a, and its outer radius is b. The inner radius of the outer cylinder is also b, and its outer radius is c. The Young's modulus and Poisson ratio of the inner cylinder are E_1 and v_1, respectively, and those of the outer cylinder are E_2 and v_2, respectively. The radial stress σ_{rr}, hoop stress $\sigma_{\theta\theta}$, and radial displacement u_r are given by, respectively,

$$\sigma_{rri}(r) = \frac{A_i}{r^2} + B_i$$

$$\sigma_{\theta\theta i}(r) = \frac{-A_i}{r^2} + B_i \quad i = 1, 2 \tag{a}$$

$$u_{ri}(r) = \frac{-(1 + v_i)}{rE_i} A_i + \frac{(1 - v_i)}{E_i} r B_i$$

where $i = 1$ refers to the inner cylinder and $i = 2$ to the outer.

If the outer surface of the outer cylinder is subjected to a compressive radial displacement U_o and the inner surface of the inner cylinder has no radial stress, then the following four boundary conditions can be used to determine A_i and B_i, where $i = 1, 2$:

$$\sigma_{rr1}(a) = 0$$
$$\sigma_{rr1}(b) = \sigma_{rr2}(b)$$
$$u_{r1}(b) = u_{r2}(b) \tag{b}$$
$$u_{r2}(c) = -U_o$$

Upon substituting Eq. a into b, the following system of equations in matrix form is obtained:

$$\begin{bmatrix} 1 & a^2 & 0 & 0 \\ 1 & b^2 & -1 & -b^2 \\ -(1 + v_1) & (1 - v_1)b^2 & (1 + v_2)E_1/E_2 & -(1 - v_2)b^2E_1/E_2 \\ 0 & 0 & -(1 + v_2) & (1 - v_2)c^2 \end{bmatrix} \begin{Bmatrix} A_1 \\ B_1 \\ A_2 \\ B_2 \end{Bmatrix} = \begin{Bmatrix} 0 \\ 0 \\ 0 \\ -U_oE_2c \end{Bmatrix}$$

Determine the hoop stress in the inner and outer cylinders at $r = b$ when $v_1 = v_2 = 0.4$, $E_1 = 3 \times 10^5$ psi, $E_2 = 3.5 \times 10^4$ psi, $U_o = 0.01$ in., $a = 0.192$ in., $b = 0.25$ in., and $c = 0.312$ in. [Answer: $\sigma_{\theta\theta 1}(b) = -9571.8$ psi, and $\sigma_{\theta\theta 2}(b) = -1989.3$ psi.]

3

Data Input/Output

Edward B. Magrab

The means of displaying annotated numerical results in the MATLAB command window and storing and retrieving data from files are presented.

3.1 STRINGS AND ANNOTATED OUTPUT

3.1.1 Creating Strings

Strings are collections of any combination of letters, numbers, and special characters. They are typically used for displaying information to the command window, for annotating data displayed to the command window, and for annotating graphs. They are created, stored, and manipulated in arrays and are defined in a manner similar to vectors and matrices. A string differs from an array of numerical values in that each character in the string occupies one element in the array, and the string is defined by enclosing all its characters between a pair of single quotes ('...').

Consider the following examples: Let *s* be the string 'testing123'. The MATLAB expression to define this string is the vector

    s = 'testing123'

or

    s = ['testing123']

where each character within the pair of single quotes is a location in the vector *s*. Thus, the length of the string is 10. To retrieve specific characters in the string *s*, we can use expressions like

    s(7) → g
    s(3:6) → stin

Strings can also be manipulated in a manner similar to numerical values. For example, consider the script

    s = 'testing123'
    fs = fliplr(s)

Its execution gives

    fs =
    321gnitset

Strings can also be concatenated (added to form a longer string) in a manner similar to numerical values. Thus,

    sc = ['testing123', 'testing123']

produces the (1×20) string

    sc =
    testing123testing123

whereas the script

    sc = ['testing123'; 'testing123']

creates the (2×10) matrix

    scs =
    testing123
    testing123

Thus,

scs(1,:) → testing123
scs(2,:) → testing123

Notice that both rows of *scs* have the same number of characters (columns).
One can also find the starting locations of strings within strings using

findstr(string1, string2)

which searches the longer of the two strings for occurrences of the shorter of the two strings. Let us find the occurrences of '123' in the concatenated string shown in the script.

sc = ['testing123', 'testing123']
Loc = findstr(sc, '123')

Upon execution, we obtain

sc =
testing123testing123
Loc =
   8   18

Thus, the first occurrence of the '123' starts at location 8, and the second occurrence starts at location 18. If the string does not exist, then *Loc* would equal a null vector—that is, [].
    If we place a string in each row of a matrix, we have a convenient way in which to access string expressions. The requirement is that each row must contain the same number of characters. This requirement can be met by employing blanks to pad the rest of the string when the individual string expressions are of unequal length. Thus, if we have the expression

lab = ['first ';'last ';'middle']

then

lab(1,:) → first*b*
lab(2,:) → last*bb*
lab(3,:) → middle

and *b* indicates a blank space. MATLAB provides a way to do this padding with the function

char

Thus, the above expression can be replaced by the easier-to-use expression

lab = char('first','last','middle')
ord = size(lab)

which, when executed, displays

```
lab =
first
last
middle
ord =
   3   6
```

where each string expression is a row in the matrix *lab* and *lab* is a (3 × 6) array. The trailing blanks are not visible in the display to the command window. The trailing blanks can be removed with

```
deblank
```

3.1.2 Converting Numerical Values to Strings and Displaying Them

To convert a numerical value to a string, we use

```
z = num2str(num)
```

where *z* is a string and *num* is either a number, an array of numbers, or an expression resulting in a number or an array of numbers. This function is most often used to place annotated numerical output in the MATLAB command window or on a figure.

A typical construct is to concatenate the converted numerical value with some identifying text. Thus, if *num* is, say, the weight in kilograms and is to be identified as such, then to display it to the MATLAB command window, we use

```
disp
```

as follows:

```
num = 12.567;
disp(['Product weight = ' num2str(num) ' kg'])
```

At least one blank space on each side of `num2str` is required. When executed, this script displays

```
Product weight = 12.567 kg
```

in the command window. Internally, this string is a vector of length 26. Notice that blank spaces are acceptable string characters and are preserved as such.

Let *num* be a vector of weights. Then, the script that displays this vector of values is

```
num = [12.567, 3.458, 9.111];
disp(['Product weight = ' num2str(num) ' kg'])
```

Upon execution, we obtain

```
Product weight = 12.567   3.458   9.111 kg
```

However, to create annotation that accompanies each value of *num*, we use the repmat function as follows:

```
num = [12.567, 3.458, 9.111];
n = length(num);
disp([repmat('Product weight = ', n, 1) num2str(num') repmat(' kg', n, 1)])
```

which upon execution displays

```
Product weight = 12.567 kg
Product weight = 3.458 kg
Product weight = 9.111 kg
```

If one were to display *num* without annotation, then the script

```
num = [12.567, 3.458, 9.111];
disp(num)
```

displays in the MATLAB command window

```
12.5670   3.4580   9.1110
```

whereas

```
num = [12.567, 3.458, 9.111];
disp(num')
```

displays

```
12.5670
3.4580
9.1110
```

MATLAB also permits one to specify the number of digits of the number to be converted to a string as follows:

```
num2str(a,N)
```

where *a* is the number being converted to a string and *N* is the number of digits. If the number of digits specified is less than the number of digits to the left of the decimal place, then MATLAB converts the number to its exponential representation with the number of significant digits equal to *N*.

Consider the following examples in which $a = 1000\pi = 3141.592653589$. Then, the various values of *N* will display the digits shown below:

```
num2str(a,1) → 3e+003
num2str(a,3) → 3.14e+003
num2str(a,4) → 3142
num2str(a,5) → 3141.5
num2str(a,8) → 3141.5927
```

Notice that the decimal point (.) does not count as a digit.

An alternative function that can be used to display formatted data to the MATLAB command window is `fprintf`, which has a slight advantage over `disp` in that it can better control the format of the numerical values. The syntax of the `fprintf` function to print to the command window is

`fprintf(1,'%....', variables)`

where the first argument, the '1', indicates that the output is to be to the command window and everything inside the quotes is the format specification pertaining to *variables*. When *variables* is a vector or a matrix, the format specification is cycled through on a column-by-column basis. The order of the format specifications corresponds to the order of the variables. The % symbol precedes each specific format specification. A commonly used format specification is of the form

x.yf

The quantity f stands for fixed-point notation and is one of several format types. (See the *Help* file for `fprintf` for other formats.) The x is an integer that specifies the total number of digits of the number and y is the number of these digits that will appear to the right of the decimal point. We illustrate the use of `fprintf` by displaying the vector

num = [12, -14, 3.458, 0.11167];

several different ways.

To display this vector on one line using `fprintf`, we have the script

num = [12, -14, 3.458, 0.11167];
fprintf(1,'%5.3f ', num)

which results in

12.000   -14.000   3.458   0.112

Notice that *num*(1) and *num*(2) had three zeros added to its representation, whereas *num*(4) was rounded to three digits after the decimal point. The numbers have two blank spaces between them, which was obtained by leaving two blank spaces between the f and the apostrophe in the `fprintf` argument. If we want to display these values as a column of four numbers, we use the delimiter \n as follows:

num = [12 -14 3.458 0.11167];
fprintf(1,'%5.3f\n', num)

which, when executed, results in

2.000
-14.000
3.458
0.112

To reproduce the four numbers with the same digital precision as given, we have to include a format specification for each quantity. Thus, the script is

```
num = [12, -14, 3.458, 0.11167];
fprintf(1,'%2.0f %2.0f %5.3f %5.5f ', num)
```

where we have placed two blank spaces between each letter *f* and the symbol % so that the numbers are separated by two spaces when displayed. The execution of this script gives

```
12 -14 3.458 0.11167
```

To annotate each number, we use the following procedure[1]:

```
num = [12, -14, 3.458, 0.11167];
fprintf(1,'weight = %2.0f kg pressure = %2.0f kPa time = %5.3f s length =
           %5.5f m', num)
```

Upon execution, this script results in

```
weight = 12 kg pressure = -14 kPa time = 3.458 s length = 0.11167 m
```

To display the values in a column, the previous script is modified as[2]

```
num = [12, -14, 3.458, 0.11167];
fprintf(1,'weight = %2.0f kg\npressure = %2.0f kPa\ntime = %5.3f s\nlength =
           %5.5f m', num)
```

The execution of this script results in

```
weight = 12 kg
pressure = -14 kPa
time = 3.458 s
length = 0.11167 m
```

If we are willing to have each number appear with the same format, then we can simplify the format specification and still generate annotated output, albeit in a somewhat less informative manner, as follows:

```
num = [12, -14, 3.458, 0.11167];
nn = 1:length(num);
fprintf(1,'x(%1.0f) = %7.5f\n',[nn; num])
```

---

[1]The `fprintf` statement cannot be broken up as shown. It has been presented in two lines because of page width restrictions.
[2]The `fprintf` statement cannot be broken up as shown. It has been presented in two lines because of page width restrictions.

Upon execution, we obtain

```
x(1) = 12.00000
x(2) = -14.00000
x(3) = 3.45800
x(4) = 0.11167
```

The `num2str` function can also employ the format specifications of `fprintf` by replacing the second argument N, the number of digits, in `num2str` with % followed by a formant specification. For example, suppose that we wanted to display a very small number as 0 instead of in exponent form. If this number were $x = 0.00045$, then the script would be

```
x = 0.00045;
disp(['x = ' num2str(x,'%2.1f')])
```

which displays

```
x = 0.0
```

whereas

```
x = 0.00045;
disp(['x = ' num2str(x, 1)])
```

displays

```
x = 0.0004
```

3.2 ENTERING DATA WITH input

Arrays of data can be solicited by a script or function and then entered by the user employing `input`. In addition, `input` can display to the MATLAB command window a message instructing the user about what is to be entered. However, the actual form of the data depends on whether the data is a scalar, vector, or matrix and whether these quantities are numbers or strings. We now illustrate these various cases. Other methods of data entry are discussed in Sections 3.3, 3.5, and 5.2.

3.2.1 Entering a Scalar

To input a single numerical quantity, we illustrate the use of `input` as follows:

```
InputData = input('Enter the temperature in degrees C: ');
```

Upon execution, we display in the command window

```
Enter the temperature in degrees C: 121.7
```

where the number 121.7 was entered by the user. The semicolon at the end of the expression in the script suppresses the echoing of the value entered. The variable *InputData* has the value of 121.7.

One can also modify user-entered values in the same expression. For example, one can convert degrees to radians as follows:

InputData = input('Enter the starting angle in degrees: ')*pi/180;

When executed, the following is displayed to the command window

Enter the starting angle in degrees: 45

where the value 45 was entered by the user. However, the value of *InputData* is 0.7854 (= 45π/180).

Now, consider the conversion of temperature from °C to °F. The script is

InputData = 1.8*input('Enter the temperature in degrees C: ')+32;

which upon execution displays

Enter the temperature in degrees C: 100

where the value 100 was entered by the user. However, the value of *InputData* is 212.

A message may be printed on several lines by including within the message's quotation delimiters a \n at the appropriate places. Thus,

InputData = input('Enter the starting angle\nin degrees: ')*pi/180;

when executed, displays

Enter the starting angle
in degrees:

Notice that in the input string, there is no space between the '\n' and the 'in'. This was done so that the two lines, when displayed, were left justified.

3.2.2 Entering a String

To input a single string quantity, we append an 's' at the end of the `input` function. Thus,

InputData = input('Enter file name, including its extension: ','s');

which displays in the MATLAB command window

Enter file name, including its extension: DataSet3.txt

where the string *DataSet3.txt* was entered by the user. Notice that no single quotation marks are required by the user. The value of *InputData* is the string *DataSet3.txt*, which is a vector of length 12.

3.2.3 Entering a Vector

To input a vector of numerical values, we use

   InputData = input('Enter four temperatures in degrees C: ');

which upon execution displays in the command window

   Enter four temperatures in degrees C: [120, 141, 169, 201]

where the vector of numbers [120, 141, 169, 201] was entered by the user. The square brackets are required. If a column vector is required, then the user's response would be either [120, 141, 169, 201]' or [120; 141; 169; 201].

3.2.4 Entering a Matrix

To input a matrix of numerical values, we use the script

   InputData = input('Enter three temperatures in degrees C\nfor levels 1 and 2: ');

which displays in the MATLAB command window

   Enter the three temperatures in degrees C
   for levels 1 and 2: [67, 35, 91;44, 51, 103]

where the array [67, 35, 91;44, 51, 103] was entered by the user. The variable *InputData* is a (2×3) array.

3.3 INPUT/OUTPUT DATA FILES

As shown in the previous sections, one method of entering data for execution by a script is to use `input`. The second means is to define data within a script using the methods discussed in Sections 2.3 and 2.4. These data creation statements can also appear in a function, which is discussed in Chapter 5. In fact, one can define a function such that it only contains data; see Section 5.2 for an example of this.

Another way to enter data is to place the data in an ASCII[3] text file and use

```
load
```

The `load` function reads data on a row-by-row basis, with each row being separated by an enter and each data value by one or more blanks or by a comma. The number of columns of data in each row must be the same. These requirements are analogous

---

[3]ASCII stands for American Standard Code for Information Interchange. It has come to signify plain text—that is, text with no formatting and is used when one wants to easily exchange data and text between different computer programs. Usually, specifying a text file means an ASCII text file.

to those that must be followed when creating matrices. Here, the carriage return is used instead of the semicolon. When creating a row vector, one enters the data without using the carriage return. When creating a column vector, each data value is followed by a carriage return.

Let us illustrate two ways to use `load`. For specificity, we shall assume that the data reside in the ASCII text file *DataSection33.txt* in the form

```
11 12 13
21 22 23
31 32 33
41 42 43
```

A useful feature of `load` is that the file name without the extension (the suffix ".txt") becomes the name of the variable whose vector or matrix elements are the data as they appear in the file. Thus, in the script, the variable named *DataSection33* is a (4×3) matrix of numbers, and it is used in the script as if a variable named *DataSection33* had been placed on the left side of an equal sign.

The load function can be used in any of the following three representations: as either

```
load DataSection33.txt
```

or

```
load 'DataSection33.txt'
```

or

```
load('DataSection33.txt')
```

The last form is, perhaps, the best one to use. It is assumed that the path to this file has been specified. If not, one uses the procedures described in Section 1.3.3. These three forms are used when the filename is known at the creation of a script and will not change. For an example, let us square each element of the matrix previously given. The script is

```
load ('DataSection33.txt')
y = DataSection33.^2
```

which upon execution results in

```
y =
      121    144    169
      441    484    529
      961   1024   1089
     1681   1764   1849
```

On the other hand, if one wanted to operate on data in different files, each having a different file name, then we would have to employ a different technique.

Here, the user will enter the file name when requested to do so by the script or function, and as before, the script will square the data residing in the file whose name is specified when the script is executed. The script is

```
FileName1 = input('Enter file name containing data (including suffix): ','s');
load(FileName1);
m = findstr(FileName1,'.');
data1 = eval(FileName1(1:m-1));
y = data1.^2
```

As discussed previously, the `findstr` function locates the position of the first occurrence in the string of characters within the apostrophes (' ')—in this case, the period (.)—and brings back its value. We have used it here to limit the string of characters comprising *FileName1* to those up to, but not including, the period; hence, the string length of interest is $m - 1$. Thus, we have stripped the suffix and the period from the file's name. Since the stripped version of *FileName1* is still unknown to the remaining expressions in the script, it must be converted to a numerical quantity. This is done by the `eval` function, which evaluates the string quantity appearing in its argument.

Upon execution of this script, we are first asked to provide the file name. We will use the file *DataSection33.txt*. Thus,

Enter file name containing data (including suffix): DataSection33.txt

is displayed in the command window and *DataSection33.txt* is the user's response. After hitting the *Enter* key, the program displays

```
y =
      121    144    169
      441    484    529
      961   1024   1089
     1681   1764   1849
```

which is what we obtained previously.

If one wants to save numerical values resulting from the execution of a script or function to a file, we use

```
save
```

Suppose that we would like to save the square of each value in *DataSection33.txt* as ASCII text. Then, the script is

```
load('DataSection33.txt')
y = DataSection33.^2;
save('SavedDataSection33.txt', 'y', '-ascii')
```

Upon execution, the script creates a text file whose contents are

```
1.2100000e+002 1.4400000e+002 1.6900000e+002
4.4100000e+002 4.8400000e+002 5.2900000e+002
9.6100000e+002 1.0240000e+003 1.0890000e+003
1.6810000e+003 1.7640000e+003 1.8490000e+003
```

When just the file name is given, MATLAB places the file in the current directory. To place the file in a specific directory, the entire path name must be given. For example, consider the script

```
load ('DataSection33.txt')
y = DataSection33.^2;
save('c:\Matlab mfiles\Matlab results\SavedDataSection33.txt', 'y', '-ascii')
```

Notice that we have to employ the form that uses the quotes around the entire path name and file name. This is necessary because of the appearance of the colon and the blank spaces in the path name.

If we want to save additional quantities in this file, we would append their respective variable names to the save statement as follows. Suppose that the above script is also to compute the square root of the values in *DataSection33.txt*. Then,

```
load('DataSection33.txt')
y = DataSection33.^2;
z = sqrt(DataSection33);
save('c:\Matlab mfiles\Matlab results\SavedDataSection331.txt', 'y', 'z', '-ascii')
```

Execution of this script creates the file *SavedDataSection331.txt*, with the contents

```
1.2100000e+002 1.4400000e+002 1.6900000e+002
4.4100000e+002 4.8400000e+002 5.2900000e+002
9.6100000e+002 1.0240000e+003 1.0890000e+003
1.6810000e+003 1.7640000e+003 1.8490000e+003
3.3166248e+000 3.4641016e+000 3.6055513e+000
4.5825757e+000 4.6904158e+000 4.7958315e+000
5.5677644e+000 5.6568542e+000 5.7445626e+000
6.4031242e+000 6.4807407e+000 6.5574385e+000
```

The data in the first four rows correspond to *y* and those in the last four rows to *z*.

3.4 CELL ARRAYS

Cell arrays are a special class of arrays whose elements consist of cells that also contain arrays. They provide an hierarchical way of storing dissimilar kinds of data. Any cell in a cell array can be accessed through matrix indexing, as is done with standard vectors and matrices. Cell notation differs from standard matrix notation in that open braces '{' and closed braces '}' are used instead of open and closed brackets. We shall now illustrate the creation and accessing of cell arrays.

Let us create four different arrays of data as shown in the following script:

```
A = ones(3,2)
B = magic(3)
C = char('Pressure', 'Temperature', 'Displacement')
D = [6+7j, 15];
```

Upon executing this script, we obtain

```
A =
    1  1
    1  1
    1  1
B =
    8  1  6
    3  5  7
    4  9  2
C =
Pressure
Temperature
Displacement
D =
   6.0000 + 7.0000i 15.0000
```

We now add to this script the cell assignment statement to create a (2×2) cell array, which is analogous to that used for standard arrays, except that we use the braces as delimiters. Thus,

```
A = ones(3,2);
B = magic(3);
C = char('Pressure', 'Temperature', 'Displacement');
D = [6+7j, 15];
Cel = {A, B; C, D}
```

After executing this script, we obtain

```
Cel =
    [3x2 double]    [3x3 double]
    [3x12 char ]    [1x2 double]
```

Notice that we do not get what is specifically in each cell, only what the size of the data arrays in each cell are and their type. To display the contents of *Cel* to the command window, we use

```
celldisp
```

Then, the script is modified as follows:

```
A = ones(3,2);
B = magic(3);
C = char('Pressure', 'Temperature', 'Displacement');
D = [6+7j, 15];
Cel = {A, B; C, D};
celldisp(Cel)
```

which upon execution gives

```
Cel{1,1} =
   1   1
   1   1
   1   1
Cel{2,1} =
Pressure
Temperature
Displacement
Cel{1,2} =
   8   1   6
   3   5   7
   4   9   2
Cel{2,2} =
   6.0000 + 7.0000i 15.0000
```

To access each cell individually, we use the index notation used for standard array variables, except that we use the braces instead of parentheses. Thus, to access the cell in the first row and second column of *Cel*, we modify our script as follows:

```
A = ones(3,2);
B = magic(3);
C = char('Pressure', 'Temperature', 'Displacement');
D = [6+7j, 15];
Cel = {A, B; C, D};
Cell_1_2 = Cel{1,2}
```

Upon execution, the following results are displayed to the command window:

```
Cell_1_2 =
   8   1   6
   3   5   7
   4   9   2
```

3.5 INPUT MICROSOFT EXCEL™ FILES

Data files created in Microsoft Excel can be read into MATLAB with the function

```
[X, Y] = xlsread('Filename')
```

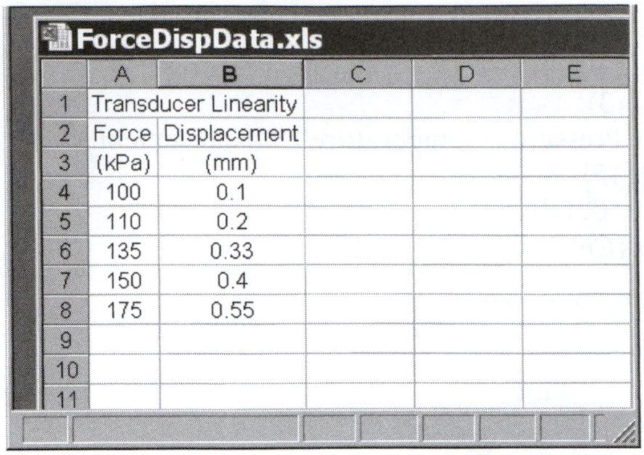
ForceDispData.xls

	A	B	C	D	E
1	Transducer Linearity				
2	Force	Displacement			
3	(kPa)	(mm)			
4	100	0.1			
5	110	0.2			
6	135	0.33			
7	150	0.4			
8	175	0.55			
9					
10					
11					

Figure 3.1 Data recorded in Microsoft Excel.

where X will be an array containing the columns and rows of data and Y will be a cell array containing any text headers that accompany the data. The file name must contain the suffix '.xls'.

To illustrate the use of this function, consider the data generated in Excel as shown in Figure 3.1. These data are saved in a file named *ForceDispData.xls*. The script to read this file is

```
[X, Y] = xlsread('ForceDispData.xls')
```

The path has been set before this statement, so that the system knows where the file resides. Upon execution, the following data are displayed to the command window:

```
X =
 100.0000 0.1000
 110.0000 0.2000
 135.0000 0.3300
 150.0000 0.4000
 175.0000 0.5500
Y =
    [1x20 char]           []
    'Force'      'Displacement'
    '(kPa)'      '(mm)'
```

The size of the cell array Y is $\{3 \times 2\}$. Since there was only a text statement in the first row of column one (Excel cell A1) and none in the second column (Excel cell B1), MATLAB does not consider this text to be part of the column headers. MATLAB collects it, but MATLAB does not display it. However, it is accessible by typing $Y\{1, 1\}$ in the command window. When this is done, we find that the system responds with

```
ans =
Transducer Linearity
```

TABLE 3.1 MATLAB Functions Introduced in Chapter 3

MATLAB function	Description
char	Places each string into a row of a matrix, and, if necessary, pads each row with blanks
celldisp	Displays to the command window the contents of a cell array
deblank	Removes trailing blanks in a string expression
eval	Executes a string containing a MATLAB expression
disp	Displays text or an array to the command window
findstr	Finds a string in another string
fprintf	Writes formatted data to a file or to the command window
input	Requests user input from the command window
load	Loads variables from a file
num2str	Converts a number or an array of numbers to a string
save	Saves specified variables to a file
xlsread	Reads a Microsoft Excel file

3.6 SUMMARY OF FUNCTIONS INTRODUCED

The functions introduced in this chapter and their descriptions are presented in Table 3.1.

EXERCISES

3.1 The Fibonacci numbers can be generated from the relation

$$F_n = \frac{1}{\sqrt{5}}\left[\left(\frac{1 + \sqrt{5}}{2}\right)^n - \left(\frac{1 - \sqrt{5}}{2}\right)^n\right] \qquad n = 0, 1, 2, \ldots$$

Generate the first 16 numbers using both fprintf and disp, and present them to the MATLAB command window as follows:

```
F 0 =  0
F 1 =  1
F 2 =  1
F 3 =  2
⋮
F15 =  610
```

3.2 Generate a script that converts from the English unit of feet to the metric unit of meters. The display of the result to the command window should look like

```
Enter the value of length in feet: 11.4
11.4 ft = 3.4747 m
```

where the value 11.4 was entered by the user.

3.3 There are 43,560 square feet per acre. Generate a script that converts the number of acres to the number of square meters. The display of the result to the command window should look like

> Enter the number of acres: 2.4
> 2.4 acres = 9712.4554 sq. m

where 2.4 was entered by the user.

3.4 Generate a script that converts a positive integer less than 2^{52} (4.5036×10^{15}) to a binary number. The MATLAB function that performs the conversion is dec2bin, whose argument is the decimal number and whose output is a string of the binary equivalent. The display to the command window should look like

> Enter a positive integer < 4.5x10^15: 37
> The binary representation of 37 is 100101

where 37 was entered by the user.

3.5 Generate a script that displays the magnitude and phase angle in degrees of a complex number. The display to the command window should look like

> The magnitude and phase of -7+13i is
>   Magnitude = 14.7648   Phase angle = 118.3008 degrees

where $-7 + 13i$ was entered by the user.

4

Program Flow Control

Edward B. Magrab

The various means of controlling the order in which a program's expressions get evaluated are presented, along with a representative set of relational and logical operators that are used to accomplish this control.

4.1 INTRODUCTION—THE LOGICAL OPERATOR

The control of the order in which a program's expressions get evaluated are achieved by four program flow control structures: while, if, for, and switch. Each time one of these statements appears, it must be followed at a later place within the program by an end statement. All expressions that appear between the control structure statement and the end statement are executed until all requirements of the structure are satisfied. Each of these control structure statements can appear as often as necessary, either within themselves or within other control structures. When this occurs, they are called nested structures.

TABLE 4.1 Several Relational and Logical Operators

Conditional	Mathematical symbol	MATLAB symbol
Relational operators		
Equal	$=$	==
Not equal	$\neq$	~=
Less than	$<$	<
Greater than	$>$	>
Less than or equal	$\leq$	<=
Greater than or equal	$\geq$	>=
Logical operators		
And	AND	&
Or	OR	|
Not	NOT	~

Control structures frequently rely on relational and logical operators to determine whether a condition has been met. When a condition has been met, the structure directs the program to a specific part of the program to execute one or more expressions. Several of MATLAB's relational and logical operators are given in Table 4.1.

When using control structures, the statements following each control structure definition up to, but not including, the end statement should be indented. This greatly improves the readability of the script or function. When the structures are nested, the entire nested structure is indented, with the nested structure's indentation being preserved. When using MATLAB's editor/debugger, this is done automatically.

One can use the relational and logical operators appearing in Table 4.1 to create a logical function whose output is 1 if the relational and logical operations are true and 0 if they are false. Suppose that we want to create a function $g(x)$ such that

$$g(x) = f(x) \quad a \leq x < b$$
$$= 0 \quad\quad x < a \text{ and } b \geq x$$

The logical operator is formed by

y = (a<=x & x<b);

where a and b have been assigned numerical values before this statement and

(a<=x & x<b)

is the logical operator that has a value of 1 (true) when $x \geq a$ and $x < b$ and 0 (false) for all other values of x. Thus, if we let $a = -1, b = 2, f(x) = e^{x/2}$, and $x = [-4 \ -1 \ 1 \ 4]$, then a script using this logical operator is

```
a = -1;  b = 2;
x = [-4, -1, 1, 4];
gofx = exp(x/2).*(a<=x & x<b)
```

which upon execution yields

```
gofx =
     0   0.6065   1.6487      0
```

Notice that dot multiplication was employed, because x is a (1×4) array.

This logical operator can be used to create the unit step function $u(t)$, which is defined as

$$u(t) = 1 \quad t \geq 0$$
$$= 0 \quad t < 0$$

For example, if t varies by increments of 0.25 in the range $-1 \leq t \leq 1$, then the following script creates the unit step function:

```
t = -1:0.25:1;
UnitStep = (t>=0);
disp(' t    UnitStep')
disp([t' UnitStep'])
```

Upon execution, the following results are displayed to the command window:

```
     t      UnitStep
-1.0000        0
-0.7500        0
-0.5000        0
-0.2500        0
      0     1.0000
 0.2500     1.0000
 0.5000     1.0000
 0.7500     1.0000
 1.0000     1.0000
```

4.2 CONTROL OF PROGRAM FLOW

Program flow control is performed by branching or looping. The branching is done with the `if` and `switch` statements, and the looping is done with either the `for` or the `while` statements. We shall now discuss these four control structures.

4.2.1 Branching—If Statement

The `if` statement is a conditional statement that branches to different parts of its structure depending on the satisfaction of certain conditional expressions. The general form of the `if` statement is

```
if condition #1
   expressions #1
elseif condition #2
```

```
      expressions #2
  else
      expressions #3
  end
```

When condition #1 is satisfied, expressions #1 are executed, followed by the next statement after the outermost end statement. When condition #1 is not satisfied, then condition #2 is examined. If condition #2 is satisfied, then expressions #2 are executed, and they are followed by the next statement after the outermost end statement. If neither condition #1 nor condition #2 is satisfied, then expressions #3 are executed, followed by the next statement after the outermost end statement. The statements elseif and else are optional, and there can be more than one elseif statement.

The following script illustrates the use of the if statement. The quantities j, x, and *nnum* have numerical values that were either assigned or determined from a computational procedure earlier in the program.

```
if j == 1
    z = sin(x);        ←──Executed only when j = 1.
    if nnum <= 4   ←──This if statement encountered only when j = 1.
        nr = 1;
        nc = 1;       ┐←──These statements executed only when j = 1 and nnum ≤ 4.
    else
        nr = 1;
        nc = 2;       ┐←──These statements executed only when j = 1 and nnum > 4.
    end
else
    nr = 2;
    nc = 1;           ┐←──These statements executed only when j ≠ 1.
end
```

It is seen that in the above script we have a nested if statement; therefore, we require a second end statement. Note how the indenting of the expressions inside the various nested structures makes the code more readable.

To terminate a script (or a function; see Chapter 5) because a specified condition has not been satisfied, one would use error. The error function generally is used to ensure that the program is using numerical values that lead to meaningful results. When the program encounters the error function, it will display the message contained within it to the command window. After displaying the message, the execution of the script or function is terminated, and control is returned to the command line in the command window. The error function can be used anywhere within a script or function and is not limited to if, for, switch, and while structures. An example of the use of error is given in Example 4.1.

Example 4.1   Fatigue strength factors

Consider the relationships that govern the correction factors used to estimate the fatigue strength of metals:

Factor	Range	Correction
Load	Bending	$C_{load} = 1$
	Axial	$C_{load} = 0.70$
Size	$d \leq 8$ mm	$C_{size} = 1$
	$8 \leq d \leq 250$ mm	$C_{size} = 1.189d^{-0.097}$
Temperature	$T < 450°C$	$C_{temp} = 1$
	$450°C \leq T$	$C_{temp} = 1 - 0.0032(T - 840)$

A portion of a script that can be used to determine these factors is given below. The values of *lode*, *d*, and *temp* have had numerical values either assigned or computed previously in the program. The quantity *lode* is a string, and it also has been assigned a value.

```
if lode == 'bending'
   cload = 1;
elseif lode == 'axial'
   cload = 0.7;
else
   error('No such loading')
end
if d < 0
   error('Negative diameter not allowed')
elseif d <= 8
   csize = 1;
else
   csize = 1.189*d^(-0.097);
end
if temp <= 450
   ctemp = 1;
else
   ctemp = 1-0.0032*(T-840);
end
```

Notice that we have included several tests to ensure that the data values are permissible. When they aren't, an error message is sent to the command window, and the program is aborted.

4.2.2 Branching—Switch Statement

The switch structure is, essentially, an alternative to using a series of if-elseif-else-end structures. The general form of the switch statement is

```
switch switch_expression
   case case_expression #1
      statements #1
   case case_expression #2
      statements #2
      ⋮
   case case_expression #n
```

```
      statements #n
   otherwise
      statements #n+1
end
```

The first *case_expression #j*, where $j = 1, 2, \ldots, n$, that is encountered in which *case_expression #j* = *switch_expression* will cause *statements #j* to be executed. Only one case is executed when the switch structure is entered. Following the execution of *statements #j*, the next statement to be executed is that statement following the end statement. If none of the *case_expression #j* is satisfied, then *statements #n+1* are executed. The otherwise statement is optional. If the otherwise statement is omitted and *case_expression #j* does not equal *switch_expression* for any *j*, then the next statement after the end statement is executed.

The following switch structure acts as indicated. The quantity k has been assigned a value or has had its value computed before encountering this structure.

```
a = 3;
switch k
  case 1
     disp('Case 1')         ◄─── This statement executed only when k = 1.
  case {2, 3}
     disp('Case 2 or 3' )   ◄─── This statement executed only when k = 2, 3.
  case a^2
     disp('Case 9')         ◄─── This statement executed only when k = 9.
  otherwise
     disp('Otherwise')      ◄─── This statement executed only when k ≠ 1, 2, 3, or 9.
end
```

Example 4.2   Selecting one of four views of a surface

Consider the situation where one wants to view a surface $z(x, y)$ in one of four orientations: regular (*reg*), top (*top*), right side (*rside*), or left side (*lside*). We will use the switch function to display the view selected. The surf function is used to plot a three-dimensional perspective of the array of values for z as a function of x and y. The view function sets the viewing angles. The script requests that the user enter the view to be displayed. The quantities x, y, and z either have been previously assigned values or have had their values previously computed. The portion of the script that uses switch is as follows:

```
surf(x, y, z)
str = input('Enter view: reg, top, rside, lside ', 's')
switch s
  case 'reg'
     view(-37.5, 30)
  case 'top'
     view(-90, 90)
  case 'rside'
     view(0, 0)
  case 'lside'
```

```
        view(-90, 0)
      otherwise
        error('No such view')
  end
```

4.2.3 For Loop

A for loop repeats a series of statements a specific number of times. Its general form is

```
for variable = expression
    statements
end
```

where one or more of the *statements* can be a function of *variable*.
 We now give several examples of the application of the for loop.

Example 4.3   Total interest on a loan

We shall compute the total interest on a loan when the amount of the loan is L, its duration is m months, and its annual percentage interest is I_a. The monthly payment p_{mon} is determined from

$$p_{mon} = \frac{iL}{1 - (1 + i)^{-m}}$$

where

$$i = I_a/1200$$

is the monthly interest rate expressed as a decimal number. Each month, as the loan is being paid off, a portion of the payment is used to pay the interest, and the remainder is applied to the unpaid loan amount. The unpaid loan amount after each payment is called the balance. Mathematically, we express these relations as follows: If $b_0 = L$, then

$$i_n = ib_{n-1}$$
$$P_n = p_{mon} - i_n \qquad n = 1, 2, 3, \ldots, m$$
$$b_n = b_{n-1} - P_n$$

where i_n is the portion of p_{mon} that goes toward the payment of the interest and P_n is the portion of the payment that goes toward the reduction of the balance b_n—that is, the amount required to pay off the loan. The total interest paid at the end of the loan's duration is

$$i_T = \sum_{i=1}^{m} i_j$$

The script to compute i_T is

```
loan = input('Enter loan amount: ');
durat = input('Enter term of loan in months: ');     ⎤ ⟵  Input
int = input('Enter annual interest rate: ')/1200;    ⎦
```

```
ints = zeros(1, durat);
prins = ints;                                          ⎤
bals = ints;                                           ⎥  ⟵  Initialization
pmon = (loan*int)/(1-(1+int)^(-durat));                ⎥
bals(1) = loan;                                        ⎦
for m = 2:durat+1                                      ⎤
   ints(m) = int*bals(m-1);                            ⎥
   prins(m) = pmon-ints(m);                            ⎥  ⟵  Computation
   bals(m) = bals(m-1)-prins(m);                       ⎥
end                                                    ⎦
fprintf(1, 'Total interest = $%8.2f', sum(ints))          ⟵  Output
```

As noted in Section 1.3.3, this script follows a program's usual structure: input, initialization, computations, and output, which in this case is to display the results to the command window. Execution of the script gives

```
Enter loan amount: 100000
Enter term of loan in months: 360
Enter annual interest rate: 8
Total interest = $164155.25
```

The first three lines are the user's response to the script's sequentially displayed queries, wherein the user entered the three numerical quantities shown after each query, and the last line is the answer. Notice that no comma was used in entering the first numerical value—100000—because the comma indicates the end of an expression.

It is recommended in MATLAB that before entering a for loop, or nested for loops, in which vectors or arrays are created by specifying their subscripts individually, one should size the array with the zeros function before entering the for loops. This greatly decreases the execution time of this portion of the script, because otherwise, MATLAB will dynamically allocate memory during the execution of the expressions in the for loop, thereby incurring substantial overhead. This initialization in this script is performed in lines 4 to 6.

Example 4.4   Equivalent implementation of **find**

We shall assume that we are given a vector g of positive and negative numbers and of arbitrary length. The objective is to create a script that performs the same function as the expression

```
indx = find(g>a)
```

where a is specified by the user. We shall check the script with $a = 4$ and with the vector $g = [4, 4, 7, 10, -6, 42, 1, 0]$.

The script is

```
g = [4, 4, 7, 10, -6, 42, 1, 0];
a = 4; k = 0;
indx = [];
for n = 1:length(g)
   if g(n) > a
      k = k+1;
```

```
      indx(k) = n;
   end
end
disp(['Element locations for g(n)>' num2str(a) ':' num2str(indx)])
```

Upon execution, the following results are displayed to the command window:

Element locations for g(n)>4: 3 4 6

An alternative way to obtain *indx* is to use column augmentation as follows (recall the summary at the end of Section 2.4):

```
g = [4, 4, 7, 10, -6, 42, 1, 0];
a = 4;  k = 0;
indx = [];
for n = 1:length(g)
   if g(n)>a
      indx = [indx, n];
   end
end
disp(['Element locations for g(n)>' num2str(a) ':' num2str(indx)])
```

Example 4.5   Equivalent implementation of cumsum

For a vector c of arbitrary length, we shall create a script that provides the same results as

Csum = cumsum(c)

We shall verify the script with the vector $c = [4, 4, 7, 10, -6, 42, 1, 0]$.
        The script is

```
c = [4, 4, 7, 10, -6, 42, 1, 0];
Csum(1) = c(1);
for k = 2:length(c)
   Csum(k) = Csum(k-1)+c(k);
end
disp(['Cumsum of c = ' num2str(Csum)])
```

Upon execution, the following results are displayed to the command window:

Cumsum of c = 4 8 15 25 19 61 62 62

An alternative way to obtain *Csum* is to employ column augmentation as follows:

```
c = [4, 4, 7, 10, -6, 42, 1, 0];
Csum(1) = c(1);
for k = 2:length(c)
   Csum = [Csum, Csum(k-1)+c(k)];
end
disp(['Cumsum of c = ' num2str(Csum)])
```

Example 4.6   Equivalent implementation of diag

For an $(n \times n)$ matrix B, we shall create a two-part script that provides the same result as

v = diag(B)

which, in the first part, extracts the diagonal elements of B and, in the second part, constructs the diagonal matrix as performed by

D = diag(v)

Here, v is that value obtained in the first part. We shall check the results using $B = $ magic(4), and we shall assume that we cannot use the colon notation and the function zeros. The script is

```
B = magic(4);
[r, c] = size(B);
for k = 1:r
    v(k) = B(k,k);
end
disp(['Diagonal elements of B = '])
disp(num2str(v'))
for n = 1:r
    for m = 1:r
        if n == m
            D(n,m) = v(n);
        else
            D(n,m) = 0.0;
        end
    end
end
disp(['Diagonal matrix D = '])
disp(num2str(D))
```

Upon execution, the following results are displayed to the command window:

```
Diagonal elements of B =
16
11
6
1
Diagonal matrix D =
16  0   0   0
 0 11   0   0
 0  0   6   0
 0  0   0   1
```

If we allow ourselves to use the colon notation and the function zeros, then the script simplifies to

```
B = magic(4);
[r, c] = size(B);
```

```
for k = 1:r
   v(k) = B(k,k);
end
disp(['Diagonal elements of B = '])
disp(num2str(v'))
D = zeros(r,c);
for n = 1:r
   D(n,n) = v(n);
end
disp(['Diagonal matrix D ='])
disp(num2str(D))
```

Example 4.7   Specification of the elements of an array

We shall create an $(n \times n)$ matrix whose elements are either $+1$ or -1 such that the sign of each element is different from its adjacent elements, both from those above and below it and from those on either side of it. The selection of n is arbitrary. Thus, we want to create the matrix

$$M = \begin{bmatrix} 1 & -1 & 1 & \cdots \\ -1 & 1 & -1 & \cdots \\ 1 & -1 & 1 & \cdots \\ \vdots & & & \end{bmatrix} \rightarrow (n \times n)$$

The script is

```
n = input('Enter the order of the square matrix: ');
k = 1:n;
M=zeros(n, n);
OddRow = (-1).^(k-1);
EvenRow = (-1).^k;
for m = 1:2:n
   M(m,:) = OddRow;
   if m+1 <= n
      M(m+1,:) = EvenRow;
   end
end
M
```

The execution of this script for $n = 3$ displays to the command window

```
Enter the order of the square matrix: 3
M =
    1   -1    1
   -1    1   -1
    1   -1    1
```

where the value 3 was entered by the user.

Example 4.8 Multiple root finding using interval halving[1]

MATLAB has a function `fzero` that is used to determine the value of x that makes $f(x)$ very closely equal to zero provided that `fzero` is given a good estimate for the location of the root (see Section 5.5.1). However, it only finds one zero at a time; to find additional zeros one must call `fzero` again with another estimate of where the next zero can be found.

Let us assume that we would like to find automatically a series of positive values of x $(x_1, x_2, \ldots)$ that make $f(x) = 0$. This assumes, of course, that $f(x)$ has multiple zeros and, therefore, that the sign of $f(x)$ alternates as x increases.

One technique to find the zeros of a function is called interval halving.[2] Referring to Figure 4.1, this technique works as follows: The independent variable x is given a starting value $x = x_{start}$ and the sign of $f(x_{start})$ is determined. The variable x is then incremented by an amount Δ, and the sign of $f(x_{start} + \Delta)$ is determined. The signs of these two values are compared. If the signs are the same (as they are in Figure 4.1), then x is again incremented by Δ, and the sign of $f(x + 2\Delta)$ is evaluated and compared to that of $f(x_{start})$. If the signs are different, then the current value of x is decremented by half the interval size—that is, by $\Delta/2$. From Figure 4.1, we see that the sign change occurs at $x = x_{start} + 3\Delta$ so that after the sign change has been detected, the next value for x is $x = x_{start} + 5\Delta/2$. The sign of $f(x_{start} + 5\Delta/2)$ is then compared to $f(x_{start})$. If it is the same, then half the current interval is added to the current value of x: otherwise, it is subtracted from the current value of x. In this example, the sign of $f(x_{start})$ is the same as $f(x_{start} + 5\Delta/2)$ so that the next point at which $f(x)$ is evaluated is $x_{start} + 11\Delta/4$. This process is repeated until the incremental change in x divided by the current value of x is

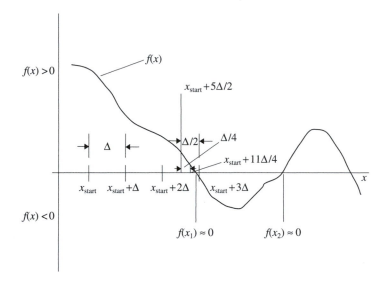

Figure 4.1 Interval halving scheme.

[1]See, for example, S. C. Chapra and R. P. Canale, *Numerical Methods for Engineers*, 2nd ed., McGraw-Hill, New York, 1988, p. 128ff.
[2]Although this method will find the roots, it is not the best way to do it, because the techniques that are used in `fzero` require two to three times fewer iterations to find a root to within a specified precision.

less than some tolerance—that is, until $\Delta_{current}/x_{current} < t_o$, the tolerance. When this tolerance criteria has been satisfied, the root $x_1 = x_{current}$. The process is continued until the desired number of x_j has been determined. After each x_j has been obtained, we reset Δ to its original value, set x_{start} to a value slightly larger than x_j (say, $x_{start} = 1.05 x_j$, and repeat the process.

The objective is to write a script using the interval halving technique to determine the first five values of x that set the function

$$f(x) = \cos(ax) \cong 0$$

where a is a constant. These x_j are said to satisfy this equation when the incremental change in x divided by x is less than $t_o = 10^{-6}$. Also, $x_j \geq x_{start} \geq 0$ for $j = 1, 2, \ldots, n$. Thus, in general, the inputs to the root-finding portion of the program are n, x_{start}, t_o, and Δ and, for this particular $f(x)$, the quantity a.

In the present case, $n = 5$ and $t_o = 10^{-6}$, and we shall let $x_{start} = 0.2$, $\Delta = 0.3$, and $a = \pi$. The script is

```
n = 5; a = pi;
increment = 0.3; tolerance = 1e-6;
xstart = 0.2;
x = xstart;
dx = increment;
for m = 1:n
    s1 = sign(cos(a*x));
    while dx/x > tolerance
        if s1 ~= sign(cos(a*(x+dx)))
            dx = dx/2;
        else
            x = x+dx;
        end
    end
    route(m) = x;
    dx = increment;
    x = 1.05*x;
end
disp(route)
```

The function sign brings back a +1, a −1, or a 0, depending on whether the sign of its argument is positive, negative, or zero, respectively. Upon execution, the following results are displayed in the command window:

    0.5000   1.5000   2.5000   3.5000   4.5000

In Section 5.3, we shall convert this script into a function so that we can determine the roots for an arbitrary $f(x)$.

4.2.4 While Loop

The while loop repeats one or more statements an indefinite number of times, leaving the loop only when a specified condition has been satisfied. Its general form is

```
while condition
    statements
end
```

where the expression defining *condition* is usually composed of one or more of the variables evaluated by *statements*.

We now present two examples of `while` loops. The first example ensures that user-entered data are within specified limits. The second example determines when certain convergence criteria have been satisfied.

Example 4.9   Ensuring that data are input correctly

The following excerpt from a program asks the user to enter a number from 1 to 8, and the program continues to request this from the user until the entry is in the specified range. The `input` function prints the message appearing in quotes to the command window and waits until the user enters a value, at which point the program sets that value to *nfnum*. The symbol "|" is the logical OR.

```
nfnum = 0;
while (nfnum < 1)|(nfnum > 8)
   nfnum = input('Enter a number from 1 to 8: ');
end
```

The quantity *nfnum* is initially set equal to a value (in this case, zero) that causes the `while` test $(nfnum < 1)|(nfnum > 8)$ to enter the `while` structure. After reaching the last expression before the `end` statement, the program returns to the `while` test expression to determine whether it is satisfied. If it is not satisfied, the program executes the next line in the structure; otherwise, it proceeds to the next statement after the `end` statement. Notice that we have employed the preferred practice of placing the structure's initializing value (in this case, *nfnum*) just before its entry into the structure.

Example 4.10   Convergence of a series

Let us determine and display the number of terms that it takes for the series

$$S_N = \sum_{n=1}^{N} \frac{1}{n^2}$$

to converge to within 0.01% of its exact value, which is $S_\infty = \pi^2/6$.

The script is

```
series = 1;  k = 2;  exact = pi^2/6;
while abs((series-exact)/exact) >= 1e-4
   series = series+1/k^2;
   k = k+1;
end
disp(['Number of terms = ' num2str(k-1)])
```

which upon execution displays to the command window

    Number of terms = 6079

The quantity *series* is initially set equal to a value (in this case, 1) that causes the `while` test abs((*series-exact*)/*exact*) to enter the `while` structure. After reaching the last expression before the `end` statement, the program returns to the `while` test expression to determine if it is satisfied. If it is not satisfied, it executes the next line in the structure; otherwise, it proceeds to the next statement after the `end` statement, which in this case displays the result to the command window.

We have used the absolute value of the test condition (*series-exact*)/*exact*) to avoid any instance when the difference *series-exact* is negative, which would be less than 10^{-4} (since it is a negative number), but whose magnitude may be greater than 10^{-4}. This avoids having to know *a priori* whether the quantity *series* approaches the limit from above or below. One must also be very careful when establishing the test criterion for the termination of the while loop, because if it is improperly or poorly stated, one may stay in the loop indefinitely—that is, until ctrl and C are pressed simultaneously by the user.

4.2.5 Early Termination of Either a `for` or a `while` Loop

The break function is used to terminate either a for or a while loop. If the break function is within nested for or while loops, then it returns to the next higher level for or while loop. Consider the following portion of a script:

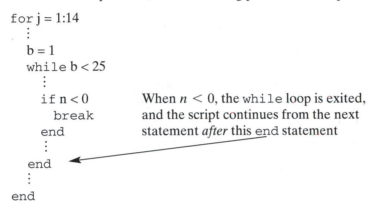

```
for j = 1:14
   ⋮
   b = 1
   while b < 25
      ⋮
      if n < 0          When n < 0, the while loop is exited,
         break          and the script continues from the next
      end               statement after this end statement
      ⋮
   end
   ⋮
end
```

4.3 SUMMARY OF FUNCTIONS INTRODUCED

Several logical and relational operators are given in Table 4.1. A summary of the additional functions introduced in the chapter is presented in Table 4.2.

TABLE 4.2   MATLAB Functions Introduced in Chapter 4

MATLAB function	Description
break	Terminates the execution of a for or a while loop
case	An alternative identifier in the switch structure
else	Executes statements based on a relational or a logical expression
elseif	Executes statements based on a relational or a logical expression
end	Terminates a for, while, if, or switch structure
error	Displays an error messages, and aborts program execution
for	Repeats statements a specific number of times
if	Executes statements based on a relational or a logical expression
sign	Signum function
switch	Switches among several cases based on a value
while	Repeats statements an indefinite number of times

EXERCISES

4.1 Create a script that performs the equivalent function of the logical operator introduced in Section 4.1 for any vector of values h such that the output vector v of the logical operator indicates which of its elements satisfy $h > a$ and $h < b$. Test your script with $h = [1\,3\,6\,-7\,-45\,12\,17\,9]$, $a = 3$, and $b = 13$. [Answer: $v = [0\,0\,1\,0\,0\,0\,1\,0\,1]$.]

4.2 The estimate of the variance of n samples x_i is determined from

$$s_n^2 = \frac{1}{n-1}\left[\sum_{j=1}^{n} x_j^2 - n\bar{x}_n^2\right] \quad n > 1$$

where

$$\bar{x}_n = \frac{1}{n}\sum_{j=1}^{n} x_j$$

is an estimate of the mean. The variance is determined from var.

Write a script that determines s_n^2 as a function of n, where $n > 1$, for the following data: $x = [45\,38\,47\,41\,35\,43]$. [Answer: [24.5000 22.3333 16.2500 24.2000 19.9000].]

4.3 For a given $a > 0$, the following relationship will determine the positive value of the $\sqrt{a}$ to within a tolerance t_0 for any starting value (guess) $x_0 > 0$:

$$x_{n+1} = \frac{1}{2}\left(x_n + \frac{a}{x_n}\right) \quad n = 0, 1, 2, \ldots$$

where $x_{n+1} \cong \sqrt{a}$. (When $x_0 < 0$ the negative square root is found.) Write a script that determines $\sqrt{a}$ to within $|x_n - x_{n+1}| < 10^{-6}$ for $a = 7$. How many iterations does it take if (a) $x_0 = 3$ and (b) $x_0 = 100$? The first iteration is the determination of x_1. [Hint: Notice that the above relationship is not an explicit function of n. Here, the subscript n is simply an indicator that the next (new) value x_{n+1} is a function of the previous (old) value x_n. Thus, each time through the loop, the old and new values keep changing. Therefore, one has to keep track of n to record the number of times this relationship is used until the convergence criterion is met.] [Answer: (a) $n_{\text{iterations}} = 4$ and (b) $n_{\text{iterations}} = 10$.]

4.4 Consider the following relation:

$$x_{n+1} = x_n^2 + 0.25 \quad n = 0, 1, 2, \ldots, N$$

For $x_0 = 0$, write two scripts that plot the values of x_n for $n = 0, 5, 10, \ldots, 200$. In the first script, use a for loop, and in the second script, use a while loop. To what value does x_N appear to converge? For the third argument of the plot function, use plot($\ldots,\ldots,$ 'ks'), which will plot the values of x_n as squares. The x-axis values are the values of n, and the y-axis values are the values of x_n. Note that all x_n, when $n = 0, 1, 2, \ldots, 200$, must be computed, but only every fifth x_n is plotted. This exercise differs from Exercise 4.3 in that the values of x_n must be saved as elements of a vector so that the appropriate elements can be subsequently displayed.

4.5 The chi-square statistic is used to perform goodness-of-fit tests (see Exercise 14.5). It is defined as

$$\chi^2 = \sum_{i=1}^{k} \frac{(x_i - e_i)^2}{e_i}$$

where e_i and x_i are independent vectors of length k.

If $e_i < 5$, then e_i and x_i must be combined with their respective e_{i+1} and x_{i+1} values. If the sum of $e_i + e_{i+1}$ is still less than 5, then e_{i+2} is added to the sum of $e_i + e_{i+1}$. This process is repeated until the sum is 5 or greater. When $e_i \geq 5$ and the sum of the remaining $e_{i+1}, e_{i+2}, \ldots, e_k$ is less than 5, then these remaining values are added to e_j.

Write a script that computes X^2 under the conditions described above. Check your results with the following vectors, which represent three different cases:

a. $x = [1, 7, 8, 6, 5, 7, 3, 5, 4]$ and $e = [2, 6, 10, 4, 3, 6, 1, 2, 3]$
b. $x = [7, 11, 13, 6]$ and $e = [6, 10, 15, 7]$
c. $x = [3, 14, 20, 25, 14, 6, 2, 0, 1, 0]$ and $e = [4, 12, 19, 19, 14, 8, 4, 2, 1, 1]$

[Hint: The most compact script will be obtained by performing tests on the elements of cumsum(e), where the length of e changes as the evaluation procedure progresses.]
[Answers:

a. $e_{\text{modified}} = [8, 10, 7, 6, 6]$, $x_{\text{modified}} = [8, 8, 11, 7, 12]$, $\chi^2 = 8.8524$
b. $e_{\text{modified}} = [6, 10, 15, 7]$, $x_{\text{modified}} = [7, 11, 13, 6]$, $\chi^2 = 0.6762$
c. $e_{\text{modified}} = [16, 19, 19, 14, 8, 8]$, $x_{\text{modified}} = [17, 20, 25, 14, 6, 3]$, $\chi^2 = 5.6349.$]

4.6 Given the two polynomials

$$y(x) = p_1 x^n + p_2 x^{n-1} + \cdots + p_n x + p_{n+1}$$

and

$$z(x) = s_1 x^m + s_2 x^{m-1} + \cdots + s_m x + s_{m+1}$$

write a script to add them—that is, $h(x) = y(x) + z(x)$ when $m = n, m < n$, and $m > n$. Polynomials are added by adding the coefficients of the terms with the same exponent. Assume that the input to the script are the vectors $p = [p_1 \, p_2 \cdots p_n \, p_{n+1}]$ and $s = [s_1 \, s_2 \cdots s_m \, s_{m+1}]$.

Check your script with the following data sets:

a. $p = [1, 2, 3, 4]$ and $s = [10, 20, 30, 40]$
b. $p = [11, 12, 13, 14]$ and $s = [101, 102]$
c. $p = [43, 54, 55]$ and $s = [77, 66, 88, 44, 33]$

[Answers:

a. $h = [11, 22, 33, 44]$
b. $h = [11, 12, 114, 116]$
c. $h = [77, 66, 131, 98, 88].$]

4.7 Write a script that computes the day of week for the years 2004, 2005, and 2006 when its input is of the form month/day/year: xx/xx/xxxx. The following information is given: January 1, 2004, is a Thursday and a leap year; January 1, 2005, is a Saturday; and January 1, 2006, is a Sunday. Have the script input and output the results in the following manner:

Enter month, day, and year in the form xx/xx/xxxx for 2004, 2005, or 2006: 11/20/2005
The date 11/20/2005 is the 324 day of the year and falls on a Sunday.

where 11/20/2005 was entered by the user. The functions str2num, deblank, and findstr should prove useful.

5

Functions

Edward B. Magrab

The creation of functions and their various uses within MATLAB are described, and several MATLAB functions that are frequently used to obtain numerical solutions to engineering problems are illustrated.

5.1 INTRODUCTION

One form of an M-file is the script file. A second type of M-file is the function file. Function files are script files that create their own local and independent workspace within MATLAB. Variables defined within a function are local to that function; they neither affect nor are affected by the same variable names being used in any script or other function file. All of MATLAB's functions are of this type. The exception is those variables that are designated global variables in user-created functions, which are discussed in Section 5.2.2. The first noncomment line of a function file must follow a prescribed format, which is given in Section 5.2.2. Typically, user-created MATLAB programs consist of a script file and employ any number of user-created functions and MATLAB functions.

5.1.1 Why Use Functions?

There are more reasons to create functions than the fact that many MATLAB functions require them (see Section 5.5). These reasons include:

1. Avoiding duplicate code
2. Limiting the effect of changes to specific sections of a program
3. Promoting program reuse
4. Reducing the complexity of the overall program by making it more readable and manageable
5. Isolating complex operations
6. Improving portability
7. Making debugging and error isolation easier
8. Improving performance, because each function can be "optimized"

The compartmentalization brought about by the use of functions also tends to minimize the unintended use of data by portions of the program, because data to each function is provided only on a need-to-know basis.

5.1.2 Naming Functions

The names of functions should be chosen so that they are meaningful and indicate what the function does. Typical lengths of function names are between 9 and 20 characters, and the names should employ standard or consistent conventions. For example, all script file names could begin with *scr* and all function names without this prefix. The proper choice of function names can also minimize the use of comments within the function itself. Recall, also, the naming conventions suggested in Section 1.3.2.

5.1.3 Length of Functions

The length of a function can vary from two lines to more than hundreds of lines of code. However, the length of a function should be governed, in part, by its functional cohesion—that is, by the degree to which it does one thing and not anything else. For example, $\sin(x)$ is 100% cohesive. A function that computes the sine and square root, however, would be less cohesive, because it does two separate things, each of which is unrelated to the other. A function can be created with numerous highly cohesive functions to create another cohesive function. An additional advantage to the creation of highly cohesive functions is their reliability—that is, a lower error rate. In addition, when functions have a low degree of cohesion, one often encounters difficulty in isolating errors.

5.1.4 Debugging Functions

During the creation of functions (and scripts), the program should be independently verified after every few expressions are written to ensure that it is working correctly. MATLAB is particularly well suited to this type of procedure, which simply involves omitting the semicolon at the end of each expression. Furthermore, one incurs very little time penalty when omitting the semicolon, except in those expressions using large vectors and matrices or iterative solution techniques. The verification should be performed with some type of independent calculation or estimation. During the verification/debugging stage, any lines of code that may be inserted to provide intermediate output should be commented out, not deleted, until the entire function has been verified to be working correctly. Only after a function is working correctly should it be improved to decrease its execution time, if necessary. Creating correctly performing programs is always the primary goal.

5.2 CREATING FUNCTIONS

5.2.1 Introduction

A function in MATLAB can be created in several ways. The most general form is the function file, which is created by the `function` command, saved in a file, and subsequently accessed by scripts and functions or from the command window. The creation of the function file is given in Section 5.2.2. A second way to create a function is with the `inline` command. This function is limited to one expression and is accessible only from the script or function in which it was created. Its creation is discussed in Section 5.2.3. A third form of the function is the subfunction. When the `function` key word is used more than once in a function file, then all the additional functions created after the first `function` key word are called subfunctions. The subfunctions are only accessible by the first function of the function file and the other subfunctions within the file. They are different from those functions created by `inline` in that they can be composed of more than one expression, and they are used to reduce function file proliferation. The subfunction is discussed in Section 5.2.4.

5.2.2 Function File

A function that is going to reside in a function file has at least two lines of program code, the first line of which has a format required by MATLAB. There is no terminating character or expression for the function program such as the `end` statement, which is required for the `for`, `while`, `if`, and `switch` structures. Furthermore, the name of the M-file should be the same as the name of the function, except that the file name has the extension *.m*.

The number of variables and their type (scalar, vector, matrix, string, or cell) that are brought in and out of the function are controlled by the function interface, which is the first noncomment line of the function program. In general, a function file will consist of the interface line, some comments, and one or more expressions as shown below. The interface has the general form given in the first line:

```
function [OutputVariables] = FunctionName(InputVariables)
% Comments
Expression(s)
```

where *OutputVariables* are the names of the output variables, each of which must be separated by a comma; *InputVariables* is the name of the input variables, each of which must be separated by a comma; and *FunctionName* is the name of the function and the function file in which the function is stored. These names must begin with an uppercase or lowercase letter and have the restrictions discussed in Section 1.3.2. The first word of this statement, `function`, is a reserved word that may only be used in this context. The function file may be stored in any directory to which a path has been or will be defined and has the file name *FunctionName.m* However, for one to have access to this function during a session, the respective paths of the function and the script must be known to the system. This is done by either having the script and function in the current directory or by placing the function in a path that has been saved using the procedure discussed regarding Figure 1.8.

The comments immediately following the function interface statement are used by MATLAB to create this function's Help information—that is, when one types at the command line

```
help FunctionName
```

all the initial contiguous comments will appear in the MATLAB command window. Any comments appearing before the `function` statement will not be part of the Help information. The Help information ends when no more contiguous comment lines are encountered—that is, when a blank line or an executable expression is encountered.

Three special cases are relevant when discussing function files:

1. Functions can also be used to create a figure, to display annotated data to the command window, or to write data to files. In these cases, no values are transferred back to the calling program (a script or another function that uses this function in one or more of its expressions). In this case, the function interface line becomes

> `function` FunctionName(InputVariables)

2. When a function is used only to store data in a prescribed manner, the function does not require any input arguments. In this case, the function interface line has the form

> `function` OutputVariables = FunctionName

This case is illustrated in Example 5.1.

3. When a function converts a script to a main function so that one can decrease the number of M-files that are normally created, the function interface line has the form

> `function` FunctionName

This form is illustrated at the end of Section 5.2.4.

Several concepts must be understood to correctly create functions. The first is that the variable names used in the function definition do not have to match the corresponding names when the function is called from the command window, a script, or another function. Instead, the locations of the input variables within the argument list inside the parentheses govern the transfer of information—that is, the first argument in the calling statement transfers its value(s) to the first argument in the function interface line, and so on.

Second, the names selected for each argument are local to the function program and have meaning only within the context of the function program. The same names can be used in an entirely different context in the script file that calls this function or in another function used by this function. However, the names appearing for each input variable of the function statement must be the same type (scalar, vector, matrix, cell, or string), in the calling program as in the function program for the function's expressions to work as intended. For example, the multiplication of two row vectors may result in an error message if the variables do not have the correct size (matrix order). Furthermore, the names used for the input variables of the function statement are equivalent to their appearing on the left side of an equal sign. Thus, if one of the input variable names is a, then a is equivalent to the expression $a = [\ldots]$. The variable names are not local to the function only when they have been assigned as global variables using `global`. (The use of `global` is discussed later).

We shall first illustrate the construction of a function and then list several of its variations. Consider the following two equations that are to be computed in a function:

$$x = \cos(at) + b$$
$$y = |x| + c$$

The values of x and y are to be returned by the function. We now create a function to compute these quantities, and we call it *ComputeXY*, which is saved as a file named *ComputeXY.m*:[1]

```
function [x, y] = ComputeXY(t, a, b, c)
% Computation of -
%    x = cos(at)+b
%    y = |x|+c
% Scalars: a,b,c
% Vector: t, x, y
x = cos(a*t)+b;
y = abs(x)+c;
```

When one types in the MATLAB command window

```
help ComputeXY
```

the following is displayed

```
Computation of -
    x = cos(at)+b
    y = |x|+c
Scalars: a, b, c
Vector: t, x, y
```

Several other variations of the function interface and how they are accessed from the calling programs are given in Table 5.1. It is seen from the examples in this table that one must ensure both the number and the type of the input and output variables are

TABLE 5.1   Several Variations of the Function Statement [u, v] = **ComputeXY**(t, a, b, c)

Function	Accessing function from script or function	Comments

`function z = ComputeXY(t,w)`
`x = cos(w(1)*t)+w(2);`
`z = [x; abs(x)+w(3)];`
	`t = 0:pi/4:pi;`
	`w = [1.4, 2, 0.75];`
	`q = ComputeXY(t, w);`
		$w(1) = a = 1.4; w(2) = b = 2;$
		$w(3) = c = 0.75; q \rightarrow (2 \times 5)$
		$x(:) = q(1,1{:}5);\ y(:) = q(2,1{:}5)$

`function z = ComputeXY(t,w)`
`x = cos(w(1)*t)+w(2);`
`z = [x abs(x)+w(3)];`
	`t = 0:pi/4:pi;`
	`w = [1.4, 2, 0.75];`
	`q = ComputeXY(t, w);`
		$w(1) = a = 1.4; w(2) = b = 2;$
		$w(3) = c = 0.75; q \rightarrow (1 \times 10)$
		$x(:) = q(1{:}5);\ y(:) = q(6{:}10)$

`function [x, y] = ComputeXY(t,w)`
`x = cos(w(1)*t)+w(2);`
`y = abs(x)+w(3);`
	`t = 0:pi/4:pi;`
	`w = [1.4, 2, 0.75];`
	`q = ComputeXY(t, w);`
		$w(1) = a = 1.4; w(2) = b = 2;$
		$w(3) = c = 0.75; q \rightarrow (1 \times 5)$
		$x = q;\ \ y$ not available[§]

[§] Many of the MATLAB functions make use of this form, as will be seen throughout the book.

---

[1]The comments are included in this example to show its usage. In most scripts and functions presented in this book, the comment lines have been omitted to make the listings themselves more readable. However, in most cases, the important features of the programs are discussed within the text accompanying each script or function, or they are obvious from its context.

correct with respect to how they are to be used by the function. These restrictions should be denoted in the function's comments intended for the response to the `help` request. In this case, we have assumed that t is a vector and that a, b, and c are scalars. We can now call this function by typing in the command window

[u, v] = **ComputeXY**(0:pi/4:pi, 1.4, 2, 0.75);

By virtue of the location within the parentheses, this means that with reference to the function, $t = [0, \text{pi}/4, \text{pi}/2, 3*\text{pi}/4, \text{pi}], a = 1.4, b = 2.0$, and $c = 0.75$. Upon executing this statement, we obtain

```
u =
    3.0000    2.4540    1.4122    1.0123    1.6910
v=
    3.7500    3.2040    2.1622    1.7623    2.4410
```

Functions normally return when the last statement of the function is reached. To force an earlier return, one uses

```
return
```

Let us modify the function **ComputeXY** so that the function is only evaluated when the variable t is a vector of length 2 or more and when the number of arguments in the calling statement is 4. This ensures that the user has entered the correct number of variables and that t is not a scalar. To determine the number of input variables that are actually used to call the function, we use `nargin`. To signify that inappropriate or insufficient data have been entered, the function returns `NaN`, which is a reserved word meaning "not a number." Then, our previous function is modified as follows (the comments have been omitted for clarity):

```
function [x, y] = ComputeXY(t, a, b, c)
if length(x) == 1|nargin ~= 4
   x = NaN;
   y = NaN;
   return
end
x = cos(a*t)+b;
y = abs(x)+c;
```

In some instances, the number of different variables that are transferred to a function can become large. In these cases, it may be beneficial for the function to share the global memory of the script or function or to create access to global variables for use by various functions. This access is provided by

```
global
```

MATLAB suggests that global variables appear in capital letters only to distinguish them from local variables.

To illustrate its usage, let us transfer the values of a, b, and c in the function **ComputeXY** as global variables. The script is modified as follows:

```
function [x, y] = ComputeXY(t)
global A B C
x = cos(A*t)+B;
y = abs(x)+C;
```

where the blank spaces between the `global` variable names must be used instead of commas. Notice that the variables a, b, and c no longer appear in the interface line.

The script required to call this function is now

```
global A B C
A = 1.4;  B = 2;  C = 0.75;
[u, v] = ComputeXY(0:pi/4:pi)
```

The same variable names must be used in both the script and the function, and it must have the same context in both. Upon execution, the following values are displayed to the command window:

```
u =
    3.0000   2.4540   1.4122   1.0123   1.6910
v =
    3.7500   3.2040   2.1622   1.7623   2.4410
```

which is what we obtained previously.

Since the arguments in the function definition are, in a sense, placeholders for the numerical values that will reside in their respective places when the function is executed, we can insert, when appropriate, any correctly constructed expression in the calling statement. To illustrate this, let us use **ComputeXY** to determine the values of x and y for

$$a = \sqrt{\frac{1.8}{(1 + k)^3}} \quad k = 1, \ldots, n$$

when t varies from 0 to π in increments of $\pi/4$, $c = 1/0.85$, b has n values that range from 1 to 1.4, and $n = 3$. Upon using the function **ComputeXY** of the form

```
function [x, y] = ComputeXY(t, a, b, c)
x = cos(a*t)+b;
y=abs(x)+c;
```

the script is

```
n = 3;
c = linspace(1, 1.4, n);
for k = 1:n
   [u, v] = ComputeXY(0:pi/4:pi, c(k), sqrt(1.8/(1+k)^3), 1/.85)
end
```

Upon execution, the following results are displayed in the command window:

```
u =
   1.4743   1.1814   0.4743  -0.2328  -0.5257
v =
   2.6508   2.3579   1.6508   1.4092   1.7021
u =
   1.2582   0.8460  -0.0508  -0.6929  -0.5508
v =
   2.4347   2.0225   1.2273   1.8693   1.7273
u =
   1.1677   0.6217  -0.4201  -0.8200  -0.1413
v =
   2.3442   1.7982   1.5966   1.9965   1.3178
```

If we repeat the above computation using global variables for a, b, and c, then the function is

```
function [x, y] = ComputeXY(t)
global A B C
x = cos(A*t)+B;
y=abs(x)+C;
```

and the script is

```
global A B C
n = 3;  C = 1/.85;
c = linspace(1, 1.4, n);
for k = 1:n
   A = c(k);
   B = sqrt(1.8/(1+k)^3);
   [u, v] = ComputeXY(0:pi/4:pi)
end
```

which upon execution produces the previously obtained results.

As a final remark, we illustrate the case where the results of a function are returned as a vector and are redefined in the script file as one row of a matrix. For simplicity, we shall assume that we are interested only in the values of x and that these values are returned inside a for loop. Thus, a segment of a program could be

```
n = 4;
c = linspace(1, 1.4, n);
t = 0:pi/4:pi;
p = zeros(n, length(t));
for k = 1:4
   p(k,:) = ComputeXY(t, c(k), sqrt(1.8/(1+k)^3), 1/.85);
      ⋮
end
      ⋮
```

It is seen that $p\ (=u=\cos(at)+b)$ in this case will be a (4×5) matrix, because $k = 1, 2, 3, 4$ and the length of the vector t is 5. Recall that the notation $p(k,:)$ means that the kth row of matrix p is to have its column elements assigned the corresponding values of the columns of the row vector returned by **ComputeXY**. The initial assignment of p using zeros to create a properly sized array is necessary; otherwise, an error message will occur.

5.2.3 `inline`

One can create a local function, either in the command window, a script, or a function, using `inline`. This function has the advantage that it doesn't have to be saved in a separate file, but it does have several limitations. It cannot call another `inline` function, but it can use a user-created function existing as a function file. It can be composed of only one expression, and it can bring back only one variable—that is, the form [u, v] is not allowed. Thus, any function requiring logic or multiple operations to arrive at the result cannot employ `inline`. However, despite these limitations, it is very convenient form to use in many situations.

The general form of `inline` is

FunctionName = `inline`('expression', 'p1','p2',...)

where *expression* is any valid MATLAB expression converted to a string and *p1,p2*, ... are the names of all the variables appearing in *expression*.

We illustrate `inline` with the following example. Let us create a function **FofX** that evaluates

$$f(x) = x^2 \cos(ax) - b$$

where a and b are scalars and x is a vector. Then,

FofX = `inline`('x.^2.*cos(a*x)-b', 'x', 'a', 'b')

displays in the MATLAB command window

```
FofX =
   Inline function:
   FofX(x,a,b) = x.^2.*cos(a*x)-b
```

The dot multiplication is required, since x is a vector. If we had ended the inline expression with a semicolon, then this display would have been suppressed.

Thus, when we enter the following expression in the command window,

g = **FofX**([pi/3, pi/3.5], 4, 1)

the system responds with

```
g =
   -1.5483   -1.7259
```

The `inline` form for functions has utility in many MATLAB functions that require one to first create a function that will subsequently be evaluated by that MATLAB function. Several examples of its usage are given in Section 5.5.

5.2.4 Sub Functions

When the `function` key word is used more than once in a function file, all the additional functions created after the first `function` key word are called sub functions. The expressions comprising the first use of the `function` key word is called the main function. It is the only function that is accessible from the command window, scripts, and other functions. The sub functions are accessible only to the main function and to other sub functions within the main function file.

We shall illustrate the use of a function and sub functions by computing the mean and standard deviation of a vector of numerical values. We shall compute this in a relatively inefficient manner to illustrate the properties and use of sub functions. The mean m and the standard deviation s are given by

$$m = \frac{1}{n}\sum_{k=1}^{n}x_k$$

$$s = \left[\frac{1}{n-1}\left(\sum_{k=1}^{n}x_k^2 - nm^2\right)\right]^{1/2}$$

We shall call the main function **MeanStdDev**, and the sub function that computes **m meen**, and that which computes the standard deviation **stdev**. The function and its sub functions are saved in a file *MeanStdDev.m*. The function and sub functions are then given by the following:

```
function [m, s] = MeanStdDev(dat)        % Main function
n = length(dat);
m = meen(dat, n);
s = stdev(dat, n);

function m = meen(v, n)                   % Sub function
m = sum(v)/n;

function sd = stdev(v, n)                  % Sub function
m = meen(v, n);                            % Calls a sub function
sd = sqrt((sum(v.^2)-n*m^2)/(n-1));
```

A script to illustrate the use of this file of functions and sub functions is

```
v = [1, 2 , 3, 4];
[m, s] = MeanStdDev(v)
```

which upon execution gives

```
m =
   2.5000
s =
   1.2910
```

It is noted that the functions **meen** and **stdev** cannot be used independently; that is, typing, for example,

$$v = [1, 2, 3, 4];$$
$$m = \textbf{meen}(v, \texttt{length}(v))$$

in the command window will produce an error message.

If one anticipates that the functions created in support of a script will not be used outside the immediate context, then one can convert the script to a function and make all functions sub functions in that function file. The form of the main function most likely will be that given by Special Case 3 in Section 5.2.2. We illustrate this procedure in Section 5.5.4.

5.3 USER-DEFINED FUNCTIONS, FUNCTION HANDLES, AND `feval`

Many MATLAB functions require the user to create functions in a form specified by that MATLAB function. These functions use the MATLAB function

    `feval`(FunctionHandle, p1, p2,..., pn)

where *FunctionHandle* is the function handle, which we will explain below, and *p1*, *p2*, ... are parameters that are to be passed to the function represented by *FunctionHandle*. Several examples of MATLAB functions that require the use of a function handle and `feval` are given in Section 5.5. In addition, there are situations when the user would also like to have this capability.

Before proceeding with an example of a script that requires the use of `feval`, we first introduce the function handle. A function handle is a means of referencing a function and is used so that it can be passed as an argument in functions, which then evaluate it using `feval`. A function handle is constructed by placing an '@' in front of the function name. An example of its construction is given in the example below.

We will explain how this procedure works with an example based on the results of Example 4.8, where a root-finding program to determine the m lowest roots of a specific function $f(x) = 0$ was presented. We now modify this script as a function whose name is **ManyZeros**, which resides in the file *ManyZeros.m*. The function $f(x)$ and its name will now be arbitrary. In addition, it will be assumed that $f(x)$ has several parameters that are part of its definition. Furthermore, we recall that the root-finding program requires four inputs: m, the number of the lowest roots desired; x_s, the starting value for search; t, the computational tolerance that determines the degree of closeness to zero of $f(x_{\text{root}})$; and Δ, the initial search increment.

For this example, we shall let

$$f(x) = \cos(\beta x) - \alpha \quad \alpha \leq 1$$

Thus, we have to transfer to the user-defined function two quantities: β and α. This user-defined function will be called **CosBeta**, and it will reside in the file *CosBeta.m*.

The function *ManyZeros* is (recall Example 4.8)

```
function nRoots = ManyZeros(zname, n, xs, toler, dxx, b, a)
x = xs;
dx = dxx;
for m = 1:n
  s1 = sign(feval(zname, x, b, a));
  while dx/x >toler
    if s1 ~= sign(feval(zname, x+dx, b, a))
      dx = dx/2;
    else
      x = x+dx;
    end
  end
  nRoots(m) = x;
  dx = dxx;
  x = 1.05*x;
end
```

The function **CosBeta** is

```
function d = CosBeta(x, beta, alpha)
d = cos(x*beta)-alpha;
```

The function **ManyZeros** requires the following input variables: the name of the function defining $f(x)$, which is the function handle **@CosBeta**, and six parameters, the first four of which correspond to m, x_s, t, and Δ and the remaining two of which, β and α, are to be transferred to the function **CosBeta**. Depending on the value of m, the result c is either a scalar ($m = 1$) or a vector of length m.

To access the function **CosBeta** and bring back its numerical value, we use the MATLAB function `feval`. The MATLAB function `sign` then evaluates the sign of the numerical value brought back by `feval`. Also, notice that the variable names defined in the function's input variables in the script file and the two function files are mostly different. This has been done to emphasize that only the locations and subsequent usage of the arguments are important, not their alphanumeric descriptors, since the variable names are local to their respective functions.

The script file that uses these functions is

```
NoRoots = 5;  xStart = 0.2;
tolerance = 1e-6;  increment = 0.3;
beta = pi/3;  a = 0.5;
c = ManyZeros(@CosBeta, NoRoots, xStart, tolerance, increment, beta, a)
```

The execution of the script displays to the command window

```
c =
    1.0000   5.0000   7.0000   11.0000  13.0000
```

5.4 MATLAB FUNCTIONS THAT OPERATE ON ARRAYS OF DATA

5.4.1 Introduction

Many general-purpose functions in MATLAB have a wide range of use in obtaining numerical solutions to engineering problems. Here, we will consider a subset of them and divide them into two groups, those that operate on arrays of data and those that require user-defined functions. In this section, we consider those functions that require arrays of data as input; in Section 5.5, we consider those that require user-defined functions.

The functions that will be introduced in this section are

polyfit	Fits a polynomial to an array of values
polyval	Evaluates a polynomial at an array of values
spline	Applies cubic spline interpolation to arrays of coordinate values
interp1	Interpolates between pairs of coordinate values
trapz	Approximates an integral from an array of amplitude values
fft/ifft	Determines the Fourier transform and its inverse from sampled data

5.4.2 Fitting Data with Polynomials—`polyfit`/`polyval`

Consider the general form of a polynomial

$$y(x) = c_1 x^n + c_2 x^{n-1} + \cdots + c_n x + c_{n+1} \tag{5.1}$$

where x is the input value and y its corresponding output. The coefficients c_k are determined from

```
c = polyfit(x, y, n)
```

where n is the order of the polynomial, $c = [c_1 \, c_2 \, \cdots \, c_n \, c_{n+1}]$ is a vector of length $n + 1$ representing the coefficients of the polynomial in Eq. 5.1 and x and y are each vectors of length $m \geq n + 1$; they are the data to which the polynomial is fitted, with x being the input and y the output.

To evaluate Eq. 5.1 once we have determined c, we use

```
y = polyval(c, xnew)
```

where c is a vector of length $n + 1$ that has been determined from `polyfit` and *xnew* is either a scalar or a vector of points at which the polynomial will be evaluated. In general, the values of *xnew* in `polyval` can be arbitrarily selected and may or may not be the same as those values given by x.

We now illustrate these functions with an example.

Example 5.1   Neuber's constant for the notch sensitivity of steel

A notch sensitivity factor q for metals can be defined in terms of a Neuber's constant $\sqrt{a}$ and the notch radius r as follows:

$$q = \left(1 + \frac{\sqrt{a}}{\sqrt{r}}\right)^{-1}$$

TABLE 5.2   Neuber's Constant for Steel

S_u (ksi)	$\sqrt{a}(\sqrt{\text{in.}})$	S_u (ksi)	$\sqrt{a}(\sqrt{\text{in.}})$
50	0.130	170	0.028
70	0.092	190	0.020
90	0.072	210	0.015
110	0.057	230	0.010
130	0.046	250	0.007
150	0.037		

The value of $\sqrt{a}$ is different for different metals and is a function of the ultimate strength S_u of the material. It can be estimated by fitting a polynomial to experimentally obtained data of $\sqrt{a}$ as a function of S_u for a given metal. Once we have this polynomial, we can determine the value of q for a given value of r and S_u.

Let us consider the data given in the Table 5.2 for steel. Using these data, we first determine the coefficients of a fourth-order polynomial that expresses $\sqrt{a}$ as a function of S_u, and then we use this polynomial to obtain q for a given r and S_u.

To fit the data appearing in Table 5.2 and to obtain the value of $\sqrt{a}$ for any value $50 \leq S_u \leq 250$ ksi and $0 < r < 0.2$ in., we use the following script. For simplicity, we assume that we enter one set of S_u and r at a time. Furthermore, we place the data appearing in Table 5.2 in a function called **NeuberData**. The generation of a set of graphs that display the values of q for a range of data is given in Figure 6.20b.

The function for the data is

```
function nd = NeuberData
nd = [50, .13; 70, .092; 90, .072; 110, .057; 130, .046; 150, .037; ...
      170, .028; 190, .020; 210, .015; 230, .010; 250, .007];
```

where $nd(:,1) = S_u$ and $nd(:,2) = \sqrt{a}$. The script is

```
ncs = NeuberData;
c = polyfit(ncs(:,1), ncs(:,2), 4);
r = input('Enter notch radius (0 < r < 0.2 in.) ');
Su = input('Enter ultimate strength of steel (50 < Su < 250 ksi) ');
q = 1/(1+polyval(c, Su)/sqrt(r));
disp(['Notch sensitivity = ' num2str(q)])
```

Executing this script yields

```
Enter notch radius (0 < r < 0.2 in.) 0.1
Enter ultimate strength of steel (50 < Su < 250 ksi) 135
Notch sensitivity = 0.87999
```

where the script displayed the first two lines sequentially and the user entered the numbers 0.1 and 135, respectively, after each line was displayed. The program then computed the value of q and displayed the third line.

5.4.3 Fitting Data with `spline`

A very powerful way to generate smooth curves that pass through a set of discrete data values is to use splines. The function that performs this curve generation is

$$Y = \text{spline}(x, y, X)$$

where y is $y(x)$, x and y are vectors of the same length that are used to create the functional relationship $y(x)$, and X is a scalar or vector for which the values of $Y = y(X)$ are desired. In general, $x \neq X$.

We shall now illustrate the use of `spline`.

Example 5.2   Fitting data to an exponentially decaying sine wave

We shall generate some exponentially decaying oscillatory data and then fit these data with a series of splines. The data will be generated by sampling the following function over a range of nondimensional times τ for $\xi < 1.0$:

$$f(\tau, \xi) = \frac{e^{-\xi\tau}}{\cos \alpha} \cos\left(\tau\sqrt{1 - \xi^2} + \alpha\right) \tag{5.2}$$

where

$$\alpha = \tan^{-1}\frac{-\xi}{\sqrt{1 - \xi^2}}$$

We shall evaluate this equation in a function called **DampedSineWave**. Thus,

```
function f = DampedSineWave(tau, xi)
alpha = atan(-xi/sqrt(1-xi^2));
f = exp(-xi*tau).*cos(tau*sqrt(1-xi^2)+alpha)/cos(alpha);
```

Let us sample 15 equally spaced points of $f(\tau, \xi)$ over the range $0 \leq \tau \leq 20$ and plot the resulting piecewise polynomial using 200 equally spaced values of τ. We shall also plot the original waveform and assume that $\xi = 0.1$. The script is

```
n = 15; xi = 0.1;
tau = linspace(0, 20, n);
data = DampedSineWave(tau, xi);
newtau = linspace(0, 20, 200);
plot(newtau, spline(tau, data, newtau), 'k--', ...
            newtau, DampedSineWave(newtau, xi), 'k-')
```

which, when executed, produces Figure 5.1. The dashed lines are the fitted data. It is seen that the results are very good, since the original curve and the fitted curve are almost visually indistinguishable from each other. A detailed discussion of `plot` is given in Section 6.2. This smooth fit over the range considered could not have been obtained using `polyfit`.

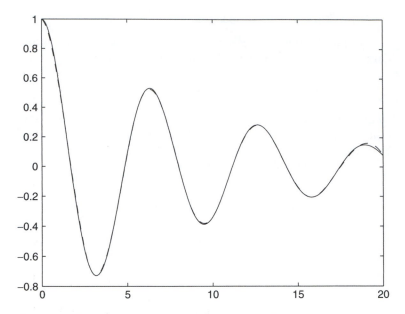

Figure 5.1   Comparison of a damped sine wave (solid line) with an approximation (dashed line) obtained with a spline using 15 equally spaced points in the
range $0 \leq \tau \leq 20$.

5.4.4 Interpolation of Data—`interp1`

To approximate the location of a value that lies between a pair of data points, we
must interpolate. The function that does this interpolation is

$$V = \texttt{interp1}(u, v, U)$$

where v is $v(u)$, u and v are vectors of the same length, and U is a scalar or vector of
values for u for which V desired. The array V has the same length as U. In general,
$u \neq U$.

   We shall now illustrate the use of `interp1`.

Example 5.3   First zero crossing of an exponentially decaying sine wave

   Let us again create a data set for the exponentially decaying sine wave given by Eq. 5.2
   and implemented with the function **DampedSineWave**. We are interested in approximating the first zero crossing from these data. From Figure 5.1, we see that this occurs
   before $\tau = 4.5$; that is, after this value, we start to get very close to the second zero
   crossing. Thus, we shall create 15 pairs of data values for the exponentially decaying
   sine wave in the range $0 \leq \tau \leq 4$ and use `interp1` to approximate the value of τ for
   which $f(\tau, \xi) \approx 0$. We assume that $\xi = 0.1$.
   The script is

```
xi = 0.1;
tau = linspace(0, 4.5, 15);
data = DampedSineWave(tau, xi);
TauZero = interp1(data, tau, 0)
```

The execution of the script gives

    TauZero =
      1.6817

The exact answer is obtained from Eq. 5.2 as

$$\tau = \frac{\pi/2 - \alpha}{\sqrt{1 - \xi^2}} = \frac{1}{\sqrt{1 - \xi^2}}\left(\pi/2 - \tan^{-1}\frac{-\xi}{\sqrt{1 - \xi^2}}\right) = 1.6794$$

5.4.5 Numerical Integration—`trapz`

One can obtain an approximation to a single integral in several ways. We shall introduce the function `trapz` in this section, which requires arrays of data. Another function, which requires the integrand to be in functional form, is `quadl`. This function is introduced in Section 5.5.2. In Section 5.6, we illustrate the use of symbolic techniques to solve integrals.

    We start with

    Area = $\text{trapz}(x, y)$

In this case, one specifies the values of x and the corresponding values of y as arrays. The function then performs the summation of the product of the average of adjacent y values and the corresponding x interval separating them.

    We now illustrate the use of this function. In these examples, we will employ the function

    `diff`

which computes the difference between successive elements of a vector; that is, for a vector $x = [x_1 \, x_2 \, \ldots \, x_n]$, a vector q with $n - 1$ elements of the form

$$q = [x_2 - x_1, x_3 - x_2, \ldots, x_n - x_{n-1}]$$

is created. For a vector x, `diff` is simply

    q = x(2:end)-x(1:end-1);

    We shall also show in Example 5.5 how `diff` can be used to obtain the length of a line in space.

Example 5.4   Area of an exponentially decaying sine wave

By using `trapz`, we shall determine the net area about the x-axis of the exponentially decaying sine wave given by Eq. 5.2 and plotted in Figure 5.1 and then show how to obtain the individual contributions of the positive and negative portions in the region $0 \le \tau \le 20$.

    The script to obtain the area of the damped sine wave, for $\xi = 0.1$ and for 200 data points, is

    xi = 0.1; N = 200;
    tau = $\text{linspace}(0, 20, N)$;
    ftau = **DampedSineWave**(tau, xi);
    Area = $\text{trapz}(\text{tau}, \text{ftau})$

Execution of this script gives

```
Area =
  0.3021
```

To determine the area of the positive and negative portions of the waveform is a little more complicated. We start in the same way that we did to determine the total area. We first generate 200 equally spaced values of τ and obtain the corresponding values of $f(\tau, \xi)$ for $\xi = 0.1$ using **DampedSineWave**. Since the positive and negative regions are separated by the x-axis, we use find and diff to obtain the indices of the values of the various portions of the positive and negative values of $f(\tau, \xi)$. We then manipulate the indices to isolate the various regions.

The diff function is used in conjunction with find to locate the beginning and end of each positive and negative region. When the values of $f(\tau, \xi)$ change from positive to negative and then back to positive, there will be a gap in the indices from find such that the difference of adjacent indices in the positive region will be 1 until there is a gap because of the negative region. When it returns to the positive region, the indicial difference will again be greater than 1. From Figure 5.1, we see that the exponentially decaying sine wave starts in the positive region. With these ideas in mind, and having the *a priori* knowledge that the last region is positive, the script is

```
xi = 0.1;  N = 200;
tau = linspace(0, 20, N);
ftau = DampedSineWave(tau, xi);
% Positive area
indx = find(ftau>=0);
reg = find(diff(indx)>1);
reg = [1 reg length(indx)];
L = length(reg);
PosArea = [];
%Negative area
indxn = find(ftau<0);
regn = find(diff(indxn)>1);
regn = [1 regn length(indxn)];
NegArea = [];
for k=1:L-1
  % Positive Area
  if  k == 1
    idx = indx(reg(k):reg(k+1));
  else
    idx = indx(reg(k)+1:reg(k+1));
  end
  PosArea = [PosArea trapz(tau(idx), ftau(idx))];
  % Negative area
  if k == 1
    idxn = indxn(regn(k):regn(k+1));
    NegArea = [NegArea trapz(tau(idxn), ftau(idxn))];
  elseif k<L-1
    idxn = indxn(regn(k)+1:regn(k+1));
```

```
        NegArea = [NegArea trapz(tau(idxn), ftau(idxn))];
    end
end
TotalPosArea = sum(PosArea)
TotalNegArea = sum(NegArea)
TotalArea = TotalPosArea+TotalNegArea
```

The execution of this script yields

```
TotalPosArea =
    2.9473
TotalNegArea =
    -2.6472
TotalArea =
    0.3001
```

We see that the total area agrees closely with the value previously obtained.

Example 5.5   Length of a line in space

Consider the following integral from which the length of a line in space can be approximated:

$$L = \int_a^b \sqrt{\left(\frac{dx}{dt}\right)^2 + \left(\frac{dy}{dt}\right)^2 + \left(\frac{dz}{dt}\right)^2}\, dt \approx \sum_{i=1}^N \sqrt{(\Delta_i x)^2 + (\Delta_i y)^2 + (\Delta_i z)^2}$$

where

$$\Delta_i x = x(t_{i+1}) - x(t_i)$$
$$\Delta_i y = y(t_{i+1}) - y(t_i)$$
$$\Delta_i z = z(t_{i+1}) - z(t_i)$$

and $t_1 = a$ and $t_{N+1} = b$.

To illustrate the approximation to L, we choose the specific parametric relations

$$x = 2t$$
$$y = t^2$$
$$z = \ln t$$

for $1 \le t \le 2$ and assume that $N = 25$. We see that the quantities $\Delta_i x$, $\Delta_i y$, and $\Delta_i z$ can each be evaluated with `diff`. Then, the script is

```
t = linspace(1, 2, 25);
L = sum(sqrt(diff(2*t).^2+diff(t.^2).^2+diff(log(t)).^2))
```

which upon execution yields

```
L =
    3.6931
```

5.4.6 Digital Signal Processing—`fft` and `ifft`

Discrete Fourier Transform

The Fourier transform of a real function $g(t)$ that is sampled every Δt over an interval $0 \le t \le T$ can be approximated by its discrete Fourier transform

$$G_n = G(n\Delta f) = \Delta t \sum_{k=0}^{N-1} g_k e^{-j2\pi nk/N} \quad n = 0, 1, \ldots, N-1$$

where $g_k = g(k\Delta t)$, $\Delta f = 1/T$, $T = N\Delta t$, and N is the number of samples (refer to Figure 5.2). In general, G_n is a complex quantity. The restriction on Δt is that

$$\alpha \Delta t < \frac{1}{f_h}$$

where f_h is the highest frequency in $g(t)$ and $\alpha \ge 2$. The quantity G_n is called the amplitude density of $g(t)$ and has the units amplitude-second or, equivalently, amplitude/Hz. The inverse transform is approximated by

$$g_k = \Delta f \sum_{n=0}^{N-1} G_n e^{j2\pi nk/N} \quad k = 0, 1, \ldots, N-1$$

To estimate the magnitude of the amplitude A_n corresponding to each G_n at its corresponding frequency $n\Delta f$, one multiplies G_n by Δf. Thus,

$$A_n = \Delta f G_n$$

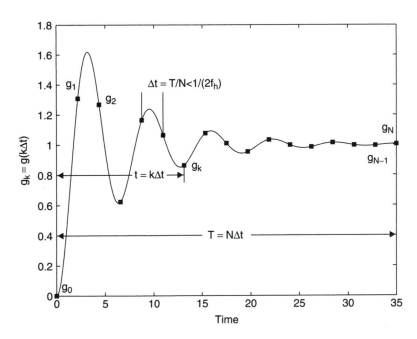

Figure 5.2 Sampled waveform.

and, therefore,

$$A_n = \frac{1}{N} \sum_{k=0}^{N-1} g_k e^{-j2\pi nk/N} \quad n = 0, 1, \ldots, N-1$$

since $\Delta f \Delta t = 1/N$. The average power in the signal is

$$P_{avg} = \sum_{n=0}^{N-1} |A_n|^2$$

One often plots $|A_n|$ as a function of $n\Delta f$ to obtain an amplitude spectral plot. In this case, we have[2]

$$|A_n|_s = 2|A_n| \quad n = 0, 1, \ldots, N/2 - 1$$

These expressions are best evaluated using the fast Fourier transform (FFT), which is a very efficient algorithm for numerically evaluating the discrete Fourier transform. It is most effective when the number of sampled data points is a power of 2—that is, $N = 2^m$, where m is a positive integer. The FFT algorithm is implemented with

G = fft(g, N)

and its inverse with

g = ifft(G, N)

where $G = G_n/\Delta t$ and $g = g_k/\Delta f$.

Weighting Functions

In many situations, it is desirable to weight $g(t)$ by a suitable function to provide better resolution or other properties in the transformed domain. The procedure is to modify the original signal before performing the discrete Fourier transform in such a way that the effects of the changes caused by the windowing function to the signal's mean value and to the signal's average power are removed. Thus, if the sampled values of the weighting function are $w_n = w(n\Delta t)$, then the corrected signal g_{cn} is given by[3]

$$g_{cn} = k_2 w_n (g_n - k_1) \quad n = 0, 1, \ldots, N-1$$

where

$$k_1 = \sum_{n=0}^{N-1} w_n g_n \Bigg/ \sum_{n=0}^{N-1} w_n$$

---

[2]See, for example, J. S. Bendat and A. G. Piersol, *Engineering Applications of Correlation and Spectral Analysis*, John Wiley & Sons, New York, 1980.
[3]E. C. Ifeachor and B. W. Jervis, *Digital Signal Processing: A Practical Approach*, Addison-Wesley, Harlow, England, 1993, p. 593.

corrects for the mean of the windowing function and

$$k_2 = \left[N \Big/ \sum_{n=0}^{N-1} w_n^2 \right]^{1/2}$$

corrects for the average power of the windowing function. One then takes the discrete Fourier transform of g_{cn}.

The Digital Signal Processing Toolbox contains eight commonly used weighting functions.

Cross-correlation

The cross-correlation of two functions $x(t)$ and $y(t)$ is given by

$$R_{xy}(\tau) = \int_{-\infty}^{\infty} x(t)y(t + \tau)\, dt \quad -\infty < \tau < \infty$$

It is current practice to evaluate this quantity from the inverse Fourier transform of the cross-spectral density function $S_{xy}(\omega)$:

$$R_{xy}(\tau) = F^{-1}[S_{xy}(\omega)]$$

where $F^{-1}(\dots)$ indicates the inverse Fourier transform and

$$S_{xy}(\omega) = X(\omega)Y^*(\omega)$$

The quantities $X(\omega)$ and $Y(\omega)$ are the Fourier transforms of $x(t)$ and $y(t)$, respectively, and the asterisk denotes the complex conjugate. To convert $R_{xy}(\tau)$ to its proper units requires that we multiply $S_{xy}(\omega)$ by $\Delta t = T/N$.

We shall illustrate these relationships with two examples.

Example 5.6   Fourier transform of a sine wave

Let us sample a sine wave of duration T. Thus,

$$g(t) = A_o \sin(2\pi f_o t) \quad 0 \le t \le T = 2^k/f_o \quad K = 0, 1, 2, \dots$$

and

$$\Delta t < 1/(2f_o) \quad \text{or} \quad m - K > 1$$

since

$$f_h = f_o = 2^K/T$$

and

$$\Delta t = 2^{-m}T$$

We assume that $g(t)$ is weighted by the Hamming function, which is given by

$$w(t) = 0.54 - 0.46 \cos(2\pi t/T) \quad 0 \le t \le T$$
$$= 0 \quad \text{otherwise}$$

The script to compute and plot the corrected weighted signal $g_c(t)$ and the amplitude spectrum A_n and display the average power in the signal, which is $P_{avg} = A_o^2/2$, is as follows: We assume that $A_o = 2.5$, $f_o = 10$ Hz, $K = 5$, and $m = 10$ ($N = 1024$). Then,

```
k = 5;  m = 10;  fo = 10;  Ao = 2.5;
N = 2^m;  T = 2^k/fo;
ts = (0:N-1)*T/N;
df = (0:N/2-1)/T;
whamm = 0.54-0.46*cos(2*pi*ts/T);
SampledSignal = Ao*sin(2*pi*fo*ts);
k1 = sum(whamm.*SampledSignal)/sum(whamm);
k2 = sqrt(N/sum(whamm.^2));
CorrectedSignal = whamm.*(SampledSignal-k1)*k2;
figure(1)
plot(ts, CorrectedSignal)
figure(2)
An = abs(fft(CorrectedSignal, N))/N;
plot(df, 2*An(1:N/2))
disp(['Average power = ' num2str(sum(An.^2))])
```

Execution of the script results in Figures 5.3 and 5.4 and the following result being displayed to the command window:

Average power = 3.125

The MATLAB function `figure` is used to provide two separate figure windows (see Section 6.1). Notice in Figure 5.4 that the amplitude of the sine wave does not equal 2.5. This value is obtained, however, when the weighting function is removed.

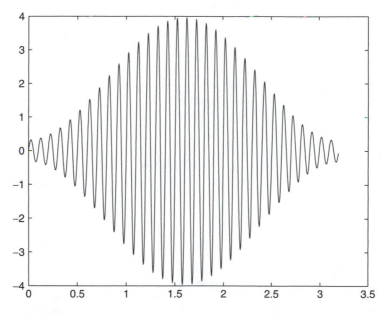

Figure 5.3   Sine wave modified by the Hamming weighting function.

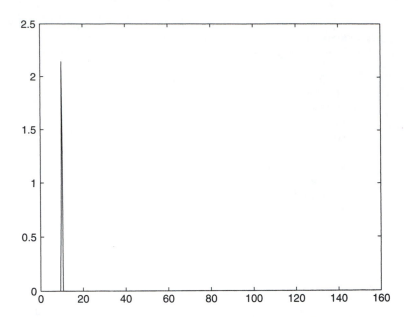

Figure 5.4   Amplitude spectrum of a sine wave using a Hamming weighting function.

Example 5.7   Cross-correlation of two pulses

We shall determine the cross-correlation function for the two rectangular pulses shown in Figure 5.5, which are expressed as

$$x(t) = A_x[u(t) - u(t - T_o)] \quad t \geq 0$$
$$y(t) = A_y[u(t - T_1) - u(t - T_1 - T_2)] \quad t \geq 0$$

where $u(t)$ is the unit step function. We assume that $A_x = A_y = 1$, $T_o = 0.01$ s, $T_1 = 2T_o$, $T_2 = T_1 + T_o$, $T = T_2 + T_o$ and $N = 2^{10}$.

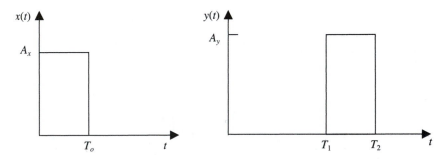

Figure 5.5   Two rectangular pulses.

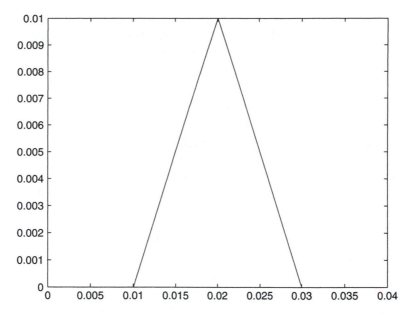

Figure 5.6   Cross-correlation function of two rectangular pulses of equal duration.

The script is

```
To = 0.01;  T1 = 2*To;  T2 = T1+To;  Tend = T2+To;
N = 2^10;  deltaT = Tend/N;  Ax = 1;  Ay = 1;
t = linspace(0, Tend, N);
PulseCrossCorr = inline('ampl*((t−Ts>=0)−(t−Te>0))', 't', 'Ts', 'Te', 'ampl');
x = PulseCrossCorr(t, 0, To, Ax);
y = PulseCrossCorr(t, T1, T2, Ay);
X = fft(x, N);
Y = conj(fft(y, N));
Rxy = ifft(X.*Y*deltaT, N);
plot(t, real(Rxy))
```

Execution of the script results in Figure 5.6. The function `real` removes residual imaginary parts because of numerical round-off errors.

5.5 MATLAB FUNCTIONS THAT REQUIRE USER-CREATED FUNCTIONS

MATLAB provides several functions that evaluate user-defined functions. The ones that we shall illustrate in this section are

`fzero`	Finds one root of $f(x) = 0$
`roots`	Finds the roots of a polynomial
`quadl`	Numerically integrates $f(x)$ in a specified interval

dblquad	Numerically integrates $f(x,y)$ in a specified region
ode45	Solves a system of ordinary differential equations with prescribed initial conditions
bvp4c	Solves a system of ordinary differential equations with prescribed boundary conditions
fminbnd	Finds a local minimum of $f(x)$ in a specified interval
fsolve	Numerically solves a system of nonlinear equations

The last function, fsolve, is from the Optimization toolbox.

When using these functions, the arguments of the user-defined functions and/or their output have to conform to specific requirements. These different requirements are illustrated in the following sections and are clearly specified in the *Help* file for that function.

5.5.1 Zeros of Functions—fzero and roots/poly

For many equations, an explicit algebraic solution to $f(x) = 0$ cannot be found. In these cases, a numerical procedure is required. The function fzero is a function that finds numerically one solution to the real function $f(x) = 0$ within a tolerance t_o in either the neighborhood of x_o or within the range $[x_1, x_2]$. It can also transfer p_j, where $j = 1, 2, \ldots$, parameters to the function defining $f(x)$. The function $f(x)$ must have a change of sign in the interval $[x_1, x_2]$; otherwise, an error message results. The general expression is

z = fzero(@**FunctionName**, x0, options, p1, p2, ...)

where z is the value of x for which $f(z) \approx 0$; **FunctionName** is the name of the function file without the extension 'm'; x0 = x_o or x0 = $[x_1\ x_2]$, p1, p2, etc., are the parameters p_j required by **FunctionName;** and *options* is set using

optimset

The function optimset is a general parameter-adjusting function that is used by several MATLAB functions, primarily from the optimization toolbox. As a minimum, it is recommended that optimset be used to turn the display off—that is,

options = optimset('Display', 'off ');

would precede each use of fzero. See the *Help* file for optimset for the types of attributes that can be altered; they are dependent on the function selected.

The interface for the function required by fzero has the form

function z = FunctionName(x, p1, p2, ...)
Expression(s)

where x is the independent variable that fzero is changing to find a value such that $f(x = z) \cong 0$. *Expressions* must be able to handle a vector of x; therefore, *Expressions* is usually expressed in dot notation. The independent variable must always appear in the first location. This requirement is true for most user-defined functions that are created for evaluation by MATLAB functions and for all functions illustrated in this chapter.

The function `fzero` can also be used with the `inline` function in either of two ways:

InlineFunctionName = `inline`('Expression', 'x', 'p1', 'p2', ...);
z = `fzero`(**InlineFunctionName**, x0, options, p1, p2, ...)

or as

z = `fzero`(`inline`('Expression', 'x', 'p1', 'p2', ...), x0, options, p1, p2, ...)

The former syntax is preferred unless *Expression* has a very simple form.

We shall now illustrate the use of `fzero` with the goal of pointing out how to avoid making a poor choice of x0. The function $f(x)$ can be either a MATLAB function or a user-created one. Let us assume that we want to determine a root of $\cos(x)$ near $x = 2\pi$. Then, selecting a guess of $x0 = 2\pi$, the script

options = `optimset`('Display', 'off ');
w = `fzero`(@cos, 2*pi, options)/pi

yields, upon execution,

w =
    1.5000

that is, $\cos(1.5\pi) = 0$. However, notice what happens when we change the initial guess slightly to $x0 = 2.04\pi$:

options = `optimset`('Display', 'off ');
w = `fzero`(@cos, 2.04*pi, options)/pi

Executing this script yields

w =
    2.5000

However, when $x0 = 2.03\pi$, the script

options = `optimset`('Display', 'off ');
w = `fzero`(@cos, 2.03*pi, options)/pi

yields, upon execution,

w =
    1.5000

Thus, for multivalued functions, one should use the form $x0 = [x_1 \ x_2]$ and specify the region explicitly. However, an error will result if the sign of $f(x_1)$ does not differ from the sign of $f(x_2)$. To show this, we rewrite the above script as

options = `optimset`('Display', 'off');
w = `fzero`(@cos, [0, 2*pi], options)/pi

When we execute this script, an error message is displayed saying that the values at the interval endpoints must differ in sign. However, when the interval is changed as given below,

```
options = optimset('Display', 'off');
w = fzero(@cos,[0.6*pi, 2*pi], options)/pi
```

we obtain, upon execution, that

```
w =
    1.5000
```

Hence, for multivalued functions whose properties are not known *a priori*, one should plot the function first to estimate the interval(s) where its zeros are.

We now determine the root of $J_1(x) = 0$ near 3, where $J_1(x)$ is the Bessel[4] function of the first kind of order 1. The Bessel function is obtained from

```
besselj(n, x)
```

where n is the order (in this case, 1) and x is the independent variable. We cannot use this function directly, because the independent variable x is not the first variable in the function (n is the first variable). Hence, we create a new function using `inline` as follows:

```
besseljx = inline('besselj(n, x)', 'x', 'n');
options = optimset('Display', 'off ');
a = fzero(besseljx, 3, options, 1)
```

Upon execution, we obtain

```
a =
    3.8317
```

Notice that to transfer the parameter $p_1 = n = 1$ to the function *besseljx*, we had to place a value of 1 in the fourth location of `fzero`.

We now present several additional examples of the use of `fzero`.

Example 5.8 Lowest five natural frequency coefficients of a clamped beam

The characteristic equation from which the natural frequency coefficients Ω of a thin beam clamped at each end is given by (see Section 9.4.1)

$$f(\Omega) = \cos(\Omega) \cosh(\Omega) - 1$$

We now use this equation to determine the lowest five roots (not including $\Omega = 0$). The procedure first is to graph the function over a range of Ω to observe the approximate locations of Ω at which $f(\Omega) = 0$. (This graph is not shown.) The resulting

---

[4]See, for example, F. B. Hildebrand, *Advanced Calculus for Applications*, Prentice-Hall, Upper Saddle River, NJ, 1976.

information is then used to obtain five ranges over which `fzero` is to search for a zero (root). The script is

```
qcc = inline('cos(x).*cosh(x)-1', 'x');
options = optimset('Display', 'off');
% Om = linspace(0, 20);
% plot(Om, qcc(Om))
% axis([0, 20, -10, 10])
xo = [3, 5];
for n = 1:5
    q(n) = fzero(qcc, xo, options);
    xo = [1.05*q(n), q(n)+4];
end
disp('Lowest five natural frequency coefficients are:')
disp(num2str(q))
```

Upon execution, the following is displayed to the command window

Lowest five natural frequency coefficients are:
4.73004   7.8532   10.9956   14.1372   17.2788

The magnitude of **qcc** varies over a very large positive and negative range; therefore, we employed `axis` to limit the values displayed, thereby greatly increasing the graph's resolution. In this case, we limited the y-axis to ±10 (see Section 6.2). From the graph, we determined that the search region for Ω could be from a value that was 5% greater than the previous root location to the previous root location plus 4, which always placed the upper limit of the search region slightly beyond the next zero location. In the actual development of the script, the last six expressions were not written until the first five expressions were executed and the results analyzed. Once this information had been determined, it was no longer needed, and the expressions were commented out.

If $f(\Omega)$ were such that a constant value (in this case, 4) didn't exist and, instead, several different values C_j, *where* $j = 1, 2, 3, 4$, were required, then the above script would become

```
qcc = inline('cos(x).*cosh(x)-1', 'x');
options = optimset('Display', 'off');
C = [ 4, 5, 6, 5, 0];
xo = [3, 5];
for n = 1:5
    q(n) = fzero(qcc, xo, options);
    xo = [1.05*q(n), q(n)+C(n)];
end
disp('Lowest five natural frequency coefficients are:')
disp(num2str(q))
```

The vector C has had added to it a fifth element 0 that is not used by the `fzero` but that is required because of the value of subscript of C.

Example 5.9   Zero of a function expressed as a series

We shall determine the value of a that satisfies the series equation

$$\sum_{j=1}^{1000} \frac{1}{j^2 - a} = 0$$

and display its annotated value to the command window. We shall used an initial guess of $\pi/2$.

The script is

```
suma = inline('sum(1./([1:1000].^2-a))', 'a');
options = optimset('Display', 'off');
fofa = fzero(suma, pi/2, options);
disp(['The value of a is ' num2str(fofa)])
```

Upon execution, we obtain

The value of a is 2.0466

When $f(x)$ is a polynomial of the form

$$f(x) = c_1 x^n + c_2 x^{n-1} + \cdots + c_n x + c_{n+1}$$

its roots can more easily be found by using

```
roots(c)
```

where

$$c = [c_1, c_2, \ldots, c_{n+1}]$$

For example, if

$$f(x) = x^4 - 10x^3 + 35x^2 - 50x + 24$$

then the script to find all the roots of the polynomial is

```
r = roots([1, -10, 35, -50, 24])
```

Executing this script gives

```
r =
    4.0000
    3.0000
    2.0000
    1.0000
```

The inverse of `roots` is

```
c = poly(r)
```

which returns c, the polynomial's coefficients, and r is a vector of roots. In the general case, r is a vector of real and/or complex numbers. Thus,

```
r = roots([1, -10, 35, -50, 24]);
c = poly(r)
```

displays upon execution

```
c =
   1.0000  -10.0000   35.0000  -50.0000   24.0000
```

Polynomials can also be multiplied using

```
conv(a, b)
```

where a and b are vectors containing the coefficients of the respective polynomials. For example, suppose we had, in addition to $f(x)$, another polynomial

$$g(x) = x^2 - 4$$

Then, the product $h(x) = g(x)f(x)$ is obtained from

```
h = conv([1, 0, -4], [1, -10, 35, -50, 24])
```

which upon execution results in

```
h =
   1  -10   31   -10  -116   200   -96
```

Thus, the resultant polynomial is

$$h(x) = x^6 - 10x^5 + 31x^4 - 10x^3 - 116x^2 + 200x - 96$$

5.5.2 Numerical Integration—`quadl` and `dblquad`

The function `quadl` numerically integrates a user-provided function $f(x)$ from a lower limit a to an upper limit b to within a tolerance t_o. It can also transfer p_j parameters to the function defining $f(x)$. The general expression for `quadl`, when $f(x)$ is represented by a function file, is

A = quadl(@**FunctionName**, a, b, t0, tc, p1, p2, …)

where **FunctionName** is the name of the function M-file without the extension '.m'; $a = a$; $b = b$; $t0 = t_o$ (when omitted, the default value is used); p1, p2, etc., are the parameters p_j; and when $tc \neq []$, `quadl` provides intermediate output. When the function is created by `inline`, then

A = quadl(**InlineFunctionName**, a, b, t0, tc, p1, p2, …)

where **InlineFunctionName** is the name of the inline function.
    The interface for the function M-file has the form

```
function z = FunctionName(x, p1, p2, …)
Expression(s)
```

where x is the independent variable over which `quadl` is integrating. The independent variable must always appear in this location. The interface for `inline` is

InlineFunctionName = inline ('Expression', 'x', 'p1', 'p2', …)

We shall now illustrate the use of `quadl`.

Example 5.10   Determination of area and centroid

Two quantities that are frequently of interest in mechanics are the area of a two-dimensional shape and the location of its centroid. Let us assume that we have two curves $y_j = f_j(x)$, where $j = 1, 2$, and that the two curves intersect at x_1 and x_2. Then, the area between the two intersection points of the curves is

$$A = \int dA = \int_{x_1}^{x_2} (y_2 - y_1)\, dx$$

and the location of the area's centroid with respect to the origin is

$$x_c = \frac{1}{A} \int x\, dA = \frac{1}{A} \int_{x_1}^{x_2} x(y_2 - y_1)\, dx$$

$$y_c = \frac{1}{A} \int y\, dA = \frac{1}{A} \int_{x_1}^{x_2} \tfrac{1}{2}(y_2 + y_1)\, dA = \frac{1}{2A} \int_{x_1}^{x_2} (y_2^2 - y_1^2)\, dx$$

Suppose that $y_2 = x + 2$ and $y_1 = x^2$, which are shown in Figure 5.7. Then, it is straightforward to show that the intersections occur at $x_1 = -1$ and $x_2 = 2$. Performing the above integrations yield $A = 4.5$, $x_c = 0.5$, and $y_c = 1.6$. We now repeat these calculations numerically.

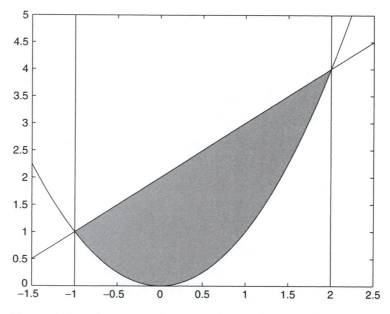

Figure 5.7   Shape for which the centroid and area are determined.

Since the expressions for these curves are relatively simple, we use `inline` to represent them. The script is

Atop = inline('x+2', 'x');
Abot = inline('x.^2', 'x');
Area = quadl(**Atop**, -1, 2)-quadl(**Abot**, -1, 2)
Mxc = inline('x.*((x+2)-x.^2)', 'x');
Myc= inline('((x+2).^2-x.^4)/2', 'x');
xc = quadl(**Mxc**, -1, 2)/Area
yc = quadl(**Myc**, -1, 2)/Area

The execution of the script gives

Area =
   4.5000
xc =
   0.5000
yc =
   1.6000

Example 5.11   Area of an exponentially decaying sine wave revisited

The damped sine wave is represented by the function **DampedSineWave**. If we again let $\xi = 0.1$ and integrate from $0 \le \tau \le 20$, then the script is

xi = 0.1;
Area = quadl(@**DampedSineWave**, 0, 20, [], [], xi)

Upon execution, we obtain

Area =
   0.3022

which agrees with what was determined in Example 5.4.

The function `dblquad` numerically integrates a user-provided function $f(x,y)$ from a lower limit x_l to an upper limit x_u in the x-direction and from a lower limit y_l to an upper limit y_u in the y-direction to within a tolerance t_o. It can also transfer p_j parameters to the function defining $f(x,y)$. The general expression for `dblquad`, when $f(x,y)$ is represented by function file, is

dblquad(@**FunctionName**, xl, xu, yl, yu, t0, meth, p1, p2, ...)

where **FunctionName** is the name of the function M-file without the extension '.m', xl = x_l; xu = x_u; yl = y_l; yu = y_u; t0 = t_o (when omitted, the default value is used); p1, p2, etc., are the parameters p_j; and when meth = [], `quadl` is used. When the function is created by `inline`, then

dblquad(**InlineFunctionName**, xl, xu, yl, yu, t0, meth, p1, p2, ...)

where **InlineFunctionName** is the name of the inline function.

The interface for the function file has the form

```
function z = FunctionName(x, y, p1, p2, ...)
Expression(s)
```

We now illustrate the use of dblquad.

Example 5.12   Probability of two correlated variables

We shall numerically integrate the following expression for the probability of two random variables that are normally distributed over the region indicated:

$$V = \frac{1}{2\pi\sqrt{1-r^2}}\int_{-2}^{2}\int_{-3}^{3} e^{-(x^2-2rxy+y^2)/2}\, dx\, dy$$

If we assume that $r = 0.5$, then the script is

```
r = 0.5;
Arg = inline('exp(-(x.^2-2*r*x.*y+y.^2))', 'x', 'y', 'r');
P = dblquad(Arg, -3, 3, -2, 2, [], [], r)/2/pi/sqrt(1-r^2)
```

Upon execution, we obtain

```
P =
    0.6570
```

5.5.3 Numerical Solutions of Ordinary Differential Equations—ode45

MATLAB can numerically solve two different types of systems of ordinary differential equations. The type of solver that is selected depends on whether one is solving an initial value problem or a boundary value problem. In the initial value problem, the conditions at $t = 0$ (or $x = 0$) are prescribed. In the boundary value problem, the conditions at both ends of the domain are prescribed—say, at $x = 0$ and $x = L$. The initial value problem is solved with

```
ode45
```

and the boundary value problem with

```
bvp4c
```

We shall discuss ode45 in this section and bvp4c in Section 5.5.4.

The function ode45 returns the numerical solution to a system of n first-order ordinary differential equations

$$\frac{dy_j}{dt} = f_j(t, y_1, y_2, \ldots, y_n) \quad j = 1, 2, \ldots, n$$

over the interval $t_0 \leq t \leq t_f$ subject to the initial conditions $y_j(t_0) = a_j$, where $j = 1, 2, \ldots, n$ and a_j are constants. The arguments and outputs of ode45 are as

[t, y] = ode45(@**FunctionName**, [t0, tf], [a1, a2, ..., an], options, p1, p2, ...)

where the output t is a column vector of the times $t_0 \leq t \leq t_f$ that are determined by ode45, the output y is the matrix of solutions such that the rows correspond to the times t, and the columns correspond to the solutions

$$y(:, 1) = y_1(t)$$
$$y(:, 2) = y_2(t)$$
$$\cdots$$
$$y(:, n) = y_n(t)$$

The first argument of `ode45` is @**FunctionName**, which is a handle to the function file *FunctionName.m*. Its form must be as follows:[5]

`function yprime = FunctionName(t, y, p1, p2, ...)`

where t is the independent variable; y is a column vector whose elements correspond to y_j, $p1$, $p2$, $\ldots$ are parameters passed to **FunctionName**; and *yprime* is a column vector of length n whose elements are $f_j(t, y_1, y_2, \ldots, y_n)$, where $j = 1, 2, \ldots, n$—that is,

$$yprime = [f_1; f_2; \ldots; f_n]$$

The variable names *yprime*, **FunctionName**, etc. are assigned by the programmer.

The second argument of `ode45` is a two-element vector giving the starting and ending times over which the numerical solution will be obtained. This quantity can, instead, be a vector of the times $[t_0 \, t_1 \, t_2 \, \ldots \, t_f]$ at which the solutions will be given. The third argument is a vector of initial conditions $y_j(t_0) = a_j$. The fourth argument, *options*, is usually set to null; however, if some of the solution method tolerances are to be changed, one does this with `odeset` (see the `odeset` *Help* file). The remaining arguments are those that are passed to **FunctionName**.

Six other ordinary differential equation solvers in MATLAB can be used to solve initial value problems, each of which has its own advantages depending on the particular properties of the differential equations. They are `ode23`, `ode113`, `ode15s`, `ode23s`, `ode23t`, and `ode23tb`. Their use is the same as described for `ode45`. (See the MATLAB users guide and their respective *Help* files for details). MATLAB recommends that one start the solution process with `ode45`.

We now illustrate the usage of `ode45` by considering the nondimensional second-order ordinary differential equation

$$\frac{d^2y}{dt^2} + 2\xi\frac{dy}{dt} + y = h(t) \tag{5.3}$$

which is subjected to the initial conditions $y(0) = a$ and $dy(0)/dt = b$. Equation 5.3 can be rewritten as a system of two first-order equations with the substitution

$$y_1 = y$$
$$y_2 = \frac{dy}{dt}$$

---

[5]One can also use `inline`; however, the number of required arguments in the interface line changes. We will not discuss the use of `inline` here, because the `inline` interface is compatible with an older MATLAB version of `ode45` and its acceptance of the "old" interface is to preserve backward compatibility.

Then, the system of equations is

$$\frac{dy_1}{dt} = y_2$$

$$\frac{dy_2}{dt} = -2\xi y_2 - y_1 + h$$

with the initial conditions $y_1(0) = a$ and $y_2(0) = b$.

Let us consider the case where $\xi = 0.15$, $y(0) = 1$, $dy(0)/dt = 0$, and

$$h(t) = \sin(\pi t/5) \qquad 0 \le t \le 5$$
$$= 0 \qquad\qquad t > 5$$

We are interested in the solution over the region $0 \le t \le 35$. Therefore, $y_1(0) = 1$, $y_2(0) = 0$, $t_0 = 0$, and $t_f = 35$. We solve this system by creating a main function called **Exampleode** and a sub function called **HalfSine**. Then, the script (functions) to solve the system of ordinary differential equations and to plot $y_1(t) = y(t)$ is

```
function Exampleode
[t, yy] = ode45(@HalfSine, [0 35], [1 0], [], 0.15); plot(t, yy(:,1))

function y = HalfSine(t, y, z)
h = sin(pi*t/5).*(t<=5);
y = [y(2); -2*z*y(2)-y(1)+h];
```

The results are shown in Figure 5.8. It is noted that $yy(:, 1) = y_1(t) = y(t)$ and $yy(:, 2) = y_2(t) = dy/dt$.

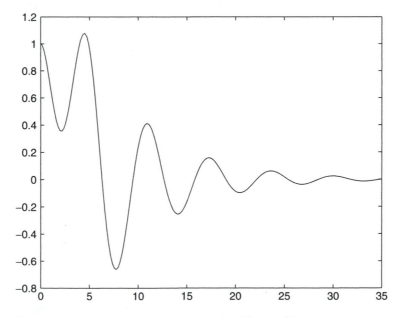

Figure 5.8   Response of Eq. 5.3 to the initial conditions $y(0) = 1$ and $dy(0)/dt = 0$ and when $h(t)$ is a half sine wave.

We now give several additional examples that show the wide range of problems that `ode45` can solve.

Example 5.13   Natural convection along a heated vertical plate

The equations describing the natural convection along a heated vertical plate in contact with a cooler fluid is given by (see Section 12.3.2)

$$\frac{d^3 f}{d\eta^3} + 3f\frac{d^2 f}{d\eta^2} - 2\left(\frac{df}{d\eta}\right)^2 + T^* = 0$$

$$\frac{d^{2*} T^*}{d\eta^2} + 3\Pr f\frac{dT^*}{d\eta} = 0$$

where Pr is the Prandtl number. When Pr $= 0.7$, the initial conditions at $\eta = 0$ are

$$f = 0 \qquad \frac{df}{d\eta} = 0 \qquad \frac{d^2 f}{d\eta^2} = 0.68$$

$$T^* = 1 \qquad \frac{dT^*}{d\eta} = -0.50$$

This coupled system of equations can be decomposed into a system of five first-order equations by introducing the following set of dependent variables:

$$y_1 = f \qquad y_4 = T^*$$

$$y_2 = \frac{df}{d\eta} \qquad y_5 = \frac{dT^*}{d\eta}$$

$$y_3 = \frac{d^2 f}{d\eta^2}$$

where y_1 is the stream function, y_2 is the velocity, y_3 is the shear in the fluid stream, y_4 is the temperature, and y_5 is the heat flux. Then, the system of first-order differential equations in terms of these new variables is

$$\frac{dy_1}{d\eta} = y_2 \qquad \frac{dy_4}{d\eta} = y_5$$

$$\frac{dy_2}{d\eta} = y_3 \qquad \frac{dy_5}{d\eta} = -3\Pr y_1 y_5$$

$$\frac{dy_3}{d\eta} = 2y_2^2 - 3y_1 y_3 - y_4$$

The corresponding initial conditions at $\eta = 0$ are

$$y_1(0) = 0 \quad y_4(0) = 1$$
$$y_2(0) = 0 \quad y_5(0) = -0.50$$
$$y_3(0) = 0.68$$

To solve this system of equations, we create the sub function **NaturalConv** to specify the column vector representing the right-hand side of the five first-order differential equations. Assuming that $0 \leq \eta \leq 20$, the script is

```
function Example 5_13 y0 = [0, 0, 0.68, 1, -0.50];
Pr = 0.7;
[eta ff] = ode45(@NaturalConv, [0 20], y0, [], Pr);

function ff = NaturalConv(x, y, Pr)
ff = [y(2); y(3); -3*y(1)*y(3)+2*y(2)^2-y(4); y(5); -3*Pr*y(1)*y(5)];
```

The results are shown in Figure 12.14.

Example 5.14   Pendulum absorber

Consider the pendulum absorber shown in Figure 5.9. It can be shown that the nondimensional equations governing the motion of the system are[6]

$$\ddot{z} + 2\zeta_x \dot{z} + z + m_r[\ddot{\varphi} \sin \varphi + \dot{\varphi}^2 \cos \varphi] = f_o \cos \Omega \tau$$

$$\ddot{\varphi} + 2\zeta_t \dot{\varphi} + (\omega_r^2 + \ddot{z}) \sin \varphi = 0$$

where the dot indicates the derivative with respect to τ, g is the gravitational constant, c and c_t are the values of damping, k is the spring constant, m and M are mass of the pendulum and the main mass, respectively, and

$$z = \frac{x}{l} \quad \tau = \omega_x t \quad \omega_r = \frac{\omega_\varphi}{\omega_x} \quad \Omega = \frac{\omega}{\omega_x} \quad f_o = \frac{F_o}{(M + m)l\omega_x^2} \quad \omega_\varphi = \sqrt{\frac{g}{l}}$$

$$2\zeta_x = \frac{c}{(M + m)\omega_x} \quad 2\zeta_i = \frac{c_t}{ml^2\omega_x} \quad m_r = \frac{m}{(M + m)} \quad \omega_x = \sqrt{\frac{k}{m + M}}$$

To put these equations in the form of a system of first order equations, we set

$$x_1 = z \quad x_3 = \varphi$$

$$x_2 = \dot{z} \quad x_4 = \dot{\varphi}$$

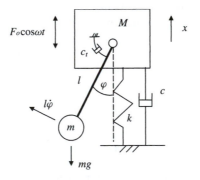

Figure 5.9   Pendulum absorber.

---

[6]B. Balachandran and E. B. Magrab, *Vibrations*, Brooks/Cole, Belmont, CA, 2004, p. 458.

Thus,

$$\dot{x}_1 = x_2 \quad \dot{x}_3 = x_4$$

To obtain the remaining two first-order equations, we use these results in the original equations to arrive at the following system of coupled equations in matrix form:

$$\begin{bmatrix} 1 & m_r \sin x_3 \\ \sin x_3 & 1 \end{bmatrix} \begin{Bmatrix} \dot{x}_2 \\ \dot{x}_4 \end{Bmatrix} = \begin{Bmatrix} A \\ B \end{Bmatrix}$$

where

$$\begin{Bmatrix} A \\ B \end{Bmatrix} = \begin{Bmatrix} f_o \cos \Omega \tau - 2\zeta_x x_2 - x_1 - x_4^2 m_r \cos x_3 \\ -2\zeta_t x_4 - \omega_r^2 \sin x_3 \end{Bmatrix}$$

Upon solving for $\dot{x}_2$ and $\dot{x}_4$, we obtain

$$\dot{x}_2 = \frac{A - Bm_r \sin x_3}{1 - m_r \sin^2 x_3}$$

$$\dot{x}_4 = \frac{B - A \sin x_3}{1 - m_r \sin^2 x_3}$$

For systems of practical interest, m_r is much less than 1; therefore, there are no singularities in these quantities.

Let us obtain a solution for the case when $\Omega = 1$, $\omega_r = 0.5$, $\zeta_x = 0.05$, $\zeta_t = 0.005$, $m_r = 0.05$, $f_o = 0.03$, and $0 \le \tau \le 300$. We shall plot the angular rotation φ when $\varphi(0) = x_3 = 0.02$ rad. In solving this system of equations, we use global, since six parameters have to be transferred to the function. In addition, the sub function for the interface required by ode45 is called **PendulumAbsorber**. The script is

```
function Example5_14
global MR WR ZX ZT OM FO
MR = 0.05;  ZX = 0.05;  ZT = 0.005;
OM = 1;  WR = 0.5;  FO = 0.03;
[t w]=ode45(@PendulumAbsorber, [0 300], [0 0 .02 0]);
plot(t, w(:,3))

function Q = PendulumAbsorber(t, w)
global MR WR ZX ZT OM FO
A = FO*cos(OM*t)-w(1)-2*ZX*w(2)-MR*w(4)^2*cos(w(3));
B = -2*ZT*w(4)-WR^2*sin(w(3));
x4dot = (B-A*sin(w(3)))/(1-MR*sin(w(3))^2);
x2dot = (A-MR*B*sin(w(3)))/(1-MR*sin(w(3))^2);
Q=[w(2); x2dot; w(4); x4dot];
```

The results are plotted in Figure 5.10.

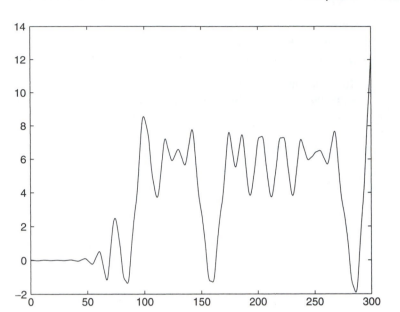

Figure 5.10   Angular rotation of the pendulum of a pendulum absorber.

5.5.4 Numerical Solutions of Ordinary Differential Equations—bvp4c

The MATLAB function bvp4c obtains numerical solutions to the two-point boundary value problem. However, unlike ode45, bvp4c requires the use of several additional MATLAB functions that were specifically created to assist in initializing bvp4c (bvpinit) and in smoothing its output for plotting (deval). In addition, several function files must be created to use bvp4c.

The function bvp4c returns the numerical solution to a system of n first-order ordinary differential equations:

$$\frac{dy_j}{dx} = f_j(x, y_1, y_2, \ldots, y_n, q) \quad j = 1, 2, \ldots, n$$

over the interval $a \leq x \leq b$ subject to the boundary conditions $y_j(a) = a_j$ and $y_j(b) = b_j$, where $j = 1, 2, \ldots, n, a_j$ and b_j are constants, and q is a vector of unknown parameters. We will not discuss the case where the system of equations contains the unknown parameters q. The arguments and outputs of bvp4c are as follows:

sol = bvp4c(@**FunctionName**, @**BCFunction**, solinit, options, p1, p2, …)

The function **FunctionName** requires the following interface

function dydx = FunctionName(x, y, p1, p2, …)

where x is a scalar corresponding to x, y is a column vector of f_j, and p1, p2, etc., are known parameters that are needed to define f_j. The output $dxdy$ is a column vector.

The function **BCFunction** contains the boundary conditions $y_j(a) = a_j$ and $y_j(b) = b_j$, where $j = 1, 2, \ldots, n$, and requires the following interface:

function Res = BCFunction(ya, yb , p1, p2, …)

where *ya* is a column vector of $y_j(a)$ and *yb* is a column vector of $y_j(b)$. The known parameters p1, p2, etc., must appear in this interface even if the boundary conditions do not require them. The output *Res* is a column vector.

The variable *solinit* is a structure[7] obtained from the function bvpinit as follows:

solinit = bvpinit(x, y)

The vector *x* is a guess for the initial mesh points. The vector *y* is a guess of the magnitude of each of the y_j. The lengths of *x* and *y* are independent of each other.

The output of bvp4c, *sol*, is a structure that contains the solution at a specific number of points. To obtain a smooth curve, values at additional intermediate points are needed. To provide these additional points, we use

sxint = deval(sol, xint)

where *xint* is a vector of points at which the solution is to be evaluated and *sol* is the output of bcp4c.

To illustrate the use of bvp4c, consider the following equation:

$$\frac{d^2y}{dx^2} + ky = x \quad 0 \le x \le 1$$

subject to the boundary conditions

$$y(0) = 0$$
$$y(1) = 0$$

First, we transform the equation into a pair of first-order differential equations with the substitution

$$y_1 = y$$
$$y_2 = \frac{dy}{dt}$$

to obtain

$$\frac{dy_1}{dx} = y_2$$
$$\frac{dy_2}{dx} = x - ky_1$$

The boundary conditions for this formulation are

$$y_1(0) = 0$$
$$y_1(1) = 0$$

We now proceed to create the required function and sub functions. The sub function that expresses the system of first-order ordinary differential equations is called **OdeBvp** and the function that records the boundary conditions is called **OdeBC**. The set of initial guesses is given in bvpinit, where it is seen that we have

---

[7]A structure will be explained by example subsequently.

selected five points between 0 and 1 and assumed that the solution for y_1 has a constant magnitude of -0.05 and that for y_2 has a constant magnitude of 0.1. Then, assuming that $k = 2$, the script is

```
function bvpExample
k = 2;
solinit = bvpinit(linspace(0, 1, 5), [-0.05, 0.1]);
exmpsol = bvp4c(@OdeBvp, @OdeBC, solinit, [], k);
x = linspace(0, 1, 50);
y = deval(exmpsol, x);
plot(x, y(1,:))

function dydx = OdeBvp(x, y, k)
dydx = [y(2); x-k*y(1)];

function res = OdeBC(ya, yb, k)
res = [ya(1); yb(1)];
```

The results are plotted in Figure 5.11.

The outputs from the various functions in the above script are now discussed. The output *exmpsol* is a structure, which permits us to access the various quantities as follows: The structure *exmpsol.y*(1, :) gives the values of y_1 at the mesh points given in the structure *exmpsol.x,* and the structure *exmpsol.y*(2, :) gives the values of y_2 at these same mesh points. All these quantities are generated by bvp4c after executing its computational procedure. In this case, the number of mesh points that bvp4c used was seven. On the other hand, the quantity y that is the output of deval looks more like that which comes from ode45. The variable y, in this case, is

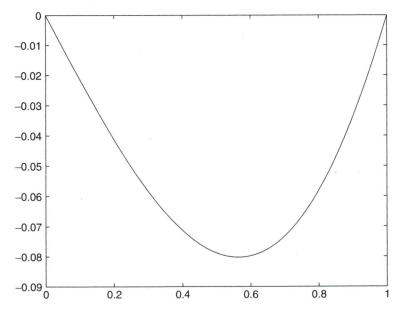

Figure 5.11 $y(x)$ for Example 5.15.

a (2×50) array, where $y(1,:) = y_1 = y$ and $y(2,:) = y_2 = dy/dx$. If we plotted the seven values from the structure $exmpsol.y(1,:)$, these values would lie on the line drawn in Figure 5.11.

In Example 5.15, we further illustrate the application of bvp4c by determining the static displacement of a uniformly loaded beam that is hinged at both ends.[8]

Example 5.15   Displacement of a uniformly loaded beam

From Section 8.2.1, the governing equation for the nondimensional displacement y of a beam subjected to a nondimensional static loading q is

$$\frac{d^4 y}{d\eta^4} = q(\eta)$$

where $0 \le \eta \le 1$ and

$$\theta = \frac{dy}{d\eta}$$

$$M = \frac{d^2 y}{d\eta^2}$$

$$V = \frac{d^3 y}{d\eta^3}$$

are the nondimensional slope, moment, and shear force, respectively.

We transform this equation in to a series of first-order ordinary differential equations through the relations

$$y_1 = y \qquad y_3 = \frac{d^2 y}{d\eta^2}$$

$$y_2 = \frac{dy}{d\eta} \qquad y_4 = \frac{d^3 y}{d\eta^3}$$

Using these relations and the original differential equation, we obtain

$$\frac{dy_1}{d\eta} = y_2 \qquad \frac{dy_3}{d\eta} = y_4$$

$$\frac{dy_2}{d\eta} = y_3 \qquad \frac{dy_4}{d\eta} = q$$

Let us consider a beam that is hinged at each end. This means that the displacements and the moments at each end are zero; that is, $y(0) = y(1) = d^2 y(0)/d\eta^2 = d^2 y(1)/d\eta^2 = 0$. In addition, let us apply an external moment M_r at the end $\eta = 1$ and apply a uniform load q_o along the length of the beam. Thus, $q(\eta) = q_o$ and the moment boundary condition at $\eta = 1$ becomes $d^2 y(1)/d\eta^2 = M_r$.

Let us assume that $M_r = 0.8$ and $q_o = 1.0$. We take 10 mesh points as our guess, and we guess that the magnitudes of the displacement, slope, moment, and shear force each have the value of 0.5. In addition, the function that is used to represent the system

---

[8]For additional examples, see L. F. Shampine, M. W. Reichelt, and J. Kierzenka, "Solving Boundary Value Problems for Ordinary Differential Equations in MATLAB with bvp4c," which is available at ftp://ftp.mathworks.com/pub/doc/papers/bvp/.

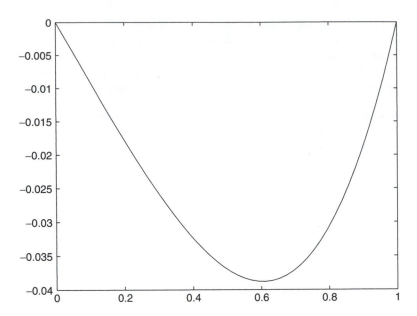

Figure 5.12 Displacement response to a uniformly loaded hinged beam with an external moment applied at $\eta = 1$.

of first-order equations is called **BeamODEqo**, and the function that represents the boundary conditions is called **BeamHingedBC**. Then, the script is

```
function Example5_15
qo = 1;  Mr = 0.8;
solinit = bvpinit(linspace(0, 1, 10), [0.5, 0.5, 0.5, 0.5]);
beamsol = bvp4c(@BeamODEqo, @BeamHingedBC, solinit, [], qo, Mr);
eta = linspace(0, 1, 50);
y = deval(beamsol, eta);
plot(eta, y(1,:))

function dydx = BeamODEqo(x, y, qo, Mr)
dydx = [y(2); y(3); y(4); qo];

function bc = BeamHingedBC(y0, y1, qo, Mr)
bc = [y0(1); y0(3); y1(1); y1(3)-Mr];
```

The results are given in Figure 5.12.

These results have been generalized to include different combinations of boundary conditions and different types of loading in Section 8.2.1.

5.5.5 Local Minimum of a Function—`fminbnd`

The function `fminbnd` finds a local minimum of the real function $f(x)$ in the interval $a \le x \le b$ within a tolerance t_o. It can also transfer p_j parameters to the function defining $f(x)$. The general expression for `fminbnd` is

[xmin fmin] = fminbnd(@**FunctionName**, a, b, options, p1, p2, …)

where **FunctionName** is the name of the function file without the extension '.m', $a = a$, $b = b$, *options* is an optional vector whose parameters are set with `optimset` (see the *Help* file for `optimset`), and p1, p2, etc., are the parameters p_j. The quantity *xmin* is the value of x that minimizes the function given in **FunctionName**, and *fmin* is the value of **FunctionName** at *xmin*.

   The interface for **FunctionName** has the form

> `function` z = FunctionName(x, p1, p2, ...)
> Expression(s)

where x is the independent variable that `fminbnd` is varying to minimize $f(x)$. The independent variable must always appear in this location.

   When $f(x)$ is an expression that can be represented by `inline` with the name **InlineFunctionName**, `fminbnd` is accessed as follows:

> [xmin, fmin] = `fminbnd`(**InlineFunctionName**, a, b, options, p1, p2, ...)

We shall now illustrate the use of `fminbnd`.

   Consider the MATLAB demonstration function `humps`, which is shown in Figure 5.13. The minimum value of the function between $0.5 \le x \le 0.8$ is determined from the script

> options = `optimset`('Display', 'off');
> [xmin, fmin] = `fminbnd`(@humps, 0.5, 0.8, options)

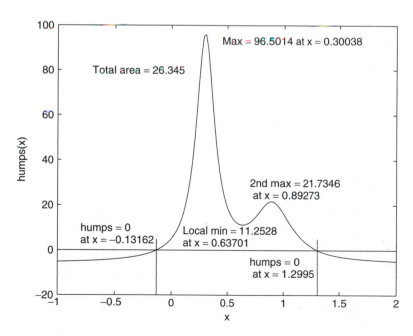

Figure 5.13   Properties of MATLAB's demonstration function `humps`.

Upon execution of this script, we obtain

```
xmin =
    0.6370
fmin =
    11.2528
```

Thus, the minimum in the interval $0.5 \leq x \leq 0.8$ occurs at $x = 0.6370$ where the magnitude of the function is 11.253.

     If, on the other hand, we want to find the maximum value of humps in the interval $0 \leq x \leq 0.5$ and where it occurs, then we have to recognize that fminbnd must operate on the negative, or the reciprocal, of the function humps. Thus, we use inline to create a function that computes the negative of humps in this region. The script is

```
options = optimset('Display', 'off');
[xmax, fmax] = fminbnd(inline('-humps(x)', 'x '), 0, 0.5, options);
disp(['Maximum value of humps in the interval 0 <= x <= 0.5 is ' num2str(-fmax)])
disp(['which occurs at x = ' num2str(xmax)])
```

which upon execution displays to the command window

```
Maximum value of humps in the interval 0 <= x <= 0.5 is 96.5014
which occurs at x = 0.30039
```

Notice that we had to compute the negative of *fmax* before displaying it, since fminbnd uses a function that is the negative of humps. The other quantities appearing in Figure 5.13 can be verified using the techniques discussed in Sections 5.5.1 and 5.5.2.

5.5.6 Numerical Solutions of Nonlinear Equations—fsolve

The function fsolve in the Optimization Toolbox finds the numerical solution to a system of n nonlinear equations $f_n(x_1, x_2, \ldots, x_n) = 0$ in the x_n unknowns using a starting guess $x_s = [x_{s1} \, x_{s2} \, \ldots \, x_{sn}]$. The output of the function is the n roots x_{roots}. The function fsolve can also transfer p_j parameters to the functions defining $f_n(x)$. The general expression for fsolve is

```
xroots = fsolve(@FunctionName, xs, options, p1, p2, ...)
```

where **FunctionName** is the name of the function file without the extension '.m', xs = x_s, *options* is an optional vector whose parameters are set with optimset (see optimset in the *Help* file), and p1, p2, etc., are the parameters p_j. The output of the function, *xroots*, is a vector of x_{roots}.

     The interface for the function whose name is **FunctionName** has the form

```
function z = FunctionName(x, p1, p2, ...)
z = [f1; f2; ...; fn];
```

where x is a vector of the n quantities to be determined, x_n, and z is a column vector composed of n MATLAB expressions for the n nonlinear equations $f_n(x_1, x_2, \ldots, x_n)$ in terms of x and the parameters p_j.

When $f_n(x_1, x_2, \ldots, x_n)$ is represented by `inline` with the name **InlineFunctionName**, `fminbnd` is accessed as follows:

xroots = `fsolve` (**InlineFunctionName**, a, b, options, p1, p2, ...)

We shall now illustrate the use of `fsolve`.

Example 5.16   Inverse kinematics

Consider the following system of equations, which results from an intermediate step in the inverse kinematics solution for the three-degree-of-freedom linkages shown in Figure 2.8:

$$r_1 - a_1 \cos(\theta_1) - a_2 \cos(\theta_1 + \theta_2) = 0$$
$$r_2 - a_1 \sin(\theta_1) - a_2 \sin(\theta_1 + \theta_2) = 0$$

To solve this system of equations, we first create a function **kinematics**, which puts these equations in the form required by `fsolve`. Thus,

```
function w = kinematics(theta, a1, a2, r1, r2)
w = [a1*cos(theta(1))+a2*cos(theta(1)+theta(2))-r1; ...
     a1*sin(theta(1))+a2*sin(theta(1)+theta(2))-r2];
```

where $theta(1) = \theta_1$ and $theta(2) = \theta_2$.

Let us assume that $r_1 = 1.8, r_2 = 2.1, a_1 = 1.0$, and $a_2 = 2$, and let our initial guesses for θ_1 and θ_2 be $\pi/6$. Then, the script is

```
options = optimset('display', 'off');
z = fsolve(@kinematics, [pi/6 pi/6], options, 1,2, 1.8, 2.1)*180/pi;
for k = 1:length(z)
   disp(['Theta(' num2str(k,1) ') = ' num2str(z(k)) ' degrees'])
end
```

which upon execution gives

```
Theta(1) = 16.6028  degrees
Theta(2) = 48.5092  degrees
```

Thus, $\theta_1 = z(1) = 16.6026°$ and $\theta_2 = z(2) = 48.5095°$. Another set of angles will be found when the initial guess is $\theta_1 = \theta_2 = \pi$. Thus, `fsolve` must be used with caution, especially if more than one solution exists.

Example 5.17   Intersection of a parabola and an ellipse

Consider the intersection of an ellipse

$$g(x, y) = x^2/4 + y^2 - 1 - 0$$

with the parabola

$$f(x, y) = y - 4x^2 + 3 - 0$$

A graph of these two functions reveals that they intersect at four points. Thus, the value returned by `fsolve` will be sensitive to the initial guess.

The function that will be used by fsolve is created with `inline`, where $xy(1) = x$ and $xy(2) = y$. The script to determine the solution with the initial guesses of $x = 0.5$ and $y = -0.5$ is

```
fgsolve = inline('[0.25*xy(1).^2+xy(2).^2-1; xy(2)-4*xy(1).^2+3]', 'xy');
options = optimset('Display', 'off');
xy = fsolve(fgsolve, [0.5, -0.5], options)
```

Upon execution, we obtain

```
xy =
   0.7188   -0.9332
```

Thus, $x = xy(1) = 0.7188$, and $y = xy(2) = -0.9332$. If, instead, we had chosen for our initial guess $x = -0.5$ and $y = 0.5$, we would have obtained $x = xy(1) = -0.9837$ and $y = xy(2) = 0.8707$.

5.6 THE SYMBOLIC TOOLBOX AND THE CREATION OF FUNCTIONS

The Symbolic Math Toolbox provides the capability of manipulating symbols to perform algebraic, matrix, and calculus operations symbolically. When one couples the results obtained from symbolic operations with MATLAB's ability to create functions, one has a very efficient means of numerically evaluating symbolically obtained expressions. In this section, we will introduce some of the basic operations that one can do with the Symbolic Math Toolbox and then illustrate how one can very straightforwardly convert these results to numerical values.

We will illustrate by example the Symbolic Toolbox syntax, the conversion of a symbolic expression to a function, symbolic differentiation and integration, the taking of limits symbolically, and obtaining the inverse Laplace transform symbolically. We will then summarize the use of many of these results with an example.

Syntax

The shorthand way to create symbolic variables is with

```
syms a b c
```

where a, b, and c are now symbolic variables. If the variables are restricted to being real variables, then we modify this statement as

```
syms a b c real
```

These symbols can be intermixed with nonsymbolic variable names, numbers, and MATLAB functions, with the result being a symbolic expression.

For example, consider the relation

$$f = 11.92e^{-a^2} + b/d$$

Assuming that $d = 4.2$, the script to represent this expression symbolically is

```
syms a b
d = 4.2;
f = 11.92*exp(-a^2)+b/d
```

which upon execution displays

```
f =
298/25*exp(-a^2)+5/21*b
```

where f is a symbolic object. Notice that $21/5 = 4.2$ and $298/25 = 11.92$. Numbers in a symbolic expression are always converted to the ratio of two integers. If the decimal representation of numbers is desired, then one uses

vpa(f, d)

where f is the symbolic expression and d is the number of digits. Thus, to revert to the decimal notation with five decimal digits, the script becomes

```
syms a b
d = 4.2;
f = vpa(11.92*exp(-a^2)+b/d, 5)
```

The execution of this script gives

```
f =
11.920*exp(-1.*a^2)+.23810*b
```

Conversion of Symbolic Expression to a Function

If we want to convert a symbolic expression f into a function, we employ `inline` and

vectorize(f)

which converts its argument to a string and converts the multiplication, division, and exponentiation operators to their dot operator counterparts. Thus, the previous script is modified to

```
syms a b
d = 4.2;
f = vpa(11.92*exp(-a^2)+b/d, 5);
g = inline(vectorize(f), 'a', 'b')
```

which upon execution displays

```
g =
    Inline function:
    g(a,b) = 11.920.*exp(-1.*a.^2)+.23810.*b
```

In other words, we have turned the symbolic expression f into the function $g(a,b)$, which can now be used as any function is used. For example, if $a = 1$ and $b = 2$, then the execution of the script

```
syms a b
d = 4.2;
f = vpa(11.92*exp(-a^2)+b/d, 5);
g = inline(vectorize(f), 'a', 'b');
z = g(1, 2)
```

displays in the command window

```
z =
    4.8613
```

Differentiation and Integration

Differentiation is performed with the function

```
diff(f, x, n)
```

where $f = f(x)$ is a symbolic expression, x is the variable with which differentiation is performed, and n is the number of differentiations to be performed. For example, when $n = 2$, the second derivative is taken.

We illustrate this function by taking the derivative of $b\cos(bt)$, first with respect to t and then with respect to b. The script is

```
syms b t
dt = diff(b*cos(b*t), t, 1)
db = diff(b*cos(b*t), b, 1)
```

Upon execution of this script, we obtain

```
dt =
-b^2*sin(b*t)
db =
cos(b*t)-b*sin(b*t)*t
```

Integration is performed with the function

```
int(f, x, c, d)
```

where $f = f(x)$ is a symbolic expression, x is the variable of integration, c is the lower limit of integration, and d is the upper limit. When c and d are omitted, the application of int results in the indefinite integral of $f(x)$.

Let us illustrate the use of int by integrating the results of the differentiation perform in the previous script. Thus,

```
syms b t
f = b*cos(b*t);
dt = diff(f, t, 1);
db = diff(f, b, 1);
it = int(dt, t)
ib = int(db, b)
```

The execution of the script results in

```
it =
b*cos(b*t)
ib =
1/t*sin(b*t)-1/t*(sin(b*t)-b*t*cos(b*t))
```

We see that *it* is our original function *f* before differentiation with respect to *t*. The second function does not look like *f* before differentiation with respect to *b*. However, if we use `simplify`, which is one of the several simplification functions, the desired results are obtained. Thus, we modify the script as

```
syms b t
f = b*cos(b*t);
dt = diff(f, t, 1);
db = diff(f, b, 1);
it = int(dt, t);
ib = int(db, b);
ib = simplify(ib)
```

Upon its execution, we obtain

```
ib =
b*cos(b*t)
```

The use of the simplification functions usually requires some experimentation with the order in which they are applied and with which ones to use. To find a list of the simplification functions and their syntax, go to *Function Reference* in *Symbolic Math Toolbox* under the *Contents* tab in the *Help* file.

Limits and Substitutions

One can take the limit of a symbolic expression as the independent variable approaches a specified value. The function that does this computation is

```
limit(f, x, z)
```

where $f = f(x)$ is the symbolic function whose limit is to be determined and x is the symbolic variable that is to assume the limiting value z.

To illustrate the use of this function, consider the expression

$$\lim_{a \to \infty} \left(\frac{2a + b}{3a - 4} \right)$$

The script is

```
syms a b
Lim = limit((2*a+b)/(3*a-4), a, inf)
```

where `inf` stands for infinity (recall Table 1.4). The execution of this script gives

```
Lim =
2/3
```

For another example, consider the limit

$$\lim_{x \to 0} \left(\frac{\sin ax}{x} \right)$$

The script to determine this limit is

```
syms a x
Lim = limit(sin(a*x)/x, x, 0)
```

Upon execution, we obtain

```
Lim =
a
```

We can also use limit to substitute a symbolic expression for a variable. For example, consider the previous case. This time, we would like to make the substitution $x = c + 2$. Thus, the previous script becomes

```
syms a x c
Lim = limit(sin(a*x)/x, x, c+2)
```

which upon execution gives

```
Lim =
sin(a*(c+2))/(c+2)
```

We make use of limit in Section 9.4.1.

Inverse Laplace Transforms

The inverse Laplace transform is determined from

```
ilaplace(F, s, t)
```

where $F = F(s)$, s is the Laplace transform parameter, and t is the variable name in the inverse domain, usually representing time.

To illustrate the use of ilaplace, consider Eq. 5.3. The Laplace transform of this equation, when $y(0) = 0$ and $dy(0)/dt = 0$, is

$$Y(s) = \frac{H(s)}{s^2 + 2\xi s + 1}$$

where $Y(s)$ is the Laplace transform of $y(t)$, $H(s)$ is the Laplace transform of $h(t)$, and $\xi < 1$ is a real constant. If we assume that $h(t) = u(t)$, where $u(t)$ is the unit step function, then $H(s) = 1/s$. Then, the script to determine $y(t)$ is

```
syms s t
syms xi real
den = s*(s^2+2*xi*s+1);
yt = ilaplace(1/den, s, t)
```

The execution of this script gives

```
yt =
1+1/(4*xi^2-4)^(1/2)*(1/(-xi+1/2*(4*xi^2-4)^(1/2))*exp((-xi+1/2*(4*xi^2-4)^(1/2))*t)
-1/(-xi-1/2*(4*xi^2-4)^(1/2))*exp((-xi-1/2*(4*xi^2-4)^(1/2))*t))
```

We now have two choices: We can convert *yt* into a function and use the resulting function to plot the result, or we can attempt to further simplify this result to obtain a more concise mathematical expression. We will show how to do both. However, before starting, we note that

$$(4*xi^2 - 4)^{\wedge}(1/2)) \rightarrow \sqrt{4\xi^2 - 4} = 2j\sqrt{1 - \xi^2}$$

since $\xi < 1$.

To convert *yt* to a function and plot it, the previous script becomes

```
syms s t
syms xi real
den = s*(s^2+2*xi*s+1);
yt = ilaplace(1/den, s, t);
yoft = inline(vectorize(yt), 't', 'xi');
t = linspace(0, 20, 200);
plot(t, real(yoft(t, 0.15)))
```

where we have assumed that $\xi = 0.15$. An examination of the numerical results indicates that the imaginary part of the solution is virtually zero. Therefore, we use `real` to remove any residual imaginary part caused by numerical round-off errors. The result is shown in Figure 5.14.

To simplify *yt*, we first set

$$(4*xi^2 - 4)^{\wedge}(1/2)) \rightarrow 2jr$$

where

$$r = \sqrt{1 - \xi^2}$$

We do this substitution with

```
subs
```

to make a literal substitution for each occurrence of $(4*xi^2 - 4)^{\wedge}(1/2)$ with $2*j*r$. To put the result in its simplest form we use

```
simple
```

The script is then modified to

```
syms s t
syms xi r real
den = s*(s^2+2*xi*s+1);
yt = ilaplace(1/den, s, t);
yt1 = subs(yt, '(4*xi^2-4)^(1/2)', '2*j*r');
yt2 = simple(yt1)
```

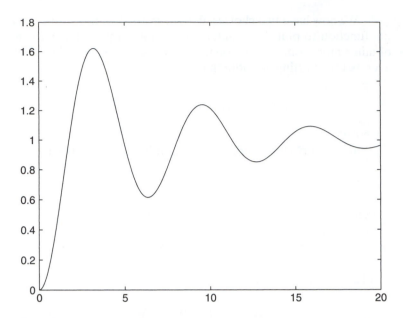

Figure 5.14 Solution to Eq. 5.3 using Laplace transforms when $h(t) = u(t)$ and $\xi = 0.15$.

Upon execution, we obtain

```
yt2 =
1-1/2*i/r*(1/(-xi+i*r)*exp((-xi+i*r)*t)-1/(-xi-i*r)*exp((-xi-i*r)*t))
```

To reduce this expression still further, we again use `subs` to make the following substitutions:

exp((-xi+i*r)*t) → exp(-xi*t)*(cos(r*t)+i*sin(r*t))
exp((-xi-i*r)*t) → exp(-xi*t)*(cos(r*t)-i*sin(r*t))

and simplify the results with `simple`. Then, the previous script becomes

```
syms s t
syms xi r real
den = s*(s^2+2*xi*s+1);
yt = ilaplace(1/den, s, t);
yt1 = subs(yt, '(4*xi^2-4)^(1/2)', '2*j*r');
yt2 = simple(yt1);
yt3 = subs(yt2, 'exp((-xi+i*r)*t)', 'exp(-xi*t)*(cos(r*t)+i*sin(r*t))');
yt4 = subs(yt3, 'exp((-xi-i*r)*t)', 'exp(-xi*t)*(cos(r*t)-i*sin(r*t))');
yt5 = simple(yt4)
```

The execution of this script gives

```
yt5 =
(r*xi^2+r^3-exp(-t*xi)*cos(r*t)*r-exp(-t*xi)*sin(r*t)*xi)/(r*xi^2+r^3)
```

We notice that

$$xi^2 + r^2 \rightarrow \xi^2 + \left(\sqrt{1 - \xi^2}\right)^2 = 1$$

Therefore,

$$r*xi^2 + r^3 \rightarrow r$$

and we simplify the result with `simple`. The final script is

```
syms s t
syms xi r real
den = s*(s^2+2*xi*s+1);
yt = ilaplace(1/den, s, t);
yt1 = subs(yt, '(4*xi^2-4)^(1/2)', '2*j*r');
yt2 = simple(yt1);
yt3 = subs(yt2, 'exp((-xi+i*r)*t)', 'exp(-xi*t)*(cos(r*t)+i*sin(r*t))');
yt4 = subs(yt3, 'exp((-xi-i*r)*t)', 'exp(-xi*t)*(cos(r*t)-i*sin(r*t))');
yt5 = simple(yt4);
yt6 = subs(yt5, 'r*xi^2+r^3', 'r');
yoft = simple(yt6)
```

Upon execution, we obtain

```
yoft =
1-1/exp(t*xi)*cos(r*t)-1/r/exp(t*xi)*sin(r*t)*xi
```

When we manually convert this result to standard algebraic form, we have

$$y(t) = 1 - e^{-\xi t}\left[\cos\left(t\sqrt{1 - \xi^2}\right) + \frac{\xi}{\sqrt{1 - \xi^2}}\sin\left(t\sqrt{1 - \xi^2}\right)\right] \qquad (5.4)$$

Example 5.18   Evaluation of a convolution integral and its characteristics

Consider the following convolution integral that results from the solution to Eq. 5.3 when $\xi < 1$ and $h(t) = u(t)$, where $u(t)$ is the unit step function:

$$y(t) = \frac{e^{-\xi t}}{\sqrt{1 - \xi^2}} \int_0^t e^{\xi \eta} \sin\left[(t - \eta)\sqrt{1 - \xi^2}\right] d\eta$$

First, we shall obtain a symbolic solution to this integral, convert it to a function, and plot it. Second, we shall determine the magnitude of its maximum response from $dy/dt = 0$ and the time at which it occurs and examine the second derivative to verify that it is a maximum. Third, we shall determine the time it takes for $y(t)$ to go from $0.1y(t)$ to $0.9y(t)$, which is called the rise time of the signal.

The script for the first part is

```
option = optimset('Display', 'off');
z = 0.15;
syms t xi n r a
r = sqrt(1- xi^2);
arg = exp(xi*n)*sin(r*(t-n));
yt = exp(-xi*t)*int(arg, n, 0, t)/r;
yoft = inline(vectorize(yt), 't', 'xi');
tt = linspace(0, 20, 200);
plot(tt, yoft(tt, z))
```

Upon execution, this script produces Figure 5.14. An examination of the symbolic expression yt will reveal that this is equivalent to Eq. 5.4.

To obtain the maximum value, we differentiate the solution $y(t)$, convert it to a function, and than use $fzero$ to determine the time t_{max} at which the derivative is zero. To verify that it is a maximum, we obtain the second derivative of $y(t)$. If the second derivative is negative at t_{max}, then the function is a maximum. The previous script then becomes

```
option = optimset('display', 'off');
z = 0.15;
syms t xi n r a
r = sqrt(1- xi^2);
arg = exp(xi*n)*sin(r*(t-n));
yt = exp(-xi*t)*int(arg, n, 0, t)/r;
yoft = inline(vectorize(yt), 't', 'xi');
tt = linspace(0, 20, 200);
plot(tt, yoft(tt, z))

% Part (2)

dydt = inline(vectorize(diff(yt, t)), 't', 'xi');
tmax = fzero(dydt, [3 5],option, z);
ymax = yoft(tmax, z);
disp(['ymax = ' num2str(ymax) '   tmax = ' num2str(tmax)])
d2ydt2 = inline(vectorize(diff(yt, t, 2)), 't', 'xi');
secder = d2ydt2(tmax, z);
disp(['Second derivative at tmax = ' num2str(secder)])
```

The execution of this script displays the following result to the command window.

```
ymax = 1.6209    tmax = 3.1775
Second derivative at tmax = -0.62087
```

To obtain the rise time, we have to create a new `inline` function to compute $y(t) - a$, where $a = 0.1$ or 0.9. Then, the previous script becomes

```
option = optimset('Display', 'off');
z = 0.15;
syms t xi n r a
r = sqrt(1- xi^2);
arg = exp(xi*n)*sin(r*(t-n));
yt = exp(-xi*t)*int(arg, n, 0, t)/r;
yoft = inline(vectorize(yt), 't', 'xi');
tt = linspace(0, 20, 200);
plot(tt, yoft(tt, z))

% Part (2)

dydt = inline(vectorize(diff(yt, t)), 't','xi');
tmax = fzero(dydt, [3 5], option, z);
ymax = yoft(tmax, z);
disp(['ymax = ' num2str(ymax) '   tmax = ' num2str(tmax)])
d2ydt2 = inline(vectorize(diff(yt, t,2)), 't', 'xi');
secder = d2ydt2(tmax, z);
disp(['Second derivative at tmax = ' num2str(secder)])

% Part (3)

ytrise = inline(vectorize(yt-a), 't', 'xi', 'a');
t9 = fzero(ytrise, [0 2], option, z, 0.9);
t1 = fzero(ytrise, [0 2], option, z, 0.1);
disp(['Rise time = ' num2str(t9-t1)])
```

Upon execution, the following is displayed to the command window

```
ymax = 1.6209    tmax = 3.1775
Second derivative at tmax = -0.62087
Rise time = 1.1518
```

5.7 SUMMARY OF FUNCTIONS INTRODUCED

A summary of the functions introduced in the chapter along with their descriptions is presented in Table 5.3, and a summary of the functions from the Symbolic Toolbox is presented in Table 5.4.

TABLE 5.3   MATLAB Functions Introduced in Chapter 5

MATLAB function	Description
bvp4c	Solves the two-point boundary value problem for a system of ODEs*
bvpinit	Forms the initial guesses for bvp4c
conv	Multiplies two polynomials
deval	Evaluates the solution from bvp4c
dblquad	Numerically evaluates a double integral
diff	Obtains differences of adjacent elements in an array
error	Displays an error message
feval	Evaluates a function
fft	Obtains the discrete Fourier transform
fminbnd	Minimizes a function of one variable in a specified interval
fsolve	Solves a system of nonlinear equations (Optimization Toolbox)
function	Creates a function m file
fzero	Finds a zero of a function of one variable
global	Defines global variables
humps	MATLAB demonstration function
ifft	Obtains the discrete inverse Fourier transform
inline	Constructs an inline function
interp1	Performs a one-dimensional interpolation
nargin	Determines the number of arguments in a function interface
ode45	Solves the initial value problem for a system of ODEs (one of six solvers)
odeset	Alters options in ODE solvers
optimset	Alters options in optimization solvers including fzero and fminbnd
poly	Creates a polynomial from its roots
polyfit	Fits data with an nth-order polynomial
polyval	Evaluates a polynomial
quadl	Numerically evaluates a single integral
return	Early return from a function
roots	Determines the roots of a polynomial
spline	Fits data with splines
trapz	Numerically integrates a single integral using trapezoidal approximation

*ODE = ordinary differential equation

TABLE 5.4   MATLAB Functions from the Symbolic Toolbox Introduced in Chapter 5

MATLAB function	Description
diff	Differentiates with respect to a symbolic variable
ilaplace	Inverse Laplace transform with respect to a symbolic variable
int	Integrates with respect to a symbolic variable
limit	Determines the limit of a symbolic expression
simple	Obtains the simplest form of a symbolic expression
simplify	Simplifies a symbolic expression
subs	Substitution of a symbolic expression
syms	Shortcut for creating symbolic variables
vectorize	Converts an expression to a string expression
vpa	Uses variable precision arithmetic on a symbolic expression

EXERCISES

Section 5.4.2

5.1 The stress concentration factor for a stepped circular shaft shown in Figure 5.15 is approximated by[9]

$$K_t = c\left(\frac{D - d}{2d}\right)^{-a}$$

where c and a are given in Table 5.5. Obtain two expressions, one for c and the other for a, as a function of D/d in two ways: with a fifth-order polynomial, and with a spline. For both methods, compare the values of K_t obtained with the two sets of fitted values to those obtained with the original values given in Table 5.5. Which is the better method to use in this case?

TABLE 5.5   Stress Concentration Factor Constants

D/d	c	a
6.00	0.88	0.33
3.00	0.89	0.31
2.00	0.91	0.29
1.50	0.94	0.26
1.20	0.97	0.22
1.10	0.95	0.24
1.07	0.98	0.21
1.05	0.98	0.20
1.03	0.98	0.18
1.01	0.92	0.17

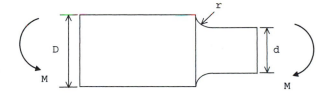

Figure 5.15   Geometry and loading for a stress concentration factor.

[9]R. L. Norton, *Machine Design: An Integrated Approach*, Prentice Hall, Upper Saddle River, NJ, 1996, p. 1,005ff.

5.2 Consider the following signal

$$f(t) = \sum_{n=1}^{4} H_n e^{-\zeta_n \omega_n} \sin\left(\sqrt{1 - \zeta_n^2}\, \omega_n t\right) \quad 0 \le t \le T$$

where the values of the constants are given in Table 5.6. For $N = 2^{10}$ and $\Delta t = 2\pi/(4\omega_4)$:

a. Plot the amplitude spectrum for this signal with and without Hamming. The results should look like those shown in Figure 5.16 but without the labels. See Chapter 6 to place axes labels and text on a figure.

b. Determine the frequencies at which the peaks occur. [Hint: Use several applications of find and diff.] [Answers: No Hamming, [4.84375 9.14063 20.0781] Hz; with Hamming, [4.92188 9.0625 9.45313 20.0781] Hz.]

TABLE 5.6   Constants Defining the Signal in Exercise 5.2

n	$\omega_n/2\pi$	ζ_n	H_n
1	5	0.1	1
2	9	0.04	1.3
3	9.4	0.04	1.3
4	20	0.03	1.8

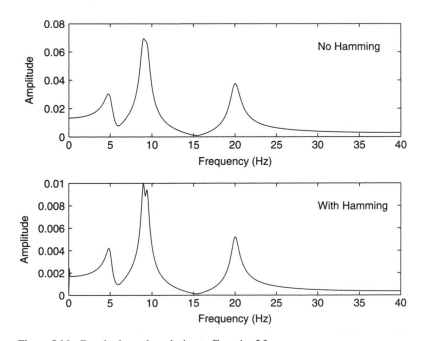

Figure 5.16   Results from the solution to Exercise 5.2a.

Section 5.5.1

5.3 The principal stresses can be determined from the roots of the polynomial[10]

$$\sigma^3 - C_2\sigma^2 - C_1\sigma - C_0 = 0$$

where

$$C_2 = \sigma_x + \sigma_y + \sigma_z$$
$$C_1 = \tau_{xy}^2 + \tau_{yz}^2 + \tau_{zx}^2 - \sigma_x\sigma_y - \sigma_y\sigma_z - \sigma_z\sigma_x$$
$$C_0 = \sigma_x\sigma_y\sigma_z + 2\tau_{xy}\tau_{yz}\tau_{zx} - \sigma_x\tau_{yx}^2 - \sigma_y\tau_{zx}^2 - \sigma_z\tau_{xy}^2$$

and $\sigma_x, \sigma_y, \sigma_z$ are the applied normal stresses and $\tau_{xy}, \tau_{yz}, \tau_{zx}$ are the applied shear stresses. If the roots of the equation are $\sigma_1, \sigma_2,$ and σ_3 (the three principal stresses), where $\sigma_1 > \sigma_2 > \sigma_3$, then the principal shear stresses are

$$\tau_{12} = (\sigma_1 - \sigma_2)/2 \quad \tau_{23} = (\sigma_2 - \sigma_3)/2 \quad \tau_{13} = (\sigma_1 - \sigma_3)/2$$

where $\tau_{max} = \tau_{13}$.

Determine the principal stresses and corresponding principal shear stresses when

$$\sigma_x = 100 \quad \tau_{xy} = -40$$
$$\sigma_y = -60 \quad \tau_{yz} = 50$$
$$\sigma_z = 80 \quad \tau_{zx} = 70$$

The root finding function does not order the roots. To accomplish this use sort in the manner discussed at the end of Example 2.2 in Section 2.5.4. [Answer: $\sigma_1 = 160.7444$, $\sigma_2 = 54.8980, \sigma_3 = -95.6424, \tau_{12} = 52.9232, \tau_{23} = 75.2702,$ and $\tau_{13} = 128.1934$.]

Note: In Exercises **5.4** to **5.16**, unless otherwise stated, find the lowest five positive roots of the given equations by using fzero. Use the form of fzero that requires the function to explore a specified region $[x_0 \ x_1]$. Plot each function before determining the roots. On occasion, it may be necessary to use axis to clip the vertical viewing area to increase the graph's resolution (see Section 6.2.2).

5.4 The following equation arises in the vibration of strings[11]:

$$\tan x = x$$

5.5 The following equation arises in the heat flow in slabs.[12] Obtain the roots for the two separate cases $p = 0.1$ and 1.

$$2 \cot x = \frac{x}{p} - \frac{p}{x}$$

5.6 The following equation[13] arises in the vibrations of annular membranes. Assume that $b = 2$.

$$J_0(x)Y_0(xb) - J_0(xb)Y_0(x) = 0$$

Use besselj and bessely, respectively, for $J_0(x)$ and $Y_0(x)$, which are the Bessel functions of the first and second kind, respectively, of order 0.

[10]See, for example, J. E. Shigley and C. R. Mischke, *Mechanical Engineering Design*, 5th ed., McGraw-Hill, New York, 1989.
[11]E. B. Magrab, *Vibration of Elastic Structural Members*, Sijthoff & Noordhoff, The Netherlands, 1979, p. 58.
[12]M. N. Ozisik, *Heat Conduction*, 2nd ed., John Wiley & Sons, New York, 1993, p. 47.
[13]E. B. Magrab, *ibid.*, p. 83.

5.7 The following equation[14] arises in the vibrations of a cantilever beam carrying a concentrated mass M_0 at its free end. Obtain the roots for the three separate cases $M_0/m_0 = 0, 0.2$, and 1.

$$(M_0/m_0)\Omega[\cos(\Omega)\sinh(\Omega) - \sin(\Omega)\cosh(\Omega)] + \cos(\Omega)\cosh(\Omega) + 1 = 0$$

5.8 The following equation[15] arises in the vibrations of a beam clamped at one end and simply supported at its other end:

$$\tanh(\Omega) - \tan(\Omega) = 0$$

5.9 The following equation[16] arises in the vibrations of a solid circular plate clamped on its outer boundary:

$$J_m(\Omega)I_{m+1}(\Omega) + I_m(\Omega)J_{m+1}(\Omega) = 0$$

where $J_m(x)$ is the Bessel function of the first kind of order m and $I_m(x)$ is the modified Bessel function of the first kind of order m. Use `besselj` and `besseli`, respectively, for $J_m(x)$ and $I_m(x)$. Find the lowest three roots for $m = 0, 1$, and 2.

5.10 The following equation[17] arises in the determination of the in-plane symmetric modes of a suspended cable. Find the lowest root when $\lambda^2 = 2\pi^2, 4\pi^2$, and $8\pi^2$. This solution must be obtained interactively by graphing the equation first. Use the `axis` function to limit the vertical axis from -10 to 20.

$$\tan \Omega = \Omega - \frac{4\Omega^3}{\lambda^2}$$

5.11 In the analysis of nonuniform flow in an open channel of trapezoidal cross-section, the ratio of the depth of the fluid to the height of the energy gradient x is determined from[18]

$$(1 + c_0x)^2(x^2 - x^3) = c_1$$

where $0 \le c_0 \le 11$ and $0.005 \le c_1 \le 12.3$ are functions of the geometry of the channel and the flow rate. However, not all combinations of c_0 and c_1 are appropriate. Find the pairs of real values of x between 0 and 1 that satisfy this equation for $c_0 = 0.4$ and $c_1 = 0.2$ and for $c_0 = 7.0$ and $c_1 = 4.0$. Use two methods: `fzero` and `roots`. To use `roots`, the equation is rewritten as

$$-c_0^2x^5 + (c_0^2 - 2c_0)x^4 + (2c_0 - 1)x^3 + x^2 - c_1 = 0$$

5.12 The wave angle $\beta(0 < \beta \le \pi/2)$ of a disturbance wave on top of a fluid in an open channel in which the velocity of the fluid is greater than the wave speed in the fluid is determined from[19]

$$2N_F^2 \sin^2(\beta)\tan^2(\beta - \theta) = \tan(\beta)\tan(\beta - \theta) + \tan^2(\beta) \quad \beta > \theta$$

[14]E. B. Magrab, *ibid.*, p. 130.
[15]E. B. Magrab, *ibid.*, p. 130.
[16]E. B. Magrab, *ibid.*, p. 252.
[17]M. Irvine, *Cable Structures*, Dover Publications, New York, 1981, p. 95.
[18]H. W. King, *Handbook of Hydraulics*, 4th ed., McGraw-Hill, New York, 1954, p. 8-1.
[19]N. H. C. Hwang and C. E. Hita, *Fundamentals of Hydraulic Engineering Systems*, 2nd ed., Prentice Hall, Englewood Cliffs, NJ, 1987, p. 222.

where θ is the wall deflection angle and $1 \leq N_F \leq 12$ is the Froude number. Determine the values of β, in degrees, in the range $\theta < \beta \leq 90°$ when $\theta = 35°$ and $N_F = 5$.

5.13 The internal rate of return i_{rr} is an accounting metric that represents the percentage interest earned on the unrecovered balance of an investment. It is determined from[20]

$$\sum_{k=0}^{n} F_k (1 + i_{rr})^{-k} = 0$$

where n is the number of periods, i_{rr} is the internal rate expressed as a decimal number, and F_k is the cash flow in each period: Positive cash flow means money is received, and negative flow means money is disbursed. Determine i_{rr} when $F_0 = -\$1000$, $F_1 = -\$800$, $F_2 = \$500$, $F_3 = \$500$, $F_4 = \$500$, and $F_5 = \$1200$.

5.14 If one invests an amount P and receives an amount A each period from an investment, then the number of periods n required for payback of P at an interest rate i per period (expressed as a decimal number) is determined from[21]

$$\frac{A}{P} = \frac{i(1 + i)^n}{(1 + i)^n - 1}$$

If $i = 12\%$ per year and $A/P = 0.16$, determine n, the number of years for payback.

5.15 An estimate of a parameter β appearing in the Weibull probability density function (see Section 14.2.2) requires the solution of[22]

$$\beta = \left[\sum_{i=1}^{n} x_i^{\beta} \ln(x_i) \Big/ \sum_{i=1}^{n} x_i^{\beta} - \frac{1}{n} \sum_{i=1}^{n} \ln(x_i) \right]^{-1}$$

where x_i are a random sample of size n. If $x = [72\ 82\ 97\ 103\ 113\ 117\ 126\ 127\ 127\ 139\ 154\ 159\ 199\ 207]$, determine the value of β.

5.16 In determining the surface contact shear stress between a sphere and a plane, which is a model of the effects of a bearing against a surface, the value of a ratio x is obtained from[23]

$$x \ln\left(\sqrt{x^2 - 1} + x\right) - \sqrt{x^2 - 1} - Cx = 0$$

where $x > 1$ and $C < 1$. For $C = 0.5$, determine x.

5.17 Find the three real roots of[24]

$$x^4 = 2^x$$

[Hint: First plot the function over the following two different regions: $-1 \leq x \leq 2$ and $2 \leq x \leq 17$.]

---

[20]G. J. Theusen and W. J. Fabrycky, *Engineering Economy*, 8th ed., Prentice Hall, Englewood Cliffs, NJ, 1993, p. 176.

[21]G. J. Theusen and W. J. Fabrycky, *ibid.*, p. 188.

[22]D. C. Montgomery and G. C. Runger, *Applied Statistics and Probability for Engineers*, John Wiley & Sons, New York, 1994, p. 299.

[23]W. Changsen, *Analysis of Rolling Element Bearings*, Mechanical Engineering Publishers, London, 1991, p. 80.

[24]Problem suggested by Prof. Jeffery M. Cooper, Department of Mathematics, University of Maryland, College Park, MD.

5.18 The computational formula for the generalized equation for the compressibility factor Z of a gas is given by[25]

$$
\begin{aligned}
Z(r, \tau) = 1 &+ r\sum_{i=1}^{6} A_i \tau^{i-1} + r^2 \sum_{i=7}^{10} A_i \tau^{i-7} + r^3 \sum_{i=11}^{13} A_i \tau^{i-11} + r^4 A_{14}\tau \\
&+ r^5(A_{15}\tau^2 + A_{16}\tau^3) + r^6 A_{17}\tau^2 + r^7(A_{18}\tau + A_{19}\tau^3) \\
&+ r^8 A_{20}\tau^3 + r^2 e^{-0.0588 r^2}[A_{21}\tau^3 + A_{22}\tau^4 + r^2(A_{23}\tau^3 + A_{24}\tau^5) \\
&+ r^4(A_{25}\tau^3 + A_{26}\tau^4) + r^6(A_{27}\tau^3 + A_{28}\tau^5) + r^8(A_{29}\tau^3 + A_{30}\tau^4) \\
&+ r^{10}(A_{31}\tau^3 + A_{32}\tau^4 + A_{33}\tau^5)]
\end{aligned}
$$

where $\tau = T_c/T$ $(0.4 \le \tau \le 1)$; $r = RT_c/P_c v$; R is the gas constant in $(\text{Mpa-m}^3)/(\text{kg-K})$; T is the temperature in K; P is the pressure in MPa; v is the volume in m^3/kg; T_c and P_c are the critical temperature and pressure, respectively; and the values of the 33 constants are given in Table 5.7.

a. Create a function to determine $Z(r, \tau)$. Check your function, using `format long e`, with the following test values:

   i. $Z(1, 1) = 0.70242396927$

  ii. $Z(1/0.3, 1) = 0.29999999980$

 iii. $Z(2.5, 0.5) = 0.99221853928$

b. The above quantity is used in the formula

$$
Z(r, \tau) = \frac{p\tau}{r} = \frac{Pv}{RT} \tag{a}
$$

TABLE 5.7   Constants in Generalized Formula for Z

j	A_j	j	A_j	j	A_j
1	0.062432384	12	−0.000727155024313	23	−0.0845194493813
2	0.12721477	13	−0.00452454652610	24	−0.00340931311928
3	−0.93633233	14	0.00130468724100	25	−0.00195127049901
4	0.70184411	15	−0.000222165128409	26	$4.93899910978 \times 10^{-5}$
5	−0.35160896	16	−0.00198140535656	27	$-4.93264612930 \times 10^{-5}$
6	0.056450032	17	$5.97573972921 \times 10^{-5}$	28	$8.85666572382 \times 10^{-7}$
7	0.0299561469907	18	$-3.64135349702 \times 10^{-6}$	29	$5.34788029553 \times 10^{-8}$
8	−0.0318174367647	19	$8.41364845386 \times 10^{-6}$	30	$-5.93420559192 \times 10^{-8}$
9	−0.0168211055517	20	$-9.82868858822 \times 10^{-9}$	31	$-9.06813326929 \times 10^{-9}$
10	1.60204060081	21	−1.57683056810	32	$1.61822407265 \times 10^{-9}$
11	−0.00109996740746	22	0.0400728988908	33	$-3.32044793915 \times 10^{-10}$

---

[25]W. C. Reynolds, "Thermodynamic Properties in SI," Department of Mechanical Engineering, Stanford University, Stanford, CA, 1979.

where $p = P/P_c$ $(1 \le p \le 6)$. Determine the value of r and $Z(r, \tau)$ using Eq. a for $p = 0.6$ and $\tau = 1/1.05$ and for $p = 2.18$ and $\tau = 1/1.2$. [Answer: $Z = 0.8013$ at $r = 0.7131$ and $Z = 0.5412$ at $r = 3.3567$.]

c. Use Eq. a to determine the value τ and $Z(r, \tau)$ when $p = 0.6$ and $r = 1/1.4$ and when $p = 2.18$ and $r = 1/0.6$. [Answer: $Z = 0.8007$ at $\tau = 0.9532$ and $Z = 0.8508$ at $\tau = 0.6505$.]

5.19 The pressure drop of a fluid flowing in a pipe is a function of the pipe's coefficient of friction λ, which can be estimated from the Colebrook formula[26]:

$$\lambda = \left[-2 \log_{10}\left(\frac{2.51}{Re\sqrt{\lambda}} + \frac{0.27}{d/k} \right) \right]^{-2} \quad Re \ge 4000$$

where Re is the Reynolds number, d is the diameter of the pipe, and k is the surface roughness. For smooth pipes ($k \cong 0$ or $d/k > 100{,}000$),

$$\lambda = \left[-2 \log_{10}\left(\frac{Re\sqrt{\lambda}}{2.51} \right) \right]^{-2} \quad Re \ge 4000$$

For fully developed turbulent flow, the coefficient of friction is given by

$$\lambda = \left[2 \log_{10}\left(3.7\frac{d}{k} \right) \right]^{-2}$$

which is independent of R_e. It is a special case of the general Colebrook formula, and it has utility in that it can be used to obtain a starting guess in iterative-type problems such as that described in Section 11.2.3.

If the values of λ range from 0.008 to 0.08, find the value of λ when $R_e = 10^5$ and, first, $d/k = 200$ and, second, $k = 0$. [Answer: $\lambda = 0.0313$ and $\lambda = 0.0180$.]

5.20 Display the real roots of the following polynomial:

$$10x^6 - 75x^3 - 190x + 21 = 0$$

Section 5.5.2

5.21 Find the area between the two sine curves shown in Figure 5.17 using `quadl` and `trapz`. The two sine waves are given by $\sin(x)$ and $|\sin(2x)|/2$.

5.22 In determining the load distribution in axial thrust bearings under an eccentric load, the following integral must be evaluated[27]:

$$I_m(\varepsilon) = \frac{1}{2\pi} \int\limits_{-a}^{a} [1 - (1 - \cos(x))] 2\varepsilon^c \cos(mx) \, dx$$

where $\varepsilon > 0$, $m = 0$ or 1,

$$a = \cos^{-1}(1 - 2\varepsilon)$$

and $c = 1.5$ for ball bearings and 1.1 for roller bearings. Determine the value of $I_1(0.6)$ for a ball bearing. [Answer: $I_1(0.6) = 0.2416$.]

---

[26]N. H. C. Hwang and C. E. Hita, *ibid.*, p. 68.
[27]W. Changsen, *ibid.*, p. 92.

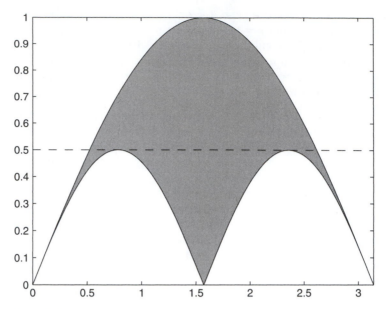

Figure 5.17   Figure for Exercise 5.21.

5.23   Given the integral

$$\int_0^\infty E_{\lambda,b}(\lambda, T)d\lambda = \sigma T^4$$

where

$$E_{\lambda,b}(\lambda, T) = \frac{C_1}{\lambda^5[\exp(C_2/\lambda T) - 1]}$$

and λ is the wavelength in μm, T is the temperature in K, $C_1 = 3.742 \times 10^8$ W · μm⁴/m², $C_2 = 1.439 \times 10^4$ μm · K, and $\sigma = 5.667 \times 10^{-8}$ W/m² · K⁴ is the Stephan-Boltzmann constant. Perform this integration numerically for $T = 300$, 400, and 500 K, and determine the percentage error of the approximate results compared to the exact value. A note of caution: Both integration limits give considerable difficulty numerically. Therefore, approximate the integral using a lower limit of 1 μm and an upper limit of 150 m. These limits were determined from the graph of $E_{\lambda,b}$ at the three temperatures and from the values of the integration limits that could be used without causing warning messages from `quad1`. [Answer: error$_{300}$ = 0.145%, error$_{400}$ = 0.061%, and error$_{500}$ = 0.030%.] (See also Exercise 12.6.)

5.24   Evaluate the following integral:

$$Z = \int_{\pi/4}^{\pi} \int_0^{\pi/2} \cos(x - y)e^{-xy/\pi^2}\, dx\, dy$$

Section 5.5.3

5.25 Consider the motion of a projectile that leaves a point $(0, 0)$ with an initial velocity v_0 and at an angle with the horizontal of α. If the projectile lands at a location (x_e, y_e) and is subjected to a drag during flight that is proportional to the square of its velocity, then the four first-order equations governing its flight are[28]

$$\frac{dv_x}{dx} = -c_d v \qquad \frac{dv_y}{dx} = \frac{-(g + c_d v v_y)}{v_x} \qquad \frac{dy}{dx} = \frac{v_y}{v_x} \qquad \frac{dt}{dx} = \frac{1}{v_x}$$

where y is the vertical height of the projectile, x is the horizontal distance of travel; t is time; v_x and v_y are the horizontal and vertical components of the velocity v, respectively; c_d is the drag coefficient; g is the gravity constant; and

$$v = \sqrt{v_x^2 + v_y^2}$$

These equations are valid only when v_0 is large enough so that v_x is greater than zero when it reaches x_e. The test for this condition can be stated as, say, $|v_x| > v_0 \times 10^{-6}$. If this condition is not satisfied, then the program's execution must be terminated. Use error to cause the termination. This check is placed in the beginning of the function that is called by ode45. The initial conditions are

$$v_{0x} = v_0 \cos(\alpha) \quad v_{0y} = v_0 \sin(\alpha) \quad y = 0 \quad t = 0$$

From the order in which the equations are written, let $y_1(x) = v_x$, $y_2(x) = v_y$, $y_3(x) = y$, and $y_4(x) = t$.

a. Plot the projectile path for $v_0 = 600$ fps, $c_d = 0.002$, and $\alpha = 45°$ until the projectile reaches $y_e = 0$—that is, plot only those points for which $y_e > 0$. Let $x_{\text{final}} = 1000$ ft in ode45.

b. What is the value of the maximum elevation of the projectile, and at what distance does this occur? Use fminbnd and spline to obtain these values. [Answer: $y_{\text{max}} = 474.8285$ ft. at $x = 648.1205$ ft.]

c. What is the value of x_e when $y_e = 0$ and the time of travel to reach this point? Use interp1 to determine these values. [Answer: $x_e = 975.3240$, and the time of travel is 10.6246 s.]

5.26 A bungee jumper is preparing to make a high-altitude jump from a hot-air balloon using a length L of bungee line. To do so safely, the peak acceleration, velocity, and total drop distance must be predicted so that the arresting force is not too great and the balloon will be high enough that the jumper doesn't hit the ground. Taking into account the aerodynamic drag forces, the governing equation is[29]

$$\frac{d^2x}{dt^2} + c_d \, \text{signum}(dx/dt)\left(\frac{dx}{dt}\right)^2 + \frac{k}{m_f}(x - L)u(x - L) = g$$

[28]H. B. Wilson and L. H. Turcotte, *Advanced Mathematics and Mechanics Applications Using* MATLAB, 2nd ed., CRC Press, Boca Raton, FL, 1997, p. 294.
[29]See, for example, D. M. Etter, *Engineering Problem Solving with MATLAB*, Prentice Hall, Upper Saddle River, NJ, 1997, pp. 220–221.

where $g = 9.8$ m/s^2 is the acceleration of gravity, c_d is proportional to the drag coefficient and has the units of m^{-1}, k is the spring constant of the bungee cord in N/m, m_j is the mass of the jumper, and $u(z)$ is the unit step function—that is, $u(z) = 0$ when $z \leq 0$, and $u(z) = 1$ when $z > 0$. The programming is greatly simplified if the logical operator described in Section 4.1 is used to describe $u(z)$.

If $L = 150$ m, $m_j = 70$ kg, $k = 10$ N/m, $c_o = 0.00324$ m^{-1}, and the initial conditions are zero, show that:

a. The maximum value of x is -308.47 m, which occurs at 11.47 s.

b. The jumper will reach 150 m in 5.988 s traveling at a velocity of -43.48 m/s.

c. The maximum acceleration will be -12.82 m/s^2($-1.308g$) at 11.18 s

Plot the displacement, velocity, and acceleration. The acceleration can be obtained by approximating the derivative of the velocity using diff. The numerical results stated above were obtained using spline on the output from ode45.

5.27 Consider an inverted pendulum that is composed of a weightless rigid rod of length L to which a mass m and a linear spring of spring constant k are attached at its free end. The pendulum is initially vertical. The unstretched length of the spring is L. The rotation of the pendulum's pivot has a damping c, and the pendulum is driven by a moment $M(t)$. The governing equation describing the angular motion is[30]

$$\frac{d^2\theta}{d\tau^2} + \alpha\frac{d\theta}{d\tau} - \sin\theta + \beta\left(1 - \frac{1}{\sqrt{5 - 4\cos\theta}}\right)\sin\theta = P(t)$$

where

$$\beta = \frac{2kL}{mg} \quad P = \frac{M}{mgL} \quad \tau = t\sqrt{\frac{g}{L}} \quad \alpha = (c/m)\sqrt{L/g}$$

and t is time.

If $M = 0$, $\beta = 10$, $\alpha = 0.1$, $\theta(0) = \pi/4$, and $d\theta(0)/d\tau = 0$, plot the rotation θ as a function of τ for 1000 equally spaced values of τ from $0 \leq \tau \leq 50$, and, in a separate figure, plot $\theta(\tau)$ versus $d\theta(\tau)/d\tau$.

5.28 The oscillations of the height Z of the separation between the fluid levels in two rectangular prismatic reservoirs connected by a long pipeline can be determined from[31]

$$\frac{d^2Z}{dt^2} + \text{signum}(dZ/dt)p\left(\frac{dZ}{dt}\right)^2 + qZ = 0$$

If $p = 0.375$ m^{-1}, $q = 7.4 \times 10^{-4}$ s^{-2}, and the initial conditions are $Z(0) = Z_n$ m and $dZ(0)/dt = 0$ m/s, determine the value of the *first* occurrence of t_n, where $n = 1, 2$, for which $Z(t_n) = 0$ when $Z_1 = 10$ m and $Z_2 = 50$ m. Use interp1 to determine t_n. The quantity signum is determined with sign. [Hint: Plot the results for one value of Z_n, and then from the characteristics of the curve, use an appropriate combination of min and find to select the middle index of the small range of values over which interp1 should perform the interpolation.] [Answers: $t_1 = 114.2692$ s, and $t_2 = 276.1428$ s.]

[30]H. B. Wilson and L. H. Turcotte, *ibid.*, p. 279.
[31]D. N. Roy, *Applied Fluid Mechanics*, Ellis Horwood Limited, Chichester, England, 1988, pp. 290–293.

5.29 Consider Eq. 5.3 and its numerical solution to a step input; that is, $h(t) = u(t)$. Determine the value of ξ that makes the following quantity a minimum:

$$f(\xi) = \sum_{n=1}^{N} (y(t_n) - 1)^2$$

Let ξ range from 0.05 to 0.95 in increments of 0.05. It should be realized that fminbnd cannot be used because $f(\xi)$ is an array of numerical values; use min to bring back the index of ξ and the value of ξ at that index.

Section 5.5.4

5.30 Consider a uniform inextensible cable of length L_o and weight per unit length w that hangs between two fixed points $x = 0$ and $x = L$ such that $L < L_o$. If the cable has no flexural rigidity and can only support tensile forces T, then the governing equation of the nondimensional deflection $z(\eta)$ of the cable is[32]

$$\frac{d^2 z}{d\eta^2} = \beta \sqrt{1 + \left(\frac{dz}{d\eta}\right)^2}$$

where $\eta = x/L$, $\beta = wL/H$, H is the horizontal component of T and a negative z indicates a downward deflection. The corresponding length L_o of the cable is equal to

$$L_o = L \int_0^l \sqrt{1 + \left(\frac{dz}{d\eta}\right)^2} \, d\eta$$

from which one can determine β and, hence, H when w, L, and L_o are given. The boundary conditions are

$$z(0) = 0 \quad \text{and} \quad z(1) = 0$$

Determine the value of β and the slope $dz(0)/d\eta$ when $L_o/L = 1.2$. The integration must be performed with trapz.

5.31 Consider the displacement $y(\eta)$ of a uniform beam clamped at $\eta = 0$ and free at $\eta = 1$. The boundary conditions are $y(0) = dy(0)/d\eta = d^2 y(1)/d\eta^2 = d^3 y(1)/d\eta^3 = 0$. Plot the displacement of the beam when there is a uniform load of unit magnitude on the beam from $\eta = 0.5$ to $\eta = 1$.

Section 5.5.5

5.32 The relationship between the lead angle of a worm gear λ; the ratio $\beta = N_1/N_2$, where N_1 is the number of teeth on the worm gear and N_2 is the number of teeth on the driven gear; the center distance C between shafts; and the normal diametral pitch P_{dn} is[33]

$$K = \frac{2P_{dn}C}{N_2} = \frac{\beta}{\sin \lambda} + \frac{1}{\cos \lambda}$$

---

[32]M. Irvine, *ibid.*, p. 4.
[33]M. F. Spotts and T. E. Shoup, *Design of Machine Elements*, Prentice Hall, Upper Saddle River, NJ, 1998, p. 613.

The ranges of practical interest are $1 \leq K \leq 2, 1° \leq \lambda \leq 40°$, and $0.02 \leq \beta \leq 0.30$. For certain combinations of values, λ can have one value, two values, or no value.

a. Find the value of λ that makes K a minimum when $\beta = 0.02, 0.05, 0.08, 0.11, 0.15, 0.18, 0.23$, and 0.30.

b. For $K = 1.5$ and $\beta = 0.16$ find the value(s) of λ.

5.33 In Exercise 1.14, the mass flow rate of a gas escaping from a tank at pressure p_0 and under reversible adiabatic conditions was proportional to

$$\psi = \sqrt{\frac{k}{k-1}} \sqrt{\left(\frac{p_e}{p_0}\right)^{2/k} - \left(\frac{p_e}{p_0}\right)^{(k+1)/k}}$$

where p_e is the pressure exterior to the tank's exit and k is the adiabatic reversible gas constant. The maximum value occurs at

$$\frac{p_e}{p_0} = \left(\frac{2}{k+1}\right)^{k/(k-1)}$$

Verify this maximum value numerically for $k = 1.4$ using `fminbnd` and using `min` with 200 equally spaced values for $0 \leq p_e/p_0 \leq 1$.

Section 5.5.6

5.34 a. Use `fsolve` to find the values of θ in degrees and k that satisfy the following equations when $a = 1$ and $b = 3$:

$$b = k(1 - \cos \theta)$$
$$a = k(\theta - \sin \theta)$$

b. The two equations in part a can be combined into the following one equation:

$$b(\theta - \sin \theta) - a(1 - \cos \theta) = 0$$

Use `fzero` to determine the value of θ when $a = 1$ and $b = 3$, and then use one of the equations in part a to determine k. [Answers: $k = 6.9189$, and $\theta = 55.4999°$.]

5.35 a. Use `fsolve` to determine from the following equations the values of Q, T_A, and T_B when $\sigma = 5.667 \times 10^{-8}, T_1 = 373$ K, and $T_2 = 293$ K:

$$T_1^4 - T_A^4 = Q/\sigma$$
$$T_A^4 - T_B^4 = Q/\sigma$$
$$T_B^4 - T_2^4 = Q/\sigma$$

b. The equations in part a can also be written as

$$\begin{bmatrix} 1 & 0 & 1/\sigma \\ 1 & -1 & -1/\sigma \\ 0 & 1 & -1/\sigma \end{bmatrix} \begin{Bmatrix} x \\ y \\ Q \end{Bmatrix} = \begin{Bmatrix} T_1^4 \\ 0 \\ T_2^4 \end{Bmatrix}$$

where $x = T_A^4$ and $y = T_B^4$. Determine the values of Q, T_A, and T_B from this system of equations using left division. [Answer: $T_A = 352.052, T_B = 326.5116$, and $Q = 226.4312$.]

Section 5.6

5.36 Use the Symbolic Toolbox to determine the limits in the expressions below at the values indicated:

a. $\lim_{x \to 0} (1 - \sin(2x))^{1/x}$

b. $\lim_{x \to 1} \dfrac{\ln x^n}{1 - x^2}$

5.37 Given that

$$f(x) = \frac{1 - e^{-x}}{1 + x^3}$$

If $x = a + b \cos(w)$, determine using the Symbolic Toolbox the value of $f(x)$ when $a = 1.2$, $b = -0.45$, and $w = \pi/3$.

5.38 Use solve to determine the value of x between $0 \le x \le \pi$ of the function given below that makes $f(x)$ an extremum. Is this extremum a maximum or a minimum?

$$f(x) = e^{\sin x}$$

5.39 Determine the value of the integral given below for 10 values of b from 0 to 4π.

$$A(b) = \int_0^b \frac{2x + 5}{x^2 + 4x + 5} dx$$

5.40 The Laplace transform with respect to the nondimensional time τ of the displacement response of one of the masses of a two-degree-of-freedom system for a particular set of numerical values is given by[34]

$$X_1(s) = \frac{0.1s^3 + 0.0282s^2 - 0.0427s + 0.0076}{s^4 + 0.282s^3 + 4.573s^2 + 0.4792s + 2.889}$$

Plot the inverse Laplace transform of $X_1(s)$ over the range $0 \le \tau \le 35$.

---

[34]B. Balachandran and E. B. Magrab, *ibid.*, p. 428.

6

2D Graphics

Edward B. Magrab

The implementation of a wide selection of two-dimensional (2D) plotting capabilities is presented.

6.1 INTRODUCTION

MATLAB provides a wide selection of very flexible and easy-to-implement 2D and three-dimensional (3D) plotting capabilities. The plotting functions can be grouped into three categories: graphics management, curve and surface generation, and annotation and graph characteristics. Although MATLAB has quite a few plotting functions, for the most part their syntax is similar and they can be annotated with the same set of functions. The functions whose usage we shall illustrate in this and the next chapter are as follows:

Management	Generation	Annotation and Characteristics
figure	**2-D**	xlabel
subplot	plot	ylabel
zoom	polar	text
hold	fill	title
	plotyy	legend
3-D	semilogx, semilogy,	box
view	loglog	set
rotate3d	stairs	grid
	stem	axis, axis equal, axis off
	bar	clabel
	3-D	**3-D**
	plot3	text3
	surf, surfc	zlabel
	mesh, meshc, meshz	colorbar
	contour, contour3,	colormap
	contourf	shading
	waterfall	
	cylinder	

When generating graphed entities, one should expend the effort so that each figure meets the solution's objective by illustrating what is important and exhibits clarity and specificity by being fully annotated with the axes labeled, the figure titled, the curves identified (if more than one), and the important numerical values displayed. However, any devices that are used to enhance the figure, such as color, line type, symbols, and text, should do so without being distracting.

A typical set of graph-creating expressions consists of management functions, followed by one or more graph-generation functions, followed by annotation functions, which may be followed in turn by additional management functions. However, except for the management functions, the order of these functions is, in most applications, arbitrary. Also, employment of the annotation and graph characteristic functions is optional. MATLAB scales the axes and labels the axes' magnitudes, even if more than one set of data is plotted. Thus, one can always obtain a partially annotated graph provided that the function's syntax has been used correctly.

Some Graph Management Functions

A graph is created in a figure window, which is a window created by MATLAB at execution time, when any one of its graph-management, -generation, or -annotation and -characteristics functions is invoked. When a program, either a script or a function, uses more than one graph-generation function, MATLAB creates a new figure window. However, any previously created window is removed before creating the new figure window. To retain each new graph in its own figure window, one must use

```
figure(n)
```

where *n* is an integer. If the argument of `figure` is omitted, then MATLAB gives it the next integer value.

One can also place several independently created graphs in one figure window with

```
subplot(i, j, k)
```

The first two arguments divide the window into sectors (rows and columns), and the third indicates in which sector a graph is to be placed. A value of 1 for this argument indicates the upper left corner, and the sum of the number of rows and columns indicates the lower right corner. As the numbers increase, they indicate the sectors from left to right, starting at the top row. Any annotation and management functions that appear in the program after `figure` and/or `subplot` apply only to the sector indicated by the third argument of `subplot`. Within each sector, any compatible set of the 2D or 3D graph-generation functions can be used. (Refer to Figure 6.1 to see several examples of how `figure` and `subplot` are used.) If only one figure window is needed, `figure` can be omitted, even if `subplot` is used.

Since each graph-generation function creates a new figure window,[1] to draw more than one curve, surface, or line (or combination of these) on a given graph, one must use

```
hold on
```

which holds the current window (or `subplot` sector) active. All figures that have been created can be copied to the Windows™ clipboard by selecting *Copy Figure* from the *Edit* pull-down menu within each figure's window. This figure can then be transferred (pasted) to a page in a word-processor program and will be in the Windows metafile format.

MATLAB provides the means to convert a figure to a format that is compatible with many common print devices. For example, if one wants to save the graphics appearing in the active figure window as a level-2 encapsulated postscript file for black-and-white printers with the name *FileName.eps*, then one uses either

```
print -deps2 'c:\path\FileName.eps'
```

or

```
print('-deps2', 'c:\path\FileName.eps')
```

where *-deps2* is a key word to indicate that a level-2 encapsulated postscript file is to be created and *path* describes the directory and subdirectory names where the file will reside. For other options, see the *Help* file for `print`. On the other hand, if one wants to insert a level-2 encapsulated postscript file into an MS Word™ document

---

[1] The MATLAB window look, management, and file management descriptions relate to a Windows environment. Equivalent procedures are used with other operating systems.

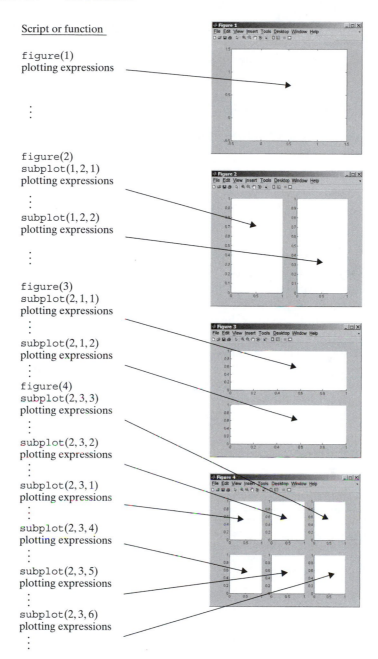

Script or function

```
figure(1)
plotting expressions
```

$\vdots$

```
figure(2)
subplot(1,2,1)
plotting expressions
```

$\vdots$

```
subplot(1,2,2)
plotting expressions
```

$\vdots$

```
figure(3)
subplot(2,1,1)
plotting expressions
```

$\vdots$

```
subplot(2,1,2)
plotting expressions
```

$\vdots$

```
figure(4)
subplot(2,3,3)
plotting expressions
```

$\vdots$

```
subplot(2,3,2)
plotting expressions
```

$\vdots$

```
subplot(2,3,1)
plotting expressions
```

$\vdots$

```
subplot(2,3,4)
plotting expressions
```

$\vdots$

```
subplot(2,3,5)
plotting expressions
```

$\vdots$

```
subplot(2,3,6)
plotting expressions
```

$\vdots$

Figure 6.1   Examples of the use of various combinations of `figure` and `subplot`.

such that a "tiff" preview image of the figure is displayed, then one uses the following expression[2]

    `print -deps2 -tiff 'c:\path\FileName.eps'`

or

    `print('-deps2', '-tiff', 'c:\path\FileName.eps')`

where *-tiff* is a key word indicating that a tiff preview is available.

6.2 BASIC 2D PLOTTING COMMANDS

The basic 2D plotting command is

    `plot(u1, v1, c1, u2, v2, c2, ...)`

where u_j and v_j are the x- and y-coordinates, respectively, of a point or a series of points. They are either a pair of numbers, vectors of the same length, matrices of the same order, or expressions that, when evaluated, result in one of these three quantities. The quantity c_j is a string of characters: One character specifies the line/point color, one character specifies the point type if points are to be plotted, and up to two characters are used to specify the line characteristics. These various line and point characteristics are given in Table 6.1. When a series of points are to be plotted, one of the characters of c_j can be, for example, an 's' to plot a square or an asterisk (*) to plot an asterisk. When the points, whether or not they are to be displayed, are to be connected with straight lines, the characters of c_j can be, for example, a '-' for a solid line and a '--' for a dashed line. When both the lines and points are to be plotted with

TABLE 6.1 Line and Point Characteristics

Line type		Line color		Point type	
Symbol	Description	Symbol	Description	Symbol	Description
-	Solid	r	Red	+	Plus sign
--	Dashed	g	Green	o	Circle
:	Dotted	b	Blue	*	Asterisk
-.	Dashed-dot	c	Cyan	.	Point
		m	Magenta	x	Cross
		y	Yellow	s	Square
		k	Black	d	Diamond
		w	White	∧	Upward-pointing triangle
				∨	Downward-pointing triangle
				>	Right-pointing triangle
				<	Left-pointing triangle
				p	Pentagram
				h	Hexagram

[2]To use this file in MS Word, the appropriate encapsulated postscript filters must be installed. These are part of MS Word but are not always installed when Word is installed. In this case, run MS Word setup, and install the desired filters.

the same color, the c_j contains both descriptors. For example, if we were to plot blue dashed lines connecting blue diamonds, c_j would be 'b--d'. The order of the three sets of characters within the single quotes is not important. When both lines and points are to be plotted but the number of points defining the line is different from the number of points that are to be plotted c_1 contains the symbol for the line type and c_2 the symbol for the point type (or vice versa). If c_j is omitted, then the system's default values are used. If more than one curve is drawn, then the line colors change according to the default sequence.

   We now describe the statements used to draw points, lines, circles, expressions, families of curves, and curves described by multiple functions.

6.2.1 Points

To place a red asterisk at the location $(2, 4)$, the plotting instruction is

   plot(2, 4, 'r*')

6.2.2 Lines

To draw a straight line that goes from $(0, 0)$ to $(1, 2)$ using the default line type (solid) and the default color (blue), the plotting instruction is

   plot([0, 1], [0, 2])

Notice that the first two-element vector $[0, 1]$ represents the values of the x-coordinates and the second two-element vector $[0, 2]$ the values of the y-coordinates. Thus, the first element of each vector defines the (x, y)-coordinates of one endpoint of the line, and the second elements of these vectors are the coordinates of the other endpoint.

   Suppose that we want to draw a set of n unconnected lines whose endpoints are (x_{1n}, y_{1n}) and (x_{2n}, y_{2n}). To accomplish this, we create four vectors:

$$x_j = [x_{j1}\ x_{j2}\ \cdots\ x_{jn}]$$
$$y_j = [y_{j1}\ y_{j2}\ \cdots\ y_{jn}] \quad j = 1, 2$$

Then, the plot instruction is

   plot([x1; x2], [y1; y2])

where $[x1; x2]$ and $[y1; y2]$ are each $(2 \times n)$ arrays.

   To illustrate this expression, let us draw four vertical lines from $y = 0$ to $y = \cos(\pi x/20)$ when $x = 2, 4, 6, 8$. The script is

   x = 2:2:8;
   y = [zeros(1, length(x)); cos(pi*x/20)];
   plot([x; x], y, 'k')

where we have used the fact that $x_1 = x_2 = x$. The color is specified so that the lines all have the same color. (In this case, black). The function zeros is used to create a vector of 0's of the same length as x. The result is shown in Figure 6.2a. Unfortunately, because of automatic scaling of the axes, the first and last lines are coincident

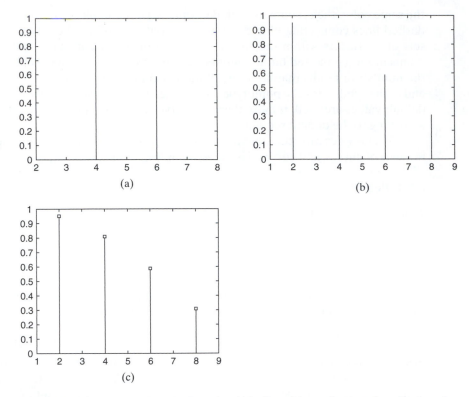

Figure 6.2   (a) Situation where the figure box hides lines; (b) use of axis to broaden the axis limits so that all lines can be seen; (c) placement of red squares at uppermost ends of lines.

with the box around the figure. Therefore, one has to adjust the axes so that these lines are visible. This adjustment is done with

$$\text{axis}([\text{xmin}, \text{xmax}, \text{ymin}, \text{ymax}])$$

where x_{min}, x_{max}, y_{min}, and y_{max} are the minimum and maximum values of the x- and y-axes, respectively. Thus, the revised script is

```
x = 2:2:8;
y = [zeros(1, length(x)); cos(pi*x/20)];
plot([x; x], y, 'k')
axis([1, 9, 0, 1])
```

The revised graph is shown in Figure 6.2b.

Obtaining the values of the axis limits and then redefining one or more of them as needed can provide additional flexibility. The limits are obtained from

$$v = \text{axis};$$

in which v is a four-element vector:

$$v(1) = x_{min} \quad v(3) = y_{min}$$
$$v(2) = x_{max} \quad v(4) = y_{max}$$

Thus, to obtain Figure 6.2b, the script could have been written as

```
x = 2:2:8;
y = [zeros(1, length(x)); cos(pi*x/20)];
plot([x; x], y, 'k')
v = axis;
v(1) = 1;
v(2) = 9;
axis(v)
```

If we want to place a red square at the end of each vertical line that is off the x-axis, then we have to add another triplet of instruction in the plot command. Thus, the script becomes[3]

```
x = 2:2:8;
y = [zeros(1, length(x)); cos(pi*x/20)];
plot([x; x], y, 'k', x, cos(pi*x/20), 'rs')
axis([1, 9, 0, 1])
```

The result is shown in Figure 6.2c.

6.2.3 Circles

To draw a circle of radius r whose center is located at (a, b) in a Cartesian coordinate system, one must first transform the radial coordinates to Cartesian coordinates (recall Figure 2.2):

$$x = a + r\cos(\theta)$$
$$y = b + r\sin(\theta)$$

where $0 \leq \theta \leq \theta_1 \leq 2\pi$. When $\theta_1 < 2\pi$, we draw an arc of a circle. If we assume that $\theta_1 = 2\pi$, $a = 1$, $b = 2$, and $r = 0.5$, then the script to draw the circle is

```
theta = linspace(0, 2*pi);
plot(1+0.5*cos(theta), 2+0.5*sin(theta))
axis equal
```

The `axis equal` function proportions the graph so that the circles appear as circles rather than as ellipses. The execution of this script is shown in Figure 6.3.

The script to draw a family of six concentric circles, whose initial radius of 0.5 increases in increments of 0.25 and whose centers are indicated by a plus sign, is

```
theta = linspace(0, 2*pi, 50);    % (1×50)
rad = 0.5:0.25:1.75;              % (1×6)
x = 1+cos(theta)'*rad;            % (50×6)
y = 2+sin(theta)'*rad;            % (50×6)
plot(x, y, 'k', 1, 2, 'k+')
axis equal
```

---

[3]This `plot` expression is, in some respects, a generalization of the plotting function `stem`, which assumes $x_1 = x_2$ and that $y_1 = 0$.

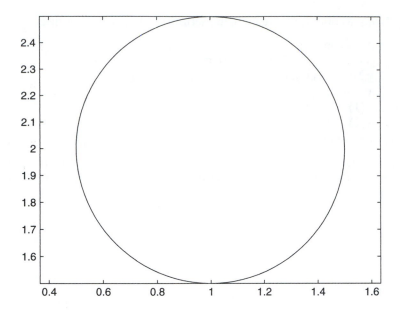

Figure 6.3   A circle.

The values in the arrays are plotted column by column. Since we wanted all 50 values of *theta* to be drawn at each value of *rad*, we formed them as (50×6) arrays. If the string 'k' were omitted, then each circle would have been drawn in a different color. The execution of this script yields Figure 6.4.

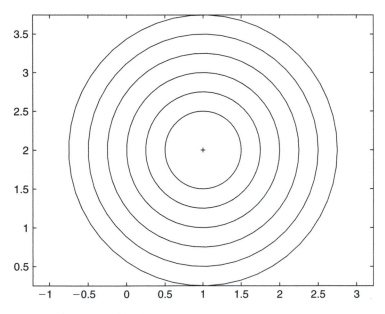

Figure 6.4   Six concentric circles.

6.2.4 Family of Curves

One way to draw a family of curves was presented for concentric circles in Section 6.2.3. In general, MATLAB allows one to have the x-axis represented by a vector and the y-axis by a matrix. It will draw the curves by drawing the vector versus either the columns or the rows of the matrix, depending on which one matches the length of the vector.

We first draw a family of parabolas

$$y = a^2 - x^2$$

for $-5 \le x \le 5$ and $a = 1, 2, \ldots, 5$. The script is

```
x = -5:0.2:5;
a = 1:5;
[xx, aa] = meshgrid(x.^2, a.^2);
plot(x, aa-xx, 'k')
```

which results in Figure 6.5.

Now, consider the visualization of the convergence of the series

$$S_N = \sum_{j=1}^{N} \frac{1}{(a + j)^2}$$

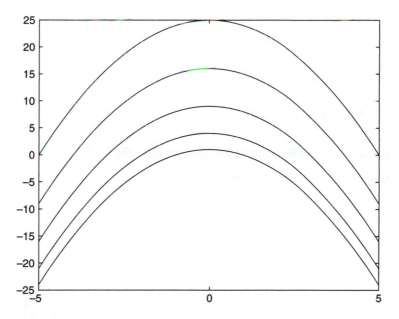

Figure 6.5 Family of parabolas.

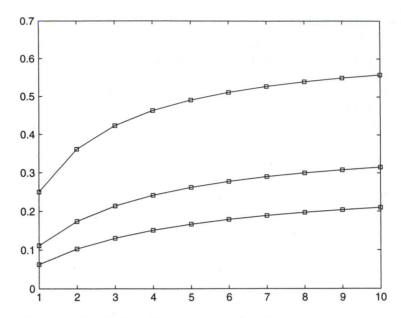

Figure 6.6   Visualization of the convergence of a series.

for $N = 1, 2, \ldots, 10$ and $a = 1, 2, 3$. In this case, we use cumsum (recall Section 2.5) to obtain the following script:

```
aa = 1:3;                    % (1×3)
N = 1:10;                    % (1×10)
[a, k] = meshgrid(aa, N);    % (10×3)
S = cumsum(1./(a+k).^2);     % (10×3)
plot(N, S, 'ks-')
```

which, when executed, results in Figure 6.6.

6.2.5 Multiple Functions Plotted on One Figure[4]

Consider the three functions

$$g_1(x) = 0.1x^2$$
$$g_2(y) = \cos^2 y$$
$$g_3(z) = e^{-0.3z}$$

---

[4]To plot two different types of graphs with two different ordinates, use plotyy (see Section 6.2.7, Figure 6.8).

where $0 \le x = y = z \le 3.5$. We can draw these three functions on one figure in either of three ways:

```
x = linspace(0, 3.5);
plot(x, [0.1*x.^2; cos(x).^2; exp(-0.3*x)], 'k')
```

or

```
x = linspace(0, 3.5);
plot(x, 0.1*x.^2, 'k', x, cos(x).^2, 'k', x, exp(-0.3*x), 'k')
```

or

```
x = linspace(0, 3.5);
plot(x, 0.1*x.^2, 'k')
hold on
plot(x, cos(x).^2, 'k')
plot(x, exp(-0.3*x), 'k')
```

Execution of any of these three scripts will produce Figure 6.7a, wherein all the curves have the same color: black.

On the other hand, if the range of the independent variable for each of these functions is different, then only the second and third scripts can be used. For example, if $0 \le x \le 3$, $1 \le y \le 4$, and $2 \le z \le 5$, then the form of the second script above is used as follows:

```
x = linspace(0, 3, 45);
y = linspace(1, 4, 55);
z = linspace(2, 5, 65);
plot(x, 0.1*x.^2, 'k-', y, cos(y).^2, 'k--', z, exp(-0.3*z), 'k-.')
```

which upon execution results in Figure 6.7b. Notice that we have plotted each function with a different line type and that each curve has been plotted with a different number of points.

6.2.6 Changing Graph Appearance

Several functions can be used to change the appearance of a graph. They are

```
axis on  or  axis off   [default — on]
box on   or  box off    [default — on]
grid on  or  grid off   [default — off]
```

The function box on only works when axis on has been selected.

We shall illustrate the effects that these functions have on the graph's appearance by plotting a Lissajous figure, which is a graph of $\sin(n\theta)$ versus $\sin(m\theta + \theta_1)$, where m and n are positive numbers, $0 \le \theta \le 2\pi$, and $0 \le \theta_1 < 2\pi$. Let us consider

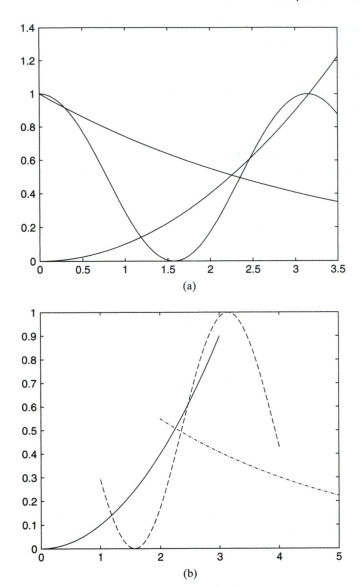

Figure 6.7 (a) Three different functions plotted over the same range; (b) three different functions plotted over three different ranges.

the case where $n = 1$, $m = 2$, and $\theta_1 = \pi/4$ ($45°$). If we take 101 equally spaced values of θ, then the script is

```
th = linspace(0, 2*pi, 101);
plot(sin(th), sin(2*th+pi/4))
```

Execution of this script and its modifications with the box, axis, and grid functions are summarized in Table 6.2.

TABLE 6.2   Illustration of box, grid, and axis

Function	Script	Graph

box on
grid on
	th = linspace(0, 2*pi, 101);
	x = sin(th);
	y = sin(2*th+pi/4);
	plot(x, y, 'k-')
	box on
	grid on	

box off
grid off
axis off
	th = linspace(0, 2*pi, 101);
	x = sin(th);
	y = sin(2*th+pi/4);
	plot(x, y, 'k-')
	box off
	grid off
	axis off	

box off
grid off
axis on
	th = linspace(0, 2*pi, 101);
	x = sin(th);
	y = sin(2*th+pi/4);
	plot(x, y, 'k-')
	box off
	grid off	

6.2.7 Some Special-Purpose Graphs

MATLAB has a library of special-purpose graphs that are applicable to a wide variety of applications. We shall briefly illustrate them by having each one plot some part of the following expression:

$$F(\Omega) = H(\Omega)e^{j\theta(\Omega)} \quad \Omega \geq 0$$

where

$$H(\Omega) = \frac{1}{\sqrt{(1 - \Omega^2)^2 + (2\zeta\Omega)^2}}$$

$$\theta(\Omega) = \tan^{-1}\frac{2\zeta\Omega}{1 - \Omega^2}$$

and $\zeta < 1$.

We first create the function **FOm** to represent this expression:

```
function [H, T] = FOm(Om, z)
T = atan2(2*z*Om, 1-Om.^2)*180/pi;
H = 1./sqrt((1-Om.^2).^2+(2*z*Om).^2);
```

where $T = \theta(\Omega)$ is expressed in degrees, $z = \zeta$, and we have used the two-argument form of the arctangent function because of the sign change in the denominator.

The first set of special-purpose graphs that we consider are `semilogx`, `semilogy`, and `loglog`. The function `semilogx` plots the x-axis on a log to the base-10 scale, `semilogy` plots the y-axis on a log to the base-10 scale, and `loglog` plots both axes on the log to the base-10 scale. These three plotting functions are summarized in Table 6.3.

Now, consider the set of plotting function `stairs`, `stem`, and `bar`. The plotting function `stairs` plots a staircase-like representation of the data points, `stem` plots the data as discrete values connected by straight lines from the x-axis, and `bar` plots the data points connected by filled rectangles (bars) from the x-axis. These three plotting functions are summarized in Table 6.4.

For our last special-purpose plotting function, we consider `plotyy`, which plots two different functions with two different ranges of x- and y-values. To illustrate the use of this function, we will plot $H(\Omega)$ and $\theta(\Omega)$ on the same graph. The script is

```
Om = linspace(0, 2, 100);
[H, T] = FOm(Om, 0.05);
plotyy(Om, H, Om, T)
```

which upon execution produces Figure 6.8.

TABLE 6.3   Illustration of `semilogx`, `semilogy`, and `loglog`

Plotting function	Script	Graph
`semilogx`	Om = linspace(0.01, 10, 200); [H, T] = **FOm**(Om, 0.05); semilogx(Om, H)	
`semilogy`	Om = linspace(0.01, 10, 200); [H, T] = **FOm**(Om, 0.05); semilogy(Om, H)	
`loglog`	Om = linspace(0.01, 10, 200); [H, T] = **FOm**(Om, 0.05); loglog(Om, H)	

TABLE 6.4   Illustration of stairs, stem, and bar

Plotting function	Script	Graph
stairs	Om = linspace(0.01, 2, 30); [H, T] = **FOm**(Om, 0.05); stairs(Om, H)	
stem	Om = linspace(0.01, 2, 30); [H, T] = **FOm**(Om, 0.05); stem(Om, H)	
bar	Om = linspace(0.01, 2, 30); [H, T] = **FOm**(Om, 0.05); bar(Om, H, 0.6)	

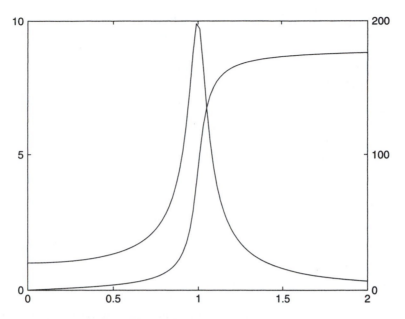

Figure 6.8   A plot of $H(\Omega)$ and $\theta(\Omega)$ using `plotyy`.

6.3 GRAPH ANNOTATIONS AND VISUAL ENHANCEMENT

6.3.1 Introduction

MATLAB has extensive graphic enhancement capabilities. In this section, we shall illustrate through example how to enhance a graph as follows:

- With axis labels, figure titles, labeled curves, legends, filled areas, and placement of text
- By altering the attributes of the axes, curve lines, and text
- By using Greek letters, mathematical symbols, subscripts, and superscripts

6.3.2 Axes and Curve Labels, Figure Titles, Legends, and Text

The functions that are used to label the x- and y-axes and to place a title above the graph are, respectively,

```
xlabel(s)
ylabel(s)
title(s)
```

where s is a string. The function that places text anywhere in the figure window is

```
text(x, y, s)
```

where x and y are the coordinates of where the text given by the string s will be placed.

Let us draw, label, title, and annotate the relationship of two intersecting curves, cos(x) and 1/cosh(x), over the range $0 \leq x \leq 6$. In this range, these two curves intersect at $x = 4.73$. (Recall Example 5.8.) We shall also draw a vertical line through the intersecting point and denote the value of x near this intersection. The script to perform these operations is

```
x = linspace(0, 6, 100);
plot(x, cos(x), 'k', x, 1./cosh(x), 'k', [4.73, 4.73], [-1, 1], 'k')
xlabel('x')
ylabel('Value of functions')
title('Visualization of two intersecting curves')
text(4.8, -0.1, 'x = 4.73')
text(2.1, 0.3, '1/cosh(x)')
text(1.2, -0.4, 'cos(x)')
```

Execution of the script results in Figure 6.9. The coordinate values for the location of the various texts are chosen only after the `plot` function is executed—that is, only after the first two lines of the script have been written and the resulting figure examined. Then, the `text` functions are added.

There is another way that we can identify the curves in Figure 6.9, and that is with

```
legend(s1, s2, ..., sn, 'Location', p)
```

where $s1$, $s2$, etc., are the strings containing the alphanumerical identifier for each line that will appear in the legend box in the order that they are given, '*Location*' is

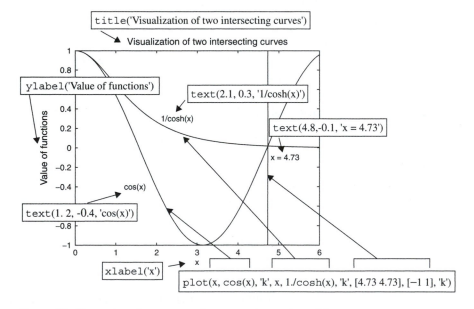

Figure 6.9 Expressions that create and annotate the graphs and figure.

a key word that tells legend that the string that follows will state where to place the legend box, and *p* is a string key word that places the legend in one of the eight predetermined locations inside the graph or in one of eight predetermined locations outside the graph. The number of arguments of legend equals the number of different lines being drawn by one or more plot functions, and the order of the strings corresponds to the order in which the various curves have been plotted. Therefore, legend has to be placed after the plot functions have been executed. The string *p* has the following values when the legend is to be placed inside the graph axes. For the key words to place the legend outside the graphs axes, see the help file for legend. To place the legend in the middle of the: (1) top of the graph, *p* = '*North*'; (2) bottom of the graph, *p* = '*South*'; (3) right side of the graph, *p* = '*East*'; (4) left side of the graph, *p* = '*West*'. To place the legend in the: (1) top right, *p* = '*NorthEast*', which is the default value; (2) top left, *p* = '*NorthWest*'; (3) bottom right, *p* = '*SouthEast*'; (4) bottom left, *p* = '*SouthWest*'. When these two strings are omitted, the legend is placed in its default location, which is the upper right. One can also use the mouse to place the legend: Simply click on the edit plot icon and with the mouse button depressed move the legend to its desired location. This placement is temporary however, in that when this figure is closed and then created at another time the legend will again appear at its default location. Lastly, the legend function differs from text in that text can be used as many times as practical, whereas legend can only be used once. In addition, legend places all the text within a box.

We shall illustrate the use of the legend function by revisiting the script that produced Figure 6.9 and replace the two text statements with legend. We shall place the legend in the lower left corner of the graph; that is, we set *p* = '*SouthWest*'. Then, the script becomes

```
x = linspace(0, 6, 100);
plot(x, cos(x), 'k-', x, 1./cosh(x), 'k--', [4.73, 4.73], [-1, 1], 'k')
xlabel('x')
ylabel('Value of functions')
title('Visualization of two intersecting curves')
text(4.8, -0.1, 'x = 4.73')
legend('cos(x) ', '1/cosh(x) ', 'Location', 'SouthWest')
```

The execution of this script produces Figure 6.10. Notice that we have employed plot to display three curves, but legend has only two strings identifiers. Therefore, only the first two curves that were plotted are identified. The third argument of each triplet in the plot function specifies that the lines are to be drawn in black, with $\cos(x)$ appearing as a solid line and $1/\cosh(x)$ as a dashed line. The legend's arguments are order dependent. The first argument relates to the first curve that is drawn and the second to the second curve. If several plot functions are used, then the order continues with the first argument of the second plot function following the last string identifying the last curve plotted in the previous plot statement. Only one legend function can be used per figure or subplot. The location key word '*South West*' in the legend function places the legend in the lower left corner of the figure.

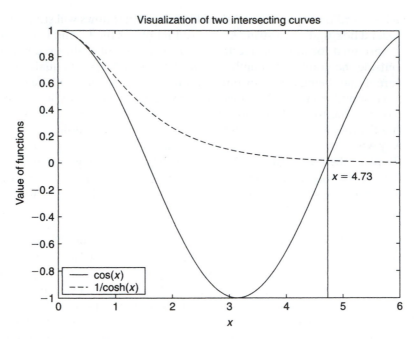

Figure 6.10   Use of the legend function.

Figure 6.10 could have also been obtained from the following script:

```
x = linspace(0, 6, 100);
plot(x, cos(x), 'k-')
hold on
plot(x, 1./cosh(x), 'k--')
plot( [4.73, 4.73], [-1, 1], 'k')
xlabel('x')
ylabel('Value of functions')
title('Visualization of two intersecting curves')
text(4.8, -0.1, 'x = 4.73')
legend('cos(x) ', '1/cosh(x) ', 'Location', 'South West')
```

When the line types and colors are not specified in the plot function, the legend function uses the default line type (solid) and the default color sequence; that is, the lines appearing in the legend are solid lines of different colors. The box around the legend can be toggled on and off with

```
legend('boxon')
```

and

```
legend('boxoff')
```

6.3.3 Filling in Areas

A region of a graph can be highlighted by coloring it or by using some geometrical element to identify it. We shall illustrate several methods that can be used to perform this highlighting.

To fill the area contained within a polygonal region, we use

`fill(x, y, c)`

where x and y are arrays of the same length that represent the endpoint of the lines that form a closed polygon and the string c is the color of the fill given by one of the letters appearing in the second column of Table 6.1.

To illustrate the use of `fill`, we modify the script used in the previous section so that the area between the two curves in the range $0 \leq x \leq 4.73$ is filled with the color cyan. The polygon that has to be created is that formed by the straight-line approximation to $1/\cosh(x)$ from $0 \leq x \leq 4.73$ and that formed by the straight-line approximation to $\cos(x)$ from $4.73 \geq x \geq 0$. Thus, the script becomes

```
x = linspace(0, 6, 100);
plot(x, cos(x), 'k-', x, 1./cosh(x), 'k--', [4.73, 4.73], [-1, 1], 'k')
xlabel('x')
ylabel('Value of functions')
title('Visualization of two intersecting curves')
text(4.8, -0.1, 'x = 4.73')
legend('cos(x) ', '1/cosh(x) ', 3)
xn = linspace(0, 4.73, 50);
hold on
fill([xn, fliplr(xn)], [1./cosh(xn), fliplr(cos(xn))], 'c');
```

The execution of this script gives Figure 6.11. The connected polygon is created by forming the vector `[1./cosh(xn) fliplr(cos(xn))]`, which is the concatenation of

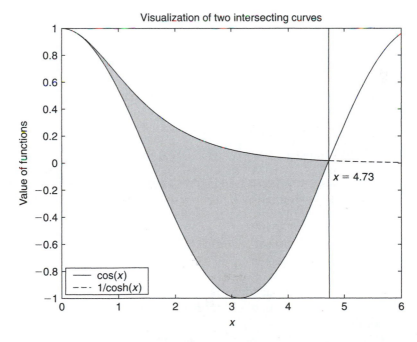

Figure 6.11   Modification of Figure 6.10 with the area between the curves filled in.

the top curve $1/\cosh(x)$ and the reversal of the vector of $\cos(x)$, the bottom curve. Corresponding to this new vector is the new x-coordinate vector [xn fliplr(xn)], which is formed by the concatenation of the new values of x and its reversed values.

Instead of using `fill`, the area between these two curves can be delineated by a series of 20 equally spaced vertical lines. In this case, the script is

```
x = linspace(0, 6, 100);
plot(x, cos(x), 'k-', x, 1./cosh(x), 'k--', [4.73, 4.73], [-1, 1], 'k')
xlabel('x')
ylabel('Value of functions')
title('Visualization of two intersecting curves')
text(4.8, -0.1, 'x = 4.73')
legend('cos(x) ', '1/cosh(x) ', 'Location', 'SouthWest')
xn = linspace(0, 4.73, 50);
hold on
xx = linspace(0, 4.73, 20);
plot([xx; xx], [cos(xx); 1./cosh(xx)], 'k-')
```

When executed, this script produces the results shown in Figure 6.12a.

To create 20 equally spaced horizontal lines, we have to work with the inverse functions $\cos^{-1}(x)$ and $\cosh^{-1}(x)$ to determine where the lines end. We see that we have to consider two separate regions. In the first region for $y > 0$, the horizontal lines at the right end at $1/\cosh(x)$, whereas, for $y < 0$, they end at $\cos(x)$. Thus, the script is

```
x = linspace(0, 6, 100);
plot(x, cos(x), 'k-', x, 1./cosh(x), 'k--', [4.73, 4.73], [-1, 1], 'k')
hold on
xlabel('x')
ylabel('Value of functions')
title('Visualization of two intersecting curves')
text(4.8, -0.1, 'x = 4.73')
legend('cos(x) ', '1/cosh(x) ', 'Location', 'SouthWest')
y1 = linspace(1, 0.01, 10);
plot([acos(y1); acosh(1./y1)], [y1; y1], 'k-')
y2 = linspace(0.01, -1, 10);
plot([acos(y2); pi+fliplr(acos(y1))], [y2; y2], 'k-')
```

which upon execution results in Figure 6.12b. Both of these scripts can be combined to form the following script to produce a hatched effect shown in Figure 6.13:

```
x = linspace(0, 6, 100);
plot(x, cos(x), 'k-', x, 1./cosh(x), 'k--', [4.73, 4.73], [-1, 1], 'k')
hold on
xlabel('x')
ylabel('Value of functions')
title('Visualization of two intersecting curves')
text(4.8, -0.1, 'x = 4.73')
legend('cos(x) ', '1/cosh(x) ', 'Location', 'SouthWest')
```

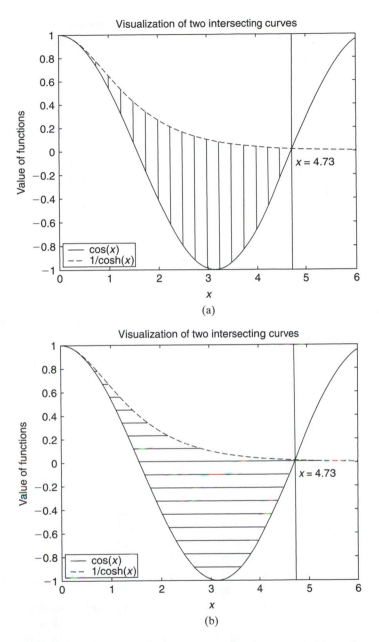

Figure 6.12   Area between two intersecting curves delineated with equally spaced (a) vertical lines or (b) horizontal lines.

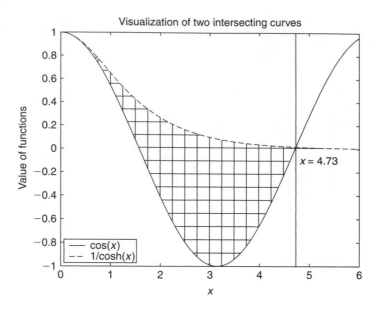

Figure 6.13   Area between two intersecting curves filled with hatched effect.

```
xx = linspace(0, 4.73, 20);
plot([xx; xx], [cos(xx); 1./cosh(xx)], 'k-')
y1 = linspace(1, 0.01, 10);
plot([acos(y1); acosh(1./y1)], [y1; y1], 'k-')
y2 = linspace(0.01, -1, 10);
plot([acos(y2); pi+fliplr(acos(y1))], [y2; y2], 'k-')
```

6.3.4 Greek Letters, Mathematical Symbols, Subscripts, and Superscripts

MATLAB provides the capability to annotate a graph with upper- and lowercase Greek letters, subscripts and superscripts, and a range of mathematical symbols. These annotations can be done within `xlabel`, `ylabel`, `text`, `legend`, and `title`. The formatting instructions follow the *LaTeX* language.[5] All the following techniques are only valid within a pair of apostrophes. None of these Greek letters, mathematical symbols, subscripts, and superscripts will work when displayed to the command window—that is, if used with `disp`.

Subscripts are created with the underscore (_) and superscripts with the exponentiation operator (^). The creation of the Greek letters is obtained by the spelling of the letter, which is preceded by a backslash (\), as shown in Table 6.5. Uppercase Greek letters are obtained by capitalizing the first letter of the spelling. However, since many of the uppercase Greek letters are the same as uppercase English letters, only those that are different are given in Table 6.5. The remaining uppercase Greek letters are obtained by using the appropriate uppercase English letters.

---

[5]See, for example, L. Lamport, *LaTeX: A Document Preparation System*, Addison-Wesley, Reading, MA, 1987.

TABLE 6.5   Uppercase and Lowercase Greek Letters and Some Mathematical Symbols

	Lowercase				Uppercase			Mathematical		
Symbol	Syntax	Symbol	Syntax	Symbol	Syntax	Symbol	Syntax	Symbol	Syntax
α	\alpha	ν	\nu	Γ	\Gamma	$\leq$	\leq	$\circ$	\circ
β	\beta	ξ	\xi	Δ	\Delta	$\geq$	\geq	$\ll$	\ll
γ	\gamma	o	o	Θ	\Theta	$\neq$	\neq	$\gg$	\gg
δ	\delta	π	\pi	Λ	\Lambda	$\pm$	\pm	$'$	\prime
ϵ	\epsilon	ρ	\rho	Ξ	\Xi	$\times$	\times	$\Leftarrow$	\Leftarrow
ζ	\zeta	σ	\sigma	Π	\Pi	∞	\infty	$\angle$	\angle
η	\eta	τ	\tau	Σ	\Sigma	$\sum$	\sum	$\surd$	\surd
θ	\theta	υ	\upsilon	Υ	\Upsilon	$\int$	\int	#	\#
ι	\iota	ϕ	\phi	Φ	\Phi	$\div$	\div	\$	\$
κ	\kappa	χ	\chi	Ψ	\Psi	$\sim$	\sim	%	\%
λ	\lambda	ψ	\psi	Ω	\Omega	$\leftarrow$	\leftarrow	&	\&
μ	\mu	ω	\omega			$\uparrow$	\uparrow	{	\{

In addition to the symbols in Table 6.5, the alphanumerical characters can be made bold by preceding the alphanumeric characters with

\bf

To make the alphanumeric characters italic, we use

\it

To return either of these changes to normal, we use

\rm

The creation of the mathematical symbols is obtained by their special spellings preceded by a backslash (\). Some of the more commonly used symbols are also given in Table 6.5. The general syntax is to place a set of concatenated instructions between a pair of apostrophes. When certain groups of symbols are to be kept together, such as an expression that is to appear in an exponent, they are placed between a pair of braces ({}). We shall now illustrate these procedures.

Let us compute and plot the function

$$g_2 = \cos(4\pi x)e^{-(1+x^\beta)}$$

for $\beta = 3$ and $1 \leq \Omega_1 \leq 2$ and then label the figure accordingly. The script is

```
x = linspace(1, 2); beta = 3;
plot(x, cos(4*pi*x).*exp(-(1+x.^beta)), 'k')
title('\itg_{\rm2} \rmversus \itx \rmfor \it\beta \rm= 3')
ylabel('\itg_{\rm2}')
xlabel('\itx')
text(1.2, 0.08, '\itg_{\rm2}\rm=cos(\itx\rm)\ite^{\rm-(1+\itx^\beta\rm)}')
```

The execution of this script results in Figure 6.14.

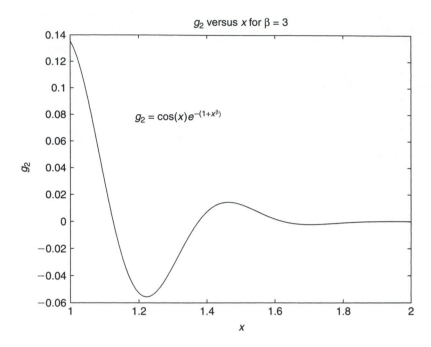

Figure 6.14 Annotation with superscripts, subscripts, and Greek letters.

6.3.5 Altering the Attributes of Axes, Curves, and Text

MATLAB provides the capability to change virtually all characteristics of the elements that comprise a graph. The ones that we shall consider are as follows: For lines, we shall discuss line width and line color. For the text in axis labels, titles, placed text, and legends, we shall discuss font, alignment, size, type, characteristics, and color. For the axes, we shall discuss line width and text attributes.

The default value of the line width for the axes and drawn curves is 0.5 pt. The default values for font size of the axis labels, placed text, and titles is 10 pt. The default font name for the axis labels and numbering, titles, and legend is Helvetica.

The manner in which changes to the attributes of lines and text are made is as follows: For `xlabel`, `ylabel`, `title`, and `text`, we add any number of pairs of key words and their values to the arguments of these functions:

   `xlabel`(s, 'Key word', KeyWordValue, …)
   `ylabel`(s, 'Key word', KeyWordValue, …)
   `title`(s, 'Key word', KeyWordValue, …)
   `text`(x, y, s, 'Key word', KeyWordValue, …)

where 'Key word' is a string containing the key word and *KeyWordValue* is the value expressed as a string or a numerical value, depending on the key word. The key words and their values for text positioning are given in Table 6.6. Additional key words and their values that we will consider for text are given in Table 6.7.

To set the attributes for curves created by `plot` and for the text appearing in `legend`, we require the function handles to `legend` and `plot`. To alter the width of

TABLE 6.6 Text Key Words and Attributes for Positioning

Key word	Key word value	Example
'Horizontal Alignment'	'Left' 'Center' 'Right'	Left Center Right
'Vertical Alignment'	'Top' 'Middle' 'Bottom'	Top Middle Bottom
'Rotation'	0 to 360° or −180° to +180°	0 or 360 · 180 or −180 · 90 or 270

TABLE 6.7   Additional Key Words and Attributes for Text

Key word	Key word value
'Linewidth'	number > 0 (default $= 0.5$)
'FontSize'	number > 0 (default $= 10$)
'FontName'	'Courier' 'Helvetica' (default) 'Times' (Times Roman)
'Color'	'Letter from 2nd column of Table 6.1'
'FontWeight'	'Normal' (default) 'Bold'

the axis line and the tick mark labels, we use `set` and `gca`. The `gca` function gets the handle for the current axis, the `set` function sets a specific property associated with a function handle. To get the function handles for `legend` and `plot`, we use

hdl = plot(...);
[lh, lo] = legend(...);

where `plot` and `legend` perform in the manner already discussed, *hdl* is the handle to the curve plotted, and *lo*(1) is the handle to the text appearing in `legend`. Note that we have ended the expression with a semicolon to suppress displaying the numerical value of the handle to the command window.

The `set` function is

set(hdl, 'Key word', KeyWordValue, ...)

where *hdl* is the handle, 'Key word' is a string containing the key word, and *KeyWordValue* is the string or numerical value that corresponds to the key word.

TABLE 6.8   Key Words and Attributes for Lines

Key word	Attribute
'Linewidth'	number > 0 (default $= 0.5$)
'Color'	'Letter from 2nd column of Table 6.1'

In Table 6.8, we give two key words that we will use for altering the characteristics of lines.

Let us return to the script that generated Figure 6.10. We shall modify that script to make the following alterations to the figure:

Title: 14 pt Courier, bold face

x-axis label: 14 pt Times Roman, italic, and bold face

y-axis label: 14 pt Helvetica

Placed text: 12 pt standard mathematical notation

Legend text: 14 pt Helvetica, red

Axes lines: 1.5 pt wide

Axes text: 14 pt Helvetica

Curve for $\cos(x)$: 4 pt line width

Curve for $\cosh(x)$: 2.5 pt line width

Vertical line at $x = 4.73$: 0.25 line width, blue

The revised script is

```
x = linspace(0, 6, 100);
hc = plot(x, cos(x), 'k-');
hold on
hch = plot(x, 1./cosh(x), 'k--');
hsl = plot( [4.73, 4.73], [-1, 1], 'k');
xlabel('\it\bfx', 'FontSize', 14, 'FontName','Times')
ylabel('Value of functions', 'FontSize', 14)
title('\bfVisualization of two intersecting curves', 'FontName', 'Courier', ...
          'FontSize', 14)
text(4.8, -0.1, '\itx \rm= 4.73','FontName', 'Times', 'FontSize', 12)
[a, b] = legend('cos(x) ', '1/cosh(x) ', 'Location', 'SouthWest');
set(hc, 'LineWidth', 4)
set(hch, 'LineWidth', 2.5)
set(hsl, 'LineWidth', 0.25, 'Color', 'b')
set(b(1), 'FontSize', 14, 'Color', 'r')
set(gca, 'FontSize', 14, 'LineWidth', 1.5)
```

The execution of this script results in Figure 6.15.

The changes to the attributes of the text, curves, and axes can also be made directly in the figure window by using the appropriate icons at its top and/or by selecting the appropriate operation from its *Tools* menu. After the changes have been made, the figure can be saved as either a Windows metafile or as a program in an M-file.

We now illustrate the results of the previous sections with several examples.

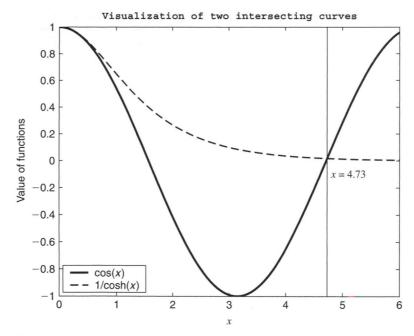

Figure 6.15   Alteration of the font sizes, font type, and line widths of Figure 6.10.

Example 6.1   Repeating curves: Display of cot(x) from $0 \le x \le m\pi$

We shall display the $\cot(x)$ from $0 < x < m\pi$, where m is any integer from 1 to 6 and is selected by the user. The choice $m = 4$ is shown in Figure 6.16. The x-axis limits vary from 0 to $m\pi$. Since $\cot(0) = \infty$ and $\cot(\pi) = -\infty$, the y-axis limits are set to ± 8, and we start and end x so as not to include these values. Also, the cotangent repeats itself every $m\pi$. Therefore, we need only to compute once for $0 < x < \pi$ and then plot these values in the region $(m - 1)\pi < x < m\pi$, where $m > 1$, by simply incrementing the x-axis values by $x + (m - 1)\pi$.

The script is

```
m = input('Enter an integer from 2 to 6): ');
the = linspace(0.12, pi-0.12, 50);
ct = cot(the);
hold on
for n = 1:m
  plot([(2*n-1)*pi/2, (2*n-1)*pi/2], [-8/40, 8/40], 'k-')
  if n == 1
    text((2*n-1)*pi/2-pi/(8*m), 0.6, '\pi/2')
  else
    text((2*n-1)*pi/2-pi/(8*m), 0.6, [num2str((2*n-1), 2) '\pi/2'])
  end

  if n == m
    plot(the+(n-1)*pi, ct, 'k-')
  else
    plot(the+(n-1)*pi, ct, 'k-', [n*pi, n*pi], [-8, 8], 'k--')
  end
end
```

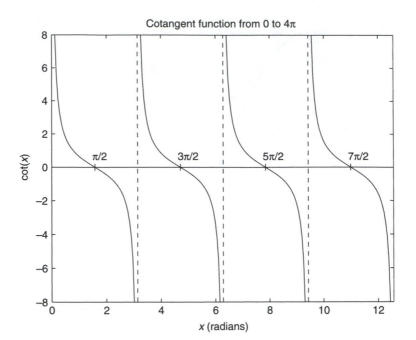

Figure 6.16   Cotangent function.

```
plot([0, m*pi], [0, 0], 'k-')
axis([0, m*pi, -8, 8])
xlabel('\itx \rm(radians)')
ylabel('cot(\itx\rm)')
title(['Cotangent function from 0 to ' num2str(m,1), '\pi'])
box on
```

It is seen that almost all the script is devoted to annotating the figure. Only two statements are used to compute $\cot(x)$.

Example 6.2   Polar plot: Far-field radiation pattern of a sound source

The normalized sound pressure at a large distance from the center of a circular piston in an infinite baffle that is vibrating at a frequency f is given by

$$p(r, \theta) = \left| \frac{J_1(ka\theta)}{ka\theta} \right| \qquad ka^2 \ll r \quad \text{and} \quad a \ll r$$

where r is the radial distance from the center of the piston, θ is the angle of r with respect to the plane of the baffle, k is the wave number, a is the radius of the piston, and $J_1(x)$ is the Bessel function of the first kind of order 1. The wave number is the reciprocal of the wavelength of the sound at frequency f; thus, ka is dimensionless. This model is a fair approximation to the angular dispersion of sound from a loudspeaker.

We shall create a polar plot of the normalized radiation pattern for $ka = 6\pi$ when θ ranges from $-\pi/2 < \theta < \pi/2$. We have chosen this solution to illustrate the use of polar, which plots results in polar coordinates. The script is

```
theta = linspace(-pi/2, pi/2, 300);
p = abs(besselj(1, 6*pi*theta)./(6*pi*theta));
polar(theta, p/max(p))
```

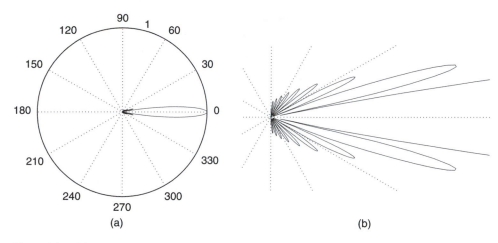

Figure 6.17   (a) Polar representation of a radiation pattern; (b) magnified region.

The execution of the script gives the curve shown in Figure 6.17a. Notice that the values of θ are such that $ka\theta \neq 0$. The max function finds the maximum value in the vector p so that the ratio $p/\mathrm{max}(p)$ is the normalized radiation pattern whose maximum value is 1. To magnify the region is the vicinity of $r < 0.1$, we have two options. The first is to depress the zoom icon in the figure window and zoom in on this region. The other is to modify the program by using view to determine the limits of the Cartesian system that is the basis of polar. Upon typing

    v = axis

in the command window immediately after the script is run, we find that

    v =
      -1.0000   1.0000 -1.1500   1.1500

Thus, the limits of the x-axis are ± 1, and those for the y-axis are ± 1.15. Therefore, we can crop the view with

    axis([-.02, 0.15, -0.05, 0.05])

Then, the modified script becomes

    theta = linspace(-pi/2, pi/2, 300);
    p = abs(besselj(1, 6*pi*theta)./(6*pi*theta));
    polar(theta, p/max(p))
    axis([-.02, 0.15, -0.05, 0.05])

which upon execution, gives the result shown in Figure 6.17b.

Example 6.3   Multiple figures: Spectral plot for a periodic pulse train and a single pulse

Consider a periodic series of rectangular pulses, shown in Figure 6.18a, whose pulse duration is d and whose period is T. This signal can be represented as (recall Example 2.11)

$$g(t) = \frac{f(t)T}{Ad} = c_0 + 2\sum_{n=1}^{\infty} c_n \cos(n\omega_0 t)$$

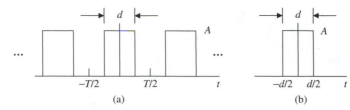

Figure 6.18 (a) Periodic rectangular pulse train; (b) single rectangular pulse.

where $\omega_0 = 2\pi/T$ and

$$c_0 = 1$$

$$c_n = \frac{\sin(n\pi d/T)}{(n\pi d/T)} \qquad n = 1, 2, \ldots$$

The c_n are the normalized amplitudes of each harmonic comprising the signal. When one plots $|c_n|$ as a function of n, the resulting plot is called the amplitude spectrum for the signal. The spectral plot has frequency content only at the harmonics of ω_0—that is, at $n\omega_0$—and is zero everywhere else. It is seen that $c_n = 0$ whenever

$$\frac{n\pi d}{T} = m\pi \quad \text{or} \quad n = \frac{m}{(d/T)}$$

On the other hand, if we have a single pulse, as shown in Figure 6.18b, its normalized frequency spectrum is

$$F(0) = 1$$

$$F(\omega) = \frac{G(\omega)}{Ad} = \frac{\sin(\omega d/2)}{(\omega d/2)} \qquad \omega > 0$$

The absolute value of $G(\omega)$ is called the amplitude density spectrum.

Let us generate two figures, one of $|c_n|$ versus n for $n = 1, 2, \ldots, 30$ when $d/T = 0.1$ and the second of $|F(\omega d)|$ versus ωd, where $0 \le \omega d \le 6\pi$. To create the first figure, we use the technique described in Section 6.2.2 to draw a series of unconnected straight lines. These two figures will be plotted one above the other using `subplot`. Note that special care has to be taken to avoid dividing by zero. The results of the following script are shown in Figure 6.19.

```
n = 1:30; dT = 0.1;
cn = [1 abs(sin(dT*pi*n)./(dT*pi*n))];
n = [0 n];
subplot(2,1,1)
plot([n;n],[zeros(1,length(cn));cn],'k')
xlabel('Harmonic number (\itn\rm) ')
ylabel('|\itc_n\rm|')
text(15,.9,['d/T = ' num2str(dT)])
title('Amplitude spectrum')
w = pi/5:pi/5:6*pi;
subplot(2,1,2)
plot([0 w],[1 abs(sin(w/2)./(w/2))],'k')
```

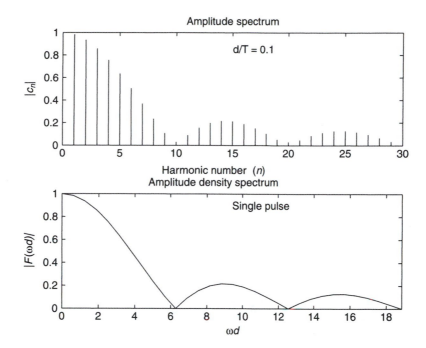

Figure 6.19 Normalized frequency spectra of (a) a periodic pulse shown in Figure 6.18a and (b) a single pulse shown in Figure 6.18b.

```
axis([0, 6*pi, 0, 1])
xlabel('\it\omegad')
ylabel('|F(\it\omegad)|')
text(3*pi, .9, 'Single pulse')
title('Amplitude density spectrum')
```

To avoid dividing by zero, we used the following technique: The harmonic number vector is initially defined as $n = 1:30$ so that we can easily compute $|c_n|$ over this range using dot division. Then, we create the two vectors that include $n = 0$ and $c_0 = 1$, respectively, as indicated in the second and third lines. The same technique is used to evaluate $|F(\omega)|$. Notice that this technique eliminates the need for any programming logic.

Example 6.4   Multiple curves: Notch sensitivity for steel

We now return to Example 5.1 and plot the notch sensitivity constant q over a range of values for $50 \leq S_u \leq 250$ and $0 < r < 0.2$. To make the script a little more readable, we create a function for the data that are to be fitted. We shall create a script that consists of two parts. The first part obtains the values of the coefficients of the fourth-order polynomial used to fit these data and then displays the data points and the polynomial that fits these points. The second part uses the polynomial to generate a family of curves of notch sensitivity q versus the notch radius for several values of the ultimate strength of steel, S_u. The execution of the following script results in Figures 6.20:

```
Su = linspace(50, 250, 50);  skip = 1:2:11;  loc = 0.25:0.08:0.65;
ncs = NeuberData;
p = polyfit(ncs(:,1), ncs(:,2), 4);
```

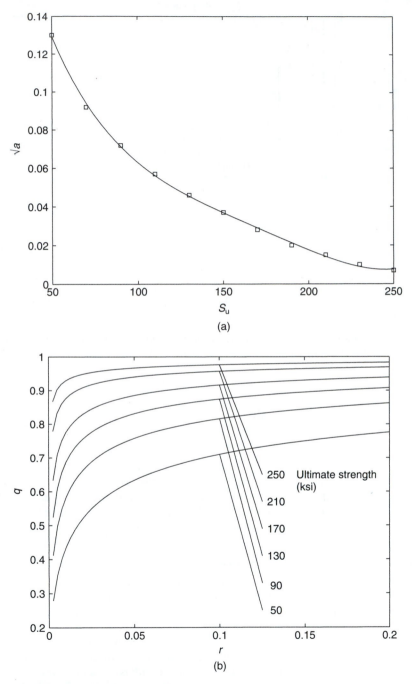

(a)

(b)

Figure 6.20   (a) Neuber's constant for steel using a fourth order fit; (b) notch sensitivity for steel as a function of notch radius r.

```
figure(1)
plot(Su, polyval(p, Su), 'k', ncs(:,1), ncs(:,2), 'ks')
xlabel('\itS_u')
ylabel('\surd\ita')
figure(2)
[s, r] = meshgrid(ncs(skip,1), linspace(0.0025, 0.2, 80));
notch = inline('1./(1+polyval(p, s)./sqrt(r))', 'p', 's', 'r');
plot(r, notch(p, s, r), 'k')
hold on
plot([repmat(0.125, 1, 6); repmat(0.1, 1, 6)], [loc; notch(p, ncs(skip, 1)', 0.1)], 'k')
text(repmat(0.13, 1, 6), loc, num2str(ncs(skip,1)))
text(0.145, 0.65, 'Ultimate strength')
text(0.145, 0.62, '(ksi)')
xlabel('\itr')
ylabel('\itq')
```

where **NeuberData** is given in Example 5.1.

The meshgrid function creates two (80×6) arrays, where the rows are the values of r and the columns are the values of S_u. Since the expressions in the inline function **notch** were written using the dot notation, we can enter these arrays for their appropriate arguments. Placement of the curve's identifying lines is done with the last plot function. We use the same techniques introduced previously to draw a series of unconnected straight lines. Note, however, that we had to transpose $ncs(:,1)$ from a column vector to a row vector. To place text adjacent to the ends of these lines we created a vector for the x and y coordinates, with the corresponding text given by converting the first column of ncs(:,1) to a string using num2str. We selected every other element of ncs by incrementing its first subscript by 2, as represented by the vector $skip$.

Example 6.5   Minimum total distance to travel to N locations

Consider N arbitrary locations, each a known distance from an origin and each residing in the upper half of a Cartesian coordinate system. If the coordinates of each location are (x_j, y_j), where $j = 1, 2, \ldots, N$, then the distance between any two locations, not including the origin, is

$$d_{ij} = \sqrt{(x_i - x_j)^2 + (y_i - y_j)^2} \quad i \neq j \quad i, j = 1, 2, \ldots, N$$

To find the total distance d_T that one has to traverse to go from one location to another location starting from the origin and ending at the origin, we have

$$d_T = d_{o1} + \sum_{j=2}^{N} d_{j-1,j} + d_{No} \tag{6.1}$$

where d_{o1} is the distance from the origin the first point and d_{No} is the distance from the Nth point to the origin. The coordinates of the origin are $(0, 0)$.

To find the minimum total distance, we have to determine the permutations of the order by which we will visit the N different locations; that is, the j in Eq. 6.1 has to have their order rearranged $N!$ times so that it assumes the N permuted combinations of $d_{j-1,j}$, where $j = 2, \ldots, N$. To incorporate this idea, we change the notation of Eq. 6.1 by introducing the quantity $p_j(k)$, where $j = 1, 2, \ldots, N$ and $k = 1, 2, \ldots, N!$, which is an ($N! \times N$) array. Each row of the array is one set of permutations of the N locations. For example, if $N = 2$, then the two possible ways that these locations can be visited is to go from the origin to location 1, then to location 2, and then to the origin. The other possible way is to go from the origin to location 2, then to location 1, and then to the origin. Thus, $p_1(1) = 1$ and $p_2(1) = 2$, and $p_1(2) = 2$ and $p_2(2) = 1$. Therefore, Eq. 6.1 becomes

$$d_T(k) = d_{o,p_1(k)} + \sum_{j=2}^{N} d_{p_j(k)-1, \, p_j(k)} + d_{p_N(k),o} \quad k = 1,\ldots, N!$$

The order of the $p_j(k)$ is determined by that value of k for which $d_T(k)$ is a minimum. The permutations are determined from

```
perms(v)
```

where v is a row vector for which the permutations are to be found. For example, if $v = [3, 15, 7]$, then the execution of

```
p = perms([3, 15, 7])
```

displays

```
p =
    7   15    3
    7    3   15
   15    7    3
   15    3    7
    3   15    7
    3    7   15
```

We shall determine the order by which one should visit the N locations for $d_T(k)$ to be a minimum and plot the results by displaying the locations and the order in which these locations are visited. To demonstrate the script, we assume that there are six locations to visit. The coordinates of these locations are given in the arrays xx and yy. We shall also assume that the location identification is given by the position in the array; that is, location 1 is represented by the first pair of coordinates, and so on. The function dT computes the total distance. The script is

```
function MinimumDistance
xx = [-6, -6, -1, 0, 2, 2];
yy = [7, 2, 5, 9, 7, 2];
N = length(xx);
p = perms(1:N);
for k = 1:factorial(N)
   TotalDist(k) = dT(xx, yy, p, k);
end
[SmalDist, indx] = min(TotalDist);
BestOrder = p(indx,:);
plot([xx], [yy], 'sk')
v = [-10, 10, 0, 10];
hold on
xplot = [zeros(1, 5); [v(2), v(4)/tan(pi/3), 0, -v(4)/tan(pi/3), v(1)]];
yplot = [zeros(1, 5); [v(2)*tan(pi/6), v(4), v(4), v(4), -v(1)*tan(pi/6)]];
plot(xplot, yplot, 'k--')
grid on
for n=1:N
   text(xx(n)+v(2)/25, yy(n), num2str(n))
end
plot([0, xx(BestOrder)], [0, yy(BestOrder)], 'k-', 'LineWidth', 2)
```

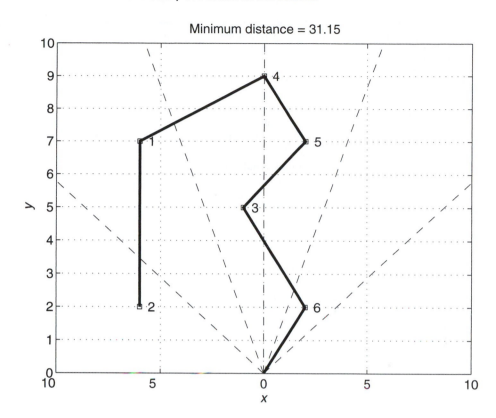

Figure 6.21 Order in which six locations should be visited to travel the minimum distance.

```
title(['Minimum distance = ' num2str(SmalDist, 4)])
xlabel('x')
ylabel('y')

function distance = dT(x, y, p, k)
dist = inline('sqrt(diff(x).^2+diff(y).^2)', 'x', 'y');
N = length(x);
dista = [dist([0, x(p(k,1))], [0, y(p(k,1))]), ...
        dist(x(p(k,1:N)), y(p(k,1:N))), ...
        dist([x(p(k,N)), 0], [y(p(k,N)), 0])];
distance = sum(dista);
```

Execution of this script results in Figure 6.21.

6.4 SUMMARY OF FUNCTIONS INTRODUCED

Attributes that can be assigned to lines and points are summarized in Table 6.1. Key words that are used to display Greek letters and a wide range of mathematical symbols are given in Table 6.5. Key words for positioning text are given in Table 6.6 and key words for additional text attributes in Table 6.7. Key words for specifying attributes of lines are given in Table 6.8. In Table 6.9, we summarize the plotting functions introduced in this chapter.

TABLE 6.9 MATLAB Functions Introduced in Chapter 6

MATLAB function	Description
axis	Scales and changes the appearance of the axes
axis equal	Sets axes so that aspect ratio units are the same in each direction
axis on/off	Turns on and off the visibility of the axes
bar	Creates a bar chart
box on/off	Turns on and off the display of the axes boundaries
factorial	Computes $N!$, where N is a positive integer
figure	Creates an individual figure window
fill	Fills a polygon
gca	Gets current axis handle for the current figure
grid on/off	Turns on and off the grid lines in 2D and 3D plots
hold on/off	When 'on', system adds new graphic object to figure; when 'off', it replaces objects in the figure
legend	Displays a legend on the graph
loglog	Creates a logarithmic x-axis and a logarithmic y-axis
perms	Computes all possible permutations
plot	Creates a linear 2D plot
plotyy	Plots a linear 2D graph with different y-axis on the left and right
polar	Creates a polar coordinate plot
print	Creates a hardcopy of the current figure
semilogx	Creates a logarithmic x-axis and a linear y-axis
semilogy	Creates a logarithmic y-axis and a linear x-axis
set	Sets object properties
stairs	Creates a stair-step plot
stem	Creates a discrete data plot with data values connected by straight lines emanating from the x-axis
subplot	Divides the current figure into a number of panes, each with its own set of axes
text	Places a text object in the current axes
title	Places a title on the current axes
xlabel	Labels the current x-axis
ylabel	Labels the current y-axis
zoom	Zooms in and out on a 2D plot

EXERCISES

Note: The actual plotting in all the exercises can be done using vector and dot operations and mesgrid. Use the for structure only to increment through a range of parameters as appropriate.

Section 6.2

6.1 Plot the following curves.[6] All of the figures require the axis equal function.

    a. *Cycloid* $(-\pi \le \varphi \le 3\pi; r_a = 0.5, 1, 1.5)$:

$$x = r_a \varphi - \sin \varphi$$
$$y = r_a - \cos \varphi$$

[6]D. von Seggern, *CRC Standard Curves and Surfaces*, CRC Press, Inc., Boca Raton, FL, 1993.

b. *Lemniscate* $(-\pi/4 \le \varphi \le \pi/4)$:

$$x = \cos\varphi\sqrt{2\cos(2\varphi)}$$
$$y = \sin\varphi\sqrt{2\cos(2\varphi)}$$

c. *Spiral* $(0 \le \varphi \le 6\pi)$:
i. Archimedean:

$$x = \varphi\cos\varphi$$
$$y = \varphi\sin\varphi$$

ii. Logarithmic $(k = 0.1)$:

$$x = e^{k\varphi}\cos\varphi$$
$$y = e^{k\varphi}\sin\varphi$$

d. *Cardioid* $(0 \le \varphi \le 2\pi)$:

$$y = 2\cos\varphi - \cos 2\varphi$$
$$y = 2\sin\varphi - \sin 2\varphi$$

e. *Astroid* $(0 \le \varphi \le 2\pi)$:

$$x = 4\cos^3\varphi$$
$$y = 4\sin^3\varphi$$

f. *Epicycloid* (case 1: $R_r = 3$; $a_r = 0.5, 1, 2$, and $0 \le \varphi \le 2\pi$; case 2: $R_r = 2.5$, $a_r = 2$, and $0 \le \varphi \le 4\pi$):

$$x = (R_r + 1)\cos\varphi - a_r\cos(\varphi(R_r + 1))$$
$$y = (R_r + 1)\sin\varphi - a_r\sin(\varphi(R_r + 1))$$

g. *Hypocycloid* ($R_r = 3$; $a_r = 0.5, 1, 2$; and $0 \le \varphi \le 2\pi$):

$$x = (R_r - 1)\cos\varphi + a_r\cos(\varphi(R_r - 1))$$
$$y = (R_r - 1)\sin\varphi - a_r\sin(\varphi(R_r - 1))$$

6.2 Plot the following curve, called the Kilroy curve,[7] for $-15 \le x \le 15$:

$$y = \ln\left|\frac{\sin x}{x}\right|$$

6.3 Consider the following polynomial from $-12 \le x \le 7$:

$$y = 0.001x^5 + 0.01x^4 + 0.2x^3 + x^2 + 4x - 5$$

Plot only its positive values. Force the values of y at the first and last points of each segment to be (almost) equal to zero. [Hint: Use `find`.]

---

[7]E. W. Weisstein, *CRC Concise Encyclopedia of Mathematics*, 2nd ed., Chapman & Hall/CRC, Boca Raton, FL, 2003, p. 1625.

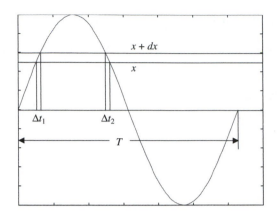

Figure 6.22   Determination of the amount of time a
sine wave spends between x and $x + dx$.

6.4 The probability density function of a time-varying signal is used to relate the probability
that, over a period of time T, the signal's amplitude has a value between x and $x + dx$.
In other words, it is used to obtain a measure of the fraction of time the signal spends
within this amplitude range. The probability density function can be approximated by

$$P(x) = \lim_{\substack{\Delta x \to 0 \\ T \to \infty}} \left[\frac{1}{T\Delta x} \sum_i \Delta t_i \right]$$

where the terms in this expression are shown for one period of the sine wave in
Figure 6.22. The probability density function $P(x)$ of a sine wave of amplitude A_o is
given by

$$P(x) = \frac{1}{\pi \sqrt{A_o^2 - x^2}} \quad |x| \le A_o$$
$$= 0 \quad\quad\quad\quad |x| > A_o$$

Estimate the probability density function for

$$y = A_o \sin t$$

for $-\pi \le t \le \pi$, and compare the results to the exact values. Let $A_o = 2$, the number
of amplitude bins equal 20, and the number data points in the time interval equal 400.
Plot the estimated values of $P(x)$ and the exact values. The results should look like
those shown in Figure 6.23.

Section 6.2.4

6.5 The force on a Belleville spring (see Figure 8.45) is proportional to C_1, where

$$C_1 = 0.5d_t^3 - 1.5h_t d_t^2 + (1 + h_t^2)d_t$$

and $h_t = h/t$, $d_t = \delta/t$, and δ is the deflection of the spring. Plot C_1 as a function of d_t
when h_t varies from 1 to 3 in increments of 0.25 and d_t varies from 0 to 5. Label the
curves and limit the y-axis to 8. The results should look like those shown in Figure 6.24.

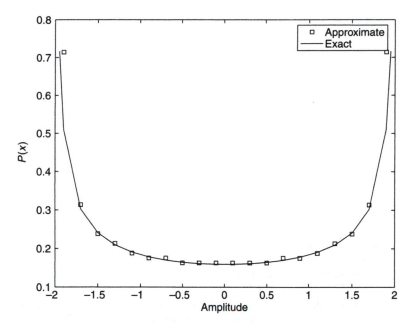

Figure 6.23 Probability density function of a sine wave.

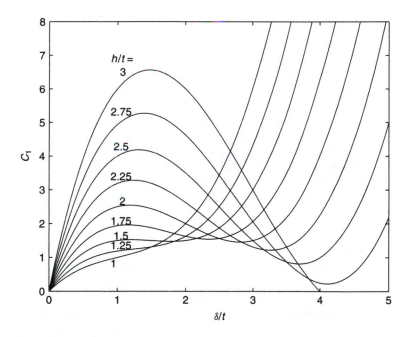

Figure 6.24 Belleville spring constant C_1.

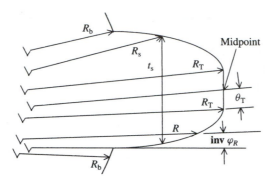

Figure 6.25   Nomenclature of a gear tooth.

6.6 Consider the gear tooth shown in Figure 6.25. It is seen that if the gear has n teeth, then each tooth appears every $2\pi/n$ radians. Let R_b be the radius of the base circle, R_T the radius of the tooth tip circle, and R ($R_b \le R \le R_T$) the radius of a point on the profile of the tooth. Then, the polar coordinates of the profile of one gear tooth (R, ϕ), including the space between an adjacent tooth, are given in Table 6.10. In Table 6.10, ϕ_s is the gear pressure angle (either $14.5°$, $20°$, or $25°$), $R_s = nm/2$ is the standard pitch radius, m is the gear module, and t_s is the tooth thickness at R_s. If a gear has 24 teeth, a pressure angle of $20°$, a module of 10 mm, a tooth thickness of 14.022 mm, a base radius of 90.21 mm, and a tip radius of 106 mm, draw the gear two ways: using polar and using plot.

6.7 The efficiency, as a percentage, of a power screw when the friction of the collar is ignored is (see Exercise 8.11)

$$e = 100\frac{\cos(\alpha) - \mu \tan(\lambda)}{\cos(\alpha) + \mu \cot(\lambda)} \quad \%$$

where μ is the coefficient of friction, λ is the lead angle of the screw, and α is the thread angle. Plot the efficiency as a function of λ for $0 < \lambda < 90°$ $\mu = 0.02, 0.05, 0.10, 0.15, 0.20, 0.25$; and for two thread angles: $\alpha = 7°$ and $14.5°$. Label the figure and the individual curves, and use the axis function to limit the efficiency to from 0% to 100%. The results should look like those shown in Figure 6.26.

TABLE 6.10   Definitions of the Various Sectors of the Gear Tooth Shown in Figure 6.25

R	ψ	Definitions
$R_b \le R \le R_T$	$\mathbf{inv}(\varphi(R))$	$\varphi(R) = \cos^{-1}(R_b/R)$
		$\mathbf{inv}(x) = \tan(x) - x$
R_T	$\mathbf{inv}(\varphi(R_T)) \le \psi \le \mathbf{inv}(\varphi(R_T)) + 2\theta_T$	$\theta_T = 0.5t_s/R_s + \mathbf{inv}(\varphi_s) - \mathbf{inv}(\varphi(R_T))$
$R_b \le R \le R_T$	$2[\theta_T + \mathbf{inv}(\varphi(R_T))] - \mathbf{inv}(\varphi(R))$	
R_b	$2[\theta_T + \mathbf{inv}(\varphi(R_T))] \le \psi \le 2\pi/n$	

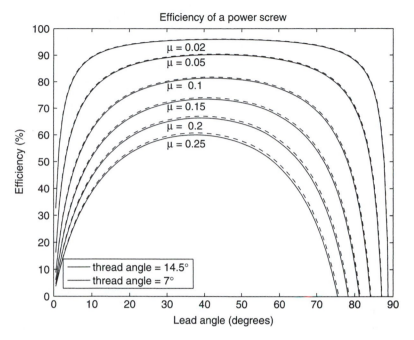

Figure 6.26   Efficiency of a power screw.

6.8 Consider the rectangle shown in Figure 6.27, where it is seen that

$$r_1 = \sqrt{d^2 + (W/2)^2} \qquad\qquad \alpha = \tan^{-1}(W/2d)$$
$$r_2 = \sqrt{(d + L)^2 + (W/2)^2} \quad \beta = \tan^{-1}(W/2(d + L))$$

If the values of L, W, and d are given, create a script that generates the maximum number of nonoverlapping replicated rectangles as shown in Figure 6.28. The values of $L = 1$, $W = 2$, and $d = 2$ were used to generate Figure 6.28. The maximum number of rectangles can be determined from `floor`(π/α). This script can be written without using a `for` loop.

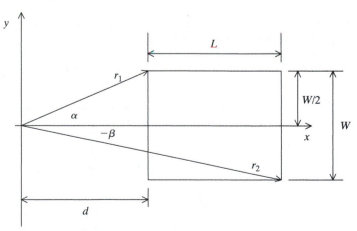

Figure 6.27   Description of a rectangle for Exercise 6.8.

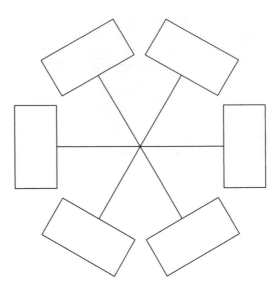

Figure 6.28   Replicated nonoverlapping rectangles.

Section 6.2.5

6.9 Using the results of Exercise 1.9, plot σ_x/p_{max}, σ_z/p_{max} and $\tau_{xz}/p_{max} = \tau_{yz}/p_{max} = 0.5(\sigma_x/p_{max} - \sigma_z/p_{max})$ as a function of z/a for $\nu_1 = 0.3$. Label the figure, and identify the curves.

6.10 Using the results of Exercise 1.10, plot σ_x/p_{max}, σ_y/p_{max}, σ_z/p_{max}, and τ_{yz}/p_{max} as a function of z/b for $\nu = 0.3$. Label the figure, and identify the curves.

6.11 The absolute viscosity of the oil in μreyn(lb-s/in.^{2}) can be estimated within $\pm 10\%$ from the relationship

$$\mu = 10^{C-1}$$

where

$$C = 10^{A_j - B_j \log_{10} T_o}$$

and $T_o = 255.2 + 5/9T$ K, where T is the temperature of the oil in °F and A_j and B_j are given in Table 6.11 as a function of the oil's SAE number. Plot, on two side-by-side figures, the $\log_{10}\log_{10}(10\mu)$ as a function of the $\log_{10}(T_o)$ and μ as a function of the T_o for the six oils given in Table 6.11. (See, also, Section 8.6.)

TABLE 6.11   Constants Used to Determine μ

SAE number	j	A_j	B_j
10	1	9.1209	3.5605
20	2	9.1067	3.5385
30	3	8.9939	3.4777
40	4	8.9133	3.4292
50	5	8.5194	3.2621
60	6	8.3666	3.1884

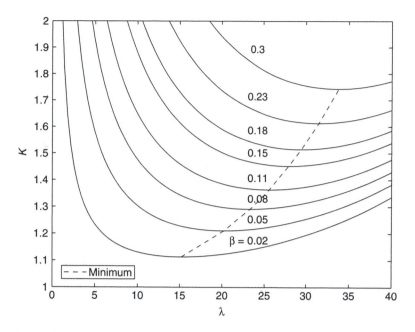

Figure 6.29   Lead angle of a worm gear.

6.12 The relationship between the lead angle of a worm gear λ, the ratio $\beta = N_1/N_2$, (where N_1 is the number of teeth on the worm gear and N_2 is the number of teeth on the driven gear), the center distance between shafts C, and the normal diametral pitch P_{dn} is

$$K = \frac{2P_{dn}C}{N_2} = \frac{\beta}{\sin \lambda} + \frac{1}{\cos \lambda}$$

Plot K versus λ for $1° \leq \lambda \leq 40°$ and $\beta = 0.02, 0.05, 0.08, 0.11, 0.15, 0.18, 0.23, 0.30$. Label the figure and the curves. Limit the range of the y-axis from 1 to 2. On the same figure, plot the results of Exercise 5.32 by drawing a line that connects the minimum values of each curve. Do this by incorporating the appropriate function(s) and portions of the script from Exercise 5.32 into the script written for this exercise. The results should look like those shown in Figure 6.29.

6.13 Write a script that produces three or more circles around a central circle of radius $r_b = 1.5$ as shown for $n = 5$ circles in Figure 6.30. The radius r_s of the outer circles is

$$r_s = \frac{r_b \sin(\pi/n)}{1 - \sin(\pi/n)}$$

Have the script ask the user for the number of circles. The script can be written without using the for loop.

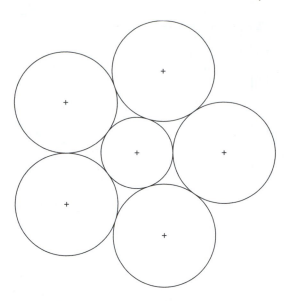

Figure 6.30   Five circles on a circle.

6.14 In Exercise 5.19, we gave the following Colebrook formula from which the pipe's coefficient of friction λ could be estimated:

$$\lambda = \left[-2 \log_{10}\left(\frac{2.51}{R_e \sqrt{\lambda}} + \frac{0.27}{d/k} \right) \right]^{-2} \qquad R_e \geq 4000$$

where R_e is the Reynolds number, d is the diameter of the pipe, and k is the surface roughness. For smooth pipes ($k \cong 0$; $d/k > 100{,}000$),

$$\lambda = \left[2 \log_{10}\left(\frac{R_e \sqrt{\lambda}}{2.51} \right) \right]^{-2} \qquad R_e \geq 4000$$

Plot $\log_{10}(\lambda)$ as a function of $\log_{10}(R_e)$, $4 \times 10^3 \leq R_e \leq 10^7$, for $d/k = 20, 50, 100, 200,$ 500, 1,000, 2,000, 5,000, 10,000, 20,000, 50,000, 100,000, and ∞ ($k = 0$). Use `semilogx` instead of `plot`. Label the figure and the curves. Place the identifiers for the curves to the right of $R_e = 10^7$—that is, outside the figure's right-hand vertical axis. The resulting figure is known as the Moody diagram of friction factors for pipe flow. The results should look like those in Figure 6.31.

Section 6.3.3

6.15 In optimization analysis, it is often beneficial to plot the function being optimized (called the objective function) and its constraints (regions in which the solution is required to reside). Consider the requirement to minimize

$$f(x_1, x_2) = (x_1 - 1)^2 + (x_2 - 1)^2$$

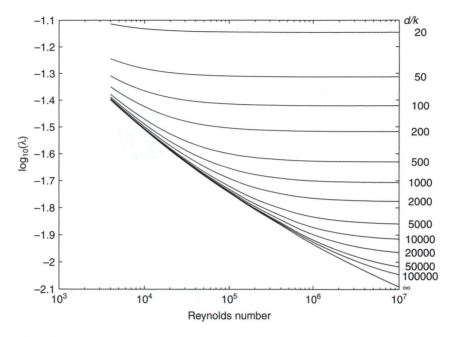

Figure 6.31   Moody diagram.

subject to the constraints

$$g_1 = (x_1 - 3)^2 + (x_2 - 1)^2 - 1 \le 0$$
$$g_2 = 2x_1 - x_2 - 5 \le 0$$

Thus, the solution x_{m1} and x_{m2} must be on the circle $f(x_1, x_2)$ and within the region specified by g_1 and g_2.

Plot the above objective function (circles) and the region in which the solution must lie. The results should be made to look like those shown in Figure 6.32. To obtain this result, the function `fill` will have to be used and applied in the proper order.

6.16 Write a script that creates Figure 5.17 of Exercise 5.21. The fill color is cyan.

Section 6.3.5

6.17 Consider a linear array of N pairs of acoustic sources shown in Figure 6.33, which are vibrating at a frequency ω and amplitude Q. The total acoustic pressure at a distance r from the array is

$$P(r, \theta) = Z_o \left[\sum_{m=1}^{N} \left(1 + \frac{md}{r} \cos \theta \right) \exp[j(-\varphi_m + mdk \cos \theta)] \right.$$
$$\left. + \sum_{m=1}^{N} \left(1 - \frac{md}{r} \cos \theta \right) \exp[j(-\varphi_{-m} - mdk \cos \theta)] \right]$$

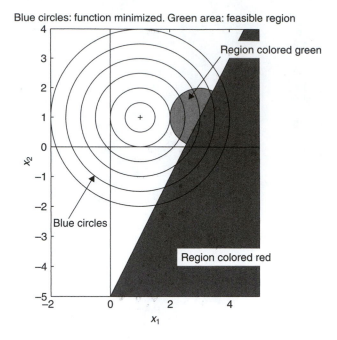

Figure 6.32   Solution to Exercise 6.15.

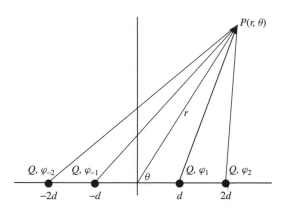

Figure 6.33   Linear array of acoustic sources.

where

$$Z_o = \frac{j\rho ckQ}{4\pi r}e^{j(\omega t - kr)}$$

and ρ is the density of the medium, c is the wave speed in the medium, $k = 2\pi\omega/c$ is the wave number, $\phi_{\pm m}$ are the phase angles with respect to $\phi_1 = 0$, $d/r \ll 1$, and $dk \ll 1$.

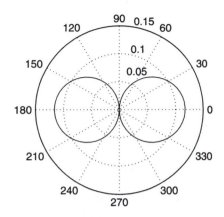

Figure 6.34 Radiation pattern of an acoustic dipole.

For the case where $N = 1$, $\phi_1 = 0$, and $\phi_{-1} = \pi$, the above equation simplifies to

$$P(r, \theta) = 2Z_o\left[jdk + \frac{d}{r}\right]\cos\theta$$

which is the expression for the far-field pressure of an acoustic dipole.

Compute $|P(r, \theta)/Z_o|$ as a function of θ, and plot the results for $0 \leq \theta \leq 2\pi$ using `polar` for $d/r = 0.05$, $dk = 0.03$, $\varphi_{-1} = \pi$, and $\varphi_1 = 0$. The results should look like those shown in Figure 6.34. Use the formula for the general case of a linear array. Also, plot the percentage difference between the exact solution and the numerically reduced solution for the dipole. Exclude the first point, $\theta = 0$, from this plot. First, create a function to compute the magnitude of the pressure as a function of an arbitrary number of pairs of sources, their phase relationships and spacing, and the far-field position in space.

7

3D Graphics

Edward B. Magrab

The implementation of a wide selection of 3D plotting capabilities is presented.

7.1 LINES IN 3D

The 3D version of `plot` is

$$\texttt{plot3}(u1, v1, w1, c1, u2, v2, w2, c2, \ldots)$$

where u_j, v_j, and w_j are the x-, y-, and z-coordinates, respectively, of a point. They are scalars, vectors of the same length, matrices of the same order, or expressions that, when evaluated, result in one of these three quantities. The quantity c_j is a string of characters, where one character specifies the color, one character specifies the point characteristics, and up to two characters specify the line type (see Table 6.1).

Suppose that we want to draw a set of n unconnected lines whose endpoints are (x_{1j}, y_{1j}, z_{1j}) and (x_{2j}, y_{2j}, z_{2j}), where $j = 1, 2, \ldots, n$. To accomplish this, we create six vectors:

$$\begin{aligned}
x_j &= [x_{j1}\, x_{j2}\, \ldots\, x_{jn}] \\
y_j &= [y_{j1}\, y_{j2}\, \ldots\, y_{jn}] \quad j = 1, 2 \\
z_j &= [z_{j1}\, z_{j2}\, \ldots\, z_{jn}]
\end{aligned}$$

Then, the `plot3` instruction is

   `plot3([x1; x2], [y1; y2], [z1; z2])`

where [x1; x2], [y1; y2], and [z1; z2] are each $(2 \times n)$ matrices. This is the 3D counterpart of the 2D procedure used with `plot`.

All annotation procedures discussed for 2D drawings in Section 6.3 are applicable to the 3D curve- and surface-generating functions, except that the arguments of
`text` become

   `text(x, y, z, s)`

where s is a string and

   `zlabel`

is used to label the z-axis.

Example 7.1   The drawing of wire-frame boxes

Consider the box of dimensions $L_x \times L_y \times L_z$ shown in Figure 7.1. We create a function called **BoxPlot3** to draw the four edges of each of the six surfaces of the box and
then use the function to draw several boxes. The location and orientation of the box are
determined by the coordinates of its two diagonally opposed corners: $\mathbf{P}(x_o, y_o, z_o)$ and
$\mathbf{P}(x_o + L_x, y_o + L_y, z_o + L_z)$:

```
function BoxPlot3(x0, y0, z0, Lx, Ly, Lz)
x = [x0     x0      x0       x0       x0+Lx  x0+Lx  x0+Lx  x0+Lx];
y = [y0     y0      y0+Ly    y0+Ly    y0     y0     y0+Ly  y0+Ly];
z = [z0     z0+Lz   z0+Lz    z0       z0     z0+Lz  z0+Lz  z0     ];
```

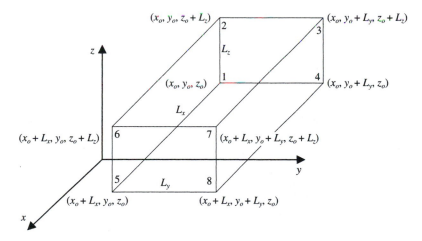

Figure 7.1   Coordinates of a box.

```
index = zeros(6,5);
index(1,:) = [1 2 3 4 1];
index(2,:) = [5 6 7 8 5];
index(3,:) = [1 2 6 5 1];
index(4,:) = [4 3 7 8 4];
index(5,:) = [2 6 7 3 2];
index(6,:) = [1 5 8 4 1];
for k = 1:6
   plot3(x(index(k,:)), y(index(k,:)), z(index(k,:)))
   hold on
end
```

Now, let us use **BoxPlot3** to generate three boxes with the following dimensions and the coordinates (x_o, y_o, z_o):

Box 1

Size: $3 \times 5 \times 7$
Location: $(1, 1, 1)$

Box 2

Size: $4 \times 5 \times 1$
Location: $(3, 4, 5)$

Box 3

Size: $1 \times 1 \times 1$
Location: $(4.5, 5.5, 6)$

The script to create and display these wire-frame boxes is

BoxPlot3$(1, 1, 1, 3, 5, 7)$
BoxPlot3$(4, 6, 8, 4, 5, 1)$
BoxPlot3$(8, 11, 9, 1, 1, 1)$

which upon execution gives Figure 7.2.

Example 7.2   Sine wave drawn on the surface of a cylinder

The coordinates of a sine wave on the surface of a cylinder are obtained from the following relations[1]:

$$x = b\cos(t)$$
$$y = b\sin(t)$$
$$z = c\cos(at)$$

If we assume that $a = 10.0$, $b = 1.0$, $c = 0.3$, and $0 \le t \le 2\pi$, then the script is

```
t = linspace(0, 2*pi, 200);
a = 10; b = 1.0; c = 0.3;
x = b*cos(t);
y = b*sin(t);
z = c*cos(a*t);
plot3(x, y, z, 'k')
axis equal
```

The execution of this script results in Figure 7.3.

---

[1]D. von Seggern, *CRC Standard Curves and Surfaces*, CRC Press, Inc., Boca Raton, FL, 1993.

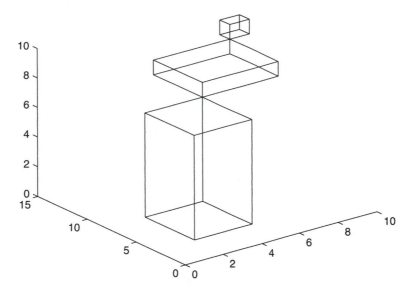

Figure 7.2   Three wire-frame boxes.

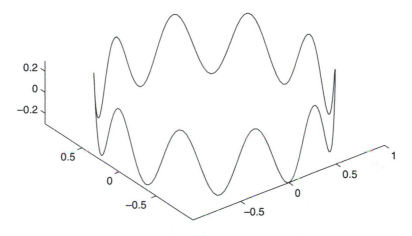

Figure 7.3   Sine wave on a cylindrical surface.

7.2 SURFACES

A set of 3D plotting functions is available to create surfaces, contours, and variations and specializations of these basic forms. A surface is defined by the expression

$$z = f(x, y)$$

where x and y are the coordinates in the xy-plane and z is the resulting height. The basic surface plotting functions are

```
surf(x, y, z)
```

and

```
mesh(x, y, z)
```

where x, y, and z are the coordinates of the points on the surface. The function `surf` draws a surface composed of colored patches, whereas `mesh` draws white surface patches that are defined by their boundary. In `surf`, the colors of the patches are determined by the magnitude of z, whereas the colors of the lines in `mesh` are determined by the magnitude of z.

We shall illustrate the use of these functions—and of several other functions—with the plotting of the surface created by

$$z(x, y) = x^4 + 3x^2 + y^2 - 2x - 2y - 2x^2y + 6$$

over the range $-3 < x < 3$ and $-3 < y < 13$. We shall place the generation of the x-, y-, and z-coordinate values in a function file so that we can use them in several examples. We call this function **SurfExample**. Thus,

```
function [x, y, z] = SurfExample
x1 = linspace(-3, 3, 15);
y1 = linspace(-3, 13, 17);
[x, y] = meshgrid(x1, y1);
z = x.^4+3*x.^2−2*x+6-2*y.*x.^2+y.^2-2*y;
```

The difference between `mesh` and `surf` upon using **SurfExample** is shown in Table 7.1.

Combining Surfaces and Lines

To show how one can combine 3D plotting functions to draw multiple surfaces and multiple lines, we create two functions. The first function, called **Corners**, draws four lines connecting the corners of the surface generated by **SurfExample** to the xy-plane passing through $z = 0$. The second function, called **Disc**, creates a circular disc that intersects this surface at $z_o = 80$, has a radius of 10 units, and has its center at $(0, 5)$. The coordinates of the corners are $(-3, -3, z(-3, -3))$, $(-3, 13, z(-3, 13))$, $(3, 13, z(3,13))$, and $(3, -3, z(3, -3))$. The script that draws the surface, the disc, and the lines to the corners of the surface is

```
function SurfDisc
[x, y, z] = SurfExample;
surf(x, y, z);
Disc(10, 80)
Corners
```

```
function Corners
xc = [-3, -3, 3, 3];
yc = [-3, 13, 13, -3];
```

TABLE 7.1   Illustration of the Difference Between `surf` and `mesh`

Plotting function	Script	Graph
surf	[x, y, z] = **SurfExample**; surf(x, y, z)	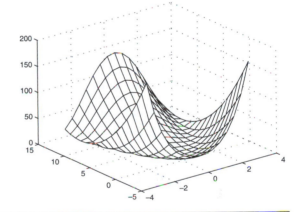
mesh	[x, y, z] = **SurfExample**; mesh(x, y, z)	

```
zc = xc.^4+3*xc.^2–2*xc+6–2*yc.*xc.^2+yc.^2–2*yc;
hold on
plot3([xc; xc], [yc; yc], [zeros(1,4); zc], 'k')

function Disc(R, zo)
r = linspace(0, R, 12);
theta = linspace(0, 2*pi, 50);
x = cos(theta')*r;
y = 5 + sin(theta')*r;
hold on
z = repmat(zo, size(x));
surf(x, y, z)
```

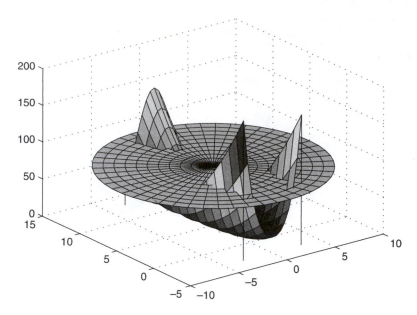

Figure 7.4   Surface with lines drawn to its corners and intersecting a disc.

The execution of this script produces Figure 7.4. The fourth line is not visible in this view.

Altering Graph Appearance

Several functions that can be used in various combinations to alter the appearance of the resulting surface plot are

```
box on  or  box off
grid on  or  grid off
axis on  or   axis off
```

The function `box on` only draws a box if `axis on` has been selected. Some examples of combinations of these functions are given in Table 7.2.

As mentioned previously, the colors of the patches are generated automatically with `surf` according to their z-value. Similarly, the colors of the lines that are generated automatically with `mesh` vary according to their z-value. The colors of either the patches or the lines can be changed to a uniform color using

```
colormap(c)
```

where c is a three-element vector, with the value of each element varying between 0 and 1. The first element corresponds to the intensity of red, the second to the intensity of green, and the third to the intensity of blue. Some commonly used combinations are listed in Table 7.3.

There are two other additional ways to visually enhance the surface generated by **SurfExample**. These are illustrated in Table 7.4.

TABLE 7.2   Illustration of box, grid, and axis

Plotting function	Script	Graph
grid off	[x, y, z] = **SurfExample**; mesh(x, y, z) grid off	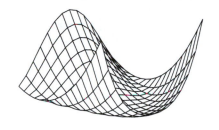
axis off grid off	[x, y, z] = **SurfExample**; mesh(x, y, z) axis off grid off	
box on axis on grid off	[x, y, z] = **SurfExample**; mesh(x, y, z) box on axis on grid off	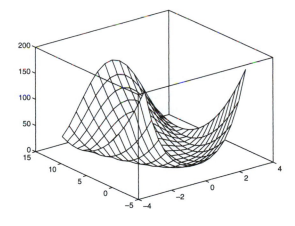

TABLE 7.3 Some Values of the
Color Vector Used in `colormap`(c)

c	Color
[0 0 0]	Black
[1 1 1]	White
[1 0 0]	Red
[0 1 0]	Green
[0 0 1]	Blue
[1 1 0]	Yellow
[1 0 1]	Magenta
[0 1 1]	Cyan
[0.5 0.5 0.5]	Gray

TABLE 7.4   Illustration of `meshz` and `waterfall`

Plotting function	Script	Graph
meshz	[x, y, z] = **SurfExample**; meshz(x, y, z)	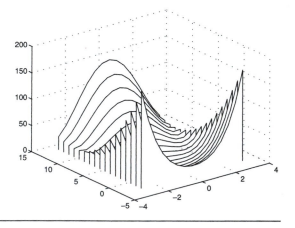
waterfall	[x, y, z] = **SurfExample**; waterfall(x, y, z)	

Contour Plots

Surfaces can also be transformed into various contour plots, which are plots of the curves formed by the intersection of the surface and a plane parallel to the xy-plane at given values of z. The functions

```
surfc(x, y, z)
meshc(x, y, z)
```

create surfaces with contours projected beneath the surface. The quantities x, y, and z are the values of the coordinates of points that define the surface. These two functions are illustrated in Table 7.5.

Various contour plots without the surfaces can be created, either with or without labels. The function

```
contour(x, y, z, v)
```

creates a 2D contour plot. The values of x, y, and z are the coordinates of the points that define the surface. The quantity v, if a scalar, is the number of contours to be displayed

---

TABLE 7.5   Illustration of `meshc` and `surfc`

Plotting function	Script	Graph
meshc	[x, y, z] = **SurfExample**; `meshc`(x, y, z) `grid off`	
surfc	[x, y, z] = **SurfExample**; `surfc`(x, y, z) `grid off`	

and, if a vector of values, the contours of the surface at those values of v. The use of v is optional. If the contour plot is to be labeled, then we use the following pair of functions:

$[C, h]$ = contour(x, y, z, v)
clabel(C, h, v)

These two functions are illustrated in Table 7.6.

Two additional contour plots are available. The first is

contour3(x, y, z, v)

which displays contours of the surface in 3D. The values of x, y, and z are the coordinates of points that define the surface. The quantity v, if a scalar, is the number of contours to be displayed and, if a vector of values, the contours of the surface at those values of v. The use of v is optional. If the contour plot is to be labeled, then we use the following pair of functions:

$[C, h]$ = contour3(x, y, z, v)
clabel(C, h, v)

The second contour function is

contourf(x, y, z, v)

which fills the region between the 2D contours with different colors. The values of the colors can be identified using

colorbar(s)

which places a bar of colors and their corresponding numerical values adjacent to the figure. The quantity s is a string equal to either 'horiz' or 'vert' to indicate the orientation the bar will appear. The default value is 'vert'. These functions are illustrated in Table 7.7.

Generation of Cylindrical Surfaces

One can also use a 2D curve as a generator to create surfaces of revolution using

$[x, y, z]$ = cylinder(r, n)

which returns the x-, y-, and z-coordinates of a cylindrical surface using the vector r to define a profile curve. The function cylinder treats each element in r as a radius at n equally spaced points around its circumference. If n is omitted, MATLAB uses a value of 20.

TABLE 7.6 Illustration of `contour` and `clabel`

Plotting function	Script	Graph
contour	[x, y, z] = **SurfExample**; contour(x, y, z)	
contour	[x, y, z] = **SurfExample**; contour(x, y, z, 4)	
contour clabel	[x, y, z] = **SurfExample**; [C, h] = contour(x, y, z); clabel(C, h)	
contour clabel	[x, y, z] = **SurfExample**; v = [10, 30:30:120]; [C, h] = contour(x, y, z, v); clabel(C, h, v)	

TABLE 7.7   Illustration of `contour3`, `contourf`, and `colorbar`

Plotting function	Script	Graph
contour3 clabel	[x, y, z] = **SurfExample**; [C, h] = contour3(x, y, z); clabel(C, h)	
contourf	[x, y, z] = **SurfExample**; contourf(x, y, z) colorbar	

To illustrate `cylinder`, consider the curve

$$r = 1.1 + \sin(z) \quad 0 \le z \le 2\pi$$

which is rotated 360° about the z-axis. Let us take 26 equally spaced increments in the z-direction and 16 equally spaced increments in the circumferential direction. The script to plot a cylindrical surface is

```
zz = linspace(0, 2*pi, 26);
[x, y, z] = cylinder(1.1+sin(zz), 16);
surf(x, y, z)
axis off
```

which upon execution gives the results shown in Figure 7.5.

Viewing Angle

In Figure 7.5, the viewing angles are the default values. In some instances, one wants to change the default viewing angle of the 3D image, either because it does

Figure 7.5   Application of `cylinder`.

not display the features of interest, several different views are to be displayed using `subplot`, or one wants to explore the surface from many different views before deciding on the final orientation. To determine the azimuth and elevation angle of the view, we use

[a, e] = `view`

where *a* is the azimuth and *e* is the elevation. To orient the object, one depresses the *Rotate 3D* icon in the figure window and orients the object until a satisfactory orientation is obtained. Upon typing the above expression in the command window, the values of the azimuth and elevation will be displayed. These values are recorded and entered in the expression

`view`(an, en)

to create the desired orientation the next time that the script is executed. In this expression, *an* and *en* are the numerical values of *a* and *e* taken from the command window.

   Using this procedure with the object shown in Figure 7.5, we find that an orientation that produces satisfactory results is one where $a = -88.5°$ and $e = -48°$. Then, the script becomes that shown in Table 7.8; the result of its execution is also shown in the table.

Shading

The surfaces created with `surf` have used the default shading property called 'faceted'. The function that changes the shading is

`shading` s

where *s* is a string equal to 'faceted', 'flat', or 'interp'. The results obtained from using these shading options are shown in Table 7.8.

   We now present several additional examples of the use of 3D plotting functions.

TABLE 7.8 Illustration of view and shading

Plotting function	Script	Graph

view
shading 'faceted'
	zz = linspace($0, 2*$pi$, 26$);
	r = $1+$sin(zz);
	[x, y, z] = cylinder(r, 16);
	surf(x, y, z)
	view(-88.5, -48)
	shading 'faceted'
	axis off	

shading 'flat'	zz = linspace($0, 2*$pi$, 26$);
	r = $1+$sin(zz);
	[x, y, z] = cylinder(r, 16);
	surf(x, y, z)
	view(-88.5, -48)
	shading 'flat'
	axis off	

shading 'interp'	zz = linspace($0, 2*$pi$, 26$);
	r = $1+$sin(zz);
	[x, y, z] = cylinder(r, 16);
	surf(x, y, z)
	view(-88.5, -48)
	shading 'interp'
	axis off	

Example 7.3   **Generation of planes and their projections**

When the coordinates of three points in space—$\mathbf{P}_o(x_o, y_o, z_o)$, $\mathbf{P}_1(x_1, y_1, z_1)$, and $\mathbf{P}_2(x_2, y_2, z_2)$—have been specified, the parametric representation of any point in a plane containing these three points is given by

$$\mathbf{P} = \mathbf{P}_o + s\mathbf{v} + t\mathbf{w}$$

where

$$\mathbf{P} = x\mathbf{i} + y\mathbf{j} + z\mathbf{k}$$
$$\mathbf{P}_o = x_o\mathbf{i} + y_o\mathbf{j} + z_o\mathbf{k}$$
$$\mathbf{v} = v_1\mathbf{i} + v_2\mathbf{j} + v_3\mathbf{k} = (x_1 - x_o)\mathbf{i} + (y_1 - y_o)\mathbf{j} + (z_1 - z_o)\mathbf{k}$$
$$\mathbf{w} = w_1\mathbf{i} + w_2\mathbf{j} + w_3\mathbf{k} = (x_2 - x_o)\mathbf{i} + (y_2 - y_o)\mathbf{j} + (z_2 - z_o)\mathbf{k}$$

and $0 \le s \le 1$ and $0 \le t \le 1$. Thus,

$$x = x_o + sv_1 + tw_1 = x_o + s(x_1 - x_o) + t(x_2 - x_o)$$
$$y = y_o + sv_2 + tw_2 = y_o + s(y_1 - y_o) + t(y_2 - y_o)$$
$$z = z_o + sv_3 + tw_3 = z_o + s(z_1 - z_o) + t(z_2 - z_o)$$

If it is assumed that we can adequately display a plane as a surface using a 5×5 grid of patches, then we can create the following function, called **PlanarSurface**, that creates the x-, y-, and z-coordinates of the planar surface:

```
function [xx, yy, zz, L] = PlanarSurface(P0, P1, P2)
v = P1-P0;
w = P2-P0;
S = 0:0.2:1;
L = length(S);
[s, t] = meshgrid(S, S);
xx = P0(1)+s*v(1)+t*w(1);
yy = P0(2)+s*v(2)+t*w(2);
zz = P0(3)+s*v(3)+t*w(3);
```

where P_o, P_1, and P_2 are each three-element vectors containing the coordinates of the points on the plane. Thus, if we execute the following script

```
[x, y, z, L] = PlanarSurface([0 0 0], [2 6 3], [7 1 5]);
surf(x, y, z)
```

we obtain the results shown in Figure 7.6.

To project this surface onto the three orthogonal coordinate reference planes, we take the appropriate vector dot products. Thus, to project the planar surface onto the xy-plane, we have

$$\mathbf{P} \cdot (\mathbf{i} + \mathbf{j} + 0\mathbf{k})$$

Similarly, we have, for the projection onto the yz-plane,

$$\mathbf{P} \cdot (0\mathbf{i} + \mathbf{j} + \mathbf{k})$$

and, for the projection onto the xz-plane,

$$\mathbf{P} \cdot (\mathbf{i} + 0\mathbf{j} + \mathbf{k})$$

Thus, we create a new function, called **PlanarSurfaceProj**, to obtain these projections:

```
function PlanarSurfaceProj(P0, P1, P2)
[xx, yy, zz, L] = PlanarSurface(P0, P1, P2);
```

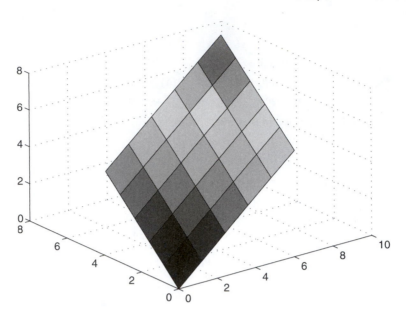

Figure 7.6   Generation of a planar surface.

```
hold on
a = axis;
c(1:L, 1:L, 1:3) = zeros(L, L, 3);
c(:,:,1) = 1;
c(:,:,2) = 1;
c(:,:,3) = 0;
surf(xx, yy, a(5)*ones(L, L), c)
surf(xx, a(4)*ones(L, L), zz, c)
surf(a(2)*ones(L, L), yy, zz, c)
```

The array c is defined such that the projections are displayed in yellow. The first two indices of array c must be of the same order as xx, yy, and zz. The last index must represent exactly three elements, each of which can have a value that varies from 0 to 1. These last three elements specify the color of each patch at each combination of the first two indices. If we execute the script

```
[x, y, z, L] = PlanarSurface([0 0 0], [2 6 3], [7 1 5]);
surf(x, y, z)
PlanarSurfaceProj([0 0 0], [2 6 3], [7 1 5])
```

we obtain the results shown in Figure 7.7. Although there is an illusion that the projections do not appear to be in their designated planes, use of the *Rotate 3D* icon in the figure window will confirm that they are.

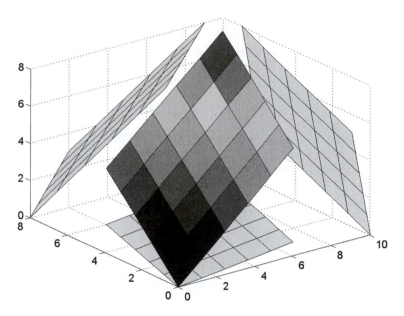

Figure 7.7   Projection of a plane onto its coordinate reference planes.

Example 7.4   Generation of boxes

We now use the results of Example 7.3 to create the surfaces of rectangular parallelepipeds (boxes) whose dimensions are $L_x \times L_y \times L_z$. Referring to Figure 7.1, we see that the boxes are composed of six planes, each of which has the following three sets of points to define it:

Surfaces perpendicular to the yz-plane

$$\mathbf{P}_o(x_o, y_o, z_o), \mathbf{P}_1(x_o, y_o, z_o + L_z), \mathbf{P}_2(x_o, y_o + L_y, z_o)$$

$$\mathbf{P}_o(x_o + L_x, y_o, z_o), \mathbf{P}_1(x_o + L_x, y_o, z_o + L_z), \mathbf{P}_2(x_o + L_x, y_o + L_y, z_o)$$

Surfaces perpendicular to the xz-plane

$$\mathbf{P}_o(x_o, y_o, z_o), \mathbf{P}_1(x_o, y_o, z_o + L_z), \mathbf{P}_2(x_o + L_x, y_o, z_o)$$

$$\mathbf{P}_o(x_o, y_o + L_y, z_o), \mathbf{P}_1(x_o, y_o + L_y, z_o + L_z), \mathbf{P}_2(x_o + L_x, y_o + L_y, z_o)$$

Surfaces perpendicular to the xy-plane

$$\mathbf{P}_o(x_o, y_o, z_o), \mathbf{P}_1(x_o + L_x, y_o, z_o), \mathbf{P}_2(x_o, y_o + L_y, z_o)$$

$$\mathbf{P}_o(x_o, y_o, z_o + L_z), \mathbf{P}_1(x_o + L_x, y_o, z_o + L_z), \mathbf{P}_2(x_o, y_o + L_y, z_o + L_z)$$

We use these set of points in the following function, called **BoxSurface**, to plot the box:

```
function BoxSurface(P0, L)
[x, y, z] = PlanarSurface(P0, P0+[0 0 L(3)], P0+[0 L(2) 0]);
```

```
surf(x, y, z)
hold on
```
[x, y, z] = **PlanarSurface**(P0+[L(1) 0 0], P0+[L(1) 0 L(3)], P0+[L(1) L(2) 0]);
```
surf(x, y, z)
```
[x, y, z] = **PlanarSurface**(P0, P0+[0 0 L(3)], P0+[L(1) 0 0]);
```
surf(x, y, z)
```
[x, y, z] = **PlanarSurface**(P0+[0 L(2) 0], P0+[0 L(2) L(3)], P0+[L(1) L(2) 0]);
```
surf(x, y, z)
```
[x, y, z] = **PlanarSurface**(P0, P0+[L(1) 0 0], P0+[0 L(2) 0]);
```
surf(x, y, z)
```
[x, y, z] = **PlanarSurface**(P0+[0 0 L(3)], P0+[L(1) 0 L(3)], P0+[0 L(2) L(3)]);
```
surf(x, y, z)
```

where $\mathbf{P}_o = [x_o, y_o, z_o]$, $L = [L_x, L_y, L_z]$, and **PlanarSurface** is given in Example 7.3.
Consider the three boxes with the following dimensions and locations of one of its corners:

Box 1

  Size: $3 \times 5 \times 7$
  Location: $(1, 1, 1)$

Box 2

  Size: $4 \times 5 \times 1$
  Location: $(3, 4, 5)$

Box 3

  Size: $1 \times 1 \times 1$
  Location: $(4.5, 5.5, 6)$

The script to create and display these boxes is

  BoxSurface([1, 1, 1], [3, 5, 7])
  BoxSurface([3, 4, 5], [4, 5, 1])
  BoxSurface([4.5, 5.5, 6], [1, 1, 1])
  view(29.5, 44)

which upon execution gives Figure 7.8.

Example 7.5   Rotation and translation of 3D objects: Euler angles

The rotation and translation of a point $p(x, y, z)$ to another location $P(X, Y, Z)$ is given by[2]

$$X = L_x + a_{11}x + a_{12}y + a_{13}z$$
$$Y = L_y + a_{21}x + a_{22}y + a_{23}z$$
$$Z = L_z + a_{21}x + a_{22}y + a_{23}z$$

---

[2]W. Gellert, H. Kustner, M. Hellwich, and H. Kastner, *The VNR Concise Encyclopedia of Mathematics*, Van Nostrand Reinhold, New York, NY, 1975, pp. 534–535.

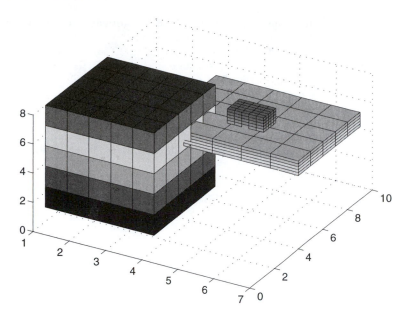

Figure 7.8   Three boxes.

where L_x, L_y, and L_z are the x-, y-, and z-components of the translation, respectively, and a_{ij}, where $i, j = 1, 2, 3$, are the elements of

$$
a = \begin{bmatrix}
\cos\psi\cos\chi & -\cos\psi\sin\chi & \sin\psi \\
\cos\phi\sin\chi + \sin\phi\sin\psi\cos\chi & \cos\phi\cos\chi - \sin\phi\sin\psi\sin\chi & -\sin\phi\cos\psi \\
\sin\phi\sin\chi - \cos\phi\sin\psi\cos\chi & \sin\phi\cos\chi + \cos\phi\sin\psi\sin\chi & \cos\phi\cos\psi
\end{bmatrix}
$$

The quantities ϕ, ψ, and χ are the ordered rotation angles (Euler angles) of the coordinate system about the origin: ϕ about the x-axis, then ψ about the y-axis, and then χ about the z-axis. In general, (x, y, z) can be scalars, vectors of the same length, or matrices of the same order.

Before we apply these relations, we create the function **EulerAngles** to implement them:

```
function [Xrt, Yrt, Zrt] = EulerAngles(psi, chi, phi, Lx, Ly, Lz, x, y, z)
a = [cos(psi)*cos(chi), -cos(psi)*sin(chi), sin(psi);
    cos(phi)*sin(chi)+sin(phi)*sin(psi)*cos(chi), cos(phi)*cos(chi)-
    sin(phi)*sin(psi)*sin(chi), -sin(phi)*cos(psi);
    sin(phi)*sin(chi)-cos(phi)*sin(psi)*cos(chi),
    sin(phi)*cos(chi)+cos(phi)*sin(psi)*sin(chi), cos(phi)*cos(psi)];
Xrt = a(1,1)*x+a(1,2)*y+a(1,3)*z+Lx;
Yrt = a(2,1)*x+a(2,2)*y+a(2,3)*z+Ly;
Zrt = a(3,1)*x+a(3,2)*y+a(3,3)*z+Lz;
```

We now illustrate the use of these transformation equations with the manipulation of a torus, whose coordinates are given by[3]

$$x = r \cos \theta$$
$$y = r \sin \theta$$
$$z = \pm \sqrt{a^2 - (\sqrt{x^2 + y^2} - b)^2}$$

where $b - a \leq r \leq b + a, 0 \leq \theta \leq 2\pi$, and $b > a$.

We first create the following function, called **Torus**, to obtain the coordinates of the torus:

```
function [X, Y, Z] = Torus(a, b)
r = linspace(b-a, b+a, 10);
th = linspace(0, 2*pi, 22);
x = r'*cos(th);
y = r'*sin(th);
z = real(sqrt(a^2-(sqrt(x.^2+y.^2)-b).^2));
X = [x x];
Y = [y y];
Z = [z -z];
```

where `real` is used to eliminate any small imaginary parts caused by numerical round-off.

We obtain four plots of the torus. The first plot is the torus without any rotations. In the second plot, the torus is rotated 60° about the x-axis ($\phi = 60°$) and then compared to the orientation of the original torus. In the third plot, the torus is rotated 60° about the y-axis ($\psi = 60°$) and then compared to the orientation of the original torus. In the last plot, the torus is rotated 60° about the x-axis ($\phi = 60°$) and 60° about the y-axis ($\psi = 60°$) and then compared to the orientation of the original torus. We assume that $a = 0.2$ and $b = 0.8$, and we use `colormap` to produce a mesh of black lines. The script is

```
a = 0.2;  b = 0.8;
[X, Y, Z] = Torus(a, b);
Lx = 0; Ly = 0; Lz = 0;
for k = 1:4
   subplot(2, 2, k)
   switch k
     case 1
       mesh(X, Y, Z)
       v = axis
       axis([v(1) v(2) v(3) v(4) -1 1])
       text(0.5, -0.5, 1, 'Torus')
     case 2
       psi = 0;  chi = 0;  phi = pi/3;
       [Xr Yr Zr] = EulerAngles(psi, chi, phi, Lx, Ly, Lz, X, Y, Z);
       mesh(X, Y, Z)
```

---

[3]D. von Seggern, *ibid.*

```
        hold on
        mesh(Xr, Yr, Zr)
        text(0.5, -0.5, 1, '\phi = 60\circ')
      case 3
        psi = pi/3;  chi = 0;  phi = 0;
        [Xr Yr Zr] = EulerAngles(psi, chi, phi, Lx, Ly, Lz, X, Y, Z);
        mesh(X, Y, Z)
        hold on
        mesh(Xr, Yr, Zr)
        text(0.5, -0.5, 1, '\psi = 60\circ')
      case 4
        psi = pi/3;  chi = 0;  phi = pi/3;
        [Xr Yr Zr] = EulerAngles(psi, chi, phi, Lx, Ly, Lz, X, Y, Z);
        mesh(X, Y, Z)
        hold on
        mesh(Xr, Yr, Zr)
        text(0.5, -0.5, 1.35, '\psi = 60\circ')
        text(0.55, -0.5, 1, '\phi = 60\circ')
    end
    colormap([0 0 0])
    axis equal
    axis off
    grid off
  end
```

The execution of this script results in Figure 7.9.

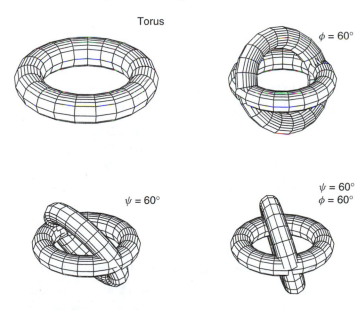

Figure 7.9   Rotations of a torus.

TABLE 7.9 MATLAB Functions Introduced in Chapter 7

MATLAB function	Description
axis on/off	Turns axes on and off
box on/off	Places box around axes borders (axis on must be selected)
clabel	Labels elevations of a contour plot
colorbar	Displays color bar with values of color scale
colormap	Sets color map; with a three-element vector, it sets all colors to one value
contour	Creates a two-dimensional contour plot
contourf	Fills regions of a 2D contour plot with colors
contour3	Creates a 3D contour plot
cylinder	Generates the coordinates of a cylinder of a specified profile
grid on/off	Turns graph grid lines on and off
mesh	Plots a surface with white patches and lines colored based on their z-value
meshc	Plots a mesh generated surface with contours shown beneath it
meshz	Draws vertical planes around the limits of the surface
plot3	Linear 3D plots
shading	Sets shading properties of surfaces created by surf
surf	Plots a surface with patches whose colors are based on their z-value
surfc	Plots a surf generated surface with contours shown beneath it
view	Changes the viewpoint specification
waterfall	Creates a waterfall effect of a surface generated by mesh
zlabel	Labels the z-axis

7.3 SUMMARY OF FUNCTIONS INTRODUCED

In Table 7.9, we have summarized the plotting functions introduced in this chapter.

EXERCISES

7.1 Plot the following three-dimensional curves.[4] Use axis equal.

a. *Spherical helix* $(c = 5.0, 0 \le t \le 10\pi)$:

$$x = \sin(t/2c) \cos(t)$$
$$y = \sin(t/2c) \sin(t)$$
$$z = \cos(t/2c)$$

b. *Sine wave on cylinder* $(a = 10.0, b = 1.0, c = 0.3, 0 \le t \le 2\pi)$:

$$x = b \cos(t)$$
$$y = b \sin(t)$$
$$z = c \cos(at)$$

c. *Sine wave on sphere* $(a = 10.0, b = 1.0, c = 0.3, 0 \le t \le 2\pi)$:

$$x = \cos(t)\sqrt{b^2 - c^2 \cos^2(at)}$$
$$y = \sin(t)\sqrt{b^2 - c^2 \cos^2(at)}$$
$$z = c \cos(at)$$

---

[4]D. von Seggern, *Ibid.*

d. *Toroidal spiral* ($a = 0.2, b = 0.8, c = 20.0, 0 \le t \le 2\pi$):

$$x = [b + a\sin(ct)]\cos(t)$$
$$y = [b + a\sin(ct)]\sin(t)$$
$$z = a\cos(ct)$$

7.2 Plot the surfaces of the following solids.[5] Use the vector form of the coordinate transformation $x = r\cos(\theta)$ and $y = r\sin(\theta)$ or $x = a\cos(\theta)$ and $y = b\sin(\theta)$ as appropriate in parts a through f, where $0 \le \theta \le 2\pi$. Let r (or a and/or b) be of length 10 and θ be of length 22. Part f requires meshgrid, and all of these shapes require axis equal.

a. *Sphere* ($r = 1$):

$$z = \sqrt{r^2 - x^2 - y^2}$$

b. *Ellipsoid* ($a = 1.0, b = 1.5, c = 2.0$):

$$z = c\sqrt{1 - x^2/a^2 - y^2/b^2}$$

c. *Oblate spheroid* (ellipsoid with $a = b > c$: $a = b = 1.0, c = 0.5$)
d. *Prolate spheroid* (ellipsoid with $a = b < c$: $a = b = 1.0, c = 1.2$)
e. *Cone* ($0 \le r \le 2$) [must use surf twice:]

$$z = \pm\sqrt{x^2 + y^2}$$

f. *Cornucopia* ($a = 0.3, b = 0.5, 0 \le u \le 2\pi, -3 \le v \le 3$) [use the *Rotate 3D* icon to explore the surface]:

$$x = e^{bv}\cos(v) + e^{av}\cos(u)\cos(v)$$
$$y = e^{bv}\sin(v) + e^{av}\cos(u)\sin(v)$$
$$z = e^{av}\sin(u)$$

7.3 Plot the following surfaces[6] using surf. Use the *rotate 3D* icon to explore them.

a. ($a = b = 1, c = 0.5, -3 \le x \le 3, -3 \le y \le 3$):

$$z = c((x/a)^4 \pm (y/b)^4)$$

b. ($a = 3, c = 0.25, -1 \le x \le 1, -1 \le y \le 1$):

$$z = c\sin(2\pi a\sqrt{x^2 + y^2})$$

c. ($a = 3, c = 0.25, -1 \le x \le 1, -1 \le y \le 1$):

$$z = c\sin(2\pi axy)$$

d. ($c = 0.2, -1 \le x \le 1, -1 \le y \le 1, x \ne 0, y \ne 0$):

$$z = c\ln(|xy|)$$

---

[5] D. von Seggern, *ibid.*
[6] D. von Seggern, *ibid.*

e. *Catenoid* ($1 \le u \le 5, 0 \le v \le 2\pi$):

$$x = u \cos(v)$$
$$y = u \sin(v)$$
$$z = \cosh^{-1}(u)$$

f. *Right helicoid* ($c = 1/2\pi, -0.5 \le u \le 0.5, -2\pi \le v \le 2\pi$):

$$x = u \cos(v)$$
$$y = u \sin(v)$$
$$z = cv$$

g. *Hyperbolic Helicoid*[7] ($\tau = 7, -\pi \le u \le \pi$ [use 150 values in this range], $0 \le v \le 0.5$ [use six values in this range]):

$$x = \frac{\sinh(v) \cos(\tau u)}{1 + \cosh(u) \cosh(v)}$$

$$y = \frac{\sinh(v) \sin(\tau u)}{1 + \cosh(u) \cosh(v)}$$

$$z = \frac{\sinh(u) \cosh(v)}{1 + \cosh(u) \cosh(v)}$$

h. *Astroidal ellipsoid*[8] ($a = b = c = 1, -\pi/2 \le u \le \pi/2, -\pi \le u \le \pi$):

$$x = (a \cos(u) \cos(v))^3$$
$$y = (b \sin(u) \cos(v))^3$$
$$x = (c \sin(v))^3$$

i. *Möbius strip*[9] ($-0.4 \le s \le 0.4, 0 \le t \le 2\pi$)

$$x = s \cos(t/2) \cos(t)$$
$$y = s \cos(t/2) \sin(t)$$
$$z = s \sin(t/2)$$

j. *Sine surface*[10] ($0 \le u \le 2\pi, 0 \le v \le 2\pi$)

$$x = a \sin(u)$$
$$y = a \sin(v)$$
$$z = a \sin(u + v)$$

k. *Whitney umbrella*[11] ($-1 \le u, v \le 1$)

$$x = uv$$
$$y = u$$
$$z = v^2$$

[7]E. W. Weisstein, *CRC Concise Encyclopedia of Mathematics*, 2nd ed., Chapman & Hall/CRC, Boca Raton, FL, 2003, p. 1421.
[8]E. W. Weisstein, *ibid*, p. 136.
[9]E. W. Weisstein, *ibid*, p. 1928.
[10]E. W. Weisstein, *ibid*, p. 2708.
[11]E. W. Weisstein, *ibid*, p. 3200.

l. *Helical spring*[12] $(r_1 = r_2 = 0.25, T = 2, n = 4, 0 \le u, v \le 2\pi.$ Use `view([-64 0]`.)

$$x = [1 - r_1 \cos(v)] \cos(nu)$$
$$y = [1 - r_1 \cos(v)] \sin(u)$$
$$z = r_2[\sin(v) + Tu/\pi]$$

m. *Crescent*[13] $(0 \le u, v \le 1)$

$$x = (2 + \sin(2\pi u) \sin(2\pi v)) \sin(3\pi v)$$
$$y = (2 + \sin(2\pi u) \sin(2\pi v)) \cos(3\pi v)$$
$$z = \cos(2\pi u) \sin(2\pi v) + 4v - 2$$

n. *Figure 8 torus*[14] $(c = 1, -\pi \le u, v \le \pi)$

$$x = \cos(u)(c + \sin(v) \cos(u) - \sin(2v) \sin(u)/2);$$
$$y = \sin(u)(c + \sin(v) \cos(u) - \sin(2v) \sin(u)/2);$$
$$z = \sin(u) \sin(v) + \cos(u) \sin(2v)/2;$$

7.4 The mode shape of a solid circular plate clamped along its outer boundary $r = b$ is[15]

$$w_{mn}(r, \theta) = [C_{mn}J_m(\Omega_{mn}r/b) + I_m(\Omega_{mn}r/b)] \cos(m\theta)$$

where $m = 0, 1, 2, \ldots,$ and $J_m(x)$ is the Bessel function of the first kind of order m and $I_m(x)$ the modified Bessel function of the first kind of order m,

$$C_{mn} = -\frac{I_m(\Omega_{mn})}{J_m(\Omega_{mn})}$$

and Ω_{mn} are the solutions to

$$J_m(\Omega_{mn})I_{m+1}(\Omega_{mn}) + I_m(\Omega_{mn})J_{m+1}(\Omega_{mn}) = 0$$

and have already been obtained in Exercise 5.9.

Using the results of Exercise 5.9, in which the lowest three natural frequency coefficients for $m = 0, 1, 2$ have been determined, plot the corresponding nine mode shapes with `surfc` on one figure using `subplot`, and at the top of each figure, place the value of $m, n,$ and the frequency coefficient. Do not draw the x- and y-axes. The first row is for $m = 0$, and so on. Normalize each mode shape using the `max` function twice (because the displacement field is a matrix) so that the maximum amplitude is 1. It is suggested that the number of radial divisions (r/b) be 15 and those for the angular divisions be 30. The results should look like those shown in Figure 7.10, which have been obtained with `meshc` and `colormap` for clarity upon reproduction.

7.5 Consider a slab of thickness $2L$ in the x-direction and of very large dimensions in the y- and z-directions. If the slab, which is initially at a uniform constant temperature T_i

---

[12] http://astronomy.swin.edu.au/pbourke/geometry/

[13] http://astronomy.swin.edu.au/pbourke/geometry/

[14] http://astronomy.swin.edu.au/pbourke/geometry/

[15] E. B. Magrab, *Vibration of Elastic Structural Members*, Sijthoff & Noordhoff, The Netherlands, 1979, p. 252.

3.1962 m=0 n=1   6.3064 m=0 n=2   9.4395 m=0 n=3

4.6109 m=1 n=1   7.7993 m=1 n=2   10.9581 m=1 n=3

5.9057 m=2 n=1   9.1969 m=2 n=2   12.4022 m=2 n=3

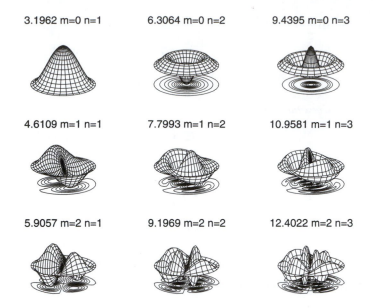

Figure 7.10   Mode shapes of a circular plate.

at $t = 0$, is suddenly exposed to a convective environment of temperature T_∞, then the temperature distribution as a function of time and position within the slab is[16]

$$\frac{\theta}{\theta_i} = 2 \sum_{n=1}^{\infty} \frac{\sin \delta_n \cos(\delta_n \eta)}{\delta_n + \sin \delta_n \cos(\delta_n)} \exp(-\delta_n^2 \tau)$$

where $\theta = \theta(\eta, \tau) = T - T_\infty$, $T = T(\eta, \tau)$ is the temperature in the slab, $\theta_i = T_i - T_\infty$, $\eta = x/L$, $\tau = \alpha^2 t/L^2$ is the nondimensional time (sometimes called the Fourier modulus), α is the thermal diffusivity, and δ_n are the solutions of

$$\cot \delta_n = \frac{\delta_n}{B_i}$$

where $B_i = \overline{h}L/k$ is the Biot number, $\overline{h}$ is the average heat transfer coefficient for convection from the entire surface, and k is the thermal conductivity of the slab.

Find the lowest 20 values of δ_n for $B_i = 0.7$, and use them to plot the surface $\theta(\eta, \tau)/\theta_i$ for $0 \le \eta \le 1$ and $0 \le \tau \le 2$. Then, use the *Rotate 3D* icon interactively to obtain an acceptable view of the surface. Label the axes, and title the figure. Also, add vertical lines as shown in Figure 7.4 to aid further in the visualization of the surface.

7.6 Plot the following mode shape and its contours for a square membrane clamped on its outer boundary using 25 grid points in each direction for $0 \le x \le 1$ and $0 \le y \le 1$:

$$w_{23}(x, y) = \sin(2\pi x) \sin(3\pi y)$$

---

[16]D. R. Pitts and L. E. Sissom, *Theory and Practice of Heat Transfer*, Schaum's Outline Series, McGraw-Hill, New York, NY, 1977, p. 79.

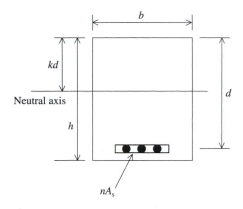

Figure 7.11 Section of a steel-reinforced concrete beam.

7.7 The mean Nusselt number for turbulent flow over a plate of length l is[17]

$$Nu = \frac{0.037\ \text{Re}^{0.8}\ \text{Pr}}{1 + 2.443\ \text{Re}^{-0.1}(\text{Pr}^{2/3} - 1)} \quad 5 \times 10^5 \leq \text{Re} \leq 10^7 \quad 0.6 \leq \text{Pr} \leq 2000$$

where Re is the Reynolds number and Pr is the Prandtl number. Plot the $\log_{10}(Nu)$ as a surface that is a function of the $\log_{10}(\text{Re})$ and $\log_{10}(\text{Pr})$ over the ranges indicated. Connect vertical lines from the boundary plane of the figure to the corners of the surface as shown in Figure 7.4.

7.8 The location of the neutral axis of the steel-reinforced concrete beam shown in Figure 7.11 is determined by the parameter k as defined below[18]

$$k = -\rho n + \sqrt{(\rho n)^2 + 2\rho n}$$

where $\rho = A_s/bd$ and $n = E_s/E_c$, which is the ratio of the Young's modulus of the steel and concrete, respectively. Plot a surface of k as a function of n and ρ for 10 values of n for $6 \leq n \leq 12$ and for nine values of ρ for $0.001 \leq \rho \leq 0.009$ plus another 10 values for $0.01 \leq \rho \leq 0.1$.

7.9 The maximum nondimensional principal shear stress τ' in a rectangular beam subjected to a torsion T is obtained from[19]

$$\tau'^2 = \tau_{xz}'^2 + \tau_{yz}'^2$$

where

$$\tau_{xz}' = \frac{\tau_{xz}J}{Ta} = -\frac{16}{\pi^2}\sum_{n=0}^{\infty}\frac{(-1)^n}{(2n+1)^2}\frac{\sinh(k_n\xi)}{\cosh(k_n b/a)}\cos(k_n\eta)$$

$$\tau_{yz}' = \frac{\tau_{yz}J}{Ta} = 2\eta - \frac{16}{\pi^2}\sum_{n=0}^{\infty}\frac{(-1)^n}{(2n+1)^2}\frac{\cosh(k_n\xi)}{\cosh(k_n b/a)}\sin(k_n\eta)$$

[17]W. Beitz and K. H. Kuttner, Eds., *Handbook of Mechanical Engineering*, Springer-Verlag, New York, NY, 1994, p. C31.

[18]L. Spiegal and G. F. Limbrunner, *Reinforced Concrete Design*, 3rd ed., Prentice Hall, Upper Saddle River, NJ, 1992, p. 196.

[19]C. T. Wang, *Applied Elasticity*, McGraw-Hill, New York, NY, 1953, p. 89.

and J is the torsional constant, $\eta = x/a\ (-1 \le \eta \le 1)$, $\xi = y/b\ (-1 \le \xi \le 1)$, and $k_n = (2n + 1)\pi/2$. Generate a surface of $\tau'^2(\eta, \xi)$ for $b/a = 1$, a square cross-section, and in a separate figure, a contour plot of $\tau'^2(\eta, \xi)$ with 30 contour lines. The results should look like those shown in Figures 7.12 and 7.13.

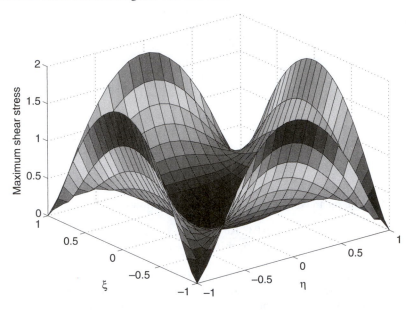

Figure 7.12   Square of the maximum shear stress from the torsion of a beam of square cross-section.

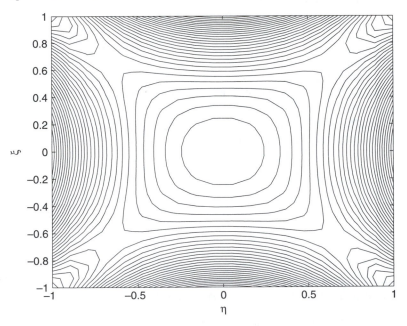

Figure 7.13   Contour representation of the maximum shear stress shown in Figure 7.12.

7.10 Consider the data in Table 7.10, which are the deviations of the output of a process about its mean value $z = 0$ for the given inputs x_1 and x_2. Use the stem3 plotting function to obtain Figure 7.14. You will have to plot the plane at $z = 0$ with a separate command. Use view(-30, 7) to obtain the orientation shown. (The function stem3 is the 3D version of stem.)

TABLE 7.10   Deviations from Process Norms

x_1	x_2	z	x_1	x_2	z
2	50	1.5713	2	360	-0.6023
8	110	-1.1460	4	205	5.8409
11	120	-2.2041	4	400	-0.3620
10	550	-1.5968	20	600	4.3341
8	295	-2.8937	1	585	-2.0368
4	200	1.1136	10	540	-1.5415
2	375	1.9297	15	250	0.0302
2	52	1.1962	15	290	-2.1809
9	100	-3.8650	16	510	1.5587
8	300	-0.4763	17	590	0.3222
4	412	-1.3223	6	100	2.1478
11	400	-0.4619	5	400	0.1537
12	500	0.4911			

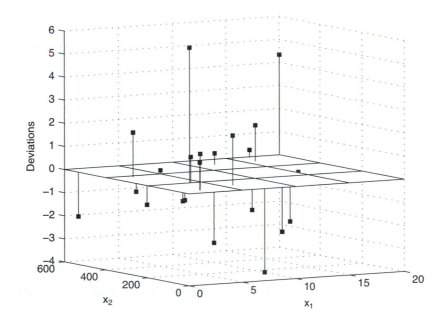

Figure 7.14   Deviations from the plane $z = 0$ using stem3.

8

Design of Machine Elements

Edward B. Magrab

Various methods to analyze different machine elements are illustrated.

274

8.1 VECTORS, FORCES, AND THE EQUILIBRIUM OF RIGID BODIES

Consider the vector

$$\mathbf{a} = a_1\mathbf{i} + a_2\mathbf{j} + a_3\mathbf{k}$$

Its dot product is defined as

$$\mathbf{a} \cdot \mathbf{a} = a_1^2 + a_2^2 + a_3^2 \tag{8.1}$$

and its magnitude is obtained from

$$a = |a| = \sqrt{\mathbf{a} \cdot \mathbf{a}} = \sqrt{a_1^2 + a_2^2 + a_3^2} \tag{8.2}$$

If **a** is given by

    a = [a1, a2, a3]

then the dot product is obtained from

    adot = dot(a, a)

and its magnitude from either

    maga = sqrt(dot(a, a))

or

    maga = norm(a)

The direction cosines of **a** are

$$\cos(\alpha_j) = \frac{a_j}{|\mathbf{a}|} \quad j = 1, 2, 3 \tag{8.3}$$

which are the components of a unit vector $\mathbf{u}_a$ in the direction of **a**; that is,

$$\mathbf{u}_a = \cos\alpha_1\mathbf{i} + \cos\alpha_2\mathbf{j} + \cos\alpha_3\mathbf{k} = \frac{a_1}{|\mathbf{a}|}\mathbf{i} + \frac{a_2}{|\mathbf{a}|}\mathbf{j} + \frac{a_3}{|\mathbf{a}|}\mathbf{k} \tag{8.4}$$

Therefore,

$$\mathbf{a} = |\mathbf{a}|\mathbf{u}_\alpha \tag{8.5}$$

and

$$\mathbf{u}_a \cdot \mathbf{u}_a = \cos^2\alpha_1 + \cos^2\alpha_2 + \cos^2\alpha_3 = \frac{a_1^2}{|\mathbf{a}|^2} + \frac{a_2^2}{|\mathbf{a}|^2} + \frac{a_3^2}{|\mathbf{a}|^2} = 1$$

where

$$\alpha_j = \cos^{-1}\frac{a_j}{|\mathbf{a}|} \quad j = 1, 2, 3 \tag{8.6}$$

The unit vector $\mathbf{u}_a$ in the direction of **a** is obtained from

    ua = a/norm(a)

and the values of the angles of its direction cosines in radians are

    alpha = acos(a/norm(a))

If we have another vector

$$\mathbf{b} = b_1\mathbf{i} + b_2\mathbf{j} + b_3\mathbf{k}$$

then the cross-product of the vectors **a** and **b** is defined as

$$\mathbf{c} = \mathbf{a} \times \mathbf{b} = \begin{vmatrix} \mathbf{i} & \mathbf{j} & \mathbf{k} \\ a_1 & a_2 & a_3 \\ b_1 & b_2 & b_3 \end{vmatrix} = (a_2b_3 - a_3b_2)\mathbf{i} + (a_1b_3 - a_3b_1)\mathbf{j} + (a_1b_2 - a_2b_1)\mathbf{k}$$

(8.7)

where **c** is perpendicular to the plane containing **a** and **b**. The cross-product can be obtained from

c = cross(a, b)

To determine the magnitude of the cross-product in the direction specified by a unit vector $\mathbf{u}_a$, we use the triple-scalar product to obtain

$$c_a = \mathbf{u}_a \cdot \mathbf{a} \times \mathbf{b}$$ (8.8)

where c_a is a scalar. Then,

ca = dot(ua, cross(a, b))

These results are now used to determine the solutions to a range of problems in the analysis of forces and moments on rigid members.

Example 8.1   Summation of forces

Consider the system of forces shown in Figure 8.1. We shall determine the magnitude of **F** and the values of the angles of the direction cosines α_i of the resultant force. Thus,

$$\mathbf{F} = \mathbf{F}_1 + \mathbf{F}_2$$

and from Eq. 8.6

$$\alpha_i = \cos^{-1}\frac{F_i}{|\mathbf{F}|}$$

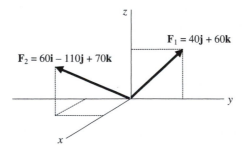

Figure 8.1   Orientation of forces for Example 8.1.

The script is

```
F1 = [0, 40, 60];  F2 = [60, -110, 70];
resultantF = norm(F2+F1)
angles = acos((F2+F1)/resultantF)*180/pi
```

When the script is executed, we obtain $|\mathbf{F}|$ = *resultant* = 159.3738 and α = *angles* = [67.8846, 116.0541, 35.3441], which are in degrees.

Example 8.2   Components of a force

Consider the force shown in Figure 8.2. We shall determine the components of the force $\mathbf{F}$ acting at D using Eqs. 8.4 and 8.5 and the values of the angles of the direction cosines α of this force using Eq. 8.6. The script is

```
r = [24, -16, -48];
ur = r/norm(r);
F = 30*ur
angles = acos(ur)*180/pi
```

When the script is executed, we obtain $\mathbf{F}$ = [12.8571, −8.5714, −25.7143] and α = *angles* = [64.6231, 106.6015, 148.9973], which are in degrees.

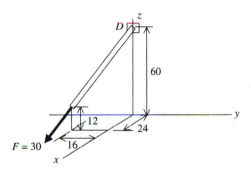

Figure 8.2   Orientation of force for Example 8.2.

Example 8.3   Magnitude of a resultant force

Consider the system of forces shown in Figure 8.3. We shall determine the components and magnitude of the resultant of forces $\mathbf{F}_L$ and $\mathbf{F}_R$, which is

$$\mathbf{F} = \mathbf{F}_L + \mathbf{F}_R$$

Using Eqs. 8.4, 8.5, and 8.2, the script is

```
rl = [2.5, 0, -3];  rr = [2.5, 0.5, -3];
F = 35*rl/norm(rl)+ 25*rr/norm(rr)
resultant = norm(F)
```

When the script is executed, we obtain $|\mathbf{F}|$ = *resultant* = 59.8818. The components of $\mathbf{F}$ are F = [38.2815, 3.1750, −45.9378].

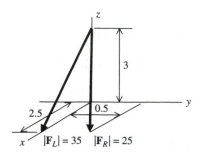

Figure 8.3   Orientation of forces for Example 8.3.

Example 8.4   Magnitude of force components in specified directions

Consider the force **F** shown in Figure 8.4. We shall determine the magnitude of the components of **F** in a direction parallel ($\mathbf{F}_{OA}$) and perpendicular ($\mathbf{F}_\perp$) to member OA and the magnitude of $\mathbf{F}_\perp$. Using Eqs. 8.4, 8.5, and 8.2 and noting that

$$\mathbf{F} = \mathbf{F}_{OA} + \mathbf{F}_\perp$$

the script is

```
r = [1, 3, 1.5];  F = [0, 125, 0];
ur = r/norm(r);
FoaPar = dot(F, ur)*ur
FoaPerp = F-FoaPar
FoaPerpMag = norm(FoaPerp)
```

When the script is executed, we obtain $\mathbf{F}_{OA} = FoaPar = [30.6122, 91.8367, 45.9184]$, $\mathbf{F}_\perp = FoaPerp = [-30.6122, 33.1633, -45.9184]$, and $|\mathbf{F}_\perp| = FoaPerpMag = 64.3848$.

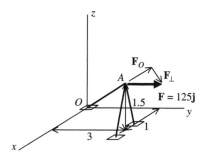

Figure 8.4   Orientation of force for Example 8.4.

Example 8.5   Equilibrium force

Consider the system of forces shown in Figure 8.5. We shall determine the components, magnitude, and values of the angles of the direction cosines α of the force required to keep this system in equilibrium:

$$\mathbf{F} = -(\mathbf{F}_1 + \mathbf{F}_2 + \mathbf{F}_3 + \mathbf{F}_4)$$

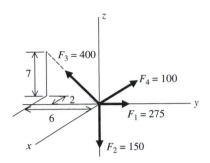

Figure 8.5   Orientation of forces for Example 8.5.

Using Eqs. 8.4, 8.5, 8.2, and 8.6, the script is

```
F1 = [0, 275, 0];   F2 = [0, 0, -150];
F4 = [-100, 0, 0];   r = [-2, -6, 7];
F3 = 400*r/norm(r);
Fequil = -(F1+F2+F3+F4)
FequilMag = norm(Fequil)
angles = acos(Fequil/FequilMag)*180/pi
```

When the script is executed, we obtain $\mathbf{F} = Fequil = [184.7998, -20.6005, -146.7994]$, $|\mathbf{F}| = FequilMag = 236.9080$, and $\alpha = angles = [38.7350, 94.9885, 128.2904]$, which are in degrees.

Example 8.6   Force magnitudes

Consider the system of forces shown in Figure 8.6. We shall determine the magnitude of $\mathbf{F_1}$, $\mathbf{F_2}$, and $\mathbf{F_3}$ when $\mathbf{W} = -85\mathbf{k}$. We first determine the components $\mathbf{F}_j = |\mathbf{F}_j|\mathbf{u}_j$, where $\mathbf{u}_j$ is the unit vector in the $\mathbf{r}_j = r_{j1}\mathbf{i} + r_{j2}\mathbf{j} + r_{j3}\mathbf{k}$ direction, $j = 1, 2, 3$, and is determined from Eqs. 8.4 and 8.5. Thus,

$$\mathbf{F_1} + \mathbf{F_2} + \mathbf{F_3} + \mathbf{W} = 0$$

or

$$H_1\mathbf{i} + H_2\mathbf{j} + H_3\mathbf{k} = 85\mathbf{k}$$

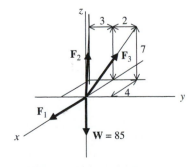

Figure 8.6   Orientation of forces for Example 8.6.

where

$$H_n = \sum_{m=1}^{3} |F_m/r_m| r_{nm} \quad n = 1, 2, 3$$

This can be written in matrix form as

$$\begin{bmatrix} r_{11}/|\mathbf{r}_1| & r_{21}/|\mathbf{r}_2| & r_{31}/|\mathbf{r}_3| \\ r_{12}/|\mathbf{r}_1| & r_{22}/|\mathbf{r}_2| & r_{32}/|\mathbf{r}_3| \\ r_{13}/|\mathbf{r}_1| & r_{23}/|\mathbf{r}_2| & r_{33}/|\mathbf{r}_3| \end{bmatrix} \begin{bmatrix} |\mathbf{F}_1| \\ |\mathbf{F}_2| \\ |\mathbf{F}_3| \end{bmatrix} = \begin{bmatrix} 0 \\ 0 \\ 85 \end{bmatrix}$$

The script is

```
r1 = [1, 0, 0]; r2 = [-4, -3, 7]; r3 = [-4, 2, 7];
u1 = r1/norm(r1);
u2 = r2/norm(r2);
u3 = r3/norm(r3);
Fmag123 = [u1', u2', u3']\[0, 0, 85]'
```

where we have used left matrix divide discussed in Section 2.6.5.

When the script is executed, we obtain $|F_j|$ = Fmag123 = [48.5714 41.7827 60.5197]'; that is, $|\mathbf{F}_1|$ = Fmag123(1, 1) = 48.5714, $|\mathbf{F}_2|$ = Fmag123(2, 1) = 41.7827, and $|\mathbf{F}_3|$ = Fmag123(3, 1) = 60.5197.

Example 8.7   Moment computation

Consider the force shown in Figure 8.7. We shall determine the magnitude of the moment created by **F** acting on member *OA* about point *O*. If $\mathbf{r}_a$ is the position vector from *O* to *A* and $\mathbf{r}_b$ is the position vector from *O* to *B*, then the components of **F** in the direction *BA* are $|\mathbf{F}|\mathbf{u}_f$, where $\mathbf{u}_f$ is the unit vector of $\mathbf{r}_a - \mathbf{r}_b$. Then, from Eq. 8.7, the moment is

$$\mathbf{M} = \mathbf{r}_a \times (|\mathbf{F}|\mathbf{u}_f)$$

and its magnitude is obtained from Eq. 8.2. The script is

```
ra = [1.5, 3.5, 3]; rb = [3.5, 5, 0];
F = 25*(ra-rb)/norm(ra-rb);
FaboutA = cross(ra, F);
Mmag = norm(FaboutA)
```

When the script is executed, we obtain $|\mathbf{M}|$ = Mmag = 121.0968.

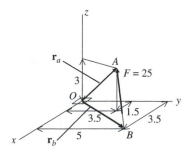

Figure 8.7   Orientation of force for Example 8.7.

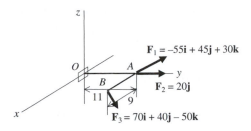

Figure 8.8   Orientation of forces for Example 8.8.

Example 8.8   Moment caused by several forces

Consider the system of forces shown in Figure 8.8, which are acting on a structural member OAB. We shall determine the magnitude of the moment $\mathbf{M}$ created by $\mathbf{F}_1$, $\mathbf{F}_2$, and $\mathbf{F}_3$ about O and the angles α of its direction cosines. Thus,

$$\mathbf{M} = \mathbf{r}_a \times \mathbf{F}_1 + \mathbf{r}_a \times \mathbf{F}_2 + \mathbf{r}_b \times \mathbf{F}_3$$

where $\mathbf{r}_a$ is the position vector OA and $\mathbf{r}_b$ is the position vector OB. The script is

```
ra = [0, 11, 0];  rb = [9, 11, 0];
F1 = [-55, 45, 30]; F2 = [0, 20, 0]; F3 = [70, 40, -50];
Mro = cross(ra, F1)+cross(ra, F2)+cross(rb, F3);
MroMag = norm(Mro)
angles = acos(Mro/MroMag)*180/pi
```

When the script is executed, we obtain $|\mathbf{M}| = MroMag = 537.5174$ and $\alpha = angles = [114.1602, 33.1563, 68.7290]$, which are in degrees.

Example 8.9   Moment causing rotation about an axis

Consider the force shown in Figure 8.9, where

$$\mathbf{F} = -30\mathbf{i} + 10\mathbf{j} - 15\mathbf{k}$$

is acting on the structural member ABC. We shall determine the moment produced by $\mathbf{F}$ that would rotate member AB about its axis, if it were not prevented from doing so. Thus,

$$|\mathbf{M}_{AB}| = \mathbf{u}_b \cdot \mathbf{r}_d \times \mathbf{F}$$

and

$$\mathbf{M}_{AB} = |\mathbf{M}_{AB}|\mathbf{u}_b$$

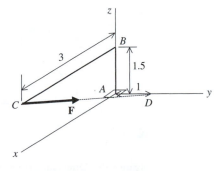

Figure 8.9   Orientation of force for Example 8.9.

where $\mathbf{u}_b$ is the unit vector in the direction of AB and $\mathbf{r}_d$ is the vector in the direction of AD. The script is

```
rb = [0, 0, 1.5]; rd = [0, 1, 0]; F = [-30, 10, -15];
ub = rb/norm(rb);
Mab = dot(ub, cross(rd,F))
MabVec = Mab*ub
```

When the script is executed, we obtain $|\mathbf{M}_{AB}| = Mab = 30$ and $\mathbf{M}_{AB} = MabVec = [0, 0, 30]$.

Example 8.10   Equivalent forces and moments

Consider the system of forces shown in Figure 8.10, where M is the moment acting about the line shown. We shall replace the forces and moment by an equivalent resultant force $\mathbf{F}_O$ and couple $\mathbf{M}_O$ acting through point O. Thus, if $\mathbf{r}_{AF}$ is a position vector representing the direction of M from A ($\alpha = 36.87°$ indicates a 3-4-5 triangle) and $\mathbf{r}_{21} = \mathbf{r}_2 - \mathbf{r}_1$, then

$$\mathbf{F}_2 = \mathbf{F}_2 \mathbf{r}_{21}/|\mathbf{r}_{21}|$$
$$\mathbf{M} = M\mathbf{r}_{AF}/|\mathbf{r}_{AF}|$$
$$\mathbf{F}_O = \mathbf{F}_1 + \mathbf{F}_2$$

and

$$\mathbf{M}_O = \mathbf{M} + \mathbf{r}_1 \times \mathbf{F}_1 + \mathbf{r}_2 \times \mathbf{F}_2$$

The script is

```
r1 = [0, 0, 12.5]; r2 = [-1.75, 1.25, 12.5];
rAF = [0, -4, 3]; F1 = [0, 0, -40];
r21 = r2-r1;
F2 = 15*r21/norm(r21);
M = 25*rAF/norm(rAF);
FatO = F1+F2
MatO = M+cross(r1, F1)+cross(r2, F2)
```

When the script is executed, we obtain $\mathbf{F}_O = FatO = [-12.2060, 8.7186, -40.0000]$ and $\mathbf{M}_O = MatO = [-108.9822, -172.5750, 15.0000]$.

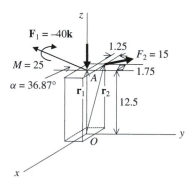

Figure 8.10   Orientation of forces for Example 8.10.

8.2 STRESSES AND DEFLECTIONS IN BEAMS, COLUMNS, AND SHAFTS

8.2.1 Statically Determinate Beams

The nondimensional equation governing the transverse displacement $w(x)$ of beams of constant cross-section, length L, Young's modulus E, moment of inertia of its cross-section I, and loading per unit length $P_o q(x)$ is

$$\frac{d^4 y}{d\eta^4} = q(\eta) \tag{8.9}$$

where $\eta = x/L$, $y = y(\eta) = w/h_o$, $h_o = P_o L^4/EI$, and P_o is a constant representing the maximum value of q. The slope θ_d, bending moment M_d about the beam's neutral axis and shear force V_d are expressed in terms of the nondimensional displacement y as follows:

$$\theta = \frac{\theta_d}{P_o L^3/EI} = \frac{dy}{d\eta} \tag{8.10}$$

$$M = \frac{M_d}{P_o L^2} = \frac{d^2 y}{d\eta^2}$$

$$V = \frac{V_d}{P_o L} = \frac{d^3 y}{d\eta^3}$$

Using these nondimensional quantities, we can generate numerical solutions that are both explicitly independent of the beam's geometric and physical properties and the maximum magnitude of the loading and just a function of the boundary conditions and shape of the load along the beam.

The maximum shear and bending stresses in the beam are, respectively,

$$\tau = \frac{\alpha V}{A} \quad \text{and} \quad \sigma = \frac{Mc}{I}$$

where A is the area of the beam's cross-section, α is a factor that is a function of the shape of the beam's cross-section, and c is the distance from the neutral axis to the top (or bottom, if asymmetrical) edge of the beam's cross-section. When the cross-section is a solid circle, $\alpha = 4/3$; when a rectangle $\alpha = 3/2$; and when a circular annulus, $\alpha = 2$.

Rather than obtain a general analytical solution to Eq. 8.9 and solve it for different combinations of the boundary conditions and loading, we shall solve it numerically using bvp4c. This function was discussed in Section 5.5.4 In addition, we will be extending the results of Example 5.15.

To convert Eq. 8.9 to the form acceptable to bvp4c, we reformulate it into four first-order equations. Thus, if

$$y_1 = y \qquad y_2 = \frac{dy}{d\eta}$$

$$y_3 = \frac{d^2 y}{d\eta^2} \qquad y_4 = \frac{d^3 y}{d\eta^3} \tag{8.11}$$

Then, Eq. 8.9 becomes

$$\frac{dy_1}{d\eta} = y_2 \qquad \frac{dy_2}{d\eta} = y_3$$
$$\frac{dy_3}{d\eta} = y_4 \qquad \frac{dy_4}{d\eta} = q \tag{8.12}$$

We see from Eqs. 8.10 and 8.11 that y_2 is the slope, y_3 is the nondimensional moment, and y_3 is the nondimensional shear force.

We shall consider the combination of four types of boundary conditions at each end of the beam: hinged, clamped, free, and hinged with an externally applied moment M_l at the left end of the beam and M_r at the right end of the beam. The mathematical representation of these boundary conditions is summarized in Table 8.1 along with their expressions according to Eq. 8.10.

To have some flexibility with the types of loading, we shall consider two types: a point load and a triangular loading that has, as a special case, a uniform loading. The types of loading are shown in Figure 8.11. The point loading is assumed to be constant over a very small region about the point of application. If the point load is applied at e_l, then q is given by

$$q = \frac{1}{0.01}[u(\eta - e_l + 0.005) - u(\eta - e_l - 0.005)]$$

TABLE 8.1   Four Common Boundary Conditions for a Beam

Type	Boundary conditions	bvp4c boundary conditions	Case number
Hinged $(y = M = 0)$	$y = d^2y/d\eta^2 = 0$	$\eta = 0, 1: y_1 = 0, y_3 = 0$	1
Clamped $(y = \theta = 0)$	$y = dy/d\eta = 0$	$\eta = 0, 1: y_1 = 0, y_2 = 0$	2
Free $(M = V = 0)$	$d^2y/d\eta^2 = d^3y/d\eta^3 = 0$	$\eta = 0, 1: y_3 = 0, y_4 = 0$	3
Hinged plus external moment $(y = 0; M = -M_l \text{ or } + M_r)$	$y = 0$ $d^2y/d\eta^2 = -M_l \text{ or } + M_r$	$\eta = 0: y_1 = 0, y_3 = -M_l$ $\eta = 1: y_1 = 0, y_3 = M_r$	4

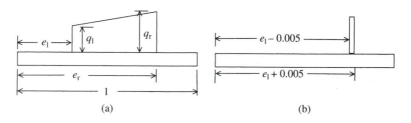

(a)

(b)

Figure 8.11   Nomenclature for (a) a general loading on the beam and (b) an approximation of a point load.

where $u(\eta)$ is the unit step function and we have arbitrarily set the 'width' of the load to 1% of the total length of the beam. The triangular loading is expressed as

$$q = \frac{q_l - q_r}{e_l - e_r}\eta + \frac{q_r e_l - q_l e_r}{e_l - e_r}$$

The values of q_l and q_r vary from 0 to 1, and either can be greater than the other. One or both of these values must have the value of 1; when they are both equal to 1 we have a uniform load. For the load locations, $e_r > e_l$.

Relying on the results of Example 5.16, we first create the function file called **StaticBeamDSMV** that obtains the solution to Eq. 8.9, subject to any combination of boundary conditions given in Table 8.1 and either a point load or a triangular load as shown in Figure 8.11. We shall use the case numbers given in Table 8.1 to select the boundary condition at each end of the beam; $k_l = 2, 3, 4$ for the left end and $k_r = 2, 3, 4$ for the right end. Case 1 is obtained from case 4 by setting M_l and/or M_r to zero. For programmatic simplicity, we shall combine case 4 and case 1 and call it case 1. The loading will be denoted 'Point', 'Triangular', or 'None' for the case when only the effects of M_l and/or M_r are considered:

```
function [y, eta] = StaticBeamDSMV
global Ltype el ql er qr kl kr Ml Mr
solinit = bvpinit(linspace(0, 1, 10), [0.5, 0.5, 0.5, 0.5]);
beamsol = bvp4c(@BeamODEq @BeamBC1, solinit, []);
eta = linspace(0, 1, 200);
y = deval(beamsol, eta);

function bc = BeamBC1(y0, y1)
global Ltype el ql er qr kl kr Ml Mr
switch kl
  case 1
  bc = [y0(1); y0(3)+Ml];
  case 2
  bc = [y0(1); y0(2)];
  case 3
  bc = [y0(3)+Ml; y0(4)];
end
switch kr
  case 1
  bc = [bc; y1(1); y1(3)-Mr];
  case 2
  bc = [bc; y1(1); y1(2)];
  case 3
  bc = [bc; y1(3)-Mr; y1(4)];
end

function dydx = BeamODEq(x, y)
global Ltype el ql er qr kl kr Ml Mr
```

```
switch Ltype
  case 'Point'
    q = (x>=el-0.005&x<=el+0.005)/0.01;
  case 'Triangular'
    q = ((ql-qr)/(el-er)*x+(qr*el-ql*er)/(el-er)).*(x>=el&x<=er);
  case 'None'
    q = 0;
end
dydx = [y(2); y(3); y(4); -q];
```

The displacement, slope, moment, and shear force will be plotted on one figure using `subplot`. In addition, we will display to the command window the type of loading, the boundary conditions, and the maximum and minimum values of the displacement, slope, moment, and shear force. We call this function **BeamDisplay**:

```
function BeamDisplay(y, eta)
global Ltype el ql er qr kl kr Ml Mr
Bc = char('Hinged', 'Clamped', 'Free');
ylab = char('Displacement', 'Slope', 'Moment', 'Shear');
disp(' ')
switch Ltype
  case 'Point'
    disp(['Load type: ' Ltype ' Applied at eta = ' num2str(el)])
  case 'Triangular'
    if ql == qr & ql ~= 0
      disp(['Load type: Uniform  Applied from eta = ' num2str(el) ' to eta = '
                num2str(er)])
    else
      disp(['Load type: ' Ltype ' Applied from eta = ' num2str(el) ' to eta = '
                num2str(er)])
      disp(['ql = ' num2str(ql) ' at eta = ' num2str(el) ' and qr = ' num2str(qr)
                ' at eta = ' num2str(er)])
    end
  case 'None'
    disp(['Load type: None'])
end
MMl = []; MMr = [];
if kl == 1
  MMl = [' (Ml = ' num2str(Ml) ')'];
end
if kr == 1
  MMr = [' (Mr = ' num2str(Mr) ')'];
end
disp(' ')
disp(['Boundary conditions:'])
disp(['  Left end: ' Bc(kl,:) MMl])
```

```
disp(['   Right end: ' Bc(kr,:) MMr])
disp(' ')
for k = 1:4
  [wmax, indx] = max(y(k,:));
  disp(['Max ' ylab(k,:) ' = ' num2str(wmax) ' at eta = ' num2str(eta(indx))])
  [wmin, indx] = min(y(k,:));
  disp(['Min ' ylab(k,:) ' = ' num2str(wmin) ' at eta = ' num2str(eta(indx))])
  disp(' ')
  subplot(2, 2, k)
  plot(eta, y(k,:), 'k-')
  xlabel('\eta')
  ylabel(ylab(k,:))
end
```

We now illustrate the use of these two functions with several examples.

Example 8.11   Hinged beam with a uniform load

Consider a beam that is hinged at both ends and subjected to a uniform load along its entire length. The script to obtain the displacement, slope, moment, and shear distributions is

```
global Ltype el ql er qr kl kr Ml Mr
Ltype = 'Triangular';
kl = 1;  kr = 1;
el = 0;  er = 1;
ql = 1;  qr = 1;
Ml = 0;  Mr = 0;
[y2 eta] = StaticBeamDSMV;
BeamDisplay(y2, eta);
```

Upon execution of this script, we obtain Figure 8.12, and the following information is displayed to the command window:

Load type: Uniform Applied from eta = 0 to eta = 1

Boundary conditions:
  Left end: Hinged (Ml = 0)
  Right end: Hinged (Mr = 0)

Max Displacement = 0 at eta = 0
Min Displacement = -0.01302 at eta = 0.49749

Max Slope   = 0.041667 at eta = 1
Min Slope   = -0.041667 at eta = 0

Max Moment   = 0.125 at eta = 0.49749
Min Moment   = 0 at eta = 1

Max Shear   = 0.5 at eta = 0
Min Shear   = -0.5 at eta = 1

The analytical solution[1] yields virtually the same values as those given above.

---

[1] R. L. Norton, *Design of Machinery*, McGraw-Hill, New York, 1992, p. 1003.

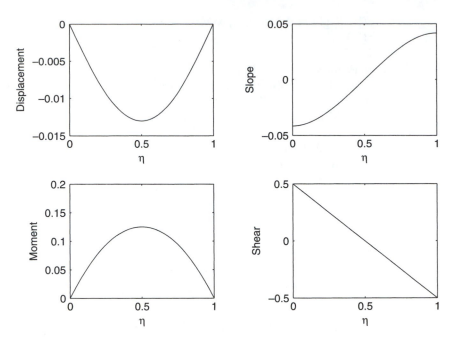

Figure 8.12   Simply supported beam subjected to a uniform load along its length.

Example 8.12   Hinged beam with a point load

Consider a beam that is hinged at both ends and subjected to a point load acting at $\eta = 0.5$. The script is

```
global Ltype el ql er qr kl kr Ml Mr
Ltype = 'Point';
kl = 1;  kr = 1;
el = 0.5;   er = 0.5;
ql = 1;  qr = 1;
Ml = 0;   Mr = 0;
[y2 eta] = StaticBeamDSMV;
BeamDisplay(y2, eta);
```

The execution of this script results in Figure 8.13, and the following information is displayed to the command window:

```
Load type: Point  Applied at eta = 0.5

Boundary conditions:
   Left end: Hinged  (Ml = 0)
   Right end: Hinged  (Mr = 0)

Max Displacement = 0 at eta = 0
Min Displacement = -0.020829 at eta = 0.50251

Max Slope      = 0.06249 at eta = 1
Min Slope      = -0.06249 at eta = 0
```

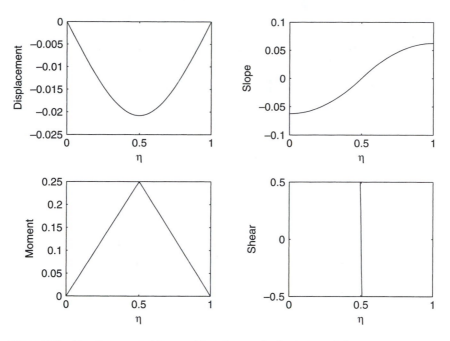

Figure 8.13   Simply supported beam subjected to a point load at $\eta = 0.5$.

Max Moment   = 0.2484 at eta = 0.50251
Min Moment   = 0 at eta = 0

Max Shear   = 0.49994 at eta = 0
Min Shear   = -0.49994 at eta = 0.50754

The analytical solution[2] yields $y_{max}(\eta = 0.5) = 0.0208$, $\theta_{max}(\eta = 1) = 0.0625$, $M_{max}(\eta = 0.5) = 0.250$, and $V_{max}(\eta = 0) = 0.500$.

Example 8.13   Cantilever beam with a uniform load

Consider a beam that is clamped at $\eta = 0$ and free at $\eta = 1$. This type of beam is called a cantilever beam. The beam is subjected to a uniform load acting from $\eta = 0.5$ to $\eta = 1$. The script is

```
global Ltype el ql er qr kl kr Ml Mr
Ltype = 'Triangular';
kl = 2;  kr = 3;
el = 0.5;  er = 1.0;
ql = 1;  qr = 1;
Ml = 0;  Mr = 0;
[y2 eta] = StaticBeamDSMV;
BeamDisplay(y2, eta);
```

---

[2]R. L. Norton, *ibid.*, p. 1003.

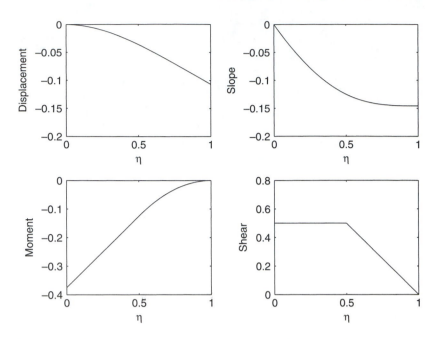

Figure 8.14   Cantilever beam subjected to a uniform load from $\eta = 0.5$ to $\eta = 1$.

The execution of the script results in Figure 8.14, and the following information is displayed to the command window:

Load type: Uniform Applied from eta = 0.5 to eta = 1

Boundary conditions:
  Left end: Clamped
  Right end: Free

Max Displacement = 0 at eta = 0
Min Displacement = -0.10677 at eta = 1

Max Slope   = 0 at eta = 0
Min Slope   = -0.14583 at eta = 1

Max Moment   = 0 at eta = 1
Min Moment   = -0.375 at eta = 0

Max Shear   = 0.5 at eta = 0
Min Shear   = 0 at eta = 1

The analytical solution[3] yields $y_{max}(\eta = 1) = 0.1068$, $\theta_{max}(\eta = 1) = 0.1458$, $M_{max}(\eta = 0) = 0.375$, and $V_{max}(\eta = 0) = 0.500$.

[3]R. L. Norton, *ibid.,* p. 1002.

Example 8.14   Cantilever beam with a point load

Consider a beam that is clamped at $\eta = 0$, free at $\eta = 1$, and subjected to a point load acting at $\eta = 0.5$. The script is

```
global Ltype el ql er qr kl kr Ml Mr
Ltype = 'Point';
kl = 2;  kr = 3;
el = 0.5;  er = 0.5;
ql = 1;  qr = 1;
Ml = 0;  Mr = 0;
[y2 eta] = StaticBeamDSMV;
BeamDisplay(y2, eta);
```

The execution of the script results in Figure 8.15, and the following information is displayed to the command window:

Load type: Point Applied at eta = 0.5

Boundary conditions:
  Left end: Clamped
  Right end: Free

Max Displacement = 0 at eta = 0
Min Displacement = -0.10416 at eta = 1

Max Slope   = 0 at eta = 0
Min Slope   = -0.12499 at eta = 0.50754

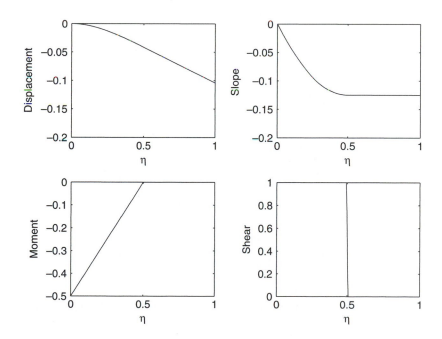

Figure 8.15   Cantilever beam subjected to a point load at $\eta = 0.5$.

Max Moment   = 0 at eta = 0.50754
Min Moment   = -0.49994 at eta = 0

Max Shear   = 0.99988 at eta = 0
Min Shear   = 0 at eta = 0.50754

The analytical solution[4] to this problem yields $y_{max}(\eta = 1) = 0.1042$, $\theta_{max}(\eta = 0.5$ to $\eta = 0.5) = 0.1250$, $M_{max}(\eta = 0) = 0.500$, and $V_{max}(\eta = 0) = 1.000$.

Example 8.15   Cantilever beam with a triangular load

Consider a beam that is clamped at $\eta = 0$, free at $\eta = 1$, and subjected to a triangular load where $q_l = 0$ at $\eta = 0$ and $q_r = 1$ at $\eta = 1$. The script is

```
global Ltype el ql er qr kl kr Ml Mr
Ltype = 'Triangular';
kl = 2;  kr = 3;
el = 0;   er = 1;
ql = 0;  qr = 1;
Ml = 0;   Mr = 0;
[y2 eta] = StaticBeamDSMV;
BeamDisplay(y2, eta);
```

The execution of the script results in Figure 8.16, and the following information is displayed to the command window:

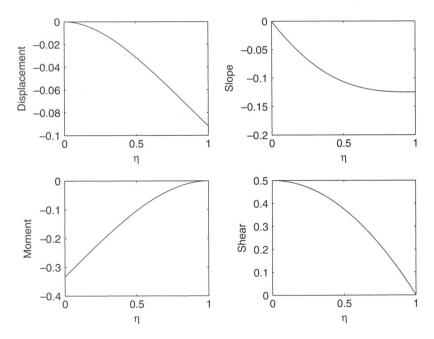

Figure 8.16   Cantilever beam subjected to a triangular load with $q_l = 0$ at $\eta = 0$ and $q_r = 1$ at $\eta = 1$.

---

[4]R. L. Norton, *ibid.*, p. 1002.

Load type: Triangular Applied from eta = 0 to eta = 1
ql = 0 at eta = 0 and qr = 1 at eta = 1

Boundary conditions:
  Left end: Clamped
  Right end: Free

Max Displacement = 0 at eta = 0
Min Displacement = -0.091666 at eta = 1

Max Slope   = 0 at eta = 0
Min Slope   = -0.125 at eta = 1

Max Moment   = 0 at eta = 1
Min Moment   = -0.33333 at eta = 0

Max Shear   = 0.5 at eta = 0
Min Shear   = 0 at eta = 1

The analytical solution[5] to this problem yields $y_{max}(\eta = 1) = -11/120 = -0.09166$, $\theta_{max}(\eta = 1) = -0.125$, $M_{max}(\eta = 0) = -1/3 = 0.333$, and $V_{max}(\eta = 0) = 0.5$.

8.2.2 Buckling of Columns

Consider a structural column of length L, cross-sectional area A, Young's modulus E, moment of inertia I, and yield strength S_y. Let the column be subjected to an axial compressive load P that is concentric with the column's axis and passes through the centroid of A. The critical value of P, denoted P_{cr}, that can cause the column to buckle is estimated by

$S_r > \pi\sqrt{2E/S_y}$:

$$P_{cr} = \frac{\pi^2 AE}{S_r^2}$$

$S_r \leq \pi\sqrt{2E/S_y}$:

$$P_{cr} = A\left[S_y - \frac{1}{E}\left(\frac{S_y S_r}{2\pi}\right)^2\right]$$

where $S_r = L_{eff}/k$, $k = \sqrt{I/A}$ is the radius of gyration of the cross-section, $L_{eff} = 2.1L$ for a cantilevered column, $L_{eff} = L$ for a column pinned at each end, $L_{eff} = 0.8L$ for a column fixed at one end and pinned at the other, and $L_{eff} = 0.65L$ for a column fixed at both ends.

For a solid rectangular cross-section, $k = h/2\sqrt{3}$, where h is the depth of the cross-section, and for a solid circular cross-section, $k = r/2$, where r is the radius of the circle. For a circular tube of inner radius r_i and outer radius r_o,

$$k = 0.5\sqrt{r_o^2 + r_i^2}$$

[5]R. J. Roark and W. C. Young, *Formulas for Stress and Strain*, McGraw-Hill, New York, NY, p. 98.

or, if $r_o = r_i + t$, then

$$k = 0.5\sqrt{r_o^2 + (r_o - t)^2}$$

If a factor of safety F_s is used, then $P = P_{cr}/F_s$.

When P is eccentrically loading the column by an offset e, then

$$P_{cr} = AS_y\left[1 + \frac{ec}{k^2}\sec\left(\frac{L_{eff}}{k}\sqrt{\frac{P_{cr}}{4AE}}\right)\right]^{-1}$$

where c is the distance from the centroid of A to the outer perimeter of A. This relationship is valid for $ec/k^2 \le 0.025$. When the cross-section is circular $c = r_o$. We see that P_{cr} appears on both sides of the equation and, therefore, must be solved using `fzero`.

We now illustrate these relationships with two examples.

Example 8.16   Determination of column diameter

A 13-ft. cantilevered steel column is to withstand a 150,000-lb. compressive axial load. If the column's cross-section is a circular tube whose wall thickness is 0.75 in., then we shall determine the minimum outside diameter d when $E = 3 \times 10^7$ psi, $S_y = 55,000$ psi, and $F_s = 3$.

We shall use `fzero` to obtain the estimate of d, which uses a sub function called **ColumnBuckling**. The script is

```
function ColumnDiameter
opt = optimset('display', 'off');
Leff = 2.1*12*13;  P = 150000;  Sy = 55000;
E = 3e+7;  Fs = 3;  t = 0.75;
d = 2*fzero(@ColumnBuckling, 5, opt, P, Sy, E, Leff, Fs, t)

function Pcr = ColumnBuckling(r, P, Sy, E, Leff, Fs, t)
Sr = 2*Leff/sqrt(r^2+(r−t)^2);
if Sr > pi*sqrt(2*E/Sy)
   Pcr = P-(pi^3*(r^2-(r-t)^2)*E/Sr^2)/Fs;
else
   Pcr = P-pi*((Sy-((Sy*Sr)/(2*pi))^2/E)*(r^2-(r-t)^2))/Fs;
end
```

which, when executed, gives $d = 8.9392$ in.

Example 8.17   Determination of diameter of an eccentrically loaded column

Consider the previous example, except now the column is eccentrically loaded at $e = 0.6$ in. For this case, we create two sub functions, one to evaluate P_{cr} at a given value of r and the other to determine the value of r that satisfies $P = P_{cr}/F_s$. The first sub function is called **SecColumnBuckling**, and the second sub function is called **EccenColumnBuckling**. The script is

```
function ColumnBucklingDia
opt = optimset('display', 'off');
```

Leff = 2.1*12*13;   P = 150000;   Sy = 55000;
E = 3e+7;   Fs = 3;   t = 0.75;   ecc = 0.6;
d = 2*fzero(@**EccenColumnBuckling**, 6, opt, P, Sy, E, Leff, Fs, t, ecc);

function Pest = SecColumnBuckling(Pcr, r, t, Sy, E, Leff, ecc)
a = (r^2−(r−t)^2)*pi;
k = 0.5*sqrt(r^2+(r−t)^2);
Pest = Pcr−a*Sy/(1+(ecc*r/k^2)*sec(Leff/k*sqrt(Pcr/4/E/a)));

function Pcr = EccenColumnBuckling(r, P, Sy, E, Leff, Fs, t, ecc)
options = optimset('display', 'off');
Pcr = P−fzero(@**SecColumnBuckling**, 50000, options, r, t, Sy, E, Leff, ecc)/Fs;

which, when executed, gives $d = 9.6616$ in.

8.2.3 Shafts Subjected to Alternating Loads

Consider a solid, circular steel shaft subjected to a fully reversed, alternating torque and bending moment T_a and M_a, respectively; a mean torque and bending moment T_m and M_m, respectively; and no axial load. Its diameter can be estimated from[6]

$$d = \sqrt[3]{\frac{32F_s}{\pi}} \ \sqrt[3]{\sqrt{(k_f M_a)^2 + 0.75(k_{fs} T_a)^2}/S_f + \sqrt{(k_{fm} M_m)^2 + 0.75(k_{fsm} T_m)^2}/S_{ut}}$$

$$(8.13)$$

where F_s is the factor of safety, S_{ut} is the ultimate strength of the material, S_f is the corrected fatigue strength, and k_α are the various stress concentration factors. This relationship is valid when M_a/M_m and T_a/T_m are constants. As will be seen subsequently, many of the quantities are themselves a function of d and are defined as follows:

Corrected Fatigue Strength—S_f

$$S_f = C_{size} C_{surf} C_{rel} S_{fu}$$

where, for circular shafts,

$C_{size} = 1$	$d < 0.3$ in.
$C_{size} = 0.869 d^{-0.097}$	$0.3 \leq d \leq 10$ in.
$C_{size} = 0.6$	$d > 10$ in.

For machined surfaces, $C_{surf} = 2.7(S_{ut})^{-0.265}$, and for 99% reliability, $C_{rel} = 0.814$. In the absence of published data, the following rough approximation for the uncorrected fatigue strength S_{fu} can be used for steels: $S_{fu} = 0.5 S_{ut}$, where $S_{ut} < 200,000$ psi. With these assumptions, we obtain

$$S_f = 1.0989 C_{size} S_{ut}^{0.735}$$

---

[6]R. L. Norton, *ibid.*, p. 575.

Stress Concentration Factors—k_α

The fatigue stress concentration factor k_f is estimated from

$$k_f = 1 + q(k_t - 1) \tag{8.14}$$

where k_t is the theoretical static stress concentration factor and q is the notch sensitivity, which is a function of the Neuber constant a (recall Example 5.1)

$$q = (1 + \sqrt{a/r})^{-1}$$

where r is the radius of the notch.

The quantity k_t is a function of the loading and geometry. Consider the case of a shaft changing abruptly from a diameter D to a smaller diameter d, as shown in Figure 8.17, in which the value for the bending fatigue stress concentration factor can be approximated by[7]

$$k_t = 1 + \left[At_r^{-k} + B\left[\frac{1 + a_r}{a_r^{3/2}}\right]^l + \frac{Ca_r}{(a_r + t_r)t_r^m} \right]^{-1/2} \tag{8.15}$$

where

$$t_r = t/r_{\text{fillet}}$$
$$a_r = d/(2r_{\text{fillet}})$$
$$r_{\text{fillet}} < (D - d)/2$$

and A, B, C, k, l, and m are given in Table 8.2 for bending and for torsion.

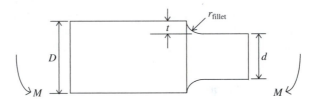

Figure 8.17   Geometry and loading for the determination of the stress concentration factor.

TABLE 8.2   Values for the Constants of the Theoretical Stress Concentration Factor k_t

Constant	Bending	Torsion
A	0.40	0.40
B	6.00	25.0
C	0.80	0.20
k	0.40	0.45
l	2.75	2.25
m	1.50	2.00

[7]W. Beitz, and K. H. Kuttner, Eds., *Handbook of Mechanical Engineering*, Springer-Verlag, New York, NY, 1994, p. D78.

The quantity k_{fm} is determined as follows:

$k_f|\sigma_{max}| < S_y$

$$k_{fm} = k_f$$

$k_f|\sigma_{max}| > S_y$

$$k_{fm} = (S_y - k_f\sigma_a)/|\sigma_m|$$

$k_f|\sigma_{max} - \sigma_{max}| > 2S_y$

$$k_{fm} = 0$$

where k_f is determined from Eqs. 8.14 and 8.15 for bending. The stresses appearing in the above equation are determined from

$$\sigma_{max} = \frac{M_{max}r_{shaft}}{I} \quad \sigma_{min} = \frac{M_{min}r_{shaft}}{I}$$

$$\sigma_a = \frac{M_a r_{shaft}}{I} \quad \sigma_m = \frac{M_m r_{shaft}}{I}$$

where $r_{shaft} = d/2$, $I = \pi d^4/64$ is the moment of inertia of the cross-section of the circular shaft, M_{max} is the maximum bending moment, M_{min} is the minimum bending moment, and

$$M_a = (M_{max} - M_{min})/2$$
$$M_m = (M_{max} + M_{min})/2$$

The quantity k_{fsm} is determined as follows:

$k_{fs}|\tau_{max}| < S_s$

$$k_{fsm} = k_{fs}$$

$k_{fs}|\tau_{max}| > S_s$

$$k_{fsm} = (S_s - k_{fs}\tau_a)/|\tau_m|$$

$k_{fs}|\tau_{max} - \tau_{max}| > 2S_s$

$$k_{fsm} = 0$$

where k_{fs} is determined from Eqs. 8.14 and 8.15 for torsion. The quantity S_s is the shear yield strength, which may be approximated by

$$S_s \approx 0.58 S_y$$

The stresses appearing in the above equations are given by

$$\tau_{max} = \frac{T_{max}r_{shaft}}{J} \quad \tau_{min} = \frac{T_{min}r_{shaft}}{J}$$

$$\tau_a = \frac{T_a r_{shaft}}{J} \quad \tau_m = \frac{T_m r_{shaft}}{J}$$

where $J = \pi d^4/32$ is the polar moment of inertia of the cross-section of the shaft, T_{max} is the maximum torque, T_{min} is the minimum torque, and

$$T_a = (T_{max} - T_{min})/2$$
$$T_m = (T_{max} + T_{min})/2$$

We now illustrate the use of these relationships with an example.

Example 8.18   Diameter of a shaft subjected to alternating loads

Consider a machined steel, circular shaft subjected to a maximum and minimum bending moment of 4000 lb.-in. and 1000 lb.-in., respectively, and a maximum and minimum torque of 1600 lb.-in. and 250 lb.-in., respectively. In addition, the factor of safety is 2.5, the yield strength of the material is 40,000 psi, its ultimate strength 70,000 psi, and the notch radius is 0.03 in. We shall determine the minimum diameter of the shaft for the case where D is 15% larger than d, the fillet radius is 10% of d, and the reliability is at the 99% level. For the circular shaft, $I = \pi d^4/64$, and $J = \pi d^4/32$.

Since many of the quantities in Eq. 8.13 are themselves a function of the shaft diameter, we create a main function **FatigueDiameter** and four sub functions for those quantities that vary with d, and we use `fzero` to estimate d. If we let $rfilletd = r_{fillet}/d$ and $Dod = D/d$, then these five functions are

FatigueDiameter—computes the shaft diameter d
neuber—computes q (see Example 5.1; note that the ultimate strength must be divided by 1000)
StressConcenB—computes k_f and k_{fs}
StressConcenM—computes k_{fm} and k_{fsm}
SsubF—determines the corrected fatigue stress S_f

The main function and the sub functions are

```
function diam = FatigueDiameter(d, rfilletd, Dod)
global Mmax Mmin Tmax Tmin Sy Su rnotch fs
Sf = SsubF(d);
D = Dod*d;
rfillet = rfilletd*d;
[kf, kfs] = StressConcenB(d, rfillet, D);
[kfm, kfsm] = StressConcenM(d, kf, kfs);
p1 = sqrt((kf*(Mmax-Mmin)/2)^2+0.75*(kfs*(Tmax-Tmin)/2)^2)/Sf;
p2 = sqrt((kfm*(Mmax+Mmin)/2)^2+0.75*(kfsm*(Tmax+Tmin)/2)^2)/Su;
diam = d-(32/pi*fs*(p1+p2))^(1/3);

function Sf = SsubF(d)
global Mmax Mmin Tmax Tmin Sy Su rnotch fs
if d<0.3;
   csize = 1;
elseif d>10;
   csize = 0.6;
else
   csize = 0.869*d^(-0.097);
end
Sf = 1.0989*csize*Su^(0.735);
```

```
function [kfm, kfsm] = StressConcenM(d, kf, kfs)
global Mmax Mmin Tmax Tmin Sy Su rnotch fs
roj = 16/pi/d^3;
roi = 2*roj;
Smax = Mmax*roi;
Smin = Mmin*roi;
if kf*abs(Smax)<=Sy
  kfm = kf;
else
  kfm = (Sy-kf*roi*(Mmax-Mmin)/2)/abs(roi*(Mmax+Mmin)/2);
end
if kf*abs(Smax-Smin)>2*Sy;
  kfm = 0;
end
Tmax = Tmax*roj;
Tmin = Tmin*roj;
if kf*abs(Tmax)<=0.58*Sy
  kfsm = kfs;
else
  kfsm = (.58*Sy-kf*roj*(Tmax-Tmin)/2)/abs(roj*(Tmax+Tmin)/2);
end
if kf*abs(Tmax-Tmin)>1.16*Sy;
  kfsm = 0;
end

function q = neuber
global Mmax Mmin Tmax Tmin Sy Su rnotch fs
ncs = [50, .13; 70, .092; 90, .072; 110, .057; 130, .046; 150, .037; ...
     170, .028; 190, .020; 210, .015; 230, .010; 250, .007];
q = 1/(1+polyval(polyfit(ncs(:,1), ncs(:,2), 4), Su/1000)/sqrt(rnotch));

function [kf, kfs] = StressConcenB(d, rfillet, D)
A = [0.4, 0.4]; B = [6, 25]; C = [0.8, 0.2];
k = [0.4, 0.45]; l = [2.75, 2.25]; m = [1.5, 2];
tr = (D-d)/2/rfillet;
ar = d/rfillet/2;
for n = 1:2
  t1 = A(n)/(tr)^k(n);
  t2 = B(n)*((1+ar)/(ar^1.5))^l(n);
  t3 = C(n)*ar/(ar+tr)/tr^m(n);
  alpha(n) = 1+1/sqrt(t1+t2+t3);
end
kf = 1+neuber*(alpha(1)-1);
kfs = 1+neuber*(alpha(2)-1);
```

The script is

```
global Mmax Mmin Tmax Tmin Sy Su rnotch fs
opt = optimset('display', 'off');
Mmax = 4000;  Mmin = 1000;
Tmax = 1600;  Tmin = 250;
```

Sy = 40000; Su = 70000;
rnotch = 0.03; fs = 2.5;
rfilletd = 0.1; Dod = 1.15;
d = fzero(@**FatigueDiameter**, 3, opt, rfilletd, Dod)

which upon execution gives $d = 2.6297$ in.

8.3 STRESSES IN SPUR GEARS

The bending stress on a gear tooth subjected to a uniform (nonvarying), tangentially transmitted load F_t is given by

$$\sigma_b = \frac{K_v K_H F_t}{mbJ_K} \quad \text{N/mm}^2$$

where b is the face width of the gear tooth, m is the module, J_K is the geometry factor for bending strength, K_v is a dynamic factor that is a function of the quality of the gear tooth and the operating pitch circle's tangential velocity v_t, and K_H is a load distribution factor.

The tangential load can be found from

$$F_t = \frac{9.549 \times 10^6 P}{nR_p} = \frac{1000T}{R_p} \quad \text{N}$$

where P is the power in kW, T is the torque in Nm, n is the rotational speed in rpm of the smaller of the two gears (pinion), and R_p is the operating pitch of the smaller of the two gears in mm.

The dynamic load factor can be estimated from

$$K_v = \left(\frac{A + \sqrt{200 v_t}}{A} \right)^B$$

where

$$v_t = \frac{2\pi R_p n}{60,000} \quad \text{m/s}$$

$$A = 50 + 56(1 - B)$$

$$B = 0.25(12 - Q_v)^{2/3}$$

and Q_v is a quality factor for the gear and is represented by an integer in the range $5 \leq Q_v \leq 11$. The upper limit is for precision gears, and the lower limit for the least precise gears. The operating pitch radius R_p is in mm, and n is the rotational speed in rpm. For each value of Q_v, there is a recommended maximum value for v_t, which is given by

$$v_{t_{max}} = (A + Q_v - 3)^2/200 \quad \text{m/s}$$

For stiff gear designs having gears mounted between bearings and relatively free from externally caused deflections, the load distribution factor can be estimated from

$$K_H = 1 + K_{Hpf} + K_{Hma}$$

where K_{Hpf} is a pinion proportion factor and K_{Hma} is a mesh alignment factor. The pinion proportion factor is estimated from

$b \leq 25$ mm

$$K_{Hpf} = k_o - 0.025$$

$25 < b \leq 432$ mm

$$K_{Hpf} = k_o - 0.0375 + 0.000492b$$

$432 < b \leq 1020$ mm

$$K_{Hpf} = k_o - 0.1109 + 0.000815b - 0.353 \times 10^{-6}b^2$$

where for $k_o \geq 0.05$,

$$k_o = 0.05b/R_p$$

and for $k_o < 0.05$,

$$k_o = 0.05$$

The quantity R_p is the operating pitch radius of the smaller of the two gears. The mesh alignment factor is estimated from

$$K_{Hma} = A + Bb + Cb^2$$

where the empirical constants A, B, and C are given in Table 8.3.

The determination of the geometry factor is very tedious and the American Gear Manufacturers Association (AGMA) provides a graphical procedure. We will follow, instead, the analytical procedure given by Colbourne,[8] who uses the same underlying theory that the AGMA uses to determine the geometry factor J_K for spur gears and differs only in the way that the critical section of the gear tooth fillet is found.

TABLE 8.3 Constants *A, B,* and *C* [†]

Type number	Type of gearing	A	B	C
1	Open	0.247	0.657×10^{-3}	-1.186×10^{-7}
2	Enclosed	0.127	0.622×10^{-3}	-1.69×10^{-7}
3	Precision enclosed	0.0675	0.504×10^{-3}	-1.44×10^{-7}
4	Extra precision enclosed	0.0380	0.402×10^{-3}	-1.27×10^{-7}

[†] AGMA Standard 2101-C95.

[8] J. R. Colbourne, *The Geometry of Involute Gears*, Springer-Verlag, New York, NY, 1987.

The procedure requires a very large number of terms and expressions. These have been listed in Tables 8.4 and 8.5 and illustrated in Figures 8.18 and 8.19. Referring to these tables and the figures, the geometry factor can be estimated from

$$J_K = \frac{\cos \varphi}{m K_J \cos \gamma_w}$$

where

$$K_J = K_f \left[\frac{1.5(x_D - x)}{y^2} - \frac{\tan \gamma_w}{2y} \right]_{max}$$

$$K_f = k_1 + \left(\frac{2y}{r_f} \right)^{k_2} \left(\frac{2y}{x_D - x} \right)^{k_3}$$

and

$$k_1 = 0.3054 - 0.00489\varphi_s - 0.000069\varphi_s^2$$
$$k_2 = 0.3620 - 0.01268\varphi_s + 0.000104\varphi_s^2$$
$$k_3 = 0.2934 + 0.00609\varphi_s + 0.000087\varphi_s^2$$

TABLE 8.4   Definition of Quantities Used to Determine the Geometry Factor of a Spur Gear J_K

Quantity	Symbol/formula
Module	m
Number of gear teeth	N
Base pitch	$p_b = m\pi \cos(\varphi_s)$
Circular pitch	$p_s = m\pi$
Diametral pitch	$p_d = 1/m$
Standard pitch radius	$R_s = N p_s/2\pi = Nm/2$
Base circle radius	$R_b = R_s \cos(\varphi_s) = N p_b/2\pi = (Nm/2)\cos(\varphi_s)$
Gear tooth tip radius (gear blank radius)	R_T
Addendum	$a = R_T - R_s$
(Standard addendum for full-depth teeth)	$(a = m)$
Radius of a point on a tooth profile	R
Operating pitch radius	$R_{p_1} = C/(1 + N_2/N_1), R_{p_2} = C/(1 + N_1/N_2)$
Root radius	R_{root}
Distance between gear centers	$C = R_{p_1} + R_{p_2}$
Gear pressure angle	φ_s
Rack pressure angle	$\varphi_r(=\varphi_s)$
Operating pressure angle	φ
Tooth thickness at R_s	t_s
Tooth thickness at R (see Figure 8.18)	$t_R = 2R\theta_R$
Tooth fillet radius	r_f
Rack addendum[*]	a_r
Tip radius of rack cutter[*]	r_{rT}
Distance between reference line and cutting pitch line. [The reference line is where tooth thickness is equal to space width ($m\pi/2$). See Figure 8.19.]	e
Involute function	$\mathbf{inv}(\varphi) = \tan(\varphi) - \varphi$

[*] The values of a_r and r_{rT} are chosen so that h, which is defined in Table 8.5, is approximately equal to m.

TABLE 8.5 Geometric Quantities Used in the Computation of $J_K{}^*$

$$e = \frac{t_s - m\pi/2}{2 \tan \varphi_s}$$

$$m_c = [\sqrt{R_{T_1}^2 - R_{b_1}^2} - \sqrt{R_{T_2}^2 - R_{b_2}^2} - (R_{b_1} + R_{b_2}) \tan \varphi]/p_b$$

$$r_f = r_{rT} + \frac{(a_r - e - r_{rT})^2}{mN_1/2 + a_r - e - r_{rT}}$$

$$R_w^2 = R_b^2 + [\sqrt{R_T^2 - R_b^2} - (m_c - 1)p_b)]^2$$

$$R_{b_j} = N_j\pi \cos \varphi_s \quad j = 1, 2$$

$$\varphi_w = \cos^{-1}(R_b/R_w)$$

$$\varphi = \cos^{-1}\left(\frac{R_{b_1} + R_{b_2}}{C}\right)$$

$$\theta_w = \frac{t_s}{Nm} + \text{inv}\varphi_s - \text{inv}\varphi_w$$

$$x_r' = -a_r + r_{rT}$$

$$\gamma_w = \varphi_w - \theta_w$$

$$y_r' = m\pi/4 + h \tan \varphi_s + r_{rT} \cos \varphi_s$$

$$x_D = R_w \cos \theta_w - R_w \sin \theta_w \tan \gamma_w$$

$$h = a_r - r_{rT} + r_{rT} \sin \varphi_s$$

$$u_{r_{min}} = \frac{e + x_r'}{\tan \varphi_s} - y_r'$$

$$u_{r_{max}} = -y_r'$$

* The subscript "1" denotes the gear for which J_K is to be determined, and the subscript "2" refers to the mating gear. The absence of either number refers only to the gear for which J_K is being computed.

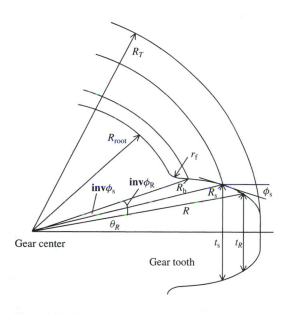

Figure 8.18   Nomenclature for a gear tooth.

where φ_s is one of the following gear pressure angles *expressed in degrees*: either 14.5°, 20°, or 25°. The quantity $[\ldots]_{max}$ indicates that K_J is the maximum value determined by varying x and y over its range of values. The values of x and y are obtained by varying u_r in the formulas given below between the limits given in Table 8.5—that is,

$$u_{r_{min}} \le u_r \le u_{r_{max}}$$

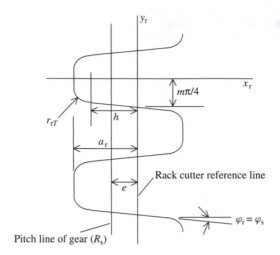

Figure 8.19   Nomenclature for a gear tooth rack cutter.

The values of x and y are given by

$$x = R \cos \theta_R$$
$$y = R \sin \theta_R$$

where

$$R = \sqrt{(N_1 m/2 + \xi)^2 + \eta^2}$$

$$\theta_R = \tan^{-1}\left(\frac{\eta}{N_1 m/2 + \xi}\right) - \frac{u_r - m\pi/2}{N_1 m/2}$$

$$\xi = s\xi' \quad \eta = s\eta'$$

$$s = 1 + \frac{r_{rT}}{\sqrt{\xi'^2 + \eta'^2}}$$

$$\xi' = e + x_r' \quad \eta' = u_r + y_r'$$

Once the stress σ_b has been computed, the permissible stress σ_F must be determined and verified that it is greater than that caused by F_t—that is, $\sigma_b \leq \sigma_F$, where the permissible stress is

$$\sigma_F = \frac{\sigma_{FP} Y_N}{F_S Y_Z}$$

for oil or gear temperatures less than 120° C. The quantity F_S is the factor of safety, Y_N is the bending stress cycle factor, and Y_Z is the reliability factor. The reliability factor has the following values: $Y_Z = 1$ for less than 1 failure in 100, $Y_Z = 1.25$ for less than 1 failure in 1000, and $Y_Z = 1.5$ for less than 1 failure in 10,000.

If n_L is the number of unidirectional tooth load cycles, then the bending stress cycle factor Y_N for steel gears at the 99% reliability level is estimated as follows:

$n_L \leq 3 \times 10^3$

$$Y_N = f(B_H)$$

where

$$f(B_H) = -9.2592 \times 10^{-6}(B_H - 160)^2 + 0.009722(B_H - 160) + 1.6$$
$$160 \leq B_H \leq 400$$

and B_H is the Brinell hardness number.

$3 \times 10^3 \leq n_L \leq 3 \times 10^6$

$$Y_N = Dn_L^E$$

where

$$D = f(B_H)10^{0.8628C_1}$$
$$E = -0.2876C_1$$
$$C_1 = \log_{10}[f(B_H)] - 0.0169$$

$n_L > 3 \times 10^6$

$$Y_N = 1.638n_L^{-0.0323}$$

which is independent of B_H.

The number of cycles is obtained from

$$n_L = 60nL$$

where L is the gear's life in hours, n is the rotation speed of the gear in rpm, and it is assumed there is one contact per revolution on the tooth.

The value for the allowable bending stress number for grade 1 hardened steel gears is

$$\sigma_{FP} = 0.533B_H + 88.3 \quad \text{N/mm}^2$$

We now present an example of the use of these relations.

Example 8.19   Bending strength of a gear tooth

Consider the following pair of gears and the geometric attributes of the rack cutter that made them:

$m = 10$ mm	$a_r = 12.5$ mm	$R_{T_1} = 153.9$ mm
$\varphi_s = 20°$	$r_{rT} = 3.8$ mm	$R_{T_2} = 391.1$ mm
$N_1 = 28$	$b = 45$ mm	$n_1 = 1800$ rpm
$N_2 = 75$	$C = 525$ mm	$B_H = 260$
$T = 2500$ Nm	$t_s = 18.51$ mm	

We note that $h = 10 = m$, which is within the recommended limits. We also assume that the factor of safety is 1.2, that the gear will be used for 4000 hours, and that the desired reliability is less than 1 failure in 100, which means that $Y_Z = 1.0$. Furthermore, we assume $Q_v = 8$ and that the gears will be in an enclosed unit—that is, type 2 in Table 8.3.

We shall obtain the stresses by creating a main function called *GearStress* that computes the stresses in spur gears and eight sub functions that compute the various intermediate factors needed in the solution. These sub functions are

GearKofV—computes K_v
GearKofH—computes K_H
involute—computes the involute of an angle
GearParameters—computes the quantities appearing in Table 8.5
GearKofF—computes K_f
GearKofJ—computes K_J
GearJofK—computes J_K
GearYofN—computes Y_N

The main function and its sub functions are

```
function [sigmab, sigmaf] = GearStress
global m phis ar rrT ts C N1 N2 rT1 rT2 torque BH fs YZ b n Qv typeg L Rp Ft
JK = GearJofK;
Kv = GearKofV;
KH = GearKofH;
sigmab = Kv*KH*Ft/m/b/JK;
sigmafp = 0.533*BH+88.3;
YN = GearYofN;
sigmaf = sigmafp*YN/fs/YZ;

function Kv = GearKofV
global Rp n Qv
vt = 2*pi*Rp*n/60000;
B = 0.25*(12-Qv)^(2/3);
A = 50+56*(1-B);
vtmax = (A+Qv-3)^2/200;
if vt>vtmax
   error('Maximum tangential velocity exceeded for given Qv')
end
Kv = ((A+sqrt(200*vt))/A)^B;

function Kh = GearKofH
global b typeg Rp
class = [0.247 0.127 0.0675 0.0380; ...
         0.657e-3 0.622e-3 0.504e-3 0.402e-3;...
         -1.186e-7 -1.69e-7 -1.44e-7 -1.27e-7];
Khma = class(1, typeg)+class(2, typeg)*b+class(3, typeg)*b^2;
ko = 0.05*b/Rp;
if ko<0.05
   ko = 0.05;
end
if b<=25
   Khpf = ko-0.025;
   elseif b<=432
      Khpf = ko-0.0375+0.000492*b;
```

```
   else
      Khpf = ko-0.1109+0.000815*b-0.353e-6*b^2;
end
Kh = 1+Khpf+Khma;

function GearParameters
global m phis ar rrT ts C N1 N2 rT1 rT2 t
global urmin urmax e xD rf xrp yrp gammaw phi
xrp = -ar+rrT;
h = ar-rrT+rrT*sin(phis);
yrp = -pi*m/4+h*tan(phis)+rrT*cos(phis);
e = (ts-pi*m/2)/tan(phis)/2;
urmin = (e+xrp)/tan(phis)-yrp;
urmax = -yrp;
Pb = m*pi*cos(phis);
Rb1 = N1*m/2*cos(phis);
Rb2 = N2*m/2*cos(phis);
phi = acos((Rb1+Rb2)/C);
mc = (sqrt(rT1^2-Rb1^2)+sqrt(rT2^2-Rb2^2)-(Rb1+Rb2)*tan(phi))/Pb;
Rw = sqrt(Rb1^2+(sqrt(rT1^2-Rb1^2)-(mc-1)*Pb)^2);
phiw = acos(Rb1/Rw);
thetaw = ts/m/N1+involute(phis)-involute(phiw);
gammaw = phiw-thetaw;
xD = Rw*cos(thetaw)-Rw*sin(thetaw)*tan(gammaw);
rf = rrT+(ar-e-rrT)^2/(N1*m/2+ar-e-rrT);

function JK = GearJofK
global m phis ar rrT ts C N1 N2 rT1 rT2 t
global urmin urmax e xD rf xrp yrp gammaw phi
GearParameters
options = optimset('display', 'off');
ur = fminbnd(@GearKofJ, urmin, urmax, options);
JK = -cos(phi)/GearKofJ(ur);

function KJ = GearKofJ(ur)
global m phis ar rrT ts C N1 N2 rT1 rT2 t
global urmin urmax e xD rf xrp yrp gammaw phi
xip = e+xrp;
etap = ur+yrp;
s = 1+rrT/sqrt(xip^2+etap^2);
xi = s*xip;
eta = s*etap;
thetaR = atan(eta/(N1*m/2+xi))-(ur-pi*m/2)/(N1*m/2);
R = sqrt((N1*m/2+xi)^2+eta^2);
x = R*cos(thetaR);
y = R*sin(thetaR);
Kf = GearKofF(x, y);
KJ = -m*cos(gammaw)*Kf*(1.5*(xD-x)/y^2-0.5*tan(gammaw)/y);

function Kf = GearKofF(x, y)
global phis rf xD
d = phis*180/pi;
```

```
k1 = 0.3054-0.00489*d-0.000069*d^2;
k2 = 0.362-0.01268*d+0.000104*d^2;
k3 = 0.2934+0.00609*d+0.000087*d^2;
Kf = k1+(2*y/rf)^k2*(2*y/(xD-x))^k3;

function inv = involute(angle)
inv = tan(angle)-angle;

function YN = GearYofN
global n L BH
nL = 60*n*L;
fBH = -9.2592e-6*(BH-160)^2+0.009722*(BH-160)+1.6;
if nL<=1e3
   YN = fBH;
elseif nL<=3e6
   D = 0.8628*(log10(fBH)-0.0169);
   E = -0.2876*(log10(fBH)-0.0169);
   YN = (fBH*10^D)* nL.^E;
else
   YN = 1.683*nL^(-0.0323);
end
```

The function **GearJofK** makes use of fminbnd to determine the maximum value of K_J as a function of u_r. For fminbnd to work properly, we have to change the sign of the value of **GearKofJ** in this function. Hence, we have to change the sign of J_K, and we do so by inserting the minus sign in the last line of the function **GearJofK**.

The script to determine the bending stress and the permissible stress is

```
global m phis ar rrT ts C N1 N2 rT1 rT2 torque BH fs YZ b n Qv typeg L Rp Ft
m = 10;  phis = 20*pi/180;  ar = 12.5;  rrT = 3.8;  ts = 18.51;
C = 525;  N1 = 28;  N2 = 75;  rT1 = 153.9;  rT2 = 391.1;  torque = 2400;
BH = 260;  fs = 1.2;  YZ = 1.0;  b = 45;  n = 1800;  Qv = 8;  typeg = 2;  L = 4000;
Rp = C/(1+N2/N1);
Ft = 1000*torque/Rp;
[sigmab, sigmaf] = GearStress;
disp(['The bending stress is ' num2str(sigmab,5) ' N/mm^2'])
disp(['The permissible level is ' num2str(sigmaf,5) ' N/mm^2'])
```

When this script is executed, the following is displayed to the command window:

```
The bending stress is 149.64 N/mm^2
The permissible level is 167.41 N/mm^2
```

8.4 KINEMATICS OF A FOUR-BAR LINKAGE

8.4.1 Position and Velocity of the Links

Consider the linkage shown in Figure 8.20. When the angles θ_1 and θ_2 are given, θ_3 and θ_4 are obtained from

$$L_2 \cos \theta_2 + L_3 \cos \theta_3 - L_4 \cos \theta_4 - L_1 \cos \theta_1 = 0$$
$$L_2 \sin \theta_2 + L_3 \sin \theta_3 - L_4 \sin \theta_4 - L_1 \sin \theta_1 = 0$$

(8.16)

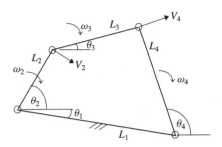

Figure 8.20 Nomenclature for a four-bar linkage.

For convenience, we set $\theta_1 = 0$. If the angular velocity of link 2 is given, then the angular velocities of links 3 and 4 are, respectively,

$$\omega_3 = \frac{L_2\omega_2 \sin(\theta_4 - \theta_2)}{L_3 \sin(\theta_3 - \theta_4)} \qquad \omega_4 = \frac{L_2\omega_2 \sin(\theta_2 - \theta_3)}{L_4 \sin(\theta_4 - \theta_3)}$$

where θ_3 and θ_4 are those obtained from Eq. 8.16. The linear velocity at the end of link 2 is $V_2 = L_2\omega_2$, and that at the end of link 4 is

$$V_4 = L_4\omega_4 = V_2 \frac{\sin(\theta_2 - \theta_3)}{\sin(\theta_4 - \theta_3)}$$

Each of these velocities is perpendicular to its respective L_j in the direction of ω_j. The angular accelerations of links 3 and 4 are[9]

$$\alpha_3 = \frac{-L_2\alpha_2 \sin(\theta_4 - \theta_2) + L_2\omega_2^2 \cos(\theta_4 - \theta_2) + L_3\omega_3^2 \cos(\theta_4 - \theta_3) - L_4\omega_4^2}{L_3 \sin(\theta_3 - \theta_4)}$$

$$\alpha_4 = \frac{L_2\alpha_2 \sin(\theta_3 - \theta_2) - L_2\omega_2^2 \cos(\theta_3 - \theta_2) + L_4\omega_4^2 \cos(\theta_3 - \theta_4) - L_3\omega_3^2}{L_4 \sin(\theta_3 - \theta_4)}$$

Algebraic solutions to obtain expressions for θ_3 are θ_4 from Eq. 8.16 are straightforward but tedious. Instead, we shall solve these equations numerically, using `fsolve` from the Optimization Toolbox, as shown in the following example.

Example 8.20   Visualization of a four-bar mechanism's position, velocity, and acceleration

We shall plot the orientation of link 3 for the case where $L_1 = 0.8$, $L_2 = 2$, $L_3 = 2$, and $L_4 = 3$. In separate graphs, we shall present the velocity ratio V_4/V_2 and the acceleration α_4 for $\omega_2 = 4$ rad/s and $\alpha_2 = 5$ rad/s^2. The sub function **FourBarPosition** is used by `fsolve` to determine θ_3 and θ_4. In this function, $th(1) = \theta_3$, $th(2) = \theta_4$, $th1 = \theta_1$, and $th2 = \theta_2$. The script to display various positions of link 3, the velocity of the end of link 4, and the accelerations of link 4 is

```
function FourBarLinakge
L2 = .8; L3 = 2; L4 = 2; L1 = 3; th1 = 0;
```

[9]A. G. Erdman and G. N. Sandor, *Mechanism Design: Analysis and Synthesis*, 2nd ed., Prentice Hall, Upper Saddle River, NJ, 1991, p. 231.

```
th2 = [1/6:1/6:2]*pi;
th34 = zeros(length(th2), 2);
opt = optimset('display', 'off');
for m = 1:length(th2)
    th34(m,:) = fsolve(@FourBarPosition, [5 5], opt, th2(m), th1, L2, L3, L4, L1);
end
y = L2*sin(th2)+L3*sin(th34(:,1)');
x = L2*cos(th2)+L3*cos(th34(:,1)');
xx = [L2*cos(th2)];
yy = [L2*sin(th2)];
figure(1)
plot([x;xx], [y;yy], 'k', [0 L1], [0 0], 'k--^', x, y, 'ko', xx, yy, 'ks')
hold on
th = linspace(0, 2*pi, 100);
plot(L2*cos(th), L2*sin(th),'k--')
xlabel('Horizontal position')
ylabel('Vertical position')
axis equal
th2 = [0:.05:2]*pi;
th34 = zeros(length(th2), 2);
for m = 1:length(th2)
    th34(m,:) = fsolve(@FourBarPosition, [5 5], opt, th2(m), th1, L2, L3, L4, L1);
end
figure(2)
y = sin(th2-th34(:,1)')./sin(th34(:,2)'- th34(:,1)');
plot(180*th2/pi, y)
v = axis;
v(2) = 360;
axis(v)
xlabel('\theta_2 (degrees)')
ylabel('V_4/V_2')
w2 = 4;  alph2 = 5;
w3 = (L2*w2*sin(th34(:,2)-th2'))./(L3*sin(th34(:,1)-th34(:,2)));
w4 = (L2*w2*sin(th2'-th34(:,1)))./(L4*sin(th34(:,2)-th34(:,1)));
s32 = th34(:,1)-th2';
s34 = th34(:,1)-th34(:,2);
alph4 = (L2*alph2*sin(s32)-L2*w2^2*cos(s32)+L4*w4.^2.*cos(s34) ...
        -L3*w3.^2)./(L4*sin(s34));
figure(3)
plot(180*th2/pi, alph4)
v = axis;
v(2) = 360;
axis(v)
xlabel('\theta_2 (degrees)')
ylabel('\alpha_4')

function t = FourBarPosition(th, th2, th1, L2, L3, L4, L1)
t = [L2*cos(th2)+L3*cos(th(1))-L4*cos(th(2))-L1*cos(th1); ...
    L2*sin(th2)+L3*sin(th(1))-L4*sin(th(2))-L1*sin(th1)];
```

The execution of the script results in Figures 8.21, 8.22, and 8.23.

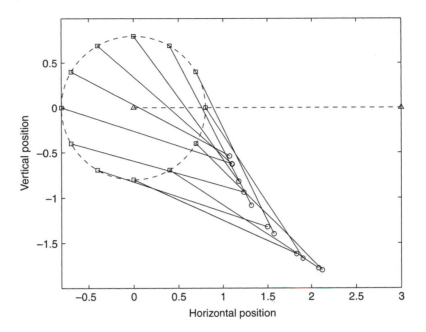

Figure 8.21   Several positions of link 3 in Figure 8.20.

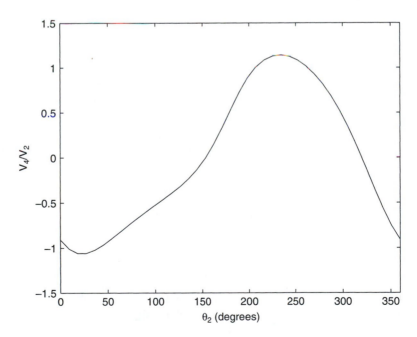

Figure 8.22   Velocity of the tip of link 4 in Figure 8.20.

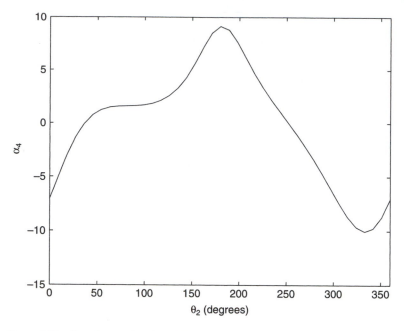

Figure 8.23   Angular acceleration of link 4 in Figure 8.20.

8.4.2 Synthesis of a Four-Bar Linkage

Synthesis of a four-bar linkage has, as one of its objective, the determination of the linkage lengths so that a specified point on the floating bar passes through three prescribed points. Consider the mechanism shown in Figure 8.24. The objective is to determine the lengths Z_k and their initial orientations so that point P passes through points P_1, P_2, and P_3. We shall assume that point P_1 is located at the origin of the coordinate system so that $R_1 = 0$.

The equations from which the six link lengths can be determined are given in terms of the two-dimensional vectors, which are most easily expressed as complex numbers. The lengths and orientation of the six vectors can be determined from the following determinants[10]

$$\mathbf{Z}_2 = \frac{1}{\mathbf{D}} \begin{vmatrix} \mathbf{R}_1 & \mathbf{d}_{12} \\ \mathbf{R}_2 & \mathbf{d}_{22} \end{vmatrix} \quad \mathbf{Z}_5 = \frac{1}{\mathbf{D}} \begin{vmatrix} \mathbf{d}_{11} & \mathbf{R}_1 \\ \mathbf{d}_{21} & \mathbf{R}_2 \end{vmatrix}$$

$$\mathbf{Z}_4 = \frac{1}{\mathbf{E}} \begin{vmatrix} \mathbf{R}_1 & \mathbf{e}_{12} \\ \mathbf{R}_2 & \mathbf{e}_{22} \end{vmatrix} \quad \mathbf{Z}_6 = \frac{1}{\mathbf{E}} \begin{vmatrix} \mathbf{e}_{11} & \mathbf{R}_1 \\ \mathbf{e}_{21} & \mathbf{R}_2 \end{vmatrix}$$

$$\mathbf{Z}_3 = \mathbf{Z}_5 - \mathbf{Z}_6 \quad \mathbf{Z}_1 = \mathbf{Z}_2 + \mathbf{Z}_3 - \mathbf{Z}_4$$

$$\mathbf{D} = \begin{vmatrix} \mathbf{d}_{11} & \mathbf{d}_{12} \\ \mathbf{d}_{21} & \mathbf{d}_{22} \end{vmatrix} = \begin{vmatrix} e^{j\phi_1} - 1 & e^{j\gamma_1} - 1 \\ e^{j\phi_2} - 1 & e^{j\gamma_2} - 1 \end{vmatrix}$$

$$\mathbf{E} = \begin{vmatrix} \mathbf{e}_{11} & \mathbf{e}_{12} \\ \mathbf{e}_{21} & \mathbf{e}_{22} \end{vmatrix} = \begin{vmatrix} e^{j\psi_1} - 1 & e^{j\gamma_1} - 1 \\ e^{j\psi_2} - 1 & e^{j\gamma_2} - 1 \end{vmatrix}$$

[10]A. G. Erdman and G. N. Sandor, *ibid.*, pp. 530–532.

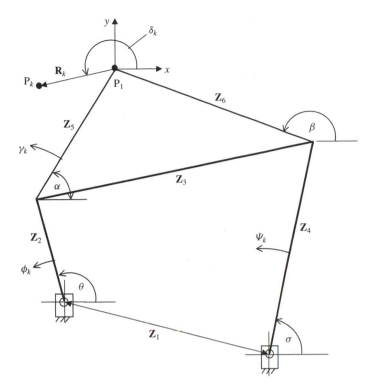

Figure 8.24   Nomenclature for three-position synthesis.

where

$$\mathbf{R}_k = |\mathbf{R}_k| e^{j\delta_k}$$

Comparing Figure 8.20 with Figure 8.24, we see that $|\mathbf{Z}_1| = L_1$, $|\mathbf{Z}_2| = L_2$, $|\mathbf{Z}_3| = L_3$, and $|\mathbf{Z}_4| = L_4$.

It is standard practice to assume values for $\mathbf{R}_k$, ϕ_k, γ_k, and ψ_k, where $k = 1, 2$. In this case, we can then determine the lengths of the six links and their original orientation angles α, β, σ, and θ. We now illustrate these results with an example.

Example 8.21   Synthesis of a four-bar linkage

We assume the following values for the system shown in Figure 8.24:

$$\phi_1 = 340° \qquad \gamma_1 = -48° \qquad \delta_1 = -31°$$
$$\phi_2 = 325° \qquad \gamma_2 = 9° \qquad \delta_2 = -15°$$
$$\psi_1 = 31° \qquad |\mathbf{P}_1| = 2.7$$
$$\psi_2 = 81° \qquad |\mathbf{P}_2| = 3.9$$

The script, which is given below, uses the sub function **FourBarSynth** to evaluate the pairs $\mathbf{Z}_2$ and $\mathbf{Z}_5$ and $\mathbf{Z}_4$ and $\mathbf{Z}_6$.

```
function FourBarLinkage2
c = pi/180; phi = [340.0 325.0]*c; gama = [−48 9.0]*c;
R = [2.7*exp(-31.0*j*c), 3.9*exp(-15.0*j*c)];
z25 = FourBarSynth(phi, gama, R);
disp(['Z2 = ' num2str(abs(z25(1))) ' theta = ' ...
```

```
                           num2str(angle(z25(1))/c) ' degrees'])
    disp(['Z5 = ' num2str(abs(z25(2)))' alpha = ' ...
                           num2str(angle(z25(2))/c) ' degrees'])
    psi = [31 80]*c;
    z46 = FourBarSynth(psi, gama, R);
    disp(['Z4 = ' num2str(abs(z46(1)))' sigma = ' ...
                           num2str(angle(z46(1))/c) ' degrees'])
    disp(['Z6 = ' num2str(abs(z46(2)))' beta = ' ...
                           num2str(angle(z46(2))/c) ' degrees'])
    Z3 = z25(2)-z46(2);
    Z1 = z25(1)+Z3-z46(1);
    disp(['Z3 = ' num2str(abs(Z3))])
    disp(['Z1 = ' num2str(abs(Z1))])

    function z = FourBarSynth(phi, gama, R)
    coeff = [exp(j*phi(1))-1 exp(j*gama(1))-1; exp(j*phi(2))-1 exp(j*gama(2))-1];
    D = det(coeff);
    z1 = det([R(1) coeff(1,2); R(2) coeff(2,2)])/D;
    z2 = det([coeff(1,1) R(1); coeff(2,1) R(2)])/D;
    z = [z1 z2];
```

Upon execution, the following is displayed to the command window:

```
    Z2 = 6.7143   theta = 90.5276 degrees
    Z5 = 1.2378   alpha = 24.8126 degrees
    Z4 = 3.1762   sigma = -143.832 degrees
    Z6 = 1.2774   beta = 95.0336 degrees
    Z3 = 1.447
    Z1 = 8.6814
```

The visualization of these results is shown in Figure 8.25; however, the script used to generate this figure has been left for Exercise 8.5.

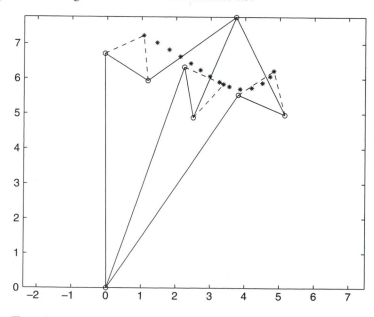

Figure 8.25   Path of point P of the synthesized four-bar linkage.

8.5 CAM PROFILES AND SYNTHESIS

8.5.1 Cam Displacement

Cams are devices for transforming one type of motion into another type of motion. A cam has either a curved or a grooved surface that mates with a follower and imparts motion to it. The cam's motion, usually rotational, is transformed into oscillation, translation, or both. We shall consider the case of cycloidal motion for the displacement profile for the follower, which is created in two types of followers: a translating flat-face follower and an offset translating roller follower. The objective is to determine the cam's profile and the coordinates of the cutter of given radius that would be used to manufacture the cam's profile.

The base circle of a cam r_b is defined as the smallest circle that can be drawn tangent to the cam's surface and is concentric to the cam's axis of rotation. The motion of the follower is

$$L(\varphi) = r_b + s(\varphi)$$

where, for cycloidal motion,

$$s(\varphi) = h\left(\frac{\varphi}{\beta} - \frac{1}{2\pi}\sin(2\pi\varphi/\beta)\right) \qquad 0 \le \varphi \le \beta$$

$$s(\varphi) = h - h\left(\frac{\varphi - \beta}{\beta} - \frac{1}{2\pi}\sin(2\pi(\varphi - \beta)/\beta)\right) \quad \beta \le \varphi \le 2\beta$$

$$s(\varphi) = 0 \qquad\qquad\qquad\qquad\qquad\qquad\qquad 2\beta \le \varphi \le 2\pi$$

is the follower's displacement profile, h is the maximum displacement of the follower, and $0 \le \beta \le \pi$.

We assume that the rotational speed of the cam $\omega = d\varphi/dt$ is constant and that v is the velocity, a is the acceleration, and j is the jerk (the time-derivative of acceleration). Then, if we define the nondimensional displacement $S = s/h$, the nondimensional velocity $V = v/(\omega h)$, the nondimensional acceleration $A = a/(h\omega^2)$, and the nondimensional jerk $J = j/(h\omega^3)$, we have the following relationships:

Displacement

$$S(\varphi) = \frac{\varphi}{\beta} - \frac{1}{2\pi}\sin(2\pi\varphi/\beta) \qquad 0 \le \varphi \le \beta$$

$$S(\varphi) = 1 - \left(\frac{\varphi - \beta}{\beta} - \frac{1}{2\pi}\sin(2\pi(\varphi - \beta)/\beta)\right) \quad \beta \le \varphi \le 2\beta$$

$$S(\varphi) = 0 \qquad\qquad\qquad\qquad\qquad\qquad\qquad 2\beta \le \varphi \le 2\pi$$

Velocity

$$V(\varphi) = \frac{1}{\beta}(1 - \cos(2\pi\varphi/\beta)) \qquad 0 \le \varphi \le \beta$$

$$V(\varphi) = -\frac{1}{\beta}(1 - \cos(2\pi(\varphi - \beta)/\beta)) \quad \beta \le \varphi \le 2\beta$$

$$V(\varphi) = 0 \qquad\qquad\qquad\qquad\qquad\qquad 2\beta \le \varphi \le 2\pi$$

Acceleration

$$A(\varphi) = \frac{2\pi}{\beta^2}\sin(2\pi\varphi/\beta) \qquad\qquad 0 \le \varphi \le \beta$$

$$A(\varphi) = -\frac{2\pi}{\beta^2}\sin(2\pi(\varphi - \beta)/\beta) \quad \beta \le \varphi \le 2\beta$$

$$A(\varphi) = 0 \qquad\qquad\qquad\qquad 2\beta \le \varphi \le 2\pi$$

Jerk

$$J(\varphi) = \frac{4\pi^2}{\beta^3}\cos(2\pi\varphi/\beta) \qquad\qquad 0 \le \varphi \le \beta$$

$$J(\varphi) = -\frac{4\pi^2}{\beta^3}\cos(2\pi(\varphi - \beta)/\beta) \quad \beta \le \varphi \le 2\beta$$

$$J(\varphi) = 0 \qquad\qquad\qquad\qquad 2\beta < \varphi < 2\pi$$

We now illustrate the use of these results with an example.

Example 8.22   Cycloidal cam displacement, velocity, acceleration, and jerk

We shall determine and plot the nondimensional cam displacement, velocity, acceleration, and jerk when $\beta = 60°$. The script is

```
beta = 60*pi/180; N = 40;
phi = linspace(0, beta, N);
phi2 = beta+phi;
ph = [phi, phi2]*180/pi;
arg = 2*pi*phi/beta;
arg2 = 2*pi*(phi2-beta)/beta;
cam = zeros(4, 2*N);
lab = char('Displacement (S)', 'Velocity (V)', 'Acceleration (A)', 'Jerk (J)');
cam(1,:) = [phi/beta-sin(arg)/2/pi, 1-(arg2-sin(arg2))/2/pi];
cam(2,:) = [(1-cos(arg))/beta, -(1-cos(arg2))/beta];
cam(3,:) = [2*pi /beta^2*sin(arg), -2*pi /beta^2*sin(arg2)];
cam(4,:) = [4*pi^2/beta^3*cos(arg), -4*pi^2/beta^3*cos(arg2)];
for k=1:4
  subplot(2,2,k)
  plot(ph, cam(k,:), 'k', [0 120], [0 0], 'k--')
  xlabel('Cam angle (degrees)')
  ylabel(lab(k,:))
  g = axis;
  g(2) = 120;
  axis(g)
end
```

The execution of this script gives the results shown in Figure 8.26.

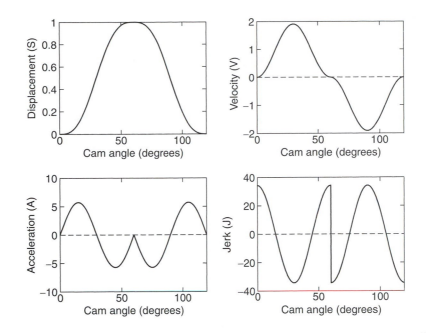

Figure 8.26   Normalized displacement, velocity, acceleration, and jerk for a cycloidal cam profile.

8.5.2 Translating Flat-Face Follower

Referring to Figure 8.27, we have the following relationships[11] for the x, y-coordinates R_x and R_y of the cam's profile and the cutter's coordinates C_x and C_y:

$$R_x = R\cos(\theta + \varphi) \quad R_y = R\sin(\theta + \varphi)$$
$$C_x = C\cos(\gamma + \varphi) \quad C_y = C\sin(\gamma + \varphi)$$

where

$$R = \frac{L}{\cos\theta} \qquad \theta = \tan^{-1}\left(\frac{1}{L}\frac{dL}{d\varphi}\right)$$

$$C = \frac{L + r_c}{\cos\gamma} \qquad \gamma = \tan^{-1}\left(\frac{dL/d\varphi}{L + r_c}\right)$$

and r_c is the radius of the cutter and $dL/d\varphi = hV(\varphi)$, where $V(\varphi)$ is given in Section 8.5.1.

We now illustrate the use of these results with an example.

---

[11]See, for example, A. G. Erdman and G. N. Sandor, *ibid.*, pp. 385–387 and H. A. Rothbart, *Cams: Design, Dynamics, Accuracy*, John Wiley & Sons, New York, NY, 1956, pp. 122–124.

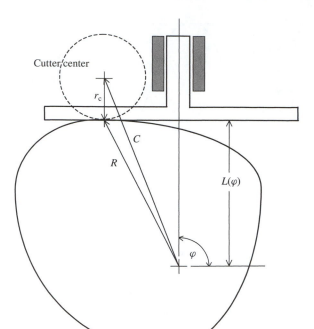

Figure 8.27   Cam with translating flat-face follower.

Example 8.23   Cam profile and cutter coordinates for a translating flat-faced follower

We shall determine R_x, R_y, C_x, and C_y when $\beta = 60°$, $r_b = 3.0$, and $h = 0.5$ and then display these results. We use two sub functions: **CamProfile**, which computes $L(\varphi)$ and $dL/d\varphi$ for a range of values for φ; and **ContourFlat**, which computes R_x, R_y, C_x, and C_y for these φ. The script is

```
function FlatFacedCam
beta = 60*pi/180;  rb = 3;
h = 0.5;  rc = 0.5;  n = 23;
phi = linspace(0, beta, n);
ph = [phi, beta+phi];
[Rx, Ry, Cx, Cy] = ContourFlat(phi, rb, h, beta, rc);
ang = linspace(2*beta, 2*pi, 40);
plot(Rx, Ry, 'k', rb*cos(ang), rb*sin(ang), 'k')
hold on
plot(Cx(1:5:2*n), Cy(1:5:2*n), 'k+')
axis equal
phd = linspace(0, 2*pi, 50);
[x, phx] = meshgrid(Cx(1:5:2*n), phd);
y = meshgrid(Cy(1:5:2*n), phd);
hold on
plot(x+rc.*cos(phx), y+rc.*sin(phx), 'k--')
```

```
function [L, dLdphi] = CamProfile(phi, rb, h, beta)
arg = 2*pi*phi/beta;
L = rb+h*(phi/beta-sin(arg)/2/pi);
dLdphi = (h/beta)*(1-cos(arg));
L = [L, fliplr(L)];
dLdphi  = [dLdphi, -dLdphi];

function [Rx, Ry, Cx, Cy] = ContourFlat(phi, rb, h, beta, rc)
[L, dLdphi] = CamProfile(phi, rb, h, beta);
theta = atan2(dLdphi, L);
R = L./cos(theta);
ph = [phi, beta+phi];
Ry = R.*sin(theta+ph);
Rx = R.*cos(theta+ph);
gama = atan(dLdphi./(L+rc));
C = (L+rc)./cos(gama);
Cy = C.*sin(gama+ph);
Cx = C.*cos(gama+ph);
```

The execution of this script results in Figure 8.28.

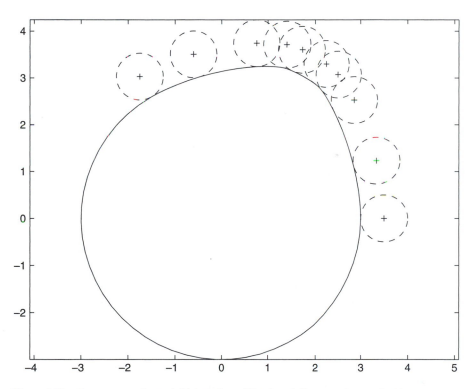

Figure 8.28   Cam contour for cycloidal motion of flat-face follower and several of its cutter positions.

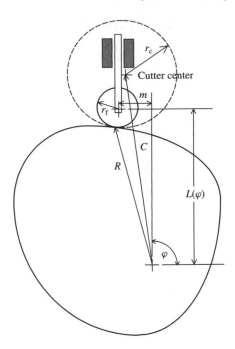

Figure 8.29   Cam with an offset translating roller follower.

8.5.3 Translating Offset Roller Follower

Referring to Figure 8.29, we have the following relationships[12] for the x,y-coordinates R_x and R_y of the cam's profile and the cutter's coordinates C_x and C_y:

$$R_x(\theta, \varphi) = R \cos(\psi + \varphi + \gamma) \quad R_y(\theta, \varphi) = R \sin(\psi + \varphi + \gamma)$$

$$C_x = C \cos(\psi + \varphi + \delta) \qquad C_y = C \sin(\psi + \varphi + \delta)$$

where

$$R^2 = (F - r_f \cos \alpha)^2 + r_f^2 \cos^2 \alpha \qquad \psi = \tan^{-1}(m/L)$$

$$C^2 = c_x^2 + c_y^2 \qquad\qquad \alpha = \tan^{-1}\left(\frac{L dL/d\varphi}{F^2 - m dL/d\varphi}\right)$$

$$c_x = F + (r_c - r_f) \cos \alpha \qquad \gamma = \tan^{-1}\left(\frac{F - r_f \cos \alpha}{r_f \sin \alpha}\right)$$

$$c_y = (r_c - r_f) \sin \alpha \qquad \delta = \tan^{-1}(c_y/c_x)$$

$$F^2 = m^2 + L^2$$

The base circle radius of the cam is

$$L(0) = r_b = \sqrt{R_x^2(\theta, 0) + R_y^2(\theta, 0)}$$

---

[12]See, for example, A. G. Erdman, and G. N. Sandor, *ibid.*, pp. 389–393, and H. A. Rothbart, *ibid.*, pp. 120–122.

which starts at $\varphi = 2\beta + \Delta$, where

$$\Delta = \tan^{-1}\left(\frac{R_y(\theta, 0)}{R_x(\theta, 0)}\right)$$

We now illustrate the use of these results with an example.

Example 8.24   Cam profile and cutter coordinates for a translating offset roller follower

We shall determine R_x, R_y, C_x, and C_y when $\beta = 60°$, $r_b = 3.0$, $h = 0.5$, $r_c = 0.5$, $r_f = 0.375$, and $m = 0.375$ and then display these results. The sub function **ContourRoller** computes R_x, R_y, C_x, and C_y for a range of values of φ, and the sub function **CamProfile** computes $L(\varphi)$ and $dL/d\varphi$ for an range of values for φ. (**CamProfile** is the same sub function that was used in Example 8.23.) The script is

```
function RollerCam
beta = 60*pi/180;  rb = 3;  h = 0.5;  rc = 0.5;
rf = 0.375;  m = .375;  n = 23;
phi = linspace(0, beta, n);
ph = [phi, beta+phi];
[Rx, Ry] = ContourRoller(0, rb, h, beta, rc, m, rf);
rb = sqrt(Rx(1)^2+Ry(1)^2);
delta = atan2(Ry(1), Rx(1));
[Rx, Ry, Cx, Cy] = ContourRoller(phi, rb, h, beta, rc, m, rf);
ang = linspace(2*beta+delta,2*pi+delta,40);
plot(Rx, Ry, 'k', Rx(1)*cos(ang), Rx(1)*sin(ang), 'k')
hold on
plot(0, 0, 'k+', Cx(1:5:2*n), Cy(1:5:2*n), 'k+')
axis equal
phd = linspace(0, 2*pi, 50);
[x, phx] = meshgrid(Cx(1:5:2*n), phd);
y = meshgrid(Cy(1:5:2*n), phd);
hold on
plot(x+rc.*cos(phx), y+rc.*sin(phx), 'k--')

function [Rx, Ry, Cx, Cy] = ContourRoller(phi, rb, h, beta, rc, m, rf)
[L, dLdphi] = CamProfile(phi, rb, h, beta);
F2 = m^2+L.^2;
F = sqrt(F2);
psi = atan2(m, L);
alpha = atan2(L.*dLdphi, F2-m*dLdphi);
gamma = atan2(rf*sin(alpha), F-rf*cos(alpha));
ph = [phi, beta+phi];
R = sqrt((F-rf*cos(alpha)).^2+(rf*sin(alpha)).^2);
Ry = R.*sin(psi+gamma+ph);
Rx = R.*cos(psi+gamma+ph);
cx = F+(rc-rf)*cos(alpha);
cy = (rc-rf)*sin(alpha);
delta = atan2(cy, cx);
C = sqrt(cx.^2+cy.^2);
Cy = C.*sin(psi+delta+ph);
Cx = C.*cos(psi+delta+ph);
```

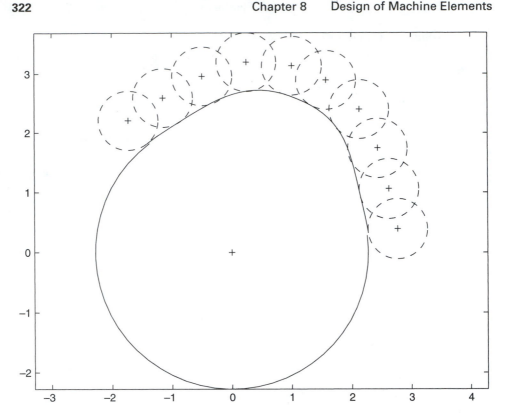

Figure 8.30   Cam contour for cycloidal motion of offset roller follower and its cutter coordinates.

When executed, this script produces the results shown in Figure 8.30.

8.5.4 Cam Radius of Curvature

The radius of curvature of the cam profile is given by

$$\rho = \frac{[(L(\varphi))^2 + (dL(\varphi)/d\varphi)^2]^{3/2}}{(L(\varphi))^2 + 2(dL(\varphi)/d\varphi)^2 - L(\varphi)d^2L(\varphi)/d\varphi^2}$$

A cam's profile should be such that the radius of curvature of a follower is always greater than the minimum radius of curvature of the profile. Thus, the quantity of interest is the minimum radius of curvature. Using the definitions in Section 8.5.1 for the nondimensional displacement, velocity, acceleration, and jerk, the radius of curvature can be written as

$$\rho/h = \frac{[(r_b/h + S)^2 + V^2]^{3/2}}{(r_b/h + S)^2 + 2V^2 - (r_b/h + S)A}$$

We now illustrate the use of this result with an example.

Example 8.25   Minimum cam radius of curvature

We shall determine the minimum (nondimensional) radius of curvature for an arbitrary value of r_b/h and β. The sub function **CamCurvature** computes ρ and uses the fact that the radius of curvature is symmetrical about β, where $0 \le \varphi \le \beta$. The script is

```
function CamRadiusCurvature
rbh = input('Enter ratio rb/h: ');
beta = input('Enter angle beta (degrees): ')*pi/180;
options = optimset('display', 'off');
phimin = fminbnd(@CamCurvature,0, beta, options, beta, rbh);
rmin = CamCurvature(phimin, beta, rbh);
disp(['When beta = ' num2str(beta*180/pi) ' degrees and rb/h = ' ...
          num2str(rbh) 'the minimum radius of curvature for a'])
disp(['cycloidal cam profile is = ' num2str(rmin) 'h, which occurs at ' ...
num2str(phimin*180/pi) ' degrees.'])
function RadiusCurve = CamCurvature(phi, beta, rbh)
arg = 2*pi*phi/beta;
S = phi/beta-sin(arg)/2/pi;
V = (1-cos(arg))/beta;
A = 2*pi /beta^2*sin(arg);
RadiusCurve = ((rbh+S)^2+V^2)^1.5/((rbh+S)^2+2*V^2-(rbh+S)*A);
```

When this script is executed, the following is displayed to the command window:

```
Enter ratio rb/h: 4
Enter angle beta (degrees): 80
When beta = 80 degrees and rb/h = 4 the minimum radius of curvature for a
cycloidal cam profile is = 2.9777h, which occurs at 58.8421 degrees.
```

where the user entered the values of 4 and 80.

8.6 HYDRODYNAMIC BEARINGS

Consider the short journal bearing shown in Figure 8.31. If $c_d = (d_b - d_j)$, then the radial clearance $c_r = c_d/2$ is the maximum value of e, the eccentricity. The eccentricity ratio is defined as $\varepsilon = e/c_r$. However, in practice, this quantity is usually obtained from the following relationship, which has been obtained from experiments:

$$\varepsilon \longrightarrow \varepsilon_x = 0.21394 + 0.38517 \log_{10} O_N - 0.0008(O_N - 60)$$

where O_N is the load factor, or Ocvirk number, given by

$$O_N = \frac{P}{nLd\eta}\left(\frac{d}{L}\right)^2\left(\frac{c_d}{d}\right)^2 = 4\pi K_\varepsilon$$

where η is the absolute viscosity of the oil and n is the rotational speed of the journal in revolutions per second. A desirable design goal is to keep $O_N < 30$.

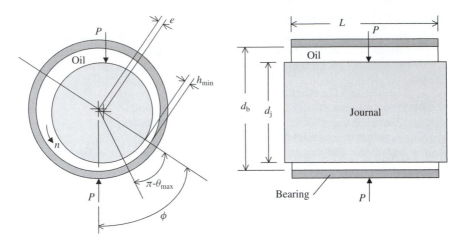

Figure 8.31 Hydrodynamic journal bearing nomenclature.

The minimum film thickness is given by

$$h_{min} = c_r(1 - \varepsilon_x)$$

which should be three to four times greater than the surface finish of the bearing and journal to greatly minimize the chance of contact of the surfaces.

The load that the bearing can support is given by

$$P = 4\pi K_\varepsilon \eta n d L^3 / c_d^2$$

and the torque needed to rotate the journal is

$$T_r = \frac{\pi^2 d^3 L n \eta}{c_d \sqrt{(1 - \varepsilon_x^2)}} + 0.5 P \varepsilon_x c_d \sin \phi$$

where the first term on the right-hand side is the stationary torque and

$$\phi = \tan^{-1}\left(\frac{\pi \sqrt{1 - \varepsilon_x^2}}{4\varepsilon_x} \right)$$

The coefficient of friction between the journal and the bearing is

$$\mu = \frac{2T_r}{Pd}$$

and the temperature rise in the oil in °F is given by

$$\Delta T = \frac{2\pi n T_r}{6600 \rho c_p Q_H}$$

where

$$Q_H = \pi d n L \varepsilon_x c_d / 2$$

TABLE 8.6   Constants Used to Determine η

SAE number	j	A_j	B_j
10	1	9.1209	3.5605
20	2	9.1067	3.5385
30	3	8.9939	3.4777
40	4	8.9133	3.4292
50	5	8.5194	3.2621
60	6	8.3666	3.1884

is the hydrodynamic oil flow in in.^{3}/s, c_p is the heat capacity of the lubricant, and ρ is its density. For lubricating oils, we have the approximate values $c_p = 0.48$ Btu/(lb.-°F) and $\rho = 0.031$ lb./in.^{3}. The temperature rise assumes that the oil is at an inlet temperature of T_{in}. However, since η (see below) and, therefore, T_r is a function of temperature, this equation has to be solved iteratively. Using these values for c_p and ρ, we have

$$\Delta T = \frac{0.0640 n T_r}{Q_H}$$

The absolute viscosity of the oil in reyn (lb.-s/in.^{2}) can be estimated within ±10% from the relationship

$$\eta = 10^{C-7}$$

where

$$C = 10^{A_j - B_j \log_{10} T_o}$$

and $T_o = 255.2 + 5/9T$ K, where T is the temperature of the oil in °F and A_j and B_j are given in Table 8.6 as a function of the oil's SAE number (see also Exercise 6.11).

We now illustrate the use of these results with an example.

Example 8.26   Load carrying capacity of a hydrodynamic journal bearing

Consider the following specifications of a hydrodynamic journal bearing:

> Oil inlet temperature = 120°F
> SAE 30 oil
> Shaft rotational speed = 3000 rpm
> Shaft diameter = 2.0 in.
> Journal length = 1.1 in.
> Radial clearance = 0.0013 in.

Let us determine the maximum load P that the bearing can support such that the Ocvirk number is less than 25 as well as the corresponding temperature rise, minimum oil film thickness, and value for the absolute viscosity.

We first create a main function **JournalLoad**, which, for a given value of the load, computes the temperature rise in the oil, the absolute viscosity of the oil, and the Ocvirk number. This function is supported by the following three sub functions:

> **AbsViscosity**—computes the absolute viscosity η
> **Ocvirk**—computes the Ocvirk number O_N
> **TempRise**—computes the temperature rise ΔT

We then use `fzero` to find a value of the maximum load P for which the Ocvirk number is equal to 25. The function file is

```
function [Omax, absvis, ex, temp] = JournalLoad(P)
global Tin SAE n d cd L
temp = Tin; Told = 0;
while abs(temp-Told)>0.1
  Told = temp;
  absvis = AbsViscosity(temp);
  ex = Ocvirk(absvis, P);
  deltaT = TempRise(temp, ex, P);
  temp = Tin+deltaT;
end
absvis = AbsViscosity(temp);
[ex, ocv] = Ocvirk(absvis, P);
Omax = 25-ocv;

function absvis = AbsViscosity(tempF)
global SAE
AandB = [9.1209 3.5605; 9.1067 3.5385; 8.9939 3.4777; 8.9133 3.4292; ...
         8.5194 3.2621; 8.3666 3.1884];
SAE10 = SAE/10;
absvis = 10^(10^(AandB(SAE10, 1)-AandB(SAE10, 2)*log10(255.2 ...
              +5/9*tempF))-7);

function [ex, ocv] = Ocvirk(vis, P)
global n d cd L
ocv = P/n/L/d/vis*(cd/L)^2;
ex = 0.21394+0.38517*log10(ocv)-0.0008*(ocv-60);

function deltaT = TempRise(temp, ex, P)
global Tin SAE n d cd L
QH = pi*d*(n)*L*ex*cd/2;
phi = atan(pi*sqrt(1-ex^2)/4/ex);
vis = AbsViscosity(temp);
Tr = pi^2*d^3*L*(n)*vis/cd/sqrt(1-ex^2)+0.5*P*ex*cd*sin(phi);
deltaT = (0.0640)*Tr*(n)/QH;
```

The script is

```
global Tin SAE n d cd L
Tin = 120;  SAE = 30;  n = 3000/60;
d = 2;  cd = .0026;  L = 1.1;
options = optimset('display', 'off');
P = fzero(@JournalLoad, 1000, options);
```

```
[Omax, absvis, ex, temp] = JournalLoad(P);
disp(['Maximum load = ' num2str(P) ' lb.'])
disp(['Temperature rise = ' num2str(temp-Tin) ' degrees F'])
disp(['Absolute viscosity = ' num2str(absvis) ' reyn'])
disp(['Minimum oil film thickness = ' num2str(0.5*cd*(1-ex)) ' inches'])
```

When executed, the script displays the following to the command window:

```
Maximum load = 1078.3427 lb.
Temperature rise = 58.6577 degrees F
Absolute viscosity = 2.1907e-006 reyn
Minimum oil film thickness = 0.0002855 inches
```

8.7 PDE TOOLBOX AND THE STRESS CONCENTRATION FACTOR FOR NOTCHES IN A THIN PLATE[13]

The Partial Differential Equation (PDE) Toolbox and its associated graphical user interface (GUI) is used to analyze several classes of two-dimensional field equations. One such class is the plane stress problem. Plane stress problems are approximations that are used to determine the stresses, strains, and displacements in thin plates of arbitrary shape and constant thickness h. For these plates, it is assumed that the stress σ_z normal to the plate's surface at $z = \pm h/2$ and the shear stresses σ_{xz} and σ_{yz} on this surface are zero and that the remaining stresses are independent of z.

We shall demonstrate the procedure for using this toolbox and GUI by determining the stress concentration factor in a rectangular steel plate in which two semicircular notches have been cut from opposing edges at the plate's middle. The plate's geometry and dimensions are shown in Figure 8.32. The plate is clamped at its left end and subjected to a force per unit length $F_x = 20$ N/cm acting in the positive x-direction at its right end. If the plate's thickness is 0.2 cm, then the stress in the positive x-direction at this edge is 100 N/cm^2. The Young's modulus for steel in the current units is 200×10^5 N/cm^2.

The PDE Toolbox requires that one describe the boundary conditions on each edge comprising its shape. Two types of boundary conditions are usually considered

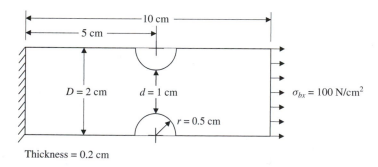

Figure 8.32   Notched plate under tension.

---

[13]See Example 11.8 of Section 11.3.3, for an application of the PDE Toolbox to flow visualization and Example 12.7 of Section 12.3.3 for an application to heat transfer.

in plane stress problems: the displacement is either zero or specified, and the boundary stress is either zero or specified. The specification of the displacements is denoted in the GUI as the *Dirichlet* boundary condition, and those for the stresses are denoted the *Neumann* boundary condition.

Consider the two components of the stress acting on a boundary segment that is at some arbitrary orientation with respect to the x,y-coordinate system. Using the notation of the GUI, if the component of the stress acting in the x-direction is g_1 and that in the y-direction is g_2, then

$$g_1 = n_x\sigma_{bx} + n_y\sigma_{bxy}$$
$$g_2 = n_y\sigma_{by} + n_x\sigma_{bxy}$$

where σ_{bx} is the stress on the boundary in the x-direction, σ_{by} is the stress on the boundary in the y-direction, and σ_{bxy} is the shear stress on the boundary. In addition, n_x and n_y are the direction cosines with respect to the x- and y-axis, respectively. Thus, on a boundary segment that is parallel to the x-axis, $n_x = 0$ and $n_y = \pm1$ (+1 is in the positive y-direction), and we specify the surface stresses as

$$g_1 = \pm\sigma_{bxy}$$
$$g_2 = \pm\sigma_{by}$$

If the shear stress on the boundary segment is zero—that is, if $\sigma_{bxy} = 0$—then $g_1 = 0$; conversely, if the normal stress $\sigma_{by} = 0$, then $g_2 = 0$. When the boundary segment is stress-free, then $g_1 = g_2 = 0$.

When we are dealing with a curved boundary segment (the arc of a circle or an ellipse), one specifies the boundary conditions as

$$g_1 = N*nx$$
$$g_2 = N*ny$$

where *nx* and *ny* are interpreted by the GUI as the direction cosines with respect to the x- and y-axis, respectively, and N is the *numerical* value for the magnitude of the stress normal to the curved boundary segment.

The process of using the PDE GUI to determine the stresses, strains, and displacements requires the following steps:

1. Set up the drawing area.
2. Specify the appropriate PDE—in this case, plane stress.
3. Draw (create) the 2D shape.
4. Specify the boundary conditions.
5. Specify the physical constants.
6. Generate the mesh.
7. Obtain the solution.
8. Display results.
9. Export arrays of numerical values generated by the GUI to the command window, if further analysis is desired.

We shall now give the detailed procedure for implementing each of these steps. At any step during this process, one can return to any previously completed step and make changes. Then, the previously completed subsequent steps must be implemented again. To access the GUI, type in the MATLAB command window

```
pdetool
```

which is a MATLAB function. This opens the PDE Toolbox GUI shown in Figure 8.33.

Set Up the Drawing Area

Based on the dimensions of the plate shown in Figure 8.32, we create a plotting area that is 12×4 units, where 1 unit = 1 cm. In addition, we show the grid lines and engage the snap-to-grid-points option by clicking on *Snap*. Thus, we click on the *Options* menu several times. First, we click on *Grid* so that a check (✓) appears. We then do the same with *Snap*. Next, we click on *Axis Limits*. In the menu window for *X-axis range,* we enter

[0 12]

and in the menu window for *Y-axis range*, we enter

[0 4]

Then, we click on *Apply* and then *Close*. Before clicking on *Apply,* make sure that the *Auto* boxes are blank. Lastly, we click on *Grid Spacing* and enter for *X-axis linear spacing*

0:0.5:12

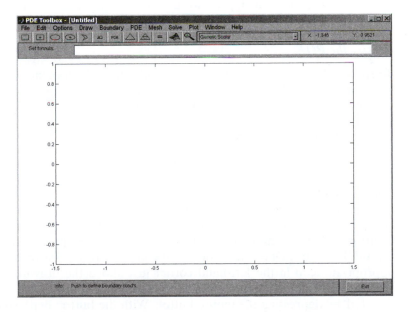

Figure 8.33   The PDE toolbox GUI.

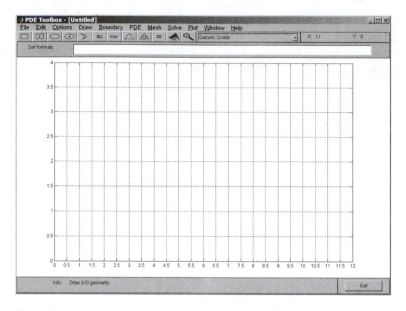

Figure 8.34   The result of setting up the drawing area.

and for *Y-axis linear spacing*

   0:0.5:4

Leave the areas for the extra tick marks blank, and make sure that the *Auto* boxes are also blank. Click on *Apply* and then on *Done*. The result of these selections is shown in Figure 8.34.

Specify the PDE

To specify the PDE, we go to the right-hand side of the toolbar; click on the arrowhead adjacent to the descriptor *Generic Scalar*, which appears when `pdetool` is first opened; and select *Structural Mech., Plane Stress*.

Draw (Create) the 2D Shape

The drawing routines use constructive solid geometry procedures to create a planar shape by performing either Boolean additions or subtractions on any combination of rectangles (squares), ellipses (circles), and *n*-sided polygons. Each of these entities can be placed anywhere within the drawing area previously created and can have any dimensions that do not exceed the bounds of the drawing area. The location of the crosshairs of the cursor is given in the upper right-hand corner of the GUI window. One selects one of the entities to be drawn by clicking on the appropriate icon in the left-hand corner just above the drawing area. Then, one places either a corner or the center of the entity, depending on which form has been selected, by depressing the mouse button. With the button depressed, the cursor is moved to the next location, and the mouse button is released. The engagement of the *Snap* option was selected to simplify this placement process.

After each entity is placed, an alphanumerical indicator appears both interior to the entity just created and in the data entry window above the drawing area and to the right of the denotation *Set formula*. The convention is *R* for a rectangle, *SQ* for a square, *E* for an ellipse, *C* for a circle, and *P* for a polygon. When an entity is placed, the sign of its alphanumeric indicator is assumed to be positive (+). To remove (subtract) an entity from another entity, one goes into this data area and changes the sign(s) of the appropriate entities to minus (−). After changing the sign(s), press *Enter* on the keyboard.

We now illustrate the steps needed to create the plate shown in Figure 8.32. First, we click on the toolbar symbol with the open rectangle. Then, we place the cursor at the coordinates (1, 1), click, and while still holding the mouse button down, drag the cursor to the coordinates (11, 3). Release of the mouse button produces a rectangle that is 10 × 2. If the placement or size is not what is desired, go to *Edit,* and select *Clear* or depress *Del* on the keyboard. When more than one entity has been placed, one must first click on the entity that is to be deleted; otherwise, all entities may be deleted. The entity selected will have a black border.

Next, we select the centered ellipse (circle), place the cursor at (6, 1), click the mouse button, and while still depressing it, move the cursor until a circle of diameter 1 appears. On the drawing area, it will appear elliptical, because the axes are unequal. The process is repeated with another circle centered at (6, 3). We also turn off the grid lines, as they are no longer needed. The result of these operations is shown in Figure 8.35.

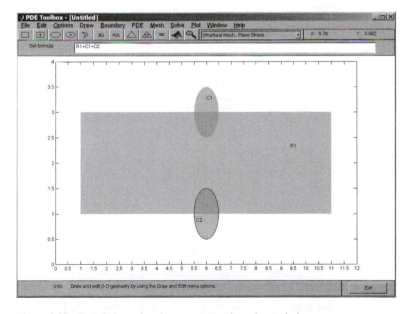

Figure 8.35   Result from drawing one rectangle and two circles.

In the *Set formula* area, we change

$R1+C1+C2$

to

$R1-C1-C2$

and hit *Enter*.

Specify the Boundary Conditions

Before we specify the boundary conditions on each boundary segment, we must instruct the GUI to perform the set operations. Thus, we first go to *Boundary* and select *Boundary Mode*. The results of this operation produce Figure 8.36. This places the figure in the drawing area in the boundary selection mode.

Next, we work our way around each of these boundary segments, which are identified as that portion of the boundary that starts from the tip of one arrowhead to the tip of an adjacent one. The boundary conditions can be specified on each segment in any order; however, it is suggested that one traverse the boundary in either a clockwise or a counterclockwise direction to minimize the possibility of missing a segment. Here, we start at segment 1 and proceed clockwise around the boundary.

When we click on segment 1, it changes color from red to black. Then, we double-click on the segment to bring up the *Boundary Conditions* window for that segment only. This edge is fixed and, therefore, will have zero displacements. As mentioned previously, the specification for the displacements is denoted the Dirichlet

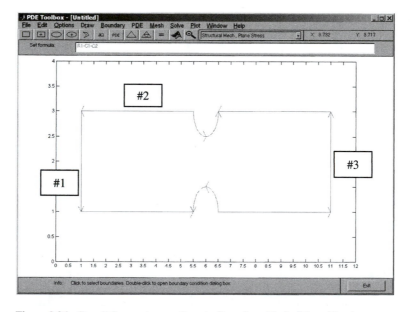

Figure 8.36   Result from set operations in *Boundary Mode*. [Note: Numbers on figure are not part of the display.]

type of boundary condition. Thus, under *Condition Type,* we select *Dirichlet*. Since the displacements are zero, we can use the default conditions: $h_{11} = h_{22} = 1$ and $h_{12} = h_{21} = r_1 = r_2 = 0$. Remember that the displacement symbol shown at the top of the menu window, u, represents two vector components: one is the displacement in the x-direction, and the other a displacement in the y-direction. Thus, r_1 is associated with the displacement in the x-direction and r_2 with the displacement in the y-direction. Click *OK* to close the boundary condition window. Notice that the color of the line segment remains red.

Since the remaining boundary segments are either stress-free or have a known stress applied to it (segment 3), they are all of the Neumann type. Thus, for segment 2 and all the other stress-free boundary segments, we employ the following procedure: Again, we double-click on the segment, and for *Condition Type,* we select *Neumann* and leave all the values at their default values, which are zeros. Click *OK* to close the boundary condition window. Notice that the line segment is now blue. This procedure is repeated for the remaining line segments, except segment 3. For segment 3, we again select *Neumann*. However, for the value of g_1, we enter the value 100, which stands for $100 \ (\text{N/cm}^2)$. The remaining default values are left as they are.

Specify the Physical Constants

To specify the physical constants for the plate, we go to *PDE* and select *PDE Specification*. For the value of E, we enter 200e5 and accept the default values of $nu = 0.3$ (Poisson's ratio) and $rho = 1$ (mass density). Since this is a static problem, density is not used. Then, we click *OK*.

Generate the Mesh

To have the system generate the mesh, we select *Initialize Mesh* from the *Mesh* menu. This results in Figure 8.37. If the mesh appears to be too coarse, then we return to the *Mesh* menu and select *Refine Mesh*. This results in Figure 8.38. Each time *Refine Mesh* is selected, the size of the mesh triangles becomes smaller.

Obtain the Solution

To obtain the solution, we can select *Solve PDE* from the *Solve* menu, or we can click on the '=' icon.

Display Results

To display the various results in a form that best illustrates them, one goes to the *Plot* menu and selects *Parameters*. The selections are reasonably self-explanatory. The distribution of σ_{xx} is shown in Figure 8.39. This was created by selecting *Color* and *Contour* under *Plot Type* and by selecting *x stress* in the first selection box under *Property*.

Figures 8.34 to 8.39 were saved as individual screen images. They could have also been saved as encapsulated postscript level 2 files with a 'tiff' image so that they could be viewed when placed in an MS Word document. This is done in the following manner. In the *File* menu, *Print* is selected. In the *Device Option* data area, we enter

```
-deps2 -tiff
```

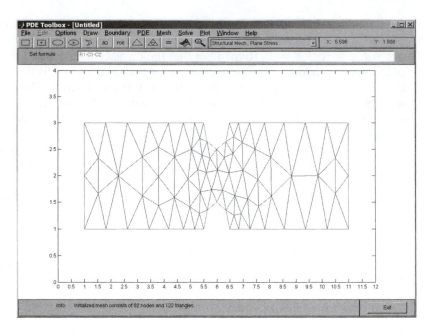

Figure 8.37   Result from *Initialize Mesh*.

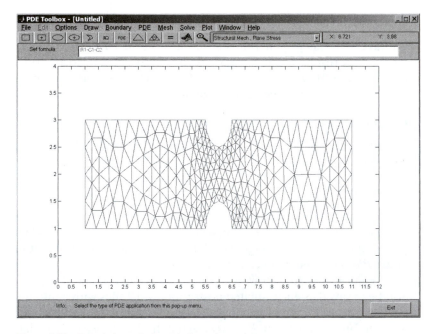

Figure 8.38   Result from *Refine Mesh* used one time.

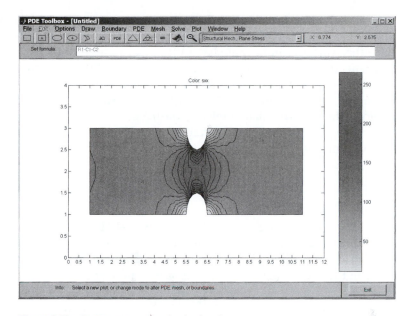

Figure 8.39   Stress contours and color bar for σ_{xx}.

and press *Enter*. In the *Send To* area, we select *File* and then click *Save*. This opens a typical *Save As* window, and the directories and file name are selected in the usual manner. The file name should end with the suffix ".eps." For other options, see the help file for `print`.

To transfer the figure to the Windows clipboard, we instead use,

    -dmeta

and then select *Printer*.

Export Arrays of Numerical Values Generated by the GUI to the Command Window

To determine the stress concentration factor, we need the value of the maximum stress σ_{xx}. Therefore, we must first transfer (export) the appropriate results to the command window. In this window, we use

    StressX = pdesmech(p, t, c, u, 'tensor', 'sxx');

to obtain an array of values for σ_{xx} and then use `max` to find the maximum value. Here, p gives the coordinates of the points in the mesh, e describes the edges of the mesh triangles, t describes the triangles, and u is the solution. See the *Help* file for `initmesh`. All these quantities are exported from the GUI in the following manner: Recall that to use the results in the command window, they must have a variable name. One can use the names provided by MATLAB, which are the names appearing in the argument list in the function statement above, or one can change them if they conflict with previously defined global variables. If they are changed, then they must also be changed in the argument list of `pdesmech`.

The parameters p and t are exported to the command window by going to the *Mesh* menu and selecting *Export Mesh*. When the window appears with the variable names, click *OK*. If one were to now go to the command window and type *p* (and press *Enter*), an array of values would appear. (This is not recommended, however, since these arrays can be quite large.) If one or more of the variable names were to be changed, they would be renamed at this time and then *OK* would be clicked.

The parameter *c* is exported to the command window by going to the *PDE* menu and selecting *Export PDE Coefficients*. Lastly, to export the solution array *u*, we go to the *Solve* menu and select *Export Solution*.

Now that the necessary variables have been exported to the command window, we employ the following two expressions to determine the maximum stress in the *x*-direction:

StressX = pdesmech(p, t, c, u, 'tensor', 'sxx');
MaxSxx = max(StressX)

which upon execution gives $MaxSxx$ = 298.3341 (N/cm^2).

To estimate the stress concentration factor, we compare σ_{xx} in an unnotched plate of cross-sectional area 0.2*d* to the maximum stress determined above. The stress in the unnotched plate σ_{xu} is approximately equal to

$$\sigma_{xu} = \frac{(100)(0.2)D}{0.2d} = 200 \quad \text{N/cm}^2$$

since D/d = 2. Then, the stress concentration factor S_{cc} is approximately

$$S_{cc} = \frac{298.3341}{200} = 1.491$$

This value compares favorably[14] with 1.37, which was obtained experimentally, and with 1.45, which is obtained from Nueber's nomograph.

A note of caution: Before using the pdetool to solve another problem, one should use clear to remove the variables *p*, *t*, *c*, and *a*. However, if new names will be assigned to these variables, then clear does not have to be used.

8.8 SUMMARY OF FUNCTIONS INTRODUCED

A summary of the functions introduced in the chapter and their descriptions are presented in Table 8.7.

TABLE 8.7   MATLAB Functions Introduced in Chapter 8

MATLAB function	Description
cross	Vector cross-product
dot	Vector dot product
norm	Vector and matrix norms
pdetool	Provides GUI for PDE Toolbox
pdesmech	Calculates structural mechanics tensor functions

[14]A. P. Boresi, R. J. Schmidt, and O. M. Sidebottom, *Advanced Mechanics of Materials*, 5th ed., John Wiley & Sons, New York, NY, 1993, pp. 582–584.

EXERCISES

Section 8.1

8.1 Referring to Figure 8.40, express the forces F_1, F_2, and F_3, and their resultant, as vectors. Determine the magnitude of the resultant and the angles of its direction cosines in degrees.   [Answers: $\mathbf{F}_1 = [56.5685 -42.4264 -70.7107]$; $\mathbf{F}_2 = [-26.9489 -33.6861 -67.3722]$; $\mathbf{F}_3 = [28.6401 \; 66.8268 -95.4669]$; $\mathbf{R} = \mathbf{F}_1 + \mathbf{F}_2 + \mathbf{F}_3 = [58.2597 - 9.2857 -233.5497]$, $|\mathbf{R}| = 240.8856$; $\alpha_R = [76.0039 \; 92.2092 \; 165.8235]$.]

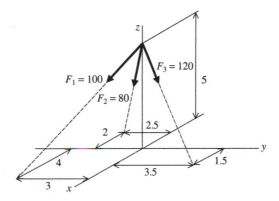

Figure 8.40   Orientation of forces for Exercise 8.1.

8.2 The system of ropes in Figure 8.41 is attached at the coordinate locations indicated. What are the magnitudes of $\mathbf{F}_1$, $\mathbf{F}_2$, and $\mathbf{F}_3$ and their respective components? [Answer: $\mathbf{F}_1 = [-44.9080 \; 44.9080 \; 67.3620]$; $|\mathbf{F}_1| = 92.5802$; $\mathbf{F}_2 = [81.2883 \; 54.1922 \; 108.3844]$; $|\mathbf{F}_2| = 145.9170$; $\mathbf{F}_3 = [0 - 74.84670]$; $|\mathbf{F}_3| = 74.8467$.]

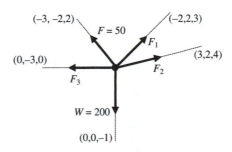

Figure 8.41   Orientation of forces for Exercise 8.2.

Section 8.2.1

8.3 Using the techniques of Section 8.2.1, plot the nondimensional deflection, slope, moment, and shear over the length of the beam, and give the maximum values and their locations for the following combinations of boundary conditions and loading:

a. Clamped at $\eta = 0$ and $\eta = 1$. Loading: Uniform across the length of the beam. [The analytical solution[15] to this set of conditions yields $y_{max}(\eta = 0.5) = -1/384$; $\theta_{max}(\eta = 0.2113$ or $0.7887) = -0.0080$; $M_{max}(\eta = 0$ or $1) = -1/12$; and $V_{max}(\eta = 0$ or $1) = 0.500.$]

b. Simply supported at $\eta = 0$ and clamped at $\eta = 1$. Loading: Uniform across the length of the beam. [The analytical solution[16] to this set of conditions yields $y_{max}(\eta = 0.4215) = -1/185$; $\theta_{max}(\eta = 0) = -1/48$; $M_{max}(\eta = 1) = -1/8$; and $V_{max}(\eta = 1) = 5/8.$]

c. Clamped at $\eta = 0$ and $\eta = 1$. Loading: Triangular, 0 at $\eta = 0$ and 1 at $\eta = 1$. [The analytical solution[17] to this set of conditions yields $y_{max}(\eta = 0.525) = -1/764$; $\theta_{max}(\eta = 0.8077) = 0.00427$; $M_{max}(\eta = 1) = -1/20$; and $V_{max}(\eta = 1) = -7/20.$]

Section 8.3

8.4 The contact stress on a gear tooth subjected to a uniform (nonvarying), tangentially transmitted load F_t is given by[18]

$$\sigma_c = Z_E \sqrt{\frac{K_v K_H F_t}{d_w b Z_I}} \quad N/mm^2$$

where Z_I is the geometry factor for pitting resistance, $d_w = 2R_{P_1}$ is the operating pitch diameter of the pinion (gear 1) and R_{P_1} is defined in Table 8.4, and Z_E is the elastic coefficient. The remaining quantities are defined in Section 8.3.

The elastic coefficient is given by

$$\frac{1}{Z_E} = \sqrt{\pi \left[\frac{1 - v_1^2}{E_1} + \frac{1 - v_2^2}{E_2} \right]}$$

where v_1 and v_2 are the Poisson's ratio for the pinion and gear, respectively, and E_1 and E_2 are the Young's modulus of the pinion and gear, respectively. When both the pinion and the gear are steel, $Z_E = 190 \ (N/mm^2)^{1/2}$.

The geometry factor for pitting resistance is given by

$$Z_I = \frac{\rho_1 \rho_2 \cot(\varphi)}{C d_p}$$

$$\rho_1 = \sqrt{R_{T_1}^2 - R_{b_1}^2} - m\pi \cos(\varphi_s)$$

$$\rho_2 = (R_{b_1} + R_{b_2}) \tan(\varphi) - \rho_1$$

[15] W. Beitz, and K. H. Kuttner, *ibid.*, p. B24.
[16] W. Beitz, and K. H. Kuttner, *ibid.*, p. B23.
[17] W. Beitz, and K. H. Kuttner, *ibid.*, p. B24.
[18] J. R. Colbourne, *ibid.*, 1987.

where $d_p = N_1 m$ is the diameter of the pinion pitch circle and the remaining quantities are defined in Tables 8.4 and 8.5.

Once the contact stress σ_c has been computed, the permissible stress σ_H must be determined and verified to be greater than that caused by F_t—that is, $\sigma_c \leq \sigma_H$, where the permissible contact stress is

$$\sigma_H = \frac{\sigma_{HP} Z_N Z_w}{F_{sc} Y_Z}$$

for oil or gear temperatures less than 120°C. The quantity F_{sc} is the factor of safety for pitting, Y_Z is the reliability factor defined in Section 8.3, Z_N is the pitting resistance stress cycle factor, σ_{HP} is the allowable contact stress number for pitting, and Z_w is the hardness ratio factor for pitting resistance.

The allowable contact stress number for pitting of through-hardened steel gears is estimated from

$$\sigma_{HP} = 2.41 B_H + 237$$

for grade 2 steel and from

$$\sigma_{HP} = 2.22 B_H + 200$$

for grade 1 steel for Brinell hardness in the range $180 \leq B_H \leq 400$.

The pitting resistance stress cycle factor is given by

$$Z_N = 1.4723 \quad n_L < 10^4$$
$$Z_N = 2.466 n_L^{-0.056} \quad n_L \geq 10^4$$

where n_L is the number of unidirectional tooth load cycles.

The hardness ratio factor for pitting resistance for surfaced hardened pinions driving through-hardened gears is estimated from

$$Z_w = 1 + 0.00075 e^{-0.448 R_z} (450 - B_{H_2}) \quad R_z \leq 1.6$$
$$Z_w = 1 \quad R_z > 1.6$$

where R_z is the surface finish of the pinion in μm and B_{H_2} is the Brinell hardness of the gear in the range $180 \leq B_{H_2} \leq 400$.

Now, consider the following pair of steel gears:

$m = 10$ mm	$b = 45$ mm	$n = 1800$ rpm	$B_{H_2} = 260$
$N_1 = 28$	$\varphi_s = 20°$	$T = 2500$ Nm	
$N_2 = 75$	$C = 525$ mm	$R_{T_1} = 153.9$ mm	

Determine the contact stress and the permissible contact stress when

The factor of safety is 1.2.
The number of unidirectional loading cycles is 4×10^8.
A grade 2 steel is used.
The surface finish of the pinion is 1.1 μm.
Less than 1 failure in 100 is desired.
$Q_v = 8$.

The gear is a type 2 gear as defined in Table 8.3. [Answer: $\sigma_c = 857.2436$ N/mm², and $\sigma_H = 636.2982$ N/mm².]

Section 8.4.2

8.5 Using the results of Example 8.21, draw the three positions of the links, and indicate the path of point P_1 as shown in Figure 8.25. The path of P_1 is determined using fsolve to obtain ψ and γ for 16 equally spaced values of ϕ ($\theta \leq \phi \leq \theta + \phi_2$) from the following equation:

$$\mathbf{Z}_2(e^{j\phi} - 1) - \mathbf{Z}_4(e^{j\psi} - 1) + (\mathbf{Z}_5 - \mathbf{Z}_6)(e^{j\gamma} - 1) = 0$$

The two required equations for fsolve are obtained by setting the real and imaginary parts of the above equation to zero. Do this numerically; that is, do not solve algebraically.

Section 8.5

8.6 Referring to the oscillating flat-faced follower shown Figure 8.42, we have the following relationships[19] for the x,y-coordinates R_x and R_y of the cam's profile and the cutter's coordinates C_x and C_y:

$$R_x = R \cos(\theta + \varphi + \xi_0) \qquad R_y = R \sin(\theta + \varphi + \xi_0)$$
$$C_x = C \cos(\theta + \varphi + \xi_0 - \gamma_0) \quad C_y = C \sin(\theta + \varphi + \xi_0 - \gamma_0)$$

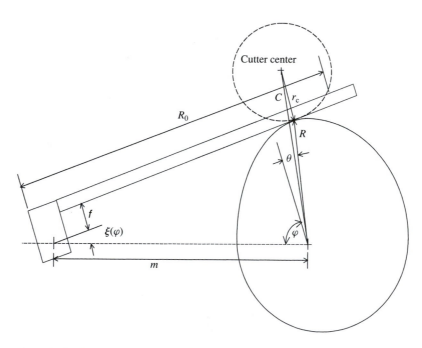

Figure 8.42   Oscillating flat-faced follower.

---

[19] A. G. Erdman and G. N. Sandor, *ibid.*, pp. 387–389.

where

$$R = \frac{f + m\sin(\xi)}{\cos(\theta)} \qquad \theta = \tan^{-1}\left[\left(\frac{d\xi/d\varphi}{1 - d\xi/d\varphi}\right)\frac{m\cos(\xi)}{f + m\sin(\xi)}\right]$$

$$C = \sqrt{c_x^2 + c_y^2} \quad c_x = r_c\sin(\theta) \qquad c_y = R + r_c\cos(\theta)$$

$$\gamma_0 = \tan^{-1}\left(\frac{c_y}{c_x}\right) \qquad \xi_0 = \sin^{-1}\left(\frac{r_b - f}{m}\right) \qquad \xi = \xi(\varphi) = \xi_0 + s(\varphi)/R_0$$

For cycloidal motion of the point R_0, $s(\varphi)$ is given in Section 8.5.1. Obtain a graph similar to those shown in Figures 8.29 and 8.31 when $\beta = 60°$, $r_b = 3.25$, $h = 0.5$, $r_c = 0.5$, $f = 0.5$, $m = 5$, and $R_0 = 9$.

Section 8.6

8.7 Consider the externally pressurized central recess thrust air bearing shown in Figure 8.43. Using the definitions given in Table 8.8, the normalized mass flow through the bearing for a given P_s is[20]

$$m' = P_s\sqrt{\left(\frac{P_1}{P_s}\right)^{2/k} - \left(\frac{P_1}{P_s}\right)^{(k+1)/k}}$$

where $m' = m/m_o$, $P_1 = p_1/p_a$, $P_s = p_s/p_a$, and P_1 is the solution to

$$P_1 = \sqrt{1 + BP_s^{(k-1)/2k}P_1^{1/k}\sqrt{P_s^{(k-1)/k} - P_1^{(k-1)/k}}}$$

when $P_1/P_s = p_1/p_s > P_c = [2/(k+1)]^{k/(k-1)}$ and P_1 is obtained from

$$P_1 = \sqrt{1 + BP_sP_c^{1/k}\sqrt{1 - P_c^{(k-1)/k}}}$$

when $P_1/P_s \le P_c$, which is the region wherein the flow is choked (the Mach number is equal to 1).

The normalized load that the bearing can support is

$$W' = \frac{\sqrt{\pi}}{2}\frac{r_1^2}{r_2^2}A_2\exp(P_1^2/A_2^2)\left[\mathrm{erf}\left(\frac{P_1}{A_2}\right) - \mathrm{erf}\left(\frac{1}{A_2}\right)\right]$$

where $W' = W/(\pi r_2^2 p_a)$, erf is the error function, and

$$A_2 = \sqrt{\frac{1 - P_1^2}{2\ln(r_1/r_2)}}$$

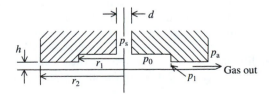

Figure 8.43　Air bearing geometry.

[20]W. A. Gross, *Gas Film Lubrication*, John Wiley & Sons, New York, NY, 1962, Chapter 5.

TABLE 8.8 Definition of Quantities in Gas Bearing Formulas

Quantity	Definition
C_D	Discharge coefficient
$A_o = \pi d^2/4$	Restrictor area
p_s	Supply pressure
p_o	Recess pressure
p_1	Inlet pressure
p_a	Ambient pressure
h	Gas film thickness
μ	Viscosity of gas
k	Ratio of specific heats (1.4 for air)
R	Gas constant (universal gas constant divided by molecular weight)
θ	Temperature (absolute scale)
$B = \dfrac{12C_D\mu A_o}{h^3 p_a \pi} \ln\!\left(\dfrac{r_2}{r_1}\right)\sqrt{\dfrac{(k-1)R\theta}{2k}}$	Bearing parameter
$m_o = \dfrac{1}{C_D A_o p_a}\sqrt{\dfrac{(k-1)R\theta}{2k}}$	Mass flow parameter
m	Mass flow
W	Bearing load

   a. Determine the values of P_1 when $B = 2$ and (i) $P_s = 2$ and (ii) $P_s = 10$. In using `fzero`, set the search range to $[0.1\ P_s]$. [Answer: (i) $P_1 = 1.4016$; (ii) $P_1 = 2.4852$.]

   b. Determine the values of m' and W' when $r_1/r_2 = 0.1$, $B = 2$, and (i) $P_s = 2$ and (ii) $P_s = 10$. [Answer: (i) $m' = 0.4822$, $W' = 0.0954$; and (ii) $m' = 2.5880$, $W' = 0.4147$.]

Section 8.7

8.8 Using the procedure outlined in Section 8.7, estimate the maximum stress for the cases of circular and elliptical holes in a plate. The three cases are shown in Figure 8.44. The boundaries of the holes are stress-free. For these three cases, let $\sigma = 1$ in the positive y-direction and $\sigma = -1$ in the negative y-direction. Also, let the Young's modulus equal 200×10^3. Use *Refine Mesh* once. For case a, let $a = 1$ (unit); for cases b and c let $b = 1$ (unit) and $a = 2$. [Answers: Case a: For the case of the circular hole, the analytically obtained[21] maximum stress ratio is $\sigma_{yy}/\sigma = 3$; the PDE solution gives 2.9122, or 2.9% lower. Case b: For an elliptical hole with the load perpendicular to the major axis, the analytical solution[22] is $\sigma_{yy}/\sigma = 1 + 2a/b$, which for our case gives $\sigma_{yy}/\sigma = 5$; the PDE solution gives $\sigma_{yy}/\sigma = 4.2264$, or 15.5% lower. Case c: For an elliptical hole with the load perpendicular to the minor axis, the analytical solution[23] is $\sigma_{yy}/\sigma = 1 + 2b/a$, which for this case gives $\sigma_{yy}/\sigma = 2$; the PDE solution gives $\sigma_{yy}/\sigma = 2.3552$, or 17.8% higher.]

---

[21] A. P. Boresi et al., *ibid.*, pp. 566–567, 569.
[22] A. P. Boresi et al., *ibid.*, pp. 568–569.
[23] A. P. Boresi et al., *ibid.*, p. 570.

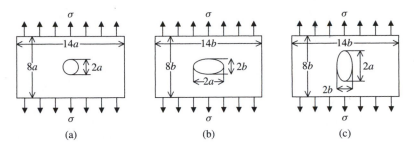

Figure 8.44 (a) Plate with circular hole; (b) plate with elliptical hole and load perpendicular to major axis; (c) plate with elliptical hole and load perpendicular to minor axis.

Additional Topics

8.9 Consider the Belleville conical spring shown in Figure 8.45. The nondimensional load P', nondimensional spring rate (spring constant) k', and nondimensional maximum compressive stress σ' as a function of the spring deflection δ are given by,[24] respectively,

$$P' = \frac{P}{P_0} = C_1 C_2 \qquad\qquad P_0 = \frac{Et^4}{(1 - \nu^2)b^2}$$

$$k' = \frac{k}{k_0} = C_2[1 + 1.5d_t^2 - 3d_t h_t + h_t^2] \quad k_0 = \frac{P_0}{t}$$

$$\sigma'_{max} = \frac{\sigma_{max}}{\sigma_0} = -d_t[C_3(h_t - 0.5d_t) + C_4] \quad \sigma_0 = \frac{P_0}{t^2}$$

where

$$C_1 = 0.5d_t^3 - 1.5h_t d_t^2 + (1 + h_t^2)d_t$$

$$C_2 = \pi\left(\frac{\alpha + 1}{\alpha - 1} - \frac{2}{\ln(\alpha)}\right)\left(\frac{\alpha}{\alpha - 1}\right)^2$$

$$C_3 = \frac{\alpha^2}{(\alpha - 1)^2}\left(\frac{\alpha - 1}{\ln(\alpha)} - 1\right)$$

$$C_4 = \frac{\alpha^2}{2(\alpha - 1)}$$

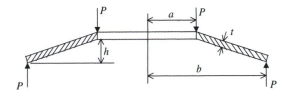

Figure 8.45 Cross-section of a Belleville conical spring.

[24]A. H. Burr and J. B. Cheatham, *Mechanical Analysis and Design*, 2nd ed., Prentice Hall, Upper Saddle River, NJ, 1995, pp. 652–656.

and v is Poisson's ratio, E is Young's modulus, $\alpha = b/a$, $h_t = h/t$, $d_t = \delta/t$. The maximum compressive stress occurs at the inner boundary a on the upper surface of the cone and is usually stipulated as $\sigma_{max} = \sigma_p/F_s$, where σ_p is the maximum permissible stress and F_s is the factor of safety.

Find the values of α and h_t and the corresponding value of k' when $d_t = 0.6667h_t$, $P' = 2.0$, and $\sigma'_{max} = -4.5$. [Answer: $\alpha = 3.3049$, $h_t = 1.5533$, and $k' = 0.2460$.]

8.10 Referring to Figure 8.46, the sizing of helical compression springs that are subjected to cyclic loading is governed by the following equations: The first is the factor of safety F_s due to stresses in the spring coils

$$F_s = \frac{S_{eL}(S_u - \sigma_L)}{S_{eL}(\sigma_m - \sigma_L) + S_u\sigma_a} > 1$$

where

$$\sigma_L = K_s F_{min} K_1 \qquad K_1 = \frac{8C}{\pi d^2} \qquad C = \frac{D}{d}$$

$$\sigma_m = K_s F_m K_1 \qquad F_m = 0.5(F_{max} + F_{min})$$

$$\sigma_a = K_w F_a K_1 \qquad F_a = 0.5(F_{max} - F_{min})$$

$$K_s = 1 + \frac{1}{2C} \qquad K_w = \frac{4C - 1}{4C - 4} + \frac{0.615}{C}$$

$$S_u = 0.67 A d^b \qquad S_e = \frac{0.707 S_{eL} S_u}{S_u - 0.707 S_{eL}}$$

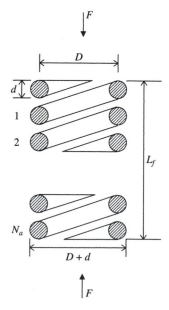

Figure 8.46 Nomenclature for a helical spring.

and F_{max} is the maximum load and F_{min} is the minimum load that is applied to the spring, S_{eL} is the endurance limit for infinite life, S_e is the endurance limit for fully reversed loading, S_u is the ultimate shear strength, D is the mean diameter of the spring, and d is the diameter of the wire. The constants a and b for cold drawn wire are $a = 141{,}040$ psi and $b = -0.1822$. For peened spring-steel wire, where $d < 0.4$ in., $S_{eL} = 67{,}500$ psi.

The second equation determines the spring rate (constant) k and is given by

$$k = \frac{dG}{8N_a C^3}$$

where G is the shear modulus of the material and N_a is the number of active coils of the spring. For steel, $G = 11.5 \times 10^6$ psi.

The last equation ensures that the unloaded spring length L_f, the coil diameter d, and the maximum applied load F_{max} are such that the steel spring doesn't buckle. Then, for both ends hinged,

$$\frac{F_{max}}{kL_f} = 0.8125\left[1 - \sqrt{1 - 6.865(Cd/L_f)^2} \right]$$

where $Cd = D$ and

$$L_f = d(N_a + 2) + 1.15 F_{max}/k - 0.15 F_{min}/k$$

which provides for 15% clash allowance.

For the peened spring-steel with $N_a = 7$, $F_{max} = 200$ lb., $F_{min} = 40$ lb., $F_s = 1.4$, and $k = 125$ lb./in., determine D and d. Will the spring buckle? [Answer: $d = 0.251$ in., $D = 1.8682$ in., and $C = 7.4432$. The spring will not buckle.]

8.11 The torque required by a power-driven screw to raise a load W is

$$T_{raise} = \frac{Wd_p}{2}\left[\frac{\mu + \tan(\lambda)\cos(\alpha)}{\cos(\alpha) - \mu\tan(\lambda)} + \mu_c \frac{d_c}{d_p} \right]$$

where λ is the lead angle obtained from

$$\tan(\lambda) = \frac{L}{\pi d_p}$$

and μ is the coefficient of friction of the threads, μ_c is the coefficient of friction of the collar (nut), d_p is the pitch diameter of the thread, d_c is the mean diameter of the collar, $L = mp$ is the lead, $p = 1/N_t$ is the pitch, N_t is the number of threads per inch, and m is the number of start threads. The angle α is the thread angle, which is $14.5°$ for an Acme thread. Also, for Acme threads, $1.9° < \lambda < 6°$. The efficiency e of the thread and collar is

$$e = \frac{WL}{2\pi T_{raise}} = \tan(\lambda)\left[\frac{\mu + \tan(\lambda)\cos(\alpha)}{\cos(\alpha) - \mu\tan(\lambda)} + \mu_c \frac{d_c}{d_p} \right]^{-1}$$

When $\mu_c = 0$,

$$e = \frac{\cos(\alpha) - \mu\tan(\lambda)}{\cos(\alpha) + \mu\cot(\lambda)}$$

The horsepower required to raise the load at a rate of v_r feet per minute is

$$hp = \frac{v_r T_{\text{raise}}}{2626 d_{\text{p}}}$$

where T_{raise} is in in.-lb.

For a single-start $(m = 1)$ Acme thread whose pitch diameter is 1.0 in. and lead angle is $4°$, find the torque and horsepower required to raise 800 lb. at a rate of 15 feet per minute when the mean diameter of the collar is 1.25 in. The coefficient of friction for the thread is 0.13 and that for the collar 0.04. What is the efficiency of the system? [Answer: $T_{\text{raise}} = 102.4558$ in.-lb., $e = 27.3003\%$, and $hp = 0.58524$.]

8.12 The power limitation based on the fatigue strength of the link plates in a link chain is

$$hp = K_s N_1^{1.08} n_1^{0.9} p^{3-0.07/p}$$

where N_1 is the number of teeth in the smaller sprocket; n_1 is the rotational speed in rpm of the smaller sprocket; p is the pitch, which the distance between the pin centers of the links; and $K_s = 0.004$ for regular weight chains. Find the pitch when $N_1 = 21$ teeth, $n_1 = 1750$ rpm, and $hp = 10$. [Answer: $p = 0.46453$.]

BIBLIOGRAPHY

"Fundamental Rating Factors and Calculation Methods for Involute Spur and Helical Gear Teeth," AGMA Standard ANSI/AGMA 2002-C95, American Gear Manufacturers Association, 1500 King Street, Alexandria, VA, 22314.

W. Beitz and K. H. Kuttner, Eds., *Handbook of Mechanical Engineering*, Springer-Verlag, New York, NY, 1994.

S. R. Bhonsle and L. J. Weinmann, *Mathematical Modeling for the Design of Machine Components*, Prentice Hall, Upper Saddle River, NJ, 1999.

A. H. Burr and J. B. Cheatham, *Mechanical Analysis and Design*, 2nd ed., Prentice Hall, Upper Saddle River, NJ, 1995.

J. R. Colbourne, *The Geometry of Involute Gears*, Springer-Verlag, New York, NY, 1987.

A. D. Dimarogonas, *Computer-Aided Machine Design*, Prentice Hall, Upper Saddle River, NJ, 1989.

A. G. Erdman and G. N. Sandor, *Mechanical Design: Analysis and Synthesis*, 2nd ed., Prentice Hall, Upper Saddle River, NJ, 1991.

R. C. Hibbeler, *Engineering Mechanics: Statics*, 8th ed., Prentice Hall, Upper Saddle River, NJ, 1998.

P. J. Jensen, *Cam Design and Manufacture*, 2nd ed., Marcel Dekker, Inc., New York, NY, 1987.

R. L. Norton, *Design of Machinery*, McGraw-Hill, New York, NY, 1992.

R. L. Norton, *Machine Design: An Integrated Approach*, Prentice Hall, Upper Saddle River, NJ, 1996.

H. A. Rothbart, *Cams: Design, Dynamics, and Accuracy*, John Wiley & Sons, New York, NY, 1956.

J. E. Shigley and C. R. Mischke, *Mechanical Engineering Design*, 5th ed., McGraw-Hill, New York, NY, 1989.

A. H. Slocum, *Precision Machine Design*, Prentice Hall, Upper Saddle River, NJ, 1992.

M. F. Spotts and T. E. Shoup, *Design of Machine Elements*, Prentice Hall, Upper Saddle River, NJ, 1998.

C. E. Wilson, *Computer Integrated Machine Design*, Prentice Hall, Upper Saddle River, NJ, 1997.

Dynamics and Vibrations

Balakumar Balachandran

Various methods are presented to analyze the dynamics of rigid bodies, the free and forced oscillations of linear and nonlinear systems with one and more degrees of freedom, and the vibrations of thin beams.

9.1 ORBITAL MOTIONS

Consider a system of two bodies in a gravitational field, shown in Figure 9.1, where the mass m_2 is fixed and the mass m_1 orbits m_2 in a plane. The coordinates describing the orbiting mass are the radial distance variable r and the angular variable θ.

For a satellite orbiting about the earth, m_2 is the mass of the earth, m_1 is the mass of the satellite, and r is the nondimensional radial distance between their centers. The radius of the earth r_e has been used to make the radial distance between centers nondimensional. The governing equations of motion are given by[1,2]

$$\frac{d^2r}{d\tau^2} - r\left(\frac{d\theta}{d\tau}\right)^2 = -\frac{4\pi^2}{r^2}$$

$$r\frac{d^2\theta}{d\tau^2} + 2\frac{dr}{d\tau}\frac{d\theta}{d\tau} = 0 \tag{9.1}$$

In Eqs. 9.1, t is time, P_c is the period of a circular orbit at the earth's surface, and the nondimensional time $\tau = t/P_c$. At the surface of m_2, $r = 1$.

Although a closed-form solution of the nonlinear system given by Eqs. 9.1 is available,[3] numerical solutions will be sought for a given set of initial conditions:

$$r(0) \quad dr(0)/d\tau \quad \theta(0) \quad d\theta(0)/d\tau$$

For compactness, this set of initial conditions will be written sometimes as

$$(r(0), dr(0)/d\tau, \theta(0), d\theta(0)/d\tau)$$

Equations 9.1, which provide an example of a differential dynamical system, describe the evolution of states r and θ with respect to τ. In general, a differential dynamical system is a set of differential equations that describes the evolution of the considered states with respect to an independent variable, such as time. When a dynamical system consists of ordinary-differential equations, such as that given by Eqs. 9.1, a solution of these equations for a given set of initial conditions can be determined through numerical integration with respect to the independent variable.

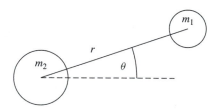

Figure 9.1   A two-body system.

[1]D. T. Greenwood, *Principles of Dynamics*, 2nd ed., Prentice Hall, Englewood Cliffs, NJ, 1988, Chapter 5.
[2]F. C. Moon, *Applied Dynamics with Applications to Multibody and Mechatronic Systems*, John Wiley & Sons, New York, NY, 1998, Chapter 7.
[3]D. T. Greenwood, *ibid.*

Example 9.1   Orbital motions for different initial conditions

We shall determine the orbits of mass m_1 for the three sets of initial conditions shown in Table 9.1. Although the type of orbit realized in each case is not known *a priori*, the orbit type that was determined after analyzing the numerical results is also shown in the last column of the table.

We first introduce the new variables,

$$x_1 = r \qquad x_3 = \theta$$
$$x_2 = \frac{dr}{d\tau}, \qquad x_4 = \frac{d\theta}{d\tau}$$

and rewrite Eqs. 9.1 as the following set of four first-order differential equations:

$$\frac{dx_1}{d\tau} = x_2$$

$$\frac{dx_2}{d\tau} = x_1 x_4^2 - \frac{4\pi^2}{x_1^2}$$

$$\frac{dx_3}{d\tau} = x_4 \tag{9.2}$$

$$\frac{dx_4}{d\tau} = -\frac{2x_2 x_4}{x_1}$$

The three orbits are obtained and plotted for the three sets of initial conditions using the following script:

```
function OrbitMotion
initcond = [2.0, 0.0, 0.0, 1.5; 1.0, 0.0, 0.0, 2.0*pi; 2.0, 0.0, 0.0, 4.0];
tspan = linspace(0, 5, 1000);
options = odeset('RelTol', 1e-6, 'AbsTol', [1e-6 1e-6 1e-6 1e-6]);
for i = 1:3
   [t, x] = ode45(@orbit, tspan, [initcond(i,:)]', options);
   polar(x(:,3), x(:,1), 'k-');
   hold on
end
text(0.50, -1.30, 'Elliptical orbit');
text(-2.10, 1.00, 'Circular orbit');
text(1.75, 2.00, 'Hyperbolic orbit');

function xdot = orbit(t, x)
xdot = [x(2); x(1)*x(4)^2-4.0*pi^2/x(1)^2; x(4); -2.0*x(2)*x(4)/x(1)];
```

TABLE 9.1   Three Sets of Initial Conditions

Set	$x_1(0)$	$x_2(0)$	$x_3(0)$	$x_4(0)$	Orbit type
1	2.0	0.0	0.0	1.5	Elliptical
2	1.0	0.0	0.0	2π	Circular
3	2.0	0.0	0.0	4.0	Hyperbolic

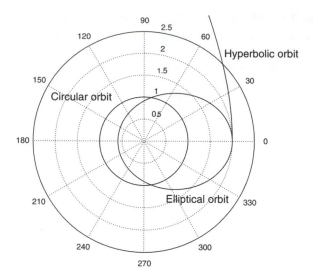

Figure 9.2   Orbits from Eq. 9.1 for three sets of initial conditions given in Table 9.1.

The three sets of initial conditions are provided in the array labeled *initcond*. A conservative spacing of 1000 equally spaced locations is used in the specified time interval to minimize numerical errors that may lead to spurious solutions. In addition, odeset is used to set the relative tolerance to 10^{-6} and the absolute tolerance for each of the four states—namely, x_j, where $j = 1, 2, 3, 4$.

Execution of the script results in Figure 9.2. The first set of initial conditions leads to an elliptical orbit, the second set of initial conditions to a circular orbit, and the third set of initial conditions to a hyperbolic orbit. This last orbit, which is an open orbit, is associated with unbounded motion.[4] Open orbits represent escape trajectories from earth and are not considered for satellite motions. In addition, the elliptical orbit is not realistic, since the satellite will crash into the earth's surface for $r < 1$.

When systems such as those given by Eqs. 9.1 are numerically integrated, one has to be aware that spurious solutions may be obtained during the integration. Usually, in problems such as the present one, there is a constant of motion (here, the angular momentum per unit mass $r^2 d\theta/d\tau$) that does not change with time. If a spurious solution were obtained, this constant would vary with time. For other systems without damping, one can determine whether the sum of the kinetic energy and potential energy remains constant during the numerical integration. It is good practice, therefore, to determine whether a different result is obtained when the step size and/or the tolerances are changed (see Exercise 9.1).

9.2 SINGLE-DEGREE-OF-FREEDOM SYSTEMS

9.2.1 Introduction

Consider a spring-mass-damper system with a mass m, a spring with linear spring constant k and nonlinear spring coefficient α, and a damper with damping coefficient c.

---

[4]D. T. Greenwood, *ibid.*, p. 211.

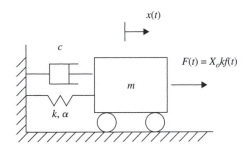

Figure 9.3   Spring-mass-damper system.

The mass is subjected to an excitation $F(t) = X_o kf(t)$. This system, which is illustrated in Figure 9.3, is a prototypical model used to study mechanical systems ranging from washing machines to vehicles.[5]

If x describes the displacement of the system, then the governing equation of motion is of the form

$$\frac{d^2 x}{d\tau^2} + 2\zeta \frac{dx}{d\tau} + x + \hat{\alpha} x^3 = X_o f(\tau) \tag{9.3}$$

where $\tau = \omega_n t$ is the nondimensional time and the damping factor ζ is given by

$$\zeta = \frac{c}{2m\omega_n} \tag{9.4}$$

In Eq. 9.4, the natural frequency ω_n is given by

$$\omega_n = \sqrt{k/m} \tag{9.5}$$

and the coefficient of the nonlinearity $\hat{\alpha}$ is given by

$$\hat{\alpha} = \frac{\alpha}{m\omega_n^2} \tag{9.6}$$

The nonlinear system given by Eq. 9.3 is said to have a softening spring when $\hat{\alpha}$ has a negative value and a hardening spring when $\hat{\alpha}$ has a positive value.[6]

---

[5]D. J. Inman, *Engineering Vibration*, Prentice Hall, Englewood Cliffs, NJ, 1994; S. S. Rao, *Mechanical Vibrations*, 3rd ed., Addison-Wesley, Reading, MA, 1995; B. H. Tongue, *Principles of Vibration*, Oxford University Press, New York, NY, 1996; B. Balachandran and E. B. Magrab, *Vibrations*, Thomson Brooks/Cole, Belmont, CA, 2003, Chapter 3.
[6]A. H. Nayfeh and B. Balachandran, *Applied Nonlinear Dynamics: Analytical, Computational, and Experimental Methods*, John Wiley & Sons, New York, NY, 1995; B. Balachandran and E. B. Magrab, *ibid.*, p. 38.

Equation 9.3 is put into state-space form by introducing the new variables:

$$x_1 = x$$

$$x_2 = \frac{dx}{d\tau}$$

Then, Eq. 9.3 becomes

$$\frac{dx_1}{d\tau} = x_2$$

$$\frac{dx_2}{d\tau} = -2\zeta x_2 - x_1 - \hat{\alpha}x_1^3 + X_o f(\tau)$$

(9.7)

Before considering several solutions to Eq. 9.7, we create a function **FreeOscillation** in a form that can be used by ode45. Thus,

```
function xdot = FreeOscillation(t, x, zeta, AlphaHat)
xdot = [x(2); -2*zeta*x(2)-x(1)-AlphaHat*x(1)^3];
```

When the function is used for a linear system, $AlphaHat = \hat{\alpha} = 0$.

9.2.2 Free Oscillations of Linear Systems

When $\hat{\alpha} = F(\tau) = 0$, we have the free motion of a linear system. Then, Eq. 9.3 becomes

$$\frac{d^2x}{d\tau^2} + 2\zeta\frac{dx}{d\tau} + x = 0$$

(9.8)

The characteristic equation of this system is

$$\lambda^2 + 2\zeta\lambda + 1 = 0$$

(9.9)

When $\zeta = 0.1$, the values of λ can be found from

```
lambda = roots([1, 0.2, 1])
```

which upon execution gives $\lambda_1 = -0.1000 + 0.9950i$ and $\lambda_2 = -0.1000 - 0.9950i$, where $i = \sqrt{-1}$. The real parts of both the roots are negative, indicating that the system is stable; this is characteristic of underdamped systems.[7] For an under-damped system,

$$|\text{Re}(\lambda_j)| = \zeta \quad \text{and} \quad |\lambda_1| = |\lambda_2| = 1$$

---

[7]D. J. Inman, *ibid.*, p. 19; S. S. Rao, *ibid.*, p. 130; B. H. Tongue, *ibid.*, p. 25; B. Balachandran and E. B. Magrab, *ibid.*, p. 155.

Example 9.2   Oscillations of a single-degree-of-freedom system for given initial velocity and initial displacement

We now determine the free response of the linear spring-mass-damper system given by Eq. 9.8 for the initial conditions

$$x(0) = x_o$$

$$\frac{dx(0)}{d\tau} = v_o$$

and for three values of the damping factor ζ: $\zeta = 0.1$, an underdamped case; $\zeta = 1$, the critically damped case; and $\zeta = 5.0$, an overdamped case. The system is set in motion from the initial conditions $x_o = 1$ and $v_o = 1$.

To determine the free response over the range $0 \leq \tau \leq 40$, the script is

```
zeta = [0.1, 1.0, 5.0];  AlphaHat = [0.0, 0.0, 0.0];
tspan = linspace(0, 40, 400);
lintyp = char('-k', '--k', '-.k');
for i = 1:3
    [t, x] = ode45(@FreeOscillation, tspan, [1 1]', [], zeta(i), AlphaHat(i));
    figure(1);
    plot(t,x(:,1),lintyp(i,:));
    hold on
    figure(2);
    plot(x(:,1), x(:,2), lintyp(i,:));
    hold on
end
figure(1)
xlabel('\tau');
ylabel('x(\tau)');
axis([0, 40, -1.5, 1.5]);
plot([0, 40], [0, 0], 'k-')
legend('\zeta=0.1', '\zeta=1.0', '\zeta=5.0')
figure(2)
xlabel('Displacement');
ylabel('Velocity');
legend('\zeta=0.1', '\zeta=1.0', '\zeta=5.0', 'Location', 'NorthWest')
axis([-1.5, 1.5, -1.5, 1.5]);
```

The results shown in Figure 9.4 are obtained by executing this script. The displacement responses are shown at the top, and the displacement-versus-velocity plots are shown at the bottom. The space $(x, \dot{x})$, which is formed using the displacement and velocity coordinates, is called the phase space. The collections of trajectories that are initiated in this space from different sets of initial conditions constitute a phase portrait. The equilibrium position of the linear system given by Eq. 9.8 corresponds to the location $x_1 = 0$ and $x_2 = 0$ [or (0.0, 0.0)] in the phase space. It is seen from the time histories that there are oscillations only in the underdamped case, which correspond to the spiral trajectory in the phase portrait. As time unfolds, this trajectory is attracted to the location (0.0, 0.0), which is the equilibrium position, and is an example of a point attractor. No oscillations are observed as the system approaches the equilibrium position in the critically damped and overdamped cases. When the system is critically damped, the trajectory reaches the equilibrium position in the shortest time.

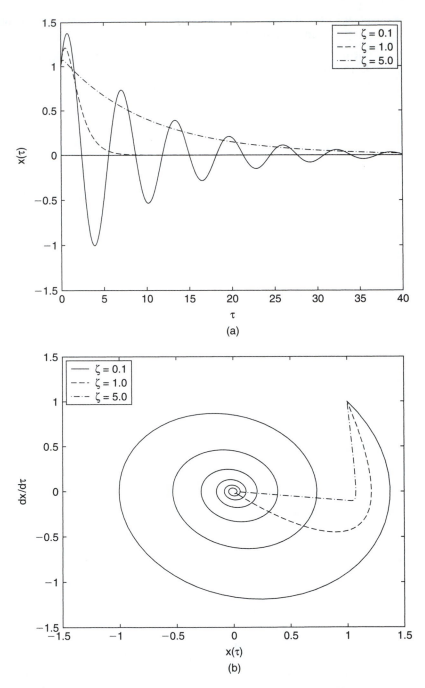

Figure 9.4   (a) Displacement histories and (b) phase portraits for the free oscillations of a damped, linear oscillator.

Logarithmic Decrement

The damping factor ζ can be obtained from the displacement response of an underdamped system on the basis of the logarithmic decrement δ; this is given by[8]

$$\delta = \frac{1}{n}\ln\left(\frac{x_j}{x_{j+n}}\right) \tag{9.10}$$

The damping is related to δ by

$$\zeta = \frac{\delta^2}{\sqrt{4\pi^2 + \delta^2}} \tag{9.11}$$

The x_j and x_{j+n} are the displacements at t_j and $t_j + nT$, respectively, where T is the period of the underdamped oscillation. One way to determine δ is to determine the magnitudes the various maxima (minima) and then determine the period T from the times at which they occur. From these results, the x_j are determined.

Example 9.3   Estimate of damping from the logarithmic decrement

Referring to Figure 9.5, which is the free response of an underdamped system, the following function is created to estimate the system's damping coefficient:

```
function [pspace, tref] = period(tdata, xdata, n, nskip)
[xmin0, tmin0] = min(xdata((1+nskip):length(xdata)));
[xmax0, tmax0] = max(xdata((1+nskip):length(xdata)));
```

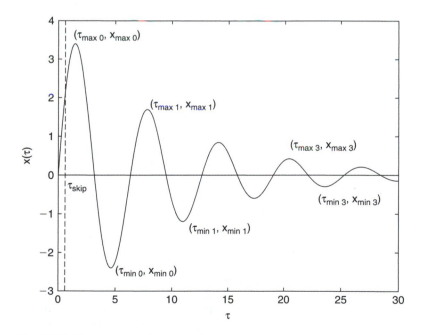

Figure 9.5   Free response of an underdamped system.

[8]D. J. Inman, *ibid.*, p. 44; S. S. Rao, *ibid.*, p. 136; B. Balachandran and E. B. Magrab, *ibid.*, p. 145.

```
tmin0 = tmin0+nskip;  tmax0 = tmax0+nskip;
m = fix(length(tdata)/(abs(tmin0-tmax0)*2.0));
while n>m
   n = n-1;
end
pspace = zeros(n, 1);
tref = zeros(n+1, 1);
for j = 1:n
   if tmin0 < tmax0
      tref(1) = tmin0;
      if j == 1
         [xmin1, tmin1] = min(xdata(tmax0:length(xdata)));
         pspace(j) = (tmax0−tmin0)+tmin1;
         tref(j+1) = tref(j)+pspace(j);
      else
         [xmaxj, tmaxj] = max(xdata(tref(j):length(xdata)));
         [xminj, tminj] = min(xdata(tref(j)+tmaxj:length(xdata)));
         pspace(j) = tmaxj+tminj;
         tref(j+1) = tref(j)+pspace(j);
      end
   else
      tref(1) = tmax0;
      if j == 1
         [xmax1, tmax1] = max(xdata(tmin0:length(xdata)));
         pspace(j) = (tmin0−tmax0)+tmax1;
         tref(j+1) = tref(j)+pspace(j);
      else
         [xminj, tminj] = min(xdata(tref(j):length(xdata)));
         [xmaxj, tmaxj] = max(xdata(tref(j)+tminj:length(xdata)));
         pspace(j) = tmaxj+tminj;
         tref(j+1) = tref(j)+pspace(j);
      end
   end
end
```

The input quantities to *period* are the time *tdata*, the corresponding response *xdata*, the number of cycles *n*, and the number of initial data points to skip *nskip*. The output from *period* comprises the arrays *pspace* and *tref*, which are, respectively, the index spacing between the peaks (or valleys) and the corresponding time indices. The functions max and min are used to determine the times at which the peaks (maxima) and the valleys (minima) occur and the time between them. The second and third lines of the function are used to determine the location of the first valley and the first peak, respectively. Since gradient is not used to ascertain the presence of extrema, errors can be made in ascertaining the extrema—in particular, the first extremum. For example, in the data shown in Figure 9.5, the first data point can be mistaken for the first minimum if the min function is used on the data starting from $\tau = 0$. To avoid this, the input parameter called *nskip* has been provided to specify the starting point of the data set.

The spacing between a maximum (minimum) and a subsequent minimum (maximum) corresponds to a half period of the damped oscillation. This fact is made use of in the fifth line to estimate the total number of cycles *m* in *xdata*. If the number of specified input cycles *n* is larger than *m*, then *n* is set to a value that is less than or equal to *m*. Following the initialization of the arrays *pspace* and *tref* in the ninth and tenth lines, respectively, the spacing between the extrema (either maximum or minimum) is determined within the for loop. Logic has been provided within this loop to distinguish between cases when the first extremum is a minimum and cases when the first extremum is a maximum. In the latter case, the index spacing between the peaks and the associated time indices are determined. For the other cases, the index spacing between the valleys and the associated time indices are determined. The extrema determined by **period** can be used as a basis to determine the period of damped oscillation over different cycles.

Although for a linear system the period of damped oscillation does not change over different cycles, this is not so for nonlinear systems. In the following script, the output from **period** is used with Eq. 9.10 to obtain an estimate of the logarithmic decrement from the response of a system given by Eq. 9.8. The system parameters are $\zeta = 0.3$ and $\hat{\alpha} = 0.0$, and the response is initiated from $x_0 = 0.0$ and $v_0 = -10.0$.

```
zeta = 0.3; AlphaHat = 0.0;
tspan = linspace(0.0, 40.0, 400);
[t, x] = ode45(@FreeOscillation, tspan, [0 -10]', [], zeta, AlphaHat);
n = input(' Enter number of cycles ');
nskip = input(' Enter number of initial points to skip ');
[pspace, tref] = period(t(:,1),x(:,1), n, nskip);
zeta = zeros(length(pspace), 1);
fprintf(1,' Cycle Number   Damping Factor\n')
for j = 1:length(pspace)
   logdec = log(x(tref(j),1)/x(tref(j+1),1));
   zeta(j) = sqrt(logdec^2/(4.0*pi^2+logdec^2));
   fprintf(1,'   %3d        %6.4f\n',j,zeta(j))
end
```

The first two lines of the script are used to generate uniformly spaced data for the system given by Eq. 9.8. The function **period** is then called to determine the damping factor. Equations 9.10 and 9.11 are implemented in the 10th and 11th lines, respectively. When one executes this script with $n = 4$ and $nskip = 4$, the following results are displayed in the MATLAB command window:

```
Enter number of cycles  4
Enter number of initial points to skip  4
Cycle Number   Damping Factor
    1               0.3008
    2               0.3006
    3               0.2992
    4               0.3004
```

As expected, for a linear system in which energy is dissipated through viscous damping, the decay is exponential, and the logarithmic decrement remains constant over each cycle of the damped oscillation.

9.2.3 Free Oscillations of Nonlinear Systems

We shall now explore the oscillations of three nonlinear systems. In the first system, there is a nonlinear cubic spring that is described by Eq. 9.3 when $F(\tau) = 0$ and $\hat{\alpha} \neq 0$. In the second system, there is nonlinear damping, and in the third system, there is an undamped, planar pendulum.

Example 9.4   System with nonlinear spring

The motion of the system given by Eq. 9.3 is examined for the three cases presented in Table 9.2. The first case corresponds to a linear system; the second and third cases correspond to a nonlinear system with a softening spring. The initial conditions are the same in the first two cases and different for the third case.

The function **FreeOscillation** (created in Section 9.2.1) is used to describe the system given by Eq. 9.3. The following script generates the responses for the three cases. In addition, the period of each cycle of the response is determined along with an estimate of its damping factor.

```
zeta = 0.2; AlphaHat = [0.00, -0.25, -0.25];
xo = [-2.00, -2.00, -2.00];  vo = [ 2.00, 2.00, 2.31];
tspan = linspace(0.0, 30.0, 401);
lintyp = char('-k', '--k', '-k');
options = odeset('RelTol', 1e-8, 'AbsTol', [1e-8 1e-8]);
d = char('Linear: x_o=-2 v_o=2 \alpha=0', ...
    'Nonlinear: x_o=-2 v_o=2 \alpha=-0.25', ...
    'Nonlinear: x_o=-2 v_o=2.31 \alpha=-0.25');
for i = 1:3
    [t, x] = ode45(@FreeOscillation, tspan, [xo(i) vo(i)]', options, zeta, AlphaHat(i));
    figure(1)
    plot(t, x(:,1), lintyp(i,:))
    hold on
    figure(2)
    plot(x(:,1), x(:,2), lintyp(i,:))
    hold on
    fprintf(1, ['Case ' num2str(i) ' ' d(i,:)])
    [pspace, tref] = period(t, x(:,1), 3, 10);
    zetaest = zeros(length(pspace), 1);
    fprintf(1, '\n Cycle No.     Period       Damping Factor\n')
    for j = 1:length(pspace)
       per(j) = t(tref(j+1))-t(tref(j));
       logdec = log(x(tref(j),1)/x(tref(j+1),1));
       zetaest(j) = sqrt(logdec^2/(4.0*pi^2+logdec^2));
       fprintf(1,'   %3d        %8.3f           %6.4f\n', j, per(j), zetaest(j))
    end
end
figure(1)
xlabel('\tau')
ylabel('x(\tau)')
axis([0.0, 30.0, -3.0, 3.0])
legend(d(1,:), d(2,:), d(3,:))
figure(2)
```

TABLE 9.2   Parameters and Initial Conditions for Three Cases

Case	System type	$\hat{\alpha}$	ζ	$x(0) = x_o$	$dx(0)/d\tau = v_o$
1	Linear	0.00	0.20	−2.00	2.00
2	Nonlinear	−0.25	0.20	−2.00	2.00
3	Nonlinear	−0.25	0.20	−2.00	2.31

```
xlabel('x(\tau)')
ylabel('dx/d\tau')
legend(d(1,:), d(2,:), d(3,:))
axis([-2.0, 3.0, -2.0, 3.0])
```

Tolerances used during the integration are specified in the fifth line, and they are provided to ensure that numerical errors do not lead to spurious solutions.

The logarithmic decrement is not strictly applicable for estimating the damping factor of a nonlinear system. Here, it is used to illustrate that its application can lead to errors when estimating the damping factor based on "large" motions of a nonlinear system and to reasonable values when estimating the damping factor based on "small" motions of a nonlinear system. In addition, the results are used to illustrate that the period of oscillation of a nonlinear system can depend upon the response amplitude. When this script is executed, the output to the command window consists of the damping factor estimate over the different cycles of oscillation in each case. Graphs of the free oscillations for these three cases are shown in Figure 9.6.

Case 1 Linear: x_o=-2 v_o=2 alpha=0

Cycle No.	Period	Damping Factor
1	6.450	0.2002
2	6.450	0.2004
3	6.375	0.1996

Case 2 Nonlinear: x_o=-2 v_o=2 alpha=-0.25

Cycle No.	Period	Damping Factor
1	7.200	0.2319
2	6.450	0.2015
3	6.450	0.2005

Case 3 Nonlinear: x_o=-2 v_o=2.31 alpha=-0.25

Cycle No.	Period	Damping Factor
1	9.000	0.2589
2	6.450	0.2017

In case 1, which corresponds to the linear system, the period of the damped oscillation remains essentially constant over each cycle. In cases 2 and 3, which correspond to a nonlinear system, both the period of the damped oscillation and the damping factor estimated from the first cycle are significantly different from those estimated from the subsequent cycles of motion. The effect of the nonlinearity is typically pronounced when the amplitudes of motion are "large," as it is in the first cycle of oscillation in case 3. The behavior of the systems in cases 2 and 3 approaches that of the linear system (case 1) as the amplitudes of motion become "smaller."

As in the corresponding linear case, the orbits of the nonlinear system initiated from these sets of the initial conditions are attracted toward the stable equilibrium position (0.0, 0.0) in the phase portrait. The spirals in the phase portrait indicate that the corresponding motions of the nonlinear system are underdamped. For "small" oscillations around the stable equilibrium position, the nonlinear system should behave like a linear system. Examining the responses initiated from the two sets of initial conditions, the feature observed for case 3 around the first extremum in the time history is not typical of the response of a linear system. In this case, the trajectory comes "close" to the unstable equilibrium position (2.00, 0.00) of the system, and the system motion is affected. Unlike a linear system, a nonlinear system can have multiple equilibrium positions, not all of which are necessarily stable.[9]

---

[9]A. H. Nayfeh and B. Balachandran, *ibid.*

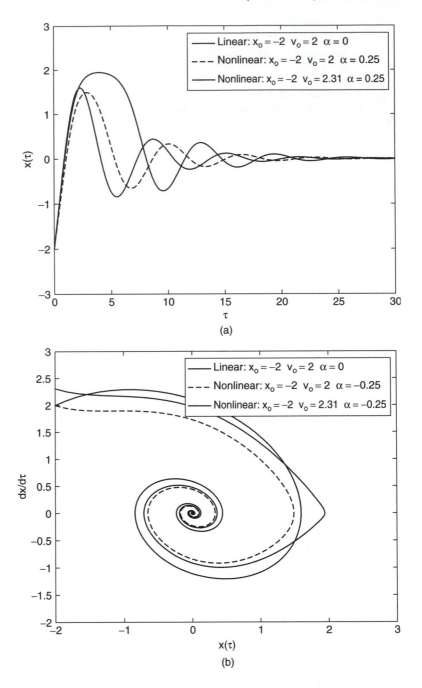

Figure 9.6   Free responses of damped, linear, and nonlinear oscillators:
(a) displacement histories; (b) phase portraits.

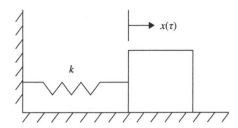

Figure 9.7 Spring-mass system with dry friction.

System with Nonlinear Damping

We now consider the spring-mass system with dry friction shown in Figure 9.7. This system is governed by

$$\frac{d^2x}{d\tau^2} + x + d\,\text{signum}(dx/d\tau) = 0 \tag{9.12}$$

where the constant $d = \mu mg/k$, μ is the friction coefficient, mg is the weight of the object, and k is the spring constant of the linear spring restraining the mass m. The dry friction force, which is a piecewise constant function of the velocity, is described by the signum function in Eq. 9.12. It has a value of $+1$ when the velocity is positive and of -1 when the velocity is negative. Since the dry friction force varies nonlinearly with respect to velocity, the system is nonlinear. When the system is set into motion, the system comes to rest when the spring force is no longer able to overcome the dry friction force. This means that the system will stop when

$$\frac{dx}{d\tau} = 0 \quad \text{and} \quad |x| \le d \tag{9.13}$$

The nonlinear system described by Eq. 9.12 has multiple equilibriums, and the locus of these equilibriums in the phase space is the straight line joining the points $(-d, 0)$ and $(d, 0)$.

Example 9.5   Response of a system with Coulomb damping

A closed-form solution of Eq. 9.12 can be obtained from the fact[10] that the system is linear in the region $dx/d\tau > 0$ and linear in the region $dx/d\tau < 0$. However, we shall obtain its numerical solution using ode45. First, Eq. 9.12 is rewritten in a state-space form by introducing the variables

$$x_1 = x$$

$$x_2 = \frac{dx}{d\tau}$$

---

[10]D. J. Inman, *ibid.*, Section 2.7; S. S. Rao, *ibid.*, Section 2.7.

This results in the following system of first-order equations:

$$\frac{dx_1}{d\tau} = x_2$$

$$\frac{dx_2}{d\tau} = -x_1 - d \, \text{signum}(x_2)$$

(9.14)

A sub function called **FreeOscillation2** is created to represent Eqs. 9.13 and 9.14. The numerical solutions of Eq. 9.12 are obtained for $d = 0.86$ and the following two sets of initial conditions: $(3.0, 0.0)$ and $(5.0, 0.0)$. The script is

```
function Coulomb
d = 0.86;  xo = [3.0, 5.0];  vo = [0.0, 0.0];
tspan = linspace(0, 12, 120);
options = odeset('AbsTol', [1e-3, 1e-3]);
lintyp = char('--k', '-k');
for i = 1:2
   [t, x] = ode45(@FreeOscillation2, tspan, [xo(i) vo(i)]', options, d);
   figure(1);
   plot(t, x(:,1), lintyp(i,:));
   hold on
   figure(2);
   plot(x(:,1), x(:,2), lintyp(i,:));
   hold on
end
figure(1)
xlabel('\tau');
ylabel('x(\tau)');
axis([0.0, 12.0, -4.0, 6.0]);
plot([0 12], [0 0], 'k-')
legend(['x_o=' num2str(xo(1))], ['x_o=' num2str(xo(2))])
plot([0, 12], [0, 0], 'k-')
figure(2)
xlabel('x(\tau)');
ylabel('dx/d\tau');
text(2.5, 0.5, '(3.0,0.0)');
text(4.5, 0.5, '(5.0,0.0)');
plot([-4 6], [0 0], 'k-', [0 0], [-6 4], 'k-')
axis([-4.0, 6.0, -6.0, 4.0]);

function xdot = FreeOscillation2(t, x, d)
if abs(x(1)) <= d & x(2) == 0.0
   xdot = [0; 0];
else
   xdot = [x(2); -d*sign(x(2))-x(1)];
end
```

The absolute tolerance specified for each state is larger than the default value of 1.0e-6 to speed up the computations. Execution of the script produces the results shown in Figure 9.8. The systems come to rest at two different positions, and the respective rest positions are reached at two different times. This example illustrates that the long time response of a nonlinear system depends upon the initial conditions. By contrast, the asymptotic response of a damped linear system is independent of the initial conditions.

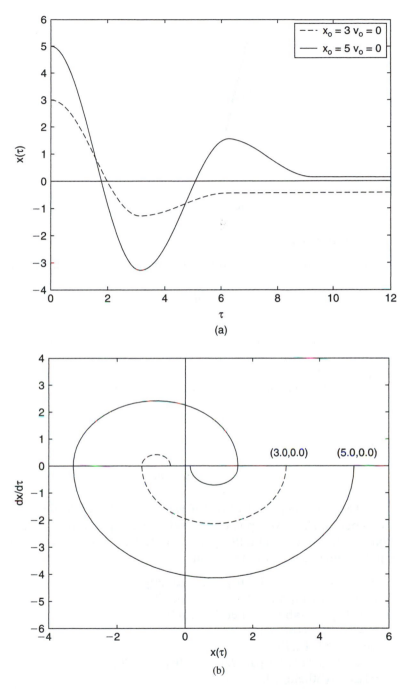

Figure 9.8 Free response of an oscillator with dry friction: (a) displacement histories; (b) phase portraits.

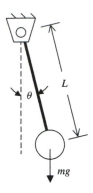

Figure 9.9   Planar pendulum.

Planar pendulum

The equation of motion of an undamped planar pendulum shown in Figure 9.9 is given by[11]

$$\frac{d^2\theta}{d\tau^2} + \sin\theta = 0 \tag{9.15}$$

where θ is the angular coordinate describing the pendulum motion, $\tau = t\sqrt{g/L}$ is the nondimensional time, g is the acceleration due to gravity, and L is the length of the pendulum.

The first integral of motion of Eq. 9.15 leads to

$$F(\theta_1, \theta_2) = \frac{1}{2}\theta_2^2 - \cos\theta_1 \tag{9.16}$$

where

$$\theta_1 = \theta \quad \text{and} \quad \theta_2 = \frac{d\theta}{d\tau}$$

The function given by Eq. 9.16 is plotted in Figure 9.10 by using the script provided below. The lowest point in the valley corresponds to a stable equilibrium position of the system and the peaks located at $\theta = \pm\pi$ correspond to unstable equilibrium positions of the system.

```
theta1 = linspace(-2.0*pi, 2.0*pi, 50];
theta2 = linspace(-2.0*pi, 2.0*pi, 50];
[T1, T2] = meshgrid(theta1, theta2);
F = T2.^2/2-cos(T1);
meshc(T1, T2, F);
axis([-2.0*pi, 2.0*pi, -2.0*pi, 2.0*pi, -5, 20]);
xlabel('\theta_1');
ylabel('\theta_2');
zlabel('F(\theta_1,\theta_2)');
```

---

[11]D. T. Greenwood, *ibid.*; B. Balachandran and E. B. Magrab, *ibid.*

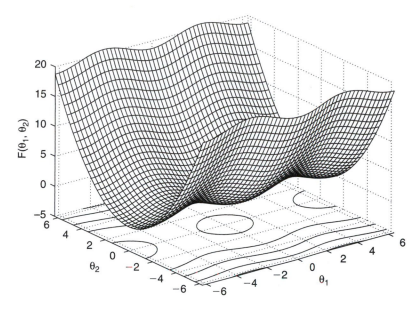

Figure 9.10   Surface $F(\theta_1, \theta_2)$ for planar pendulum.

9.2.4 Forced Oscillations of Linear and Nonlinear Systems

Responses of linear and nonlinear systems to harmonic excitations will be determined in the time domain using `ode45`. The corresponding information in the frequency domain will be determined with `fft`. (Recall Section 5.4.6.)

Consider the system given by Eq. 9.3. Let the forcing be harmonic—that is,

$$F(\tau) = X_o \cos(\Omega\tau) \tag{9.17}$$

where Ω is the nondimensional excitation frequency and X_o is a measure of the forcing amplitude. At a excitation frequency and excitation amplitude, we determine the steady-state response of the system given by Eq. 9.3—that is,

$$\lim_{t \to \infty} x(t)$$

and examine the spectral content of this response for the following cases: $\hat{\alpha} = 0$ (linear system) and $\hat{\alpha} \neq 0$ (nonlinear system).

Equation 9.3 is numerically integrated by `ode45` for the forcing function given by Eq. 9.17 and the following parameters: the initial conditions (0, 0); $\zeta = 0.4$; $\hat{\alpha} = 1.5$ (in the nonlinear case); $\Omega = 3.0$; and $X_o = 5.0$. The excitation frequency Ω has been chosen to be three times the natural frequency of the system. The data from this analysis are saved for use in the subsequent example. The script is

```
function NonlinearResponse
zeta = 0.4; AlphaHat = [0 1.5];
Omega = 3.0; Xo = 50.0;
```

```
tspan = linspace(0, 30, 6000);
sampint = tspan(2);
options = odeset('RelTol', 1e-8, 'AbsTol', [1e-8 1e-8]);
for m = 1:2
  [t, x] = ode45(@ForcedOscillator1, tspan, [0 0]', options, zeta, AlphaHat(m),
            Omega, Xo);
  if m == 1
    figure(1);
    plot(t, x(:,1));
    axis([0, 30, -8, 8]);
    xlabel('\tau');
    ylabel('x(\tau)');
    yy = x(:,1);
    save 'c:\path\ForcedOscLin.txt' yy -ascii;
  else
    figure(2);
    plot(t, x(:,1));
    axis([0, 30, -8, 8]);
    xlabel('\tau');
    ylabel('x(\tau)');
    yy = x(:,1);
    save 'c:\path\ForcedOscNonLin.txt' yy -ascii;
  end
end

function xdot = ForcedOscillator1(t, x, zeta, AlphaHat, Omega, Xo)
xdot = [x(2); -2*zeta*x(2)-x(1)-AlphaHat*x(1)^3+Xo*cos(Omega*t)];
```

where *path* is defined by the user.

Execution of the script results in Figure 9.11, where it is seen that the responses of both the linear and nonlinear systems reach steady state when $\tau \geq 8$. This time corresponds to an index $N_{start} = 1600$. Although both of the steady-state responses have a period equal to the period of the harmonic forcing function, they have different characteristics that can be more clearly distinguished in the frequency domain.

To obtain the information in the frequency domain, we will use `fft` on portions of the linear and nonlinear time histories saved in *ForcedOscLin.txt* and *ForcedOscNonLin.txt*, respectively. Then, using the results in Section 5.4.6, we determine the amplitude spectrum of each signal for $\tau \geq 8$. The sampling rate at which the data in *ForcedOscLin.txt* and *ForcedOscNonLin.txt* are acquired is $\tau_s = 30/6000$ $= 0.005$. Therefore, the (dimensionless) sampling frequency is $f_s = 1/\tau_s = 200$. This is far in excess of what is necessary to sample the response based on the excitation frequency $\Omega = 3$. The consequences are that we have to truncate the spectrum plot; thus, we shall display only the first 40 values. Also, we let $N_{start} = 3200$ and $N = 2^{11} = 2048$. The script is

```
load 'c:\path\ForcedOscLin.txt';
load 'c:\path\ForcedOscNonLin.txt';
```

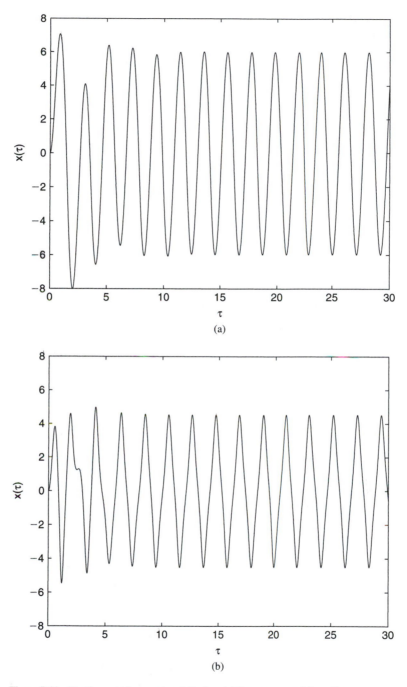

Figure 9.11 Response to harmonic exicitation: (a) linear system; (b) nonlinear system.

```
N = 2048; Nstart = 3200; Fs = 200;
f = (Fs*(0:N-1)/N)*2.0*pi;
figure(1)
AmpLin = abs(fft(ForcedOscLin(Nstart:Nstart+N), N))/N;
semilogy(f(1:40), 2*AmpLin(1:40));
xlabel('Frequency');
ylabel('Amplitude');
text(3.1, 10^4.5, '\Omega');
figure(2);
AmpNonLin = abs(fft(ForcedOscNonLin(Nstart:Nstart+N), N))/N;
semilogy(f(1:40), 2*AmpNonLin(1:40));
v = axis;
xlabel('Frequency');
ylabel('Amplitude');
text(3.1, 0.5*v(4), '\Omega');
text(9.1, 0.2*v(4), 3\Omega');
```

where *path* is defined by the user.

The execution of the script results in Figure 9.12, where it is seen that the amplitude spectrum of the displacement response in the nonlinear case shows spectral peaks at the forcing frequency Ω and integer multiples of it. The additional peaks are due to the cubic nonlinearity of the spring. In the linear case, there is only one spectral peak, which corresponds to the excitation frequency. The above example illustrates that the response of a nonlinear system can have spectral components different from the excitation frequency.

9.2.5 Frequency Response and the Responses to Step and Impulse Excitations

We now illustrate how to compute and display the frequency response curves for linear systems. Although the material of this section does not differ in principle from that presented in Section 9.2.4, it is presented to demonstrate the use of the functions

```
bode, tf, step, impulse, damp
```

from the Controls Toolbox. The transfer function of a linear time-invariant system (i.e., a system described by a differential equation with constant coefficients) can be represented in the form

$$G(s) = \frac{N(s)}{D(s)}$$

where $N(s)$ and $D(s)$ are polynomials in the complex variable s. The function

```
sys = tf(N, D)
```

is used to specify the system's transfer function when the arrays of coefficients for $N(s)$ and $D(s)$ are known.

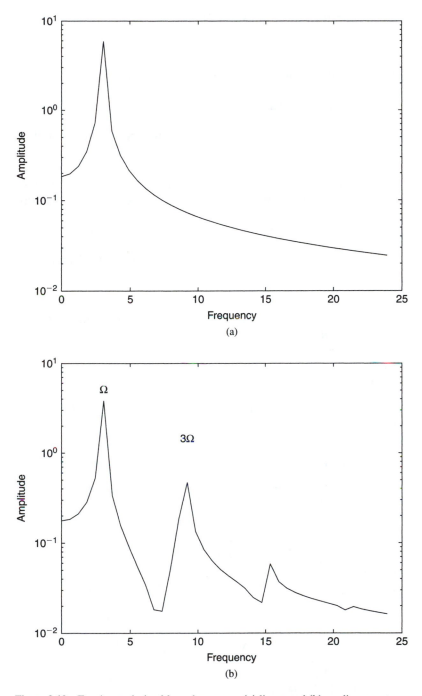

Figure 9.12   Fourier analysis of forced response: (a) linear and (b) nonlinear system.

The frequency response function $G(i\omega)$ can be computed and plotted with

```
bode(tf(N, D), w)
```

which plots the magnitude and phase of $G(i\omega)$, or with

```
[magnitude, phase] = bode(tf(N, D), w)
```

which provides arrays of numerical values for the magnitude and phase. The array w is either a two-element cell that specifies the minimum and maximum values of the frequency range of interest or an array of radian frequency values.

The functions impulse and step can be used to determine the impulse and step responses, respectively, of linear time-invariant systems set into motion from rest. Thus,

```
impulse(tf(N, D))
```

plots the impulse response of the system described by tf and

```
step(tf(N, D))
```

plots the response of a system to a unit step function applied at $t = 0$. (See Chapter 10 for additional applications of these functions.)

The function

```
[wn, zeta] = damp(tf(N, D))
```

is used to determine the damping factors ζ and natural frequencies ω_n of a linear time-invariant system from its transfer function.

Example 9.6   Frequency response—Bode plots

To illustrate these functions, consider again the system described by Eq. 9.3 with $\hat{\alpha} = 0$. Taking the Laplace transform,[12] the (nondimensional) transfer function for this system is

$$\frac{\bar{x}(s)}{X_o f(s)} = G(s) = \frac{1}{s^2 + 2\zeta s + 1} \tag{9.18}$$

Thus,

$$N(s) = 1$$
$$D(s) = s^2 + 2\zeta s + 1$$

and the arrays defining N and D are, respectively,

```
N = [0 0 1];
D = [1 2*zeta 1];
```

---

[12]L. Meirovitch, *ibid.*, Appendix B; B. Balachandran and E. B. Magrab, *ibid.*, p. 116.

The transfer function given by Eq. 9.18 is now used to construct the frequency response curves using tf and bode. The script is

```
zeta = 0.2:0.2:1.0;
omega = 0.0:0.01:3.0;
for i = 1:length(zeta)
   sys = tf([0, 0, 1], [1, 2*zeta(i), 1]);
   [mag, phas] = bode(sys, omega);
   figure(1)
   plot(omega, mag(1,:));
   hold on;
   figure(2)
   plot(omega, phas(1,:));
   hold on;
end
figure(1)
xlabel('Frequency ratio');
ylabel('Magnitude');
text(0.8, 2.7, '\zeta = 0.2');
text(0.8, 1.55, '\zeta = 0.4');
text(0.8, 0.4, '\zeta = 1.0');
hold on;
plot([0.0, 3.0], [1.0, 1.0], '-k');
v = axis;  v(2) = 2.5;
axis(v)
figure(2)
xlabel('Frequency ratio');
ylabel('Phase (degrees)');
text(0.7, -15.0, '\zeta = 0.2');
text(0.5, -80.0, '\zeta = 1.0');
hold on;
v = axis;  v(2) = 2.5;
axis(v)
plot([0.0, 3.0], [-90, -90], '-k');
plot([1.0, 1.0], [-200, 0], '-k');
```

The execution of this script results in Figure 9.13. The magnitude of the nondimensional transfer function is sometimes referred to as the magnification factor.

Example 9.7   Impulse response

We determine the impulse response of the system described by Eq. 9.18 for $\zeta = 0.1$, 1.0, and 3.0, which represent an underdamped system, a critically damped system, and an overdamped system, respectively. The script is

```
zeta = [0.2, 1.0, 3.0];  tfinal = 30;
tdata = linspace(0, tfinal, 100);
for i = 1:length(zeta)
   xdata = impulse([0 0 1], [1 2*zeta(i) 1], tdata);
```

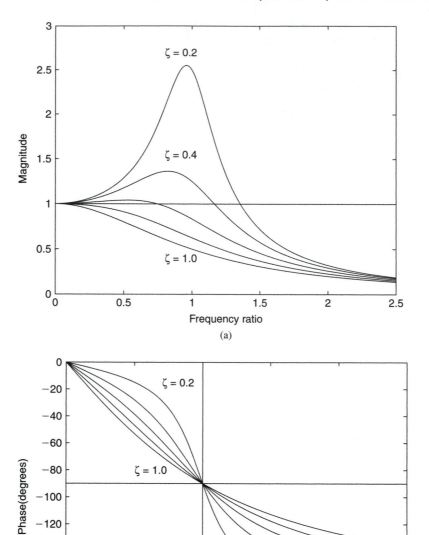

Figure 9.13 (a) Amplitude and (b) phase responses of a directly excited spring-mass-damper system.

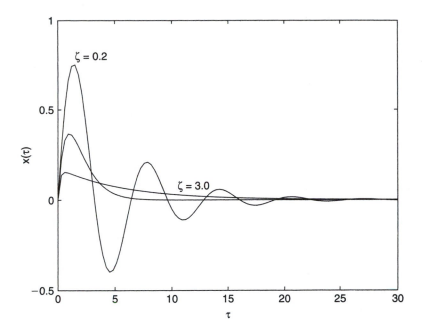

Figure 9.14 Impulse responses of underdamped, critically damped, and over-damped systems.

```
    plot(tdata, xdata);
    hold on;
end
axis([0.0, 30.0, -0.5, 1.0]);
xlabel('\tau');
ylabel('x(\tau)');
text(1.5, 0.8, '\zeta = 0.2');
text(10.5, 0.08, '\zeta = 3.0');
```

The results, which are shown in Figure 9.14, can also be obtained from the free-vibration response by integrating the time-domain counterpart of Eq. 9.18 from the set of initial conditions $(0, 1)$.

Example 9.8   Step response

We determine the step response of the system described by Eq. 9.18 for $\zeta = 0.2$, 1.0, and 3.0, which represent an underdamped system, a critically damped system, and an overdamped system, respectively. The script is

```
zeta = [0.2, 1.0, 3.0];  tfinal = 30;
tdata = linspace(0, tfinal, 100);
for i = 1:length(zeta)
    xdata = step([0, 0, 1], [1, 2*zeta(i), 1], tdata);
    plot(tdata, xdata, 'k-');
    hold on;
end
```

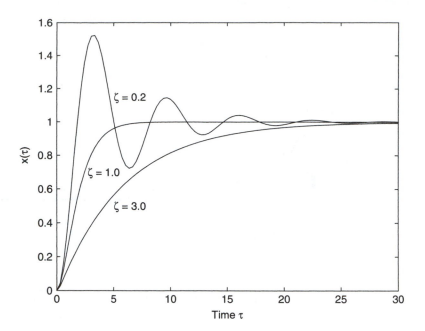

Figure 9.15 Step responses of underdamped, critically damped, and overdamped systems.

```
xlabel('\tau');
ylabel('x(\tau)');
text(5.0, 1.15, '\zeta = 0.2');
text(2.7, 0.70, '\zeta = 1.0');
text(5.0, 0.50, '\zeta = 3.0');
```

The results are shown in Figure 9.15. The response of the underdamped system oscillates about the steady-state position before settling down; the responses in the critically damped and overdamped cases are not oscillatory. In the critically damped case, the system settles to the steady-state position in the shortest amount of time.

Example 9.9   Estimation of ω_n and ζ for a damped oscillator

We shall determine the natural frequency and the damping for the system described by Eq. 9.18 for $\zeta = 0.3$. First, we model the system with $\zeta = 0.3$, and then we use damp to determine this value. The function damp determines the damping factors and associated natural frequencies from the poles of the transfer function. The script is

```
sys = tf([0 0 1], [1 2*0.3 1]);
[w, zeta] = damp(sys)
```

which upon execution gives $\omega_n = 1$ and $\zeta = 0.3$.

Example 9.10   Curve fitting of the frequency response function

From Eq. 9.18, the frequency response function is determined to be

$$G(i\omega) = \frac{A_o}{(1 - \omega^2) + 2i\zeta\omega} \tag{9.19}$$

whose magnitude is given by

$$|G(i\omega)| = \frac{A_o}{\sqrt{(1 - \omega^2)^2 + (2\zeta\omega)^2}} \tag{9.20}$$

In Figure 9.16, we show experimentally obtained data that has been fitted using Eq. 9.20. The data are shown with open circles, and the fitted curve is shown with a solid line. The MATLAB function `lsqcurvefit` from the Optimization Toolbox has been used. The estimated parameters are found to be $\zeta = 0.15$ and $\omega_n = 1.5$ rad/s. The script that is used to carry out the parameter estimation through curve fitting is

```
hh = inline('x(3)./sqrt((1-(w/x(1)).^2).^2+(2*x(2)*w/x(1)).^2)', 'x', 'w');
xo = [1.3, 0.1, 0.01];
ww = [0.0, 0.0769, 0.1538, 0.2308, 0.3077, 0.3846, 0.4615, 0.5385, ...
      0.6154, 0.6923, 0.7692, 0.8461, 0.9231, 1.000, 1.077, 1.154, ...
      1.231, 1.308, 1.385, 1.462, 1.538, 1.615, 1.692, 1.769, 1.846, ...
      1.923, 2.000, 2.077, 2.154, 2.231, 2.308, 2.384, 2.461, 2.538, ...
      2.615, 2.692, 2.769, 2.846, 2.923, 3.000];
hr = [0.0141, 0.01383, 0.01414, 0.01418, 0.01468, 0.01504, 0.01532, ...
      0.01550, 0.01666, 0.01784, 0.01879, 0.01958, 0.02156, 0.02354, ...
```

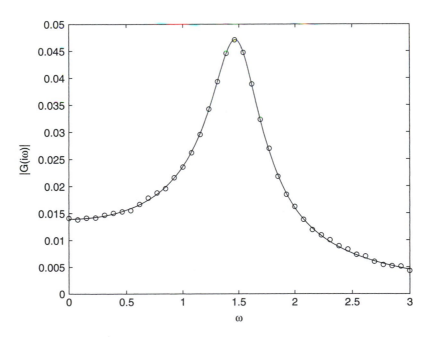

Figure 9.16   Curve fitting of frequency response.

0.02616, 0.02956, 0.03425, 0.03931, 0.04456, 0.04707, 0.04472, ...
0.03888, 0.03232, 0.02696, 0.02179, 0.01844, 0.01621, 0.01381, ...
0.01191, 0.0109, 0.01002, 0.0089, 0.0083, 0.0073, 0.0070, 0.0060, ...
0.0054, 0.0052, 0.00514, 0.0043];

```
x = lsqcurvefit(hh, xo, ww, hr);
w = linspace(0, 3, 200);
plot(w, hh(x, w), 'k-', ww, hr, 'ko')
xlabel('\omega')
ylabel('|G(i\omega)|')
```

In this script, the function to be curve fit; that is, Eq. 9.20, is represented by **hh**. The quantity x_o contains the initial guesses for ω_n, ζ, and A_o.

In Examples 9.7 through 9.10, different functions from the Controls Toolbox have been used for studying single-degree-of-freedom systems. They can also be used to study multidegree-of-freedom systems, as illustrated in Section 9.3.

9.2.6 Machine Tool Chatter

The vibration of the tool shown in Figure 9.17 can be described by[13]

$$\frac{d^2x}{d\tau^2} + \left(\frac{1}{Q} + \frac{K}{k\Omega}\right)\frac{dx}{d\tau} + \left(1 + \frac{k_1}{k}\right)x - \mu\frac{k_1}{k}x(\tau - 1/\Omega) = 0 \qquad (9.21)$$

where the nondimensional time $\tau = \omega_n t$ and

$$\Omega = \frac{N}{2\pi\omega_n} \quad \omega_n = \sqrt{\frac{k}{m}} \quad Q = \frac{1}{2\zeta} \quad 2\zeta = \frac{c}{m\omega_n} \qquad (9.22)$$

To study the possibility of chatter, a solution of the form

$$x = Ae^{\lambda\tau}$$

is assumed and introduced into Eq. 9.21 to obtain the characteristic equation

$$\lambda^2 + \left(\frac{1}{Q} + \frac{K}{k\Omega}\right)\lambda + 1 + \frac{k_1}{k}(1 - \mu e^{-\lambda/\Omega}) = 0 \qquad (9.23)$$

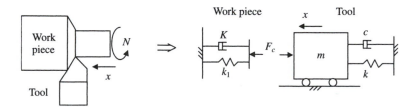

Figure 9.17   Model of a tool and work piece during turning.

---

[13]B. Balachandran and E. B. Magrab, *ibid.*, Section 4.5.

To find the stability boundary, we let $\lambda = i\omega$ and substitute into Eq. 9.23 to obtain the equations

$$\frac{1}{Q} + \frac{K}{k\Omega} + \frac{\mu k_1}{k}\frac{\sin(\omega/\Omega)}{\omega} = 0$$

$$\omega^2 = 1 + \frac{k_1}{k}(1 - \mu\cos(\omega/\Omega)) \tag{9.24}$$

In Eqs. 9.24, the quantities K/k, μ, and k_1/k are known, and the values of the non-dimensional spindle speed Ω are varied over a specified range. At each value of Ω, the value of ω is determined numerically from the second of Eqs. 9.24 by using `fzero`. The values for Ω and ω are then used in the first of Eqs. 9.24 to determine the positive values of Q that satisfy the equation—that is, those values of Ω and ω for which

$$\frac{1}{Q} = -\frac{K}{k\Omega} - \frac{\mu k_1}{k}\frac{\sin(\omega/\Omega)}{\omega}$$

Example 9.11   Stability charts for turning operations

In the plot of Ω versus Q, we can show the regions for which the system is either stable or unstable. For $K/k = 0.0029$, $k_1/k = 0.0785$, and $\mu = 1$, Eqs. 9.24 are solved numerically by using the script below. The results of the execution of the script are shown in Figure 9.18.

```
chat = inline('1-w.^2+k1k*(1-u*cos(w/Ob))', 'w', 'u', 'k1k', 'Ob');
k1k = 0.0785; Kk = 0.0029; u = 1;
```

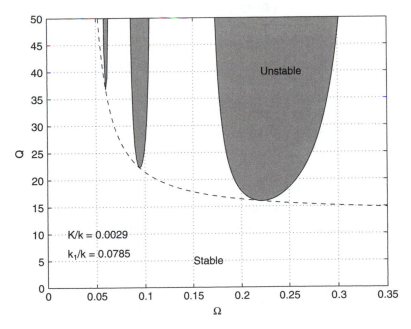

Figure 9.18   Stability chart for $K/k = 0.0029$, $k_1/k = 0.0785$, and $\mu = 1$.

```
Ob = linspace(0.03, 0.5, 300);
opt = optimset('Display', 'off');
L = length(Ob);
for n = 1:L
   w(n) = fzero(chat, [0.8 1.2], opt, u, k1k, Ob(n));
end
xx = -1./(Kk./Ob+u*sin(w./Ob)./w*k1k);
indx = find(xx>=0);
plot(Ob(indx), xx(indx), 'k-')
hold on
a = axis; a(4) = 50;
axis(a)
fill(Ob(indx), xx(indx), 'c')
B = sqrt(2)*sqrt(1+k1k-sqrt(1+2*k1k+(k1k^2)*(1-u^2)));
Qm = 1./(B-Kk./Ob);
ind = find(Ob<0.05);
plot(Ob(ind(end):L), Qm(ind(end):L), 'k--')
xlabel('\Omega')
ylabel('Q')
text(.22, 40, 'Unstable')
text(.15, 5, 'Stable')
text(0.02, 10, ['K/k=' num2str(Kk, 5)])
text(0.02, 6, ['k_1/k=' num2str(k1k, 5)])
grid on
```

9.3 MULTI-DEGREE-OF-FREEDOM SYSTEMS

9.3.1 Free Oscillations

We shall consider three different classes of problems that require the determination of the system's eigenvalues:

1. Principal moments of inertia
2. Stability of a rotating rigid body
3. Natural frequencies of a multidegree-of-freedom system

Principal Moments of Inertia

Consider the rigid body shown in Figure 9.19, which has three rotational degrees of freedom. The associated rotational inertia matrix has the form

$$I_{\text{rot}} = \begin{bmatrix} I_{xx} & I_{xy} & I_{xz} \\ I_{yx} & I_{yy} & I_{yz} \\ I_{zx} & I_{zy} & I_{zz} \end{bmatrix} \tag{9.25}$$

where the various moments of inertia are defined with respect to the coordinate system shown in Figure 9.19.

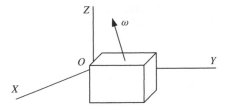

Figure 9.19   Rotation of a rigid body in a frame with Cartesian axes.

Example 9.12   Principal moments of inertia

We shall determine a new set of orthogonal axes such that the inertia matrix is diagonal. These axes are called the principal axes, and the associated moments of inertia are called the principal moments of inertia. The eigenvalues of Eq. 9.25 provide the principal moments of inertia, and the associated eigenvectors define the principal axes.[14] These two quantities are determined with eig as shown below. We also note that the sum of the eigenvalues of a matrix is equal to the trace of the matrix. The trace of a matrix is the sum of the diagonal elements of the matrix, and it is determined with trace. Furthermore, let

$$[I] = \begin{bmatrix} 150 & 0 & -100 \\ 0 & 250 & 0 \\ -100 & 0 & 500 \end{bmatrix} \text{kg} \cdot \text{m}^2 \tag{9.26}$$

The script is

```
Irot = [150, 0, -100; 0, 250, 0; -100, 0, 500];
[PrincipalDirections, PrincipalMoments] = eig(Irot)
TraceIrot = trace(Irot)
TracePM = trace(PrincipalMoments)
```

which upon execution produces

```
PrincipalDirections =
  -0.9665      0  -0.2567
       0  1.0000       0
  -0.2567      0   0.9665
PrincipalMoments =
  123.4436       0        0
         0  250.0000       0
         0        0  526.5564
TraceIrot =
  900
TracePM =
  900
```

Although the first eigenvector corresponds to the first eigenvalue, the second eigenvector corresponds to the second eigenvalue, and so forth, the eigenvalues (in this case, principal moments) are not in any particular order. This is typical of the results

---

[14]D. T. Greenwood, *ibid.*

obtained from eig. When the inertia matrix is examined, it is found that in this case, the y-axis is a principal axis and, hence, one of the eigenvalues is equal to I_{yy}. The matrix of principal directions defines a direction cosine matrix that can be used to transform the x,y,z-axes to the principal axes.

Stability of a Rigid Body

Consider the rigid body shown in Figure 9.19. Let I_1, I_2, and I_3, respectively, represent the second mass moments of inertia about the x-, y-, and z-axes that are chosen to be along the respective principal axes of the body—that is, the principal moments of inertia in the previous example. Let ω_1, ω_2, and ω_3 represent the respective angular velocities about these axes, and let M_1, M_2, and M_3 represent the respective external moments about these axes. The equations of motion, which are known as Euler's equations, are of the form[15]

$$
\begin{aligned}
I_1\dot{\omega}_1 + (I_3 - I_2)\omega_2\omega_3 &= M_1 \\
I_2\dot{\omega}_2 + (I_1 - I_3)\omega_3\omega_1 &= M_2 \\
I_3\dot{\omega}_3 + (I_2 - I_1)\omega_1\omega_2 &= M_3
\end{aligned}
\tag{9.27}
$$

where

$$
\dot{\omega}_j = \frac{d\omega_j}{dt} \quad j = 1, 2, 3
$$

In the moment-free case—that is, when $M_1 = M_2 = M_3 = 0$—there are three types of solutions where ω_j are constant with respect to time. These solutions, which are called the constant solutions, are as follows:

1. $(\omega_{10} \neq 0, \omega_{20} = 0, \omega_{30} = 0)$
2. $(\omega_{10} = 0, \omega_{20} \neq 0, \omega_{30} = 0)$
3. $(\omega_{10} = 0, \omega_{20} = 0, \omega_{30} \neq 0)$

Each of these solutions corresponds to pure rotational motions about one of the principal axes. We are interested in determining the stability of these three types of motions. To this end, we let ξ_j, where $j = 1, 2, 3$, represent the disturbances provided to the system about the respective axes—that is,

$$
\begin{aligned}
\omega_1(t) &= \omega_{10} + \xi_1(t) \\
\omega_2(t) &= \omega_{20} + \xi_2(t) \\
\omega_3(t) &= \omega_{30} + \xi_3(t)
\end{aligned}
\tag{9.28}
$$

After substituting Eqs. 9.28 into Eqs. 9.27 and assuming that the magnitudes of the disturbances are "small," one can linearize[16] Eqs. 9.27 and study the associated eigenvalue problem. This results in the following system of equations:

$$
\begin{bmatrix}
0 & (I_3 - I_2)\omega_{30}/I_1 & (I_3 - I_2)\omega_{20}/I_1 \\
(I_1 - I_3)\omega_{30}/I_2 & 0 & (I_1 - I_3)\omega_{10}/I_2 \\
(I_2 - I_1)\omega_{20}/I_3 & (I_2 - I_1)\omega_{10}/I_3 & 0
\end{bmatrix}
\begin{Bmatrix} \xi_1 \\ \xi_2 \\ \xi_3 \end{Bmatrix}
= \lambda \begin{Bmatrix} \xi_1 \\ \xi_2 \\ \xi_3 \end{Bmatrix}
\tag{9.29}
$$

---

[15]D. T. Greenwood, *Ibid.*, p. 392; F. C. Moon, *Ibid.*, p. 192.
[16]A. H. Nayfeh and B. Balachandran, *ibid.*

If one or more of the three eigenvalues of Eqs. 9.29 has a positive real part, then the disturbances will grow in magnitude and the associated motion will be unstable. Since the trace of Eqs. 9.29 is zero, the sum of its eigenvalues will also be zero.

Example 9.13   Stability of a rigid body

Let us consider a rigid body with $I_1 = 150 \text{ kg} \cdot \text{m}^2$, $I_2 = 50 \text{ kg} \cdot \text{m}^2$, and $I_3 = 300 \text{ kg} \cdot \text{m}^2$ and determine the stability of each of the three constant solutions. The script shown below determines the eigenvalues λ for disturbances provided to the rotational motions along the axis of maximum inertia, the axis of minimum inertia, and the other axis.

```
I = [150, 50, 300];
omega10 = [1, 0, 0];
omega20 = [0, 1, 0];
omega30 = [0, 0, 1];
for i = 1:length(omega10)
    A = [0, (I(3)-I(2))*omega30(i)/I(1), (I(3)-I(2))*omega20(i)/I(1); ...
            (I(1)-I(3))*omega30(i)/I(2), 0, (I(1)-I(3))*omega10(i)/I(2); ...
            (I(2)-I(1))*omega20(i)/I(3), (I(2)-I(1))*omega10(i)/I(3), 0];
    fprintf(1, '\nCase %3d: Eigenvalues\n', i);
    lambda = eig(A)
    SumLambda = sum(lambda)
end
```

Execution of the script displays the following to the MATLAB command window:

```
Case  1: Eigenvalues
lambda =
    1
   -1
    0
sum_lambda =
    0
Case  2: Eigenvalues
lambda =
        0 + 0.7454i
        0 - 0.7454i
        0
sum_lambda =
0
Case  3: Eigenvalues
lambda =
        0 + 2.2361i
        0 - 2.2361i
        0
sum_lambda =
    0
```

In each of the three cases, one of the eigenvalues is always zero, and the sum of the eigenvalues is always zero. In the first case, where the initial rotational motion is along the axis with the intermediate value of inertia, one of the eigenvalues has a positive real part indicating that the motion is unstable. The associated physical motions are wobbly. In the second case, which corresponds to an initial rotational motion about the axis of minimum rotational inertia, two of the eigenvalues form a purely imaginary pair. In the third case, which corresponds to an initial rotational motion about the axis of maximum rotational inertia, two of the eigenvalues form a purely imaginary pair. In the second and third cases, the respective disturbances to the system do not grow, because none of the eigenvalues has a positive real part. Hence, the motions in these cases are stable. If one further explores the solutions of Eqs. 9.27 by numerically integrating the last two cases, the motions will be found to correspond to circular orbits in the 3D space defined by the three states ω_1, ω_2, and ω_3. These orbits lie on an ellipsoid called Poinsot's ellipsoid.[17]

Natural Frequencies and Mode Shapes of a Three-Degree-of-Freedom System

Consider the system shown in Figure 9.20. Let the displacements x_1, x_2, and x_3 be measured from the static-equilibrium position of the system. The governing system of equations is given by

$$\begin{bmatrix} m_1 & 0 & 0 \\ 0 & m_2 & 0 \\ 0 & 0 & m_3 \end{bmatrix} \begin{Bmatrix} \ddot{x}_1 \\ \ddot{x}_2 \\ \ddot{x}_3 \end{Bmatrix} + \begin{bmatrix} k_1 & -k_1 & 0 \\ -k_1 & (k_1 + k_2) & -k_2 \\ 0 & -k_2 & k_2 \end{bmatrix} \begin{Bmatrix} x_1 \\ x_2 \\ x_3 \end{Bmatrix} = \begin{Bmatrix} 0 \\ 0 \\ 0 \end{Bmatrix} \qquad (9.30)$$

where

$$\ddot{x}_j = \frac{d^2 x_j}{dt^2}$$

The associated eigenvalue problem has the following form:

$$\begin{bmatrix} k_1 & -k_1 & 0 \\ -k_1 & (k_1 + k_2) & -k_2 \\ 0 & -k_2 & k_2 \end{bmatrix} \begin{Bmatrix} v_1 \\ v_2 \\ v_3 \end{Bmatrix} = \lambda \begin{bmatrix} m_1 & 0 & 0 \\ 0 & m_2 & 0 \\ 0 & 0 & m_3 \end{bmatrix} \begin{Bmatrix} v_1 \\ v_2 \\ v_3 \end{Bmatrix} \qquad (9.31)$$

where $\lambda = \omega^2$.

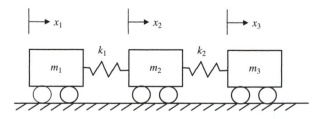

Figure 9.20   System with three degrees of freedom.

[17]D. T. Greenwood, *ibid.*, Section 8.4.

Example 9.14   Natural frequencies and mode shapes of a three-degree-of-freedom system

We assume that $k_1 = 100$ N/m, $k_2 = 50$ N/m, and $m_1 = m_2 = m_3 = 100$ kg. The script that determines the eigenvalues and associated eigenvectors is

```
k = [100, -100, 0; -100, 150, -50; 0, -50, 50];
m = diag([100, 100, 100]);
[VibrationModes, Eigenvalues] = eig(k, m)
```

Execution of the script gives

```
VibrationModes =
   0.5774    0.5774   -0.5774
  -0.7887    0.5774   -0.2113
   0.2113    0.5774    0.7887
Eigenvalues =
   2.3660       0        0
       0   0.0000        0
       0        0   0.6340
```

When the system shown in Figure 9.20 is examined, it is found that since the masses at each end are not restrained, a rigid-body mode in which all masses move in the same direction by the same amount is possible. This is reflected in the corresponding vibration mode, which is depicted by the second column of the matrix of vibration modes. The springs are neither stretched nor compressed in this case. This motion is associated with the zero eigenvalue.

When a square matrix has a zero eigenvalue, the determinant of the matrix is zero. To ascertain whether a matrix has zero eigenvalues, the rank of a matrix can be determined. The rank of a matrix, which is the order of the largest square matrix for which the determinant is nonzero, can be determined from

```
rank(K)
```

where K is a matrix. The script for determining whether the stiffness matrix in Eq. 9.30 has a zero eigenvalue is

```
k = [100, -100, 0; -100, 150, -50; 0, -50, 50];
rnk = rank(k);
[m n] = size(k);
disp(['Number of zero eigenvalues is ' num2str(m-rnk, 2)])
```

Execution of the script produces the following output

```
Number of zero eigenvalues is 1
```

Here, the rank of the stiffness matrix is 2, indicating that one can form a (2×2) matrix with a nonzero determinant from the (3×3) stiffness matrix.

9.3.2 Forced Oscillations and the Vibration Absorber

A two-degree-of-freedom system subjected to a forcing function $F(t)$ is shown in Figure 9.21, where the mass m_2, the spring k_2, and the damper c_2 comprise the secondary system and the mass m_1, the spring k_1, and the damper c_1 comprise the primary system. When the secondary system is added to the forced primary system to attenuate its motions, it is called an absorber.

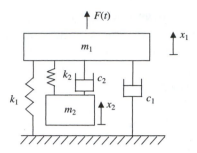

Figure 9.21   A two-degree-of-freedom system subjected to an external force $F(t)$.

The transfer functions for this system are given by[18]

$$\frac{\bar{x}_1(s)}{F(s)} = \frac{m_2 s^2 + c_2 s + k_2}{D(s)}$$

$$\frac{\bar{x}_2(s)}{F(s)} = \frac{c_2 s + k_2}{D(s)}$$

(9.32)

where

$$D(s) = m_1 m_2 s^4 + [(c_1 + c_2)m_2 + c_2 m_1]s^3 + [(k_1 + k_2)m_2 + k_2 m_1 + c_1 c_2]s^2$$
$$+ (k_1 c_2 + k_2 c_1)s + k_1 k_2$$

(9.33)

Since these two transfer functions will be used several times in the following examples, the following function called **Transferab** is created:

```
function sys = Transferab(m, k, c)
N = {[m(2) c(2) k(2)]; [c(2) k(2)]};
D = [m(1)*m(2) ((c(1)+c(2))*m(2)+c(2)*m(1)) ...
    ((k(1)+k(2))*m(2)+k(2)*m(1)+c(1)*c(2)) ...
    (k(1)*c(2)+c(1)*k(2)) k(1)*k(2)];
sys = tf(N, D);
```

Example 9.15   Impulse response of a two-degree-of-freedom system

We shall determine the responses of masses m_1 and m_2 when an impulse of unit magnitude is applied at time $t = 0$ to mass m_1. We assume that

$$m_1 = 50 \text{ kg} \qquad k_1 = 200 \text{ N/m} \qquad c_1 = 10 \text{ Ns/m}$$
$$m_2 = 10 \text{ kg} \qquad k_2 = 40 \text{ N/m} \qquad c_2 = 6 \text{ Ns/m}$$

---

[18]B. Balachandran and E. B. Magrab, *ibid.*

The script to determine the response is

```
m = [50, 10];  k = [200, 40];  c = [10, 6];
[y, t] = impulse(Transferab(m, k, c), 20);
figure(1)
plot(t, y(:,1), 'k-' , [0 20], [0 0], 'k-')
ylabel('x_1(t)')
xlabel('t')
figure(2)
plot(t, y(:,2), 'k-' , [0 20], [0 0], 'k-');
xlabel('t');
ylabel('x_2(t)');
```

The execution of the script results in Figure 9.22, where it is seen that the initial transient motions of both the masses are different. Although the impulse is applied to mass m_1, the response amplitude of the secondary mass m_2 is initially larger than that of m_1. After the first 7s or so, the two masses appear to be oscillating with the same period.

The step responses of the system can be obtained in a similar manner by replacing `impulse` with `step`.

Example 9.16   Vibration absorber

We now determine the frequency response functions for the displacement responses of masses m_1 and m_2 when a force is applied to mass m_1. This type of analysis is used to design vibration absorbers to attenuate the displacement response of the primary mass at the disturbance frequency.[19] Using the same system parameters given in Example 9.15, the script is

```
m = [50 10];  k = [200 40];  c = [10 6];
omega = linspace(0, 4, 300);
sys = tf([1], [m(1) c(1) k(1)]);
[mag, phas] = bode(sys, omega);
plot(omega, mag(1,:), '--k');
hold on;
sys = Transferab(m, k, c);
[mag, phas] = bode(sys, omega);
plot(omega, mag(1,:), 'k-');
xlabel('Excitation frequency (rad/s)');
ylabel('|x_1|');
text(2.1, 0.045, 'No vibration absorber');
text(0.3, 0.02, 'With vibration absorber');
```

Executing the script produces Figure 9.23. It is seen that the response of m_1 is attenuated in the frequency range around 2 rad/s, which is the undamped natural frequency of the primary system—that is, when $m_2 = 0$. In the system with the absorber, there are two degrees of freedom, and the associated system behavior indicates the presence of two resonance frequencies.

---

[19]D. J. Inman, *ibid.*; Section 5.3; S. S. Rao, *ibid.*, Section 9.10; B. H. Tongue, *ibid.*, Section 4.4; B. Balachandran and E. B, Magrab, *ibid.*, Section 8.6.

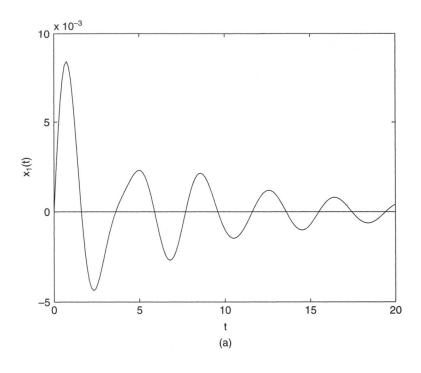

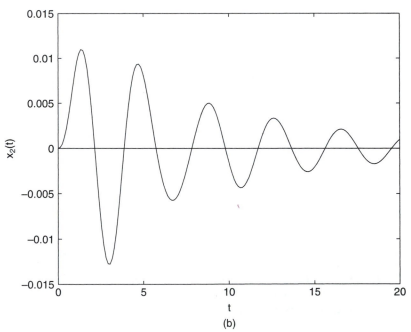

Figure 9.22   Impulse responses of a two-degree-of-freedom system when the impulse is applied to m_1: (a) response of m_1; (b) response of m_2.

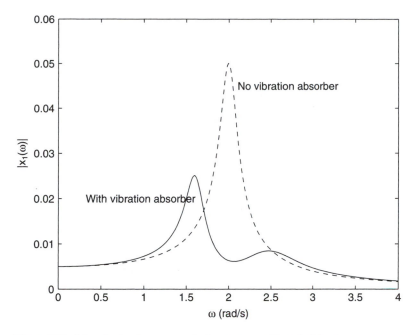

Figure 9.23   Magnitude of response of primary mass with and without a vibration absorber.

Example 9.17   Optimal parameters for a vibration absorber

Starting from Eqs. 9.32 and 9.33, we first introduce the frequency response function

$$G_{11}(i\Omega) = \frac{\bar{x}_1(i\Omega)}{F(i\Omega)} \tag{9.34a}$$

and define the magnitude of this function as

$$H_{11}(\Omega) = |G_{11}(i\Omega)| \tag{9.34b}$$

where $\Omega = \omega/\omega_n$, $\omega_n = \sqrt{k_1/m_1}$. In Figure 9.24, a representative graph of the function $H_{11}(\Omega)$ is shown for an absorber system. For convenience, we introduce the following nondimensional quantities:

$$\omega_r = \frac{\omega_{n2}}{\omega_{n1}} = \frac{1}{\sqrt{m_r}}\sqrt{\frac{k_2}{k_1}}, \quad m_r = \frac{m_2}{m_1}$$

$$\omega_{nj}^2 = \frac{k_j}{m_j}, \quad 2\zeta_j = \frac{c_j}{m_j\omega_{nj}} \quad j = 1, 2$$

Then, from the first of Eqs. 9.32 and Eq. 9.33, we obtain

$$H_{11}(\Omega) = \left| \frac{E_2(i\Omega)}{k_1 D_2(i\Omega)} \right|$$

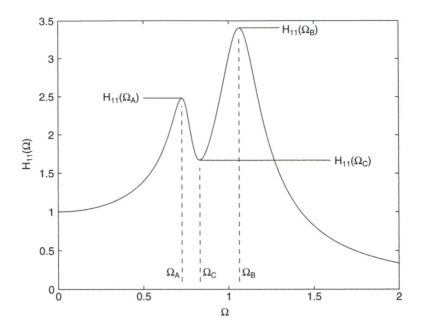

Figure 9.24   Representative amplitude response of an absorber system.

where

$$E_2(j\Omega) = -\Omega^2 + 2\zeta_2\omega_r j\Omega + \omega_r^2$$

$$D_2(j\Omega) = \Omega^4 - j[2\zeta_1 + 2\zeta_2\omega_r m_r + 2\zeta_2\omega_r]\Omega^3 - [1 + m_r\omega_r^2 + \omega_r^2$$
$$+ 4\zeta_1\zeta_2\omega_r]\Omega^2 + j[2\zeta_2\omega_r + 2\zeta_1\omega_r^2]\Omega + \omega_r^2$$

The objective is to determine an optimal set of parameters for the absorber so that there is an operating region including $\Omega = 1$ wherein the variation of the amplitude of the primary system m_1 with respect to the frequency is minimal. With respect to Figure 9.24, the goal is to find the absorber parameters for which the peak amplitudes A and B are equal and as "small" as possible while the minimum between these peaks C is as close to A and B as possible in terms of magnitude. In other words, we would like to find the system parameters that minimize each of the following three maximum values simultaneously: $H_{11}(\Omega_A)$, $H_{11}(\Omega_B)$, and $1/H_{11}(\Omega_C)$. This can be stated as follows:

$$\begin{aligned}
&\min_{\omega_r, \zeta_2}\{H_{11}(\Omega_A)\} \\
&\min_{\omega_r, \zeta_2}\{H_{11}(\Omega_B)\} \\
&\min_{\omega_r, \zeta_2}\{1/H_{11}(\Omega_C)\} \\
&\text{subject to: } \omega_r > 0 \\
&\hspace{4.5em} \zeta_2 \geq 0
\end{aligned} \tag{9.35}$$

For $\zeta_1 = 0.1$ and mass ratios $m_r = 0.1, 0.2, 0.3, 0.4$, the script used to determine the optimum values of $\zeta_{2,\text{opt}}$ and $\omega_{r,\text{opt}}$ is shown below. The responses corresponding to these optimal values is shown in Figure 9.25.

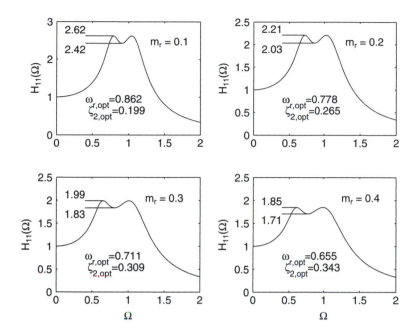

Figure 9.25 Optimum values for the parameters of a vibration absorber and the resulting amplitude responses of m_1 for $\zeta_1 = 0.1$.

```
function VibAbsorbOptPara
OM = linspace(0, 2, 100);
Lbnd = [0.1, 0];
Ubnd = [2 1];
xo = [.8, 0.35];
opt = optimset('Display', 'off');
mr = [.1 .2 .3 .4];
z1 = [.1 .1 .1 .1];
for k = 1:4
  subplot(2, 2, k)
  [xopt, fopt] = fminimax(@objfun2doflinconstr, xo, [], [], [], [], Lbnd, Ubnd, [], ...
                    opt, mr(k), z1(k));
  plot(OM, Ha1(OM, xopt(1), mr(k), z1(k), xopt(2)), 'k-')
  hold on
  ax = axis;
  if k~=1
    ax(4) = 2.5;
    axis(ax)
  end
  text(.2*ax(2),.3*ax(4),['\omega_{r,opt}=' num2str(xopt(1),3)])
  text(.2*ax(2),.2*ax(4),['\zeta_{2,opt}=' num2str(xopt(2),3)])
  text(1.3,.8*ax(4),['m_r=' num2str(mr(k))])
  if k>2
    xlabel('\Omega')
  end
```

```
ylabel('H_{11}(\Omega)')
[z, xx] = objfun2doflinconstr([xopt(1), xopt(2)], mr(k), z1(k));
hold on
plot([xx(1), 0.2*ax(2)], [fopt(1) fopt(1)], 'k-')
text(.14*ax(2), fopt(1), num2str(fopt(1), 3))
plot([xx(3), 0.2*ax(2)], [fopt(3) fopt(3)], 'k-')
text(.14*ax(2), fopt(3), num2str(fopt(3), 3))
end

function [z, xx] = objfun2doflinconstr(x, mr, z1)
wr = x(1);
z2 = x(2);
opt = optimset('Display', 'off');
a1 = 1+(1+mr)*wr^2;
a2 = wr^2;
O1 = sqrt(0.5*(a1-sqrt(a1^2-4*a2)));
O2 = sqrt(0.5*(a1+sqrt(a1^2-4*a2)));
[x1, f1] = fminsearch(@Min2dof, O1, opt, wr, mr, z1, z2);
[x2, f2] = fminsearch(@Min2dof, O2, opt, wr, mr, z1, z2);
[x3, z(3)] = fminsearch(@Ha1, (O2+O1)/2, opt, wr, mr, z1, z2);
z(1) = 1/f1;
z(2) = 1/f2;
xx = [x1 x2 x3];

function h = Ha1(Om, wr, mr, z1, z2)
realpart = Om.^4-(1+mr*wr^2+wr^2+4*z1*z2*wr)*Om.^2+wr^2;
imagpart = -2*(z1+z2*wr*mr+z2*wr)*Om.^3+2*(z2*wr+z1*wr^2)*Om;
nrealpart = wr^2-Om.^2;
nimagpart = 2*z2*wr*Om;
h = sqrt(nrealpart.^2+nimagpart.^2)./sqrt(realpart.^2+imagpart.^2);

function m = Min2dof(Om, wr, mr, z1, z2)
m = 1./Ha1(Om, wr, mr, z1, z2);
```

9.4 VIBRATIONS OF THIN BEAMS[20]

9.4.1 Natural Frequencies and Mode Shapes of Beams with Uniform Cross-Section

The governing nondimensional equation of motion for the transverse deflection $w'(x, t)$ of an undamped beam of length L, cross-sectional area A, moment of inertia I, density ρ, and Young's modulus E subjected to a dynamic force $F(x, t)$ is

$$\frac{\partial^4 w}{\partial \eta^4} + \frac{\partial^2 w}{\partial \tau^2} = F_o(\eta, \tau) \quad 0 \le \eta \le 1 \quad \tau > 0 \tag{9.36}$$

---

[20]This section has been adapted, in part, from B. Balachandran and E. B. Magrab, *Vibrations*, Brooks/Cole, Belmont, CA, 2002, Chapter 9.

where $\eta = x/L, \tau = t/t_o, w(\eta, \tau) = w'(x/L, t/t_o)/L, F_o(\eta, \tau) = F(x/L, t/t_o)L^3/EI,$ and

$$t_o^2 = \frac{\rho A L^4}{EI}$$

For the configuration shown in Figure 9.26, the beam has the following boundary conditions:

$\eta = 0$

$$\frac{\partial^3 w}{\partial \eta^3} = -K_1 w$$

$$\frac{\partial^2 w}{\partial \eta^2} = B_1 \frac{\partial w}{\partial \eta}$$

(9.37a)

$\eta = 1$

$$\frac{\partial^3 w}{\partial \eta^3} = K_2 w + M \frac{\partial^2 w}{\partial \tau^2}$$

$$\frac{\partial^2 w}{\partial \eta^2} = -B_2 \frac{\partial w}{\partial \eta} - J \frac{\partial^3 w}{\partial \eta \partial \tau^2}$$

(9.37b)

In Eqs. 9.37, $M = M_o/m_o, J = J_o/j_o, M_o$ is the magnitude of an attached mass, J_o is the magnitude of the mass moment of inertia of an attached mass, $m_o = \rho A L$ is the mass of the beam, $j_o = m_o L^2$, and the nondimensional translation and torsion spring constants are, respectively,

$$K_j = \frac{k_j L^3}{EI} \quad \text{and} \quad B_j = \frac{k_{tj} L}{EI} \quad j = 1, 2$$

where k_j is the linear spring constant and k_{tj} is the torsion spring constant.

To determine the natural frequencies and mode shapes, we set $F_o = 0$ in Eq. 9.36 and assume harmonic free oscillations of the form

$$w(\eta, \tau) = W(\eta)\cos(\Omega^2 \tau)$$

(9.38)

In Eq. 9.38, the frequency coefficient is given by

$$\Omega = \sqrt{\omega t_o}$$

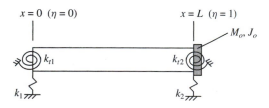

$x = 0 \ (\eta = 0)$ $x = L \ (\eta = 1)$

M_o, J_o

k_{t1} k_{t2}

k_1 k_2

Figure 9.26   Beam with spring elements at the left and right boundaries and an inertia element at the right boundary.

and $\omega = 2\pi f$ is the radian frequency. After substituting Eq. 9.38 into Eqs. 9.37, we obtain

$\eta = 0$

$$\frac{d^3W}{d\eta^3} = -K_1 W$$

$$\frac{d^2W}{d\eta^2} = B_1\frac{dW}{d\eta}$$

(9.39a)

$\eta = 1$

$$\frac{d^3W}{d\eta^3} = (K_2 - M\Omega^4)W$$

$$\frac{d^2W}{d\eta^2} = (-B_2 + J\Omega^4)\frac{dW}{d\eta}$$

(9.39b)

We substitute Eq. 9.38 into Eq. 9.36 with $F_o = 0$ to obtain the general solution to the resulting equation, and then we apply the boundary conditions given by Eqs. 9.39 to obtain the following characteristic equation from which the natural frequency coefficients Ω_n and corresponding modes shapes $W_n(\eta)$ are determined. The characteristic equation is

$$z_1[\cos \Omega_n \sinh \Omega_n + \sin \Omega_n \cosh \Omega_n] + z_2[\cos \Omega_n \sinh \Omega_n - \sin \Omega_n \cosh \Omega_n]$$

$$- 2z_3 \sin \Omega_n \sinh \Omega_n + z_4(\cos \Omega_n \cosh \Omega_n - 1)$$

$$+ z_5(\cos \Omega_n \cosh \Omega_n + 1) + 2z_6 \cos \Omega_n \cosh \Omega_n = 0$$

(9.40)

where

$$z_1 = [b_{1n}b_{2n}(a_{1n} + a_{2n}) + (b_{1n} - b_{2n})]$$
$$z_2 = [a_{1n}a_{2n}(b_{1n} - b_{2n}) - (a_{1n} + a_{2n})]$$
$$z_3 = (a_{1n}a_{2n} + b_{1n}b_{2n})$$
$$z_4 = (1 - a_{1n}a_{2n}b_{1n}b_{2n})$$
$$z_5 = (a_{2n}b_{2n} - a_{1n}b_{1n})$$
$$z_6 = (a_{1n}b_{2n} - a_{2n}b_{1n})$$

(9.41)

and

$$a_{1n} = \frac{K_1}{\Omega_n^3} \quad a_{2n} = \frac{1}{\Omega_n^3}(K_2 - M\Omega_n^4)$$

$$b_{1n} = \frac{B_1}{\Omega_n} \quad b_{2n} = \frac{1}{\Omega_n}(-B_2 + J\Omega_n^4)$$

(9.42)

The mode shapes depend on the range of values of b_{1n} as follows:

Case 1—$0 \leq a_{jn} \leq \infty, 0 \leq b_{2n} \leq \infty$, and $0 \leq b_{1n} < \infty$

The mode shape is

$$W_n(\eta) = C_n[Q(\Omega_n\eta) - a_{1n}T(\Omega_n\eta)] + R(\Omega_n\eta) + b_{1n}S(\Omega_n\eta) \quad (9.43a)$$

where the nondimensional coefficient C_n is given by

$$C_n = \frac{a_{2n}R(\Omega_n) + (a_{2n}b_{1n} - 1)S(\Omega_n) - b_{1n}T(\Omega_n)}{R(\Omega_n) - (a_{1n} + a_{2n})Q(\Omega_n) + a_{1n}a_{2n}T(\Omega_n)} \quad (9.43b)$$

Case 2—$0 \leq a_{jn} \leq \infty, 0 \leq b_{2n} \leq \infty$, and $b_{1n} \rightarrow \infty$ (infinite torsion stiffness at $\eta = 0$)

The mode shape is

$$W_n(\eta) = C_n[Q(\Omega_n\eta) - a_{1n}T(\Omega_n\eta)] + S(\Omega_n\eta) \quad (9.44a)$$

where the nondimensional coefficient C_n is given by

$$C_n = \frac{a_{2n}S(\Omega_n) - T(\Omega_n)}{R(\Omega_n) - (a_{1n} + a_{2n})Q(\Omega_n) + a_{1n}a_{2n}T(\Omega_n)} \quad (9.44b)$$

The different functions appearing in Eqs. 9.43 and 9.44 are given by

$$Q(u) = [\cos(u) + \cosh(u)]/2$$
$$R(u) = [\sin(u) + \sinh(u)]/2$$
$$S(u) = [\cosh(u) - \cos(u)]/2$$
$$T(u) = [\sinh(u) - \sin(u)]/2$$

These expressions depend the boundary conditions, which have been chosen so that numerous special cases can be considered. These special cases are obtained by setting the quantities a_{1n}, a_{2n}, b_{1n}, and b_{2n} either to the limiting value of 0 or ∞ or to some intermediate values, as the case may be. Many boundary conditions and the corresponding values of a_{1n}, a_{2n}, b_{1n}, and b_{2n} are summarized in Table 9.3. Upon taking the

TABLE 9.3   Parameter Values for Special Cases of Eqs. 9.41 through 9.44

Boundary condition	$\eta = 0$		$\eta = 1$	
	a_{1n}	b_{1n}	a_{2n}	b_{2n}
Hinged	∞	0	∞	0
Clamped	∞	∞	∞	∞
Free	0	0	0	0
Free with M_o	—	—	$-M\Omega_n$	0
Free with J_o	—	—	0	$J\Omega_n^3$
Free with k_j	K_1/Ω_n^3	0	K_2/Ω_n^3	0
Free with k_{tj}	0	B_1/Ω_n	0	$-B_2/\Omega_n$
Hinged with k_{tj}	∞	B_1/Ω_n	∞	$-B_2/\Omega_n$

TABLE 9.4 Several Special Cases of Eq. 9.40

Boundary conditions		
$\eta = 0$	$\eta = 1$	Eq. 9.40 becomes
Hinged	Hinged	$\sin(\Omega_n) = 0$
Clamped	Clamped	$\cos(\Omega_n)\cosh(\Omega_n) - 1 = 0$
Clamped	Free with $M_o \neq 0$ and $J_o = 0$	$M\Omega_n[\cos(\Omega_n)\sinh(\Omega_n) - \sin(\Omega_n)\cosh(\Omega_n)]$ $+ \cos(\Omega_n)\cosh(\Omega_n) + 1 = 0$
Clamped	Free	$\cos(\Omega_n)\cosh(\Omega_n) + 1 = 0$
Clamped	Hinged	$\tanh(\Omega_n) - \tan(\Omega_n) = 0$

limits indicated in Table 9.3, Eq. 9.40 reduces to the relations shown in Table 9.4 for several combinations of boundary conditions.

We shall use Eqs. 9.40 through 9.44 to determine the natural frequencies and mode functions for any combination of boundary conditions given by Eqs. 9.39. To do this, we shall first create a function that combines the ability to take limits using the Symbolic Toolbox with those of MATLAB to create functions from the resulting symbolic expressions. The function will be called **BeamFreqMode**, which is given below. Following the presentation of this function, two examples are provided to illustrate its use. In determining the roots of the characteristic equation, we have done some preliminary work to determine the appropriate search regions for fzero.

```
function [Omeg, Mshape] = BeamFreqMode
global Bn1 Kn1 Bn2 Kn2 M J Nfreq BCtypeLeft BCtypeRight Neta
syms a1 a2 b1 b2 x K1 K2 B1 B2 Mm Jj et
z1 = b1*b2*(a1+a2)+b1-b2;
z2 = a1*a2*(b1-b2)-a1-a2;
z3 = a1*a2+b1*b2;
z4 = 1-a1*a2*b1*b2;
z5 = a2*b2-a1*b1;
z6 = a1*b2-a2*b1;
chareqn = z1*(cos(x)*sinh(x)+sin(x)*cosh(x)) ...
        +z2*(cos(x)*sinh(x)-sin(x)*cosh(x)) ...
        -2*z3*sin(x)*sinh(x)+z4*(cos(x)*cosh(x)-1) ...
        +z5*(cos(x)*cosh(x)+1)+2*z6*cos(x)*cosh(x);
Q = (cosh(x)+cos(x))/2;
S = (cosh(x)-cos(x))/2;
R = (sinh(x)+sin(x))/2;
T = (sinh(x)-sin(x))/2;
Cn = (a2*R+(a2*b1-1)*S-b1*T)/(R-(a1+a2)*Q+a1*a2*T);
Qo = (cosh(et*x)+cos(et*x))/2;
So = (cosh(et*x)-cos(et*x))/2;
Ro = (sinh(et*x)+sin(et*x))/2;
To = (sinh(et*x)-sin(et*x))/2;
```

```
Wn = Cn*(Qo-a1*To)+Ro+b1*So;
switch BCtypeLeft
   case 'clamped'
      chareqn = limit(limit(chareqn/a1, a1, inf)/b1, b1, inf);
      Cnb1 = (a2*S-T)/(R-(a1+a2)*Q+a1*a2*T);
      Wn = limit(Cnb1*(Qo-a1*To)+So, a1, inf);
   case 'hinged'
      chareqn = limit(limit(chareqn/a1, a1, inf),b1, B1/x);
      Wn = limit(limit(Wn, a1, inf), b1, B1/x );
   case 'free'
      chareqn = limit(limit(chareqn, b1, B1/x), a1, K1/x^3);
      Wn = limit(limit(Wn, b1, B1/x), a1, K1/x^3);
end
switch BCtypeRight
   case 'clamped'
      chareqn = limit(limit(chareqn/a2, a2, inf)/b2, b2, inf);
      Wn = limit(Wn, a2, inf);
      ul = 1.7*pi;
   case 'hinged'
      chareqn = limit(limit(chareqn/a2, a2, inf), b2, -B2/x);
      Wn = limit(Wn, a2, inf);
      ul = 1.7*pi;
   case 'free'
      chareqn = limit(limit(chareqn, b2, -B2/x+Jj*x^3), a2, K2/x^3-Mm*x);
      Wn = limit(Wn, a2, K2/x^3-Mm*x);
      if length(BCtypeLeft)==4
         ul = 1.7*pi;
      else
         ul = pi;
      end
end
charist = inline(vectorize(chareqn), 'x', 'K1', 'K2', 'B1', 'B2', 'Mm', 'Jj');
modes = inline(vectorize(Wn), 'x', 'et', 'K1', 'K2', 'B1', 'B2', 'Mm', 'Jj');
ll = 0.1*pi;
eta = linspace(0, 1, Neta);
opt = optimset('Display', 'off');
Omeg = zeros(1, Nfreq);
Mshape = zeros(Nfreq, Neta);
for k=1:Nfreq
   Omeg(k) = fzero(charist, [ll, ul], opt, Kn1, Kn2, Bn1, Bn2, M, J);
   ll = pi*(Omeg(k)/pi+0.1);
   ul = pi*(Omeg(k)/pi+1.2);
   z = modes(Omeg(k), eta, Kn1, Kn2, Bn1, Bn2, M, J);
   Mshape(k,:) = z/max(z);
end
```

**Example 9.18   Natural frequencies and modes shapes of a clamped-hinged beam
with a torsion spring**

Consider a beam that is clamped at $\eta = 0$ and hinged at $\eta = 1$. In addition, at $\eta = 1$ there is a torsion spring attached such that the nondimensional torsion stiffness $B_2 = 10$. We shall determine the first four natural frequencies and mode shapes and plot the results shown in Figure 9.27 by using the following script:

```
global Bn1 Kn1 Bn2 Kn2 M J Nfreq BCtypeLeft BCtypeRight Neta
md = char('1st mode: ', '2nd mode: ', '3rd mode: ', '4th mode: ');
Kn1 = 0;  Bn1 = 0;
Kn2 = 0;  Bn2 = 10;
M = 0;  J = 0;
Nfreq = 4;  Neta = 100;
BCtypeLeft = 'clamped';
BCtypeRight = 'hinged';
[Omeg, Mshape] = BeamFreqMode;
eta = linspace(0, 1, Neta);
for k=1:Nfreq
  subplot(2,2,k)
  plot(eta, Mshape(k,:), 'k-', [0, 1], [0, 0], 'k--')
  title([md(k,:) ' \Omega_' num2str(k) '/\pi = ' num2str(Omeg(k)/pi)])
  axis off
end
```

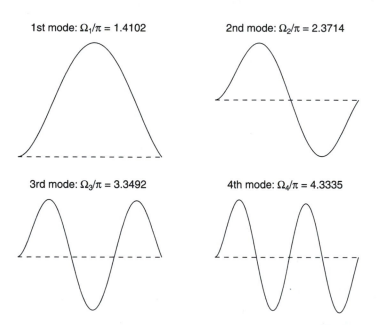

1st mode: $\Omega_1/\pi = 1.4102$

2nd mode: $\Omega_2/\pi = 2.3714$

3rd mode: $\Omega_3/\pi = 3.3492$

4th mode: $\Omega_4/\pi = 4.3335$

Figure 9.27 First four mode shapes of a beam clamped at one end and hinged at the other end with $B_2 = 10$.

Example 9.19   Natural frequencies of a clamped-free beam with an attached mass

Consider a beam that is clamped at $\eta = 0$ and free at $\eta = 1$. In addition, at $\eta = 1$ there is a mass attached whose nondimensional mass ratio M varies in the range $0.01 \leq M \leq 100$. We shall determine the first two natural frequencies as a function of M and plot the results shown in Figure 9.28 by using the following script:

```
global Bn1 Kn1 Bn2 Kn2 M J Nfreq BCtypeLeft BCtypeRight Neta
Kn1 = 0;  Bn1 = 0;
Kn2 = 0;  Bn2 = 0;
J = 0;
Nfreq = 2;  Neta = 100;
BCtypeLeft = 'clamped';
BCtypeRight = 'free';
Mm = logspace(-2, 2, 40);
LM = length(Mm);
omeg = zeros(LM, Nfreq);
for k=1:LM
    M = Mm(k);
    Omeg(k,:) = BeamFreqMode/pi;
end
for k=1:Nfreq
    semilogx(Mm, Omeg(:,k), 'k-')
    hold on
```

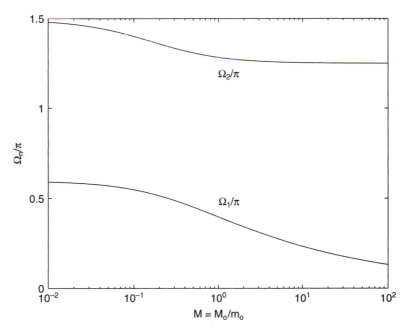

Figure 9.28   First two natural frequencies of a beam clamped at one end and free at the other end as a function of M.

```
        text(1, 0.8*Omeg(1,k), ['\Omega_' num2str(k) '/\pi'])
    end
    xlabel('M = M_o/m_0')
    ylabel('\Omega_n/\pi')
```

9.4.2 Forced Vibrations of Beams

When the initial conditions are zero, the solution of Eq. 9.36, subject to the boundary conditions given by Eqs. 9.37, is

$$w(\eta, \tau) = \sum_{n=1}^{\infty} \frac{W_n(\eta)}{\Omega_n^2 N_n} \int_0^1 \int_0^\tau F_o(\eta, \tau') W_n(\eta) \sin[\Omega_m^2(\tau - \tau')] d\tau' d\eta \qquad (9.45)$$

where $W_n(\eta)$ is the nondimensional modal function given by Eqs. 9.43a or 9.44a,

$$\Omega_n = \sqrt{\omega_n t_o}$$

$\omega_n = 2\pi f_n$ is the radian natural frequency, and the normalization constant is

$$N_n = \int_0^1 W_n^2(\eta) d\eta$$

We shall now illustrate the numerical evaluation of this result with an example.

Example 9.20   Impulse response of a cantilever beam with a mass at its free end

The beam is subjected to an impulse load of magnitude f_o at $\eta = \xi \neq (0 < \xi < 1)$; that is,

$$F_o(\eta, \tau) = f_o \delta(\eta - \xi) \delta(\tau)$$

For this loading, Eq. 9.45 becomes

$$w(\eta, \tau) = f_o \sum_{n=1}^{\infty} \frac{W_n(\eta) W_n(\xi)}{\Omega_n^2 N_n} \sin(\Omega_n^2 \tau)$$

We shall plot the beam response at 14 instants of time in the range $0.05 \leq \tau \leq 1.35$ when $\xi = 0.4$ and $f_o = 1$. We shall sum only the first 14 terms of this series; that is, only the first 14 beam modes will be considered. The following script is used to produce the results shown in Figure 9.29:

```
global Bn1 Kn1 Bn2 Kn2 M J Nfreq BCtypeLeft BCtypeRight Neta
Kn1 = 0;  Bn1 = 0;
Kn2 = 0;  Bn2 = 0;
M = 0.2;  J = 0;
Nfreq = 11;  Neta = 100;
BCtypeLeft = 'clamped';
BCtypeRight = 'free';
[Omeg, Mshape] = BeamFreqMode;
eta = linspace(0, 1, Neta);
tau = 0.05:0.1:1.35;  xi = 0.4;
[v indx] = min(abs(eta-xi));
```

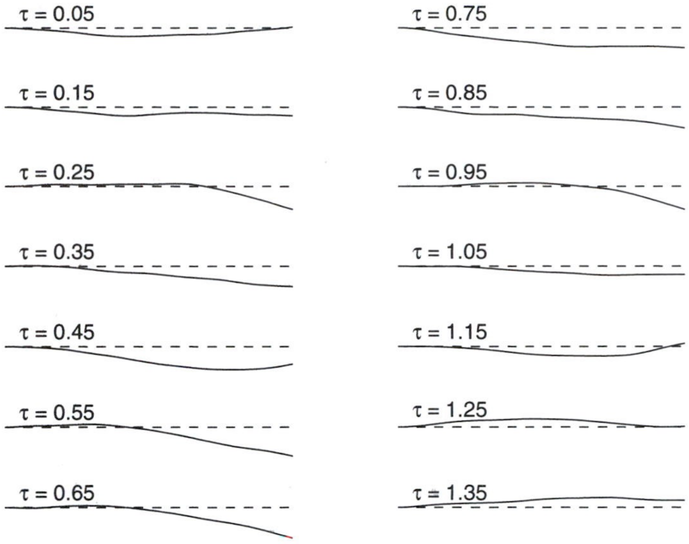

Figure 9.29   Response of a beam clamped at one end and free at the other end with $M = M_o/m_o = 0.2$ when an impulse is applied at $\xi = 0.4$.

```
for k = 1:Nfreq
    Nn(k) = trapz(eta, Mshape(k,:).^2);
    Wnxi(k) = Mshape(k,indx);
end
C = Wnxi./Nn./Omeg.^2;
w = repmat(C, Neta, 1).*Mshape'*sin(Omeg.^2'*tau);
Ntau = length(tau);
for k = 1:Ntau/2
    subplot(Ntau/2, 2, 2*k-1)
    plot(eta, -w(:,k), 'k-', [0 1], [0 0], 'k--')
    axis([0 1 -0.4 0.4])
    text(0.05, 0.2, ['\tau = ' num2str(tau(k))])
    axis off
    subplot(Ntau/2, 2, 2*k)
    plot(eta, -w(:,k+Ntau/2), 'k-', [0 1], [0 0], 'k--')
    axis([0 1 -0.4 0.4])
    text(0.05, 0.2, ['\tau = ' num2str(tau(k+Ntau/2))])
    axis off
end
```

9.4.3 Beams with Variable Cross-Section

A beam with variable cross-section is shown in Figure 9.30. This type of beam is called a double-tapered beam. The nondimensional equation of motion of this beam undergoing free harmonic oscillations in the z-direction is

$$\frac{d^2}{d\eta^2}\left[I(\eta)\frac{d^2w}{d\eta^2}\right] - \Omega'^4 A(\eta)w = 0 \tag{9.46}$$

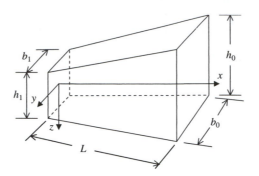

Figure 9.30   Nomenclature for a tapered beam.

where

$$I(\eta) = [\alpha + (1 - \alpha)\eta]^3[\beta + (1 - \beta)\eta^{n-1}]$$
$$A(\eta) = [\alpha + (1 - \alpha)\eta][\beta + (1 - \beta)\eta^{n-1}]$$
$$\Omega'^4 = \omega^2 L^4/c_b^2 r_0^2$$
$$c_b^2 = E/\rho$$

and r_0 is the radius of gyration of the cross-section at $\eta = 1$, $\alpha = h_1/h_0 \leq 1$ is the depth taper ratio, $\beta = b_1/b_0 \leq 1$ is the thickness taper ratio, and n is a positive constant. When $\beta = 0$, the beam tapers to a point at $\eta = 0$ in the xy-plane, and when $\alpha = 0$, the beam tapers to a point at $\eta = 0$ in the xz-plane. When $\beta = \alpha = 1$, we have a beam of constant cross-section. When the thickness taper ratio and the depth taper ratio are linearly proportional to η, then $n = 2$. When the beam has a constant thickness ($\beta = 1$), then $n = 1$. When the thickness and depth taper ratios are equal, then $\beta = \alpha$.

We shall confine the discussion to a double-tapered beam for which $\beta = \alpha$ and $n = 2$. Then, Eq. 9.46 can be written as

$$\frac{d^2}{d\varphi^2}\left[\varphi^4\frac{d^2W}{d\varphi^2}\right] - \lambda^4\varphi^2W = 0 \qquad (9.47)$$

where

$$\varphi = [\alpha + (1 - \alpha)\eta]$$
$$\lambda = \Omega'/(1 - \alpha)$$

The solution of Eq. 9.47 is

$$W(\varphi) = \varphi^{-1}\left[AJ_2(2\lambda\sqrt{\varphi}) + BY_2(2\lambda\sqrt{\varphi}) + CI_2(2\lambda\sqrt{\varphi}) + DK_2(2\lambda\sqrt{\varphi})\right] \quad (9.48)$$

where $J_2(z)$ and $Y_2(z)$ are the Bessel functions of the first and second kind, respectively, of order 2 and $I_2(z)$ and $K_2(z)$ are the modified Bessel functions of the first and second kind, respectively, of order 2. The boundary conditions can be obtained from Eqs. 9.39 by noting that $d\varphi/d\eta = (1 - \alpha)$.

Example 9.21   Lowest natural frequencies of a double-tapered cantilever beam

We shall determine the first three natural frequency coefficients for a cantilever beam that is clamped at $\eta = 1$ and free at $\eta = 0$ for a range of values of α. The boundary conditions are as follows:

$$\eta = 1 \; (\varphi = 1)$$

$$W = 0 \quad \text{and} \quad \frac{dW}{d\varphi} = 0 \tag{9.49a}$$

$$\eta = 0 \; (\varphi = \alpha)$$

$$\frac{d^2W}{d\varphi^2} = 0 \quad \text{and} \quad \frac{d^3W}{d\varphi^3} = 0 \tag{9.49b}$$

Upon substituting Eq. 9.48 into Eqs. 9.49, we obtain the following equation from which the natural frequency coefficients λ_n can be determined:

$$\begin{vmatrix} J_5(2\lambda\sqrt{\alpha}) & Y_5(2\lambda\sqrt{\alpha}) & -I_5(2\lambda\sqrt{\alpha}) & K_5(2\lambda\sqrt{\alpha}) \\ J_4(2\lambda\sqrt{\alpha}) & Y_4(2\lambda\sqrt{\alpha}) & I_4(2\lambda\sqrt{\alpha}) & K_4(2\lambda\sqrt{\alpha}) \\ J_2(2\lambda) & Y_2(2\lambda) & I_2(2\lambda) & K_2(2\lambda) \\ J_3(2\lambda) & Y_3(2\lambda) & -I_3(2\lambda) & K_3(2\lambda) \end{vmatrix} = 0 \tag{9.50}$$

To obtain Eq. 9.50, we used the following relations:

$$\frac{d}{d\varphi}\left[\varphi^{-n/2}J_n(2\lambda\sqrt{\varphi})\right] = -\lambda\varphi^{-(n+1)/2}J_{n+1}(2\lambda\sqrt{\varphi})$$

$$\frac{d}{d\varphi}\left[\varphi^{-n/2}Y_n(2\lambda\sqrt{\varphi})\right] = -\lambda\varphi^{-(n+1)/2}Y_{n+1}(2\lambda\sqrt{\varphi})$$

$$\frac{d}{d\varphi}\left[\varphi^{-n/2}I_n(2\lambda\sqrt{\varphi})\right] = \lambda\varphi^{-(n+1)/2}I_{n+1}(2\lambda\sqrt{\varphi})$$

$$\frac{d}{d\varphi}\left[\varphi^{-n/2}K_n(2\lambda\sqrt{\varphi})\right] = -\lambda\varphi^{-(n+1)/2}K_{n+1}(2\lambda\sqrt{\varphi})$$

For the special case when $\beta = \alpha = 1$, the solution for λ_1 is obtained by executing the function **BeamFreqMode** for the case of a cantilever beam. The result is $\lambda_1 = \Omega'_1 = 1.8751$. The following script generates Figure 9.31, where the function **TaperedBeam** represents Eq. 9.50.

```
function TaperedBeamFreq
a = logspace(-1, 0, 20);
opt = optimset('Display', 'off');
for k=1:length(a)-1
    b(k) = fzero(@TaperedBeam, [1.5/(1-a(k)), 4/(1-a(k))], opt, a(k))*(1-a(k));
end
b(length(a)) = 1.8751;
semilogx(a, b, 'k-')
xlabel('\alpha')
ylabel('\Omega\prime_1')
axis([.1 1 1.8 2.8])

function r = TaperedBeam(x, alpha)
a1 = 2*x;
a2 = a1*sqrt(alpha);
```

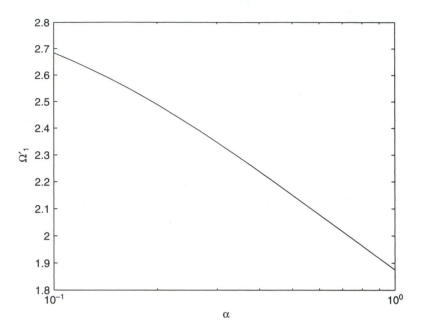

Figure 9.31   First natural frequency coefficient for a double-tapered cantilever beam.

```
r = det([besselj(5,a2) bessely(5,a2) -besseli(5,a2) besselk(5,a2); ...
         besselj(4,a2) bessely(4,a2) besseli(4,a2) besselk(4,a2); ...
         besselj(2,a1) bessely(2,a1) besseli(2,a1) besselk(2,a1); ...
         besselj(3,a1) bessely(3,a1) -besseli(3,a1) besselk(3,a1)]);
```

9.4.4 Beam Carrying a Concentrated Mass

Let a uniform, undamped beam carry a concentrated mass M_0' at $\eta = \xi$. The non-dimensional equation of motion for free harmonic oscillations is

$$\frac{d^4W}{d\eta^4} - \Omega^4\left[1 + \frac{M_0'}{m_o}\delta(\eta - \xi)\right]W = 0 \tag{9.51}$$

where $W \equiv W(\eta)$. The boundary conditions are given by Eqs. 9.39. The general solution to Eq. 9.51 is

$$W(\eta)/W(\xi) = AQ(\Omega\eta) + BR(\Omega\eta) + CS(\Omega\eta) + DT(\Omega\eta)$$
$$+ \frac{M_0'}{m_0}\Omega T(\Omega(\eta - \xi))u(\eta - \xi) \tag{9.52}$$

where $u(\eta - \xi)$ is the unit step function. The natural frequency coefficients Ω_n are determined from Eq. 9.52 when evaluated at $\eta = \xi$. This results in

$$1 = AQ(\Omega_n\xi) + BR(\Omega_n\xi) + CS(\Omega_n\xi) + DT(\Omega_n\xi) \tag{9.53}$$

since $T(0) = 0$. The constants A, B, C, and D are determined from the substitution of Eq. 9.52 into the boundary conditions given by Eqs. 9.39. The corresponding mode shape is

$$w_n(\eta) = A_n Q(\Omega_n \eta) + B_n R(\Omega_n \eta) + C_n S(\Omega_n \eta) + D_n T(\Omega_n \eta)$$

$$+ \frac{M_0'}{m_0} \Omega_n T(\Omega_n(\eta - \xi))u(\eta - \xi) \tag{9.54}$$

where the constants A_n, B_n, C_n, and D_n are the constants A, B, C, and D evaluated at $\Omega = \Omega_n$, respectively. We now illustrate these results with an example.

Example 9.22   Natural frequencies and mode shapes of a beam hinged at both ends that is carrying a mass

We determine and plot the first three natural frequency coefficients of a beam simply supported at both ends as the position of the mass ξ varies from 0.05 to 0.5 and the ratio M_0'/m_0 takes each of the following three values: 0.1, 1, and 10. Since the beam's boundary conditions are the same at each end, the values of Ω_n will be symmetrical around $\xi = 0.5$. In addition, we plot the mode shapes and compare them to those of a beam hinged at both ends without the attached mass.

The boundary conditions are

$$W(0) = \frac{d^2W(0)}{d\eta^2} = 0$$

$$W(1) = \frac{d^2(1)}{d\eta^2} = 0 \tag{9.55}$$

Substituting Eq. 9.52 into Eq. 9.54, we find that $A = C = 0$ and that

$$B = \frac{M_0'\Omega}{G_0 m_0}[T(\Omega)R(\Omega\varepsilon) - R(\Omega)T(\Omega\varepsilon)]$$

$$D = \frac{M_0'\Omega}{G_0 m_0}[T(\Omega)T(\Omega\varepsilon)] - R(\Omega)R(\Omega\varepsilon)] \tag{9.56}$$

$$G_0 = R^2(\Omega) - T^2(\Omega)$$

where $\varepsilon = 1 - \xi$. Then, Eq. 9.53, the characteristic equation, becomes

$$R^2(\Omega_n) - T^2(\Omega_n) - \frac{M_0'}{m_0}\Omega_n\{R(\Omega_n\xi)[T(\Omega_n)R(\Omega_n\varepsilon) - R(\Omega_n)T(\Omega_n\varepsilon)]$$

$$+ T(\Omega_n\xi)[T(\Omega_n)T(\Omega_n\varepsilon) - R(\Omega_n)R(\Omega_n\varepsilon)]\} = 0 \tag{9.57}$$

Thus, the mode shape is

$$W_n(u) = B_n V(\Omega_n u) + D_n T(\Omega_n u) + \frac{M_0'}{m_0}\Omega_n T(\Omega_n(u - \xi))H(u - \xi) \tag{9.58}$$

where B_n and D_n are given by Eq. 9.54 with $\Omega = \Omega_n$.

For a hinged beam without an attached mass, it can be shown that (see also Table 9.4)

$$\Omega_n = n\pi$$
$$W_n(\eta) = \sin(n\pi\eta)$$

The following main function contains two sub functions. The first sub function, called **BeamMassCharEqn**, represents Eq. 9.57, the characteristic equation. The second sub function, called **BeamMassMode**, computes the mode shape given by Eq. 9.58. The execution of the following script produces Figures 9.32 and 9.33.

```
function BeamWithMass
Mom = [.1, 1, 10];
opt = optimset('Display', 'off');
xi = linspace(0.05, 0.5, 15);
Ll = [0.4, 1.2, 2.3]*pi;
Ul = [1.1, 2.1, 3.1]*pi;
for m = 1:length(Mom)
  for k = 1:length(xi)
    for n=1:3
      coeff(m, k, n) = fzero(@BeamMassCharEqn, [Ll(n), Ul(n)], opt, xi(k), ...
        Mom(m))/pi;
    end
  end
end
lab = char('first', 'second', 'third');
figure(1)
for kk = 1:3
  plot(xi, coeff(1,:,kk), 'k-', xi, coeff(2,:,kk), 'k--', xi, coeff(3,:,kk), 'k-.')
  hold on
  text(.4, kk+.1, lab(kk,:))
end
axis([0.05, 0.5, 0, 3.5])
xlabel('Mass position, \xi')
ylabel('\Omega_n/\pi')
legend(['M\prime_0/m_0 = ' num2str(Mom(1))], ...
        ['M\prime_0/m_0 = ' num2str(Mom(2))], ...
        ['M\prime_0/m_0 = ' num2str(Mom(3))], 'Location', 'SouthWest')
figure(2)
sig = 1;
lab = char('First mode', 'Second mode', 'Third mode');
for k = 1:3
  if k == 3
    sig = -1;
  end
  for kk = 1:3
    subplot(3, 3, 3*(k-1)+kk)
    [shape, u] = BeamMassMode(coeff(kk,2,k)*pi, 0.4);
    plot(u, shape, 'k-', u, sig*sin(k*u*pi), 'k--', [0 1], [0 0], 'k-')
    axis([0 1 -1 1])
    axis off
    if k == 1
      title(['M\prime_0/m_0 = ' num2str(Mom(kk))])
    end
```

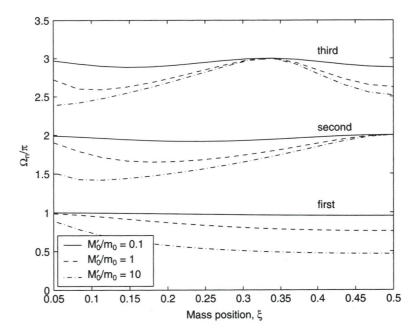

Figure 9.32   Lowest three natural frequency coefficients of a beam simply supported at each end as a function of the position and magnitude of an attached mass.

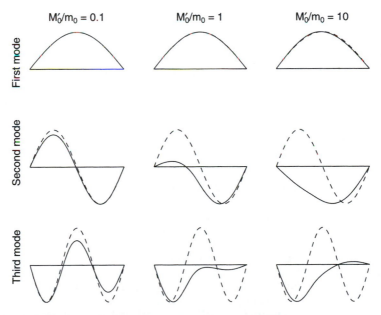

Figure 9.33   Mode shapes of a beam simply supported at each end with a mass attached at $\xi = 0.4$: solid line—beam with mass; dashed line—beam without mass.

```
          if kk == 1
             text(-.15, -.5, lab(k,: ), 'rotation', 90)
          end
       end
    end

function Omn = BeamMassCharEqn(Om, xi, Mom)
ep = 1-xi;
R = inline('(sinh(x)+sin(x))/2', 'x');
T = inline('(sinh(x)-sin(x))/2', 'x');
p1 = R(Om)^2-T(Om)^2;
p2 = R(Om*xi)*(T(Om)*R(Om*ep)-R(Om)*T(Om*ep));
p3 = T(Om*xi)*(T(Om)*T(Om*ep)-R(Om)*R(Om*ep));
Omn = p1-Mom*Om*(p2+p3);

function [modeshape, etat] = BeamMassMode(Om, xi)
ep = 1-xi;
R = inline('(sinh(x)+sin(x))/2', 'x');
T = inline('(sinh(x)-sin(x))/2', 'x');
p1 = R(Om)^2-T(Om)^2;
p2 = (T(Om)*R(Om*ep)-R(Om)*T(Om*ep))/p1;
p3 = (T(Om)*T(Om*ep)-R(Om)*R(Om*ep))/p1;
eta1 = 0:0.01:xi;
modeshape1 = R(Om*eta1)*p2+T(Om*eta1)*p3;
eta = xi+0.01:0.01:1;
modeshape2 = R(Om*eta)*p2+T(Om*eta)*p3+T(Om*(eta-xi));
modeshape = [modeshape1, modeshape2];
modeshape = modeshape/max(abs(modeshape));
etat = [eta1, eta];
```

9.5 SUMMARY OF FUNCTIONS INTRODUCED

A summary of the functions introduced in the chapter is presented in Table 9.5.

TABLE 9.5   MATLAB Functions Introduced in Chapter 9

MATLAB function	Description
besseli	Modified Bessel function of the first kind
besselj	Bessel function of the first kind
besselk	Modified Bessel function of the second kind
bessely	Bessel function of the second kind
bode	Bode frequency response of a linear time-invariant model
damp	Damping factors and natural frequencies of a linear time-invariant model
fminimax	Solves minimax problem
fminsearch	Finds a minimum of an unconstrained multivariable function
impulse	Impulse response of a linear time-invariant model
rank	Estimates the number of linearly independent rows or columns of a full matrix
step	Step response of a linear time-invariant model
tf	Specifies transfer function of a linear time-invariant model
trace	Sum of the diagonal elements of a matrix

EXERCISES

9.1 For the two-mass system given by Eqs. 9.1, numerically determine the corresponding orbit in the (r, θ) plane for the initial conditions $r(0) = 2.0$, $dr(0)/d\tau = 0.0$, $\theta(0) = 0.0$, and $d\theta(0)/d\tau = 0.5$. Use ode45 with the following sets of parameter values: time span of 20 units, step size of 20/400, relative tolerance of 10^{-3}, and absolute tolerance of 10^{-3} for each of the states; and time span of 20 units, step size of 20/4000, relative tolerance of 10^{-6}, and absolute tolerance of 10^{-6} for each of the states.

Determine whether the angular momentum per unit mass $r^2\dot{\theta}$ is conserved in each case throughout the time span of 20 units and display graphs of orbits and angular momentum per unit mass versus time.

9.2 Let $r(0) = r_o$ and $d\theta(0)/d\tau = \theta_o$. Then, Eqs. 9.1 can be reduced to the single equation

$$\frac{1}{2}\left(\frac{dr}{d\tau}\right)^2 + \frac{r_o^2\theta_o^2}{2r^2} - \frac{4\pi^2}{r} = \frac{\theta_o^2}{2} - \frac{4\pi^2}{r_o}$$

The maximum and minimum values of the radial distance r can be determined by setting $dr/d\tau = 0$ in the above equation. Determine if a satellite orbiting the earth will crash on the earth's surface for the following initial conditions:

a. Initial conditions 1:

$$r(0) = 2.0 \quad \frac{dr(0)}{d\tau} = 0 \quad \theta(0) = 0.0 \quad \frac{d\theta(0)}{d\tau} = 2.0$$

b. Initial conditions 2:

$$r(0) = 2.0 \quad \frac{dr(0)}{d\tau} = 0 \quad \theta(0) = 0.0 \quad \frac{d\theta(0)}{d\tau} = 0.2$$

9.3 For the free response of a spring-mass-damper system given by Eq. 9.8, use the function **freeosc** to numerically determine the responses for selected underdamped ($\zeta = 0.1$), overdamped ($\zeta = 2.0$), and critically damped ($\zeta = 1$) cases. Let $x_0 = 1.0$ and $v_0 = 1.0$ for all cases. Compare these responses with those computed from the following equations:[21]

Underdamped

$$x(\tau) = e^{-\zeta\tau}\left\{ x_o \cos\left(\sqrt{1 - \zeta^2}\tau\right) + \frac{v_o + \zeta x_o}{\sqrt{1 - \zeta^2}} \sin\left(\sqrt{1 - \zeta^2}\tau\right) \right\}$$

Critically damped

$$x(\tau) = [x_o + (v_o + x_o)\tau]e^{-\tau}$$

Overdamped

$$x(\tau) = C_1 e^{(-\zeta + \sqrt{\zeta^2 - 1})\tau} + C_2 e^{(-\zeta - \sqrt{\zeta^2 - 1})\tau}$$

---

[21] D. J. Inman, *ibid.*, Section 1.3; S. S. Rao, *ibid.*, Section 2.6; B. Balachandran and E. B. Magrab, *ibid.*, Section 4.2.

where $\tau = \omega_n t$ and

$$C_1 = \frac{x_o\left(\zeta + \sqrt{\zeta^2 - 1}\right) + v_o}{2\sqrt{\zeta^2 - 1}}$$

$$C_2 = \frac{-x_o\left(\zeta - \sqrt{\zeta^2 - 1}\right) - v_o}{2\sqrt{\zeta^2 - 1}}$$

9.4 Consider free oscillation data shown in Table 9.6. Curve fit these data assuming that the response is of the form

$$x(t) = \frac{X_o e^{-\zeta \omega_n}}{\sqrt{1 - \zeta^2}} \sin\left(\omega_n t \sqrt{1 - \zeta^2} + \varphi\right)$$

where

$$\varphi = \tan^{-1}\frac{\sqrt{1 - \zeta^2}}{\zeta}$$

and determine X_o, ζ, and ω_n.

9.5 A mass m slides along a rough rod of length l, which is pivoted at the end O. The angular orientation of the rod with respect to the horizontal is given by $\theta(t)$, and the location of the mass along the rod from its pivot point is given by r. When the rod rotates in the horizontal plane with a constant angular speed $d\theta/dt = \omega$, the equation of motion of mass m is

$$\ddot{r} + 2\mu\,\omega\dot{r} - \omega^2 r = 0$$

where μ is the coefficient of friction between the rod and the mass. For $\mu = 0.2$, $l = 3.0$ m, $\omega = 6$ rad/s, and initial conditions $r(0) = 1.0$ m, $\theta(0) = 0.0$ rad/s, and $\dot{r}(0) = 0.0$ m/s, graph the path of the mass in the (r, θ) plane until it leaves the rod.

TABLE 9.6 Free Oscillation Data

Time	Amplitude	Time	Amplitude	Time	Amplitude
0.000	0.801	10.00	-0.0151	20.77	0.0379
0.692	0.365	10.77	-0.00688	21.54	0.0167
1.538	-0.386	11.54	0.118	22.31	-0.0184
2.308	-0.562	12.31	0.0882	23.08	-0.0259
3.077	-0.114	13.07	-0.028	23.85	-0.0141
3.846	0.349	13.85	-0.0871	24.61	0.0149
4.615	0.338	14.15	-0.0551	25.38	0.0115
5.385	-0.301	15.85	0.0220	26.15	0.00367
6.154	-0.204	16.23	0.0687	26.92	-0.0148
6.923	0.104	17.92	0.0376	27.69	-0.0125
7.692	0.228	18.46	-0.040	28.46	0.0157
8.461	0.008	19.23	-0.0514	29.23	0.00263
9.231	-0.010	20.00	-0.00641	30.00	-0.00727

9.6 The ratio of the measured amplitude to the true acceleration amplitude for an accelerometer is

$$\frac{A_m}{A_t} = \frac{1}{\sqrt{(1 - r^2)^2 + 4\zeta^2 r^2}}$$

where $r = \omega/\omega_n$, ω is the acceleration frequency, ω_n is the accelerometer's natural frequency, and ζ is the accelerometer's damping factor. Obtain the following:

a. A plot of A_m/A_t as a function of r and ζ.
b. The damping factor of an accelerometer with a mass $m = 0.01$ kg and natural frequency of 150 Hz that is to measure accelerations at 6000 rpm with an error e of $\pm 2.0\%$[22] where

$$e = 100\left(1 - \frac{A_m}{A_t}\right) \ \%$$

9.7 The ratio of the measured amplitude to the true displacement amplitude of a seismometer is[23]

$$\frac{d_m}{d_t} = \frac{r^2}{\sqrt{(1 - r^2)^2 + 4\zeta^2 r^2}}$$

where $r = \omega/\omega_n$, ω is the acceleration frequency, ω_n is the seismometer's natural frequency, and ζ is the seismometer's damping factor. Obtain the following:

a. A plot of d_m/d_t as a function of r and ζ.
b. Determine the minimum natural frequency of the seismometer to measure vibrations at 1500 rpm with an error less than $\pm 2.0\%$. Let $\zeta = 0.1$.

9.8 A single-degree-of-freedom system is shown in Figure 9.34 with a dead zone of width $2b$ centered on its equilibrium position. The governing equations of the system are

$$m\ddot{x} + k(x + b) + 2c\dot{x} = F(t) \quad x < -b$$
$$m\ddot{x} + 2c\dot{x} = F(t) \quad -b \leq x \leq b$$
$$m\ddot{x} + k(x - b) + 2c\dot{x} = F(t) \quad x \geq b$$

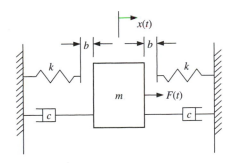

Figure 9.34 Spring-mass-damper system with dead zone.

[22]D. J. Inman, *ibid.*, Section 2.6; S. S. Rao, *ibid.*, Section 10.3; B. Balachandran and E. B. Magrab, *ibid.*
[23]S. S. Rao, *ibid.*, Section 10.3; B. Balachandran and E. B. Magrab, *ibid.*

Determine the free response of a system with $m = 10.0$ kg, $k = 150 \times 10^3$ N/m, and $c = 50$ Ns/m when the motion is initiated from $x(0) = 0$ m and $dx(0)/dt = 2$ m/s in the following cases: dead zone $b = 1.0\,\mu$m and dead zone $b = 1000\,\mu$m. Also, for $b = 5.0\,\mu$m, $x(0) = 0$ m, and $dx(0)/dt = 0$ m/s, determine the forced response of the system when $F(t) = 20\cos(12t)u(t)$ N, where $u(t)$ is the unit step function.

9.9 The transfer function for the mechanical system shown in Figure 9.35 when subjected to base excitation $x_b(t)$ is

$$G(s) = \frac{x_m(s)}{x_b(s)} = \frac{2\zeta\omega_n s + \omega_n^2}{s^2 + 2\zeta\omega_n s + \omega_n^2}$$

Let $\zeta = 0.1$ and $\omega_n = 4$ rad/s. Use bode to determine the amplitude and phase response of this system. Compare these results with those obtained from the analytical solution:

$$G(\omega) = \sqrt{\frac{\omega_n^4 + (2\zeta\omega\omega_n)^2}{(\omega_n^2 - \omega^2)^2 + (2\zeta\omega\omega_n)^2}}$$

$$\phi(\omega) = \tan^{-1}\left(\frac{2\zeta\omega}{\omega_n}\right) - \tan^{-1}\left(\frac{2\zeta\omega\omega_n}{\omega_n^2 - \omega^2}\right)$$

9.10 Consider the vibration absorber discussed in Section 9.3.2 for the undamped case— that is, when $c_1 = c_2 = 0$. Let the primary mass be 1.0 unit, the ratio of the secondary mass to the primary mass be 0.2, the natural frequency of the primary system be 1.0, and the ratio of the natural frequency of the secondary mass to the natural frequency of the primary mass be 1.0. Plot the nondimensional frequency response functions for mass m_1 and mass m_2, and verify that the resonance (pole) locations coincide in both plots and that there is an antiresonance (zero) in the response curve of mass m_1 at the absorber natural frequency.

9.11 Consider the vibration absorber discussed in Section 9.3.2. Set $c_1 = 0$, and fix the ratio of the secondary mass to the primary mass at 0.05. Let the primary mass be 1.0 unit, the natural frequency of the primary system be 1 rad/s, and the ratio of natural frequency of the absorber to the natural frequency of the primary mass be 1.0. For various values of the absorber's damping factor ζ, plot the frequency response curves for the primary mass, and verify that the different graphs intersect at two frequency locations.[24]

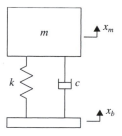

Figure 9.35 Spring-mass-damper system excited at its base.

[24]S. S. Rao, *ibid.*, Section 9.10.

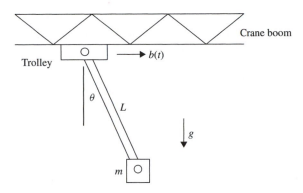

Figure 9.36 Trolley on an overhead crane carrying a swinging load m.

9.12 An overhead crane's trolley is carrying, via a cable, a load of mass m as shown in Figure 9.36. When the trolley is moved with an acceleration $b(t)$, the governing equation of motion of the crane load is

$$L\frac{d^2\theta}{dt^2} + g \sin \theta = -b(t)\cos \theta$$

where $g = 9.8$ m/s^2 is the gravity constant. If the cable length is 2 m, graph the swing motion $\theta(t)$ for the following accelerations of the trolley over the time interval $0 \le t \le 10$ s:

a. $b(t) = 10u(t)$ m/s^2, $\theta(0) = 0.2$ rad, and $d\theta(0)/dt = 0$ rad/s

b. $b(t) = 0.2u(t)$ m/s^2, $\theta(0) = 0.2$ rad, and $d\theta(0)/dt = 0$ rad/s. ($u(t)$ is the unit step function).

9.13 A model that is frequently used to study the bounce-pitch motion of a vehicle is shown in Figure 9.37. The equations governing the free oscillations of the undamped system are

$$m\frac{d^2x}{dt^2} + (k_1 + k_2)x + (L_2 k_2 - L_1 k_1)\theta = 0$$

$$I_c\frac{d^2\theta}{dt^2} + (k_1 L_1^2 + k_2 L_2^2)\theta + (L_2 k_2 - L_1 k_1)x = 0$$

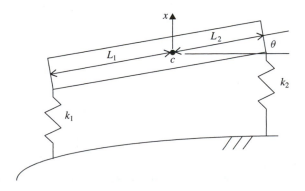

Figure 9.37 Two-degree-of-freedom model of a vehicle.

If $k_1 = 1000$ lb./ft., $k_2 = 1500$ lb./ft., $L_1 = 5$ ft., $L_2 = 4$ ft., $m = 50$ slug, and $I_c = 1000$ slug $\cdot$ ft.^{2}, then by using the associated eigenvalue problem, find the natural frequencies, mode shapes, and node locations.

9.14 A vehicle suspension system can be modeled as shown in Figure 9.38. The governing equations of this system are

$$m_1 \frac{d^2 x_1}{dt^2} + c_1\left(\frac{dx_1}{dt} - \frac{dx_2}{dt}\right) + k_1(x_1 - x_2) = 0$$

$$m_2 \frac{d^2 x_2}{dt^2} + c_1\left(\frac{dx_2}{dt} - \frac{dx_1}{dt}\right) + k_1(x_2 - x_1) + k_2 x_2 + c_2 x_2 = k_2 y + c_2 \frac{dy}{dt}$$

Determine the free response of the system when its initial conditions are $x_1(0) = 0.5$ m, $dx_1(0)/dt = 0$ m/s, $x_2(0) = 0.2$ m, and $dx_2(0)/dt = 0$ m/s. Let $m_1 = 1$ kg, $m_2 = 2$ kg, $c_1 = 1$ N/m/s, $c_2 = 5$ N/m/s, $k_1 = 10$ N/m, and $k_2 = 30$ N/m. Also, take the Laplace transform the equations of motion and, assuming that the initial conditions are zero, plot the frequency response curves for the system.

9.15 Consider a spinning rigid circular shaft that is elastically supported at each end as shown in Figure 9.39. The rotor is spinning at an angular speed of ω rad/s about its axis.

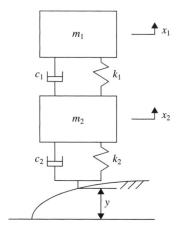

Figure 9.38   One-quarter-car model of a vehicle suspension system.

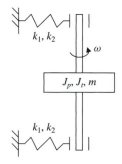

Figure 9.39   Rigid spinning rotor on an elastic support.

Furthermore, the rotor has a polar moment of inertia J_p about the axis of rotation, a transverse moment of inertia J_t about any axis in the plane of rotation, and support stiffness k_1 and k_2 in their respective horizontal directions. The free whirling speeds Ω can be determined from the solution to the eigenvalue problem

$$K'w = \lambda M'w$$

where, $\lambda = \Omega^2$,

$$K' = \begin{bmatrix} KM^{-1}K & KM^{-1}G \\ G'M^{-1}K & K + G'M^{-1}G \end{bmatrix} \quad M' = \begin{bmatrix} K & 0 \\ 0 & M \end{bmatrix}$$

and

$$M = \begin{bmatrix} m & 0 & 0 & 0 \\ 0 & J_t & 0 & 0 \\ 0 & 0 & m & 0 \\ 0 & 0 & 0 & J_t \end{bmatrix} \quad G = \begin{bmatrix} 0 & 0 & 0 & 0 \\ 0 & 0 & 0 & -J_p\omega \\ 0 & 0 & 0 & 0 \\ 0 & J_p\omega & 0 & 0 \end{bmatrix}$$

$$K = \begin{bmatrix} k_1 & 0 & 0 & 0 \\ 0 & k_2 & 0 & 0 \\ 0 & 0 & k_1 & 0 \\ 0 & 0 & 0 & k_2 \end{bmatrix}$$

If $m = 10$ kg, $J_p = 2$ kg·m², $J_t = 1.2$ kg·m², $k_1 = k_2 = 2.5 \times 10^6$ N/m, then plot the value of Ω as a function of ω in the range $0 \le \omega \le 1500$ rad/s. This graph is an example of a Campbell diagram.[25] The speed at which $\Omega = \omega$ is called the critical speed. The results should look like those shown in Figure 9.40.

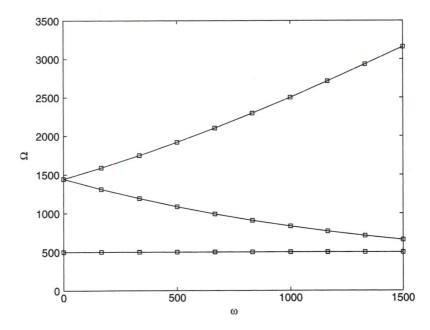

Figure 9.40 Campbell diagram for a spinning rigid rotor on an elastic support.

[25]G. Genta, *Vibration of Structures and Machines: Practical Aspects*, Springer-Verlag, New York, NY, 1993, Section 4.3.

BIBLIOGRAPHY

B. Balachandran and E. B. Magrab, *Vibrations*, Thomson Brooks/Cole, Belmont CA, 2003.

D. T. Greenwood, *Principles of Dynamics*, 2nd ed., Prentice Hall, Englewood Cliffs, NJ, 1988.

F. J. Hale, *Introduction to Space Flight*, Prentice Hall, Englewood Cliffs, NJ, 1994.

D. J. Inman, *Engineering Vibration*, Prentice Hall, Englewood Cliffs, NJ, 1994.

E. B. Magrab, *Vibrations of Elastic Structural Members*, Sijthoff & Noordhoff, Alphen aah den Rijn, The Netherlands, 1979.

L. Meirovitch, *Elements of Vibration Analysis*, McGraw-Hill, New York, NY, 1986.

F. C. Moon, *Applied Dynamics with Applications to Multibody and Mechatronic Systems*, John Wiley & Sons, New York, NY, 1998.

A. H. Nayfeh and B. Balachandran, *Applied Nonlinear Dynamics: Analytical, Computational, and Experimental Methods*, John Wiley & Sons, New York, NY, 1995.

S. S. Rao, *Mechanical Vibrations*, 3rd ed., Addison-Wesley, Reading, MA, 1995.

B. H. Tongue, *Principles of Vibration*, Oxford University Press, New York, NY, 1996.

10

Control Systems

Gregory C. Walsh

The representation, design, and evaluation of control systems using MATLAB's Controls Toolbox and SIMULINK are presented.

10.1 INTRODUCTION TO CONTROL SYSTEM DESIGN

Consider the system shown in Figure 10.1. We find that control systems typically involve a device modeled with differential equations (the plant), with one or more operator-controlled variables (the inputs $u(t)$) and one or more outputs $y(t)$. For all of the systems, an algorithm (the controller), using both the operator's commands (the reference $r(t)$) and the plant outputs, computes the controlled variables. Figure 10.1 represents schematically a cascade-control system in a block diagram. In a cascade-control system, the controller takes the difference between the reference and the output, forming the error signal $e(t) = r(t) - y(t)$. The error signal is then used in the algorithm to produce the input to the plant, $u(t)$. The controller is typically a computer, though in some (older) systems, analog circuits or mechanical devices may be found.

In control systems, one knows from the outset how he or she wants the system to behave. The control design problem therefore involves changing the physical system so that the desired behavior occurs. This requires not only the ability to predict what will happen to a given model of the system but also what changes in the system model are needed to obtain the desired behavior. Thus, control system design is an inverse problem. A control system designer will obtain an inverse model by inferring a system model from experimental data.

Control system design objectives fall into three categories: performance, safety, and robustness. For example, the responsiveness of a servomotor to commands can be quantified with transient design goals, while the eventual fidelity to a given command can be quantified with steady-state design goals. The control designer is usually tasked with ensuring that the system does not enter dangerous conditions or damage itself. Finally, uncertainty enters the control design problem, because sometimes not every input to the system is measured or controlled and because the system to be controlled may change in an unmeasured way over time, over production, or over operating conditions. The aforementioned servomotor may be buffeted by winds one day and a baking sun the next, and it must continue to function. A successfully designed control system is invisible to the user and is never the limiting factor in performance, safety, or robustness.

The control design problem is usually addressed by using feedback. Feedback is the natural idea of using the output of the system as a correction to the input. In addition to the obvious advantage of making a system work without human intervention, feedback also can be used to reduce the effect of nonlinearity, increase system robustness, and enhance stability. Feedback is the most powerful (but not the only)

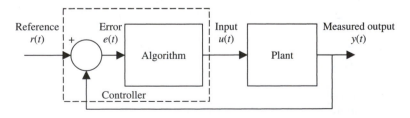

Figure 10.1   Schematic diagram of a feedback loop.

tool in the control engineer's toolbox. Other useful tools include embedded system programming, digital signal processing, and system identification.

In this chapter, we emphasize how one uses the many tools available in MATLAB for solving classes of control problems. In Section 10.2, we detail how control systems are represented in MATLAB using transfer functions, block diagrams, and state-space models. The representation of these models in discrete time—that is, as an embedded computer control system would view them—is also reviewed. In Section 10.3, both methods for computing the response of system models and methods for computing system models from the response are explained. In Section 10.4, design tools, such as Bode plots, the root locus, and LQR/LQG, are detailed. The last section, Section 10.5, is devoted to design examples.

10.1.1 Tools for Controller Design

Controller design demands a good understanding of the solutions of ordinary differential equations, which are required to describe the behavior of physical systems. Before the advent of computational tools like MATLAB, this understanding had to be gained by solving hundreds of differential equations. Linear, time-invariant, ordinary differential equations are represented in three different formats in MATLAB:

1. State-space equations
2. Transfer functions
3. Block diagrams

State-space representations are time-domain based and use matrices. Transfer functions are Laplace-domain based and use polynomials of the complex variable s. Block-diagram representations, available through the SIMULINK toolbox in MATLAB, visually depict the input and output connections. Conversion between the various representations is facilitated by built-in functions provided by MATLAB.

For this chapter, we will consider three types of control objectives:

1. Transient
2. Steady state
3. Stability

Transient design requirements focus on the short-term behavior of the system and address concerns such as responsiveness and stiffness. Steady-state requirements focus on the long-term behavior of the system, answering questions about how the system will perform over long periods of time. Standard input signals, such as steps, ramps, and sinusoids, are applied to test whether the system meets transient and steady-state design requirements. MATLAB provides functions for finding the response of systems to the standard test signals. Transient and steady-state requirements are performance oriented, while feedback stability has more to do with safety. Feedback has the potential to both remove and introduce instability into otherwise well-behaved physical processes, and instability must always be avoided. Transient and steady-state design requirements are typically in conflict, forcing one to make a design trade-off. In practice, limitations in control performance come from inherent limitations in the sensors, actuators, and the plant.

Graphical tools used to solve control problems include Bode plots, Nyquist plots, and root locus plots. Linear algebra–based tools are used in more advanced design techniques, such as LQG (linear quadratic Gaussian), H_∞, and μ-synthesis. For most single-input, single-output control designs, one of five controllers that are presented in this chapter will solve the design problem.

10.1.2 Naming and File Conventions

In the course of this chapter, we use a standard set of naming conventions. Because the description of even a simple differential equation requires multiple vectors and matrices, MATLAB provides a method for gathering the necessary matrices and vectors under a single name. These collections of matrices, vectors, and even strings are called systems. We will use the name *Plant* to label systems whose structure is fixed during the controller design and the name *Control* to label the part we will be able to choose. The final closed-loop system, consisting of the *Plant* connected with the *Control,* we will label *clSys*. If the feedback connection is broken, we will call the resulting system *olSys*. The MATLAB functions used in this chapter to assemble and analyze control systems take systems, instead of vectors and matrices, as arguments.

Several example systems are considered in this chapter. For convenience, we will create function files that return these model systems. The functions will return a system object. The examples covered include:

- A permanent magnet motor with a load (**MotorSS**)
- A pointer with a flexible shaft (**Pointer**)
- A magnetic levitator (**MagLev**)
- An inverted pendulum (**Pend**)
- A flywheel (**Fly**).

Controllers, such as lead, lag, PI, and PD, are generated as needed.

10.2 REPRESENTATION OF SYSTEMS IN MATLAB

The input to a control system is described by a real-valued function of time $r(t)$. This quantity typically represents some physical variable under control, such as a force, voltage, or temperature. The output of a control system is also described by a real-valued function of time $y(t)$. The value of this function is some measured quantity, such as angle, pressure, or velocity. The relationship between the input function $u(t)$ and the output function $y(t)$ in control systems is represented by a linear, time-invariant, ordinary differential equation, which has the general form

$$a_n \frac{d^n y(t)}{dt^n} + a_{n-1} \frac{d^{n-1} y(t)}{dt^{n-1}} + \cdots + a_0 y(t)$$

$$= b_m \frac{d^m u(t)}{dt^m} + b_{m-1} \frac{d^{m-1} u(t)}{dt^{m-1}} + \cdots + b_0 u(t)$$

(10.1)

where $n \geq m$. The coefficients of the equation, a_j and b_j, are constant real-valued numbers. System models in MATLAB are stored as objects, and much like the graphics objects of Chapters 6 and 7, the properties of these models are accessible though the use of get and set. Introductory control topics typically focus on differential equations of the form shown in Eq. 10.1, and MATLAB provides three classes to represent this type of input–output relationship:

- Transfer function representation (class tf)
- State-space representation (class ss)
- Zero-pole-gain representation (class zpk)

   Discrete-time linear systems are also of great practical interest, since control loops are often implemented on computers. All three representations also have discrete-time versions, where the additional information concerning the sampling time is appended. Having the system models encapsulated as objects allows the user to attach auxiliary data to the representation. Examples of data fields attached to system objects include InputName, OutputName, and Notes.

   To illustrate the three primary representations, consider the simple model of a DC permanent-magnet servomotor shown in Figure 10.2. The input voltage $v(t)$ is applied to the windings of the motor producing electrical current $i(t)$. The current in the windings produces a torque on the rotor that is proportional to its magnitude. The effective inertia J is the sum of the load inertia J_1 and the rotor inertia J_m. The rotor with angle $\theta(t)$ acts like a generator, producing a back voltage proportional to the angular velocity of the rotor. A torque balance and circuit analysis yields the following coupled linear ordinary differential equations[1] describing the relationship between the input voltage $v(t)$ and the output angle $\theta(t)$:

$$L\frac{di(t)}{dt} + k_b\frac{d\theta(t)}{dt} + Ri(t) = v(t)$$

$$J\frac{d^2\theta(t)}{dt^2} + b\frac{d\theta(t)}{dt} - k_\tau i(t) = 0$$

(10.2)

The electrical constants are R, L, k_τ, and k_b, where R is the motor resistance, L is the winding inductance, k_τ is the conversion factor from current to torque, and k_b is the

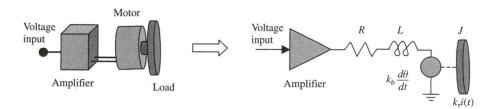

Figure 10.2   A common electric servomotor.

[1]D. K. Anand and R. B. Zmood, *Introduction to Control Systems*, 3rd ed., Butterworth-Heinemann Ltd. Oxford, England, 1995.

back emf generator constant. The total inertia J is usually dominated by the load inertia J_1. The motor friction b is generally small if there is no gearbox. We shall now convert these equations into the three system representations.

10.2.1 State-Space Models

State-space models gained popularity with the widespread use of computers, since they can be made more numerically reliable than transfer functions. State-space models are first order–coupled differential equations. The model of the motor in Eqs. 10.2 is not first order. In particular, there is a second time derivative of $\theta(t)$. To represent the motor as a state-space model, we first have to convert the equations to first order, as was done in Section 5.5.3. Let

$$x_1(t) = \theta(t)$$

$$x_2(t) = \frac{d\theta(t)}{dt} = \omega(t)$$

$$x_3(t) = i(t)$$

Then, Eqs. 10.2 become

$$\frac{dx_1}{dt} = x_2$$

$$\frac{dx_2}{dt} = -\frac{b}{J}x_2 + \frac{k_\tau}{J}x_3$$

$$\frac{dx_3}{dt} = -\frac{k_b}{L}x_2 - \frac{R}{L}x_3 + \frac{v(t)}{L}$$

If we let

$$x(t) = [x_1(t), x_2(t), x_3(t)]'$$

$$u(t) = v(t)$$

$$y(t) = \theta(t) = x_1(t)$$

then the state-space representation for the motor system is

$$\frac{dx(t)}{dt} = Ax(t) + Bu(t)$$

$$y(t) = Cx(t) + Du(t)$$

(10.3)

where

$$A = \begin{bmatrix} 0 & 1 & 0 \\ 0 & -b/J & k_\tau/J \\ 0 & -k_b/L & -R/L \end{bmatrix}$$

$$B = [0 \quad 0 \quad 1/L]'$$

$$C = [1 \quad 0 \quad 0]$$

$$D = [0]$$

The matrices A, B, C, and D are the essential data needed to describe the differential equations in MATLAB.

We now illustrate these results with several examples.

Example 10.1   State-space model of a servomotor

We shall create a function **MotorSS** that will return a state-space system model of the servomotor shown in Figure 10.2. The values assumed for the constants are $L = 5$ mH (motor inductance), $R = 5\ \Omega$ (motor resistance), $k_b = 0.125$ V/rad/s (back emf constant), $k_\tau = 15$ Nm/A (motor torque constant), $J = 0.03$ kg·m^2 (rotor inertia), and $B = 0.01$ Nm/rad/s (rotor friction).

The function is given as follows:

```
function Plant = MotorSS(Jl)
if nargin < 1
    Jl = 0;
end;
L = 5e-3;  R = 5;  kb = 12.5e-2;
ki = 15;  J = 3e-2 + Jl;  b = 1e-2;
A = [0, 1, 0; 0, -b/J, ki/J; 0, -kb/L, -R/L];
B = [0; 0; 1/L];
C = [1, 0, 0];
D = 0;
Plant = ss(A, B, C, D);
set(Plant, 'InputName', 'volts','OutputName', '\theta');
set(Plant, 'StateName', {'\theta', '\omega','i'});
set(Plant, 'Notes', 'Small DC servomotor');
```

The function ss collects the matrices A, B, C, and D into a single system object. Typing

MotorSS

in the MATLAB command window displays

```
a =
            \theta      \omega       i
   \theta      0          1          0
   \omega      0      -0.33333     500
       i      0        -25       -1000
b =
            volts
   \theta      0
   \omega      0
       i      200
c =
            \theta      \omega       i
   \theta      1          0          0
d =
            volts
   \theta      0
Continuous-time model.
```

The input is labeled by default $u1$, the output $y1$, and the interior states $x1$, $x2$, and $x3$. We preferred to label these using our own labels, which was done using `set`. Thus, we have named the state-space variables θ, ω, and i. In addition, we have included a note to remind us what the model represents. Without labeling the model, the following would have been displayed in the MATLAB command window:

```
a =
               x1        x2        x3
       x1       0         1         0
       x2       0      -0.33333    500
       x3       0        -25      -1000
b =
               u1
       x1       0
       x2       0
       x3      200
c =
               x1        x2        x3
       y1       1         0         0
d =
               u1
       y1       0
Continuous-time system.
```

When the function **MotorSS** is called, only the system object is returned, not any of the constants. If we wish to recover the matrices A, B, C, and D, we use

[A, B, C, D] = ssdata(**MotorSS**)

which displays to the command window the following matrices A, B, C, and D:

```
A =
  1.0e+003 *
        0    0.0010        0
        0   -0.0003    0.5000
        0   -0.0250   -1.0000
B =
     0
     0
   200
C =
     1    0    0
D =
     0
```

MATLAB provides functions that take system objects such as **MotorSS** as an argument. Suppose we wish to examine the behavior of the motor when it is connected

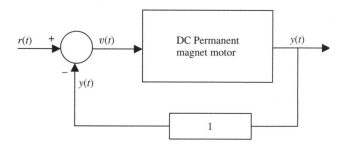

Figure 10.3   A simple unity gain feedback control system for controlling the servomotor.

in a simple feedback configuration as shown in Figure 10.3. From the schematic, we have

$$v(t) = r(t) - y(t) = r(t) - Cx(t)$$

and consequently, Eqs. 10.3 become

$$\frac{dx(t)}{dt} = (A - BC)x(t) + Br(t)$$

$$y(t) = Cx(t) + Dr(t)$$

which amounts to replacing A in Eqs. 10.3 with $A - BC$. MATLAB provides a function for the operation we have just described mathematically. The command is

clSys = feedback(**MotorSS**, 1);

which returns the closed-loop system. The number 1 in the second argument describes the transfer function of the feedback loop, which we have assumed is 1. Note that A of *clSys* is equal to $A - BC$ of **MotorSS**. One can check this by typing in the command window

clSys = feedback(**MotorSS**, 1);
Plant = **MotorSS**;
clSys.a- (Plant.a - Plant.b*Plant.c)

which returns a (3×3) matrix of zeros.

The function feedback performed the algebra necessary to connect the motor system into a new configuration. Other MATLAB functions, which take systems as arguments, solve the differential equations when inputs are applied. In the next example, we use step to compute the response of the system to a step input signal.

Example 10.2   Step response of a servomotor

We shall determine the response of the servomotor shown in Figure 10.2 to a step input. The script is

```
[y, t] = step(feedback(MotorSS, 1));
plot(t, y, 'k-');
xlabel('Time (s)');
ylabel('Rotor angle \theta(t)  (radians)');
```

Upon execution, we obtain the results shown in Figure 10.4.

We now extend the previous script to generate the step response of the servomotor for a variety of load inertias. The script is

```
t = 0:0.05:2;
Jload = 0:0.01:0.1;
data = zeros(length(t), length(Jload));
for i = 1:length(Jload)
    data(:,i) = step(feedback(MotorSS(Jload(i)), 1), t);
end;
mesh(Jload, t, data);
view([45, 30]);
xlabel('Load inertia J_l (kg m^2)');
ylabel('Time (s)');
zlabel('Rotor angle \theta(t) (radians)')
```

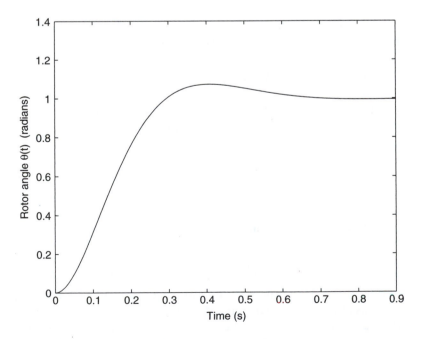

Figure 10.4   Step response of the servomotor control system.

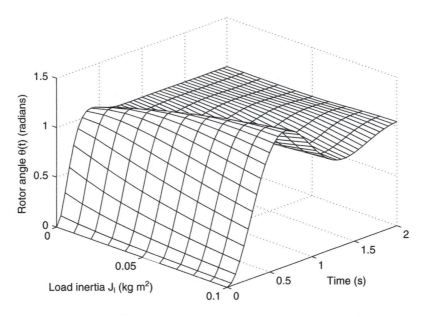

Figure 10.5   Response of the closed-loop servomotor to a step command in position as a function of load inertia.

The results are shown in Figure 10.5. The response overshoots the goal more as the load inertia J_{load} is increased. In Section 10.3, we shall develop a similar set of expectations for system responses as a function of pole and zero locations.

10.2.2 Transfer-Function Representation

The transfer-function representation is the Laplace transform of the output divided by the Laplace transform of the input, assuming zero initial conditions. Although this representation is less general and more sensitive to numerical errors than the state-space approach,[2] it remains popular for the intuition it provides the designer. For a general ordinary differential equation of the form given by Eq. 10.1, the transfer function is given by

$$H(s) = \frac{Y(s)}{R(s)} = \frac{b_m s^m + b_{m-1} s^{m-1} + \cdots + b_0}{a_n s^n + a_{n-1} s^{n-1} + \cdots + a_1 s + a_0} \tag{10.4}$$

where $a_n \neq 0$ and $n \geq m$. The roots of the denominator's polynomial are called the poles of the system, and the roots of the numerator are called the zeros. A transfer function is represented in MATLAB as two vectors, each containing the coefficients of s. The coefficients of the numerator polynomial are

Num = [bm, ..., b1, b0]

---

[2]*MATLAB Control System Toolbox, User's Guide*, Version 4, The Math Works, Natick, MA, 1992.

and those of the denominator polynomial are

Den = [an, ..., a1, a0]

The coefficient a_n is often set to 1 by dividing all coefficients by it, but doing so is not required. To find the transfer function, one takes the Laplace transform of the equations of motion and does the algebra needed to find the ratio $H(s)$. Taking a Laplace transformation of Eqs. 10.2 yields

$$k_b s \Theta(s) + (sL - R)I(s) = V(s)$$
$$(Js^2 + bs)\Theta(s) - k_\tau I(s) = 0$$

where we have assumed that the initial conditions are zero. Solving for $\Theta(s)$ gives

$$\Theta(s) = \frac{k_\tau}{(sL + R)(Js^2 + bs) + k_\tau k_b s} V(s) \qquad (10.5)$$

The system transfer-function model is now generated with the following script. It is the transfer-function representation of the state-space model generated by **MotorSS**:

```
function PlantTF = MotorTF
L = 5e-3;  R = 5;  kb = 12.5e-2;
ki = 15;  J = 3e-2;  b = 1e-2;
Num = ki;
Den = conv([L, R], [J, b, 0]) + [0, 0, kb*ki, 0];
PlantTF = tf(Num, Den);
```

When one types

MotorTF

in the command window, the following is displayed:

```
Transfer function:
            15
-----------------------------------
0.00015 s^3 + 0.15 s^2 + 1.925 s
```

The coefficients of the numerator and denominator polynomials, *Num* and *Den*, are the essential data for the transfer-function realization, just as the matrices *A*, *B*, *C*, and *D* were the essential data for the state-space realization. Names of the input, output, and other descriptive fields can be set as before by using set and get. To extract the coefficients of the numerator and denominator polynomials, we use

[Num, Den] = tfdata(**MotorTF**, 'v')

The character v tells the function to return *Num* and *Den* as row vectors. If v is omitted, the numerator will be returned in a cell array, which is used to represent multiple-input, multiple-output (MIMO) systems. For the most part, we confine our discussion to single-input, single-output (SISO) systems. Upon execution, we obtain

```
Num =
   0   0   0   15
Den =
   0.0001   0.1500   1.9250      0
```

As with state-space systems, MATLAB functions accept transfer-function systems as input arguments. For example, the command

```
step(feedback(MotorTF, 1))
```

will compute and plot the response of the controlled motor subjected to a step input command. Notice that `step` and `feedback` are the same commands used for the state-space models. These functions will work with any representation of a system object.

Two other useful functions are `pole` and `tzero`. The function `pole` returns the poles (roots of the denominator polynomial in the case of transfer functions). For example,

```
p = pole(feedback(MotorTF, 1))
```

displays

```
p =
1.0e+02 *
-9.8744
-0.0645 + 0.0773i
-0.0645 - 0.0773i
```

which are the closed-loop poles of the simple control system. The function `tzero` returns the transmission zeros of a plant. Thus,

```
z = tzero(feedback(MotorTF, 1));
```

sets z to an empty matrix; that is, the system has no zeros. Both `pole` and `tzero` may be applied to state-space systems as well. The transfer function is related to the state-space model through the equation

$$H(s) = C(sI - A)^{-1}B$$

where I is the unit matrix. From this equation, it is seen that the roots of the denominator equation, the poles, are equal to the roots of the determinant of $(sI - A)$, which are the eigenvalues of the matrix A. The concepts of poles, zeros, and eigenvalues are frequently used to develop understanding of the behavior of a control system.

One representation of a transfer function is the zero-pole-gain format, which is parameterized by the poles and zeros. In general, because the transfer function is a rational polynomial function, its numerator and denominator can both be factored to give

$$H(s) = k \frac{(s - z_1)(s - z_2)\dots(s - z_m)}{(s - p_1)(s - p_2)\dots(s - p_n)} \qquad (10.6)$$

The transfer function is uniquely defined by its list of poles and zeros together with the constant gain k. We now generate a zero-pole-gain model of the closed-loop control system shown in Figure 10.3. First, we generate the lists of the poles and zeros and set the gain to 1 by dividing by the DC gain. The script is

```
Poles = pole(feedback(MotorTF, 1));
Z = tzero(feedback(MotorTF, 1));
PlantZPK = zpk(Z, Poles, 1);
PlantZPK = dcgain(feedback(MotorTF, 1))/dcgain(PlantZPK)*PlantZPK;
step(PlantZPK);
```

which upon execution also yields Figure 10.4. The commands feedback, pole, and tzero also apply to this model.

10.2.3 Discrete-Time Models

Discrete-time versions of the state-space, transfer-function, and zero-pole-gain models can be generated using

```
c2d
```

The function c2d uses, by default, the zero-order-hold approximation. Functions such as step, impulse, and feedback support discrete-time system models. The sampling time of the various components must be the same when combining elements. If

```
c2d(MotorSS, 0.001)
```

is typed in the MATLAB command window, the following system description is displayed:

```
a =
            \theta      \omega          i
   \theta       1   0.00099818   0.00018374
   \omega       0      0.99507      0.31535
        i       0     -0.015768     0.36458
```

b =
```
              volts
    \theta    1.3203e-05
    \omega    0.036748
       i      0.12617
```
c =
```
              \theta    \omega     i
    \theta      1         0         0
```
d =
```
              volts
    \theta      0
```

Note that the matrices a and b of the discrete-time model are substantially different from those of the continuous time models. The state equations for discrete-time models evolve using difference equations, not differential equations. In the case of state-space models, we have, for time indexed by k,

$$x[k + 1] = A_d x[k] + B_d u[k]$$
$$y[k] = Cx[k] + Du[k]$$

which are matrix multiplications. These matrix multiplications match the behavior of the continuous-time differential equations given by Eqs. 10.3 at sample times $t = k\Delta$, where Δ is the sampling interval as long as the matrices A_d and B_d are chosen properly. With a zero-order-hold approximation, we have[3]

$$A_d = e^{A\Delta}$$

$$B_d = \int_0^\Delta e^{A(\Delta - \tau)} B d\tau$$

which maps all left-half complex plane eigenvalues into the unit circle. The triangle approximation, the bilinear approximation (Tustin), the prewarped Tustin approximation, and the matched approximation are also available in MATLAB.

If the command

c2d(**MotorTF**, 0.001)

---

[3]See, for example, T. Kailith, *Linear Systems Theory*, Prentice Hall, Englewood Cliffs, NJ, 1980; or K. Astrom and B. Wittenmark, *Computer Controlled Systems*, 3rd ed., Prentice Hall, Upper Saddle River, NJ, 1997.

is typed in the command window, then the following polynomial representation of a discrete time system is displayed:

Transfer function:
1.32e-005 z^2 + 4.191e-005 z + 8.023e-006
----
  z^3 - 2.36 z^2 + 1.727 z - 0.3678

Sampling time: 0.001

Example 10.3   Conversion of a continuous-time model to a discrete-time model

We convert a continuous-time model to a discrete-time model with a sampling time of 1 ms. For clarity in the graphical output of the script, we plot the results with a small offset added to the continuous system response to separate it from the discrete-time response.

```
[ydiscrete, time] = step(feedback(c2d(MotorSS, 0.001), 1));
ycontinous = step(feedback(MotorSS, 1), time);
plot(time, ycontinous, 'k-.', time, ydiscrete+0.1, 'k-');
grid;
xlabel('Time (s)');
ylabel('Response');
legend('Continuous', 'Discrete', 4)
```

The result of executing this script is shown in Figure 10.6. Since the sampling time chosen was so small, there is no observable difference between the two step responses.

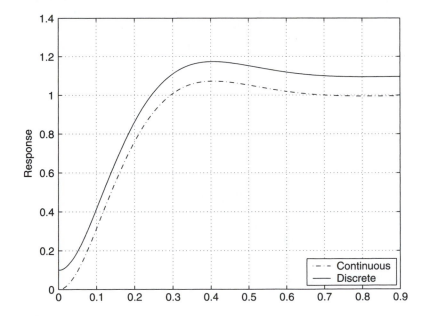

Figure 10.6   Comparison of the discrete-time step response and the continuous-time step response. (A vertical shift of 0.1 in the discrete-time response has been arbitrarily introduced.)

In discrete time, transfer functions are polynomials of the complex variable z instead of the complex variable s. The variable z is used to represent one sample delay, instead of the transform of a derivative. Consider a generic discrete-time transfer function:

$$H(z) = \frac{Y(z)}{R(z)} = \frac{b_m z^m + b_{m-1} z^{m-1} + \cdots + b_0}{a_n z^n + a_{n-1} z^{n-1} + \cdots + a_1 z + a_0} \tag{10.7}$$

By multiplying both sides of Eq. 10.7 by $R(z)$, we obtain

$$a_n z^n Y(z) + a_{n-1} z^{n-1} Y(z) + \cdots + a_0 Y(z)$$
$$= b_m z^m R(z) + b_{m-1} z^{m-1} R(z) + \cdots + b_0 R(z)$$

This can be converted to discrete sample times as follows:

$$a_n y[j+n] + a_{n-1} y[j+n-1] + \cdots + a_0 y[j]$$
$$= b_m r[j+m] + b_{m-1} r[j+m-1] + \cdots + b_0 r[j]$$

Setting $k = j + n$ and $p = n - m$, we solve for $y[k]$ and obtain

$$y[k] = \frac{1}{a_{n-1}} (-a_{n-1} y[k-1] - \cdots - a_0 y[k-n] + b_m r[k-p]$$
$$+ b_{m-1} r[k-p-1] + \cdots + b_0 r[k-p-m]) \tag{10.8}$$

Implementing control and filtering algorithms in an embedded system often involve at their core a computation such as Eq. 10.8, which is known as an infinite impulse response (IIR) filter. A computer can implement this type of algorithm at each sample time with a series of multiplications and additions as long as the computer stores previous values of the computed output and measured inputs. Special-purpose computer architectures for embedded control and filtering systems have been developed to implement this equation and other similar equations quickly.

10.2.4 Block Diagrams and SIMULINK®

A typical control system is composed of several distinct units, such as the plant and the controller. More complicated structures involving many distinct subsystems are often studied, and these input-output maps are sketched by system designers using block diagrams, the basic elements of which are shown in Figure 10.7. MATLAB has provided a collection of built-in functions and operators to compute their transfer functions, a process referred to as block-diagram algebra. MATLAB supplies standard operators (+, −, *, and /) and provides feedback, series, and connect, among others, so that the block diagrams may be implemented and simulated from the command line. The SIMULINK Toolbox provides a graphical user interface from which one can literally sketch the block diagram and simulate the characteristics of the resulting system.

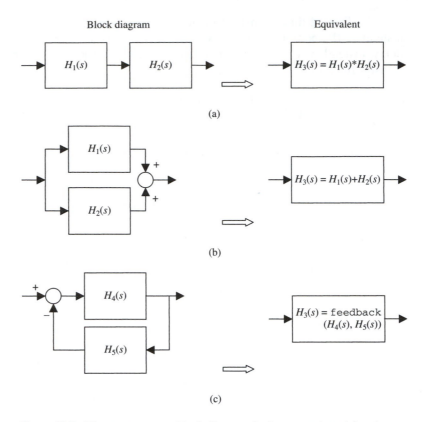

Figure 10.7 The most common block-diagram algebra operations: (a) series (cascade); (b) parallel; (c) feedback.

The cascade connection of two systems shown in Figure 10.7a can be determined using the multiplication operator. For example, if system objects H1 and H2 represent the transfer functions $H_1(s)$ and $H_2(s)$, respectively, then the resulting cascaded system $H_3(s)$ can be obtained by

H3 = H1*H2

Division is also supported, but it is applicable only to strictly proper models and will not be considered here.

The parallel connection of two systems illustrated in Figure 10.7b can be found using the addition and subtraction operators. If systems $H1$ and $H2$ are connected in parallel, then the resulting system is

H3 = H1 + H2

Subtraction is obtained by changing the sign in the above equation to minus.

The feedback connection shown in Figure 10.7c differs from the other two operations in that a function, instead of an operator, implements the operation. If systems $H4$ and $H5$ are connected in feedback, then the resulting closed loop system is given by

H3 = feedback($H4, H5$);

Negative feedback is assumed; if positive feedback is desired, then $H_3(s)$ is obtained from

H3 = feedback($H4, H5,+1$);

One common control configuration is called cascade feedback, which was shown in Figure 10.1. This configuration is the combination of Figure 10.7a, the cascade, with Figure 10.7c, feedback. In this case, the output of the *Plant* (H_2) is subtracted from the input, and the resulting error signal is fed to the *Controller* (H_1). To build the closed-loop model, we set

H4 = Controller*Plant

and

H5 = 1

The closed-loop system *clSys* is then obtained from

clSys = feedback(Controller*Plant, 1);

The functions feedback and series and the operators *, +, and − also support MIMO systems by allowing vector-valued inputs and outputs. In addition, matrix operations allow the quick construction of MIMO systems. For example, a two-input, one-output system $H3$ can be created from two SISO plants, $H1$ and $H2$, using

H3 = [H1, H2]

A one-input, two-output system can be created with

H3 = [H1; H2]

The subsystems $H1$ and $H2$ can be extracted from $H3$ using the same operations used to extract sub matrices discussed in Section 2.4. Cascade, parallel, and feedback connections require specifications as to which inputs are connected to which outputs when working with MIMO systems. The functions series and parallel are provided for these purposes. More complicated MIMO structures may be formed using ift and connect. In this chapter, we consider SISO control systems almost exclusively.

If the system objects $H1$ and $H2$ are different types, then an implicit conversion is performed so that the resulting model is homogeneous. MATLAB favors state-space models above all others; therefore, if any one of the models in a computation is a state-space model, the result will be in state-space form. Between transfer-function and zero-pole-gain models, transfer-function models are favored.

SIMULINK

SIMULINK allows a designer to model and simulate systems by constructing them from a large library of components. The components are selected from the library, dragged to a modeling window, and connected, after which their individual parameters are specified. Then, the model is run and the results displayed.

SIMULINK is invoked by typing

```
simulink
```

at the MATLAB command line. Variables defined in the MATLAB command window are accessible from the SIMULINK window.

We shall illustrate how to model the DC servomotor with SIMULINK. The final result is shown in Figure 10.8. To generate the plant model, we first define it in the MATLAB command window and extract the system matrices. Then, we start SIMULINK. Thus,

```
[A, B, C, D] = ssdata(MotorSS);
simulink
```

This brings up the SIMULINK library browser window, which displays a list of available libraries and includes the SIMULINK main library. First, we click on the new page icon (white rectangle) to open a SIMULINK modeling window. Then, we return to the browser window and double-click on SIMULINK, which displays the following directory of SIMULINK component libraries:

Continuous
Discontinuities
Discrete
Look Up Tables
Math Operations
Model Verification

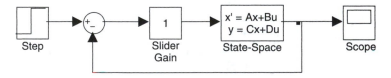

Figure 10.8   A block-diagram model of a DC servomotor created in SIMULINK.

Model Wide Utilities

Ports and Subsystems

Signal Attributes

Signal Routing

Sinks

Sources

User-Defined Functions

   To open the components (blocks) of any of these libraries, click on the library name of interest. We start by displaying the *Continuous* library. Next, we click on *State-Space* and, keeping the mouse button depressed, drag a copy of this library component to the modeling window. We place the component at its desired location and release the mouse button. Next, we go to the *Math Operations* library and sequentially select *Slider Gain* and *Sum,* dragging them one at a time to the model window, and placing each, respectively, to the left of the *State-Space* component. Then, we go to the *Sources* library, select *Step,* and place it in the modeling window to the left of all the components placed so far. The last component we select is *Scope,* from the *Sinks* library. It is placed to the right of all the components selected.

   The next steps are to specify the parameters of the components. We start with the *State-Space* block and double-click on it. This brings up a *State-Space* parameter window with five places to enter data: A, B, C, D, and *Initial Condition*. Since these matrices have been defined in the MATLAB command window, we type A, B, C, and D, respectively, for each of the four quantities. Had we selected different names in the MATLAB command window, we would have entered those names in their appropriate places. We leave the initial condition at 0. The signs of the summation are changed in the same manner; the second sign is changed to negative. The range of gains for the slider may also be selected. A range of 0 for the smallest and 15 for the largest is recommended. The center selection of 1 is left as is. We use the default values for the *Step* block except for *Step Time* (time offset or delay), which we set to 0. Double-clicking on *Scope* brings up a simulation of an oscilloscope display. There are no parameters to select at this point.

   We now connect the components to form a feedback control system. Each of the components in the project window may be moved and resized using the mouse, if desired. Connections are made at the small protrusions on the exterior of the blocks; by default, inputs are on the left and outputs on the right. Connections are made by using the mouse and dragging a line from an output to an input. Place the crosshairs at the output of the *Step* block, and with the left button depressed, move the crosshairs to the plus ($+$) input of the *Sum* component. Continue this process until the connected block diagram looks like that shown in Figure 10.8. The line that goes from the middle of the *State-Space* block and the *Scope* to the negative input of the summing device is created as follows: Place the cursor (arrowhead) on the existing line between these two blocks, and while maintaining this position, depress the *Ctrl* key on the keyboard and then the left mouse button. While holding both of these down, move the crosshairs to the negative input of the summing device, and release the mouse and *Ctrl* key. To adjust the line, simply click on it, and with the mouse button depressed, move it up or down to its desired position.

The placement and size of each component is not material; only the connections are. There will be models in which, before making these connections, we will have to flip one or more of the blocks around so that the inputs are on the right and the outputs on the left. This operation is performed by selecting (clicking on) the block and then going to the *Format* pull-down menu and selecting *Flip Block*. Also from the *Format* menu, one can suppress the display of the block identifier beneath the block. Select the block, and then select *Hide Name*. To put the identifier back, select the block, and then select *Show Name*. These two choices do not appear together.

To run the simulation, we go to the *Simulation* menu and select *Start*. After the simulation has executed, double-click on *Scope* to see the results. Use the *x*- and *y*-axis zoom icons to obtain the desired resolution for the image. Note that under the *Simulation* menu, one may adjust the parameters of the simulation, such as the integration method used, by selecting *Parameters*. If the diagram is not completely or correctly connected, the simulation will not run, and MATLAB will send error messages to the MATLAB command window and to a special pop-up window. When rendered as indicated in Figure 10.8, the results shown in *Scope* are those given in Figure 10.4.

10.2.5 Conversion Between Representations

MATLAB provides functions for converting between the three representations using the system constructor functions `ss`, `tf`, and `zpk`. For example, the transfer-function model can be generated from the state-space model by using the state-space model **MotorSS** in `tf`.

> PlantTF = `tf`(**MotorSS**)

Slight differences in the coefficients of system models result from numerical errors in the conversion process.

The state-space model can be generated from the transfer-function model by using `ss`. Thus,

> PlantTF = `tf`(**MotorSS**);
> PlantSS = `ss`(PlantTF)

The resulting system matrices A, B, C, and D are not the same matrices that were defined in **MotorSS**, which points out that unlike the transfer-function model, there is no unique state-space representation for a given system. One typically uses

> `ssbal`

to scale the input, state, and output quantities to make the simulation as well conditioned as possible. Thus,

> PlantTF = `tf`(**MotorSS**);
> PlantSS = `ss`(PlantTF)
> PlantBal = `ssbal`(PlantSS)

attempts to find the best-conditioned representation of the system.

The zero-pole-gain model can also be converted from state-space or transfer-function models. For example, the zero-pole-gain model could have been generated from the state-space model using

```
PlantTF = tf(MotorSS);
PlantSS = ss(PlantTF)
PlantZ = zpk(PlantSS)
```

This (and the other conversion methods) make use of the numerical root-finding algorithms within MATLAB and are sometimes subject to large numerical errors, especially for systems of order 10 and higher.[4] In practical situations, it is recommended that one resist changing representations often.

10.3 RESPONSE OF SYSTEMS

In this section, we illustrate the use of a number of tools available for estimating the response of a system and, conversely, for estimating a system given its response. Functions for computing the response of a system applicable to all three representations in both continuous and discrete time include `step`, `impulse`, `initial`, and `lsim`. The SIMULINK toolbox also supplies a number of built-in signal sources that simplify simulation when using block diagrams. For estimating a system from its response, we will use the function `arx`.

The locations of the poles and zeros, either in a transfer-function or state-space representation, are a shorthand notation that control engineers use to estimate the responses of a system. Many design specifications can be translated into pole and zero location constraints. The controller design problem often becomes one of designing feedback so that the closed-loop poles lie in desired regions of the complex plane. Zeros cannot be moved by feedback.

10.3.1 Estimating Response from Systems

The response of a control system to a step input is the most commonly used benchmark to compare different controller designs. The MATLAB function `step` computes the step response and, if the return values are not requested, plots it as well. The function automatically determines a suitable range of times in which to compute the simulation. Thus, the script

```
[theta, t] = step(MotorSS);
plot(t, theta)
xlabel('Time (s)')
ylabel('\theta(t)')
```

Upon execution of the script, we obtain Figure 10.9. From this figure, it is seen that the step response of the motor is a ramp, because if a constant voltage is applied to the windings, eventually a constant speed will be reached.

---

[4]N. E. Leonard and W. S. Levine, *Using MATLAB to Analyze and Design Control Systems*, Benjamin/Cummings, Redwood City, CA, 1992.

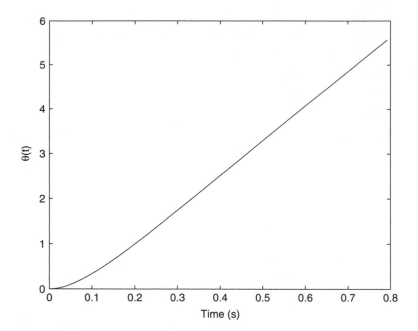

Figure 10.9   Step response of the motor without feedback.

On the other hand, we can specify the range of times t rather than accept what `step` provides. In this case, we replace the first line of the previous script as follows:

```
t = linspace(0, 100, 100);
theta = step(MotorSS, t);
plot(t, theta)
xlabel('Time  (s)')
ylabel('\theta(t)')
```

where time now spans $0 \leq t \leq 100$.

The MATLAB function `impulse` is used in the same manner as `step`, except that it computes the response of the system to an impulse.

MATLAB does not supply functions for all standard test inputs. However, it does provide the capability of determining the response of a system to an arbitrary input using

```
lsim (sys, u, t)
```

where *sys* is the system under consideration and *u* is a vector representing the amplitude of the input as a function of time, *t*. The lengths of *u* and *t* must be equal.

Example 10.4   Tracking error of a motor control system

We shall determine the steady-state tracking error of the motor control system given in Figure 10.3. The steady-state tracking error is the eventual difference between the desired position and the actual position when the input is a ramp. We will use a ramp

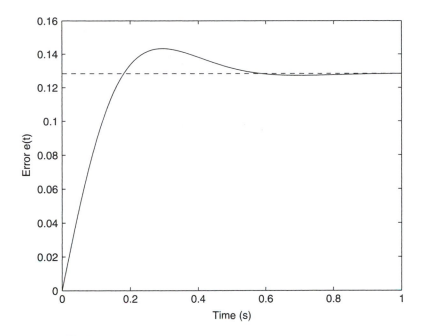

Figure 10.10   Tracking error of a control system as a function of time.

with a slope of 1 over the range $0 \leq t \leq 1$. For the DC servomotor, the error is $e(t) = \theta(t) - t$ for $0 \leq t \leq 1$. The script is

```
t = linspace(0, 1, 100);
theta = lsim(feedback(MotorSS, 1), t, t);
plot(t, t'-theta, 'k-');
error = t(end) - theta(end);
hold on;
plot([0, t(end)], [error, error], 'k--');
xlabel('Time (s)');
ylabel('Error e(t)');
```

which upon execution generates Figure 10.10. Note that after an initial transient, the error settles to approximately 0.13. A control system design objective could be to reduce this steady-state error to less than 0.05.

For a state-space system, the MATLAB function

```
initial(sys, x0)
```

runs a simulation with nonzero initial conditions, where *sys* is the system under consideration and *x0* is a vector of initial conditions.

Example 10.5   Response of a DC motor to initial conditions

Consider the DC motor given in Figure 10.3 with an initial position $\theta(0) = 0$, an initial current $i(0) = 0$, and an initial angular velocity of $\omega(0) = 5$ rad/s. In addition, we assume a gain of 2. If the voltage across the windings is kept at zero (possibly by

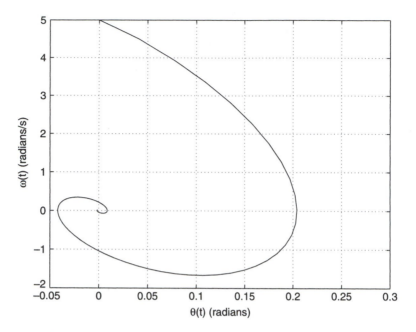

Figure 10.11   Phase plot of the rotor with an initial angular velocity $\omega(t) = 5$ rad/s.

shorting them), the following script will compute the response of the motor to these initial conditions:

```
x0 = [0; 5; 0];
[theta, t, x] = initial(feedback(2*MotorSS, 1), x0);
plot(x(:,1), x(:,2), 'k-');
grid on;
xlabel('\theta(t) (radians)');
ylabel('\omega(t) (radians/s)');
```

where $x(:, 1) = \theta(t)$, $x(:, 2) = \omega(t)$, and $x(:, 3) = i(t)$. The result of executing this script is shown in Figure 10.11.

10.3.2 Estimating Response from Poles and Zeros

When using MATLAB to solve control problems, it is important to have a qualitative understanding of the solution of differential equations. Since controller design is an inverse process, having this qualitative understanding allows one to know what the system should be like to achieve some desired behavior. MATLAB can be used to help develop this important qualitative understanding of the solutions to differential equations by solving many equations of particular types.

In this section, we shall compute the step response to a number of systems characterized by their pole and zero locations. First, we consider a first-order system with one pole and no zeros. We assume that the pole is located at $-\sigma$; therefore, the transfer function is

$$H(s) = \frac{\sigma}{s + \sigma}$$

The numerator is set to σ to keep the DC gain of the system at 1. We now obtain the response of this system to a step input.

Example 10.6   Step response of a first-order system to a range of pole locations

We shall generate a series of step responses for a series of pole locations ranging from slow ($\sigma = 0.1$) to quick ($\sigma = 2$). The script is

```
t = 0:0.1:10;
polevect = 0.1:0.1:2;
hold on;
for i = 1:length(polevect)
   y = step(tf([polevect(i)], [1, polevect(i)]), t);
   plot(t, y, 'k-');
end
xlabel('Time');
ylabel('Step response');
text(0.2, 0.95, 'p = 2');
text(3, 0.1, 'p = 0.1  (\Deltap = 0.1)')
```

The results from executing this script are shown in Figure 10.12.

As the pole of a first-order system approaches the imaginary axis (i.e., as σ becomes small), the control system becomes more sluggish. Sluggishness is usually not a good characteristic of a control system, but sometimes, if the slow response is with respect to some disturbance that needs to be rejected, this slowness is a good characteristic. The best location of the system poles will depend on the objective of the control system.

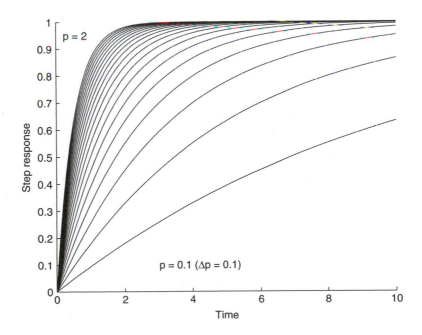

Figure 10.12   Response of a first-order system for a variety of pole locations p.

If two first-order systems are cascaded, then the system becomes a second-order system. Many mechanical systems are second order, so a good understanding of second-order systems is important. Consider the following second-order system:

$$H(s) = \frac{\sigma^2 + \omega^2}{s^2 + 2s\sigma + \sigma^2 + \omega^2} \tag{10.9}$$

The system has complex poles located at $-\sigma \pm j\omega$, where σ is the real part of the pole locations and ω is the complex part. In general, σ represents the amount of damping in the system, and ω specifies the strength of the storage mechanism, or spring. However, since we are interested in relating the system's response to the location of the pole, the transfer function is parameterized by the pole location. We shall now evaluate Eq. 10.9 as a function of its pole locations.

Example 10.7   Step response of a second-order system to a range of pole locations

We shall explore the response of the system represented by Eq. 10.9 to a variety of pole locations. First, we plot the step response as a function of σ with $\omega = 1.0$. Then, we plot the step response as a function of ω with $\sigma = 0.5$. We also sketch the locus of pole locations next to each response plot.
     The script is

```
t = 0:0.4:10; sigma = linspace(0.05, 1.0, 10);
data = zeros(length(t), length(sigma));
omega = 1.0;
for i = 1:length(sigma)
   data(:,i) = step(tf([sigma(i)^2 + omega^2], ...
                    [1, 2*sigma(i) sigma(i)^2+omega^2]), t);
end;
subplot(2, 2, 1);
mesh(t, -sigma, data');
ylabel('\sigma');
xlabel('Time');
zlabel('Response');
title('Response as a function of \sigma: \omega = 1.0');
data = zeros(length(t), length(omega));
sigma = 0.5; omega = linspace(0.3, 2.0, 10);
for i = 1:length(omega)
   data(:,i) = step(tf([sigma^2 + omega(i)^2], [1 2*sigma sigma^2+omega(i)^2]), t);
end;
subplot(2, 2, 3);
mesh(t, omega, data');
ylabel('\omega');
xlabel('Time');
zlabel('Response');
title('Response as a function of \omega: \sigma = 0.5');
subplot(2, 2, 2);
hold on;
plot([-0.1, -0.1], [1.0, -1], 'x');
plot([-0.1, -1], [1.0, 1.0]);
```

```
plot([-0.1, -1], [-1.0, -1.0]);
plot ([-1, -1], [1.0, -1], '<');
plot ([-2, 1], [0, 0], 'k');
plot ([0, 0], [-2, 2], 'k');
axis([-2, 1, -2, 2]);
xlabel('Real axis');
ylabel('Imaginary axis');
title('Pole location');
subplot(2, 2, 4);
hold on;
plot ([-0.5, -0.5], [0.3, -0.3], 'x');
plot ([-0.5, -0.5], [0.3, 1.5]);
plot ([-0.5, -0.5], [-0.3, -1.5]);
plot (-0.5, 1.5, '^');
plot (-0.5, -1.5], 'v');
plot ([-2, 1], [0, 0], 'k');
plot ([0, 0], [-2, 2], 'k');
axis([-2, 1, -2, 2]);
xlabel('Real axis');
ylabel('Imaginary axis');
title('Pole location');
```

The results from executing this script are shown in Figure 10.13.

Like the first-order system, the steady-state response is $H(0) = 1$. As seen in Figure 10.13, when σ is fixed and ω is increased, the system response becomes less

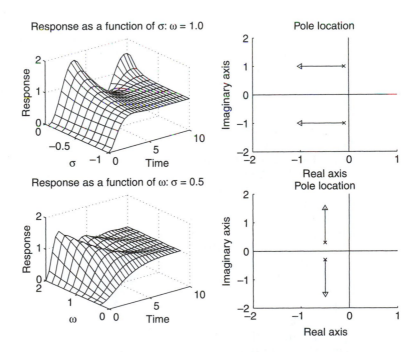

Figure 10.13   Response of a second-order system as a function of pole location.

damped. When ω is held constant and σ is increased, the response becomes more damped. If the real part of the pole approaches the imaginary axis, then the system becomes less damped. If the pole crosses into the right half of the complex plane, then the response becomes unbounded.

Systems of higher order, like the electric motor, often behave like a second- and, sometimes, a first-order system. The system poles with the greatest real part dominate the input-output behavior of the system if they are much greater than the real part of the closest poles—as long as there are no transmission zeros near them. This allows the designer to approximate the closed-loop behavior of a system with that of either a first- or second-order system. To understand why this is true, consider the velocity control of a DC permanent magnet motor. The equations of motion are the same as Eqs. 10.2, except the output is now rotor angular velocity $d\theta(t)/dt = \omega(t)$ instead of rotor angle $\theta(t)$. The following script makes the needed changes:

```
PlantRPM = MotorSS;
PlantRPM.c = [0, 1, 0];
PlantRPM = minreal(PlantRPM);
set(PlantRPM, 'OutputName', '\omega');
pole(PlantRPM)/(2*pi)
```

The first line of the script creates a system *PlantRPM* and then sets the readout matrix C to select $\omega(t)$ instead of $\theta(t)$. Since the rotor angle $\theta(t)$ is now unobservable, `minreal` is called to eliminate that state from the equations. The last line returns the poles of the system: one fast pole at approximately 160 Hz, which is related to the electronic coil, and one slow pole at approximately 2 Hz, which is related to the rotor dynamics. The slow pole related to the rotor dynamics dominates the open-loop response of the system, since the fast pole is more than 10 times the speed of the slow pole. The following script runs simulations with initial conditions for the rotor speed $\omega(t)$ and coil current i ranging between -1 and 1, and it plots the results together in a phase plot—that is, a graph of $\omega(t)$ versus $i(t)$. Time is not explicitly marked in a phase plot, so a circle is placed on the trajectory when 5% of the total trajectory time has passed.

```
PlantRPM = MotorSS;
PlantRPM.c = [0, 1, 0];
PlantRPM = minreal(PlantRPM);
set(PlantRPM, 'OutputName', '\omega');
t = linspace(0, 0.05, 500);
hold on;
for i = 0:13;
   x0 = [-1.4+0.2*i, 1];
   [y, t, x] = initial(PlantRPM, x0, t);
   plot(x(:,2), x(:,1), 'k-');
   k = floor(0.05*length(t));
   plot(x(k,2), x(k,1),'ro');
end;
for i = 0:13;
   x0 = [-1+0.2*i, -1];
   [y, t, x] = initial(PlantRPM, x0, t);
```

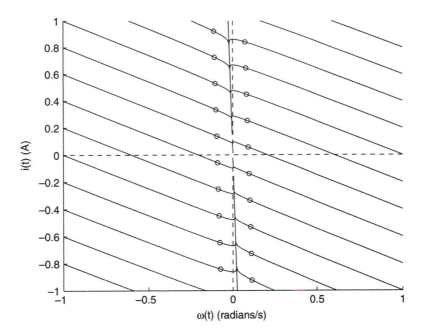

Figure 10.14   Phase portrait of a DC electric motor.

```
plot(x(:,2), x(:,1), 'k-');
k = floor(0.05*length(t));
plot(x(k,2), x(k,1), 'ko');
end
plot([1, -1], [0, 0], 'k--');
plot([0 0], [,1 -1], 'k--');
axis([-1, 1, -1, 1]);
ylabel('i(t) (A)');
xlabel('\omega(t) (radians/s)');
```

The resulting phase portrait of the system is shown in Figure 10.14. Note that the vast majority of the time for every trajectory is spent about a one-dimensional subspace. The subspace is associated with the slow pole. In general, those poles with the larger real part will dominate the step response of a system.

Example 10.8   Effects of zeros near poles of a second-order system

Consider the second-order plant

$$H(s) = \frac{-(s - z)}{z(s^2 + 0.5s + 1)}$$

where z is the location of the zero. Although zeros cannot be moved by feedback, the effect of their positions can be profound if they are near poles or near the imaginary axis. To show this, we examine the step response of a family of plants with a zero approaching and crossing the imaginary axis. We select four values of z: ± 5 and ± 1. The script is

```
t = linspace(0, 25, 200);
Z = [-5, -1, 1, 5];
Den = [1, 0.5, 1];
y = zeros(length(t), length(Z));
for i = 1:length(Z)
    y(:,i) = step(-1/Z(i)*tf([1, -Z(i)], Den), t);
end
plot(t, y(:,1), 'k-')
hold on
plot(t, y(:,2), 'k--')
plot(t, y(:,3), 'k-o')
plot(t, y(:,4), 'k-+')
legend('zero at -5', 'zero at -1', 'zero at 1', 'zero at 5')
xlabel('Time')
ylabel('Step response')
```

The execution of this script results in Figure 10.15. The zeros are stable at $z = -5$ and $z = -1$; however, for the cases where $z = 1$ and $z = 5$, the zero is unstable. Unstable zeros do not destabilize a system, but they do limit the amount of feedback that can be applied. The hallmark of an unstable zero is the system's tendency to go the wrong way initially, as seen with the plot with the zero at 1. A system with one or more unstable zeros is called nonminimum phase.

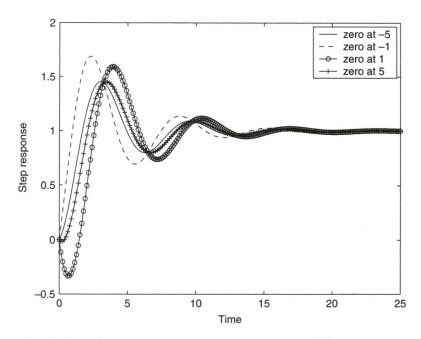

Figure 10.15 Effect of a zero approaching and crossing the imaginary axis on the step response.

Example 10.9   Masking of modal dynamics

Consider the first- through fourth-order systems given by

$$G_1 = \frac{1}{s+1} \qquad\qquad G_3 = G_1(s)*G_2(s)$$

$$G_2 = \frac{100}{s^2+10s+100} \qquad G_4 = \frac{19.8s+20}{s+20}G_3(s)$$

The step response of the plant G_3 is very similar to the response of the first-order plant G_1, because the pole at -1 dominates the complex poles, as discussed previously. However, if a zero were near the pole at -1, then that pole would no longer dominate. The system given by G_4 places a zero near the dominant pole at -1 in G_3, thereby masking its effect. However, this is not generally practical to do, since to force G_3 to move quickly, G_4 will initially produce a large output, which may saturate or damage the actuators. This can be observed in the step response of G_4. The step responses of G_3 and G_4 are obtained with the following script and are shown in Figure 10.16:

```
G1 = tf([1], [1, 1]);
G2 = tf([100], [1, 10, 100]);
G3 = G1*G2;
G4 = tf([19.8, 20], [1, 20])*G3;
t = linspace(0, 6, 200);
yG3 = step(G3, t);
yG4 = step(G4, t);
```

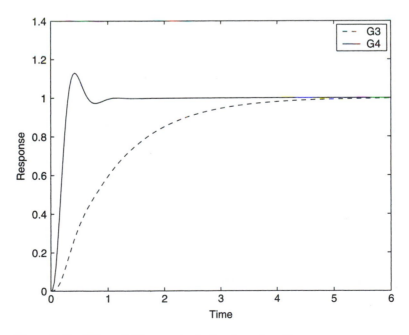

Figure 10.16   Effect of hiding a system's slow dynamics with a zero.

```
plot(t, yG3, 'k--', t, yG4, 'k-')
legend('G3', 'G4')
xlabel('Time')
ylabel('Response')
```

The distance between a zero and a pole measures how perpendicular the input or output matrices are to the mode eigenvector. If a zero is directly on top of a pole, then the mode is either not excitable or not seeable in the output. The terms controllability and observability are also used to describe this phenomenon.

10.3.3 Estimating Systems from Response

In this section, we introduce a technique known as system identification. The MATLAB System Identification Toolbox can be accessed with `ident`, which provides a number of system identification tools. First principle models, such as the motor used throughout this chapter, are developed during the system design process. When implementing the control algorithm, however, estimating this model from experimental data provides validation to the first principles modeling effort and can uncover unexpected phenomena—for example, a resonance in the motor shaft that is slow enough to interact with the control loop. To introduce this topic, we focus on parametric identification using an autoregressive model with external input (`arx`).

We simulate taking data from an experiment by using the motor model example system under feedback control. We generate a random input for the discrete-time version of the system and then determine the response. The input must richly excite the system for effective identification. All linear systems, for example, look the same with zero input.[5] The experiment generates a series of inputs $u[k]$ (commands), and the resulting responses are $y[k]$ (angles). The sampling interval is T_s. In practice, the data set would be less clean, since noise and unmeasured disturbances can contaminate the signals. The data are then collected into an identification data object using `iddata` from the System Identification Toolbox and split into an identification data set and a validation data set. The results are plotted in Figure 10.17. Three different `arx` models of differing degree are created, and their ability to predict the response is shown in Figure 10.18. The ARX estimation function requires the user to supply the orders of the numerator and denominator polynomials as well as a net delay. Because we have simulated the data, we know in advance that the system has three poles; in practice, however, this is not certain. That command `detrend` is used to set the mean of the outputs and inputs to zero to satisfy linearity and initial condition assumptions of the ARX technique. The results of the three models are then compared using the System Identification Toolbox function `compare`.

```
Ts = 5e-2; N = 1000;
u = zeros(N, 1);
Jmodel = rand;
clSys = feedback(c2d(MotorSS(Jmodel), Ts), 0.4);
```

---

[5]See, for example, L. Lyung, *System Identification: Theory for the User,* 2nd ed., Prentice Hall, Upper Saddle River, NJ, 1999.

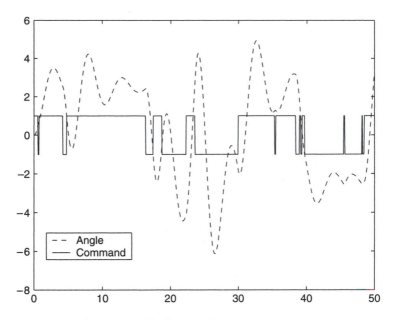

Figure 10.17   System identification data set.

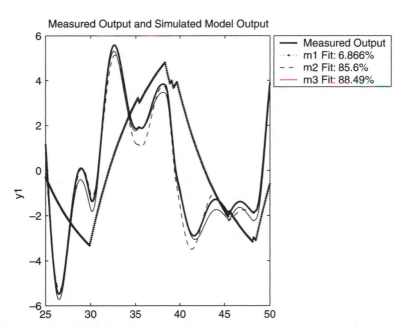

Figure 10.18   Comparison of the three system responses to the validation data set.

```
r = 1;
for i=1:length(u)
    if  rand < 2.5e-2
        r = -1*r;
    end
    u(i) = r;
end
t = Ts*(1:N);
y = lsim(clSys, u);
figure(1)
plot(t, y, 'k--', t, u, 'k-')
legend('Angle', 'Command', 'Location', 'SouthWest')
motorExp = iddata(y, u, Ts);
motorId = detrend(motorExp(1:N/2));
motorVal = detrend(motorExp(N/2:N));
m1 = arx(motorId, [1, 1, 0]);
m2 = arx(motorId, [2, 1, 0]);
m3 = arx(motorId, [3, 1, 0]);
figure(2)
compare(motorVal, m1, m2, m3)
```

It is seen that little improvement is made between the second-order model $m2$ and the third-order model $m3$. The system itself has three poles, however, two are dominant in determining the response and are, hence, the first to be identified.

A number of parametric model identification techniques are implemented in the MATLAB toolbox, such as Box-Jenkins, Output Error, and Prediction Error, each differentiated by the model structure and their treatment of noise. The frequency response of systems can be estimated directly from experimental data using nonparametric identification methods.

10.4 DESIGN TOOLS

In this section, we consider design tools in MATLAB and the criteria by which designs are evaluated. Many design techniques are graphical, because they were developed before computers were in general use. The graphical design tools include

> bode—creates Bode plots
> nyquist—creates Nyquist plots
> rlocus—creates root locus plots

A computer-based modern design tool employing lqr and lqe is also introduced.

Design criteria for control systems involve three requirements:

1. Stability
2. Transient response
3. Steady-state response

The need for stability is clear when solving differential equations. Each root of the denominator polynomial corresponds to a component of the solution, and any root with a positive real part will contribute a term that grows exponentially. A system with a pole on the imaginary axis is labeled marginally stable. The other two categories of design criteria assume that the system is stable. Transient response requirements look at the short-term response of the system to a unit step input. Steady-state response requirements look at the long-term error in tracking either a step or ramp input and, on rare occasions, a parabola. The stability criteria must always be met. Some systems are initially unstable and must be stabilized; examples of such systems include an inverted pendulum and a magnetic bearing. Many systems can be destabilized by the application of feedback. Stability of a closed-loop control system can easily be checked using `pole` on the closed-loop transfer function. Any roots with a positive real part indicate instability of the closed-loop system.

10.4.1 Design Criteria

We now return to the DC motor to study design tools, and we consider the stability of a closed-loop system with the DC motor as the plant. A proportional controller, which takes the error between the desired position and the actual position and multiplies it by its gain, is used. The designer using the proportional controller must choose which gain to use. The following script generates Figure 10.19, which is a plot of the real part of the right-most pole as a function of the design parameter gain, which ranges from 1 to 200. For small gains, the system is stable. By the time the gain

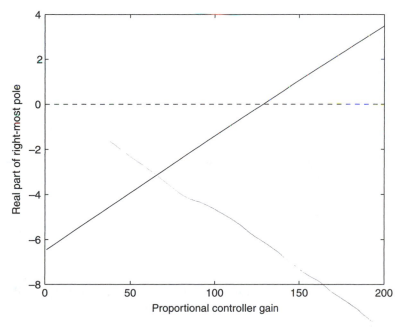

Figure 10.19   Real part of the right-most system pole of the closed-loop system as a function of controller gain.

is greater than approximately 128, however, the response of the closed-loop system is unbounded, and the motor might be damaged.

```
gains = linspace(1, 200, 50);  y = [];
for i = 1:length(gains)
   y = [y, max(real(pole(feedback(gains(i)*MotorSS, 1))))];
end;
plot(gains, y, 'k-', [0, 200], [0, 0], 'k--');
xlabel('Proportional controller gain');
ylabel('Real part of right-most pole');
```

The Bode plot in Figure 10.20 is generated by

```
bode(MotorSS)
```

and can also be used to determine at which gain the system becomes unstable. The command is

```
[gm, pm, wgm, wpm] = margin(MotorSS);
```

which computes the gain margins (*gm*) and phase margins (*pm*) and the frequencies at which they occur—that is, *wgm* and *wpm*, respectively. In this case, the gain margin (the amount of gain that may be applied before the system becomes unstable) is $gm = 128.37$, or 42.2 dB.

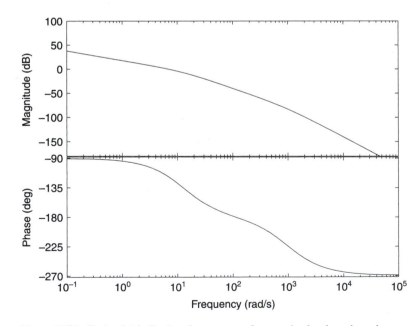

Figure 10.20   Bode plot indicating the crossover frequencies for the gain and phase margin.

Even if the closed-loop system is stable, the behavior may not be acceptable. Consider the step response of the DC permanent magnet motor system for a range of stable gains, as shown in Figure 10.21. Time ranges between 0 and 1 s, and four gains are chosen at equally spaced points between 1 and 10 on a logarithmic scale. The script to obtain Figure 10.21 is

```
t = linspace(0, 1, 100);
gains = logspace (0, 1, 4);
hold on;
for i = 1:length(gains)
  [y, t] = step(feedback(gains(i)*MotorSS, 1));
  plot(t, y);
end;
xlabel('Time');
ylabel('Response');
text(0.16, 1.5, 'Gain = 10');
text(0.16, 0.4, 'Gain = 1');
```

The response to commands quickens as the gain is increased, but the high-gain controllers overshoot the goal angle and tend to oscillate about the target position of one radian. There are many metrics by which these observations are quantified; here, we will consider rise time, overshoot, and settling time.

Transient requirements are measured from the response of the system to a step input. Rise time is the amount of time the system takes to go from 10% to 90%

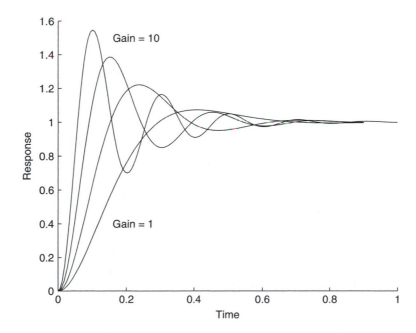

Figure 10.21   Step response of a motor system under proportional control.

of its final value. A related value is peak time—that is, the time of the first maximum. In this particular system, rise time and peak time are in conflict with the next criteria, which is overshoot. Percentage overshoot is the amount by which the system overshoots its goal. Settling time is typically defined as the amount of time it takes for the system to come to and stay within a 2% envelope of the final value. These quantities are calculated in the function **transient** given below. The function returns $[-1, -1, -1]$ if the system is not stable.

```
function criteria = transient(system)
criteria = [-1 -1 -1];
maxP = max(real(pole(system)));
if maxP >= 0
  return
end
MaxTime = -6*(1/maxP);
Time = linspace(0, MaxTime, 500);
Response = step(system, Time);
[ResponseMax, IndexMax] = max(Response);
FinalValue = Response(end);
TimeLow = interp1(Response(1:IndexMax), Time (1:IndexMax),
                  0.1*FinalValue);
TimeHigh = interp1(Response(1:IndexMax), Time (1:IndexMax),
                   0.9*FinalValue);
criteria(1) = TimeHigh-TimeLow;
k = length(Time);
while (k>0) & (0.02 > abs((FinalValue - Response(k))/FinalValue));
   k = k-1;
end
criteria(2) = Time(k);
criteria(3) = 100*(max(Response)-FinalValue)/FinalValue;
```

where $criteria(1)$ = rise time, $criteria(2)$ = settling time, and $criteria(3)$ = percentage overshoot.

We use this function to evaluate controllers for the DC motor. Thus,

transient(feedback(**MotorSS**, 1))

displays the vector $[0.1935, 0.6080, 7.6136]$, where 0.1935 is the rise time, 0.6080 the settling time, and 7.6136 is the percentage overshoot.

10.4.2 Design Tools

For the design criteria discussed in Section 10.4.1, we introduce a collection of design tools and illustrate their application to the motor controller. Typically, one of three different tools will be applied:

1. Frequency-based
2. Root locus
3. LQG based

Frequency-based design does not require an explicit model, only the results from a collection of experiments. The last two methods require very good models of the plant.

We now illustrate these design tools.

Example 10.10   Controller design to meet rise time and percentage overshoot criteria

We again consider the motor controller. The design criteria require that we keep the overshoot under 20%; thus, many of the design gains shown in Figure 10.19 are unacceptable. Furthermore, we want the closed-loop system to be very quick, having a rise time less than 0.05 s. Using a straight proportional controller, we see that we are in a deadlocked situation. To obtain a rise time under 0.05 s, a gain greater than 3 must be used. To have an overshoot under 20%, we must use a gain smaller than 2. The following script generates Figure 10.22, which graphs the overshoot and rise time as functions of gain for the proportional controller:

```
kp = 0.4*logspace(0, 1, 20);
result = [];
for i = 1:length(kp)
    result = [result; transient(feedback(kp(i)*MotorSS, 1))];
end;
[ax, h1, h2] = plotyy(kp, result(:,3), kp, result(:,1));
xlabel('Controller gain');
ylabel('Percentage overshoot');
v = axis;
set(get(ax(2), 'Ylabel'), 'String', 'Rise time (s)')
```

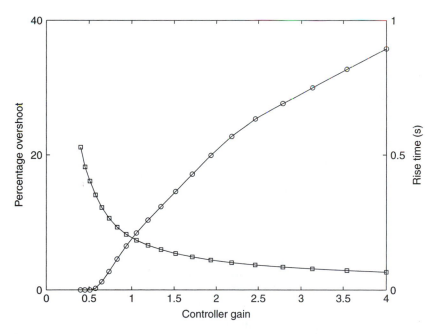

Figure 10.22   Percentage overshoot (circles) and rise time (squares) as a function of controller gain.

```
set(h2, 'Marker', 'ks');
set(h1 , 'Marker', 'ko');
```

First we attempt a frequency-based design. The overshoot requirement can be translated into a phase-margin minimum. For this system, a phase margin of 45° is needed to meet the overshoot requirements. Looking at the Bode plot in Figure 10.18, we see that at a phase of −135°; (45° phase margin), a gain of approximately 2.0 is allowed. To compute the gain more precisely, we use fzero with **transient**. The script is

```
function Gain
options = optimset('display', 'off');
gain = fzero(@PEcontrol, 2, options)
transresp = transient(feedback(gain*MotorSS, 1))

function s = PEcontrol(gain)
rval = transient(feedback(gain*MotorSS, 1));
s = rval(3)-20;
```

From the execution of this script, we obtain *gain* = 1.9384 for a 20% overshoot and *transresp*(1) = rise time = 0.1111 s, more than twice as slow as the design specification.

A lead controller is typically used to improve the transient response of a system. A properly designed lead controller increases the phase for a short range of frequencies; this boost in phase allows more gain to be applied. The zero of the lead controller is chosen to be at −15, just to the left of the second open-loop pole at −13. This ensures that the lead controller's phase boost starts about where the phase of the DC motor starts to roll off. The lead controller pole is at −100, nearly 10 times the zero location. In theory, the further to the left, the better, but having the pole very far to the left makes the controller sensitive to noise. As a rule of thumb, the pole cannot be located further left than 10 times the location of the zero. The resulting controller transfer function is

$$C(s) = \frac{100}{15} \frac{s + 15}{s + 100} = \frac{6.667s + 100}{s + 100}$$

where we have multiplied the transfer function by 100/15 to set the DC gain to 1.

The following script generates Figure 10.23, which compares the frequency response of the uncompensated and compensated system:

```
Control = tf([6.667 100], [1 100]);
bode(MotorSS, 'k-', Control*MotorSS, 'k--')
```

Note how the phase roll-off is delayed to higher frequencies. Again, we use the Bode plot to find an initial guess for the correct feedback gain—that is, approximately 10. To compute the exact value of the gain at which an overshoot of 20% is reached and the corresponding rise time, we use the following script:

```
function Gain2
options = optimset('display', 'off');
gain = fzero(@LDcontrol, [10], options)
transresp = transient(feedback(13.0108*tf([6.667, 100], [1, 100])*MotorSS, 1))

function s = LDcontrol(gain)
rval = transient(feedback(gain*tf([6.667, 100], [1, 100])*MotorSS, 1));
s = rval(3)-20;
```

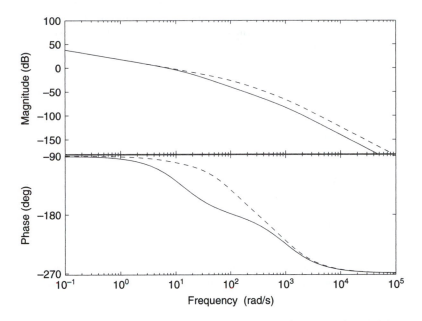

Figure 10.23 Bode plots of the lead compensated system (dashed line) and of the uncompensated system (solid line).

Upon execution, we find that *gain* = 13.01 for a 20% overshoot and *transresp*(1) = rise time = 0.017 s, nearly three times faster than the target value. The graphs of the step responses for both the proportional and lead-controlled systems are shown subsequently in Figure 10.26.

By using the lead compensator, one is able to meet both the overshoot and the rise-time requirements. Frequency-based design requires data from a Bode plot, but it does not depend on an explicit model. The other frequency-based tools include the Nyquist plot and the Nichols plot, which are used in a similar manner.

The root locus is another commonly applied tool. The same lead compensator may be applied, but the approach differs. Given that the complex poles subtend an angle ξ from the imaginary axis and have radius ω_n, we have [6]

$$M_p = \exp\left(-\frac{\pi\xi}{\sqrt{1 - \xi^2}}\right)$$

$$T_r \approx \frac{1}{\omega_n}(1 + 1.4\xi)$$

where M_p is the peak magnitude and T_r is the rise time. Inverting these formulas constrains where the closed-loop poles may be located in the complex plane to meet the transient design requirements. Hence, an overshoot requirement of less than 20% constrains ξ, requiring that the dominant poles be located within a 120° wedge centered along the negative imaginary axis. A 0.05-s rise time corresponds roughly to a minimum

---

[6]D. K. Anand and R. B. Zmood, *ibid.*, 1995.

pole radius ω_n of 20. These formulas are rules of thumb, but they serve as a good starting point. In the following script, we shade the region of the complex plane in which all closed-loop poles must lie. Then, we plot the root locus to see if this condition is met at any gain.

```
theta = linspace(-2/3*pi, -4/3*pi, 15);
X = [20*cos(theta), 200*cos(-4/3*pi), 200*cos(-2/3*pi), 20*cos(2/3*pi)];
Y = [20*sin(theta), 200*sin(-4/3*pi), 200*sin(-2/3*pi), 20*sin(-2/3*pi)];
hold on;
h=fill(X, Y, 'c');
alpha(h, 0.2);
sgrid;
rlocus(MotorSS);
axis(100*[-1, 0, -1, 1]);
ylabel('Imaginary axis');
xlabel('Real axis');
```

The results are shown in Figure 10.24a. Notice that the controller and the plant, **MotorSS**, have had their order switched. In theory, this produces the same root-locus plot. However, when the root-locus command with the lead controller precedes the plant, the calculations run much slower and may cause some systems to lock because of the controller's zero being near the plant pole. The transformation to controller form, which simplifies the computation of the closed-loop poles, is nearly singular when the lead controller precedes the plant; that is, the cascade is nearly uncontrollable. By switching the order, we make the system nearly unobservable and do not compromise the transformation.

A similar plot can be generated for the lead-controlled system using the following script:

```
theta = linspace(-2/3*pi, -4/3*pi, 15);
X = [20*cos(theta), 200*cos(-4/3*pi), 200*cos(-2/3*pi), 20*cos(2/3*pi)];
Y = [20*sin(theta), 200*sin(-4/3*pi), 200*sin(-2/3*pi), 20*sin(-2/3*pi)];
hold on;
h=fill(X, Y, 'c');
alpha(h, 0.2);
sgrid;
rlocus(MotorSS*tf([6.667, 100] ,[1, 100]));
axis(90*[-1, 0, -0.5, 0.5]);
ylabel('Imaginary axis');
xlabel('Real axis');
```

Execution of the script results in the graph shown in Figure 10.24b. Notice that for the proportional controller, there is no gain where all the closed-loop roots are located in the acceptable region. The net effect of the lead controller is to bend the root-locus lines back into the acceptable region.

To find the correct gain, we use

```
rlocus(MotorSS*tf([6.667, 100], [1 100]))
[k, p] = rlocfind(MotorSS*tf([6.667, 100], [1 100]))
```

and place the crosshairs where the root locus crosses the edge of the acceptable region. The function rlocus precedes rlocfind, because rlocfind does not draw the root

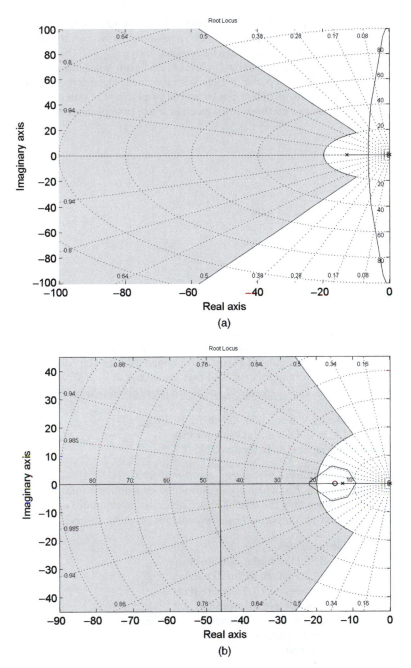

Figure 10.24 Root-locus plots of the motor positioning system: (a) proportional controlled, (b) lead controlled.

locus. This procedure yields a gain of 12. These regions are approximate, so it is a good practice to fine-tune the gain by simulation. Thus, from a simulation, it will be found that a gain as high as 13 can be applied.

In the root-locus design, the objective is to place the poles of the closed-loop system into the acceptable region. With the linear algebra tools developed for state-space models, such a problem can be solved by placing the poles directly in the desired locations. The two methods introduced here are pole placement with

```
place
```

and

```
acker
```

and LQG design with

```
lqr
lqe
```

and

```
reg
```

To meet the design specifications, we choose the pole locations $-30, -20+30i$, $-20-30i$. These pole locations are chosen arbitrarily but are safely inside the acceptable shaded region of Figures 10.24a and 10.24b. The following script uses place to compute the gain matrix K so that the matrix $A - BK$ has eigenvalues in the desired locations. The quantities A and B are those given by Eqs. 10.3:

```
DesiredPoles = [-30, -20+30*i, -20-30*i];
[A, B, C, D] = ssdata(MotorSS);
K = place(A, B, DesiredPoles)
```

The execution of the script gives $K = [0.3900, -0.1002, -4.6517]$. The feedback needed is then $u = Kx$, which assumes we have available the internal state of the system given by x. Since only the output is available, a state estimator needs to be designed. A complete script computing both the controller and the observer is

```
DesiredPoles = [-30, -20+30*i, -20-30*i];
[A, B, C, D] = ssdata(MotorSS);
K = place(A, B, DesiredPoles)
L = (place(A', C', 3*DesiredPoles))';
ControlSS = reg(MotorSS, K, L);
clSys = feedback(MotorSS, ControlSS, +1);
clSys = 1/dcgain(clSys)*clSys;
step(clSys);
```

The result of this script is plotted subsequently in Figure 10.26 as the state-space controller. The first three lines of the script generate the feedback gain matrix K. Using duality through the transpose between observability and controllability, place is used to compute the observer feedback gain matrix L. This matrix depends on the system matrices A and C and a set of desired observer pole locations, which we set to 3 times the feedback pole locations. The function reg then creates the estimator, which, using the plant output, estimates the internal state and outputs the corrective command. Since the command signal has the correct sign, we employ positive feedback in `feedback`.

Pole locations in the previous example were chosen to satisfy the transient requirements. These requirements are inequalities in nature, so a range of pole locations is acceptable. We arbitrarily chose a set of pole locations within the acceptable region. The linear quadratic Gaussian controller design method follows similar steps but offers the designer a systematic method for assigning pole locations. Poles are chosen to minimize the integral[7]

$$J = \int [x'(t)Qx(t) + u'(t)Ru(t)] \, dt \qquad (10.10)$$

where $x(t)$ is the internal system state at time t, $u(t)$ is the input vector at time t, Q is a positive semidefinite matrix, and R is a positive definite matrix. The matrix Q is often chosen as $C'C$ so that the first term reduces to the square of the output error.

The designer may adjust the relative importance of the state error to the input by modifying the relative magnitudes of Q and R. In our particular case, the plant has only one input, so R is a positive scalar. With $Q = C'C$, the following script plots the location of the optimal poles as a function of R and, in addition, the region in which the poles must lie to satisfy the transient design requirements:

```
[A, B, C, D] = ssdata(MotorSS);
clPoles = [];
R = logspace(-4, 1, 60);
for i = 1:length(R)
   [K, S, E] = lqr(A, B, C'*C, R(i));
   clPoles = [clPoles, E];
end;
theta = linspace(-2/3*pi, -4/3*pi, 15);
X = [20*cos(theta), 200*cos(-4/3*pi), 200*cos(-2/3*pi), 20*cos(-2/3*pi)];
Y = [20*sin(theta), 200*sin(-4/3*pi), 200*sin(-2/3*pi), 20*sin(-2/3*pi)];
h = fill(X, Y, 'c');
alpha(h, 0.2);
hold on;
plot(real(clPoles), imag(clPoles), 'x');
axis(40*[-1, 0, -0.5, 0.5]);
sgrid;
ylabel('Imaginary axis');
xlabel('Real axis');
```

Figure 10.25 shows the resulting root locus, which plots discrete root location with an 'x', instead of using lines. For large values of R, the cost of the input is large relative to the cost of the output error, and, consequently, little control effort is applied. The closed-loop poles are close to the open-loop poles. As the cost of the input is made less expensive, the optimal closed-loop poles move further into the left half of the complex plane. More control action is being applied, and the response of the system is much faster. Since we want to meet both an optimality condition and the transient requirements, we must select R so that the optimal closed-loop poles lie within the shaded region.

---

[7]T. Kailith, *ibid.*, 1980.

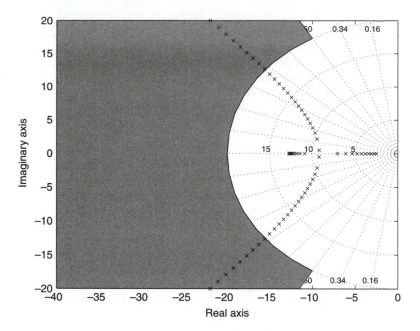

Figure 10.25   Closed-loop poles of the optimal controller as a function of the input cost weight R.

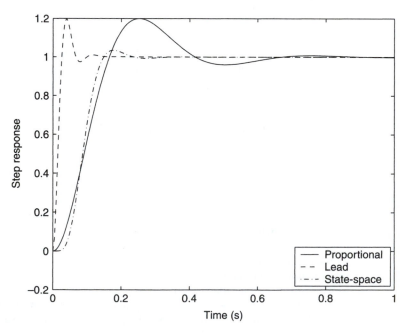

Figure 10.26   Comparison of a proportional, lead, and state-space controller to a step input.

The step responses of the three major controller designs discussed so far are generated in the following script and are compared in Figure 10.26. The proportional controller fails to meet the rise-time design criteria. Using pole placement, both the lead controller and the state-space controller meet the design criteria. The state-space controller has the additional benefit of having almost no overshoot.

```
t = linspace(0, 1, 200);
yp = step(feedback(1.9416*MotorSS, 1), t);
yl = step(feedback(13.0108*tf([6.667, 100], [1 100])*MotorSS, 1), t);
DesiredPoles = [-30, -20+30*i, -20-30*i];
[A, B, C, D] = ssdata(MotorSS);
K = place(A, B, DesiredPoles);
L = (place(A', C', 3*DesiredPoles))';
ControlSS = reg(MotorSS, K, L);
clSys = feedback(MotorSS, ControlSS, +1);
clSys = clSys/dcgain(clSys);
ys = step(clSys, t);
plot(t, yp, 'k-', t, yl, 'k--', t, ys, 'k-.');
xlabel('Time (s)');
ylabel('Step response');
legend('Proportional', 'Lead', 'State-space', 'Location', 'SouthEast');
```

10.5 DESIGN EXAMPLES

In this section, we shall use MATLAB tools to design controllers for four different physical systems:

1. *DC motor with a flexible shaft*—design a notch controller to suppress the flexible shaft's vibration mode.
2. *Single-axis magnetic suspension system*—design a PID controller to keep the mass positioned at its equilibrium location.
3. *Inverted pendulum*—design multiple-input, single-output (MISO) controller to keep a pendulum vertical.
4. *Magnetically suspended flywheel*—design a MIMO controller to keep a flywheel suspended.

There are four steps in the controller design process:

1. Specify the controller requirements.
2. Develop a model of the plant.
3. Design the controller to meet the requirements.
4. Simulate and test the controller design.

Plant models in the following sections are derived from first principles, but they are not tested against experimental data. It cannot be overemphasized that validating and refining the model is of great importance in controller design and must not be ignored. The latter three plant models described above are nonlinear, but only slightly; each can be linearized about an operating point, which is stabilized. Frequency-based design using open-loop data from Bode plots is possible only for the DC motor with a flexible shaft, since all the other systems are open-loop unstable.

Controllers used in the subsequent sections include the following:

- Lead (Lag)
- Notch
- PID
- LQG

With each of these methods, the root locus is the primary design tool. In practice, the PID controller is by far the most common type of controller used for SISO control systems.

10.5.1 Notch Control of a Flexible Pointer

Consider the read-write head on a hard drive. The objective is for the head to move as fast as possible to a desired location and, once there, to provide a steady platform for the read or write operation. With limited actuation, typically a voice coil, the way to go faster is to remove material from the swing arm holding the read–write head. Removing material tends to reduce the stiffness of the arm; hence, moving quickly is more likely to excite the vibration modes of the arm.

As a model of this design, we consider the DC motor mounted with a flexible shaft as shown in Figure 10.27. The user specifies a desired angle θ_d and the control system, and by measuring the angle of inclination of the rod θ attempts to match the command in as quick a manner as possible. However, if the pointer gets to the desired position and then oscillates for a long time, the head will not function properly.

The equations of motion for the flexible pointer are[8]

$$L\frac{di(t)}{dt} + k_b\frac{d\theta(t)}{dt} + Ri = v(t)$$

$$J_m\frac{d^2\theta(t)}{dt^2} - k_r i(t) = b\left(\frac{d\phi(t)}{dt} - \frac{d\theta(t)}{dt}\right) + k[\phi(t) - \theta(t)] \tag{10.11}$$

$$J_l\frac{d^2\phi(t)}{dt^2} = -b\left(\frac{d\phi(t)}{dt} - \frac{d\theta(t)}{dt}\right) - k[\phi(t) - \theta(t)]$$

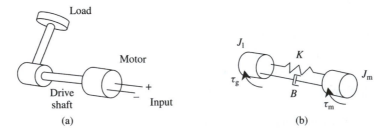

Figure 10.27   (a) Pointer with a flexible drive shaft and (b) its equivalent model.

[8]R. C. Dorf and R. H. Bishop, *Modern Control Systems*, Addison-Wesley, Reading, MA, 1998.

where θ is the angle of the rotor, ϕ is the orientation of the pointer, $J_m = 0.03 \text{ kg} \cdot \text{m}^2$ is the rotor inertia, $J_1 = 0.015 \text{ kg} \cdot \text{m}^2$ is the load inertia, $b = 0.01 \text{ Nm/rad/s}$ is the flexible shaft damping, and $k = 10 \text{ Nm/rad}$ is the flexible shaft spring constant. The values for the inductance L, resistance R, back emf constant k_b, and the motor torque constant k_τ are defined in Section 10.2.1.

The coupled second-order differential equations can be converted to linear coupled first-order equations by introducing the state variables

$$
\begin{aligned}
x_1 &= \theta & x_4 &= \phi \\
x_2 &= \frac{d\theta}{dt} & x_5 &= \frac{d\phi}{dt} \\
x_3 &= i
\end{aligned}
$$

Then, Eqs. 10.11 become

$$
\frac{dx}{dt} = x_2
$$

$$
\frac{dx_2}{dt} = -\frac{k}{J_m}x_1 - \frac{b}{J_m}x_2 + \frac{k_2}{J_m}x_3 + \frac{k}{J_m}x_4 + \frac{b}{J_m}x_5
$$

$$
\frac{dx_3}{dt} = -\frac{k_b}{L}x_2 - \frac{R}{L}x_3 + v
$$

$$
\frac{dx_4}{dt} = x_5
$$

$$
\frac{dx_5}{dt} = \frac{k}{J_1}x_1 + \frac{b}{J_1}x_2 - \frac{k}{J_1}x_4 - \frac{b}{J_1}x_5
$$

The following function **Pointer** computes the system matrices for the coupled first-order equations and returns a state-space system object model:

```
function Plant = Pointer
L = 5e-3;  R = 5;  kb = 0.125;
ki = 15;  Jm = 3e-2;
Jl = 0.5*Jm;  k = 10;  b = 0.01;
A = [0, 1, 0, 0, 0;
     -k/Jm, -b/Jm, ki/Jm, k/Jm, b/Jm;
     0, -kb/L, -R/L, 0, 0;
     0, 0, 0, 0, 1;
     k/Jl, b/Jl, 0, -k/Jl, -b/Jl];
B = [0; 0; 1/L; 0; 0];
C = [0, 0, 0, 1, 0];
D = 0;
Plant = ss(A, B, C, D);
```

The output of the system is the angular position of the pointer $\phi(t)$. Typing

```
pole(Pointer)
```

in the MATLAB command window gives

```
1.0e+002 *
 -9.8734
 -0.0248 + 0.3104i
 -0.0248 - 0.3104i
  0.0000
 -0.0871
```

which shows that the flexible pointer system has five poles, three of which are on the real axis: one at the origin, one at nearly -1000 rad/s because of the motor coil electronics, and a pole at -8.7 rad/s because of the rotor dynamics. The flexible attachment adds a pair of complex poles at $-2.5 \pm 31.0i$. As before, a lead controller could be applied to improve the transient response; however, the poorly damped poles will frustrate this approach.

To illustrate the limitation of lead control for this system, we shall generate the root locus of the proportional and lead-controlled systems. We place the lead zero at -6, which is just to the right of the first stable pole. The lead pole is placed at -50, nearly 10 times the location of the zero. Then, the transfer function is

$$H(s) = \frac{s + 6}{s + 50}$$

The script is

```
rlocus(Pointer);
axis(70*[-1, 1, -0.5, 0.5]);
sgrid;
xlabel('Real axis');
ylabel('Imaginary axis');
figure(2);
rlocus(tf([1, 6], [1, 50])*Pointer);
axis(70*[-1, 1, -0.5, 0.5]);
sgrid;
xlabel('Real axis');
ylabel('Imaginary axis');
```

The result of executing this script is shown in Figure 10.28. The allowable gain for both designs is limited not by the real-axis open-loop poles, as it was in the case of the DC motor, but by the complex poles because of the flexible shaft. The performance of the lead controller will be only a little better than the performance of the proportional controller. By entering

```
rlocus(tf([1, 6], [1, 50])*Pointer)
[k, p] = rlocfind(tf([1, 6], [1, 50])*Pointer)
```

in the MATLAB command window, we can pick the best gains for the lead-controlled system and, similarly, the proportional-controlled system. The crosshairs must be placed

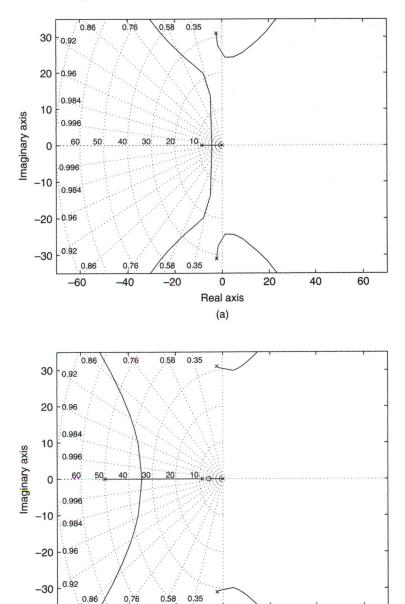

Figure 10.28   Root locus of the flexible pointer under (a) proportional control
and (b) lead control.

near the complex poles that are caused by the flexible shaft, because they primarily limit the gain. A gain of 3 for each is stable and has fair performance, as shown subsequently by their closed-loop step responses in Figure 10.30. The undamped complex poles block further performance improvement, because standard controllers will unwittingly excite the flexible mode.

Not exciting the flexible mode is the key to further improving the closed-loop performance. Recall from Section 10.3.2 that if a zero happens to be near a pole, then that mode is difficult to excite. We will use a notch controller whose zeros are chosen close to the flexible mode locations at $-3 \pm 30i$. To keep the transfer strictly proper, we choose both notch poles at -60. There is no realistic hope of being directly on top of the poles and canceling them, because to be close requires a good model that most likely has been derived from a set of experiments on the system.

The following script plots the root locus of the notch-controlled system:

```
Notch = zpk([-3+30i, -3-30i], [-60, -60], 1);
rlocus(tf([1 6], [1 50])*Notch*Pointer);
axis(70*[-1, 1, -0.5, 0.5]);
sgrid;
xlabel('Real axis');
ylabel('Imaginary axis');
```

The result of executing this script is shown in Figure 10.29. The zeros are very close to the poles because of the flexible mode, and the root-locus plot is very similar to a system without the flexible modes.

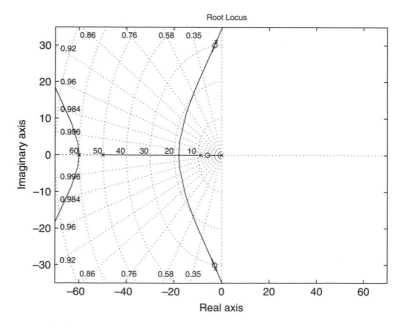

Figure 10.29   Root locus of the notch-lead compensated flexible pointer.

Using

```
Notch = zpk([-3+30i, -3-30i], [-60, -60], 1);
rlocus(tf([1, 6], [1, 50])*Notch*Pointer)
rlocfind(tf([1, 6], [1, 50])*Notch*Pointer)
```

a gain of 40.0 is found to produce a stable closed-loop system. The crosshairs are placed along the root-locus lines that cross the imaginary axis. Placing them inside a 120° wedge centered about the negative real axis will yield good transient performance.

The following script computes the step response of all three types of control schemes previously described.

```
Lead = tf([1, 6], [1, 50]);
Notch = zpk([-3+30i, -3-30i], [-60, -60], 1);
t = linspace(0, 3, 200);
yp = step(feedback(3.0*Pointer, 1), t);
yl = step(feedback(3.0*Lead*Pointer, 1), t);
yn = step(feedback(40.0*Notch*Lead*Pointer, 1), t);
plot(t, yp, 'k--', t, yl, 'k-.', t, yn, 'k-');
legend('Proportional', 'Lead', 'Notch');
xlabel('Time');
ylabel('Step response');
```

The results of executing this script are shown in Figure 10.30. The notch controller has the rise time of the proportional controller, but it doesn't excite the flexible mode of the shaft.

The controllers resulting from the preceding design are analog; however, the final controller most likely will be implemented using an embedded controller, which is a small, inexpensive computer. The embedded controller, perhaps using an optical encoder, periodically measures the position of the pointer and compares to its desired position. After some computation, a digital-to-analog converter or a pulse-width modulator sets the effective amplifier voltage. In the following example, the computer reads the encoder and updates the output of the voltage amplifier 100 times a second. Because of the small sampling interval, the computation done at every sampling instance must be kept to a minimum. The following script designs the controller for the discretized version of the plant and then compares the digital design to that obtained from the previous continuous notch design. The zeros of the digital notch filter are set at $0.92 \pm 0.3i$, close to the poles of the discretized version of the plant, and the poles are placed at 0.6. A digital transfer function does not have to be strictly proper to be implemented. The zero of the digital lead is placed at 0.95, just to the right of the first stable pole of the discretized plant—that is, the pole at 0.5. Using

```
Ts = 0.01;
DNotch = zpk([0.92+0.3i, 0.92-0.3i], [0.6 0.6], 1, Ts);
DLead = tf([1, -0.95], [1, -0.5], Ts);
rlocus(DNotch*DLead*c2d(Pointer, Ts))
rlocfind(DNotch*DLead*c2d(Pointer, Ts))
```

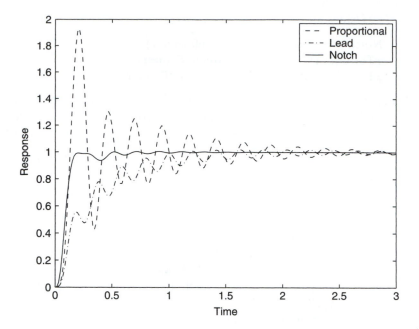

Figure 10.30 Comparison of the step responses of the proportional, lead, and notch controllers.

one places the crosshairs on the root-locus line that leaves the unit circle and finds a gain of 15. Then the script is

```
Ts = 0.01;
DNotch = zpk([0.92+0.3i, 0.92-0.3i], [0.6 0.6], 1, Ts);
DLead = tf([1, -0.95], [1, -0.5], Ts);
rlocus(DNotch*DLead*c2d(Pointer, Ts))
axis(1.2*[-1, 1, -1, 1]);
zgrid;
figure(2);
[yd, t]= step(feedback(15*DNotch*DLead*c2d(Pointer, Ts), 1));
Lead = tf([1, 6], [1, 50]);
Notch = zpk([-3+30i, -3-30i], [-60, -60], 1);
yn = step(feedback(40.0*Notch*Lead*Pointer, 1), t);
plot(t, yd, 'k-', t, yn, 'k:');
legend('Discrete control', 'Continuous control', 'Location', 'SouthEast');
xlabel('Time (s)');
ylabel('Response');
axis(1.2*[0, 1, 0, 1]);
```

The results from executing this script are shown in Figure 10.31.

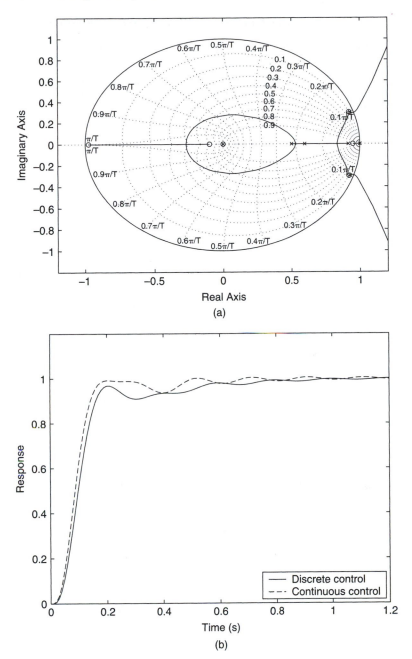

(a)

(b)

Figure 10.31   Digital implementation of the flexible pointer system:
(a) root locus; (b) step response.

10.5.2 PID Control of a Magnetic Suspension System

Consider the magnetic suspension system[9] shown in Figure 10.32. The objective is to keep the ball floating at a desired height when it is subjected to external disturbances. The height of the ball is $h(t)$, and the current in the coil is $i(t)$. The equations of motion for the magnetic suspension are

$$m\frac{d^2h(t)}{dt^2} = mg - k\left(\frac{i(t)}{h(t)}\right)^2$$

$$L\frac{di(t)}{dt} = v(t) - Ri(t)$$

(10.12)

where m is the mass of the ball, g is the gravitational constant, L is the inductance of the coil, R the coil resistance, and k the coupling factor between the magnetic fields and the ball. The input to the system is the coil voltage $v(t)$, and the measured output is the height of the ball $h(t)$. The equations are nonlinear.

The magnetic fields are stronger the closer the ball is to the electromagnet, which tends to destabilize the system. Ideally, the ball is located far enough away so that the magnetic force cancels the pull of gravity. If the ball drops too far, then the magnetic fields are weaker and the ball drops away completely. If the ball is too close to the magnet, then the magnetic fields are stronger and the ball will be pulled to the magnet. Our first step is to compute the point where the gravitational pull equals the attractive magnetic force. This point is called an equilibrium point. Given a desired position h_0, the current that is required to maintain that position can be found by setting the acceleration equal to zero. Hence,

$$i_0^2 = \frac{mg}{k}h_0^2$$

Knowing the equilibrium point, the model can be linearized about it. This linearization simplifies Eqs. 10.12 to give a set of linear equations.

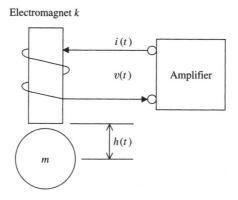

Figure 10.32   A magnetic suspension system.

---

[9]B. Friedland, *Advanced Control System Design*, Prentice Hall, Englewood Cliffs, NJ, 1996.

First, we introduce the state variables

$$x_1 = h \quad x_2 = \frac{dh}{dt} \quad x_3 = i$$

Then, Eqs. 10.12 become

$$\frac{dx_1}{dt} = x_2$$

$$\frac{dx_2}{dt} = g - \frac{k}{m}\left(\frac{x_3}{x_1}\right)^2 \tag{10.13}$$

$$\frac{dx_3}{dt} = \frac{v}{L} - \frac{R}{L}x_3$$

Equations 10.13 can be linearized by taking a Taylor's series expansion around the operating points $x_3 = i_0$ and $x_1 = h_0$. The linearization results in dx_2/dt being modified. The linearized result is

$$\begin{bmatrix} dx_1/dt \\ dx_2/dt \\ dx_3/dt \end{bmatrix} = \begin{bmatrix} 0 & 1 & 0 \\ \dfrac{2k}{m}\dfrac{i_0^2}{h_0^3} & 0 & \dfrac{-2k}{m}\dfrac{i_0}{h_0^2} \\ 0 & 0 & -R/L \end{bmatrix} \begin{bmatrix} x_1 \\ x_2 \\ x_3 \end{bmatrix} + v \begin{bmatrix} 0 \\ 0 \\ 1/L \end{bmatrix}$$

We assume the mass of the ball is 100 gm, the resistance of the coil is 5 Ω, the inductance of the coil is 40 mH, the coupling constant is 0.01 Nm²/A, and the desired height is 2 cm. We first create the function **MagLev** to represent the state-space model of the system.

```
function Plant = MagLev
m = 0.1; g = 9.82; R = 5;
L = 0.04; k = 0.01; h0 = 0.02;
i0 = h0*sqrt(m*g/k);
A = [0, 1, 0; 2*k*i0^2/(m*h0^3), 0, -2*k*i0/(m*h0^2); 0, 0, -R/L];
B = [0; 0; 1/L];
C = [1, 0, 0];
D = 0;
Plant = ss(A, B, C, D)
```

Typing in the MATLAB command window

MagPoles = pole(**MagLev**)

we obtain

```
MagPoles =
   31.3369
  -31.3369
 -125.0000
```

We see that the poles of the linearized system are located at ± 31.3 for the suspension and -125 for the amplifier. Thus, a proportional derivative (PD) controller to stabilize the system is needed. Theoretically, the transfer function for a PD controller is given by

$$C_0(s) = k_p + sk_d$$

where k_p is the proportional gain and k_d is the derivative gain. The controller output involves the derivative of the input, which is hard to realize in practice because of high-frequency noise. Typically, the derivative is approximated and then filtered to remove the noise, resulting in

$$C_1(s) = k_p + k_d\frac{s}{\tau_f s + 1} = k_p\frac{(\tau_f + k_d/k_p)s + 1}{\tau_f s + 1}$$

The transfer function $C_1(s)$ is equivalent to a lead controller with the zero time constant $\tau_f + k_d/k_p$ and the pole (filter) time constant τ_f. The controller is a lead controller, because the zero is always slower than the pole. We select the controller zero at -20, which is just to the right of the first stable pole of the magnetic levitation system, and the filter pole at -50, which results in $\tau_f = 20$ ms. This system requires positive feedback to be stabilized, so we include the sign change in the controller. Thus, the transfer function is

$$C_1(s) = -\frac{s + 20}{s + 50}$$

The script is

```
PD = tf(-1*[1, 20], [1, 50]);
rlocus(PD*MagLev);
sgrid
xlabel('Real axis');
ylabel('Imaginary axis');
```

The resulting root locus plot is shown in Figure 10.33.

The plot shows that at some low gain, the unstable pole is pulled into the left half plane, and at a higher gain, a complex conjugate pair cross over into the right half plane. A stabilizing gain can be determined from this figure by typing

```
rlocus(tf(-1*[1, 20], [1, 50])*MagLev)
rlocfind(tf(-1*[1, 20], [1, 50])*MagLev)
```

in the command window and then placing the crosshairs on the real-axis root-locus line between the unstable pole and the controller zero. A point approximately halfway between the imaginary axis and the controller zero yields a gain of 150. Hence, $k_p = -60$, $k_d = -1.8$, and the filter time constant is 20 ms.

Measurement and modeling errors are likely to produce errors in determining $v_0 = Ri_0$. This will cause a steady-state error in the position of the ball, $h(t)$. While the PD portion of the control shapes the instability and transient behavior of the

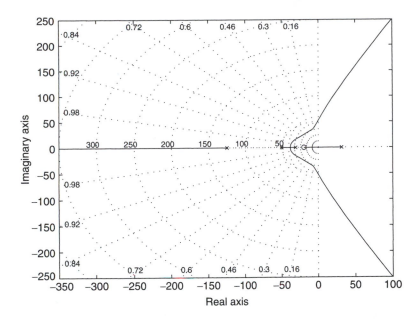

Figure 10.33   Root-locus plot of the PD cascade-control magnetic-levitation system.

system, the PI portion typically is used to improve the steady-state behavior. Consider the PI controller

$$C_2(s) = k_p + \frac{k_i}{s} = \frac{k_p s + k_i/k_p}{k_i} \frac{s}{s}$$

with parameters k_p and k_i. The PI controller has one pole at the origin and a zero at $-k_i/k_p$. If the zero is close to the pole relative to the locations of the other poles and zeros of the system, then the effect of the PI controller on the closed-loop transient behavior is negligible when it is cascaded with the PD controller to form a PID controller. Hence, the feedback gain of 150 may still be used. The effect of the PI controller on the steady-state error is large. For this control system, we choose $k_p = k_i = 1$. The following script simulates the impulse response of the closed-loop system with the linearized model of the magnetic levitator:

```
PD = tf(-1*[1, 20], [1, 50]);
PI = tf([1, 1], [1, 0]);
[y, t] = impulse(feedback(150*PI*PD*MagLev, 1));
plot(t, y, 'k-');
grid;
xlabel('Time');
ylabel('Impulse response');
```

The result of executing this script is shown in Figure 10.34, which is the closed-loop system of the linearized plant model. However, determining the stability of the system with the nonlinear model in the loop is of far greater interest.

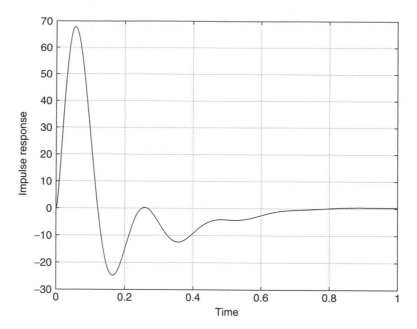

Figure 10.34 Impulse response of the linear approximation to the magnetic-levitation system.

The nonlinear system will now be simulated using SIMULINK. We will require a block called *S-Function*, which is a user-defined function. We will call this user-defined function **MagModel**. There are four parameters to be passed to **MagModel** in the following order as specified by SIMULINK's *S-Function*: time t, state variables x, inputs u, and an integer *flag*. Hybrid models with both discrete and continuous states may be constructed using *S-Function*; we consider those parts that enable continuous nonlinear models. SIMULINK queries the user function to determine everything about the nonlinear model; *flag* determines the purpose of the query. When $flag = 1$, the function returns the derivatives of x using time t, states x, and input u given by Eqs. 10.11. When $flag = 3$, the function returns the outputs. Finally, when $flag = 0$, the function returns a vector *sys*, whose components are, in order, the number of continuous states, the number of discrete states, the number of outputs, the number of inputs, the number of roots, and a final flag that is set to 1 if the system has direct feedthrough. In the case of the magnetic levitator, $sys = [3\ 0\ 1\ 1\ 0\ 0]$, which indicates three continuous states, no discrete states, one input, one output, no roots, and no feedthrough. When $flag = 0$, we also return the initial conditions of the continuous states—that is, the state of the system when it is first started. The equilibrium of the system is $x(0) = [h(0)\ 0\ i(0)]'$. We will start the system near, but not at, the equilibrium position by setting the initial value $h(0)$ 10% larger than the equilibrium value. With such an initial condition, the controller must take action, or the ball will drop away from the magnet. The deviation for the equilibrium position must be small, because the controller is based on a linearized model of the system.

```
function [sys, x0] = MagModel(t, x, u, flag)
m = 0.1; g = 9.82; R = 5; L = 0.040;
k = 0.01; h0 = 0.02;
i0 = h0*sqrt(m*g/k);
switch flag
  case 1
    xdot = zeros(3, 1);
    xdot(1) = x(2);
    xdot(2) = m*g-k*x(3)^2/x(1)^2;
    xdot(3) = −R/L*x(3) + 1/L*u(1);
    sys = xdot;
  case 3
    sys = x(1);
  case 0
    sys = [3 0 1 1 0 0];
    x0 = [h0+0.1*h0; 0; i0];
  otherwise
    sys = [];
end
```

The controller will be specified using variable names rather than numerical values; therefore, these variables must be defined in the command window before running the simulation in SIMULINK. To generate these variables and start SIMULINK, we run the following script:

```
PD = tf(-1*[,1 20], [1, 50]);
PI = tf([1, 1], [1, 0]);
v0 = 0.991; h0 = 0.02;
[num, den] = tfdata(150*PD*PI, 'v');
simulink;
```

The values of $v0$ and $h0$ were computed from the values given.

We now use SIMULINK to generate the block diagram shown in Figure 10.35. From the *Math* library, we use *Sum* and *Gain*. From the *User Defined Functions* library, we use *S-Function*, which, in turn, will use **MagModel**. This assignment is done by double-clicking on the *S-Function* block in the modeling window and entering **MagModel** for the *S-Function* name.

From the *Continuous* library, we use *Transfer Fnc*. Then, we double-click on this block and, in our case, enter the variable names *num* and *den* for the numerator and denominator, respectively, since these two quantities have been specified in the third line in the script we ran before entering SIMULINK.

From the *Sources* library, we use *Constant* to enter a voltage offset and a height offset. These quantities are used to represent errors. Their values are defined by double-clicking on the block and entering either numerical values or variable names, if the variable names have been or will be assigned numerical values in the

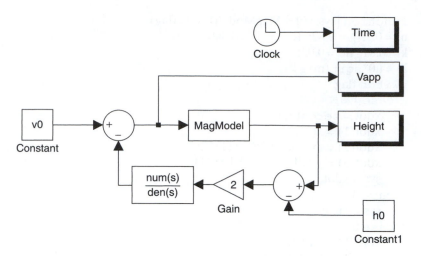

Figure 10.35 SIMULINK block diagram for the nonlinear magnetic-levitation system.

command window. We choose the latter method, since *v0* and *h0* have been defined in our previously run script.

Lastly, we use *To Workspace* from the *Sinks* library to record the bearing's height (*Height*) and the magnitude of the magnet's coil voltage (*Vapp*) as a function of time. The values of time are stored in the array *Time* by *Clock*, which is from the *Sources* library. The shadows around these three blocks are obtained using *Show Drop Shadow* from the *Format* pull-down menu. The quantities *Vapp* and *Height* are saved to the workspace each time the simulation is run and can then be displayed with `plot`. Figure 10.36 shows the quantities *Vapp* and *Height* as a function of *Time*, which were obtained with the following script run in the MATLAB command window. The values of *Height* have been scaled by a factor of 50.

```
plot(Time, 50*Height, 'k-', Time, Vapp, 'k-.')
legend('50h(t)', 'v(t)')
text(1, 1.5, 'Initial conditions')
text(1.2, 1.45, 'h(0) = 0.022 m')
text(1.2, 1.4, 'v(0) = 0.991 V')
xlabel('Time (s)')
ylabel('V_{app} and h(t)')
axis([0 4 .7 1.6])
```

10.5.3 Lead Control of an Inverted Pendulum

We shall design a lead controller for an inverted pendulum using root-locus techniques. Consider an inverted pendulum mounted on a disk, as shown in Figure 10.37.

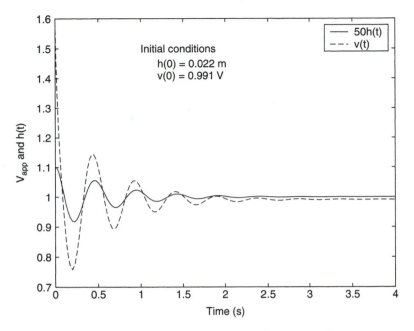

Figure 10.36 Response under PID control of the nonlinear magnetic suspension system to initial conditions and modeling errors.

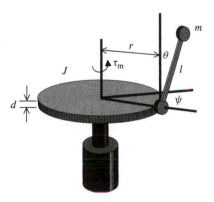

Figure 10.37 Inverted pendulum on a disk.

The objective of the control system is to command the position of the disk while keeping the pendulum upright. Both the angle of the disk ψ and the angle of the pendulum θ are measured. The equations of motion are

$$
\begin{aligned}
ml^2\frac{d^2\theta}{dt^2} + mrl\cos(\theta)\frac{d^2\psi}{dt^2} &= mgl\sin(\theta) + b_1\frac{d\theta}{dt} \\
mrl\cos(\theta)\frac{d^2\theta}{dt^2} + (J + mr^2)\frac{d^2\psi}{dt^2} &= mrl\sin(\theta)\left(\frac{d\theta}{dt}\right)^2 + b_2\frac{d\psi}{dt} + \tau_m
\end{aligned}
\tag{10.14}
$$

where m is the mass of the bob, l the length of the pendulum, r is the radius of the disk (which is also the radius of the bob attachment), d is the thickness of the disk, $J = \rho\pi dr^4/4$ is the inertia of the disk, b_1 is the friction coefficient of the revolute joint of the pendulum, b_2 is the friction in the revolute joint of the disk, and τ_m is the torque applied by the motor attached to the base of the disk. As with the magnetic bearing, the equations of motion may be linearized about the operating point when θ and $d\theta/dt$ are very small.

We define the elements of the state vector x as

$$x_1(t) = \theta(t) \quad x_3(t) = \frac{d\theta}{dt}$$

$$x_2(t) = \psi(t) \quad x_4(t) = \frac{d\psi}{dt}$$

Substituting these equations into Eqs. 10.14 and assuming that θ and $d\theta/dt$ are very small and, hence, that we can neglect all terms of order 2 and higher, we obtain

$$\frac{dx_1}{dt} = x_3$$

$$\frac{dx_2}{dt} = x_4$$

$$ml^2\frac{dx_3}{dt} + mlr\frac{dx_4}{dt} = mglx_1 + b_1x_3$$

$$mlr\frac{dx_3}{dt} + (J + mr^2)\frac{dx_4}{dt} = b_2x_4 + \tau_m$$

or, in matrix form,

$$M\dot{x} = Qx + Wu$$

where

$$W = [0 \quad 0 \quad 0 \quad 1]' \qquad x = [x_1 \quad x_2 \quad x_3 \quad x_4]' \qquad \dot{x} = dx/dt$$

$$M = \begin{bmatrix} 1 & 0 & 0 & 0 \\ 0 & 1 & 0 & 0 \\ 0 & 0 & ml^2 & mlr \\ 0 & 0 & mlr & J + mr^2 \end{bmatrix} \quad Q = \begin{bmatrix} 0 & 0 & 1 & 0 \\ 0 & 0 & 0 & 1 \\ mgl & 0 & b_1 & 0 \\ 0 & 0 & 0 & b_2 \end{bmatrix} \quad u = \tau_m$$

The upright position corresponding to $x(t) = 0$ is an equilibrium point of the system at which $u = \tau_m = 0$. The linearized equations of the inverted pendulum system about the upright position are represented as a state-space system in the following function called **Pendulum**. This system has the angle of the pendulum θ and the angle of the disk ψ as the outputs. Therefore, the output *Plant* of **Pendulum** is a system with two outputs and one input, which can be accessed as follows: *Plant*(1, 1) is the transfer function from τ_m to θ, and *Plant*(2, 1) is the transfer function from τ_m to ψ. We assume the length of the pendulum is 30 cm, the mass of the bob 0.2 kg, the radius of the disk 15 cm, the thickness of the disk 1 cm, and its density 2,500 kg/m³.

The friction in the systems is set to zero; thus, $b_1 = b_2 = 0$.

```
function Plant = Pendulum
l = 0.3; g = 9.81; m = 0.2; r = 0.15;
d = 0.01; rho = 2500; b1 = 0; b2 = 0;
J = 0.25*pi*rho*d*r^4;
M = [1, 0, 0, 0; 0, 1, 0, 0; 0, 0, m*l^2 m*r*l; 0, 0, m*r*l, J+m*r^2];
Q = [0, 0, 1, 0; 0, 0, 0, 1; m*g*l, 0, b1, 0; 0, 0, 0, b2];
W = [0; 0; 0; 1];
A = inv(M)*Q;
B = inv(M)*W;
C = [1, 0, 0, 0; 0, 1, 0, 0];
D = [0];
Plant = ss(A, B, C, D);
```

The poles of the system are found by typing

pole(**Pendulum**)

in the MATLAB command window. This displays

```
0
0
6.8923
-6.8923
```

Thus, there are two poles at the origin and a pair on the real axis mirrored about the imaginary axis at ±6.9 rad/s. The system is, therefore, open-loop unstable. The transmission zeros of the inverted pendulum from the perspective of θ, the angle of the pendulum, is found by typing in the MATLAB command window

Plant = **Pendulum**;
tzero(Plant(1, 1))

which displays two zeros. The system with only the first output θ and first input τ_m may be addressed using matrix notation; hence, the (1, 1) subscript on *Plant*. Thus, there are two zeros right on top of the poles. This indicates that using only the output θ to control the inverted pendulum will ignore some of the dynamics. In particular, the angle of the pendulum contains insufficient information to discern the position and velocity of the disk. Thus, the outputs of a sensor measuring this angular motion can be zero even when the disk is rotating at a uniform angular velocity. The dynamics, which are not at rest while the output is zero, are sometimes referred to as zero dynamics. These (unobservable) zero dynamics will not be stabilized by feedback from θ alone. The zeros of the pendulum from the perspective of the disk angle ψ are found by typing

Plant = **Pendulum**;
tzero(Plant(2, 1))

in the command window. Since the plant has two outputs, we address the subsystem with the second output and the first input with the subscript $(2, 1)$. It is found from these results that the zeros are located at ± 5.72, which are close to the open-loop poles of the pendulum, which are ± 6.9. This indicates that while the behavior of the pendulum is observable from the disk position, it is just barely so. A SISO controller designed using either output will perform badly.

A MISO controller that is dependent on both outputs would perform much better than a SISO controller and, thus, will be the focus of the rest of our effort. We shall design this controller shown in Figure 10.38 in two steps. First, we shall design a controller using the output θ to keep the pendulum upright. Wrapped around this control loop will be a controller that uses ψ to keep the angle of the disk at the commanded position.

We start the design process with a lead controller that keeps the pendulum upright. Such a controller will use the output θ to determine which correction to apply. Recall that the open-loop poles are located at ± 6.9. We put the lead zero at -5, just to the right of the stable pole in the pair to pull the unstable pole into the left half of the complex plane. The lead pole is placed at -10. Hence,

$$C_\theta(s) = -\frac{s + 5}{s + 10}$$

Since positive feedback is required, a negative sign appears in $C_\theta(s)$.

The following script generates the root-locus plot of the θ control loop. MATLAB automatically picks a range of gains to apply, but in this case, we select a range of $0.1 \le \theta \le 10$ equally spaced on a logarithmic scale.

```
Plant = Pendulum;
PlantTheta = minreal(Plant(1,1));
ControlTheta = tf(-1*[1, 5], [1, 10]);
rlocus(ControlTheta*PlantTheta, logspace(-1, 1, 60));
sgrid;
xlabel('Real axis');
ylabel('Imaginary axis');
```

Executing the script results in Figure 10.39a.

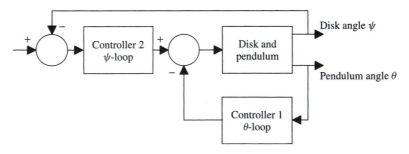

Figure 10.38   Block diagram for the inverted pendulum control system.

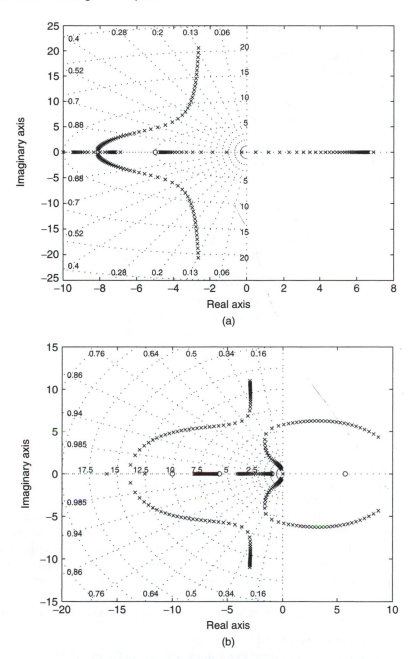

Figure 10.39   Root locus of the control loops in feedback for (a) the θ control loop and (b) the ψ control loop.

A suitable gain can be found with

```
Plant = Pendulum;
PlantTheta = minreal(Plant(1, 1));
ControlTheta = tf(-1*[1, 5], [1, 10]);
rlocus(ControlTheta*PlantTheta)
rlocfind(ControlTheta*PlantTheta)
```

Placing the crosshairs on the real axis between the imaginary axis and the lead zero, we find that a gain of 4 stabilizes the θ loop. The resulting closed-loop poles of the theta control system are found from the following script:

```
Plant = Pendulum;
PlantTheta = minreal(Plant(1, 1));
ControlTheta = tf(-1*[1, 5], [1, 10]);
pole(feedback(4*ControlTheta*PlantTheta,1))
```

It is found from the execution of this script that the closed-loop poles are approximately -4, $-3 \pm 11i$, which, although stable, are not well damped.

Now we design the outer feedback loop for the disk position ψ. The outer feedback loop is designed with the inner θ loop in place, so we first form the closed-loop system by wrapping the first controller inside a loop employing θ. We do this with the following script:

```
ControlTheta = tf(-[1, 5], [1, 10]);
PlantPsi = feedback(Pendulum, 4*ControlTheta, [1], [1]);
pole(PlantPsi(2,1))
tzero(PlantPsi(2,1))
```

Note that we have to specify which inputs and outputs to use since the plant is MIMO and the controller is SISO. The results show that *PlantPsi* has two additional poles at the origin, which is representative of a double integrator. These poles need to be moved to the left; however, complicating that objective is an unstable zero at 5.72. The inverted pendulum is an example of a system that is nonminimum phase. To move the disk, the controller first must move in the opposite direction to keep the pendulum upright during the transition from its current position to the desired position. The unstable zero attracts one of the poles of the double integrator. To solve this problem, we again use a lead controller whose zero is just inside the left half of the complex plane. The following script plots the root locus of the ψ control loop:

```
ControlTheta = tf(-[1, 5], [1, 10]);
PlantPsi = feedback(Pendulum, 4*ControlTheta, [1], [1]);
ControlPsi = tf(-[1, 1], [1, 8]);
k = 0.35*logspace(-1, 1, 60);
rlocus(ControlPsi*PlantPsi(2,1), k);
sgrid;
xlabel('Real axis')
ylabel('Imaginary axis')
```

The execution of this script results in Figure 10.39b. To find the appropriate gain, we type

```
ControlTheta = tf(-[1, 5], [1, 10]);
PlantPsi = feedback(Pendulum, 4*ControlTheta, [1], [1]);
ControlPsi = tf(-[1, 1], [1, 8]);
rlocus(ControlPsi*PlantPsi(2,1))
rlocfind(ControlPsi*PlantPsi(2,1))
```

in the command window and place the crosshairs near the lower half of the root-locus lines that loop into the complex plane. It is found that a gain of 0.3 places all the poles inside the left half complex plane.

The step response of the final control system is computed from the following script:

```
ControlTheta = tf(-[1, 5], [1, 10]);
PlantPsi = feedback(Pendulum, 4*ControlTheta, [1], [1]);
ControlPsi = tf(-[1, 1], [1, 8]);
[y, t] = step(feedback(0.3*ControlPsi*PlantPsi, 1, [1], [2]));
plot(t, y(:,1), 'k-', t, y(:,2), 'k--');
xlabel('Time');
ylabel('Step response');
legend('\theta(t)', '\psi(t)');
```

The resulting step-response plot is shown in Figure 10.40, which reveals the nonminimum phase behavior of the controller and the plant.

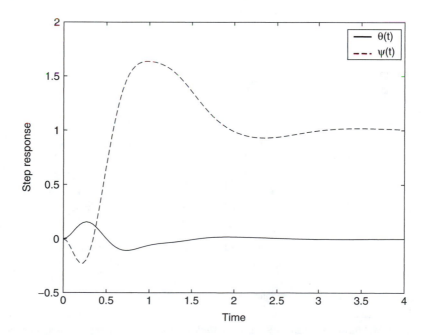

Figure 10.40   Step response of the inverted pendulum.

10.5.4 Control of a Magnetically Suspended Flywheel

Consider the magnetically suspended flywheel system shown in Figure 10.41. Magnetic coils are used to float the wheel so that the wheel can be run at high speeds without the losses associated with friction. The objective of the control system is to keep the wheel suspended. Like the magnetic suspension described in Section 10.5.2, the system is naturally unstable. Four distances are measured as outputs. These distances correspond to the x- and y-positions of the top and bottom shafts as measured in the inertial frame. Four coil currents may be selected to control the magnetic fields about the shaft; these coils are co-located with the sensors. The linearized equations of motion are

$$\frac{d^2 x_{cm}}{dt^2} = \frac{f_1 + f_3}{m}$$

$$\frac{d^2 y_{cm}}{dt^2} = \frac{f_2 + f_4}{m}$$

$$\frac{d^2 \phi}{dt^2} = -\beta\omega\frac{d\psi}{dt} + \frac{h}{J_{xx}}(f_4 - f_2)$$

$$\frac{d^2 \psi}{dt^2} = \beta\omega\frac{d\phi}{dt} + \frac{h}{J_{xx}}(f_1 - f_3)$$

where x_{cm} and y_{cm} are the location of the center of mass of the flywheel as measured in the inertial frame; (ϕ, ψ) give the orientation of the flywheel frame with respect to the inertial frame using roll (ϕ), pitch (ψ), and yaw orientation[10]; m is the mass of the flywheel; J_{xx} is the rotational inertia of the flywheel about the nonspinning axis; $\beta = J_{zz}/J_{xx}$; and h is the distance from the center of mass to the actuators. The inputs f_i are the forces applied by the magnetic bearings and obey the following relationships:

$$f_i = k_1 y_i + k_2 u_i$$

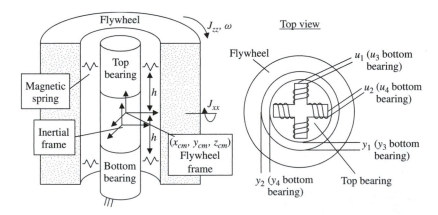

Figure 10.41 A magnetically suspended flywheel.

---

[10]R. M. Murray, X. Li, and S. S. Sastry, *A Mathematical Introduction to Robotic Manipulation*, CRC Press, Boca Raton, FL, 1994.

where y_i is the distance from the wheel to the actuator and is the system's output. The bearings are composed of a permanent magnet surrounded by coils. The negative spring constant k_1 is caused by the permanent magnet and the gain k_2 by the field generated by the current u_i in the coils. The operating speed of the wheel is ω rad/s.

The output values y_i for small ϕ and ψ are given by

$$y_1 = x_{cm} + h\psi$$
$$y_2 = y_{cm} - h\phi$$
$$y_3 = x_{cm} + h\psi$$
$$y_4 = y_{cm} - h\phi$$

If we let

$$q(t) = [x_{cm}, y_{cm}, \phi(t), \psi(t)]'$$

and

$$u(t) = [u_1\, u_2\, u_3\, u_4]'$$

then the linearized equations can be written as

$$\ddot{q} = \omega P_a \dot{q} + k_1 B_a C_a q + k_2 B_a u$$
$$y = C_a q$$

where

$$P_a = \begin{bmatrix} 0 & 0 & 0 & 0 \\ 0 & 0 & 0 & 0 \\ 0 & 0 & 0 & \beta \\ 0 & 0 & -\beta & 0 \end{bmatrix}$$

$$B_a = \begin{bmatrix} 1/m & 0 & 1/m & 0 \\ 0 & 1/m & 0 & 1/m \\ 0 & -h/J_{xx} & 0 & h/J_{xx} \\ h/J_{xx} & 0 & -h/J_{xx} & 0 \end{bmatrix} \tag{10.15}$$

$$C_a = \begin{bmatrix} 1 & 0 & 0 & h \\ 0 & 1 & -h & 0 \\ 1 & 0 & 0 & -h \\ 0 & 1 & h & 0 \end{bmatrix}$$

Hence, if we set

$$z = \begin{bmatrix} q \\ \dot{q} \end{bmatrix}$$

we have the following matrix equations

$$\dot{z} = \begin{bmatrix} 0 & I \\ k_1 B_a C_a & \omega P_a \end{bmatrix} z + \begin{bmatrix} 0 \\ k_2 B_a \end{bmatrix} u$$

$$y = [C_a \quad 0]z + [0]u$$

where I is the unit matrix.

The following function **Flywheel** generates the linearized model as a function of rotational speed in revolutions per minute (rpm) and is used in the subsequent design evaluations. If no arguments are supplied to this function, it is assumed the operating speed is 0 rpm. For the flywheel under consideration, the rotational inertia about the x and y body-axes of the flywheel is 1.563×10^{-4} Nm·s^2, and the rotational inertia about the z-axis is 1.141×10^{-4} Nm·s^2. The dimensionless shape factor β is approximately 1. The mass of the wheel is 340 gm, and the height from the center of mass is 3 cm. The coil constants are $k_1 = 4.8 \times 10^4$ N/m and $k_2 = 3.75$ N/A.

```
function Plant = Flywheel(rpm)
if nargin < 1, rpm = 0; end;
Jxx = 1.563e-4; Jzz = 1.141e-4;
beta = Jzz/Jxx; m = 0.34;
h = 0.03; k1 = 4.8e4; k2 = 3.75;
omega = rpm/60*2*pi;
Pa = [zeros(1,4); zeros(1,4); 0, 0, 0, -beta; 0, 0, beta, 0];
Ba = [1/m, 0, 1/m, 0; 0, 1/m, 0, 1/m; 0, -h/Jxx, 0, h/Jxx; h/Jxx, 0, -h/Jxx, 0];
Ca = [1, 0, 0, h; 0, 1, -h, 0; 1, 0, 0, -h; 0, 1, h, 0];
A = [zeros(4), eye(4); k1*Ba*Ca, omega*Pa];
B = [zeros(4); k2*Ba];
C = [Ca, zeros (4)];
D = [zeros(4)];
Plant = ss(A, B, C, D);
```

The open-loop poles change as a function of *rpm*. Execution of the following script plots the open-loop poles for a range of typical operating speeds:

```
rpm = [0:100:16000, 16100:10:20000];
result = zeros(8, length(rpm));
for j = 1:length(rpm)
   result(:,j) = pole(Flywheel(rpm(j)));
end
plot(real(result(:,1)), imag(result(:,1)), 'x');
hold on;
for j = 1:8;
```

```
    x = real(result(j,:));
    y = imag(result(j,:));
    plot(x, y);
end;
grid;
xlabel('Real axis');
ylabel('Imaginary axis');
```

The result of executing this script is shown in Figure 10.42. There are two sets of poles (but no zeros) mirrored about the imaginary axis. One set, located at ±530 rad/s (85 Hz), is caused by the translational modes and does not change with operating speed. The other set, located at ±740 rad/s (120 Hz), is caused by the two rotational modes and is affected by the gyroscopic coupling.

In summary, there are four unstable and four stable poles, and half of the poles change location with the operating speed. From an examination of Eqs. 10.15, we see that at $\omega = 0$ rpm, P does not affect the solution. This suggests that the flywheel at 0 rpm may be statically decoupled, resulting in two rotational and two translational SISO systems. Thus, traditional lead-control design techniques, such as a root locus, can now be used to generate a stabilizing controller.

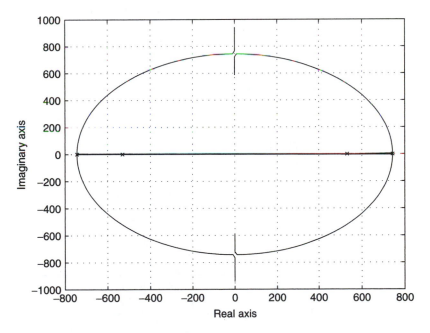

Figure 10.42   Root locus of the flywheel as a function of operating speed from 0 to 20,000 rpm.

Consider the matrix T, which forms the sums and differences between input channels:

$$T = \begin{bmatrix} 1 & 0 & 0 & 1 \\ 0 & 1 & -1 & 0 \\ 1 & 0 & 0 & -1 \\ 0 & 1 & 1 & 0 \end{bmatrix}$$

Note that the matrix T diagonalizes the input and output matrices of Eqs. 10.15, as shown in the following:

$$BT = \begin{bmatrix} 2/m & 0 & 0 & 0 \\ 0 & 2/m & 0 & 0 \\ 0 & 0 & 2h/J_{xx} & 0 \\ 0 & 0 & 0 & 2h/J_{xx} \end{bmatrix}$$

$$T^{-1}C = \begin{bmatrix} 1 & 0 & 0 & 0 \\ 0 & 1 & 0 & 0 \\ 0 & 0 & h & 0 \\ 0 & 0 & 0 & h \end{bmatrix}$$

After performing a static decoupling using T, we can perform our lead design on the four resulting SISO plants. Figure 10.43 shows how the matrices T would be inserted in practice. The following script generates the decoupled SISO plants and computes a root locus of the result:

```
T = [1, 0, 0, 1; 0, 1, -1, 0; 1, 0, 0, -1; 0, 1, 1, 0];
decoupFly = inv(T)*Flywheel(0)*T;
```

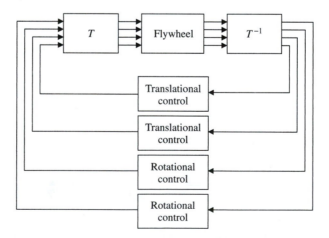

Figure 10.43 Static decoupling of the flywheel.

```
transFly = minreal(decoupFly(1, 1));
rotFly = minreal(decoupFly(3, 3));
Lead = tf([1, 400], [1, 1000]);
rlocus(Lead*transFly);
sgrid;
xlabel('Real axis');
ylabel('Imaginary axis');
figure(2);
rlocus(Lead*rotFly);
sgrid;
xlabel('Real axis');
ylabel('Imaginary axis');
```

The result of executing this script is shown in Figure 10.44.

The script

```
T = [1, 0, 0, 1; 0, 1, -1, 0; 1, 0, 0, -1; 0, 1, 1, 0];
decoupFly = inv(T)*Flywheel(0)*T;
transFly = minreal(decoupFly(1, 1));
Lead = tf([1, 400], [1, 1000]);
rlocus(Lead*transFly)
rlocfind(Lead*transFly)
```

is used to find a stabilizing gain for the translational system, and the script

```
T = [1, 0, 0, 1; 0, 1, -1, 0; 1, 0, 0, -1; 0, 1, 1, 0];
decoupFly = inv(T)*Flywheel(0)*T;
rotFly = minreal(decoupFly(3, 3));
Lead = tf([1, 400], [1, 1000]);
rlocus(Lead*rotFly)
rlocfind(Lead*rotFly)
```

is used similarly for the rotational system. By design, the same gain (5) stabilizes both the translational and rotational components of the system. Since the gain for the translational and rotational control is the same, the controllers are identical. Also, decoupling is not needed in the implementation, because the matrix T commutes with the transfer function of the controller. This fact makes the implementation easier.

We now design an LQG controller for the flywheel. The design involves choosing the appropriate penalty R for the cost function. The following script computes the optimal closed-loop poles for $10^{-10} \le R \le 10^{-6}$. The result of its execution is shown in Figure 10.45.

```
[A, B, C, D] = ssdata(Flywheel);
clPoles = [];
R = logspace(-10, -6, 60);
```

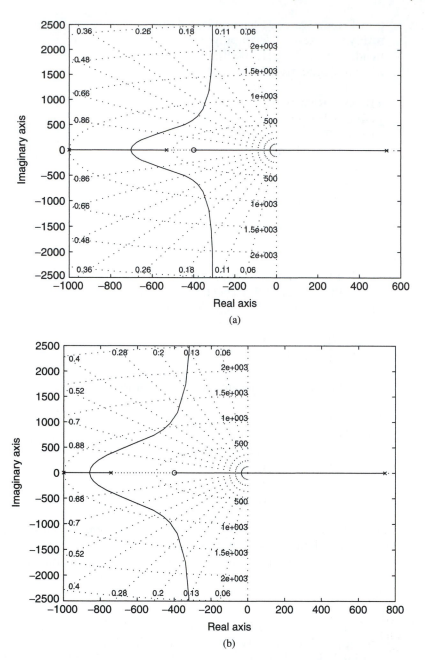

Figure 10.44 Root locus of the control loops for (a) the translational motion and (b) the rotational motion.

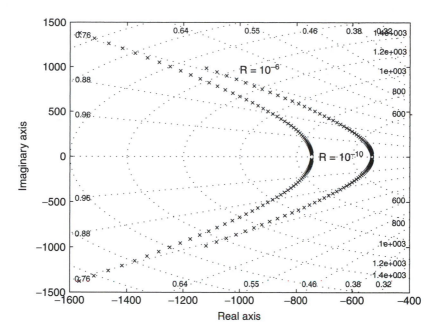

Figure 10.45 Optimal root locus for the flywheel for $10^{-10} \leq R \leq 10^{-6}$.

```
for i = 1:length(R)
   [K, S, E] = lqr(A, B, C'*C, R(i)*eye(4));
   clPoles = [clPoles, E];
end;
plot(real(clPoles), imag(clPoles), 'kx');
sgrid;
ylabel('Imaginary axis');
xlabel('Real axis');
text(-700, 0, 'R = 10^{-10}');
text(-1000, 1000, 'R = 10^{-6}');
```

To compare the two different control schemes, the following script computes the response of the two different controllers with the same initial conditions. The initial conditions are all zero, except that the flywheel is slightly tilted such that $\phi(0) = 0.001$ radians. The flywheel spins at 10,000 rpm, even though the controllers were designed for 0 rpm. The LQG controller is designed with penalty factor $R = 10^{-6}$.

```
Control = 4e4*eye(4)*tf([1, 400], [1, 1000]);
x0 = zeros(12, 1); x0(3) = 1e-3; t = linspace(0, 0.25, 1000);
yl = initial(feedback(Flywheel(10000), Control), x0, t);
```

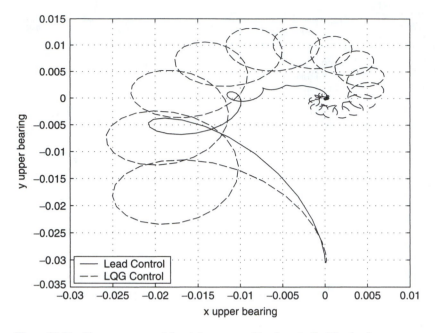

Figure 10.46   Phase response of the state-space and lead-controlled flywheels.

```
[A, B, C , D] = ssdata(Flywheel);
K = lqr(A, B, C'*C, 1e-6*eye(4));
L = (lqr(A', C', B*B', 1e-6*eye(4)))';
ControlSS = reg(Flywheel, K, L);
x0 = zeros(16, 1);  x0(3) = 1e-3;
ys= initial(feedback(Flywheel(10000), ControlSS, +1), x0, t);
plot(1000*yl(:,1), 1000*yl(:,2), 'k-', 1000*ys(:,1), 1000*ys(:,2), 'k--');
grid;
xlabel('x upper bearing');
ylabel('y upper bearing');
legend('Lead Control', 'LQG Control', 'Location', 'SouthWest')
```

The results from the execution of the script are the phase plots shown in Figure
10.46. Both controllers keep the flywheel suspended with comparable levels of
performance.

10.6 SUMMARY OF FUNCTIONS INTRODUCED

A summary of the functions introduced in this chapter is presented in Table 10.1.

TABLE 10.1   MATLAB Functions Introduced in Chapter 10

MATLAB function	Description
acker	Pole placement for single-input systems
alpha	Sets transparency properties for objects
arx*	Estimates parameters of an ARX model
bode	Bode frequency response
c2d	Makes continuous-time systems discrete
compare*	Compares measured outputs with model outputs
connect	Obtains state-space model from block diagram description
conv	Convolution and polynomial multiplication
dcgain	DC gain
detrend*	Remove trends from output–input data
feedback	Feedback connection of two LTI (linear time invariant) models
iddata*	Packages input–output data into the iddata object
ident*	Opens the GUI
ift	Redheffer star product of two LTI models
impulse	Impulse response of LTI model
initial	Response of state-space models to initial conditions
lqe	Kalman estimator design for continuous-time systems
lqr	Linear-quadratic state-feedback regulator for continuous plant
lsim	Simulates response of LTI model to arbitrary input
margin	Gain and phase margins and associated crossover frequencies
mineral	Minimal realization of pole-zero cancellation
nyquist	Nyquist frequency response of LTI model
parallel	Parallel connection of two LTI models
place	Pole placement
pole	Poles of an LTI system
reg	Form regulator given state-feedback and estimator gain
rlocfind	Finds root-locus gains for a given set of roots
rlocus	Root locus
series	Series connection of two LTI models
sgrid	s-Plane grid of constant damping factors and natural frequencies
simulink	Starts SIMULINK
ss	State-space model
ssbal	Balances state-space models using a diagonal similarity transformation
ssdata	Accesses state-space model data
step	Step response of LTI systems
tf	Transfer function model
tfdata	Accesses transfer function data
tzero	Transmission zeros of LTI system
zgrid	z-Plane grid of constant damping factors and natural frequencies
zpk	Specifies zero-pole-gain model

* System Identification Toolbox

EXERCISES

10.1 The suspension system[11] shown in Figure 10.47 has the level of the road surface as the input $y(t)$ and absolute position of m_1 as the output $x(t)$. The transfer function of the system is

$$\frac{y(s)}{r(s)} = \frac{sbk_2 + k_1k_2}{m_1m_2s^4 + b(m_1 + m_2)s^3 + k_1(m_1 + m_2)s^2 + k_2m_1s^2 + k_2bs + k_1k_2}$$

Assume that $m_1 = 500$ kg, $m_2 = 100$ kg, $b = 1000$ Ns/m, $k_1 = 2000$ N/m, and $k_2 = 10^4$ N/m.

a. A washboard-like road surface can be approximated by

$$r(t) = \epsilon \sin \omega t$$

Determine the value of ω such that the amplitude of the induced response amplitude of the ride $y(t)$ is 10% of the amplitude of $r(t)$.

b. Depending on its usage, the mass of the car may double. Generate a meshed surface of the magnitude of the Bode plot as a function of m_1 for $500 \le m_1 \le 1000$ kg.

c. Plot the value of ω for which the attenuation of the road variation $r(t)$ is 90% as a function of b and m_1.

10.2 Construct a fifth-order system with five equally spaced poles on a circle of radius $2\pi k$ in the left half of the complex plane and five zeros in the right half plane at the mirror-image locations. Set the DC gain to 1 and $k = 1$.

a. Cascade the fifth-order system with a simple first-order plant with a pole at -1 and a DC gain of 1. Plot the step response of the system for 4 s and the step response of the plant without the fifth-order system on the same graph.

b. Compute the percentage overshoot and the rise time.

c. Repeat parts a and b for $k = 0.5$ and $k = 2.0$. Notice how the response delay grows with increasing k.

d. Repeat parts a and b for three and seven equally spaced poles. Notice how the oscillations increase with an increase in the number of poles.

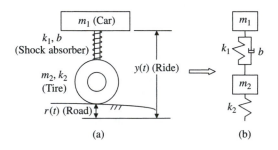

(a)   (b)

Figure 10.47 (a) Simplified model of an automotive wheel suspension; (b) mass and spring equivalent.

[11]U. Ozguner, H. Goktas, and H. Chan, "Automotive Suspension Control Through a Computer Communication Network," *Proceedings of 1st IEEE Conference on Control Application*, Vol. 2, 1992, pp. 895–900.

10.3 Suppose a controller is designed using a simple nominal plant model, such as[12]

$$G_0(s) = \frac{1}{s + 1}$$

The plant may not be accurately modeled. For each of the following alternate models, plot the open-loop step response of the nominal plant $G_0(s)$ with the open-loop step response of the alternate plant. Also, plot the closed-loop step response of both systems with proportional error control and a gain of 20. Use a maximum time of 2 s. Notice that while the open-loop responses are very different, the closed-loop responses are nearly identical.

a.
$$G_1(s) = \frac{3.7}{0.75s + 0.6}$$

b.
$$G_2(s) = \frac{1.63}{0.94s + 0.92}$$

c.
$$G_3(s) = \frac{0.7s^2 + 7s + 17}{s^3 + 2s^2 + 5.2s + 4}$$

10.4 Consider the flexible drive-shaft system discussed in Section 10.5.1 with the configuration shown in Figure 10.27. As mentioned in that section, it is difficult to know the exact frequency of the resonant mode. The question is whether it is better to overestimate or to underestimate this frequency. To investigate this, plot together the Bode plots of the uncompensated pointer with the following two compensators:

Notch Filter #1: $\dfrac{(s + 3 + 28i)(s + 3 - 28i)}{(s + 60)^2}$

Notch Filter #2: $\dfrac{(s + 3 + 34i)(s + 3 - 34i)}{(s + 60)^2}$

Set the gain of each notch filter to 1 before plotting, and draw your conclusions from the plotted results.

10.5 The appearances of nonlinear characteristics in systems are very common in practice. Consider a feedback system with an input nonlinearity, as shown in Figure 10.48. The nonlinearity obeys the relationship $u(t) = f(e(t))$, where $e(t)$ is the input signal and $u(t)$ is the nonlinear output signal. The plant is given by

$$G_0(s) = \frac{1}{s + 1}$$

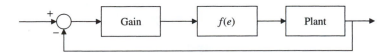

Figure 10.48   Block diagram for simple system with a nonlinear input.

---

[12]R. Jurgen, *Electronic Engine Control Technologies*, SAE International, Troy, MI, 1999.

Find the steady-state response of the system as a function of the magnitude of a step input signal for the three controller gains $k = 1$, $k = 10$, and $k = 100$ for the following nonlinear functions:

a.
$$f(e) = 0.2(e^3 - e)$$

b.
$$f(e) = e + \sin(e) \quad |e| > 1$$
$$= 0 \quad |e| \le 1$$

c.
$$f(e) = \tan^{-1}(e)$$

10.6 Consider the guided missile in Figure 10.49. The lateral force of the air rotates a missile about its center of gravity. The force applied by the air can be considered as a point force applied to the center of pressure. If this center of pressure is ahead of the center of mass, the guided missile is unstable.

   The input to the system is the angle of thrust $\psi(t)$, and the output of the system is $\theta(t)$. The force applied by the air drag can be modeled as $F_d = k_d \sin(\theta)$, where k_d depends on the shape and velocity of the rocket. The off-axis force applied by the rocket engines is given by $F_r \sin(\psi)$. The other relevant parameters are l_1, the distance from the rocket engine to the center of mass of the missile; l_2, the distance from the center of mass of the missile to the center of pressure; and J, the rotational inertia of the rocket.

   For a fixed k_d and F_r, the effective transfer function from ψ to θ, when ψ to θ are small, is[13]

$$G(s) = \frac{l_1 F_r / J}{s^2 - l_2 k_d / J}$$

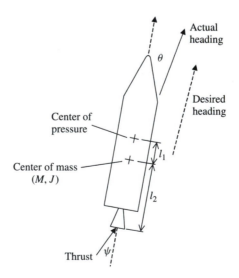

Figure 10.49   Attitude control of a missile.

[13]M. Driels, *Linear Control Systems*, McGraw-Hill, New York, NY, 1996.

Assume that $l_1 F_r/J = l_2 k_d/J = 9$ is an operating point of interest.

a. Using a lead-control structure

$$C(s) = k\frac{s + z}{z + p}$$

find the values of k, z, and p such that the closed-loop system response is stable.

b. As the velocity of the rocket changes, k_d changes. The operating speed changes enormously over the life of the rocket, effectively changing k_d. For the fixed controller designed in a, use a root-locus plot to determine the range of k_d for which the system remains stable.

10.7 Consider the design of a cruise controller for an automobile. The car is modeled as a mass with a damper that limits the forward motion. The open-loop transfer function $G(s)$ from the engine throttle angle to the car's velocity is

$$G(s) = \frac{1}{ms + b}$$

The controller $C(s)$ is PI, with transfer function

$$C(s) = k_p + k_i/s$$

Assume that the car's mass m is 1200 kg and the friction coefficient b is 70 Ns/m. The grade (slope) of the road acts as a disturbance into the plant. The block diagram for this system is shown in Figure 10.50. The desired speed is $r(t)$, the input for the motor (a throttle angle) is $u(t)$, and the speed of the vehicle is $y(t)$, as measured by a speedometer. The disturbance $d(t)$ represents the effect of the road grade.

a. The transfer function from the disturbance $d(t)$ to the speed $y(t)$ is

$$G_{CL}(s) = \frac{G(s)}{1 + C(s)G(s)}$$

where $G(s)$ is the open-loop response and $C(s)$ is the PI transfer function defined previously. Plot the step response of the open-loop system and closed-loop system on the same figure for $k_p = 100$ and $k_i = 0$. Note that as the gain is increased, the disturbance is reduced.

b. The transfer function from the velocity command $r(t)$ to speed $y(t)$ is

$$G_{ry}(s) = \frac{C(s)G(s)}{1 + C(s)G(s)}$$

Plot the step response for $k_p = 100$ and $k_i = 0$.

c. Plot the steady-state output for the systems in parts a and b to a step response as a function of the proportional gain P in the range 50 to 150. It is seen that the integrator eliminates the steady-state error, and its speed is determined by the gain k_i.

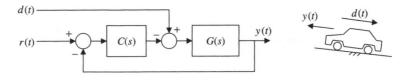

Figure 10.50 Block diagram of the automobile cruise control.

10.8 An automotive suspension typically is passive, being composed of springs and dampers. To improve the suspension of cars, active suspensions systems have been proposed. Figure 10.51 depicts a simplified model of an active automobile suspension system in which $y(t)$ represents the input of the road surface and $x(t)$ is the vertical position of the passenger compartment. Assume that the mass of the tire is negligible and that velocity feedback is used so that $u(t) = C\,dx(t)/dt$. The actuator applies a force to the rod and the passenger compartment that is proportional to their relative velocity: $C(dx/dt - dy/dt)$. The velocity transfer function from the road $y(t)$ to the ride $r(t)$ is

$$G(s) = \frac{(c + b)s + k}{ms^2 + (c + b)s + k}$$

a. Use `rlocus` and `rlocfind` to determine the value of c needed to set the damping ratio to 1—that is, to make the system critically damped. To use `rlocus`, notice that the denominator can be written as $ms^2 + bs + k + cs$. Hence, it is now in standard form for `rlocus`, with the numerator $[1\ 0]$ and the denominator $[m\ b\ k]$. The value determined by `rlocfind` will be c. Place the crosshairs at the point where the closed-loop poles first cross the real axis.

b. Plot the step response and Bode diagrams for the system with and without active control ($c = 0$). Assume that $m = 5000$ kg, $k = 8 \times 10^5$ N/m, and $b = 12{,}000$ Ns/m.

c. In this problem, the spring is accounted for in k. Using the design in part b, and for k ranging between 4×10^5 to 10×10^5 N/m, create a meshed surface of the step response. Which car would you prefer to ride in?

10.9 Consider the task of designing an autopilot for a large, slowly moving ship in which the output of a compass provides the feedback. The controller sends commands to a rudder mechanism, which, with delay, turns it to the desired position, thereby turning the ship. The following equations have been linearized from Nomoto's equation[14] for a ship at cruising speed. The open-loop transfer function of the steering system without the controller is[15]:

$$G(s) = \frac{s + 0.03}{s(s + 0.09)(s + 0.04)(s - 0.0004)}$$

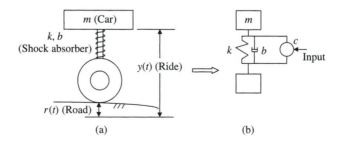

(a)   (b)

Figure 10.51 (a) A simplified model of the quarter-car model with an active suspension and (b) its mass and spring equivalent.

---

[14]M. Driels, *ibid.*
[15]C. L. Phillips and R. D. Harbor, *Feedback Control Systems*, 3rd ed., Prentice Hall, Englewood Cliffs, NJ, 1996.

a. The plant has an unstable pole. Plot the root locus of the steering system.

b. Using the lead-control structure

$$C(s) = k\frac{s + z}{z + p}$$

find the values of k, z, and p that stabilize the closed-loop system response while maintaining less than 30% overshoot.

c. Using a new sensor that provides velocity information, one can now use PD control. Thus,

$$C(s) = k_p + sk_d$$

Find k_p and k_d such that the closed-loop response is stable, has less than 5% overshoot, and has a settling time less than 275 s.

10.10 A recent-model automobile has a catalytic converter to meet exhaust-emission standards. The catalytic converter requires tight control of the engine air/fuel ratio (A/F), the ignition-spark timing, and exhaust-gas recirculation. We consider the A/F regulation task. The transfer function of the carburetor with the effective A/F as output is[16]

$$G(s) = \frac{4e^{-T_d s}}{s + 4}$$

where the time delay T_d is 0.2 s. The function pade may be used to generate an approximation of the time delay, or one may set the output delay property of the transfer function to 0.2. However, using pade is less difficult, because it is one of MATLAB's few functions that support time delay.

a. Suppose that the time delay is neglected in the design of the controller and we let the controller be a PI controller so that

$$C(s) = k_p + \frac{k_i}{s}$$

Set $k_i = 2$, and select the value of k_p so that the rise time for the unit-step response is smaller than 0.4 s. Determine the step response of the system.

b. Consider feeding a time-delayed signal back into the controller, as shown in Figure 10.52. The extra compensation element in the controller contains a model

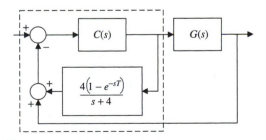

Figure 10.52 Exhaust emission control system using a Smith predictor.

[16]B. Kuo, *Automatic Control Systems*, 7th ed., Prentice Hall, Englewood Cliffs, NJ, 1995, p. 815.

of the plant and its time delay and is called a Smith predictor. Using a lead-control structure

$$C(s) = k\frac{s + z}{z + p}$$

find the values of k, z, and p that stabilize the closed-loop system response while having no overshoot and a rise time less than 0.2 s. Compare the results to the PI controller in part a.

c. Suppose that the time delay and the plant are not modeled correctly. Determine the step responses for system time delays of 0.3 and 0.1 s with the controller generated in part b and a plant model with a DC gain of 1.2 and a pole at -5 instead of at -4. From the results, is it better to overestimate or to underestimate the time delay?

10.11 Consider the automatic motorized bicycle whose block diagram is shown in Figure 10.53. An inclinometer detects the angle of the bicycle body from vertical, $y(t)$. The inclinometer's output is compared to the desired angle from vertical $r(t)$, and the error is input to the controller to generate a steering signal. Any disturbances to the system $d(t)$ are modeled as entering with the input to the bicycle. The transfer functions for the blocks shown in Figure 10.53 are

$$G(s) = \frac{9}{s^2 + 9}$$

$$F(s) = \frac{\omega^2}{s^2 + 2\xi\omega s + \omega^2}$$

$$C(s) = k\frac{s + z}{s + p}$$

where $C(s)$ is a lead controller.

a. A micromachined inclinometer has a settling time of 0.2 s and a bandwidth of 125 Hz. The sensor's parameters are $\omega = 250\pi$ and $\xi = 20/\omega$. Find k, z, and p such that the overshoot for unit step response is no more than 20% and the setting time is less than 4 s.

b. Suppose that there is another type of inclinometer to choose, one that is based on the principle of a pendulum. Its resonant frequency is 7.4 Hz ($\omega = 14.8\pi$), and its damping coefficient $\xi = 0.4$. Can this inclinometer also be used?

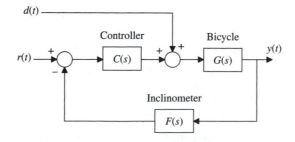

Figure 10.53   Block diagram of an automatic motorized bicycle.

BIBLIOGRAPHY

D. K. Anand and R. B. Zmood, *Introduction to Control Systems*, Butterworth and Heinmann, Ltd., Oxford, England, 1995.

E. Chowanietz, *Automobile Electronics*, SAE International, Troy, MI, 1995.

R. Dorf and R. Bishop, *Modern Control Systems*, Addison-Wesley, Reading, MA, 1997.

M. Driels, *Linear Control System Engineering*, McGraw-Hill, New York, NY, 1996.

G. Franklin, J. Powell, and A. Emami-Naeini, *Feedback Control of Dynamic Systems*, 3rd ed., Addison-Wesley, Reading, MA, 1994.

B. Friedland, *Advanced Control System Design*, Prentice Hall, Englewood Cliffs, NJ, 1996.

R. Jurgen, *Electronic Engine Control Technologies*, SAE International, Troy, MI, 1999.

B. Kuo, *Automatic Control Systems*, Prentice Hall, Englewood Cliffs, NJ, 1995.

W. Levine, *The Control Handbook*, CRC Press, Boca Raton, FL, 1996.

L. Ljung, *System Identification: Theory for the User*, Prentice Hall, Upper Saddle River, NJ, 1999.

N. Nise, *Control Systems Engineering*, Addison-Wesley, Reading, MA, 1995.

U. Ozguner, H. Goktas, and H. Chan, "Automotive Suspension Control Through a Computer Communication Network," *Proceedings of First IEEE Conference on Control Application*, Vol. 2, 1992, pp. 895–900.

C. Phillips and R. Harbor, *Feedback Control Systems*, Prentice Hall, Englewood Cliffs, NJ, 1996.

11

Fluid Mechanics

James H. Duncan

Several classes of problems in fluid mechanics and aerodynamics are analyzed, and several flow fields are presented using a variety of visualization techniques.

11.1 HYDROSTATICS

In hydrostatics, the pressure is constant on any surface of constant height in a single fluid, and the pressure varies with height according to

$$\frac{dP}{dz} = -\rho g \tag{11.1}$$

TABLE 11.1 Temperature of the Standard
Atmosphere as a Function of Elevation

Elevation (m)	Temperature (°C)
0.0	15.0
11,000.0	−56.5
20,100.0	−56.5
32,200.0	−44.5
47,300.0	−2.5

where $\rho = \rho(z)$ is the density distribution, g is the acceleration of gravity
(9.81 m/s^2), P is the pressure, and z is the vertical Cartesian coordinate, with positive being up. We now use Eq. 11.1 to solve two hydrostatics problems.

11.1.1 Pressure Distribution in the Standard Atmosphere

If the atmosphere is a perfect gas, then

$$\rho = P/(RT)$$

where $R = 287.13$ J/(kg °K) is the perfect gas constant and T is the temperature in degrees Kelvin. With this assumption, Eq. 11.1 can be integrated to obtain

$$P(z) = P_0 \exp\left[-\frac{g}{R}\int_0^z \frac{dz}{T}\right] \qquad (11.2)$$

where $P_0 = 101{,}330$ Pa is the pressure at $z = 0$. We assume that the temperature distribution in the standard atmosphere varies linearly between the temperatures at the elevations given in Table 11.1.

Example 11.1   Temperature and pressure variation as a function of altitude

Equation 11.2 is easily integrated analytically; however, we shall do the evaluation numerically. A script that integrates Eq. 11.2 and plots both P and T as a function of z is given below. We use interp1 to perform the linear interpolation between the temperature values given in Table 11.1. Because of numerical difficulties, we start the integration at 0.1 m. The results are shown in Figure 11.1.

```
gravity = 9.81;  p0 = 101330;  R = 287.13;
tempC = [15, -56.5, -56.5, -44.5, -2.5];
z = [0, 11000, 20100, 32200, 47300];
invertemp = 1./(tempC+273.15);
np = 18;
goverR = gravity/R;
elevation = linspace(0, z(end), np);
```

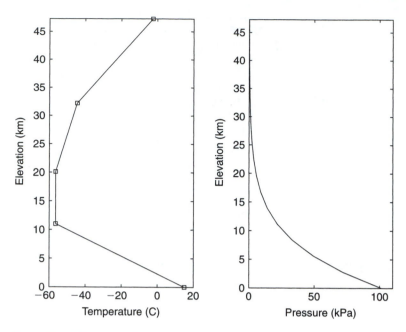

Figure 11.1 The standard atmosphere: (a) temperature from Table 11.1 versus elevation; (b) pressure from Eq. 11.2 versus elevation.

```
pressure = zeros(1, np);
intarg = inline('interp1(z, invertemp, elevation)', 'elevation', 'z', 'invertemp');
for i = 1:np
    pressure(i) = p0*exp(-goverR*quadl(intarg, 0.1, elevation(i), [], [], z, ...
                                        invertemp));
end
subplot(1, 2, 1)
plot(tempC, z/1000.0, 'k-s')
axis([-60, 20, 0, elevation(end)/1000.0])
xlabel('Temperature (C)')
ylabel('Elevation (km)')
subplot(1, 2, 2)
plot(pressure/1000.0, elevation/1000.0, 'k')
axis([0, 110, 0, elevation(end)/1000.0])
ylabel('Elevation (km)')
xlabel('Pressure (kPa)')
```

11.1.2 Force on a Planar Gate

Consider the reservoir shown in Figure 11.2. One wall of the reservoir is a tiltable metal gate that is hinged at the bottom and has weight W and length L. The width of the reservoir in the direction normal to the page is B. Initially, the gate is vertical, and the water level reaches the top of the gate. The total volume of water is $V_w = aLB$. A rod holds the gate closed, and the force of the rod on the gate F_{rod} is directed along the rod.

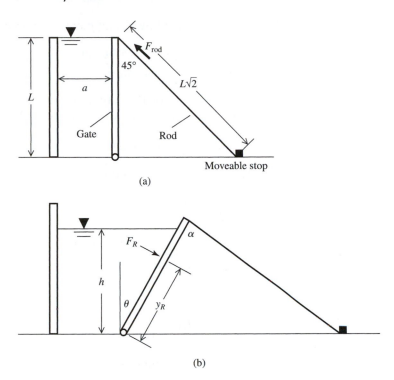

Figure 11.2   Reservoir with tiltable gate: (a) gate vertical; (b) gate opened to an angle θ.

A stop holds the opposite end of the rod in place. This stop can be moved to the right, thus letting the gate rotate clockwise about its hinge. For gate angles θ that are less than or equal to some critical angle θ_{max}, the water level is at or below the top of the gate; however, for $\theta > \theta_{max}$, the water spills over the top.

The volume bounded by the bottom, the fixed walls, the gate, and a level surface at the top of the gate is

$$\frac{V}{V_w} = \cos\theta + \frac{L}{2a}\cos\theta\sin\theta \qquad (11.3)$$

The water will spill over the dam when

$$\frac{V}{V_w} < 1.0$$

An equation for the water level h versus θ is obtained by equating V_w to an equation for the water volume at any θ. Thus,

$$\frac{V_w}{B} = aL = ah + 0.5h^2\tan\theta \qquad (11.4)$$

The magnitude of F_{rod} is obtained by taking moments about the hinge. Thus,

$$F_{rod} = \frac{F_R y_R + 0.5WL \sin \theta}{L \sin \alpha} \tag{11.5}$$

where F_R is the total force of the water on the gate, y_R is the distance from the hinge to the center of pressure, and the angle α is shown in Figure 11.2b and is given by

$$\alpha = \theta + \cos^{-1}\left(\cos \theta / \sqrt{2}\right)$$

From the hydrostatics equations, we find that

$$F_R = \frac{B\rho g h^2}{2 \cos \theta}$$

$$y_R = \frac{h}{2 \cos \theta} - \frac{2I_{xx} \cos^2 \theta}{Bh^2}$$

where

$$I_{xx} = \frac{Bh^3}{12 \cos^3 \theta}$$

is the second moment of area about the hinge of the submerged portion of the gate. Thus, Eq. 11.5 becomes

$$F_{rod} = \frac{1}{L \sin \alpha}\left[\frac{B\rho g h^3}{6 \cos^2 \theta} + \frac{WL}{2}\sin \theta\right] \tag{11.6}$$

We now illustrate these results.

Example 11.2   Properties of a reservoir

We shall determine θ_{max} and plot the depth of the water h and F_{rod} for $0 \le \theta \le \theta_{max}$. The results are shown in Figure 11.3. We assume that $L = 10$ m, $a = 5$ m, $B = 10$ m, and $W = 100,000$ N. In addition, V/V_w is computed from Eq. 11.3 and plotted versus θ. The function fzero is used to determine θ_{max}, the location of which is denoted in Figure 11.3a. In the computation of θ_{max}, the inline function **MaxTheta**, which returns $1 - V/V_w$, is created. To obtain a graph of h as a function of θ, the quadratic equation in h given by Eq. 11.4 is solved using roots. Only the positive root is used. It is also of interest to determine the value of θ for which the reservoir is capable of holding the most water. This is obtained from fminbnd, which also calls **MaxTheta**. The result is $\theta = 30°$ as shown in Figure 11.3. The script to determine these values and to display the results, including F_{rod} versus θ, as shown in Figure 11.4, is

```
a = 5.0;  L = 10.0;  B = 10.0;  rho = 1000.0;
grav = 9.81;  W = 100000.0;  ratio = L/a;
theta = linspace(0.0, pi/2.0);
VoverVw = cos(theta)+0.5*ratio*cos(theta).*sin(theta);
options = optimset('display', 'off');
```

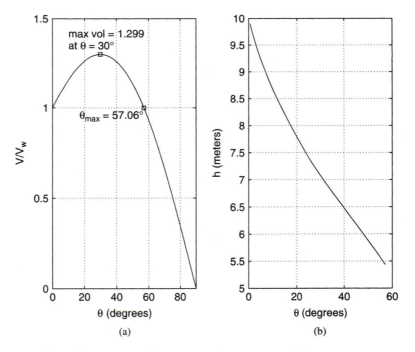

Figure 11.3   Results for the hinged gate configuration: (a) V/V_w versus θ; (b) h versus θ.

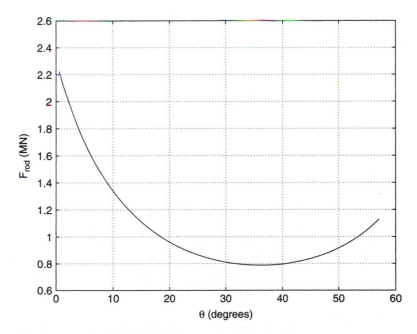

Figure 11.4   Force needed to keep the gate closed versus θ.

```
figure(1)
subplot(1, 2, 1)
plot(theta*180/pi, VoverVw, 'k')
axis([0.0, 90.0, 0.0, 1.5])
ylabel('V/V_w')
xlabel('\theta (degrees)')
grid on
hold on
MaxTheta = inline('1-(cos(theta)+0.5*ratio*cos(theta).*sin(theta))', 'theta', ...
                  'ratio');
ThetaMaxDeg = fzero(MaxTheta, [0.01, pi/2.0], options, ratio)*180/pi;
plot(ThetaMaxDeg, 1.0, 'sk')
text(19, 0.95, ['\theta_{max}= ', num2str(ThetaMaxDeg, 4) '\circ'])
ThetaMaxVol = fminbnd(MaxTheta, 0.0, ThetaMaxDeg*pi/180, options, ratio);
MaxVol = 1-MaxTheta(ThetaMaxVol, ratio);
plot(ThetaMaxVol*180/pi, MaxVol, 'ks')
text(10, MaxVol+0.1, ['max vol = ' num2str(MaxVol, 4)])
text(10, MaxVol+0.05, [' at \theta = ' num2str(ThetaMaxVol*180/pi, 4) '\circ'])
subplot(1, 2, 2)
theta = linspace(0.01, ThetaMaxDeg*pi/180);
h = zeros(1, length(theta));
for i = 1:length(theta)
   r = roots([tan(theta(i))*0.5, a, -a*L]);
   h(i) = r(2);
end
plot(theta*180.0/pi, h, 'k-')
ylabel('h (meters)')
xlabel('\theta (degrees)')
grid on
figure(2)
Frod = ((B*rho*grav*h.^3)./(6*cos(theta).^2)+0.5*W*L*sin(theta))./...
          (L*sin(theta+acos(cos(theta)/sqrt(2))));
plot(theta*180.0/pi, Frod*1e-6, 'k-')
ylabel('F_{rod} (MN)')
xlabel('\theta (degrees)')
grid on
```

11.2 INTERNAL VISCOUS FLOW

There is a large class of problems that concern laminar and turbulent viscous flow in pipes and ducts. The solutions to several of these problems are given below. For low Reynolds numbers, the flow is laminar, and the PDE Toolbox is used to compute the flow field and the pressure drop along the pipe. For higher Reynolds numbers, the flow is turbulent, and the flow and pressure drop are computed with the aid of the Colebrook equation.[1]

---

[1] C. E. Colebrook, "Turbulent Flow in Pipes with Particular Reference to the Transition Region Between Smooth and Rough Pipe Laws," *Journal of the Institute of Civil Engineers*, London, Vol. 11, 1939, pp. 133–156.

11.2.1 Laminar Flow in a Horizontal Pipe with Various Cross-Sections

With the PDE Toolbox, it is relatively straightforward to compute the fully developed laminar flow field in a horizontal pipe with various cross-sectional shapes. The analytical solution for a circular pipe is available in most textbooks.[2] Therefore, we begin by computing this flow field and comparing the computed maximum and average velocities to the analytically determined values. We assume that the pipe radius is $R = 5.0$ mm, the dynamic viscosity of the fluid is $\mu = 0.38$ N·s/m^2, and the pressure gradient in the axial direction is $dP/dz = 1.0 \times 10^6$ Pa/m.

The differential equation for the axial flow field is

$$\frac{\partial^2 u}{\partial y^2} + \frac{\partial^2 u}{\partial z^2} = \frac{1}{\mu}\frac{dP}{dx} \tag{11.7}$$

where $u(y, z)$ is the axial velocity in the x-direction and y and z are the Cartesian coordinates of the pipe cross-section, with the point $(0, 0)$ being at the center of the pipe. The y, z-coordinates of the wall of the pipe are given by

$$y^2 + z^2 = R^2$$

and the no-slip boundary condition on the wall requires that $u = 0$.

We shall solve the problem using `pdetool`.[3] Once in `pdetool`, we create a circle of radius 1.0 centered at $(0, 0)$. This implies that we have created the dimensionless coordinates $y' = y/R$ and $z' = z/R$, and Eq. 11.7 becomes

$$\frac{\partial^2 u}{\partial y'^2} + \frac{\partial^2 u}{\partial z'^2} = \frac{R^2}{\mu}\frac{dP}{dx} = f$$

In `pdetool`, we select the *Boundary Mode* from the *Boundary* pull-down menu and specify the Dirichlet boundary conditions ($u = 0$) on each of the four arcs comprising the circle. We then select the elliptic partial differential equation with the parameters $c = 1$, $a = 0$, and $f = 65.79$ m/s $((0.005^2/0.38) \times 10^6)$. Next, we initialize the mesh and refine it two times. The resulting solution is plotted in contour form in Figure 11.5.

To obtain additional quantitative data from the solution, we export the solution u and the mesh descriptors p, e, and t to the command window. The maximum value of the velocity occurs at the center of the pipe cross-section and can be found by typing

    umax = max(u)

in the command window. The result is *umax* = 16.435, which is very close to the theoretically predicted value of 16.447.

---

[2]B. R. Munson, D. F. Young, and T. H. Okiishi, *Fundamental of Fluid Mechanics*, John Wiley & Sons, New York, NY, 1998.
[3]See Section 8.7 for more details on how to use `pdetool`.

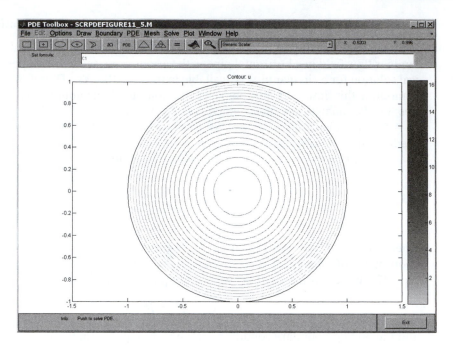

Figure 11.5   Axial flow field in a circular pipe. The value of the innermost contour is 16.

The flux of volume Q is given by

$$Q = \iint_A u\,dA \approx \sum_{i=1}^{N_t} u_i \Delta A_i$$

where A is the cross-sectional area of the pipe, N_t is the number of triangles in the mesh, u_i is the value of the velocity at the center of each triangular grid, and ΔA_i is the area of each triangle. In the following script, u_i is determined by pdeintrp and ΔA_i by pdetrg:

```
ui = pdeintrp(p, t, u);
DeltaAi = pdetrg(p, t);
Q = sum(DeltaAi.*ui)
```

Executing this script—after exporting u, p, e, and t to the MATLAB window—gives $Q = 25.806$. The resulting average velocity is $u_{avg} = Q/A = 25.806/\pi = 8.214$, which is very close to the theoretical value of half the maximum velocity, or $16.447/2 = 8.224$. Further refinement of the mesh will bring the computed and theoretical values to closer agreement.

It is also possible to plot the velocity as a function of distance along a pipe diameter: $y' = 0$ and $-1 \le z' \le 1$. To do this, it is first necessary to use tri2grid to interpolate the triangular mesh data onto points that lie on a diameter of the pipe

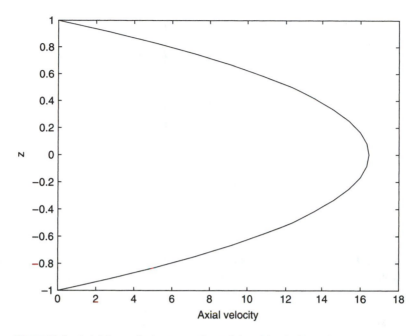

Figure 11.6   Axial flow velocity versus the radial position inside a pipe.

cross-section. The result is shown in Figure 11.6 and has the parabolic profile that is obtained from the theory. The script is

```
z = linspace(-1, 1, 25);
uyz = tri2grid(p, t, u, 0, z);
plot(uyz, z)
axis([0, 1800, -1.0, 1.0])
ylabel('z')
xlabel('Axial velocity')
```

11.2.2 Downward Flow in a Vertical Pipe

Consider a vertically oriented smooth pipe of length L and diameter D in which a fluid of density ρ and kinematic viscosity v is flowing downward, as shown in Figure 11.7. For a particular flow rate, the pressure drop caused by the downward flow of the fluid is balanced by the pressure gain caused by gravity; that is, at this flow rate, the static pressure in the pipe is independent of the distance along the pipe.

The head loss equation is

$$\frac{P_1}{\rho g} + \frac{V_1^2}{2g} + z_1 = \frac{P_2}{\rho g} + \frac{V_2^2}{2g} + z_2 + \frac{\lambda L V^2}{2gD} \qquad (11.8)$$

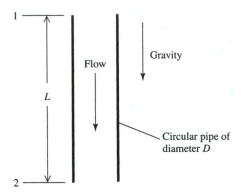

Figure 11.7   Flow in a vertically oriented pipe
of diameter D.

where P is the pressure, V is the average flow speed, z is the height, and λ is the friction factor. In the present problem, $P_1 = P_2$, $V_1 = V_2$, and $z_1 - z_2 = L$; therefore, Eq. 11.8 reduces to

$$\lambda = \frac{2gD^3}{v^2 R_e^2} \tag{11.9}$$

where R_e is the Reynolds number defined as

$$R_e = \frac{VD}{v} \tag{11.10}$$

The Colebrook formula for λ versus R_e in pipes of varying roughness factors k/D is given by (recall Exercise 5.19)

$$\frac{1}{\sqrt{\lambda}} = -2 \log_{10}\left(\frac{2.51}{R_e \sqrt{\lambda}} + \frac{k/D}{3.7} \right) \quad R_e \geq 4000 \tag{11.11}$$

In the present case, $k = 0$. Substituting λ from Eq. 11.9 into Eq. 11.11 yields a transcendental equation for the Reynolds number of the pipe flow and, therefore, the desired flow rate.

We shall now illustrate these results with an example.

Example 11.3   Flow rate in a pipe

Consider a vertically oriented smooth pipe of diameter $D = 4.0$ cm in which water of density $\rho = 1000.0$ Kg/m^3 and kinematic viscosity $v = 1.2 \times 10^{-6}$ m^2/s is flowing downward. We shall find the flow rate for which the pressure drop caused by the downward flow is balanced by the pressure gain caused by gravity. The Colebrook expression is evaluated in **ColebrookFriction**. The script is

```
function Colebrook
diameter = 0.04; gravity  = 9.81;
nu = 1.2e-6; kOverD = 0.000;
options = optimset('display', 'off');
Re = fzero(@ColebrookFriction, [1e3, 1e7], options, nu, kOverD, gravity, ...
            diameter);
```

```
disp(['Re = ',num2str(Re)])
disp(['Flow Rate = ' num2str(pi*diameter*Re*nu/4) ' m^3/s'])

function value = ColebrookFriction(Re, nu, kOverD, gravity, diameter)
lambda = 2*gravity*diameter^3/(nu*Re)^2;
value = 1/sqrt(lambda)+2*log10(kOverD/3.7+2.51/(Re*sqrt(lambda)));
```

which, when executed, gives

```
Re = 240405.8408
Flow Rate = 0.0090631 m^3/s
```

where the flow rate $Q = \pi D^2 V/4$.

11.2.3 Three-Reservoir Problem

Consider the classical three-reservoir problem[4] in which three reservoirs of different elevations are connected to a common junction at location J as shown in Figure 11.8. If we are given the length L_j, diameter d_j, and roughness k_j of the pipes meeting at J and the elevations of each reservoir h_j, then we can determine the corresponding flow rates Q_j and the direction of flow in each pipe. The method is as follows: If an open-ended tube were installed at the junction, then the water's elevation in the tube would rise to the elevation h_p, which is unknown. The difference between the elevations at P and J is the pressure head at the junction. Second, at J, the sum of the flows from each pipe must be zero—that is,

$$\sum_{j=1}^{3} Q_j = 0 \tag{11.12}$$

with a positive value of Q_j indicating flow toward the junction and a negative value indicating flow out of the junction.

The flow in each pipe is determined from

$$Q_j = 0.25\pi d_j^2 V_j s_j \quad j = 1, 2, 3$$

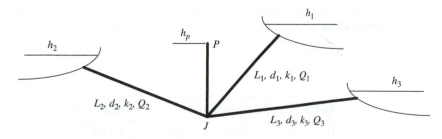

Figure 11.8   Pipes connecting three reservoirs at junction J.

---

[4]N. H. C. Hwang and C. E. Hita, *Fundamentals of Hydraulic Engineering Systems*, 2nd ed., Prentice Hall, Englewood Cliffs, NJ, 1987, pp. 106–110.

where

$$V_j = s_j\sqrt{\frac{2gd_j|\Delta h_j|}{\lambda_j L_j}} \qquad \Delta h_j = h_j - h_p \quad j = 1, 2, 3$$

and s_j is the sign of Δh_j, $g = 9.81$ m/s^2 is the gravity constant, and λ_j is the pipe friction coefficient as determined from Eq. 11.11 and is a function of R_{ej}—that is, recall Eq. 11.10

$$R_{ej} = \frac{V_j d_j}{v} \quad j = 1, 2, 3$$

where $v = 1.002 \times 10^{-6}$ m^2/s is the kinematic viscosity of water at 20°C. Thus, the objective is to determine the value of h_p that satisfies Eq. 11.12.

The solution is obtained as follows: We assume a value for h_p, which we know lies somewhere between the minimum and maximum values of h_j. Then, we compute a value for each V_j by first assuming a value for λ_j that is obtained from Eq. 11.11 for very large R_e—that is,

$$\lambda_j = \left[2\log_{10}\left(3.7\frac{d_j}{k_j}\right)\right]^{-2}$$

We use these values of V_j to determine values for R_{ej}, which are then used to determine λ_j from the general Colebrook formula given by Eq. 11.11. We continue this process until the values of V_j are within an acceptable tolerance.

After each V_j has been determined, we compute each Q_j and determine whether Eq. 11.12 has been satisfied. If it hasn't, then another value of h_p is selected, and new values of V_j are computed as just described. It should be noted that when $\Delta h_j = 0, Q_j = 0$ and the value of λ_j cannot be computed, since $R_{ej} = 0$. In the scripts and functions that implement this procedure, we use nested applications of fzero, an inner one to determine V_j and an outer one to determine h_p.

We now illustrate these results with the following example.

Example 11.4   Flow rates from three reservoirs

Using the solution method described above, we shall determine the flow rates for the values are given in Table 11.2. We create three sub functions. The first sub function determines Q_j and evaluates Eq. 11.12. It is called **ReservoirSumQ**. The second subfunction, called **PipeFrictionCoeff**, evaluates Eq. 11.11. The third sub function, called **ResFriction**, determines λ_j at each value of V_j. The script is

```
function Reservoir
d = [0.3, 0.5, 0.4];
```

TABLE 11.2   Parameters for Reservoir in Figure 11.8

Reservoir	d_j(m)	L_j(m)	k_j(m)	h_j(m)
1	0.30	1000	0.00060	120
2	0.50	4000	0.00060	100
3	0.40	2000	0.00060	80

```
el = [1000, 4000, 2000];
k = [0.6, 0.6, 0.6]*1e-3;
h = [120, 100, 80];
options = optimset('display', 'off');
hg = fzero(@ReservoirSumQ, 110, options, d, el, k, h);
[sq, q] = ReservoirSumQ(hg, d, el, k, h);
disp(['Elevation h_sub_p = ' num2str(hg) ' m'])
disp(['Q1 = ' num2str(q(1)) ' m^3/s   Q2 = ' num2str(q(2)) ' m^3/s   Q3 = ' ...
           num2str(q(3)) ' m^3/s'])

function [sq, q] = ReservoirSumQ(hg, d, el, k, h)
cv = 2*9.81*d./el;
ro = d/1.002e-6;
dk = d./k;
qd = 0.25*pi*d.^2;
frictguess = (2*log10(3.7*dk)).^-2;
hh = h-hg;
options = optimset('display', 'off');
for n = 1:length(d)
  if hh(n) == 0
    q(n) = 0;
  else
    lambda = fzero(@ResFriction, frictguess(n), options, dk(n), hh(n), cv(n), ...
                      ro(n));
    q(n) = sign(hh(n))*sqrt(cv(n)*abs(hh(n))/lambda)*qd(n);
  end
end
sq = sum(q);

function x = PipeFrictionCoeff(el, re, dk)
if dk>100000|dk == 0
  x = el-(2*log10(re*sqrt(el)/2.51))^-2;
else
  x = el-(2*log10(2.51/re/sqrt(el)+0.27/dk))^-2;
end

function lamb = ResFriction(lambda, dk, dh, cv, ro)
ren = sqrt(cv*abs(dh)/lambda)*ro;
lamb = PipeFrictionCoeff(lambda, ren, dk);
```

Execution of the script gives

```
Elevation h_sub_p = 98.904 m
Q1 = 0.16185 m^3/s   Q2 = 0.068728 m^3/s   Q3 = -0.23058 m^3/s
```

11.3 EXTERNAL FLOW

11.3.1 Boundary Layer on an Infinite Plate Started Suddenly from Rest

Consider a layer of liquid of thickness $h = 10.0$ cm that extends to infinity in the x,z-plane and is bounded by a rigid plate at $y = 0$ and a free surface at $y = h$. The plate and the fluid are initially at rest. At $t = 0$, the plate is instantaneously accelerated to a speed U in the positive x-direction. The resulting fluid motion is only in the x-direction and is a function only of time and the y-coordinate—that is, $u = u(y, t)$. We shall determine u for $U = 5.0$ cm/s and for a fluid with kinematic viscosity $v_{vis} = 1.0$ cm^2/s.

The solution is obtained by solving the x-component of the Navier-Stokes equations, which in the present case reduces to

$$\frac{\partial u}{\partial t} = v_{vis} \frac{\partial^2 u}{\partial y^2} \tag{11.13}$$

The initial condition is

$$u(y, 0) = 0$$

The boundary condition at the surface of the plate is the no-slip condition,

$$u(0, t) = U$$

while the boundary condition at the free surface, $y = 10.0$ cm, is zero shear stress—that is,

$$v_{vis} \frac{du}{dy}\bigg|_{y=10.0} = 0$$

We shall solve this problem with pdetool. In the pdetool window, we use *Axes Limits* in the *Options* menu to create a window with dimensions -1.5 to 1.5 in the x-direction and 0.0 to 10.0 in the y-direction. Then, we create a rectangle extending from -0.25 to 0.25 in the x-direction and from 0.0 to 10.0 in the y-direction. The PDE Toolbox solves equations in the x,y-domain, whereas the present computation will be independent of x. Thus, the computation time is decreased if, as we have done above, the x-dimension of the computational domain is a small fraction of the total dimension of the y-direction.

The boundary conditions on the rectangle are set as follows: On the bottom of the rectangle, which is the surface of the plate, the Dirichlet boundary condition is $u = U = 5.0$ ($h = 1, r = 5$). On the top of the rectangle, which is the free surface, the Neumann boundary condition is $\partial u / \partial x = 0$ ($q = g = 0$). The Neumann boundary conditions $\partial u / \partial x = 0$ are also used on the two vertical boundaries of the rectangle to make the solution independent of x. The solution was obtained with a mesh that was refined twice. To specify Eq. 11.13 in pdetool, we use the *Parabolic* option in the *PDE Specification* window of the *PDE* pull-down menu. For this choice, we set $c = 1, a = 0, f = 0$, and $d = 1$. Finally, to select times for which the solution will be displayed, we use the *Parameters* option from the *Solve* pull-down menu. In the input area for *Time*, we enter 0:0.5:10. After solving the equation, we export the solution u and the mesh parameters p, e, and t to the command window. The size of the solution array u is $(n_m \times n_t)$, where n_m is the number of mesh points and n_t is the number of times for which the solution is given—in this case, $n_t = 21$. The following script extracts the data along the line

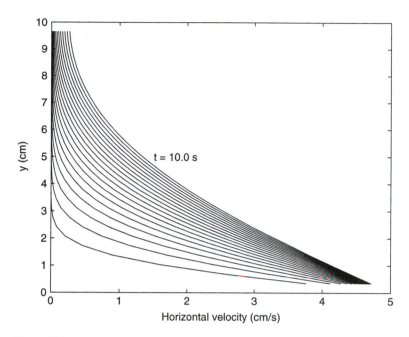

Figure 11.9   Horizontal velocity in a fluid layer of depth 10.0 cm that is suddenly accelerated to a speed $U = 5.0$ cm/s.

$x = 0$ and produces the plot given in Figure 11.9, where the Δt between the contours is 0.5 s:

```
ymin = 0.0;  ymax = 10.0;
y = linspace(ymin, ymax, 30);
[nm, nt] = size(u);
for i = 1:nt
    plot(tri2grid(p, t, u(:,i), 0, y), y)
    hold on
end
axis([0, 5, ymin, ymax])
ylabel('y (cm)')
xlabel('Horizontal velocity (cm/s)')
text(1.5, 5, 't=10.0 s')
```

11.3.2 Blasius Boundary Layer

The incompressible flow field in a laminar boundary layer on a flat plate is given by the solution to the boundary layer equations

$$\frac{\partial u}{\partial x} + \frac{\partial v}{\partial y} = 0$$

$$u\frac{\partial u}{\partial x} + v\frac{\partial u}{\partial y} = v_{\text{vis}}\frac{\partial^2 u}{\partial y^2}$$

(11.14)

where x and y are the coordinates parallel to and perpendicular to the plate surface, respectively; u and v are the corresponding fluid velocity components, respectively; and v_{vis} the kinematic viscosity. The boundary conditions are that both u and v are zero on the plate surface and that $u \rightarrow U$ as $y \rightarrow \infty$.[5]

A similarity solution is proposed where

$$\frac{df}{d\eta} = \frac{u}{U} \tag{11.15a}$$

and

$$\eta = y \sqrt{\frac{U}{xv_{vis}}} \tag{11.15b}$$

The quantity f is proportional to the stream function of the flow, and $d^2f/d\eta^2$ is proportional to the shear. The similarity solution transforms the boundary layer equation into the ordinary nonlinear differential equation

$$2\frac{d^3f}{d\eta^3} + f\frac{d^2f}{d\eta^2} = 0 \tag{11.16}$$

where, at $\eta = 0$,

$$f = 0 \qquad \frac{df}{d\eta} = 0 \tag{11.17a}$$

and, as $\eta \rightarrow \infty$,

$$\frac{df}{d\eta} \rightarrow 1 \tag{11.17b}$$

To solve Eq. 11.16, we reduce it to three first-order equations using the definitions

$$f_1 = f$$
$$f_2 = \frac{df}{d\eta} \tag{11.18}$$
$$f_3 = \frac{d^2f}{d\eta^2}$$

to obtain

$$\frac{df_1}{d\eta} = f_2$$
$$\frac{df_2}{d\eta} = f_3 \tag{11.19}$$
$$\frac{df_3}{d\eta} = -0.5f_1f_3$$

---

[5]Full details can be found in R. L. Panton, *Incompressible Flow*, 2nd ed., John Wiley & Sons, New York, NY, 1996, p. 516.

The boundary conditions at $\eta = 0$ become

$$f_1(0) = f_2(0) = 0 \qquad\qquad (11.20a)$$

and, as $\eta \to \infty$,

$$f_2(\eta \to \infty) \to 1 \qquad\qquad (11.20b)$$

We shall now illustrate these results with an example.

Example 11.5   Laminar boundary layer on a flat plate

We solve the differential equations, Eqs. 11.19, by using bvp4c. Following the procedure discussed in Section 5.5.4, the script is

```
function BlasiusSolution
solinit = bvpinit(linspace(0, 8, 8), @BlasiusTguess);
sol = bvp4c(@BlasiusT, @BlasiusTbc, solinit);
x = linspace(0, 8);
y = deval(sol, x);
plot(x, y(1,:), 'k-', x, y(2,:), 'k--', x, y(3,:), 'k-.')
xlabel('\eta')
ylabel('f, df/d\eta, d^2f/d\eta^2')
legend('f', 'df/d\eta', 'd^2f/d\eta^2', 'Location', 'NorthWest')
axis([0, 4, 0, 3])

function dydx = Blasius(x, y)
dydx = [y(2); y(3); -0.5*y(1)*y(3)];

function  F = BlasiusT(x, y, flag, Pr)
Pr = 0.07;
F = [Blasius(x, y(1:3)); y(5); -Pr*0.5*y(1)*y(5)];

function  res = BlasiusTbc(ya, yb)
res = [ya(1); ya(2); ya(4); yb(2)-1; yb(4)-1];

function y = BlasiusTguess(x)
y(1) = x;
y(2) = x^0.5;
y(3) = 5-x;
y(4) = x/10;
y(5) = 0.5*(1-x/10);
```

When this script is executed, we find that the shear stress is 0.3321 at $\eta = 0$, and we obtain the results shown in Figure 11.10.

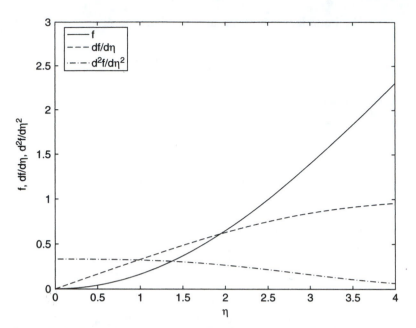

Figure 11.10 Blasius boundary layer profiles of the stream function $f_1 = f$, streamwise component of velocity $f_2 = df/d\eta$, and shear $f_3 = d^2f/d\eta^2$.

11.3.3 Incompressible Potential Flow

In incompressible potential flows, the velocity fields $\vec{u}$ are governed by

$$\nabla \cdot \vec{u} = 0$$

and

$$\nabla \times \vec{u} = 0$$

These conditions dictate that the velocity can be expressed as the gradient of a potential field, ϕ,

$$\vec{u} = \nabla\phi$$

where ϕ satisfies Laplace's equation,

$$\nabla^2 \phi = 0 \tag{11.21}$$

An alternative mathematical description for two-dimensional flows is obtained using the stream function ψ, where

$$u = \frac{\partial \psi}{\partial y}$$

$$v = -\frac{\partial \psi}{\partial x}$$

The stream function also satisfies Laplace's equation. Boundary conditions consist of the Neumann conditions, where the component of the velocity normal to a boundary is specified, or the Dirichlet conditions, where the value of ϕ is specified. At solid boundaries, the Neumann condition is $\vec{u} \cdot \hat{n} = 0$, where $\hat{n}$ is the unit normal to the boundary. In the following examples, several methods for obtaining flow fields for two-dimensional potential flows are discussed. In two of these methods, the flows are constructed by adding together known potentials or stream functions. We now give four such quantities:

Sources and Sinks

$$\phi_M = \frac{m}{2\pi}\ln r_M \qquad\qquad \psi_M = \frac{m}{2\pi}\theta_M$$

$$r_M^2 = (x - x_M)^2 + (y - y_M)^2 \quad \theta_M = \tan^{-1}\frac{y - y_M}{x - x_M}$$

where (x_M, y_M) is the location of the source or sink and m is the source strength.

Doublets (Dipoles)

$$\phi_K = \frac{K\cos\theta_K}{r_K} \qquad\qquad \psi_K = -\frac{K\sin\theta_K}{r_K}$$

$$r_K^2 = (x - x_K)^2 + (y - y_K)^2 \quad \theta_K = \tan^{-1}\frac{y - y_K}{x - x_K}$$

where (x_K, y_K) is the location of the dipole and K is the dipole strength.

Vortices

$$\phi_\Gamma = \frac{\Gamma}{2\pi}\theta_\Gamma \qquad\qquad \psi_\Gamma = -\frac{\Gamma\ln r_\Gamma}{2\pi}$$

$$r_\Gamma^2 = (x - x_\Gamma)^2 + (y - y_\Gamma)^2 \quad \theta_\Gamma = \tan^{-1}\frac{y - y_\Gamma}{x - x_\Gamma}$$

where (x_Γ, y_Γ) is the location of the vortex and Γ is the vortex strength.

Uniform Flow Field

$$\phi_U = Ux \quad \psi_U = Uy$$

where U is the flow speed.

Thus, in general, one can form an additive combination of these different stream functions to simulate different flows around different shapes. Then, if ψ_s is the new streamline function,

$$\psi_s = \psi_M + \psi_K + \psi_\Gamma + \psi_U$$

Example 11.6   Streamline Pattern Using contour

The easiest method of determining the streamline pattern of a flow is to plot the streamlines with contour. The following script plots the streamline ψ_s for a flow consisting of a uniform flow of speed U, a dipole of strength K located at (x_K, y_K), and a vortex of strength Γ located at (x_Γ, y_Γ). To illustrate this result, we choose the location of the dipole and vortex at $(-1, -1)$ and give the strengths of each of these quantities the following values:

$$K = 5.0 \quad (x_K, y_K) = (-1, -1)$$
$$\Gamma = 8\pi \quad (x_\Gamma, y_\Gamma) = (-1, -1)$$
$$U = 5.0$$

As illustrated in Figure 11.11, the resulting streamlines show flow about a cylinder with circulation. The main difficulty in obtaining these results is how to choose the contour

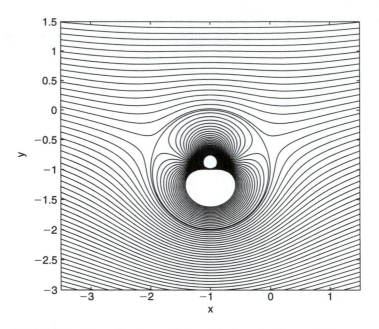

Figure 11.11   Streamlines for a cylinder with circulation in cross flow obtained from a contour plot of ψ_s.

levels to obtain a complete description of the flow. This can be accomplished using the value of ψ_s at the lower left corner of the domain for the minimum value and the value of ψ_s at the top middle of the domain for the maximum value. In Figure 11.11, the surface of a cylinder, which is also a streamline, has been superimposed on the streamlines.

The script that generated Figure 11.11 is

```
nx =100; xmin = -3.5; xmax = 1.5;
ny = 100; ymin = -3.0; ymax = 1.5;
[x, y] = meshgrid(linspace(xmin, xmax, nx), linspace(ymin, ymax, ny));
U0 = 5.0;
Gamma = 8*pi; xGamma = -1.0; yGamma = -1.0;
K = 5.0; xK = -1.0; yK = -1.0;
radius = inline('sqrt((x-x1).^2+(y-y1).^2)', 'x', 'y', 'x1', 'y1');
PsiK = K*sin(atan2(y-yK, x-xK))./radius(x, y, xK, yK);
PsiGamma = Gamma*log(radius(x, y, xGamma, yGamma))/2/pi;
StreamFunction = U0*y-PsiGamma-PsiK;
levmin = StreamFunction(1, nx);
levmax = StreamFunction(ny, nx/2);
levels = linspace(levmin, levmax, 50)';
contour(x, y, StreamFunction, levels)
hold on
theta = linspace (0, 2*pi);
plot(xGamma+cos(theta), yGamma+sin(theta), 'k-')
axis equal
axis([xmin, xmax, ymin, ymax])
ylabel('y')
xlabel('x')
```

Example 11.7   Direct calculation of streamlines

A second method to obtain flow patterns is to use `fzero` to find specific streamlines. As an example, we assume that the flow consists of a uniform stream of $U = 1$ in the positive y-direction, a source of strength $m = 4.0$ at $(0, -1)$, and a source of strength $m = -4.0$ at $(0, 1)$. Thus,

$$\psi_{\text{oval}} = +\psi_U + \psi_{M_1} + \psi_{M_2}$$

These components produce a uniform flow over an oval-shaped body given by[6]

$$\frac{2xa}{x^2 + y^2 - a^2} = \tan\frac{xU}{m/2\pi} \tag{11.22}$$

where U is the flow speed, m is the source strength, and a is a characteristic dimension.

A difficulty in using `fzero` in this example is the need to find a good starting guess. In the following script, this is done by finding the value of the stream function ψ_{oval} at a set of x locations along $y = -2.0a$. Given these initial data, a streamline is computed by marching along it, starting at $y = -2.0a$. At each successive y-location, `fzero` uses function **StreamFun** to determine the x-location of the stream function; the value of x at the previous y-location is used as the initial guess. A plot from the output of the script is given in Figure 11.12, where we have assumed that $a = 1$. The graph has been rotated 90° so that the flow is horizontal, which is the traditional way of presenting

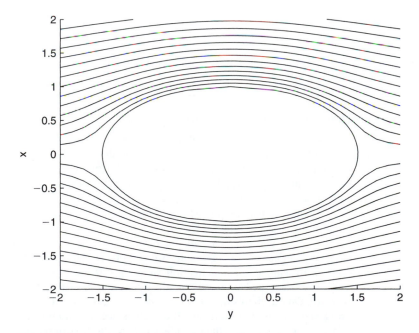

Figure 11.12   Streamlines for the oval given by Eq. 11.22.

---

[6]L. M. Milne-Thomson, *Theoretical Hydrodynamics*, Dover, Mineola, NY, 1996, p. 216.

it. The streamline that coincides with the boundary of the oval was not computed in this manner; it was plotted directly from Eq. 11.22. The script is

```
U = 1.0; a = 1.0; m = 4.0; co = m/(2*pi);
nPsi = 15; n = 30; yStart = -2.0*a;
xStart = linspace(0, 2*a, nPsi);
y = linspace(-2*a, 2*a, n);
x = zeros(1, n);
StreamFun = inline('-U*x-co*(atan2(x, y+a)-atan2(x, y-a))-psi', 'x', 'y', ...
                   'psi', 'U', 'co', 'a');
Psi = StreamFun(xStart, yStart, 0, U, co, a);
options = optimset('display', 'off');
for j = 1:nPsi
   guess = xStart(j);
   for i = 1:n
      x(i) = fzero(StreamFun, guess, options, y(i), Psi(j), U, co, a);
      guess = x(i);
   end
   if j>1
      plot(y, x, 'k-', y, -x, 'k-')
   end
   hold on
end
axis([-2*a, 2*a, -2*a, 2*a])
ylabel('x')
xlabel('y')
xx = linspace(-1, 1, 40);
yy = sqrt(1-xx.^2+2*xx./tan(xx/co));
plot(yy, xx, 'k-', -yy, xx, 'k-')
```

where *nPsi* is the number of streamlines and *n* is the number of points computed along each streamline.

Example 11.8　Solving for the flow field with pdetool

A third method to obtain potential flow solutions is to use pdetool to solve Eq. 11.21 directly. Let us compute the flow field for a cylinder of radius 1.0 that is placed in the center of a duct in which the flow speed is 10.0. In the pdetool window, we select the axes of the window to extend from −3.5 to 3.5 in the *x*-direction and from −2.5 to 2.5 in the *y*-direction. We then create a circle (*C*1) of radius 1.0 centered at $(0, 0)$ and a rectangle (*R*1) of dimensions 6.0 wide by 5.0 high, also centered at $(0, 0)$. We alter the *Set Formula* to $R1 - C1$ and then select *Boundary Mode*.

Next, we select *Specify Boundary Conditions*, and on the circle and the top and bottom boundaries of the rectangle, we select the Neumann boundary condition $\hat{n} \cdot \nabla\phi = 0$. To achieve this specification, we set $q = 0$ and $g = 0$. On the left side of the rectangle, we select the Neumann boundary condition $\hat{n} \cdot \nabla\phi = 10$; that is, we set $q = 0$ and $g = 10$. On the right side, we set $\hat{n} \cdot \nabla\phi = -10$; that is, we set $q = 0$ and $g = -10$. This makes the mean flow go from left to right, since the unit normal $\hat{n}$ to the boundary in pdetool is directed from the boundary toward the flow domain.

At this point, we initialize the mesh and refine it twice. The partial differential equation is specified by selecting *Elliptic* from *PDE Specification* in the *PDE* pull-down menu. Our equation is $\nabla^2 u = 0$, where, in the present case, the variable *u* represents ϕ;

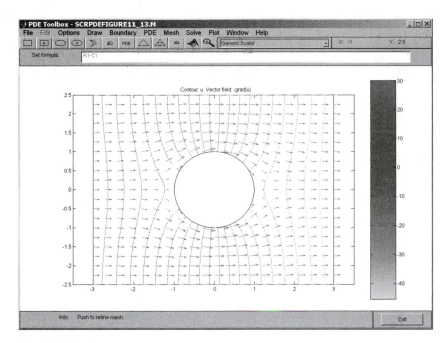

Figure 11.13   Velocity potential (contours) and velocity vectors from the direct solution of Eq. 11.21.

therefore, we set $c = 1$, $a = 0$, and $f = 0$. We solve for u and produce a vector plot of the velocity ∇u on top of a contour plot of u, as shown in Figure 11.13.

To obtain more detailed results, we export the solution u and the mesh coordinates p, e, and t to the command window. A plot of the velocity along any vertical or horizontal line can be obtained in the following manner: Consider the horizontal velocity along the vertical line $x = 0$ extending from the top of the cylinder to the top of the rectangle. To obtain a plot of this velocity distribution, the script given below is used. In this script, we first create a rectangular grid in the area of interest—say, $-0.5 \le x \le 0.5$ ($n_x = 9$ points) and $0.5 \le y \le 2.5$ ($n_y = 25$ points) with `tri2grid`. We then use `gradient` to obtain the difference field. Finally, the horizontal component of the gradient is obtained along the line $x = 0$ by dividing the appropriate differences by the grid spacing in the x-direction. The resulting array of velocities is called ux in the script. A plot of ux versus y is given in Figure 11.14. For a cylinder in an infinite flow field, the maximum velocity, which occurs on the top and bottom of the cylinder ($\pm 90°$ from the flow direction), is $2U$. In the present case, the cylinder is in a duct created by the top and bottom of the rectangle. The maximum velocity is again at the $90°$ position on the cylinder, and the value is $ux(1) = 22.64U$.

```
nx = 9; xmin = -0.5; xmax = 0.5;
x = linspace(xmin, xmax, nx);
ny = 25; ymin = 0.5; ymax = 2.5;
y = linspace(ymin, ymax, ny);
uxy = tri2grid(p, t, u, x, y);
[DX, DY] = gradient(uxy);
ux = -DX(:,(nx-1)/2)/((xmax-xmin)/(nx-1));
plot(ux, y, 'k-')
```

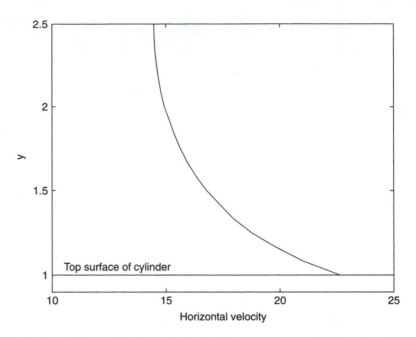

Figure 11.14 Horizontal velocity distribution along a vertical line extending from the top surface of a cylinder.

```
axis([10, 25, 0.9, 2.5])
ylabel('y')
xlabel('Horizontal velocity')
hold on
plot([10, 25], [1, 1] , 'k-')
text(10.5, 1.05, 'Top surface of cylinder')
ux1 = max(ux)
```

11.3.4 Joukowski Airfoils

The potential flow over a Joukowski airfoil in the complex z-plane ($z = x + iy$, where $i = \sqrt{-1}$) is obtained by conformal transformation of the flow over a cylinder with circulation in the ζ-plane ($\zeta = \xi + i\eta$). For a uniform incoming flow with speed Q and angle α relative to the ξ-axis over a cylinder with radius R, center at $\zeta_{\text{off}} = \xi_{\text{off}} + i\eta_{\text{off}}$, and circulation Γ, the complex potential is given by[7]

$$F(\zeta) = \phi + i\psi = Qe^{-i\alpha}(\zeta - \zeta_{\text{off}}) + Qe^{i\alpha}R^2/(\zeta - \zeta_{\text{off}}) + \frac{i\Gamma}{2\pi}\ln[(\zeta - \zeta_{\text{off}})/R]$$

where ϕ and ψ are the velocity potential and the stream function, respectively.

Referring to Figure 11.15, the Joukowski transformation is given by

$$z = \zeta + \lambda^2/\zeta \tag{11.23}$$

---

[7]R. L. Panton, *ibid.*, p. 516.

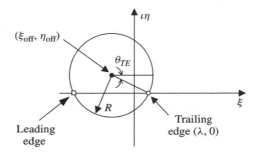

Figure 11.15   Geometry for flow over a cylinder in the ζ-plane.

where

$$\lambda = \xi_{\mathrm{off}} + \sqrt{R^2 - \eta_{\mathrm{off}}^2}$$

is a real parameter determined by the position of the center of the cylinder relative to the origin of the ξ,η-coordinate system.

The Joukowski transformation maps each point in the ζ-plane to a point in the z-plane and transfers the value of F according to $F(\zeta(z))$; that is, the value of F is the same at ζ and the corresponding point z. The transformation leaves both the circulation and the uniform flow far from the cylinder/airfoil unchanged. The circulation is adjusted so that in the ζ-plane, the stagnation point on the downwind side of the cylinder is moved to the point $(\lambda, 0)$, labeled as TE in Figure 11.15, which becomes that trailing edge of the airfoil in the z-plane. This value of Γ can be found either by trial and error from plots of the streamlines in the cylinder plane using a MATLAB program or by using the theoretical value

$$\Gamma = 4\pi QR \sin(\alpha - \theta_{TE})$$

as is done in the script given below. (See Figure 11.15 for the definition of θ_{TE}, where θ_{TE} as shown is negative.) The lift per unit span on either the cylinder or the airfoil is $F_{\mathrm{L}} = \rho Q\Gamma$, where ρ is the density of the fluid.

An important quantity in the airfoil flow field is the pressure, which is usually represented by the pressure coefficient

$$C_{\mathrm{p}} = \frac{P - P_\infty}{\rho Q^2/2} = 1 - \frac{q^2}{Q^2} \tag{11.24}$$

where P is the local pressure, P_∞ is the pressure at infinity, ρ is the density of the fluid, and

$$q = \sqrt{u^2 + v^2}$$

is the local flow speed, where u and v are the x- and y-components of the fluid velocity, respectively. The local flow speed in the z-plane is computed from the complex velocity

$$w = u - iv$$

Hence,

$$ww^* = u^2 + v^2 = q^2$$

where the * denotes the complex conjugate. The complex velocity in the airfoil flow field is given by the derivative of F with respect to z—that is,

$$w = \frac{dF}{dz} = \frac{dF}{d\zeta}\frac{d\zeta}{dz} = \left[Qe^{-i\alpha} - Qe^{i\alpha}R^2/(\zeta - \zeta_{\text{off}})^2 + \frac{i\Gamma}{2\pi(\zeta - \zeta_{\text{off}})} \right]\frac{d\zeta}{dz}$$

where, from the above Joukowski transformation (Eq. 11.23),

$$\frac{d\zeta}{dz} = \frac{1}{1 - \lambda^2/\zeta^2}$$

As an example for the use of these equations, we will calculate the streamlines and pressure field around a Joukowski airfoil. We assume that the cylinder has a radius $R = 1.0$ m and that the flow comes from the lower left with an angle of 8° relative to the horizontal. The offset of the cylinder is given by $(\xi_{\text{off}}, \eta_{\text{off}}) = (-0.093R, 0.08R)$. The following script first evaluates the complex potential F in the ζ-plane and plots the streamlines (lines of constant ψ), as shown in Figure 11.16. The points on the cylinder corresponding to the leading and trailing edges of the airfoil are marked in the figure. The coordinates are then transformed to the z-plane, and the streamlines are plotted in the z-plane as shown in Figure 11.17. Finally, the pressure contours are calculated and plotted in Figure 11.18. In all cases, contours are plotted using `contour`. The program is complicated by the fact that Eq. 11.23 transforms the flow outside the cylinder to the flow outside the airfoil but the flow inside the cylinder to the flow over the entire z-plane. Thus, to obtain only the desired streamlines and pressure contours outside

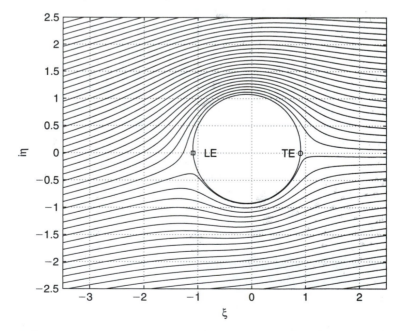

Figure 11.16 Streamline pattern around a circular cylinder with circulation Γ in the ζ-plane. Cylinder radius $R = 1$ m, $\alpha = 8°$, and $(\xi_{\text{off}}, \eta_{\text{off}}) = (-0.093R, 0.08R)$.

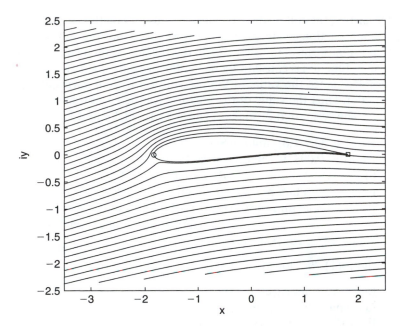

Figure 11.17   The Joukowski airfoil and streamlines obtained by transforming the cylinder and flow pattern shown in Figure 11.16. The square and circle correspond to the square and circle in Figure 11.16. This case is for $R = 1$ m, $\alpha = 8°$, and $(\xi_{\text{off}}, \eta_{\text{off}}) = (-0.093R, 0.08R)$.

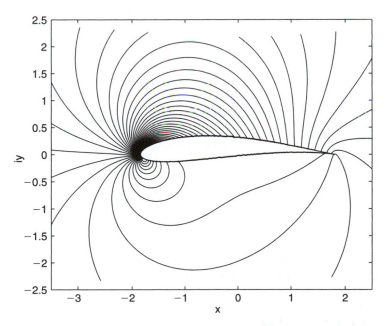

Figure 11.18   Contours of constant pressure coefficient in the vicinity of the Joukowski airfoil shown in Figure 11.17. This case is for $R = 1$ m, $\alpha = 8°$, and $(\xi_{\text{off}}, \eta_{\text{off}}) = (-0.093R, 0.08R)$.

the airfoil, the following procedure was used: For the streamlines, the values of the stream function inside the cylinder were set to the constant value of the stream function on its surface. In other words, the surface of the cylinder is a streamline, so the stream function is constant there. For the pressure coefficient, this procedure must be modified since the value of the pressure coefficient varies along the surface of the cylinder. Thus, the value of the pressure coefficient inside was set arbitrarily to zero.

The script that produces Figures 11.16, 11.17, and 11.18 is

```
R = 1.0;  Q = 1.0;  alpha = 8.0*pi/180;
ksioff = -0.093*R;  etaoff = 0.08*R;  zetaoff = complex(ksioff, etaoff);
nksi = 800;  ksimin = -3.5*R;  ksimax = 2.5*R;
neta = 800;  etamin = -2.5*R;  etamax = 2.5*R;
[ksi, eta] = meshgrid(linspace(ksimin, ksimax, nksi), ...
                      linspace(etamin, etamax, neta));
zeta = complex(ksi, eta);

figure(1)  % Flow over cylinder

thetaTE = -asin(etaoff/R);
Gamma = 4*pi*Q*R*sin(alpha-thetaTE);
F = Q*exp(-i*alpha)*(zeta-zetaoff)+ Q*exp(i*alpha)*R^2./
         (zeta-zetaoff)+ ... i*Gamma/(2*pi).*log((zeta-zetaoff)/R);
StreamFunction = imag(F);
zetapt = complex(R+ksioff, etaoff);
Fpt = Q*exp(-i*alpha)*(zetapt-zetaoff)+Q*exp(i*alpha)*R^2./
         (zetapt-zetaoff)+ ... i*Gamma/(2*pi).*log((zetapt-zetaoff)/R);
StreamFunctionpt = imag(Fpt);
rad = sqrt((ksi-ksioff).^2+(eta-etaoff).^2);
indx = find(rad<=R);
StreamFunction(indx) = StreamFunctionpt;
levmin = StreamFunction(1,nksi);
levmax = StreamFunction(neta,1);
levels = linspace(levmin, levmax, 50);
contour(ksi, eta, StreamFunction, levels)
axis equal
grid
axis([ksimin, ksimax, etamin, etamax])
xlabel('\xi')
ylabel('i\eta')
hold on
theta = linspace(0, 2*pi, 1000);
zetac = R*exp(i*theta)+zetaoff;
plot(zetac, 'k-')
hold on
ksiTE = ksioff+sqrt(R^2-etaoff^2);
ksiLE = ksioff-sqrt(R^2-etaoff^2);
plot(ksiTE, 0, 'or')
plot(ksiLE, 0, 'sr')
```

```
text(ksiTE-0.35*R, 0, 'TE')
text(ksiLE+0.2*R, 0, 'LE')
```

figure(2) % Joukowski airfoil

```
lambda = ksioff+sqrt(R^2-etaoff^2);
zeta = complex(ksi, eta);
z = zeta+lambda^2./zeta;
x = real(z);
y = imag(z);
contour(x, y, StreamFunction, levels)
axis equal
axis([ksimin, ksimax, etamin, etamax])
xlabel('x')
ylabel('iy')
hold on
zair = zetac+lambda^2./zetac;
xair = real(zair);
yair = imag(zair);
[xle, ile] = min(xair);
[xte, ite] = max(xair);
plot(zair, 'k')
zetaTE = complex(ksiTE, 0);
zetaLE = complex(ksiLE, 0);
zTE = zetaTE+lambda^2/zetaTE;
zLE = zetaLE+lambda^2/zetaLE;
plot(zTE, 0, 'or')
plot(zLE, 0, 'sr')
chord = real(zTE-zLE);
```

figure(3) % Pressure field around airfoil

```
w = (Q*exp(-i*alpha)-Q*exp(i*alpha)*R^2./(zeta-zetaoff).^2+ ...
            i*Gamma/(2*pi)./(zeta-zetaoff))./(1.0-lambda^2./zeta.^2);
Cp = 1.0-w.*conj(w)/Q^2;
Cp(indx) = 0.0;
levels = linspace(-10, 1, 150);
contour(x, y, Cp, levels)
hold on
zair = zetac+lambda^2./zetac;
xair = real(zair);
yair = imag(zair);
[xle, ile] = min(xair);
[xte, ite] = max(xair);
plot(zair, 'k-')
axis equal
axis([ksimin, ksimax, etamin, etamax])
xlabel('x')
ylabel('iy')
```

11.4 OPEN-CHANNEL FLOW

Consider gradually varying flow in a channel with the constant prismatic cross-section shown in Figure 11.19 and streamwise slope S_0. The water depth above the bottom of the channel at any streamwise location z is given by y. The cross-sectional area of the water in the channel is

$$A = by(2 + y/(bm))$$

and the wet portion of the perimeter of the channel is

$$P = 2\left(b + y\sqrt{1 + 1/m^2}\right)$$

Thus, the hydraulic radius is

$$R_h = A/P = \frac{by(2 + y/(bm))}{2\left(b + y\sqrt{1 + 1/m^2}\right)}$$

Let the volume flow rate in the channel be Q. Two physically important water depths are the uniform flow depth y_0 and the critical flow depth y_c[8]. The uniform flow depth is the depth at which the water depth and flow conditions do not vary along the length of the channel. This depth is obtained by solving the Manning equation:

$$Q = 1.486\frac{AR_h^{2/3}S_0}{n} \tag{11.25}$$

where S_0 is the streamwise slope of the channel and n is a constant. The above equation is valid for English units; for metric units, the value of 1.486 should be replaced by 1.0. The critical flow depth is the depth at which the Froude number ($v/\sqrt{gA/B}$, where v is the average flow velocity and B is the surface width ($2b + 2y_c/m$)) is equal to unity. In terms of the flow rate, this condition is written

$$Q^2 = g\frac{A^3}{B} = g\frac{(by_c(2 + y_c/(bm)))^3}{2b + 2y_c/m} \tag{11.26}$$

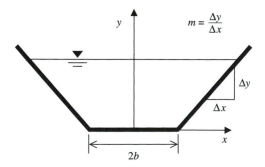

Figure 11.19   Cross-section of a prismatic channel with water depth y.

[8]J. B. Franzini and E. J. Finnemore, *Fluid Mechanics with Engineering Applications*, McGraw-Hill, New York, NY, 1997, pp. 427–449.

where g is the gravity constant. For constant flow rate but nonuniform flow conditions along a channel of uniform slope S_0, the water depth y is given by the first-order differential equation[9]

$$\frac{dy}{dx} = S_0 \frac{1 - (y_0/y)^{3.333}}{1 - (y_c/y)^3} \tag{11.27}$$

We shall now illustrate the use of these results with two examples.

Example 11.9   Uniform channel with an overfall

Consider a uniform channel with $Q = 1000$ ft./s, $n = 0.025$, $m = 0.6667$, $b = 10.0$, and four different slopes $S_0 = 0.0010, 0.0015, 0.0020$, and 0.0025. In each case, the outlet of the channel is a free overfall. The presence of the overfall at the downstream end of the channel requires that the flow reach the critical condition, $y = y_c$, at that point. The water surface height in the channel will increase with distance upstream of the overfall, eventually reaching the uniform flow depth y_0. For each channel slope, we shall find the water surface height profile along the channel upstream of the overfall to the point where $y = 0.975 y_0$. This problem is solved by integrating Eq. 11.27; however, since the right-hand side tends to infinity at the overfall where $y \to y_c$, it is most convenient to invert the equation and integrate dx/dy over the interval from $0.975 y_0$ to y_c. This is accomplished with the following script, and the results are shown in Figure 11.20.

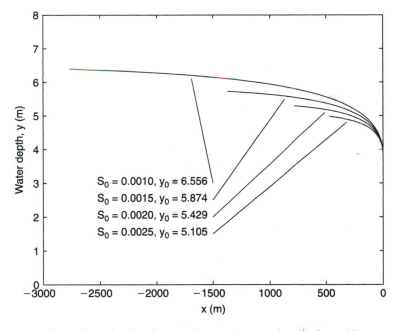

Figure 11.20   Water height (y) versus distance along a prismatic channel for $m = 0.6667$, $b = 10.0$ ft., $n = 0.025$, $Q = 1000.0$ ft³/s and for several values of slopes S_0. There is a free overfall at $x = 0$, where the flow reaches the critical condition.

---

[9]F. M. Henderson, *Open Channel Flow*, MacMillan Publishing Company, New York, NY, 1966, p. 131.

```
function OpenChannel
grav = 32.2;  m = 0.6667;  b = 10.0;
n = 0.025;  Q = 1000;  nS = 4;
slopearr = linspace(0.0010, 0.0025, nS);
xmin = -3000;  ylegend = 3.0;  dyl = 0.5;
opt = optimset('display', 'off');
for iS = 1:nS
  slope = slopearr(iS);
  y0 = fzero(@Manning, 6, opt, Q, n, b, m, slope);
  A_0 = b*y0*(2+y0/(b*m));
  P_0 = 2*(b+y0*sqrt(1+1/m^2));
  Rhd_0 = A_0/P_0;
  yc = fzero(@Q26, 3, opt, Q, grav, b, m);
  [y, x] = ode45(@dchannel, [yc, 0.975*y0], 0, [], yc, y0, slope);
  plot(x, y, 'k-')
  axis([xmin, 0, 0, 8])
  xlabel('x (m)')
  ylabel('Water depth, y (m)')
  hold on
  text(-1550, ylegend, ['S_0 = ' num2str(slope, '%6.4f') ...
         ', y_0 = ' num2str(y0, 4)])
  nx = size(x);
  plot([-1500, x(nx(1)-3)], [ylegend, y(nx(1)-3)-0.1], 'k-')
  ylegend = ylegend-dyl;
end

function dydx = dchannel(y, x, yc, y0, slope)
dydx(1) = 1/slope*(1-(yc/y(1))^3)/(1-(y0/y(1))^3.333);

function A = Manning(y, Q, n, b, m, slope)
A = Q-1.486/n*b*y*(2+y/(b*m))*(b*y*(2+y/(b*m))) ...
           /(2*(b+y*sqrt(1+1/m^2))))^0.667*slope^0.5;

function B = Q26(y, Q, grav, b, m)
B = Q^2-grav*(b*y*(2+y/(b*m)))^3/(2*b+2*y/m);
```

Example 11.10   Reservoir discharge

A reservoir is connected to a long uniform prismatic channel with constant slope via a weir, as shown in Figure 11.21. The change in elevation between the top of the weir and the water free surface in the center of the reservoir is y_R. We shall calculate the flow rate in the channel. The solution to the problem uses the specific energy

$$E = y + v^2/(2g)$$

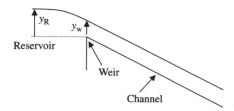

Figure 11.21   Schematic of reservoir and discharge channel.

which, by Bernoulli's equation, is constant along the free surface streamline from the center of the reservoir, where the flow speed is zero, to the point on the free surface directly over the lip of the weir, where the water depth above the weir is y_w. In the center of the reservoir, we have $E = E_0 = y_R$. Thus, the specific energy equation reduces to

$$y_R = y_w + v_w^2/(2g)$$

In terms of the flow rate Q,

$$y_R = y_w + Q^2/(2gA^2) = y_w + Q^2/(2gb^2y_w^2(2 + y_w/(bm))^2) \tag{11.28}$$

The critical depth over the weir y_{wc} occurs when the Froude number $v/\sqrt{gA/B}$ equals one at that point. Thus, at the critical condition, the specific energy equation becomes

$$y_{wc} + \frac{A_{wc}}{2B_{wc}} = y_R$$

where

$$A_{wc} = by_{wc}(2 + y_{wc}/(bm))$$
$$B_{wc} = 2b + 2y_{wc}/m$$

The value of Q that satisfies both the Manning equation (Eq. 11.25) and the specific energy equation (Eq. 11.28) is the flow rate for all $y_w > y_{wc}$. As the slope of the channel increases, so does Q—until the critical condition is reached at the weir. For higher channel slopes, the flow rate remains constant at the critical value.

We shall now calculate Q and y_w for $y_R = 10.0$ ft., $n = 0.014$, $m = 30.0$, $b = 5.0$ ft., and $S_0 = 0.001$. The execution of the script below results in Figure 11.22 where both the Manning equation and the specific energy equation are plotted. In this case, the flow condition at the weir is subcritical, and the intersection of the two curves gives the flow rate and the water depth.

```
function Discharge
yr = 10.0; g = 32.2; b = 5.0; m = 30; S0 = 0.001; n = 0.014;
yw = linspace(0, yr, 100);
Qbernoulli = sqrt(2*g*b^2*(yr-yw).*(2*yw+yw.^2/(b*m)).^2);
plot(Qbernoulli, yw, 'k-')
hold on
xlabel('Volume flow rate (ft^3/s)')
ylabel('y_w (ft)')
text(500, 2, 'Bernoulli Equation')
A = b*yw.*(2+yw/(b*m));
P = 2*(b+yw*sqrt(1+1/m^2));
Rh = A./P;
Qmanning = 1.486*A.*(Rh.^0.6666*sqrt(S0))/n;
plot(Qmanning, yw, 'k-');
hold on
```

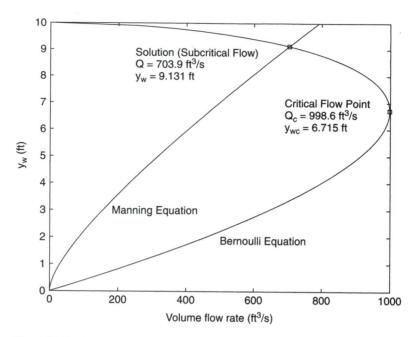

Figure 11.22   Reservoir discharge calculation for $y_R = 10.0$ ft, $b = 5.0$ ft., $m = 30.0$, $S_0 = 0.001$, and $n = 0.014$.

```
text(180, 3, 'Manning Equation')
opt = optimset('display', 'off');
ywflow = fzero(@Q2526, [8.5,9.5], opt, b, m, S0, n, g, yr)
Awflow = b*ywflow*(2+ywflow/(b*m));
Qflow = Awflow*sqrt(2*g*(yr-ywflow))
text(260, 8.9, 'Solution (Subcritical Flow)')
text(260, 8.2, ['Q = ' num2str(Qflow, 4) ' ft^3/s'])
text(260, 7.3, ['y_{w} = ' num2str(ywflow, 4) ' ft'] )
plot(Qflow, ywflow, 'ks')
ywcrit = fzero(@Q26, 6, opt, b, m, yr);
Awcrit = b*ywcrit*(2+ywcrit/(b*m));
Qcrit = Awcrit*sqrt(2*g*(yr-ywcrit));
hold on
text(690, 7, 'Critical Flow Point')
text(690, 6.3, ['Q_{c} = ' num2str(Qcrit, 4) ' ft^3/s'])
text(690, 5.5, ['y_{wc} = ' num2str(ywcrit, 4) ' ft'] )
plot([Qcrit, ywcrit, 'ks')

function A = Q2526(y, b, m, S0, n, g, yr)
A = 1.486*(b*y*(2+y/(b*m)))*(((b*y*(2+y/(b*m))) ...
    /(2*(b+y*sqrt(1+1/m^2))))^0.6666*sqrt(S0))/n- ...
    sqrt(2*g*b^2*(yr-y)*(2*y+y^2/(b*m))^2);

function B = Q26(ywc, b, m, yr)
B = ywc+0.5*b*ywc*(2+ywc/(b*m))/(2*b+2*ywc/m)-yr;
```

TABLE 11.3   MATLAB Functions Introduced in Chapter 11

MATLAB function	Description
gradient	Numerical gradient
pdeintrp	Interpolates from node data to triangle midpoint data in pdetool
pdetrg	Area of each triangle formed by mesh in pdetool
trigrid	Interpolates from triangular mesh to rectangular grid in pdetool

11.5 SUMMARY OF FUNCTIONS INTRODUCED

A summary of the functions introduced in this chapter is presented in Table 11.3.

EXERCISES

Section 11.2.1

11.1 Obtain the flow fields in two ducts with the same cross-sectional area but with one whose cross-sectional shape is square and one whose shape is rectangular. The rectangular-shaped cross-section has the length of one side four times that of the other. Compare the volume flow rates of the two ducts using pdetool. The governing equation is that given by Eq. 11.7. Assume that the right-hand side of Eq. 11.7 is the same for each duct—say, 1.0. Also, the boundary condition at the duct wall is $u = 0$. Export each solution to the command window, and use the procedure illustrated in Section 11.2.1 to obtain

$$Q_{sq}/Q_{rect} \approx 2$$

where Q is the flow rate.

11.2 Consider laminar, steady, pressure-driven flow in a channel of height $2h$, as depicted in Figure 11.23. The velocity is given by

$$u(y) = -\frac{h^2}{2\mu} \frac{dP}{dx} \left(1 - \frac{y^2}{h^2}\right)$$

where dP/dx is the pressure gradient and μ is the dynamic viscosity of the fluid. Using pdetool, compare this velocity distribution to the velocity distribution along the center plane of a duct with the same height as the channel and a width that is twice the height.

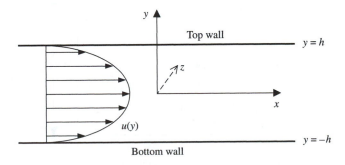

Figure 11.23   A channel extending from $\pm\infty$ in the z-direction. (For the duct, two additional vertical walls are placed at $z = \pm 2h$.)

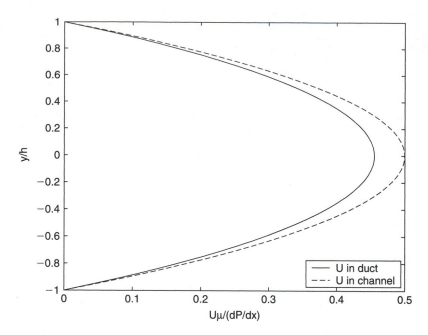

Figure 11.24 Comparison of the velocity distribution through a cross section of the duct and velocity distribution in the channel of same height.

Assume the same pressure gradient and viscosity. The differential equation to be solved is given by Eq. 11.7. The results should look like those presented in Figure 11.24.

11.3 Consider the laminar, steady, fully developed, pressure-driven flow of oil in a duct, as shown in Figure 11.25. The duct has a rectangular cross-section, which is 1 cm high and 0.5 cm wide. The right wall is moving at a velocity of 0.5 m/s in the direction of the flow driven by the pressure gradient (out of the plane of the page in Figure 11.25), while the other three walls are stationary. Assume that the pressure gradient is 10 kPa/m and that the dynamic viscosity of the oil is 0.1 kg/m · s. Using `pdetool`, plot the distributions of velocity along the horizontal and vertical center planes of the duct. The differential equation to be solved is given by Eq. 11.7. The results should look like those shown in Figures 11.26 and 11.27.

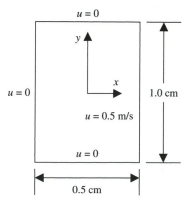

Figure 11.25 Duct cross-section for Exercise 11.3.

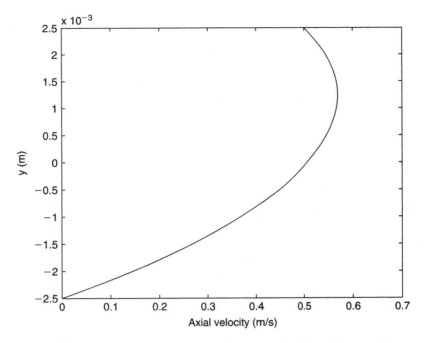

Figure 11.26 Axial velocity in the center plane connecting the stationary and moving 1-cm-long walls.

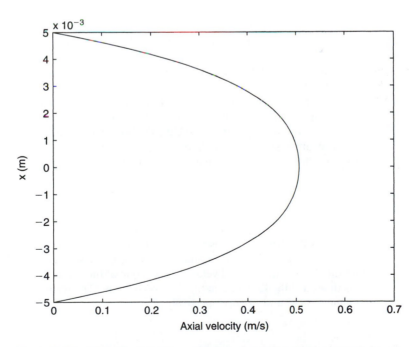

Figure 11.27 Axial velocity in the center plane connecting the two stationary, 0.5-cm-long walls.

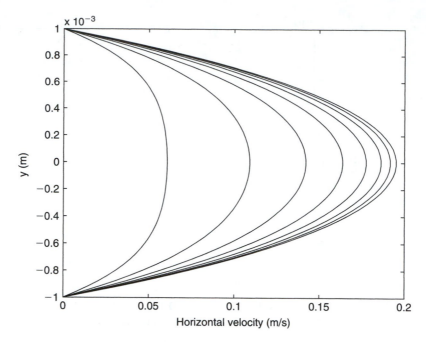

Figure 11.28   Axial velocity in the center plane connecting the two 0.3-cm-long walls.

11.4 Consider a viscous fluid with $\mu = 0.02$ kg/m·s and $\rho = 800$ kg/m³ in a rectangular duct with dimensions 0.2 cm × 0.3 cm. The fluid is initially at rest. At $t = 0$, a pressure gradient of magnitude 10 kPa/m in the direction along the axis of the duct is turned on. For times from 0 to 0.04 s, in steps of 0.005 s, plot the velocity profile across the center plane connecting the 0.3-cm-long walls of the duct. The results should look like those shown in Figure 11.28.

11.5 Consider the viscous, fully developed flow along a duct with a square cross-section of dimensions $a \times a$. At $t = 0$, the velocity distribution is uniform with magnitude 1 m/s over the cross-section. For $t > 0$, the no-slip boundary condition at the walls is applied and an axial pressure gradient dP/dx is imposed[10] such that the final steady flow rate Q_f attained after a long time is equal to the flow rate Q_0 at $t = 0$:

$$\frac{dP}{dx} = \frac{28.46\mu Q_0}{d^4}$$

where μ is the dynamic viscosity of the fluid. Assume that $a = 1$ cm and that the fluid is an oil with $\mu = 0.2$ kg/m·s and $\rho = 800$ kg/m³. Use the results from `pdetool` to plot the distribution of axial velocity across one of the center planes of the duct at various times and the flow rate in the duct versus time. The results should look like those in Figures 11.29 and 11.30, respectively.

---

[10]F. M. White, *Fluid Mechanics*, 4th ed., McGraw-Hill, New York, NY, 1999, p. 365.

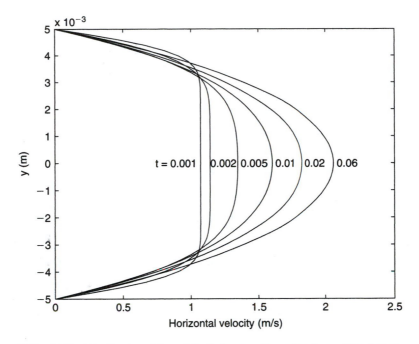

Figure 11.29   Distribution of the axial velocity over the center plane of the duct at various times.

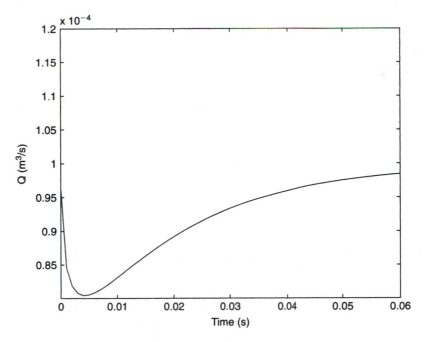

Figure 11.30   Flow rate in the duct versus time.

Section 11.2.2

11.6 Water is to flow from reservoir A to reservoir B through the piping system shown in Figure 11.31. The flow rate when the valve is completely open is to be 0.003 m³/s. The generalized head loss equation is

$$\frac{P_1}{\rho g} + \frac{V_1^2}{2g} + z_1 = \frac{P_2}{\rho g} + \frac{V_2^2}{2g} + z_2 + \frac{\lambda L V^2}{2gD} + \sum_{m=1}^{5} K_{Lm} \frac{V^2}{2g}$$

where K_{Lm} are the minor loss coefficients at the locations shown in Figure 11.31, λ is the pipe friction coefficient, and $V = 4Q/\pi D^2$ is the average velocity in the pipe. If $v_{vis} = 1.3 \times 10^{-6}$ m²/s and $\rho = 1000$ kg/m³, then determine the pipe diameter. [Answer: $D = 0.04698$ m.]

11.7 The oscillations caused by a suddenly released fluid from a height Z that separates the fluid levels in two rectangular prismatic reservoirs connected by a long pipeline of length L, as shown in Figure 11.32, can be determined from[11]

$$\frac{d^2 Z}{dt^2} + \text{signum}(dZ/dt) p \left(\frac{dZ}{dt}\right)^2 + qZ = 0$$

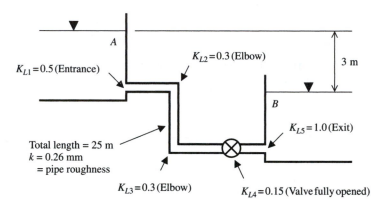

Figure 11.31   Piping system between two reservoirs.

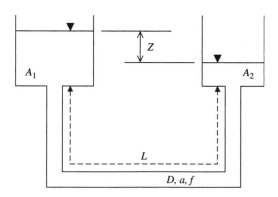

Figure 11.32   Interconnected reservoirs.

[11]D. N. Roy, *Applied Fluid Mechanics*, Ellis Horwood Limited, Chichester, England, 1988, pp. 290–293.

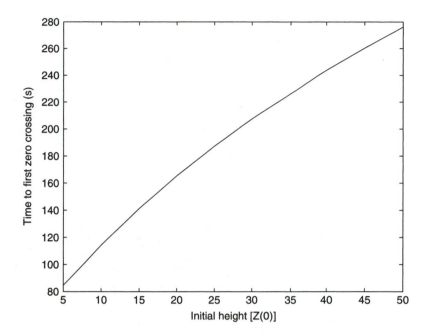

Figure 11.33 Values of the first occurrence of t_n for which $Z(t_n) = 0$ as a function of $Z(0) = Z_n$.

where

$$p = \frac{f A_1 A_2 L_e}{2 D a L (A_1 + A_2)} \qquad q = \frac{g a (A_1 + A_2)}{A_1 A_2 L}$$

and it has been assumed that the motion of the liquid is mostly turbulent so that the head loss is proportional to the square of the velocity. The quantity L_e is the equivalent length of the pipe incorporating minor losses, g is the gravitational constant, f is the friction coefficient in the pipe, A_1 and A_2 are the water surface areas of the two reservoirs, a is the cross-sectional area of the pipeline, and D is its diameter.

If $p = 0.375$ m^{-1}, $q = 7.4 \times 10^{-4}$ s^{-2}, and the initial conditions are $Z(0) = Z_n$ m and $dZ(0)/dt = 0$ m/s, determine the value of the first occurrence of t_n for which $Z(t_n) = 0$ when $Z_n = 5, 10, \ldots, 50$. Plot the results, which should look like those shown in Figure 11.33. Use interp1 to determine t_n.

Section 11.3.3

11.8 The flow about a thin, symmetrical airfoil can be approximated by potential flow theory.[12] The chord of the airfoil extends along the x-axis from $x = 0$ to $x = c$ and is represented by a vortex sheet whose strength $\gamma(x)$ is given by

$$\gamma(\theta) = 2 \alpha V_\infty \frac{1 + \cos \theta}{\sin \theta}$$

---

[12]See, for example, J. D. Anderson, *Fundamentals of Aerodynamics*, McGraw-Hill, New York, NY 1991, Chapter 4.

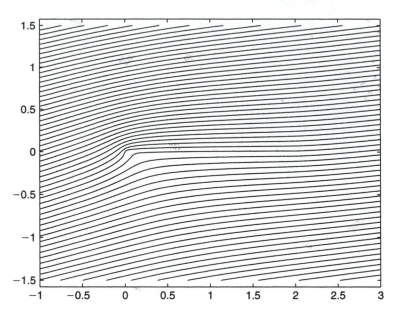

Figure 11.34   Stream lines for a thin airfoil with a 2-m chord and an angle of attack of $10°$. The flow is from left to right, and the foil extends horizontally from $(0,0)$ to $(2,0)$.

where

$$x = \frac{c}{2}(1 - \cos \theta) \quad 0 \le \theta \le \pi$$

α is the angle of attack (in radians) of the incoming flow relative to the x-axis and V_∞ is the flow speed. Consider the vortex sheet to be approximated by a set of N discrete vortices separated by a distance $\Delta x = c/N$ with strength $\Gamma_i = \gamma(\theta_i)\Delta x$. Using method 1 of Section 11.3.3, which constructs flows by adding known potentials, draw the streamlines of this flow for $\alpha = 10°, c = 2$ m, and $V_\infty = 100$ m/s. The results should look like those shown in Figure 11.34.

11.9   Consider the flow field around a cylinder in a duct, as shown in Figure 11.35. Assume potential flow, and use pdetool to compute the streamlines. Export the mesh and solution variables to the MATLAB command window, and compute the velocity distribution along the bottom wall of the channel. The results should look like those presented in Figure 11.36.

11.10   Consider a potential flow over a cylinder that is placed near a wall, as shown in Figure 11.37. Represent the flow over the cylinder and wall with a uniform flow of speed $U = 1.0$ m/s and two dipoles of strength $m = 2\pi UD^2/4$ located at $(x, y) = (0, 0.75D)$ and $(0, -0.75D)$. Plot the streamline pattern. Note that the closed streamline around each dipole

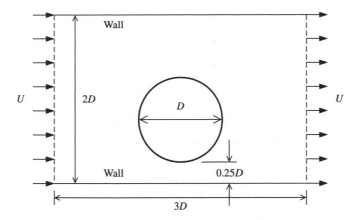

Figure 11.35 The flow enters the duct on the left and leaves the duct on the right with a uniform horizontal velocity profile of $U = 1$ m/s. The cylinder has a diameter of $D = 1.0$ m, and its center is located at $(x, y) = (0.0, 0.75)$ m.

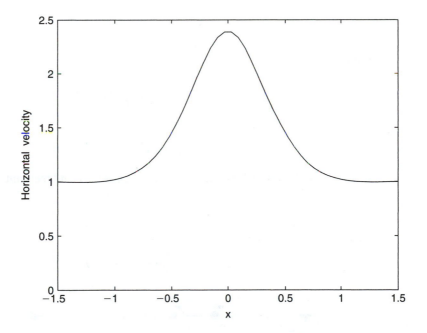

Figure 11.36 Horizontal velocity along the bottom wall of the duct.

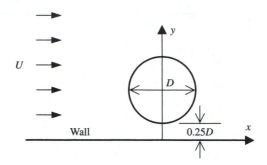

Figure 11.37   Cylinder near a wall with a uniform
horizontal flow upstream.

is not circular. Plot the velocity distribution along the wall, and compare it to the solution
obtained in Exercise 11.9.

11.11   The flow about a thin, cambered airfoil, as shown in Figure 11.38, can be approximated
by potential flow theory.[13] The chord of the airfoil extends along the x-axis from $x = 0$
to $x = c$ and is represented by a vortex sheet placed along the chord. The strength $\gamma(x)$
of this vortex sheet is given by

$$\gamma(\theta) = 2V_\infty\left(A_0\frac{1 + \cos\theta}{\sin\theta} + \sum_{n=1}^{\infty} A_n \sin(n\theta) \right)$$

where

$$\frac{x}{c} = \frac{1}{2}(1 - \cos\theta) \quad 0 \le \theta \le \pi$$

α is the angle of attack (in radians) of the incoming flow relative to the x-axis and V_∞
is the flow speed. The constants A_n are given by

$$A_0 = \alpha - \frac{1}{\pi}\int_0^\pi \frac{dz}{dx}d\theta_o$$

$$A_n = \frac{2}{\pi}\int_0^\pi \frac{dz}{dx}\cos(n\theta_o)d\theta_o$$

where $z(x)$ is the vertical distance between the chord line and the camber line.

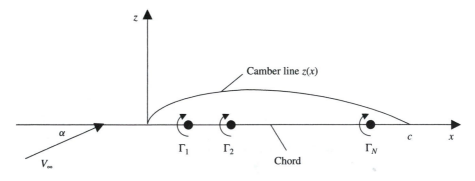

Figure 11.38   Placement of a vortex sheet on the chord line.

---

[13]J. D. Anderson, *ibid.*

Let the camber line be

$$\frac{z}{c} = 2.6595\frac{x}{c}\left[\left(\frac{x}{c}\right)^2 - 0.6075\frac{x}{c} + 0.1147\right] \quad 0 \le x/c \le 0.2025$$

$$= 0.02208\left(1 - \frac{x}{c}\right) \quad 0.2025 \le x/c \le 1.0$$

where the distance z is normal to the chord. Compute A_n for $n = 0, 1, \ldots, 20$. Let the vortex sheet be approximated by a set of N_v discrete vortices (see Section 11.3.3) along the x-axis in the region $0 \le x/c \le 1$. The vortices are separated by a distance $\Delta x = c/N$ and have the strengths $\Gamma_i = \gamma(\theta_i)\Delta x$. Use contour to draw the streamlines of this flow for $\alpha = 4°$, $c = 2$ m, and $V_\infty = 100$ m/s. In the streamline plot, the camber line should closely follow a streamline. [Partial answers: $A_0 = 0.0412$, $A_1 = 0.0955$, $A_2 = 0.0792$, $A_3 = 0.0568$.]

Section 11.3.4

11.12 Let the chord L of a Joukowski airfoil be the distance following a straight line along the x-axis from leading edge to trailing edge in the z-plane. Let the thickness t of the foil be the maximum vertical distance along the y-axis between the lower and upper surfaces of the foil, as shown in Figure 11.39. Let the camber b of the foil be the maximum distance between the chord line (the x-axis) and the midline of the foil. (A point on the midline is located with equal vertical distance to the upper and lower surfaces of the foil.) It is found that t/L is primarily a function of ξ_{off}, and b/L is primarily a function of η_{off}. Plot t/L versus ξ_{off} over the range $-0.2R$ to $0R$ for $\eta_{off}/R = [0.01, 0.02, 0.03, 0.04]$, and plot b/L versus η_{off} over the range $0.0R$ to $0.04R$ for $\xi_{off}/R = [-0.2, -0.15, -0.10, -0.05, 0]$. The plots should look like those in Figure 11.40.

11.13 Plot the pressure coefficient distribution (see Eq. 11.24) on the upper and lower surfaces of a Joukowski airfoil for $R = 1.0$, $\alpha = 6°$, $\xi_{off} = -0.093R$, $\eta_{off} = 0.08R$ (i.e., $t/L = 0.1215$, and $b/L = 0.0401$). The results should look like those given in Figure 11.41.

11.14 The lift coefficient of the foil is given by

$$C_L = \frac{F_L}{\rho Q^2 L/2}$$

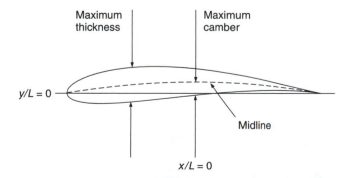

Maximum thickness   Maximum camber

$y/L = 0$

Midline

$x/L = 0$

Figure 11.39 Definitions of maximum foil thickness and maximum foil camber.

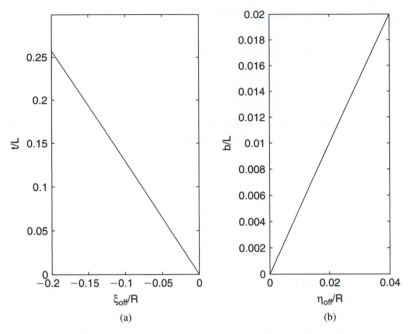

Figure 11.40　(a) Foil thickness versus ξ offset and (b) foil camber versus η offset. In part a, five curves are drawn for $\eta_{\text{off}}/R = 0, 0.01, 0.02, 0.03$, and 0.04. In part b, five curves are drawn for $\xi_{\text{off}}/R = -0.2, -0.15, -0.10, -0.05$, and 0.0. Note that in each plot, the five curves are virtually on top of one another.

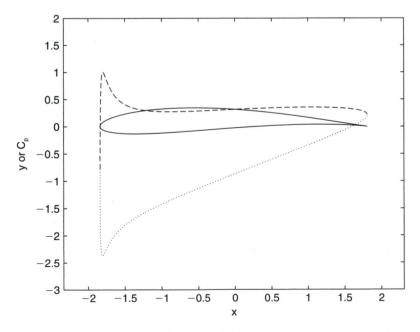

Figure 11.41　Foil and pressure coefficient distribution on upper surface (dotted line) and lower surface (dashed line) for $R = 1.0, Q = 1.0, a = 6°, \xi_{\text{off}} = -0.093R$, $\eta_{\text{off}} = 0.08R$ ($t/L = 0.1215$ and $b/L = 0.0401$).

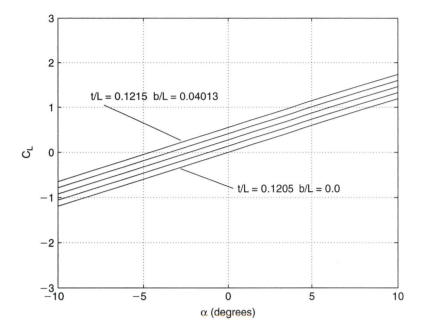

Figure 11.42   Lift coefficient C_L versus angle of attack α for $\xi_{\text{off}} = -0.093R$ and $\eta_{\text{off}} = 0, 0.02R, 0.04R, 0.06R$, and $0.08R$.

where $F_L = \rho Q \Gamma$ is the lift force per unit span. Plot C_L versus angle of attack α (range $-10°$ to $10°$) for $\xi_{\text{off}} = -0.093R$ and $\eta_{\text{off}} = [0, 0.02R, 0.04R, 0.06R, 0.08R]$. The results should look like the one shown in Figure 11.42. For convenience, let $R = 1$.

Section 11.4

11.15 Find the reservoir discharge flow rate as a function of channel slope when the vertical distance between the top of the weir and the free surface in the reservoir is $y_R = 10.0$ ft. and the long prismatic channel is described by $n = 0.014$, $b = 5.0$ ft., and $m = 1.0$. The result should look like that shown in Figure 11.43.

11.16 Consider discharge from a reservoir into a prismatic channel with conditions $y_R = 10.0$ ft., $n = 0.014$, $b = 5.0$ ft., and $S_0 = 0.001$. Make a plot of the flow rate versus m, the slope of the channel sidewalls. The plot should look like the one shown in Figure 11.44.

11.17 Flow discharges from a reservoir into a prismatic channel with conditions $y_R = 10.0$ ft., $n = 0.014$, $b = 5.0$ ft., $m = 1.0$, and $S_0 = 0.003$. Note from Figure 11.43 that S_0 is above the critical slope, indicating that the flow rate is 1666 ft^3/s, the maximum value. Compute the surface height profile in the channel assuming that the channel is long enough for the flow to gradually reach the supercritical normal flow depth. The results should look like those given in Figure 11.45.

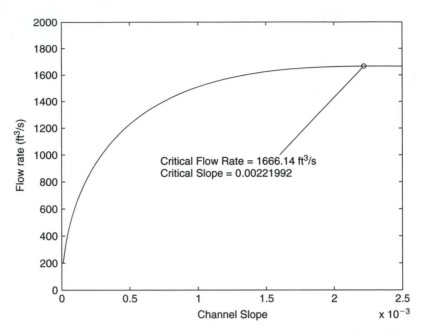

Figure 11.43   Flow rate versus channel slope for a reservoir discharge problem with $y_R = 10.0$ ft., $n = 0.014$, $b = 5.0$ ft., and $m = 1.0$.

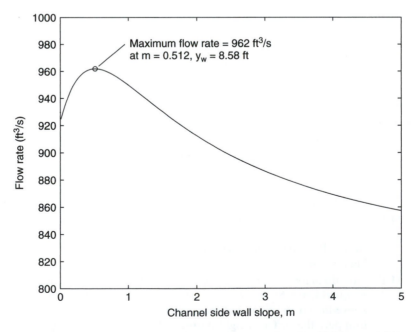

Figure 11.44   Flow rate versus channel sidewall slope m for $y_R = 10.0$ ft., $n = 0.014$, $b = 5.0$ ft., and $S_0 = 0.001$.

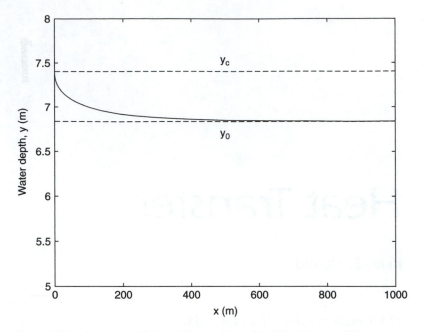

Figure 11.45 Surface profile in a channel with a critical flow inlet condition at $x = 0$ and a slope that creates a supercritical flow for $n = 0.014$, $b = 5.0$ ft., $m = 1.0$, and $S_0 = 0.003$.

BIBLIOGRAPHY

B. R. Munson, D. F. Young, and T. H. Okiishi, *Fundamentals of Fluid Mechanics*, 3rd ed., John Wiley & Sons, New York, NY, 1998.

J. D. Anderson, *Fundamentals of Aerodynamics*, 2nd ed., McGraw-Hill, New York, NY, 1991.

V. L. Streeter, E. B. Wylie, and K. W. Bedford, *Fluid Mechanics*, 9th ed., McGraw-Hill, New York, NY, 1998.

R. W. Fox and A. McDonald, *Introduction to Fluid Mechanics*, 5th ed., John Wiley & Sons, New York, NY, 1998.

12

Heat Transfer

Keith E. Herold

Several techniques for analyzing and visualizing conduction, convection, and radiation heat transfer are presented.

12.1 CONDUCTION HEAT TRANSFER

12.1.1 Transient Heat Conduction in a Semi-Infinite Slab with Surface Convection

The transient temperature distribution in a semi-infinite solid that is initially at a uniform temperature T_i and that has convection at the boundary surface $\eta = 0$ is given by[1]

$$\theta(\eta, \tau) = \text{erfc}\left[\frac{\eta}{2\tau}\right] - \exp[\eta + \tau^2]\text{erfc}\left[\frac{\eta}{2\tau} + \tau\right]$$

where erfc is the complementary error function,

$$\theta(\eta, \tau) = \frac{T(\eta, \tau) - T_\infty}{T_\infty - T_i}$$

$$\tau = \frac{h}{k}\sqrt{\alpha t}$$

$$\eta = \frac{hx}{k}$$

and x is the spatial coordinate, t is time, h is the heat-transfer coefficient, k is the thermal conductivity of the solid, T_∞ is the ambient air temperature, and α is the thermal diffusivity of the solid.

> **Example 12.1   Transient heat conduction time and temperature distributions in a semi-infinite solid**
>
> We shall plot the temperature in the semi-infinite solid two ways. In the first way, the temperature is plotted over the range $0 \leq \eta \leq 5$ and $0.01 \leq \tau \leq 3$. The results are shown in Figure 12.1. In the second way, the temperature is plotted as a function of τ for $0.01 \leq \tau \leq 4$ at six different locations: $\eta = 0, 1, \ldots, 5$. These results are shown in Figure 12.2. The script is
>
> ```
> tau = linspace(0.01, 3, 30); eta = linspace(0, 5, 20);
> [x, t] = meshgrid(eta, tau);
> theta = inline('erfc(0.5*x./t)-exp(x+t.^2).*erfc(0.5*x./t+t) ', 'x', 't');
> figure(1)
> mesh(x, t, theta(x, t))
> xlabel('\eta')
> ylabel('\tau')
> zlabel('\theta')
> figure(2)
> eta = linspace(0, 5, 6);
> tau = linspace(0.01, 4, 40);
> ```

---

[1]F. P. Incropera and D. P. DeWitt, *Fundamentals of Heat and Mass Transfer*, 4th ed., John Wiley & Sons, New York, NY, 1996, p. 239.

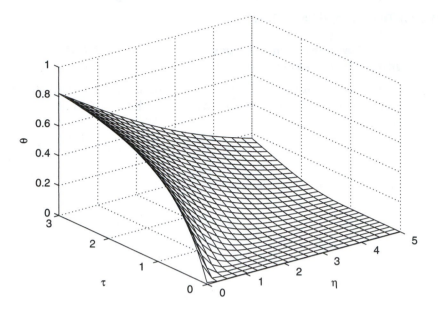

Figure 12.1   Temperature in a semi-infinite solid as a function of position η and time τ.

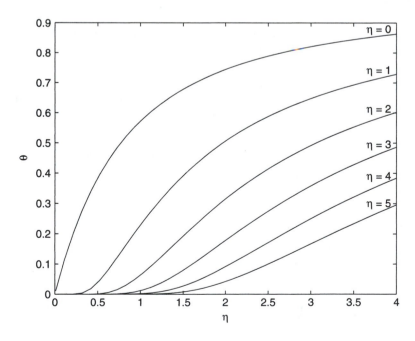

Figure 12.2   Temperature in a semi-infinite solid as a function of time τ at several locations η.

```
for k = 1:6
    thet = theta(eta(k), tau);
    plot(tau, thet)
    text(.92*4,1.02*thet(end), ['\eta = ' num2str(eta(k))])
    hold on
end
xlabel('\eta')
ylabel('\theta')
```

12.1.2 Transient Heat Conduction in an Infinite Solid Cylinder with Convection

The transient temperature distribution in an infinitely long solid circular cylinder, which is initially at a uniform temperature and has convection at the surface, is given by[2]

$$\theta(\xi, \tau) = \sum_{n=1}^{\infty} C_n \exp(-\zeta_n^2 \tau) J_0(\zeta_n \xi)$$

where

$$\theta(\xi, \tau) = \frac{T(\xi, \tau) - T_\infty}{T(\xi, 0) - T_\infty}$$

and

$$C_n = \frac{2}{\zeta_n} \frac{J_1(\zeta_n)}{J_0^2(\zeta_n) + J_1^2(\zeta_n)}$$

The quantity $J_m(x)$ is the Bessel function of the first kind of order m, $\tau = \alpha t/a^2$, α is the thermal diffusivity, a is the radius of the cylinder, t is time, $\xi = r/a$, r is the radial location in the cylinder, T_∞ is the ambient air temperature, and ζ_n are the positive roots of

$$\frac{J_1(\zeta_n)}{J_0(\zeta_n)} - \frac{Bi}{\zeta_n} = 0$$

where $Bi = ha/k$ is the Biot number, h is the heat-transfer coefficient, and k is the thermal conductivity of the cylinder.

Example 12.2   Transient heat conduction in an infinite solid cylinder with convection

We shall plot $\theta(\xi, \tau)$ for $0 \le \xi \le 1$, $0 \le \tau \le 1.5$, and $Bi = 0.5$ using the lowest 15 positive roots of ζ_n. The script is

```
Bi = 0.5; nroots = 15; r = zeros(1, nroots);
guess = 0.01;
CylinderRoots = inline('x.*besselj(1, x)-Bi*besselj(0, x)', 'x', 'Bi');
```

---

[2]F. P. Incropera and D. P. DeWitt, *ibid.*, p. 229.

```
options = optimset('Display', 'off');
for k = 1:nroots
    r(k) = fzero(CylinderRoots, [guess, guess+1.1*pi], options, Bi);
    guess = 1.05*r(k);
end
tau = linspace(0, 1.5, 20);
[t, rt] = meshgrid(tau, r);
Fn = exp(−t.*rt.^2);
cn = 2*besselj(1, r)./(r.*(besselj(0, r).^2+besselj(1, r).^2));
ccn = meshgrid(cn, tau);
pro = ccn'.*Fn;
rstar = linspace(0, 1, 20);
[R, rx] = meshgrid(rstar, r);
Jo = besselj(0, rx.*R);
the = Jo'*pro;
[rr, tt] = meshgrid(rstar, tau);
mesh(rr, tt, the')
xlabel('\xi')
ylabel('\tau')
zlabel('\theta')
view(49.5, -34)
```

where the values of *guess* are determined from a plot of **CylinderRoots**. Execution of this script results in Figure 12.3.

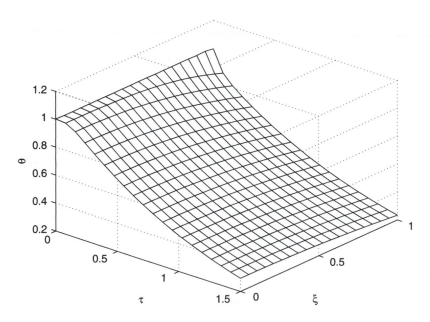

Figure 12.3 Temperature distribution in a cylinder as a function of time τ and radial position ξ.

12.1.3 Transient One-Dimensional Conduction with a Heat Source

One-dimensional, transient conduction is governed by

$$\frac{1}{\alpha}\frac{dT}{dt} = \frac{d^2T}{dx^2} + \frac{q}{k}$$

where T is the temperature, t is time, x is the spatial coordinate, α is the thermal diffusivity, k the thermal conductivity, and q the volumetric heat source. We convert this equation to a dimensionless form by introducing the following nondimensional quantities:

$$\xi = \frac{x}{L} \qquad \tau = \frac{\alpha t}{L^2} \qquad Bi = \frac{hL}{k}$$

$$\theta = \frac{T - T_\infty}{T_i - T_\infty} \qquad \Sigma = \frac{L^2 q}{k(T_i - T_\infty)} \qquad X = \frac{-q''L}{k(T_i - T_\infty)}$$

where L is the length of the domain, T_i is an arbitrary temperature that usually represents the initial temperature, q'' is the heat flux, and T_∞ is the fluid temperature for a convective boundary. For cases where a convective boundary condition is not used, T_∞ is an arbitrary temperature, but with the requirement that it must be different from T_i. In terms of these variables, the governing equation becomes

$$\frac{\partial \theta}{\partial \tau} = \frac{\partial^2 \theta}{\partial \xi^2} + \Sigma \tag{12.1}$$

The domain is illustrated in Figure 12.4. Typical boundary conditions at each end of the domain are

Fixed temperature

$$\theta = \theta_w$$

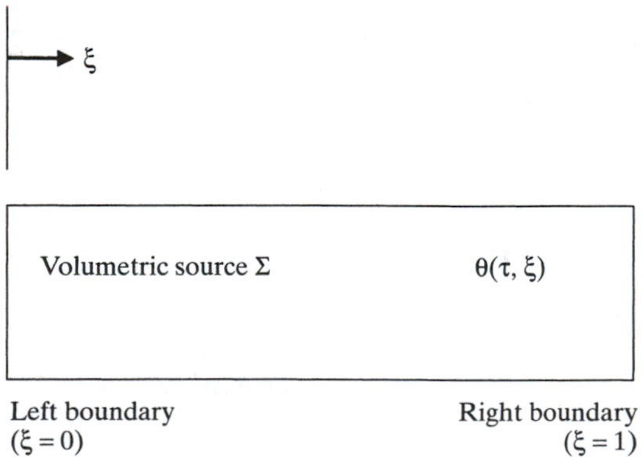

Figure 12.4   Geometry of a one-dimensional transient heat transfer with source Σ.

Specified flux

$$\frac{\partial \theta}{\partial \xi} = \chi_w$$

Convective

$$\frac{\partial \theta}{\partial \xi} = -Bi\theta_w$$

where the negative sign in the convective condition is correct for the left boundary and the subscript w represents the wall values.

Equation 12.1 is a partial differential equation of the parabolic type with one spatial dimension. One method of solution, applicable to a restricted set of boundary conditions, is separation of variables. An example of this type of solution was used to obtain the result given in Section 12.1.2. The Partial Differential Equation (PDE) Toolbox provides a numerical solution method, but it is not designed to handle only one spatial variable and, therefore, is cumbersome to use for this type of problem. The function pdepe, which solves parabolic PDE's with one spatial variable, provides the needed capability. We now illustrate the use of pdepe to obtain a solution to this problem.

Example 12.3   One-dimensional transient heat transfer with source

Consider the data in Table 12.1, which describes a one-dimensional system subjected to a transient source. We shall determine the nondimensional temperature as a function of nondimensional time at five locations in a solid: $\xi = 0.0, 0.25, 0.5, 0.75,$ and 1.0. In obtaining the solution, we note that pdepe requires three functions: one to define the PDE, which we call **pdetran**; one to define the initial conditions, which we call **pdeIC**; and one to define the boundary conditions, which we call **pdeBC**. The syntax for these functions can be obtained from the online Help for pdepe. The inputs to the main function and the subfunctions given below are also given in Table 12.1:

```
function Transient1D
Bi = 0.1; Tr = 0.55; Sigma = 1; L = 21; Lt = 101;
```

TABLE 12.1   Input Values Used to Obtain Figure 12.5

Parameter	Value
Boundary conditions and source	
Dimensionless source strength, Σ	1
Left-boundary Biot number	0.1
Right-boundary dimensionless temperature, $\theta(1)$	0.55
Initial conditions	
Left boundary, $\theta_i(0)$	1
Linear distribution between $\theta_i(0) = 1$ and $\theta_i(1) = 0.55$	
Numerical grid parameters	
Number of equally spaced grid points in $0 < \xi < 1$	21
Number of equally spaced time steps	101
Extent of nondimensional integration time	1

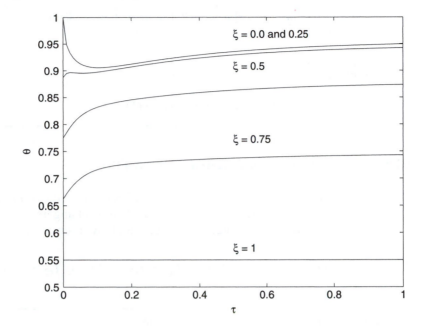

Figure 12.5   One-dimensional heat conduction using the data in Table 12.1.

```
xi = linspace(0, 1, L);
tau = linspace(0, 1, Lt);
options = odeset;
sol = pdepe(0, @pdetran1D, @pdeIC, @pdeBC, xi, tau, options, Bi, Tr, Sigma);
theta = sol(:,:,1);
g = [1, 6, 11, 16, L];
for k = 1:5
  plot(tau, theta(:,g(k)), 'k-')
  hold on
  if k==1
    text(0.5, 1.02*theta(Lt,g(k)),'\xi = 0.0 and 0.25')
  elseif k>2
    text(0.5, 1.04*theta(Lt, g(k)), ['\xi = ' num2str(xi(g(k)))])
  end
end
axis([0 1 0.5 1])
xlabel('\tau')
ylabel('\theta')

function [c, f, s] = pdetran1D(x, t, u, DuDx, Bi, Tr, Sigma)
c = 1;
f = DuDx;
s = Sigma;

function T0 = pdeIC(x, Bi, Tr, Sigma)
T0 = 1-0.45*x;
```

```
function [pl, ql, pr, qr] = pdeBC(xl, ul, xr, ur, t, Bi, Tr, Sigma)
pr = ur-Tr;
qr = 0;
pl = -Bi*ul;
ql = 1;
```

The execution of the script function results in Figure 12.5.

12.2 SIZING OF SHELL AND TUBE HEAT EXCHANGERS

Using the definitions in Table 12.2 and Figure 12.6, we have the following equations that govern the characteristics of shell and tube heat exchangers.

The energy balance on a heat exchanger can be written as

$$Q = UAF\Delta T_{\mathrm{m}} = (\dot{m}c_{\mathrm{p}})_{\mathrm{h}}(T_{\mathrm{h}1} - T_{\mathrm{h}2}) = (\dot{m}c_{\mathrm{p}})_{\mathrm{c}}(T_{\mathrm{c}2} - T_{\mathrm{c}1})$$

TABLE 12.2 Definitions of Terms in Heat-Exchanger Relations

Symbol	Units	Description
c_{p}	J/(kg K)	Specific heat at constant pressure
d_{o}	m	Tube outside diameter
d_{i}	m	Tube inside diameter
f		Tube flow friction factor
f_{s}		Friction factor shell side
h_{o}	W/(m^2 K)	Heat-transfer coefficient outside tube
h_{i}	W/(m^2 K)	Heat-transfer coefficient inside tube
k	W/(m K)	Thermal conductivity of fluids
k_{tube}	W/(m K)	Thermal conductivity of tubes
$\dot{m}_{\mathrm{t}}$	kg/s	Tube-side mass flow rate
$\dot{m}_{\mathrm{s}}$	kg/s	Shell-side mass flow rate
Δp_{s}	Pa	Shell-side pressure drop
Δp_{t}	Pa	Tube-side pressure drop
u_{t}	M/s	Mean axial velocity of fluid in tube ($\dot{m}_{\mathrm{t}}/\rho A_{\mathrm{t}}$)
A_{o}	m^2	Tube outside surface area per pass ($\pi d_{\mathrm{o}}^4 L N_{\mathrm{T}}/N_{\mathrm{P}}$)
A_{i}	m^2	Tube inside surface area per pass ($\pi d_{\mathrm{i}} L N_{\mathrm{T}}/N_{\mathrm{P}}$)
A_{s}	m^2	Cross-flow area at or near shell centerline
A_{t}	m^2	Total cross-sectional area of tubes per pass ($\pi d_{\mathrm{i}}^2 N_{\mathrm{T}}/(4N_{\mathrm{P}})$)
B	m	Baffle spacing
C	m	Clearance between adjacent tubes (see Figure 12.7)
C_{L}		Tube layout constant
C_{TP}		Tube count calculation constant
D_{e}	m	Equivalent diameter of shell
D_{s}	m	Shell inside diameter
F		Log mean temperature difference (LMTD)-correction factor for counter-flow arrangements

TABLE 12.2 (*Continued*)

Symbol	Units	Description
L	m	Tube length
N_b		Number of baffles (Integer(L/B))
N_T		Number of tubes
N_p		Number of tube passes
P_T	m	Pitch size (see Figure 12.7)
P_P	W	Pumping power of fluid in tubes
Pr		Prandtl number
Q	W	Heat-transfer rate
R_{fo}	(m² K)/W	Fouling resistance on outside of tube
R_{fi}	(m² K)/W	Fouling resistance on inside of tube
Re_b		Reynolds number at T_b
Re_s		Shell-side Reynolds number at T_b
ΔT_m	°C, K	LMTD
T_{h_1}	°C, K	Inlet temperature of hot fluid
T_{h_2}	°C, K	Outlet temperature of hot fluid
T_{c_1}	°C, K	Inlet temperature of cold fluid
T_{c_2}	°C, K	Outlet temperature of cold fluid
T_b	°C, K	Bulk temperature
T_w	°C, K	Wall temperature
U	W/(m² K)	Average overall heat-transfer coefficient based on A
η_p		Pump efficiency ($0.80 \leq \eta_p \leq 0.85$)
ϕ_s		Viscosity correction factor
μ	kg/(s m)	Dynamic viscosity
μ_b	kg/(s m)	Dynamic viscosity at T_b
μ_w	kg/(s m)	Dynamic viscosity at T_w
ρ	kg/m³	Density

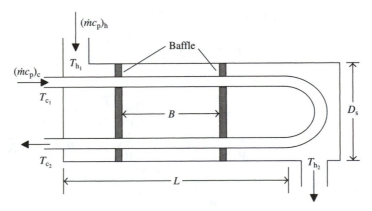

Note: The choice of which fluid to place on the shell side is arbitrary and is usually governed by other design considerations.

Figure 12.6 Typical one-shell, two-tube-pass, heat exchanger arrangement.

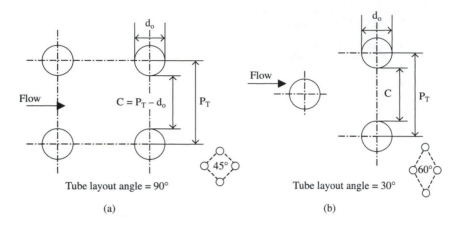

Figure 12.7 Two-tube layouts: (a) layout angle equals 90°; (b) layout angle equal 30°.

where the subscript 1 denotes the temperature of the fluid entering, the subscript 2 denotes the temperature of the fluid leaving, the subscript h denotes the hot fluid, and the subscript c denotes the cold fluid, and

$$\Delta T_{\mathrm{m}} = \frac{\Delta T_1 - \Delta T_2}{\ln(\Delta T_1/\Delta T_2)}$$
$$\Delta T_1 = T_{h1} - T_{c2}$$
$$\Delta T_2 = T_{h2} - T_{c1}$$

is the log mean temperature difference, assuming a counter-flow arrangement.

For one-shell pass and two, four, ... tube passes[3]

$$F = R_s C_o \left[\log_{10} \frac{C_1 + R_s}{C_1 - R_s} \right]^{-1}$$

and for two-shell passes and four, eight, ... tube passes

$$F = 0.5 R_s C_o \left[\log_{10} \frac{C_1 + C_2 + R_s}{C_1 + C_2 - R_s} \right]^{-1}$$

where

$$R_s = \sqrt{R^2 + 1} \quad P = \frac{T_{c2} - T_{c1}}{T_{h1} - T_{c1}} \quad R = \frac{T_{h1} - T_{h2}}{T_{c2} - T_{c1}}$$
$$C_1 = \frac{2}{P} - 1 - R \quad C_2 = \frac{2}{P}\sqrt{(1 - P)(1 - PR)}$$
$$C_o = \frac{1}{R - 1}\log_{10}\frac{1 - P}{1 - PR} \quad R \neq 1$$
$$= \frac{P}{2.3(1 - P)} \quad R = 1$$

[3]R. A. Bowman, A. C. Mueller, and W. M. Nagle, "Mean Temperature Difference in Design," *Transaction of American Society of Mechanical Engineers*, Vol. 62, May, 1940, pp. 283–293.

The overall heat-transfer coefficient U is given by

$$U = \left[\frac{d_o}{d_i}\frac{1}{h_i} + \frac{d_o}{d_i}R_{fi} + \frac{d_o}{2k_{tube}}\ln\frac{d_o}{d_i} + R_{fo} + \frac{1}{h_o} \right]^{-1}$$

The value of the heat-transfer coefficient inside the tube is approximated from

$$h_i = \frac{k}{d_i}Nu_b$$

where, for fully developed, turbulent forced convection through a circular pipe with constant properties,[4]

$$Nu_b = \frac{0.125f(Re_b - 1000)Pr_b}{1 + 12.7\sqrt{0.125f}((Pr_b)^{2/3} - 1)} \quad 0.5 < Pr_b < 2000 \quad 3000 < Re_b < 5 \times 10^6$$

The subscript b indicates that the quantities are evaluated at the average temperature of the fluid inside the pipe, which is called the bulk temperature.

The quantity f is the friction factor for flow in smooth pipes given by

$$f = (0.790 \ln Re_b - 1.64)^{-2} \quad 3000 \le Re_b \le 10^6$$

For rough tubes, the results of Exercise 5.19 are used with $\lambda = f$.

The Reynolds number Re_b is given by

$$Re_b = \frac{\rho u_t d_i}{\mu} = \frac{4\dot{m}_t}{\pi d_i \mu N_T/N_P}$$

since

$$u_t = \dot{m}_t/(0.25\rho\pi d_i^2 N_T/N_p)$$

and Pr_b is the Prandtl number given by

$$Pr_b = \frac{c_p \mu}{k}$$

The shell-side heat-transfer coefficient is estimated from

$$h_o = 0.36\frac{k\phi_s}{D_e}(Re_s)^{0.55}(Pr)^{1/3} \quad 2000 < Re_s < 10^6$$

$$\phi_s = \left(\frac{\mu_b}{\mu_w}\right)^{0.14} \quad T_w = (T_{c1} + T_{c2} + T_{h1} + T_{h2})/4$$

---

[4]F. P. Incropera and D. P. DeWitt, *ibid.*, p. 424.

where the quantities are evaluated at the average temperature of the shell-side fluid, except for ϕ_s, where μ_w is evaluated at T_w. The equivalent diameter D_e of the shell with tubes laid out on a square pitch, as shown in Figure 12.7, is given by

$$D_e = 4(P_T^2 - \pi d_0^2/4)/\pi d_o$$

and for tubes on a triangular pitch by

$$D_e = 8\left(P_T^2\sqrt{3}/4 - \pi d_0^2/8\right)/\pi d_o$$

The shell-side Reynolds number Re_s is given by

$$\mathrm{Re}_s = \frac{\dot{m}_s D_e}{A_s \mu}$$

$$A_s = 1.128 C B \sqrt{\frac{N_T C_L}{C_{TP}}} = \frac{D_s C B}{P_T}$$

where D_s is the shell inside diameter given by

$$D_s = 1.128 P_T \sqrt{\frac{N_T C_L}{C_{TP}}}$$

Suggested values for C_{TP} are

> One-tube pass ($N_P = 1$): $C_{TP} = 0.93$
> Two-tube pass ($N_P = 2$): $C_{TP} = 0.90$
> Three-tube pass ($N_P = 3$): $C_{TP} = 0.85$

and for C_L (see Figure 12.7)

$C_L = 1$ for 90° and 45°
$C_L = 0.87$ for 30° and 60°

There are standard tube layout tables that tabulate the number of tubes (N_T) that are used with a given shell inside diameter (D_s) as a function of the tube outside diameter (d_o), tube pitch (square or triangular), and number of tube passes (N_P).[5] Therefore, the appropriate results from the numerical calculations are usually adjusted to assume a value nearest to these standard values.

The shell-side pressure drop is given by

$$\Delta p_s = \frac{f_s \dot{m}_s^2 (N_b + 1) D_s}{2 A_s^2 \rho D_e \phi_s}$$

where

$$f_s = \exp(0.576 - 0.19 \ln \mathrm{Re}_s)$$

---

[5]See, for example, S. Kakaç and H. Liu, *Heat Exchangers: Selection, Rating, and Thermal Design*, CRC Press, Boca Raton, FL, 1998, pp. 258–261.

and the properties are evaluated at T_b. The tube-side pressure drop is given by

$$\Delta p_t = f\left(\frac{LN_p}{d_i}\right)\left(\frac{\rho u_t^2}{2}\right)$$

where the properties are evaluated at T_b and the effects of any tube bends have been neglected, which is a good assumption for low-speed flow of liquids.

The pumping power is

$$P_P = \frac{\dot{m}_t \Delta p_t}{\rho \eta_p}$$

We now illustrate these results with an example.

Example 12.4   Determining tube length and pressure drops in a heat exchanger

A preliminary analysis is performed to size a one-shell, two-pass, water-to-water heat exchanger to remove approximately 800 kW. Cold water is in the tubes, and the hot water is on the shell side. The results of the preliminary analysis are summarized in Table 12.3. The objective is to determine whether the length of the heat exchanger is less than 4.5 m and that both the shell-side and tube-side pressure drops are less than 4000 Pa. Rearrangement of several of the preceding equations results in the following equations that govern this analysis:

$$T_{h_2} = T_{h_1} - \frac{(\dot{m}c_p)_t}{(\dot{m}c_p)_s}(T_{c_2} - T_{c_1})$$

$$\Delta p_t = C_o \frac{f\dot{m}_t^3}{UFAT_m}$$

$$\Delta p_s = \frac{f_s \dot{m}_s^2 (N_b + 1) D_s}{2A_s^2 \rho D_e \phi_s}$$

$$L = \frac{(\dot{m}c_p)_t (T_{c_2} - T_{c_1})}{\pi d_o N_T UFAT_m}$$

TABLE 12.3   Parameters from a Preliminary Analysis of a Heat Exchanger

Geometric	Physical
$D_s = 0.39$ m	$T_{c_1} = 18°C$
$N_T = 124$	$T_{c_2} = 42°C$
$N_P = 2$	$T_{h_1} = 65°C$
$P_T = 0.024$ m	$\dot{m}_s = \dot{m}_h = 14$ kg/s
$B = 0.5$ m	$\dot{m}_t = \dot{m}_c = 8.5$ kg/s
$N_b = 4$	$R_{fi} = 0.00015$
$d_i = 16$ mm (0.016 m)	$R_{fo} = 0.00015$
$d_o = 19$ mm (0.019 m)	
$k_{tube} = 60$ W/m^2 K (carbon steel)	
90° tube layout	
Tubes are on a square pitch	
Tubes are smooth	

TABLE 12.4   Sub Functions for Example 12.1

Function name	Purpose
LMTDcorrFacto	Computes F
TubeFF	Computes f for smooth pipes
WaterProperties	Computes k, ρ, μ, c_p, and Pr at a temperature between 0° and 100°C, based on the data in Table 12.5
LMTD	Computes the LMTD
hTubeOutside	Computes h_o and Δp_s
hTubeInside	Computes h_i
PressureDropLength	Computes Δp_t and L
T2HotSide	Computes T_{h_2} using `fzero`

TABLE 12.5   Thermophysical Properties of Water

T (K)	k (W/m K)	ρ (kg/m^3)	μ (N s/m^2)	c_p(J/kg K)	Pr
273	0.569	1000.0	1750×10^{-6}	4217	12.99
285	0.590	1000.0	1225×10^{-6}	4189	8.81
300	0.613	998.0	855×10^{-6}	4179	5.83
315	0.634	991.1	631×10^{-6}	4179	4.16
330	0.650	984.3	489×10^{-6}	4184	3.15
345	0.668	976.6	389×10^{-6}	4191	2.45
360	0.674	967.1	324×10^{-6}	4203	2.02
373	0.680	957.9	279×10^{-6}	4217	1.76

where

$$C_o = \frac{N_P(T_{c_2} - T_{c_1})(c_p)_t}{2\pi d_i d_o N_T \rho_t A_t^2}$$

$$A_t = \frac{\pi d_i^2}{4}\frac{N_T}{N_P}$$

The solution is implemented with the function **HeatExchanger**, which contains the eight subfunctions listed in Table 12.4. The thermophysical properties of water are obtained from the data given in Table 12.5.

```
function HeatExchanger
global Tc1 Tc2 Th1 ms mt
global Ds C B PT pitch
global NP NT
global di do kTube Rfi Rfo Nb
Ds = 0.39; NT = 124; NP = 2; B = 0.5; PT = 0.024;
di = 0.016; do = 0.019; kTube = 60;
Rfi = 0.00015; Rfo = 0.00015;
pitch = 'square'; C = PT-do; ms = 14; mt = 8.5;
Tc1 = 18; Tc2 = 42; Th1 = 65; Nb = 4;
```

```
options = optimset('Display', 'off');
Th2 = fzero(@T2HotSide, Th1+15, options);
[DeltaPt, DeltaPs, L] = PressureDropLength(Th2);
disp(['Shell-side exit temperature = ' num2str(Th2) ' deg C'])
disp(['Tube-side pressure drop = ' num2str(DeltaPt) ' Pa'])
disp(['Shell-side pressure drop = ' num2str(DeltaPs) ' Pa'])
disp(['Tube length = ' num2str(L) ' m'])

function F = LMTDcorrFactor(Th2)
global Tc1 Tc2 Th1 ms mt
global NP NT
P = (Tc2-Tc1)/(Th1-Tc1);
R = (Th1-Th2)/(Tc2-Tc1);
C1 = 2/P-1-R;
C2 = 2*sqrt((1-P)*(1-P*R))/P;
Rs = sqrt(R^2+1);
if R == 1
    Co = P/2.3/(1-P);
else
    Co = log10((1-P)/(1-P*R))/(R-1);
end
if NP == 1
    F = Rs*Co/log10((C1+Rs)/( C1-Rs));
else
    F = 0.5*Rs*Co/log10((C1+C2+Rs)/( C1+C2-Rs));
end

function f = TubeFF (Re)
f = 1/(0.79*log(Re)-1.64)^2;

function [cp, mu, k, rho, Pr] = WaterProperties(Temp)
Temp = Temp+273;
T = [273, 285, 300, 315, 330, 345, 360, 373];
cpp = [4217, 4189, 4179, 4179, 4184, 4191, 4203, 4217];
muu = [1750, 1225, 855, 631, 489, 389, 324, 279]*1e-6;
kk = [569, 590, 613, 634, 650, 668, 674, 680]*0.001;
rhoo = [1000, 1000, 998, 991.1, 984.3, 976.6, 967.1, 957.9];
Prr = [12.99, 8.81, 5.83, 4.16, 3.15, 2.45, 2.02, 1.76];
cp = spline(T, cpp, Temp);
mu = spline(T, muu, Temp);
k = spline(T, kk, Temp);
rho = spline(T, rhoo, Temp);
Pr = spline(T, Prr, Temp);

function Tm = LMTD(Th2)
global Tc1 Tc2 Th1 ms mt
DT1 = Th1-Tc2;
DT2 = Th2-Tc1;
Tm = (DT1-DT2)/log(DT1/DT2);

function hi = hTubeInside(Reb, Prb, kb)
global di do kTube Rfi Rfo Nb
```

```
f = TubeFF(Reb);
Nub = 0.125*f*(Reb-1000)*Prb/(1+12.7*sqrt(0.125*f)*(Prb^(2/3)-1));
hi = Nub*kb/di;

function [ho, DeltaPs] = hTubeOutside(Tb, Tw)
global Ds C B PT pitch
global di do kTube Rfi Rfo Nb
global Tc1 Tc2 Th1 ms mt
[cpb, mub, kb, rhob, Prb] = WaterProperties(Tb);
[cpw, muw, kw, rhow, Prw] = WaterProperties(Tw);
phis = (mub/muw)^0.14;
if pitch == 'square'
   De = 4*(PT^2-pi*do^2/4)/pi/do;
else
   De = 8*(PT^(sqrt(3)/4)-pi*do^2/8)/pi/do;
end
As = Ds*C*B/PT;
Res = ms*De/mub/As;
ho = 0.36*kb*phis*Res^0.55*Prb^(1/3)/De;
fs = exp(0.576-0.19*log(Res));
DeltaPs = fs*ms^2*(Nb+1)*Ds/(2*As^2*rhob*De*phis);

function Th = T2HotSide(Th2)
global Tc1 Tc2 Th1 ms mt
cph = WaterProperties((Th2+Th1)/2);
cpc = WaterProperties((Tc1+Tc2)/2);
Th = Th1-mt*cpc*(Tc2-Tc1)/ms/cph-Th2;

function [DeltaPt, DeltaPs, L] = PressureDropLength(Th2)
global Tc1 Tc2 Th1 ms mt
global Ds C B PT pitch
global NP NT
global di do kTube Rfi Rfo Nb
Tcb = (Tc1+Tc2)/2;
[cpc, muc, kc, rhoc, Prc] = WaterProperties(Tcb);
[cph, muh, kh, rhoh, Prh] = WaterProperties((Th1+Th2)/2);
Th2 = Th1-mt*cpc*(Tc2-Tc1)/ms/cph;
Thb = (Th1+Th2)/2;
At = 0.25*pi*di^2*NT/NP;
Co = 2*NP*(Tc2-Tc1)*cpc/pi/di/do/NT/rhoc/At^2;
Tm = LMTD(Th2);
F = LMTDcorrFactor(Th2);
Tw = (Th1+Th2+Tc1+Tc2)/4;
[ho, DeltaPs] = hTubeOutside(Thb, Tw);
Rec = 4*mt*NP/pi/di/muc/NT;
hi = hTubeInside(Rec,Prc,kc);
U = 1/(do/di/hi+do*Rfi/di+do/2/kTube*log(do/di)+Rfo+1/ho);
f = TubeFF(Rec);
DeltaPt = Co*f*mt^3/U/F/Tm;
Q = mt*cpc*(Tc2-Tc1);
L=Q/pi/do/NT/U/F/Tm;
```

Execution of the script displays the following results to the command window:

```
Shell-side exit temperature = 50.45 deg C
Tube-side pressure drop = 14274.54 Pa
Shell-side pressure drop = 1799.40 Pa
Tube length = 4.232 m
```

We see that the tube-side pressure drop exceeds our design limits.

12.3 CONVECTION HEAT TRANSFER

12.3.1 Thermal Boundary Layer on a Flat Plate—Similarity Solution

The determination of the velocity profiles for laminar boundary layer flow over the flat plate shown in Figure 12.8 is obtained from the solution of the following Blasius equation[6]:

$$\frac{d^3f}{d\eta^3} + \frac{f}{2}\frac{d^2f}{d\eta^2} = 0$$

where f is a modified stream function

$$f = \frac{\psi}{u_\infty\sqrt{v_{vis}x/u_\infty}}$$

The stream function ψ is defined such that

$$u = \partial\psi/\partial y$$
$$v = -\partial\psi/\partial x$$

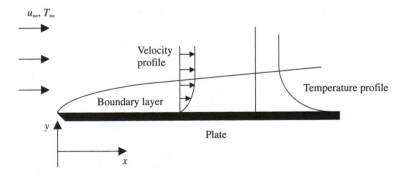

Figure 12.8   Flow over a flat plate.

---

[6]F. P. Incropera and D. P. DeWitt, *ibid.*, pp. 350–352.

where u and v are the velocities in the x- and y-directions, respectively, and η is the similarity variable

$$\eta = y\sqrt{u_\infty/v_{vis}x}$$

The free stream velocity is u_∞, and v_{vis} is the kinematic viscosity of the fluid. Solution of the Blasius equation gives the velocity at any location within the boundary layer. A numerical solution of the Blasius equation is described in Section 11.3.2.

Under conditions of constant fluid properties and certain boundary layer assumptions, the thermal energy equation for the fluid can be expressed in terms of the similarity variable as[7]

$$\frac{d^2T^*}{d\eta^2} + \text{Pr}\frac{f}{2}\frac{dT^*}{d\eta} = 0$$

where T^* is the dimensionless temperature

$$T^* = \frac{T - T_s}{T_\infty - T_s}$$

T is the fluid temperature, T_s is the plate surface temperature, T_∞ is the fluid free stream temperature, and the Prandtl number is $\text{Pr} = v_{vis}/\alpha$, where α is the thermal diffusivity of the fluid. Note that T^* is coupled to the velocity solution through the presence of f in the energy equation.

The boundary conditions are

$$f(0) = 0 \quad \frac{df}{d\eta}\bigg|_{\eta=0} = 0 \quad \frac{df}{d\eta}\bigg|_{\eta\to\infty} \to 1$$
$$T^*(0) = 0 \quad T^*(\eta\to\infty) \to 1$$

Example 12.5   Flow over a flat plate: Blasius formulation

We shall obtain a solution to the Blasius formulation of flow over a flat plate for $\text{Pr} = 0.07$, 0.7, and 7.0. The solution is obtained with bvp4c, with the boundary conditions at $\eta\to\infty$ being approximated by assuming a large value for η called η_{max}. The two coupled nonlinear equations are decomposed into a set of five coupled first-order ordinary differential equations by introducing the following set of dependent variables:

$$y_1 = f \quad\quad y_4 = T^*$$
$$y_2 = \frac{df}{d\eta} \quad y_5 = \frac{dT^*}{d\eta}$$
$$y_3 = \frac{d^2f}{d\eta^2}$$

---

[7]F. P. Incropera and D. P. DeWitt, *ibid.*

where y_1 represents the stream function, y_2 the velocity, y_3 the shear, y_4 the temperature, and y_5 the heat flux. These quantities are governed by the five first-order differential equations

$$\frac{dy_1}{d\eta} = y_2 \qquad \frac{dy_4}{d\eta} = y_5$$

$$\frac{dy_2}{d\eta} = y_3 \qquad \frac{dy_5}{d\eta} = -\frac{\mathrm{Pr}}{2} y_1 y_5$$

$$\frac{dy_3}{d\eta} = -\frac{1}{2} y_1 y_3$$

with the corresponding boundary conditions

$$y_1(0) = 0 \qquad y_4(\eta \to \infty) \to 1$$
$$y_2(0) = 0 \qquad y_4(0) = 0$$
$$y_2(\eta \to \infty) \to 1$$

We create a main function **BlasiusX**, which includes two sub functions that support bvp4c. The function **BlasiusT** defines the five first-order differential equations,
and the function **BlasiusTbc** defines the boundary conditions. To approximate $\eta \to \infty$,
we use a value of $\eta_{max} = 8$ for $\mathrm{Pr} = 0.7$ and 7.0 and a value of $\eta_{max} = 20$ for $\mathrm{Pr} = 0.07$.

```
function BlasiusX
Pr = [0.07, 0.7, 7.0]; etaMax = [15, 8, 8]; xm = [15, 5, 5];
for k=1:3
   figure(k)
   solinit = bvpinit(linspace(0, etaMax(k), 8), [0, 0, 0, 0, 0]);
   sol = bvp4c(@BlasiusT, @BlasiusTbc, solinit, [], Pr(k));
   eta = linspace(0, etaMax(k));
   y = deval(sol, eta);
   subplot(2, 1, 1)
   plot(eta, y(1,:), '-.k', eta, y(2,:), '-k', eta, y(3,:), '--k')
   xlabel('\eta')
   ylabel('y_i (i = 1, 2, 3)')
   legend('Stream function, f = y_1', 'Velocity, df/d\eta = y_2',
      'Shear, d_2f/d\eta_2 = y_3')
    axis([0 xm(k) 0 2])
   subplot(2, 1, 2)
   plot(eta, y(4,:), '-k', eta, y(5,:), '--k')
   axis([0 xm(k) 0 2])
   legend('Temperature, T_^* = y_4', 'Heat flux, dT_^*/d\eta = y_5')
   xlabel('\eta')
   ylabel('y_i (i = 4, 5)')
end

function F = BlasiusT(eta, y, Pr)
F = [y(2);  y(3); -0.5*y(1)*y(3); y(5); -Pr*0.5*y(1)*y(5)];

function res = BlasiusTbc(ya, yb, Pr)
res = [ya(1); ya(2); ya(4); yb(2)-1; yb(4)-1];
```

The results from executing this script are shown in Figures 12.9 to 12.11.

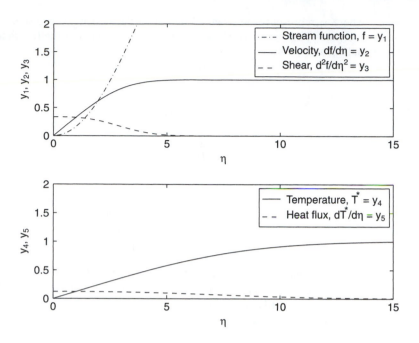

Figure 12.9   Extended Blasius solution for Pr $= 0.07$.

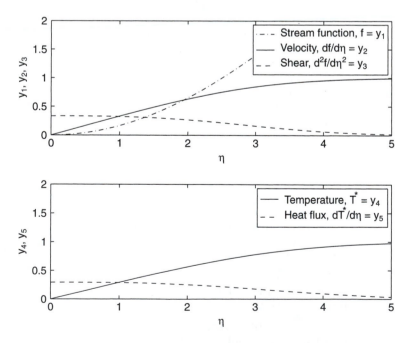

Figure 12.10   Extended Blasius solution for Pr $= 0.7$.

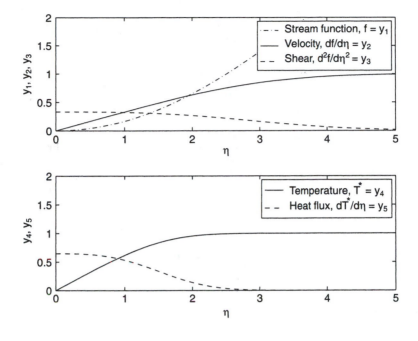

Figure 12.11   Extended Blasius solution for Pr = 7.

12.3.2 Natural Convection Similarity Solution

Natural convection along a heated vertical plate in contact with a cooler fluid is shown in Figure 12.12. The bulk fluid is quiescent, but the heat transfer from the plate causes buoyancy-driven flow. This flow is described by the following two coupled nonlinear ordinary differential equations[8]

$$\frac{d^3 f}{d\eta^3} + 3f\frac{d^2 f}{d\eta^2} - 2\left(\frac{df}{d\eta}\right)^2 + T^* = 0$$

$$\frac{d^{2*}T^*}{d\eta^2} + 3\,\mathrm{Pr}\,f\frac{dT^*}{d\eta} = 0$$

where f is the modified stream function

$$f = \frac{\psi}{4v_{vis}(Gr_x/4)^{0.25}}$$

The stream function ψ is defined such that

$$u = \partial\psi/\partial y$$
$$v = -\partial\psi/\partial x$$

---

[8]F. P. Incropera and D. P. DeWitt, *ibid.*, pp. 487–490.

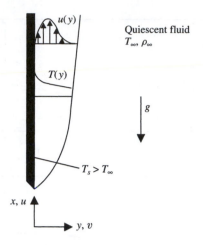

Figure 12.12   Natural convection
plume along a heated plate.

where u and v are the velocities in the x- and y-directions, respectively. The quantity η is the similarity variable

$$\eta = \frac{y}{x}\left(\frac{Gr_x}{4}\right)^{0.25}$$

defined in terms of the Grashof number

$$Gr_x = g\beta(T_s - T_\infty)x^3/v_{vis}^2$$

where g is the acceleration of gravity, β is the coefficient of thermal expansion

$$\beta = \frac{-1}{\rho}\left(\frac{\partial\rho}{\partial T}\right)_p$$

and v_{vis} is the kinematic viscosity. The quantity Pr is the Prandtl number defined previously, and the quantity T^* is the dimensionless temperature given by

$$T^* = \frac{T - T_\infty}{T_s - T_\infty}$$

The boundary conditions for this system are

$\eta = 0$:

$$f = 0, \quad \frac{df}{d\eta} = 0, \quad T^* = 1$$

$\eta \rightarrow \infty$:

$$\frac{df}{d\eta} \rightarrow 0 \quad T^* \rightarrow 0$$

This system can be decomposed into a system of five first-order equations by introducing the following set of dependent variables:

$$y_1 = f \qquad y_4 = T^*$$
$$y_2 = \frac{df}{d\eta} \qquad y_5 = \frac{dT^*}{d\eta}$$
$$y_3 = \frac{d^2f}{d\eta^2}$$

The differential equations in terms of these new variables are

$$\frac{dy_1}{d\eta} = y_2 \qquad \frac{dy_4}{d\eta} = y_5$$
$$\frac{dy_2}{d\eta} = y_3 \qquad \frac{dy_5}{d\eta} = -3\,\text{Pr}\,y_1 y_5$$
$$\frac{dy_3}{d\eta} = 2y_2^2 - 3y_1 y_3 - y_4$$

The corresponding boundary conditions are

$$y_1(0) = 0 \qquad y_4(0) = 1$$
$$y_2(0) = 0 \qquad y_4(\eta \rightarrow \infty) \rightarrow 0$$
$$y_2(\eta \rightarrow \infty) \rightarrow 0$$

Example 12.6   Natural convection along a heated plate

We shall obtain a solution to the system of equations describing natural convection along a heated plate for $\text{Pr} = 0.07, 0.7$, and 7.0. The value of η that is used to approximate the condition as $\eta \rightarrow \infty$ is denoted η_{max}. The appropriate value of η_{max} depends on the Prandtl number, with larger Prandtl numbers requiring smaller values of η_{max}. A reasonably accurate solution is found when the solution becomes independent of the choice of η_{max}. In this case, η_{max} was set equal to 8 for $\text{Pr} = 0.7$ and 7 and equal to 11 for $\text{Pr} = 0.07$.

To solve this boundary value problem, we use bvp4c, which requires two functions: **NaturalConv**, which defines the various coefficients in the five ordinary differential equations, and **NaturalConvbc** which defines the boundary conditions. The main function and subfunctions to obtain the solution are given below:

```
function NaturalConvection
Pr = [.07 .7 7]; eta_max = [11 8 8]; xm = [10 5 5]; ym = [2 0.8 0.5];
guess = [0 0 0 0 0];
    for k = 1:3
        figure(k);;
        solinit = bvpinit(linspace(0, eta_max(k), 5), guess);
        sol = bvp4c(@NatConv, @NatConvBC, solinit, [], Pr(k));
        eta = linspace(0, eta_max(k), 300);
        y = deval(sol, eta);
```

```
subplot(2, 1, 1)
plot(eta, y(1,:), '-.k', eta, y(2,:), eta, y(3,:), '--k')
legend('Stream function, f = y_1', 'Velocity, df/d\eta = y_2,',
   'Shear d_2f/d\eta_2 = y_3, ')
axis([0 xm(k) -0.2 ym(k)])
xlabel('\eta')
ylabel('y_1, y_2, y_3')
subplot(2, 1, 2)
plot(eta, y(4,:), '-k', eta, y(5,:), '--k')
legend('Temperature, T_^* = y_4', 'Heat flux, dT_^*/d\eta = y_5')
axis([0 xm(k) -1.2 1])
xlabel('\eta')
ylabel('y_4, y_5')
end

function ff = NatConv(eta, y, Pr)
ff = [y(2); y(3); -3*y(1)*y(3)+2*y(2)^2-y(4); y(5); -3*Pr*y(1)*y(5)];

function res = NatConvBC(ya, yb, Pr)
res = [ya(1); ya(2); ya(4)-1; yb(2); yb(4)];
```

The results of the execution of this script are shown in Figures 12.13 through 12.15. Referring to these figures, which are for Prandtl numbers 0.07, 0.7, and 7.0, respectively, we see that in all three cases, there is a wall plume where the velocity

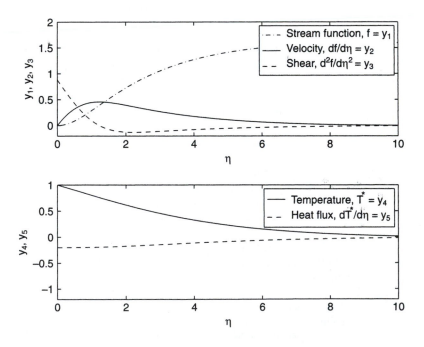

Figure 12.13   Natural convection solution for Pr = 0.07.

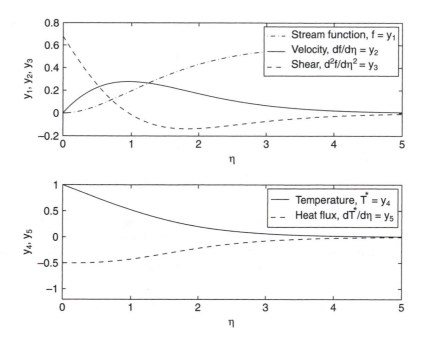

Figure 12.14   Natural convection solution for Pr = 0.7.

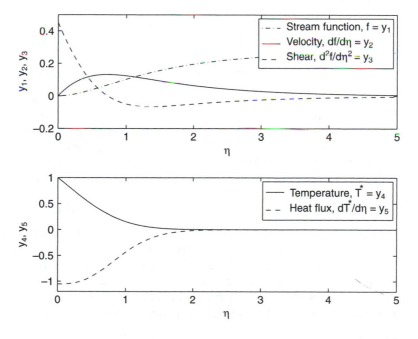

Figure 12.15   Natural convection solution for Pr = 7.

attains a maximum around a value of $\eta = 1$. The shear stress in the fluid in a direction parallel to the wall is

$$\tau_s = \frac{\sqrt{2}v^2\rho}{x^2} Gr_x^{3/4} \frac{d^2f}{d\eta^2}$$

which goes to zero at the location where the velocity is maximum.

The thermal effects drive the flow. As a result, for a thermally driven wall plume, the velocity boundary layer thickness is never less than the temperature boundary layer thickness. This is different from the result obtained for the corresponding case for forced flow over a flat plate in Section 12.3.1, where the thickness of the velocity boundary layer is much less than the thickness of the temperature boundary layer for the case $Pr = 0.07$.

The maximum value of the stream function is a measure of the pumping action provided by the heating of the fluid, which is a strong function of Pr. High values of Pr yield low values of the modified stream function f. The maximum value of the modified stream function is related to the total volumetric flow rate in the plume. However, to interpret this for a particular fluid, one must compute the dimensional stream function using

$$\psi(x, y) = 4f(\eta)v\left(\frac{Gr_x}{4}\right)^{0.25}$$

When this is done, it is found that the volumetric flow rate for air, at the same temperature difference, is significantly greater than it is for water.

Since the flow carries energy away from the surface, a similar analysis is of interest for the heat flux, which is determined from

$$q_s'' = -\frac{k(T_s - T_\infty)}{x}\left(\frac{Gr_x}{4}\right)^{0.25}\frac{dT^*}{d\eta}\bigg|_{\eta=0}$$

When the heat flux is computed for both air and water, it is found that the heat flux for water is on the order of 100 times greater than that for air. This is primarily because of the roles of thermal conductivity, specific heat, and density, which determine the magnitude of the heat flux. At atmospheric pressure and 300 K, the thermal conductivity is approximately 30 times greater for water as compared with that for air, the specific heat is 4 times greater, and the density is 1000 times greater. Thus, even though the volumetric flow rate in the plume is larger for air, the heat flux is larger for water.

12.3.3 Temperature Distribution in a Printed Circuit Board[9]

Consider the printed circuit board shown in Figure 12.16, on which four electronic devices that are flush-mounted and that dissipate energy in the amounts indicated. The board is mounted in a rack such that the y-axis is vertical. In such situations, the heat-transfer coefficient h varies in the y-direction. To simplify the model somewhat, we assume that the heat-transfer coefficient is constant in the x-direction. To approximate the variation of the heat-transfer coefficient in the y-direction, the

---

[9]Topic suggested by Professor Yogendra Joshi, Department of Mechanical Engineering, Georgia Institute of Technology, Atlanta, GA.

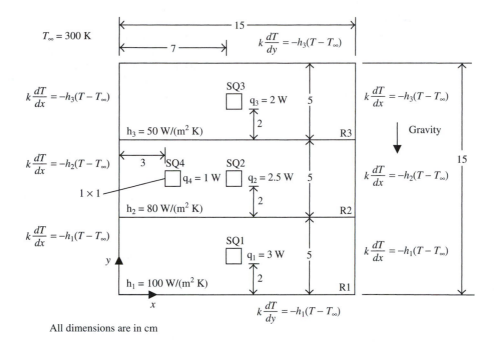

Figure 12.16   Geometry and constants describing a printed circuit board.

board is considered to be composed of three equal-sized contiguous boards, each having different heat-transfer coefficients, as shown in Figure 12.16. However, the thermal conductivity k of the boards and components is assumed to be the same and independent of location. For simplification, it is also assumed that the four heating elements have the same thermal conductivity as the board on which they are placed.

The governing equation for each of the three boards and electronic components is

$$\nabla(k\nabla T) + q''' - H(T - T_\infty) = 0$$

where q''' is the power per unit volume of the heat source (W/m^3), $H = 2h/t$ $(\text{W/m}^3\,\text{K})$, t is the thickness of the board, and T_∞ is the ambient temperature of the surroundings. The factor of 2 in the definition of H is because the heat is convected from both sides of the board.

Example 12.7   Temperature and flux determination in a printed circuit board

We shall determine an estimate of the temperature distribution throughout the board using the PDE Toolbox. First, we create the appropriate drawing environment by going to the *Options* menu and setting the *Axis Limits* to [0 17] with the grid spacing of 1 for both axes and then selecting *Snap*. Next, we change *Generic Scalar* to *Heat Transfer*. Then, we draw three rectangles and four squares with the dimensions and locations shown in Figure 12.16. This results in the set formula $R1 + R2 + R3 + SQ1 + SQ2 + SQ3 + SQ4$. Each of these regions will be governed by the heat-conduction equation. However, we have to specify boundary conditions only for the edges of the rectangular regions indicated in Table 12.6. This is because the combination of the plus (+) signs in the set formula and the fact that each SQn resides completely within a previously defined region (Rn) indicates to the PDE tool that no new boundaries have been created. Notice that the units for $k, h,$ and Q are W/(cm K), W/(cm^2 K), and W/cm^3, respectively, to be consistent with the units of the dimensions of the board.

Next, we go the *Boundary Mode* and then *Specify Boundary Conditions*. The boundary conditions on the edges that are indicated in Table 12.6 are each of the Neumann type. These boundaries appear as red lines terminated by an arrowhead. After double-clicking each line, the values given in Table 12.6 are entered in the appropriate places. Then *PDE Mode* is selected. Placing the cursor in one of the seven regions and double-clicking brings up the *PDE Specification* window. In each of the seven appearances of this window, the appropriate values from Table 12.6 are entered.

The mesh is initialized and refined once. Then, the solution is obtained, and both the temperature distribution and the heat flux are plotted. The results are shown in Figures 12.17 and 12.18, respectively.

TABLE 12.6   Numerical Values Used in the Description of the Printed Circuit Board and Their Corresponding pdetool Notation

	Region						
	$R1$	$R2$	$R3$	$SQ1$	$SQ2$	$SQ3$	$SQ4$
Boundary Conditions							
Left							
$\quad g \rightarrow hT_\infty$ (W/cm^2)	3	2.4	1.5	—	—	—	—
$\quad q \rightarrow h$ (W/cm^2 K)	0.01	0.008	0.005	—	—	—	—
Right							
$\quad g \rightarrow hT_\infty$ (W/cm^2)	3	2.4	1.5	—	—	—	—
$\quad q \rightarrow h$ (W/cm^2 K)	0.01	0.008	0.005	—	—	—	—
Top							
$\quad g \rightarrow hT_\infty$ (W/cm^2)	—	—	1.5	—	—	—	—
$\quad q \rightarrow h$ (W/cm^2 K)	—	—	0.005	—	—	—	—
Bottom							
$\quad g \rightarrow hT_\infty$ (W/cm^2)	3	—	—	—	—	—	—
$\quad q \rightarrow h$ (W/cm^2 K)	0.01	—	—	—	—	—	—
PDE Specification							
$\quad k \rightarrow k$ (W/cm K)	0.003	0.003	0.003	0.003	0.003	0.003	0.003
$\quad Q \rightarrow Q$ (W/cm^3)	0	0	0	30	25	20	10
$\quad h \rightarrow H$ (W/cm^3 K)	0.1	0.08	0.05	0.1	0.08	0.05	0.08
$\quad Text \rightarrow T_\infty$ (K)	300	300	300	300	300	300	300

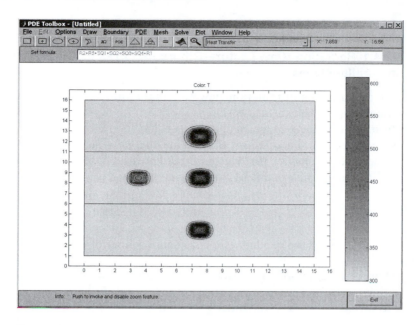

Figure 12.17 Temperature distribution in the printed circuit board shown in Figure 12.16.

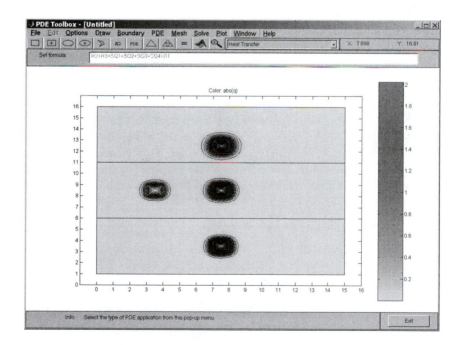

Figure 12.18 Heat flux in the printed circuit board shown in Figure 12.16.

12.4 RADIATION HEAT TRANSFER

12.4.1 Radiation View Factor—Differential Area to Arbitrary Rectangle in Parallel Planes

The computation of radiation view factors is required when analyzing the radiation in enclosures with diffuse surfaces. There are numerous techniques for evaluating these factors, many of which apply to specific geometries. A more general approach is to start from the relations that define the view factor and then integrate them numerically. Consider first the general expression[10] for the view factor between a differential area element dA_1 and a finite area A_2:

$$dF_{2-d_1} = \frac{dA_1}{A_2} \int_{A_2} \frac{\cos\theta_1 \cos\theta_2}{\pi S^2} dA_2 \qquad (12.2)$$

where S is the line-of-sight distance between dA_1 and some position on A_2 as shown in Figure 12.19. The angles θ_j, where $j = 1, 2$, are measured between the normal to the surface and S. The reciprocity relation for the view factors is

$$A_2 dF_{2-d_1} = dA_1 F_{d_1-2} \qquad (12.3)$$

Thus, F_{d_1-2} can be written as

$$F_{d_1-2} = \int_{A_2} \frac{\cos\theta_1 \cos\theta_2}{\pi S^2} dA_2 \qquad (12.4)$$

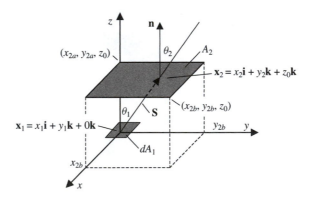

Figure 12.19 Geometry when the differential area and the finite rectangle are in parallel planes.

---

[10]R. Siegel and J. R. Howell, *Thermal Radiation Heat Transfer*, 3rd ed., Hemisphere Pub., Washington, DC, 1992, pp. 189–252.

We shall perform the integration numerically. Consider the case where dA_1 and A_2 are in parallel planes and A_2 is a rectangle. Both of these restrictions could be removed with additional programming effort. For this case, Eq. 12.4 can be written as

$$F_{d_1-2} = \frac{1}{\pi} \int_{y_{2a}}^{y_{2b}} \int_{x_{2a}}^{x_{2b}} \frac{\cos \theta_1 \cos \theta_2}{S^2} dx_2 dy_2$$

where the line-of-sight vector **S** is

$$\mathbf{S} = \mathbf{x}_2 - \mathbf{x}_1 = (x_2 - x_1)\mathbf{i} + (y_2 - y_1)\mathbf{j} + (z_2 - z_1)\mathbf{k}$$

and

$$S = |\mathbf{S}|$$

The angles can be expressed in terms of the line-of-sight vector and a normal vector to the rectangle $\mathbf{n} = \mathbf{k}$:

$$\cos \theta_1 = \cos \theta_2 = \frac{\mathbf{n} \cdot \mathbf{S}}{|\mathbf{S}|}$$

Since the two surfaces are parallel, $\theta_1 = \theta_2 = \theta$. Then,

$$F_{d_1-2} = \frac{1}{\pi} \int_{y_{2a}}^{y_{2b}} I_{x2}(y_2) dy_2 \qquad (12.5)$$

where

$$I_{x2}(y_2) = \int_{x_{2a}}^{x_{2b}} f(x_2, y_2) dx_2$$

and

$$f(x_2, y_2) = \frac{\cos^2 \theta}{|\mathbf{S}|^2} = \frac{(\mathbf{n} \cdot \mathbf{S})^2}{|\mathbf{S}|^4}$$

Example 12.8   View factor for a differential area and a finite rectangle in parallel planes

To illustrate the numerical integration of Eq. 12.5, we consider the two sets of data given in Table 12.7. In the first case, we shall obtain the view factors shown in the last row of the table. In the second case, we shall obtain a plot of the view factor for data set 1 as a function of the separation distance of the surfaces.

We create a main function called **Fd1_2** and a sub function called **kernel2** to define the kernel $f(x_2, y_2)$ at any location on surface A_2. The functions are given below. The function uses a vector-based formulation to determine the length S and $\cos \theta$. It is noted that for compatibility with dblquad, **kernel2** must return a vector whose length equals the length of the input vector x. This allows dblquad to minimize the number of calls to the integrand function while still providing the needed data.

TABLE 12.7   Example Configurations and View Factor Results

Parameter	Set 1	Set 2
Geometry of A_2		
$\quad$ x-Coordinate of first corner point, x_{2a}	-1	-1
$\quad$ y-Coordinate of first corner point, y_{2a}	-1	-1
$\quad$ x-Coordinate of opposite corner point, x_{2b}	0	1
$\quad$ y-Coordinate of opposite corner point, y_{2b}	0	1
Separation distance between planes, z_0	5	1
Computed view factor, F_{d_1-2}	0.0121	0.5541

This capability is implemented in **kernel2** by using `length` to determine the number of elements in *x:*

```
function F = Fd1_2(x_2a, x_2b, y_2a, y_2b, dz)
F = dblquad(@kernel2, x_2a, x_2b, y_2a, y_2b, [], [], dz)/pi;

function f = kernel2(x, y, dist)
L = length(x);
S = [x; linspace(y, y, length(x)); dist*ones(1, length(x))];
n = repmat([0, 0, 1]', 1, L);
f = dot(n, S).^2./dot(S, S).^2;
```

We now use these functions to evaluate the two data sets given in Table 12.7. The script is

```
Set1 = Fd1_2(-1, 0, -1, 0, 5)
Set2 = Fd1_2(-1, 1, -1, 1, 1)
```

which upon execution gives the results shown in the last row of Table 12.7.

Next, we plot the view factor as a function of the separation distance for data set 1 given in Table 12.7. The script is

```
x_2a = 0;  x_2b = 1;  y_2a = 0;  y_2b = 1;
dz = linspace(0.1, 5, 100);
for i = 1:length(dz)
    Fd12(i) = Fd1_2(x_2a, x_2b, y_2a, y_2b, dz(i));
end
plot(dz, Fd12, 'k-')
xlabel('Separation distance of surfaces')
ylabel('View factor')
```

which upon execution gives the result shown in Figure 12.20. It is interesting to note that F_{d_1-2} goes to a limiting value of 0.25 as the separation distance between the two parallel planes goes to zero. This is because the point dA_1 is aligned with one of the corners of the square area A_2. Thus, as the two parallel planes approach each other, A_2 cuts off one-quarter of the total hemispherical view from dA_1. In the geometry of data set 2, dA_1 is aligned with the center point of A_2, and the limiting value on F_{d_1-2} as the planes approach each other is 1.0.

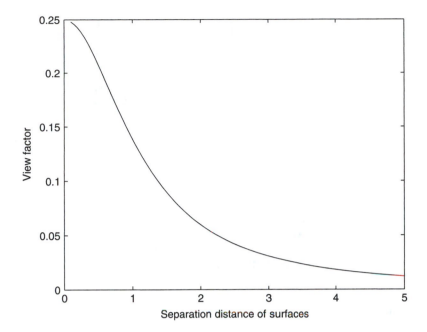

Figure 12.20   View factor versus separation distance between two parallel planes for the geometry shown in Figure 12.19. The areas are in parallel planes, and the differential area is aligned with a corner of the finite area.

12.4.2 View Factor Between Two Rectangles in Parallel Planes

The view factor computed previously was from an infinitesimal area to a finite area. The infinitesimal area can be integrated over a second finite area to obtain the view factor between two finite areas. The equation defining such a view factor is

$$
F_{2-1} = \frac{1}{\pi A_2} \int_{A_1} \int_{A_2} \frac{\cos \theta_1 \cos \theta_2}{S^2} dA_2 dA_1
$$

$$
= \frac{1}{\pi A_2} \int_{y_{1a}}^{y_{1b}} \int_{x_{1a}}^{x_{1b}} \int_{y_{2a}}^{y_{2b}} \int_{x_{2a}}^{x_{2b}} \frac{\cos \theta_1 \cos \theta_2}{S^2} dx_2 dy_2 dx_1 dy_1
$$

(12.6)

where the variables are defined in the previous section and those variables specific to this quadruple integral are defined in Figure 12.21. There are numerous methods to evaluate this integral. The approach used here is again direct integration. Since the two plates are in parallel planes and their edges are parallel, Eq. 12.6 can be written as

$$
F_{2-1} = \frac{1}{\pi A_2} \int_{y_{1a}}^{y_{1b}} I_{x1}(y_1) dy_1
$$

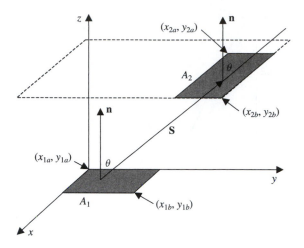

Figure 12.21   Geometry for the determination of the view factors between two finite rectangles in parallel planes.

where

$$I_{x1}(y_1) = \int_{x_{1a}}^{x_{1b}} I_{y2}(x_1, y_1)dx_1$$

$$I_{y2}(x_1, y_1) = \int_{y_{2a}}^{y_{2b}} I_{x2}(x_1, y_1, y_2)dy_2$$

$$I_{x2}(x_1, y_1, y_2) = \int_{x_{2a}}^{x_{2b}} f(x_1, y_1, x_2, y_2)dx_2$$

$$f(x_1, y_1, x_2, y_2) = \frac{\cos^2 \theta}{|\mathbf{S}|^2} = \frac{(\mathbf{n} \cdot \mathbf{s})^2}{|\mathbf{S}|^4}$$

$$\mathbf{S} = (x_1 - x_2)\mathbf{i} + (y_1 - y_2)\mathbf{j} + (z_1 - z_2)\mathbf{k}$$

and $\mathbf{n} = \mathbf{k}$, $z_1 = 0$, and $z_2 = z_0$.

Example 12.9   View factor between two parallel rectangles

We shall obtain the view factors for the two sets of data shown in Table 12.8. The method used is to nest two calls to dblquad . This is implemented in the function **F1_2**, given below, which contains two kernel sub functions. The function **InnerKernel** evaluates $f(x_1, y_1, x_2, y_2)$, and the function **OuterKernel** evaluates $I_{y2}(x_1, y_1)$; that is, it integrates f over A_2 for a particular point on A_1. The use of dblquad in the main function performs the integration over all the points on A_1.

```
function F1_2(x1a, x1b, y1a, y1b, x2a, x2b, y2a, y2b, dz)
F12 = dblquad(@OuterKernel, x_1a, x1b, y1a, y1b, [], [], x2a, x2b, y2a, y2b, ...
          dz)/(A2*pi)
```

TABLE 12.8   Data Used to Compute the View Factors

Parameter	Set 1	Set 2
Geometry of A_1		
x-Coordinate of first corner point, Area 1, x_{1a}	−1	−2
y-Coordinate of first corner point, Area 1, y_{1a}	−1	−2
x-Coordinate of opposite corner point, Area 1, x_{1b}	1	0
y-Coordinate of opposite corner point, Area 1, y_{1b}	1	0
Geometry of A_2		
x-Coordinate of first corner point, Area 2, x_{2a}	−1	2
y-Coordinate of first corner point, Area 2, y_{2a}	−1	2
x-Coordinate of opposite corner point, Area 2, x_{2b}	1	0
y-Coordinate of opposite corner point, Area 2, y_{2b}	1	0
Separation distance between planes	2	2
Computed view factor (F_{2-1})	0.1998	0.0433

```
function f = OuterKernel(x1, y1, x2a, x2b, y2a ,y2b, dz)
for i = 1:length(x1)
    f(i) = dblquad(@InnerKernel, x2a, x2b, y2a, y2b, [], [], dz, x1(i), y1);
end

function f = InnerKernel(x, y, dz, x2, y2)
L = length(x);
S = [x-x2*ones(1, L); (y-y2)*ones(1, L); dz*ones(1, L)];
n = repmat([0, 0, 1]', 1, L);
f = dot(n, S).^2./dot(S, S).^2;
```

The view factors between two arbitrarily located rectangles in parallel planes for the two data sets listed in Table 12.8 are computed using the following script:

```
Set1 = F1_2(-1, 1, -1, 1, -1, 1, -1, 1, 2)
Set2 = F1_2(-2, 0, -2, 0, 2, 0, 2, 0, 2)
```

Upon execution, we obtain the results shown in the last row of Table 12.8. The areas of the two rectangles and the spacing between the parallel planes are the same for both data sets. However, the rectangles in set 1 are directly opposed to each other, while the rectangles of those in set 2 are offset from each other. The result of set 1 in Table 12.8 was verified by comparison with an available analytical solution for the case of directly opposed rectangles[11] and was found to be identical to four significant digits.

12.4.3 Enclosure Radiation with Diffuse Gray Walls

A common problem in radiation heat transfer is to determine the temperatures and heat-transfer rates because of radiation in an enclosure with diffuse gray surfaces enclosing a nonparticipating medium. These situations occur in ovens, rooms, and other enclosed spaces. Making the diffuse gray surface assumptions considerably

---

[11]R. Siegel and J. R. Howell, *ibid.*, p. 1030.

reduces the complexity of the model compared with the general radiation model. The diffuse specification means that the intensity of the radiation leaving and arriving at all surfaces is independent of direction. The gray specification means that the emissivity and absorptivity are independent of wavelength. However, even with these simplifications, enclosure problems still require considerable effort to set up and solve. Such problems are naturally expressed in matrix notation; thus, MATLAB provides an ideal environment for their formulation and solution. The equations that result from such analyses are[12]

$$\frac{Q_k}{A_k} = q_k = \frac{\varepsilon_k}{1 - \varepsilon_k}(\sigma T_k^4 - q_{0,k}) \tag{12.7}$$

$$\frac{Q_k}{A_k} = q_k = q_{0,k} - \sum_{j=1}^{N} F_{k-j} q_{0,j} = \sum_{j=1}^{N} F_{k-j}(q_{0,k} - q_{0,j}) \tag{12.8}$$

where Q_k is the heat-transfer rate from surface k, A_k is its area, q_k is its heat flux, $q_{0,k}$ is its radiosity, F_{k-j} is the view factor representing the fraction of the energy leaving surface k that is intercepted by surface j, N is the number of surfaces in the enclosure, and $\sigma = 5.67 \times 10^{-8}$ W/(m² K⁴) is the Stefan-Boltzmann constant. The formulation of these equations assumes that both the incoming and the outgoing radiation from each of the surfaces is uniform over that surface and that the intensity is independent of direction. This assumption should be evaluated for a given problem by subdividing the surfaces of the enclosure until results are obtained that are independent of the area subdivision scheme.

For a general enclosure problem, one must specify either the heat-transfer rate or the temperature of each of the surfaces. Once such a specification has been made, Eqs. 12.7 and 12.8 yield a single independent relation for each surface. For a specified temperature, Eqs. 12.7 and 12.8 are equated to yield

$$q_{0,k} - \sum_{j=1}^{N} F_{k-j} q_{0,j} = \frac{\varepsilon_k}{1 - \varepsilon_k}(\sigma T_k^4 - q_{0,k}) \tag{12.9}$$

When the heat-transfer rate is specified, Eq. 12.9 is written as

$$\frac{Q_k}{A_k} = q_{0,k} - \sum_{j=1}^{N} F_{k-j} q_{0,j} \tag{12.10}$$

These equations can be written in matrix form as

$$\begin{bmatrix} d_1 - F_{1-1} & -F_{1-2} & \cdots & -F_{1-N} \\ -F_{2-1} & d_2 - F_{2-2} & & -F_{1-2} \\ \vdots & & & \vdots \\ -F_{N-1} & -F_{N-2} & & d_N - F_{N-N} \end{bmatrix} \begin{bmatrix} q_{0,1} \\ q_{0,2} \\ \vdots \\ q_{0,N} \end{bmatrix} = \begin{bmatrix} b_1 \\ b_2 \\ \vdots \\ b_N \end{bmatrix}$$

---

[12]R. Siegel and J. R. Howell, *ibid.*, pp. 189–252.

where, when the temperatures are specified,

$$d_k = 1/(1 - \varepsilon_k)$$

$$b_k = \frac{\varepsilon_k}{1 - \varepsilon_k} \sigma T_k^4$$

and, when the heat-transfer rates are specified,

$$d_k = 1$$

$$b_k = \frac{Q_k}{A_k}$$

Each row of the matrix represents one surface whose form depends on whether the temperature or the heat-transfer rate is specified for that surface. In either case, the radiosity associated with the surface is the unknown. Thus, the resulting system of equations consists of N equations in the N unknown radiosities. Once the radiosities are known, the unknown temperature or heat-transfer rate for a given surface can be determined from either Eqs. 12.7 or 12.8. Equation 12.7 is somewhat simpler to evaluate except for the special case where the emmissivity equals 1, in which case Eq. 12.8 is used.

Example 12.10   Total heat transfer rate of a rectangular enclosure

Consider an oven that is assumed to be infinitely long into the plane of the page and that has a rectangular cross-section. The geometry of the cross-section is defined in Figure 12.22, and the corresponding view factors are defined in Table 12.9. These view factors can be computed using Hottel's crossed-string method.[13] The values shown in boldface in Table 12.9 are those that were chosen, and the remaining values are those that were computed from view-factor algebra based on these chosen values and their areas.

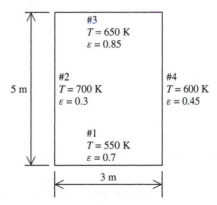

Figure 12.22   Enclosure geometry and surface properties for radiation in an enclosure with gray walls.

---

[13]R. Siegel and J. R. Howell, *ibid.*

TABLE 12.9 View Factors F_{i-j} for the Enclosure Shown in Figure 12.22

i\j	1	2	3	4
1	**0**	**0.3615**	**0.2770**	0.3615
2	0.2169	**0**	**0.2169**	0.5662
3	0.2770	0.3615	**0**	0.3615
4	0.2169	0.5662	0.2169	0

The following script makes use of an identifier c_k, where $k = 1, 2, \ldots, N$, which equals 0 when the temperature is given and equals 1 when the heat-transfer rate is given. It is then used to select the appropriate values for d_k and b_k. Furthermore, all vectors must be of length N and, the matrix F is $(N \times N)$. The script is

```
sigma = 5.6693e-8; N = 4;
A = [3, 5, 3, 5]; epsilon = [0.7, 0.3, 0.85, 0.45];
T = [550, 700, 650, 600];
F = -[0, 0.3615, 0.277, 0.3615;...
      0.2169, 0, 0.2169, 0.5662;...
      0.277, 0.3615, 0, 0.3615;...
      0.2169, 0.5662, 0.2169, 0];
Q = [0, 0, 0, 0];
c = [0, 0, 0, 0];
b = sigma*epsilon./(1-epsilon).*(1-c).*T.^4+c.*Q./A;
d = (1-c).*1./(1-epsilon)+c;
for k = 1:N
   F(k, k) = d(k)+F(k, k);
end
q0 = F\b';
Q = A.*epsilon./(1-epsilon).*(1-c).*(sigma*T.^4-q0')
q = Q./A
```

Execution of the script gives $Q = [-8627.9 \ 8061.1 \ 4525.9 -3959.1]$ W and $q = [-2876 \ 1612.2 \ 1508.6 -791.8]$ W/m^2. It is seen that the heat-transfer rates Q correctly sum to zero.

12.4.4 Transient Radiation Heating of a Plate in a Furnace[14]

Consider a vertically suspended flat plate in a furnace. One wall of the furnace that is parallel to the plate's surface contains heating elements. The furnace and the plate are initially at room temperature. The amount of heating power Q required in the heating elements to raise the plate's temperature to T_e in time t_h can be determined

---

[14]Topic suggested by Professor Yogendra Joshi, Department of Mechanical Engineering, Georgia Institute of Technology, Atlanta, GA.

from energy balances on the plate and the furnace walls, which yield the following coupled equations:

$$\frac{dT_w}{dt} = P_1 Q - P_2(T_w^4 - T_p^4)$$

$$\frac{dT_p}{dt} = -P_3(T_p^4 - T_w^4)$$

where the plate and wall are modeled as lumped masses, T_w is the temperature of the wall, and T_p is the temperature of the plate. If we assume that this setup can be modeled as a two-surface enclosure with gray diffuse surfaces, then[15]

$$P_1 = \frac{1}{m_w c_w}$$

$$P_2 = \frac{\sigma}{m_w c_w} \left[\frac{1 - \varepsilon_p}{\varepsilon_p A_p} + \frac{1}{A_w F_{wp}} + \frac{1 - \varepsilon_w}{\varepsilon_w A_w} \right]^{-1}$$

$$P_3 = \frac{\sigma}{m_p c_p} \left[\frac{1 - \varepsilon_p}{\varepsilon_p A_p} + \frac{1}{A_p F_{pw}} + \frac{1 - \varepsilon_w}{\varepsilon_w A_w} \right]^{-1}$$

where m_p and m_w are the masses of the plate and wall, respectively; c_p and c_w are the specific heats of the plate and wall, respectively; ε_p and ε_w are the emissivities of the plate and wall, respectively; A_p and A_w are the areas of the plate and wall, respectively; F_{pw} and F_{wp} are the view factors; and $\sigma = 5.67 \times 10^{-8}$ W/(m^2 K^4) is the Stefan-Boltzmann constant.

Example 12.11   Transient radiation heating of a plate in a furnace

Let us assume that for a certain configuration we have determined that $P_1 = 1.67 \times 10^{-5}$ K/J, $P_2 = 8.8 \times 10^{-14}$ s^{-1} K^{-3}, and $P_3 = 6.3 \times 0^{-13}$ s^{-1} K^{-3}. We want to determine the value of Q required by the heating elements to raise the plate's temperature to $T_e = 1100$ K in $t_h = 10$ min (600 s). It is assumed that both the plate and the furnace are initially at 300 K.

To obtain a solution, we create the following main function **TranRadHeat** and two sub functions: **RadTemp**, which uses ode45 to solve the two coupled first-order ordinary differential equations, and **Qgen**, which uses fzero to determine the value of Q. In **QGen**, we have denoted T1o = $T_w(0)$ and T2o = $T_p(0)$, and we have used interp1 to locate the time at which the temperature T_e = Te = 1100 K.

```
function TranRadHeat
global Te th P1 P2 P3 T1o T2o tend
P1 = 1.67e-5; P2 = 8.8e-14; P3 = 6.3e-13;
Qguess = 100000; Te = 1100; th = 600; tend = 660;
```

---

[15]F. P. Incropera and D. P. DeWitt, *ibid.*, Chapter 13.

```
T1o = 300;  T2o = 300;
options = optimset('display', 'off');
Q = fzero(@Qgen, Qguess, options);
[t, T] = ode45(@RadTemp, [0, tend], [T1o; T2o], [], Q);
plot(t, T(:,1), 'k-', t, T(:,2), 'k--')
z = axis;
hold on
plot([0, z(2)], [Te, Te], 'k', [th, th], [z(3), z(4)], 'k')
xlabel('Time (s)')
text(0.05*z(2), 0.85*z(4), ['Q = ' num2str(Q,6) ' W'])
ylabel('Temperature (K)')
legend('Wall temperature', 'Plate temperature', 'Location', 'NorthWest')

function dTdt = RadTemp(t, T)
dTdt = [P1*Q-P2*(T(1)^4-T(2)^4); -P3*(T(2)^4-T(1)^4)];

function PlateTempDev = QGen(Q)
global Te th P1 P2 P3 T1o T2o tend
[t, T] = ode45(@RadTemp, [0, tend], [T1o; T2o], [], Q);
PlateTempDev = Te-interp1(t, T(:,2), th, 'spline');
```

When the script is executed, we obtain Figure 12.23.

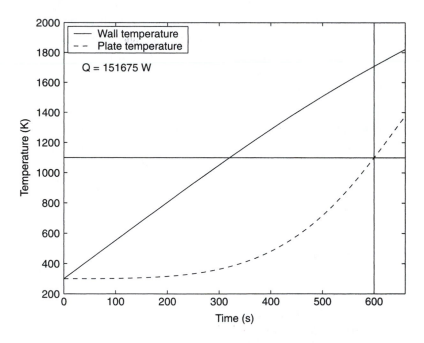

Figure 12.23   Temperature as a function time in the plate and in the furnace.

EXERCISES

12.1 One-dimensional conduction in a plane wall can be represented by

$$-k(T)\frac{dT}{dx} = q$$

where q is the heat flux, $k(T)$ is the temperature-dependent thermal conductivity, T is the temperature, and x is the spatial coordinate. If we assume that the wall is composed of mineral wool insulation, then the thermal conductivity varies as

$$k(T) = -k_0 + k_s T \quad 240 < T < 365 \text{ K}$$

where $k_0 = 0.48$, $k_s = 0.00032$, k is in W/m K, and T is in K. Determine the temperature at $x = 0$ when the heat flux is $q = 12.5$ W/m^2, the wall thickness is 0.1 m, and the temperature of the surface at $x = 0.1$ m is 300 K. Compare the results with the analytical solution

$$k_0(T - T_L) + \frac{k_s}{2}(T^2 - T_L^2) = q(x - L)$$

where $T(0) = T_L$. It is noted that the heat flux computed from an average value of the thermal conductivity will give an excellent prediction of the true value.

12.2 A standard plastic milk jug can be represented as a lumped capacitance for the purpose of estimating the time required to heat (or to cool) the milk. The governing equation for such a situation is

$$\frac{dT}{dt} = \frac{Q}{mc_v}$$

where $Q = hA(T_{amb} - T)$ is the heat transfer to the jug from the surroundings, m is the mass of the jug, and c_v is the specific heat. For a simple radiation model

$$Q = A\sigma\varepsilon(T^4 - T_{amb}^4)$$

where $\sigma = 5.667 \times 10^{-8}$ W/m^2 K^4 is the Stephan-Boltzmann constant, ε is the emissivity, A is the surface area, T is the jug temperature, and T_{amb} is the ambient temperature.

Determine the time constant for this system with and without radiation. The time constant τ is the time required for the temperature difference between the jug's temperature and the ambient temperature to decrease by 63.2% from its initial value—that is,

$$\frac{T_{amb} - T(\tau)}{T_{amb} - T(0)} = 0.368$$

The jug has a mass of $m = 3.5$ kg and specific heat of $c_v = 4.2$ J/g K. The surface area of the jug is 0.3 m^2, and the initial temperature is $T(0) = 5°C$. The jug interacts with an environment at $T_{amb} = 30°C$. With no radiation, natural convection occurs from the jug surface, with a heat-transfer coefficient of $h = 2$ W/K m^2. With combined convection plus radiation, assume that $\varepsilon = 0.5$. [Answers: For the case without radiation, $\tau = 6.8$ h ($= mc_v/(hA)$); with radiation present, $\tau = 2.78$ h, and is a function of the initial temperature.]

12.3 The heat loss by convection from the outer surface of the insulation of an insulated pipe is determined from

$$q = \frac{2\pi L(T_i - T_\infty)}{\dfrac{1}{k}\ln(r_o/r_i) + \dfrac{1}{r_o h}}$$

where L is the pipe length, r_o is the outer diameter of the insulation, r_i is its inner diameter, k is its thermal conductivity, and h is the heat-transfer coefficient. For small values of r_o, additional insulation has the effect of increasing the heat-transfer rate. Demonstrate this effect by plotting q as a function of r_o for a range of r_o that spans $r_o = k/h$. Let $h = 5$ W/m^2 K, $k = 0.1$ W/m K, $r_i = 0.01$ m, $L = 1$ m, $T_i = 100°$C, and $T_\infty = 20°$C. Although the usual experience is that adding insulation reduces the heat-transfer rate, this is an exception.

12.4 A temperature sensor is used to measure the temperature of a flowing fluid. The sensor is mounted on a small-diameter, cylindrical probe that protrudes through a duct wall into the flow normal to the direction of flow. The probe can be modeled as a fin whose temperature distribution is given by

$$\frac{T(x) - T_\infty}{T_b - T_\infty} = \frac{\cosh m(L - x)}{\cosh mL}$$

where

$$m^2 = \frac{hP}{kA_c}$$

and T_b is the wall temperature, T_∞ is the fluid temperature, $P = \pi d$ is the perimeter of the probe of diameter d, $A_c = \pi d^2/4$ is the cross-sectional area, k is the thermal conductivity, h is the heat-transfer coefficient, and L is the length of the probe.

The error e in the sensed temperature resulting from conduction along the probe is, therefore,

$$e = T(L) - T_\infty = \frac{T_b - T_\infty}{\cosh mL}$$

Plot the error as a function of probe length for $0.005 \le L \le 0.1$ m for several values of k in the range $20 \le k \le 400$ W/m K. Assume that probe diameter is 0.005 m, the fluid temperature is 100°C and the wall temperature is 80°C. The heat-transfer coefficient between the fluid and the probe is 25 W/m^2 K.

12.5 Because of the nonlinear nature of radiation heat transfer, the placement of shields in the radiation path reduces heat transfer. Thus, for insulation applications, the use of radiation shields is important. The effect of radiation shields can be illustrated by considering the heat transfer between two infinite parallel plates at temperatures T_1 and T_2 that are separated by an evacuated space. When the surfaces radiate as black bodies, the heat-transfer rate q with no shield is obtained from

$$q = \sigma(T_1^4 - T_2^4)$$

When we have one shield, the heat-transfer rate is determined from

$$q = \sigma(T_1^4 - T_m^4)$$
$$q = \sigma(T_m^4 - T_2^4)$$

where T_m is the temperature of the shield. The heat-transfer rate with two shields is obtained from

$$q = \sigma(T_1^4 - T_{m1}^4)$$
$$q = \sigma(T_{m1}^4 - T_{m2}^4)$$
$$q = \sigma(T_{m2}^4 - T_2^4)$$

where $\sigma = 5.667 \times 10^{-8}$ W/m^2 K^4 is the Stephan-Boltzmann constant and T_{m1} and T_{m2} are the temperatures of shields 1 and 2, respectively. If the temperatures of the two plates are 100°C and 20°C, then determine the heat-transfer rate with no shield, one shield, and two shields. [Answers: With no shield, $q = 680$ W/m^2; with one shield, $q = 340.1$ W/m^2 and $T_m = 340.15$ K; and with two shields, $q = 226.7$ W/m^2, $T_{m1} = 352.2$ K, and $T_{m2} = 326.7$ K.]

12.6 The Planck distribution represents the power spectral density of black-body radiation at a particular temperature and is given by

$$E_{\lambda, b}(\lambda, T) = \frac{C_1}{\lambda^5 [\exp(C_2/\lambda T) - 1]}$$

where λ is the wavelength, T is the temperature, $E_{\lambda, b}$ is the spectral emissive power, and $C_1 = 3.742 \times 10^8$ W μm^4/m^2, and $C_2 = 1.439 \times 10^4$ μm K. A common need in radiation calculations is to integrate this function over some range of wavelengths. When integrated over all wavelengths, we have that

$$\int_0^\infty E_{\lambda, b} d\lambda = \sigma T^4$$

where $\sigma = 5.667 \times 10^{-8}$ W/m^2 K^4 is the Stephan-Boltzmann constant. Perform this integration numerically for $T = 300, 400$, and 500 K, and compare the result with the exact value. A note of caution: Both integration limits give considerable difficulty numerically. Approximate the integral by using a very small, nonzero lower limit, such as 0.5 μm. For the upper limit, use a value of 300 μm, which will vary depending on the value of T.

12.7 Use the solution method introduced in Section 12.3.1 to determine the thickness of the temperature and velocity boundary layers for Pr $= 0.07, 0.7$, and 7.0. In the notation of Section 12.3.1, the boundary layer thickness for the temperature δ_T is defined as that value of η for which $y_4 = T^*(\eta = \delta_T) = 0.99$, and the boundary layer thickness for the velocity δ_u is defined as that value of η for which $y_2 = u(\eta = \delta_u) = 0.99$. At each value of the Prandtl number, compare the ratio δ_u/δ_T to that predicted by the relation Pr$^{1/3}$. [Answers are given in Table 12.10.]

TABLE 12.10 Answers to Exercise 12.7

Pr	δ_u	δ_T	δ_u/δ_T	Pr$^{1/3}$
0.07	4.92	13.66	0.36	0.41
0.7	4.92	5.63	0.87	0.89
7.0	4.92	2.45	2.01	1.91

12.8 Consider air flowing over a flat plate at $u_\infty = 1$ m/s for which $Pr = 0.7$ and $\nu_{vis} = 1.5 \times 10^{-5}$ m/s^2. Use the formulation of Section 12.3.1 to compute $T(x, y)$ over the full laminar domain $0 < x < x_{crit}$ and $0 < y < 10x_{crit}/(Re_{crit})^{1/2}$ where

$$Re_{crit} = \frac{u_\infty x_{crit}}{\nu_{vis}} = 5 \times 10^{-5}$$

Create a contour plot of $T(x, y)$ over this domain. In the notation of Section 12.3.2, $T(x, y) = y_4$, and

$$\eta = y\sqrt{u_\infty/\nu_{vis}x}$$

12.9 For the same conditions defined in Exercise 12.8, create a contour plot of the stream function

$$\psi = fu_\infty\sqrt{\frac{\nu_{vis}x}{u_\infty}}$$

12.10 For the natural convection solution of Section 12.3.2, find the value of η at which the velocity u is a maximum for $Pr = 0.07, 0.7$, and 7.0. In the notation of Section 12.3.2, $u = y_2$. Use fminbnd on the negative of u, and select the search region based on the curves in Figures 12.13 to 12.15. [Answer: For $Pr = 0.7, u_{max} = 0.2784$ at $\eta_{max} = 0.9632$. See Table 12.11.]

12.11 For the natural convection solution of Section 12.3.2, determine the thickness of the thermal and velocity boundary layers for $Pr = 0.07, 0.7$, and 7.0. In the notation of Section 12.3.2, the boundary layer thickness for the temperature δ_T is defined as that value of η for which $y_4 = T^*(\eta = \delta_T) = 0.01$, and the boundary layer thickness for the velocity δ_u is defined as that value of η for which $y_2 = u(\eta = \delta_u)/u_{max} = 0.01$, where u_{max} are those values found in Exercise 12.4. [Answers are given in Table 12.11.]

12.12 Consider the natural convection of air over a heated plate as described in Section 12.3.2. The dimensional velocities can be expressed in terms of the nondimensional solution as

$$u = \frac{2\nu_{vis}}{x}Gr_x^{1/2}\frac{df}{d\eta}$$

$$v = \frac{\nu_{vis}}{x}\left(\frac{Gr_x}{4}\right)^{1/4}\left(\eta\frac{df}{d\eta} - 3f\right)$$

For quiescent air at 300 K, compute the velocity components $u(x, y)$ and $v(x, y)$ over the domain $0 < x < 1$ m and $0 < y < 0.25$ m. Plot u and v at five evenly spaced x locations from $x = 0.1$ to $x = 0.5$. Refer to Figure 12.12 for the definitions of x and y.

TABLE 12.11   Answers to Exercises 12.10 and 12.11

Pr	0.07	0.7	7.0
η_{max}	1.21	0.96	0.728
u_{max}	0.455	0.278	0.131
δ_u	9.48	5.65	6.41
δ_T	10.27	4.47	1.78

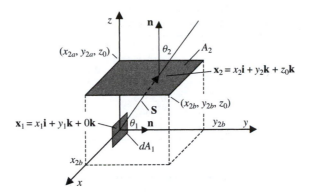

Figure 12.24 Geometry when the differential area and the finite rectangle are in perpendicular planes.

12.13 The steam function was defined in Section 12.3.2 as

$$\psi = 4vf\left(\frac{Gr_x}{4}\right)^{1/4}$$

For air at 300 K, create a contour plot of the stream function over the domain $0 < x < 1$ m and $0 < y < 0.25$ m. Refer to Figure 12.12 for the definitions of x and y.

12.14 Based on the analysis given in Section 12.4.1, alter the formulation for the view factors to evaluate the case where the rectangles are in two perpendicular planes. As shown in Figure 12.24, the differential area element is located a distance from a perpendicular plane in which a finite rectangular area exists. For simplicity, we consider only the case where the differential element can see the entire finite rectangle. In other words, the line of intersection of the perpendicular planes cannot pass through the finite rectangle. Using data given in Table 12.12, determine the view factor for the surfaces shown in Figure 12.24. Note that in this case, $\cos\theta_1 \neq \cos\theta_2$.

12.15 Based on the enclosure analysis of Section 12.4.3, recalculate the example given with surface 4 split into two equal size surfaces—that is, the system will now have five surfaces. Assume that the surface properties are the same as those used in the original example. Calculate the heat-transfer rate from each of the surfaces, and compare it with the more coarse calculation done originally. Using the surface numbering scheme given in Section 12.4.3, surface 4 is now split in two, and surface 4 refers to the upper half and

TABLE 12.12 Parameters and Answers for Exercise 12.14

Parameter	Set 1
Geometry of finite rectangle	
$\quad$ x-Coordinate of first corner point	−1
$\quad$ y-Coordinate of first corner point	−1
$\quad$ x-Coordinate of opposite corner point	0
$\quad$ y-Coordinate of opposite corner point	0
Separation distance between the differential element and the perpendicular plane	5
Computed view factor (F_{d_1-2})	0.0012

TABLE 12.13   View Factors for Exercise 12.15

i\j	1	2	3	4	5
1	0	0.3615	0.2770	0.0957	0.2658
2	0.2169	0	0.2169	0.2831	0.2831
3	0.2770	0.3615	0	0.2658	0.0957
4	0.1148	0.5662	0.3190	0	0
5	0.3190	0.5662	0.1148	0	0

TABLE 12.14   Answers to Exercise 12.15

Surface	1	2	3	4	5
Q (kW)	-8560	8064	4451	-2373	-1582
T (K)	550	700	650	600	600
q (kW/m^2)	-2853	1613	1484	-949	-633

surface 5 to the lower half. The view factors for this geometry were calculated and are given in Table 12.13. These values were obtained from Hottel's crossed-string method. The results of the enclosure calculation are summarized in Table 12.14.

It is noted that the energy balance is satisfied—that is, the Qs sum to zero. Comparing these results with those in the text, it is seen that the heat-transfer rates (Q) and the fluxes (q) are similar between the two calculations for surfaces 1 through 3. However, for the surface that was split, it is seen that the flux varies considerably over the length. It is interesting to note that the overall heat-transfer rate (the sum for surfaces 4 and 5) matches reasonably closely with the originally calculated heat-transfer rate.

12.16 The transient temperature distribution in a solid sphere, which is initially at a uniform temperature and has convection at the boundary surface, is given by[16]

$$\theta(\xi, \tau) = \sum_{n=1}^{\infty} C_u \exp(-\zeta_{rt}^2 \tau) \frac{\sin(\zeta_n \xi)}{\zeta_n \xi}$$

where

$$\theta(\xi, \tau) = \frac{T(\xi, \tau) - T_\infty}{T(\xi, 0) - T_\infty}$$

and $\tau = \alpha t / a^2$, α is the thermal diffusivity, a is the radius of the sphere, t is time, $\xi = r/a$, r is the radial location in the sphere, T_∞ is the ambient air temperature,

$$C_n = \frac{4[\sin \zeta_n - \zeta_n \cos \zeta_n]}{2\zeta_n - \sin 2\zeta_n}$$

and ζ_n are the positive roots of

$$1 - \zeta_n \cot \zeta_n = Bi$$

where $Bi = ha/k$ is the Biot number, h is the heat-transfer coefficient, and k is the thermal conductivity of the sphere.

Plot $\theta(\xi, \tau)$ as a function of ξ and τ for $0 \le \xi \le 1, 0 \le \tau \le 1.5$ and $Bi = 0.5$.

---

[16]F. P. Incropera and D. P. DeWitt, *ibid.*, p. 229.

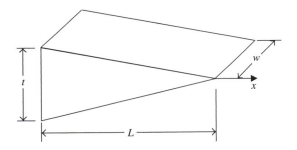

Figure 12.25 Triangular fin geometry.

12.17 The steady-state temperature distribution in the triangular fin shown in Figure 12.25 is determined from

$$(1 - \eta)\frac{d^2\theta}{d\eta^2} - \frac{d\theta}{d\eta} - M^2\theta = 0$$

where $\eta = x/L$,

$$\theta(\eta) = \frac{T(\eta) - T_\infty}{T_b - T_\infty}$$

$$M^2 = \frac{2hL^2}{kt}\sqrt{1 + \left(\frac{t}{2L}\right)^2}$$

h is the heat-transfer coefficient, k is the thermal conductivity, and it is assumed that $t/w \ll 1$.

Assume that the boundary condition at $\eta = 0$ is $T(0) = T_b$—that is,

$$\theta(0) = 1$$

and that at $\eta = 1$ the boundary condition is

$$\left.\frac{d\theta}{d\eta}\right|_{\eta=1} = 0$$

The fin efficiency η_f for this fin is obtained from

$$\eta_f = \left.\frac{-1}{M^2}\frac{d\theta}{d\eta}\right|_{\eta=0}$$

Determine the fin efficiency for 10 logarithmically equally spaced values from $0.01 < M^2 < 100$, and plot the results using `semilogx`. Compare these results with those from the analytically obtained expression[17]

$$\eta_f = \frac{1}{M}\frac{I_1(2M)}{I_0(2M)}$$

where $I_n(x)$ in the modified Bessel function of the first kind of order n and is determined from `besseli`.

---

[17]F. P. Incropera and D. P. DeWitt, *ibid.*, p. 125.

BIBLIOGRAPHY

J. P. Holman, *Heat Transfer*, 7th ed. McGraw-Hill, New York, NY, 1990.

F. P. Incropera and D. P. DeWitt, *Fundamentals of Heat and Mass Transfer*, 4th ed. John Wiley & Sons, New York, NY, 1996.

S. Kakaç and H. Liu, *Heat Exchangers: Selection, Rating, and Thermal Design*, CRC Press, Boca Raton, FL, 1998.

F. Krieth and M. S. Bohn, *Principles of Heat Transfer*, 5th ed. West Publishing Co., New York, NY, 1993.

A. F. Mills, *Heat Transfer*, Irwin, Boston, MA, 1992.

R. Siegel and J. R. Howell, *Thermal Radiation Heat Transfer*, 3rd ed. Hemisphere Publishing Co., Washington, DC, 1992.

N. V. Suryanarayana, *Engineering Heat Transfer*, West Publishing Co., New York, NY, 1995.

13

Optimization

Shapour Azarm

Representative examples from a range of engineering optimization problems are solved using the Optimization Toolbox.

13.1 DEFINITION, FORMULATION, AND GRAPHICAL SOLUTIONS

13.1.1 Introduction

Optimization in engineering refers to the process of finding the "best" possible values for a set of variables for a system while satisfying various constraints. The term "best" indicates that the decision maker wishes to optimize one or more design objectives by

603

either minimizing or maximizing. For example, one might want to design a product by maximizing its reliability while minimizing its weight and cost. In an optimization process, variables are selected to describe the system such as size, shape, material type, and operational characteristics. An objective refers to a quantity that the decision maker wants to be made as high (a maximum) or as low (a minimum) as possible. A "constraint" refers to a quantity that indicates a restriction or limitation on an aspect of the system's capabilities.

Generally speaking, an optimization problem involves minimizing one or more objective functions subject to some constraints and is stated as

$$\underset{x \in D}{\text{minimize}} \ \{f_1(x), f_2(x), \ldots, f_m(x)\} \tag{13.1}$$

where $f_i, i = 1, \ldots, m$, is a scalar objective function that maps a variable vector x into the objective space. The n-dimensional design variable vector x is constrained to lie in a region D, called the feasible domain. Constraints to the above problem are included in the specification of the feasible domain. In general, the feasible domain is constrained by J-inequality constraints and/or K-equality constraints as

$$D = \{x : g_j(x) \leq 0, h_k(x) = 0, j = 1, \ldots, J, k = 1, \ldots, K\} \tag{13.2}$$

An optimization problem in which the objective and constraint functions are linear functions of their variables is referred to as a linear programming problem.

TABLE 13.1 Classification of Optimization Problems, MATLAB Functions, and Examples Given in Chapter 13

Problem class	MATLAB function	Example	
Linear programming	linprog	13.2	Production planning
		13.3	Oil refinery
Nonlinear programming: Single-objective unconstrained			
Multiple variable	fminunc	13.1	and 13.4 Two-spring system
	fminsearch	13.5	Bottom of a bottle
Curve fitting	lsqcurvefit	13.6	Stress–strain relationship
Least squares	lsqnonlin	13.7	Stress–strain relationship
		13.8	Semiempirical P-v-T relationship
		13.9	Mineral exploration
Single-objective constrained			
Single variable	fminbnd	13.10	Piping cost in a plant
		13.11	Closed box
Multiple variable	fmincon	13.12	Two-bar truss
		13.13	Helical compression spring
		13.14	Gear reducer
Quadratic	quadprog	13.15	Production planning
Semi-infinite	fseminf	13.16	Planar two-link manipulator
Multiobjective	fminimax	13.17	Vibrating platform
	fgoalattain	13.18	Production planning

On the other hand, if at least one of the objective or constraint functions is nonlinear, then it is referred to as a nonlinear programming problem.

The classes of optimization problems, the MATLAB solution functions, and the examples appearing in this chapter for continuous variable optimization problems are summarized in Table 13.1.

13.1.2 Graphical Solution

Solutions to optimization problems with two variables can be visualized with MATLAB's plotting capabilities. This is demonstrated with the following example.

Example 13.1   Two-spring system

Consider a two-spring system[1] shown in Figure 13.1. The system in Figure 13.1 shows, with springs depicted in dashed lines, an unloaded and undeformed spring system. After the loads are applied at joint A, the system is deformed until it is in equilibrium at point B, with springs shown with solid lines. We are interested in finding the equilibrium state of the loaded system—that is, the location (x_1, x_2) of joint B.

The equilibrium state of the system is obtained by deriving the potential energy (PE) for the system and then minimizing it with respect to the design variables x_1 and x_2 to obtain the location of point B. The potential energy is computed from the difference between the strain energies of the springs, which is given by the first two terms in the Eq. 13.3, and the work done by external forces, which is given by the last two terms in Eq. 13.3. The quantities k_1, k_2, L_1, L_2, F_1, and F_2 are constants whose values are shown in Figure 13.1. Hence, the objective function of the unconstrained optimization problem is

$$\begin{aligned}
\underset{x_1, x_2}{\text{minimize PE}}(x_1, x_2) = {} & 0.5k_1\left(\sqrt{x_1^2 + (L_1 - x_2)^2} - L_1\right)^2 \\
& + 0.5k_2\left(\sqrt{x_1^2 + (L_2 + x_2)^2} - L_2\right)^2 - F_1x_1 - F_2x_2
\end{aligned} \tag{13.3}$$

There are two variables, x_1 and x_2, in the objective function; hence, their values can be estimated graphically.

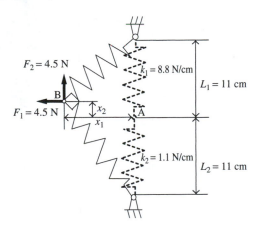

Figure 13.1   Two-spring system.

---

[1]G. Vanderplaats, *Numerical Optimization Techniques for Engineering Design*, McGraw-Hill, New York, NY, 1984, pp. 72–73.

The script is

```
k1 = 8.8;  k2 = 1.1;  L1 = 11;  L2 = 11;  F1 = 4.5;  F2 = 4.5;
[x1, x2] = meshgrid(linspace(-5, 15, 15), linspace(-5, 15, 15));
PE1 = 1/2*k1*(sqrt(x1.^2+(L1-x2).^2)-L1).^2;
PE2 = 1/2*k2*(sqrt(x1.^2+(L2+x2).^2)-L2).^2;
PE = PE1+PE2-F1*x1-F2*x2;
subplot(1, 2, 1);
h = contour(x1, x2, PE, [-40:20:20, 50:100:500], 'k');
clabel(h);
axis([-5, 15, -5, 15])
xlabel('x_1');
ylabel('x_2');
subplot(1, 2, 2);
surfc(x1, x2, PE);
axis([-10, 15, -10, 15, -100, 500]);
zlabel('PE');
xlabel('x_1');
ylabel('x_2')
```

The execution of the above script produces the results shown in Figure 13.2, wherein Figure 13.2a shows a contour plot of PE. The contours are labeled with their numerical

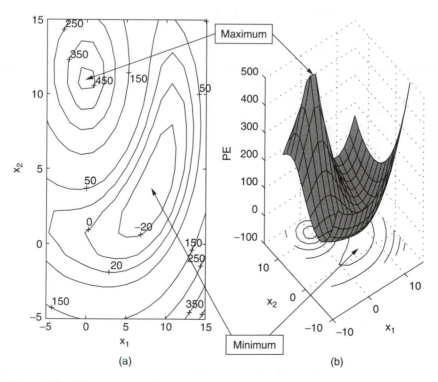

Figure 13.2   (a) Contour and (b) surface plots of the PE function for the two-spring system shown in Figure 13.1.

values so that the approximate location of the minimum/maximum point can be visually located. Figure 13.2b shows the surface plot of PE with the contours shown below the surface. It also shows the approximate location of the minimum or maximum point, the point where the PE function reaches its minimum or maximum values. The exact location of the minimum or maximum point for this example is obtained in Section 13.3.1 using an unconstrained minimization technique is implemented in `fminunc`.

13.2 LINEAR PROGRAMMING

Linear programming (LP) refers to an optimization method applicable to the solution of problems in which the objective and constraint functions are linear functions of the design variables. An LP problem can be stated as follows:

$$\text{minimize } f^T x$$
$$x$$

$$\text{subject to: } Ax \leq b$$
$$A_{eq}x = b_{eq} \tag{13.4}$$
$$lb \leq x \leq ub$$

where $f, b, b_{eq}, lb,$ and ub are vectors and A and A_{eq} are matrices. The quantity x is a vector of design variables, and the superscript T indicates the transpose. The matrix A and the vector b are the coefficients of the linear inequality constraints, and A_{eq} and b_{eq} are the coefficients of the equality constraints. The MATLAB linear programming solver is `linprog`, which is used to solve the problem given by Eq. 13.4. The basic command is

[xopt, fopt] = `linprog` (f, A, b, Aeq, beq, lb, ub, x0, options)

which returns a vector $xopt = [x_{1opt}, x_{2opt}, \ldots]$ of the design variables and the scalar $fopt$, which is $f(x_{opt})$. The quantity $x0$ sets the starting points of x, and *options* sets the parameters described in `optimset`. If no equality constraints exist set $A_{eq} = []$ and $b_{eq} = []$.

We now demonstrate the use of `linprog` with the following example.

Example 13.2   Production planning

Consider two liquid products, A and B, that require production time in two departments. Product A requires 1 h in the first department and 1.25 h in the second department. Product B requires 1 h in the first department and 0.75 h in the second department. The available hours in each department are 200 h. Furthermore, there is a maximum market potential of 150 units for product B. Assume that the profits are $4 and $5 per unit of product A and B, respectively. We shall determine the number of units of products A and B that should be produced so that the producer's profit is maximized.

We first assume that x_1 represents the number of units of product A to be produced, and x_2 the number of units of product B. Then, the objective function and the constraints are[2]

$$\text{minimize } f(x_1, x_2) = -4x_1 - 5x_2$$

subject to:

$$g_1: x_1 + x_2 \le 200$$
$$g_2: 1.25x_1 + 0.75x_2 \le 200 \tag{13.5}$$
$$g_3: x_2 \le 150$$
$$(x_1, x_2) \ge 0$$

Thus,

$$f^T = [-4 \ -5] \tag{13.6}$$

and the inequality constraints are expressed as

$$\begin{bmatrix} 1 & 1 \\ 1.25 & 0.75 \\ 0 & 1 \end{bmatrix} \begin{bmatrix} x_1 \\ x_2 \end{bmatrix} \le \begin{bmatrix} 200 \\ 200 \\ 150 \end{bmatrix} \tag{13.7}$$

The script is

```
f = [-4, -5];
A = [1, 1; 1.25, 0.75; 0, 1];
b = [200, 200, 150];
lb = [0, 0];
x = linprog(f, A, b, [], [], lb, [])
```

which upon execution gives the optimum number of units of product A and B, respectively: $x_1 = 50$ and $x_2 = 150$.

Example 13.3   Oil refinery

A refinery has three types of crude oil: C1, C2, and C3. Crude oil C1 costs \$0.40/gallon, and there are, at most, 10,000 gallons/day of it available. Crude oil C2 costs \$0.20/gallon, and there are, at most, 12,000 gallons/day of it available. Crude oil C3 costs \$0.10/gallon, and there are, at most, 15,000 gallons/day of it available. The refinery can convert each type of crude oil to gasoline and could produce three types of gasoline: regular, plus, and premium. The maximum market demand for the regular, plus, and premium gasoline is 9000, 8000, and 7000 gallons/day, respectively. The refinery can sell its gasoline to a distributor for \$0.70/gallon for regular, \$0.80/gallon for plus, and \$0.90/gallon for premium gasoline. Assume that 1 gallon of crude oil C1 yields 0.2 gallons of regular, 0.3 gallons of plus, and 0.5 gallons of premium gasoline. Also, assume that 1 gallon of crude oil C2 yields 0.5 gallons of regular, 0.3 gallons of plus gasoline, and 0.2 gallons of premium gasoline. For crude oil C3, assume that 1 gallon of it yields 0.7 gallons of regular, 0.3 gallons of plus, and no premium gasoline. We shall determine the number of gallons of each of the crude oils C1, C2, and C3 that the refinery should purchase to maximize its daily profit.

---

[2]A. Osyczka, *Multicriterion Optimization in Engineering with Fortran Programs*, Ellis Horwood Limited, West Sussex, England, 1984, p. 4.

We first assume that x_1, x_2, and x_3 represent the number of gallons for crude oils C1, C2, and C3, respectively, to be purchased. Then, the objective function f (the negative of the profit) and constraints on crude oil and gasoline demands availability are

$$\text{minimize } f(x_1, x_2, x_3) = -[0.7(0.2x_1 + 0.5x_2 + 0.7x_3)$$
$$+ 0.8(0.3x_1 + 0.3x_2 + 0.3x_3)$$
$$+ 0.9(0.5x_1 + 0.2x_2) - 0.4x_1 - 0.2x_2 - 0.1x_3]$$
$$= -0.43x_1 - 0.57x_2 - 0.62x_3$$

subject to:

$$g_1: 0.2x_1 + 0.5x_2 + 0.7x_3 \leq 9000$$
$$g_2: 0.3x_1 + 0.3x_2 + 0.3x_3 \leq 8000 \qquad (13.8)$$
$$g_3: 0.5x_1 + 0.2x_2 \leq 7000$$
$$g_3: x_1 \leq 10{,}000$$
$$g_3: x_2 \leq 12{,}000$$
$$g_3: x_3 \leq 15{,}000$$

$$(x_1, x_2, x_3) \geq 0$$

The script is

```
f = [-0.43, -0.57, -0.62];
A = [0.2, 0.5, 0.7; 0.3, 0.3, 0.3; 0.5, 0.2, 0;1, 0, 0; 0, 1, 0; 0, 0, 1];
b = [9000, 8000, 7000, 10000, 12000, 15000];
lb = [0, 0, 0];
[x, f] = linprog(f, A, b, [], [], lb, [])
```

which upon execution gives the optimum number of gallons for the crude oils C1, C2, and C3, respectively: $x_1 = 9{,}200$, $x_2 = 12{,}000$, and $x_3 = 1{,}657$, for a daily profit of $11,840.

13.3 NONLINEAR PROGRAMMING

Nonlinear programming (NLP) refers to an optimization method in which the objective or constraint function (or both) is a nonlinear function of the design variables. The NLP problems and the corresponding methods are divided into two classes: the unconstrained methods, and the constrained methods.

13.3.1 Unconstrained Methods

Unconstrained NLP methods find the minimum of an unconstrained multivariable function formulated as

$$\text{minimize } f(x) \qquad (13.9)$$
$$x$$

where x is a vector of design variables and f is a scalar objective function. There are two functions that can be used to solve the problem of Eq. 13.9: `fminunc`, and fminsearch, which are, respectively, based on derivative and nonderivative optimization solution techniques. The command to invoke fminunc is

[xopt, fopt] = fminunc(@**UserFunction**, x0, options, p1, p2, ...)

where **UserFunction** is a function that computes the objective function f evaluated at x. The quantity $x0$ is the vector of starting values for x, and *options* sets the parameters described in optimset. The quantities $p1$, $p2$, ... are parameters that are passed to **UserFunction**.

The command to invoke fminsearch is

x = fminsearch(@**UserFunction**, x0, options, p1, p2, ...)

where the definitions of its arguments are the same as for fminunc.

We now illustrate the use of fminunc and fminsearch.

Example 13.4   Two-spring system revisited

The two-spring system of Example 13.1 is now solved numerically as an unconstrained optimization problem with the script below. The unconstrained objective function is created with the design variables x_1 and x_2 in sub function **SpringEquilibrium**.

```
function Twospring
x0 = [0.5, 5];
k1 = 8.8;  k2 = 1.1;  L1 = 11;  L2 = 11;  F1 = 4.5;  F2 = 4.5;
options = optimset('LargeScale', 'off');
[x, f] = fminunc(@SpringEquilibrium, x0, options, k1, k2, L1, L2, F1, F2)

function PE = SpringEquilibrium(x, k1 ,k2, L1, L2, F1, F2)
PE1 = 1/2*k1*(sqrt(x(1)^2+(L1-x(2))^2)-L1)^2;
PE2 = 1/2*k2*(sqrt(x(1)^2+(L2+x(2))^2)-L2)^2;
PE = PE1+PE2-F1*x(1)-F2*x(2);
```

which gives the optimum solution $x = [8.4251, 3.6331]$ and $f = PE = -35.0507$. This solution agrees with the approximate location of the solution shown in Figure 13.2. Note that by default, fminunc chooses a large scale optimization algorithm; however, with *options* 'LargeScale' set to 'off', it uses a medium-scale optimization algorithm. To obtain the maximum value of the PE function, one can either minimize the inverse, 1/PE, or the negative, $-PE$. Thus, we create the function **SpringEquilibriumMax,** and the script is

```
function Twospring2
x0 = [0.5, 5];
k1 = 8.8;  k2 = 1.1;  L1 = 11;  L2 = 11;  F1 = 4.5;  F2 = 4.5;
options = optimset('LargeScale', 'off');
[x, f] = fminunc(@SpringEquilibriumMax, x0, options, k1, k2, L1, L2, F1, F2)

function PE = SpringEquilibriumMax(x, k1, k2, L1, L2, F1, F2)
PE1 = 1/2*k1*(sqrt(x(1)^2+(L1-x(2))^2)-L1)^2;
PE2 = 1/2*k2*(sqrt(x(1)^2+(L2+x(2))^2)-L2)^2;
PE = -(PE1+PE2-F1*x(1)-F2*x(2));
```

Upon execution, we find that $x = [0\ 11]$ and PE = 549.45. We see that the solution agrees with the approximate location of the maximum shown in Figure 13.2.

It is pointed out that both `fminunc` and `fminsearch`—and almost all other techniques in this chapter (except `linprog`)—obtain only a local optimum solution and are dependent upon the choice of the initial point x0. In some cases, depending on the problem, if the location of the initial point is changed, the location of the solution might change, too. We illustrate this occurrence in the next example.

Example 13.5   Bottom of a bottle

Consider the following two-variable function[3]

$$\text{minimize } f(x_1, x_2) = (C + 1)/8$$

where

$$C = \frac{1}{2}(A^2 + B^2 + 3) + \sin(A^2 + B^2 + 2)$$
$$A = 6x_1 - 3$$
$$B = 6x_2 - 3 \qquad\qquad (13.10)$$
$$0 \le (x_1, x_2) \le 1$$

First, we use the following script to create Figure 13.3, which is a surface of the function:

```
[x1, x2] = meshgrid(linspace(0, 1, 50), linspace(0, 1, 50));
A = 6*x1-3;  B = 6*x2-3;
C = (A.^2+B.^2+3)./2+sin(A.^2+B.^2+2);
bottle = (C+1)/8;
colormap([1 1 1]);
surf(x1, x2, bottle);
zlabel('f')
xlabel('x_1')
ylabel('x_2');
view(-10, 45)
```

As shown in Figure 13.3, the function is axially symmetric and has a dome-like region in the center whose shape resembles the bottom of a bottle. Figure 13.3 shows three regions, each having an infinite number of local maxima located on a circle: the central dome-like local region, the middle maximum region, and further above them, the four regions that are on a circle.

Next, `fminsearch` is used in the following script to obtain a local maximum for the above function:

```
x0 = [0.2, 0.8];
bottle = inline('-(((6*x(1)-3)^2+(6*x(2)-3)^2+3)/2+sin((6*x(1)-3)^2+...
        (6*x(2)-3)^2+2)+1)/8','x');
options = optimset('Large', 'off');
[x, f] = fminsearch(bottle, x0, options)
```

---

[3]Revised from: D. A. Van Veldhuizen and G. B. Lamont, "Multi-Objective Evolutionary Algorithm Research: A History and Analysis," Technical Report TR-98-03, Air Force Institute of Technology, Wright Patterson AFB, OH, 1998.

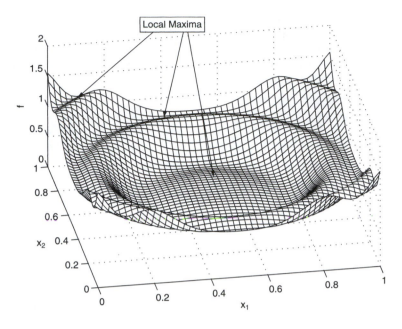

Figure 13.3   Surface plot of the bottom-of-a-bottle function.

Upon execution, we find that the local maximum is at $x = [0.2068, 0.802]$ and $f = 0.8194$. However, if the initial point is changed to $x0 = [0.2, 0.9]$, then we find that the local maximum is at $x = [0.1803, 0.9995]$ and $f = 1.2121$. If the initial point is changed to $x0 = [0.3, 0.6]$, then we find that the local maximum is at $x = [0.4526, 0.4806]$ and $f = 0.4267$. In fact, this problem has an infinite number of local maxima, and the location of the local optimum obtained from `fminsearch` is dependent upon the initial point.

13.3.2 Fitting Curves to Data

Nonlinear curve fitting can be performed in a least-squares sense with `lsqcurvefit`. Given a set of input values *xdata* and a corresponding set of output values *ydata*, this function finds the coefficients x for the "best-fit" of the equation $f(x, xdata_i)$—that is,

$$\text{minimize}_{x} \frac{1}{2} \sum_{i} [f(x, xdata_i) - ydata_i]^2 \qquad (13.11)$$

With *options* 'LargeScale' set to 'off', MATLAB uses two optimization methods for solving the problem of the type shown in Eq. 13.11. The basic command is

[xopt, resnorm] = `lsqcurvefit` (@**UserFunction**, x0, xdata, ydata,
                                lb, ub, options, p1, p2, ...)

where *xopt* is the optimum value of *x* and *resnorm* is the Euclidean norm of the residual

$$\sum (f(x_{\text{data}}) - y_{\text{data}})^2$$

UserFunction is the name of the function that computes the objective function. One could also generate functions of more than one argument with `inline` by specifying the names of the input arguments along with the string expression, as shown in the next example. The quantity *x0* is the vector of starting values, *xdata* and *ydata* are, respectively, vectors of the input and output data, and *options* set the parameters described in `optimset`. The quantities *lb* and *ub*, respectively, are vectors representing the lower and upper bounds on *x*—that is, $lb \le x \le ub$.

An empty matrix [] is used for *lb* and *ub* when they are not used and for *options* to indicate that the default quantities are used. The quantities $p1, p2, \ldots$ are parameters that are passed to **UserFunction**.

The `lsqcurvefit` function is now demonstrated.

Example 13.6   Stress–strain relationship

Stress–strain data are given for a plastic material in Table 13.2, where σ is the stress in ksi and ε is the strain. Assume that the relationship between the stress and strain is of the form

$$\varepsilon = a + b \ln \sigma \qquad (13.12)$$

The objective is to find the design variables *a* and *b* that produce the best-fit function based on the data values given in Table 13.2. The function required by `lsqcurvefit` is given by the inline function **SigmaEpsilonFit**. The script is

```
sigma = [925, 1125, 1625, 2125, 2625, 3125, 3625];
epsilon = [0.11, 0.16, 0.35, 0.48, 0.61, 0.71, 0.85];
x0 = [0.1, 0.1];
SigmaEpsilonFit = inline('x(1)+x(2)*log(sigma)', 'x', 'sigma');
[x, resnorm] = lsqcurvefit(SigmaEpsilonFit, x0, sigma, epsilon)
```

which upon execution gives $x(1) = a = -3.581$ and $x(2) = b = 0.5344$, with the norm of the residual *resnorm* = 0.0064. Thus, the best-fit function is

$$\varepsilon = -3.581 + 0.5344 \ln \sigma \qquad (13.13)$$

TABLE 13.2   Stress-Strain
Data for a Plastic Material

σ	ε
925	0.11
1125	0.16
1620	0.35
2125	0.48
2625	0.61
3125	0.71
3625	0.85

13.3.3 Least Squares

Nonlinear least-squares data fitting are obtained with lsqnonlin. This function can also be used for curve fitting, as shown in Example 13.7. However, lsqnonlin is mainly used for problems with multiple sets of input data and a single set of observed output data, as shown in Example 13.8. The lsqnonlin function finds x such that

$$\text{minimize}_x \sum_i [f_i(x)]^2 \tag{13.14}$$

The lsqnonlin function is

[xopt, resnorm] = lsqnonlin(@**UserFunction**, x0, lb, ub, options, p1, p2, …)

where

$$\text{resnorm} = \sum_i f_i^2(x_{opt})$$

UserFunction is the name of the function that computes the objective functions $f_i(x)$, not $f_i^2(x)$. Note that the sum of squares

$$\sum_i f_i^2$$

should not be formed explicitly (see the example below). The quantity $x0$ is the vector of starting values; lb and ub are the lower and upper bounds on x, respectively; *options* sets the parameters described in optimset; and $p1, p2, \ldots$ are parameters passed to **UserFunction.** Use the pair of brackets [] when lb and ub are not specified and when the default values are used for *options*.

The lsqnonlin function is now demonstrated.

Example 13.7   Stress–strain relationship revisited

The stress–strain relationship of Example 13.6 is now solved with lsqnonlin. The design variables a and b are determined by minimizing

$$\text{minimize}_{a, b} \sum_{i=1}^{7} [\varepsilon_i - (a + b \ln \sigma_i)]^2 \tag{13.15}$$

where ε_i and σ_i correspond to the seven experimentally obtained values in Table 13.2. The script is

sigma = [925, 1125, 1625, 2125, 2625, 3125, 3625];
epsilon = [0.11, 0.16, 0.35, 0.48, 0.61, 0.71, 0.85];
x0 = [0.1, 0.1];
SigmaEpsilonLeastSq = inline('epsilon-(x(1)+x(2)*log(sigma))', 'x', 'sigma', …
        'epsilon');
[x, resnorm] = lsqnonlin(**SigmaEpsilonLeastSq**, x0, [], [], [], sigma, epsilon)

which upon execution, gives $x(1) = a = -3.581$, $x(2) = b = 0.5344$, and *resnorm* = 0.0064. These results are the same as those obtained in Example 13.6.

Example 13.8   Semi-empirical $P-v-T$ relationship

It is well known that the $P-v-T$ relationship of real gases deviates from that estimated by the ideal gas

$$Pv = RT \qquad (13.16)$$

where P is the pressure in atmospheres (atm), v is the molar volume in cm^3/g mol, T is the temperature in K, and R is a gas constant equal to 82.06 atm cm^3/g mol K. A semi-empirical relationship used to correct the departure from the ideal gas is[4]

$$P = \frac{RT}{v - b} - \frac{a}{v(v + b)\sqrt{T}} \qquad (13.17)$$

where the values of a and b are obtained from experimental data. Listed in Table 13.3 are the $P-v-T$ experimental measurements obtained for the gas. The design variables a and b are determined by minimizing the following least-squares objective function:

$$\underset{a,b}{\text{minimize}} \sum_{i=1}^{8} \left[P_i - \frac{RT_i}{v_i - b} + \frac{a}{v_i(v_i + b)\sqrt{T_i}} \right]^2 \qquad (13.18)$$

where P_i, v_i, and T_i correspond to the values at the ith experimentally obtained conditions shown in Table 13.3. If the semi-empirical relationship given by Eq. 13.17 is to exactly match the experimental data, then at the optimum the objective function of Eq. 13.18 would be equal to zero. However, because of the experimental error and the simplicity of the semi-empirical relationship to model the gas nonlinearities, the objective function of Eq. 13.18 will not be equal to zero at the optimum.

The script is

```
x0 = [8000, 40];  R = 82.06;
T = [283, 313, 375, 283, 313, 375, 283, 375];
v = [480, 480, 576, 672, 576, 672, 384, 384];
P = [32.7, 42.6, 44.5, 25.7, 36.6, 38.6, 37.6, 63.0];
pvt = inline('P-R*T./(v-x(2))+x(1)./(sqrt(T).*v.*(v+x(2)))', 'x', 'R', 'T', 'v', 'P');
format long e;
options = optimset('MaxFunEvals', 600);
[x, resnorm] = lsqnonlin(pvt, x0, [], [], options, R, T, v, P)
format short
```

TABLE 13.3   *P-v-T* Data for a Gas

Run i	P (atm)	$v(cm^3$/g mol)	T (K)
1	32.7	480	283
2	42.6	480	313
3	44.5	576	375
4	25.7	672	283
5	36.6	576	313
6	38.6	672	375
7	37.6	384	283
8	63.0	384	375

[4]G. V. Reklaitis et al., *Engineering Optimization*, John Wiley & Sons, New York, NY, 1983, pp. 20–22.

which upon execution gives $a = x(1) = 7.422 \times 10^7$ and $b = x(2) = 30.682$, with *resnorm* = 13.8. Thus, the best-fit function is

$$P = \frac{RT}{v - 30.682} - \frac{7.442 \times 10^7}{v(v + 30.682)\sqrt{T}} \tag{13.19}$$

For this example, the solution is sensitive to the initial point *x0*, which affects the value of *resnorm*. We are looking for a solution that gives the smallest value for *resnorm*. Ideally, the solution with *resnorm* = 0 provides the best fit.

Example 13.9   Mineral exploration

A 2- $\times$ 2-km site is believed to overlay a thick layer of mineral deposits. To create a model of the mineral deposit profile and establish the economic viability of mining the site, a preliminary subsurface exploration consisting of 16 boreholes is conducted. Each borehole is drilled to approximately 45 m, with the upper and lower boundaries of mineral deposits being recorded. The borehole data are given in Table 13.4, where the coordinate and depth of the borehole are in meters.[5] With the borehole data collected, the next step is to create a simplified three-dimensional computer model of the subsurface mineral deposits. The four vertical sides are defined by the 2- $\times$ 2-km boundaries of the site. The top and bottom planes are defined by the surface

$$z(x, y) = a_0 + a_1 x + a_2 y \tag{13.20}$$

We use lsqnonlin in the script below to obtain the best possible fit and to create the top and bottom planes according to the data in Table 13.4.

TABLE 13.4   Subsurface Mineral Exploration Data

Borehole number	Coordinates $[x, y]$	Depth (z) [top, bottom]
1	[10, 10]	[−30.5, −40.5]
2	[750, 10]	[−29, −39.8]
3	[1250, 10]	[−28, −39.3]
4	[1990, 10]	[−26.6, −38.5]
5	[10, 750]	[−34.2, −41.4]
6	[750, 750]	[−32.8, −40.6]
7	[1250, 750]	[−31.8, −40.1]
8	[1990, 750]	[−30.3, −39.4]
9	[10, 1250]	[−36.7, −42]
10	[750, 1250]	[−35.2, −41.2]
11	[1250, 1250]	[−34.2, −40.7]
12	[1990, 1250]	[−32.8, −40]
13	[10, 1990]	[−40.4, −42.8]
14	[750, 1990]	[−39, −42.1]
15	[1250, 1990]	[−38, −41.6]
16	[1990, 1990]	[−36.5, −40.9]

---

[5]M. Austin and D. Chancogne, *Engineering Programming in C, MATLAB, and JAVA*, John Wiley & Sons, New York, NY, 1998, p. 461.

```
xb = [10.0, 750.0, 1250.0, 1990.0, 10.0, 750.0, 1250.0, 1990.0,...
      10.0, 750.0, 1250.0, 1990.0, 10.0, 750.0, 1250.0, 1990.0];
yb = [10.0, 10.0, 10.0, 10.0, 750.0, 750.0, 750.0, 750.0, 1250.0,...
      1250.0, 1250.0, 1250.0, 1990.0, 1990.0, 1990.0, 1990.0];
zbtop = [-30.5, -29.0, -28.0, -26.6, -34.2, -32.8, -31.8, -30.3,...
      -36.7, -35.2, -34.2, -32.8, -40.4, -39.0, -38.0, -36.5];
zbbot =[-40.5, -39.8, -39.3, -38.5, -41.4, -40.6, -40.1, -39.4,...
      -42.0, -41.2, -40.7, -40.0, -42.8, -42.1, -41.6, -40.9];
x0 = [1, 1, 1];
MinrlDepErrTop = inline('zbtop-(x(1)+x(2)*xb+x(3)*yb)', 'x', 'xb', 'yb' ,'zbtop');
[xtop, Errornormtop] = lsqnonlin(MinrlDepErrTop, x0, [], [], [], xb, yb, zbtop)
MinrlDepErrBot =inline('zbbot-(x(1)+x(2)*xb+x(3)*yb)', 'x', 'xb', 'yb', 'zbbot');
[xbot, Errornormbot] = lsqnonlin(MinrlDepErrBot, x0, [] ,[], [], xb, yb, zbbot)
[xb, yb] = meshgrid(linspace(0, 2000, 20), linspace(0, 2000, 20));
zb = xtop(1)+xtop(2)*xb+xtop(3)*yb;
mesh(xb, yb, zb);
hold on
zb = xbot(1)+xbot(2)*xb+xbot(3)*yb;
mesh(xb, yb, zb);
xlabel('x');
ylabel('y');
zlabel('z');
```

Upon execution, we obtain the two best-fit planes shown in Figure 13.4. The fitting error for both the top and bottom planes is 0.0122.

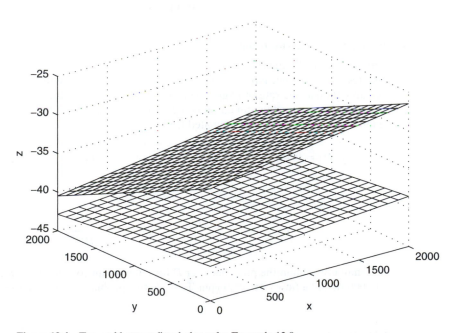

Figure 13.4   Top and bottom fitted planes for Example 13.9.

13.4 SINGLE-OBJECTIVE CONSTRAINED METHODS

Constrained nonlinear optimization methods find the minimum of a constrained function as formulated by Eqs. 13.1 and 13.2 for the case of a single objective function—that is, $m = 1$.

13.4.1 Constrained Single-Variable Method

The constrained single-variable method finds the minimum of a function of one variable on a fixed interval

$$\underset{x}{\text{minimize }} f(x)$$

$$\text{subject to: } x_1 \leq x \leq x_2 \tag{13.21}$$

The function is

$$[\text{xopt, fxopt}] = \texttt{fminbnd}(@\textbf{UserFunction}, \text{x1}, \text{x2}, \text{options}, \text{p1}, \text{p2}, \ldots)$$

where $xopt = x_{opt}$ is the optimum value of x, $fxopt = f(x_{opt})$, and **UserFunction** is the name of the function that computes the objective function. The quantities $x1$ and $x2$ define the interval over which **UserFunction** is minimized with respect to x, *options* sets parameters described in $\texttt{optimset}$, and $p1, p2, \ldots$ are additional parameters passed to **UserFunction**.

The $\texttt{fminbnd}$ function is now demonstrated.

Example 13.10   Piping cost in a plant

Piping costs, including the fittings and pumping costs, are important considerations in the design of a chemical plant. Consider the design of a pipeline that is L-ft. long and is to carry fluid at the rate of Q gpm. The objective is to determine the pipe diameter D (in.) that minimizes the annual pumping cost. For a standard carbon steel pump, the annual pumping cost can be estimated from[6]

$$f(D) = 0.45L + 0.245LD^{1.5} + 325(hp)^{0.5} + 61.6(hp)^{0.925} + 102 \tag{13.22}$$

where

$$hp = 4.4 \times 10^{-8}\frac{LQ^3}{D^5} + 1.92 \times 10^{-9}\frac{LQ^{2.68}}{D^{4.68}} \tag{13.23}$$

We shall now obtain the pipe diameter D for a minimum cost of a pipe with the length of 1000 ft. and a flow rate of 20 gpm. To solve this problem, we create the sub function

---

[6]G.V. Reklaitis et al., *ibid.*, pp.66–67.

PipeLineCost. Then, the pipe diameter for the minimum piping cost is determined
from the following script:

```
function PipeLine
L = 1000;  Q = 20;
[D, fD] = fminbnd(@PipeLineCost, 0.25, 6, [], L, Q)

function f = PipeLineCost(D, L, Q)
hp = 4.4*10^(-8)*L*Q^3/D^5+(1.92*10^(-9)*L*Q^2.68)/(D^4.68);
f = 0.45*L+0.245*L*D^1.5+325*hp^0.5+61.6*hp^0.925+102;
```

which upon execution gives $D = 1.1173$ in. and $fD = f(D) = 1003$ \$/yr.

Example 13.11   Closed box

We shall determine the dimensions of a closed box with maximum volume V that is
constructed from one piece of cardboard 90- $\times$ 90-cm by cutting four squares from its
four corners, as shown in Figure 13.5. The lower and upper values of the height of the
box, x, are assumed to be 8 cm and 12 cm, respectively.

The volume of the closed box, with $y = 90 - 3x$, is

$$\text{maximize } V(x) = xy^2 = x(90 - 3x)^2$$
$$\text{subject to:} \quad 8 \le x \le 12 \tag{13.24}$$

The script is

```
L = 90;
Volume = inline('-(L-3*x)^2*x', 'x', 'L');
[x, V] = fminbnd(Volume, 8, 12, [], L)
```

which upon execution gives $x = 10$ cm and $V = 36,000$ cm^3.

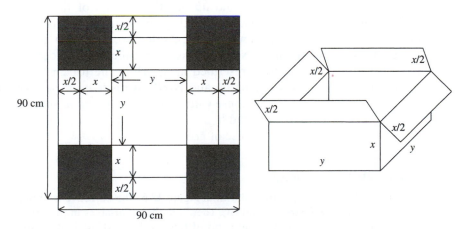

Figure 13.5   Construction of a closed box.

13.4.2 Constrained Multiple-Variable Method

The constrained multivariable method is invoked by `fmincon`, which finds the minimum of a nonlinear multiple-variable constrained optimization problem. Both equality and inequality constraints can be considered. Also, both the objective and/or the constraint functions can be nonlinear. A nonlinear multiple-variable constrained optimization problem is stated as

$$\underset{x}{\text{minimize }} f(x)$$

$$
\begin{aligned}
\text{subject to: } & Ax \leq b & \text{(linear inequality constraints)} \\
& A_{eq}x = b_{eq} & \text{(linear equality contraints)} \\
& C(x) \leq 0 & \text{(nonlinear inequality constraints)} \\
& C_{eq}(x) = 0 & \text{(nonlinear equality constraints)} \\
& lb \leq x \leq ub, \quad \ldots
\end{aligned}
\tag{13.25}
$$

The basic command is

$$[xopt, fxopt] = \texttt{fmincon}(@\textbf{UserFunction}, x0, A, b, Aeq, beq, lb, ub,$$
$$@\textbf{NonLinConstr}, \text{options}, p1, p2, \ldots)$$

where $xopt = x_{opt}$ is the optimum value of x, $fxopt = f(x_{opt})$, and **UserFunction** is the name of the function that computes the objective function. It must create an output in the order specified in the *Help* file for `fmincon`. The quantity $x0$ is the vector of starting values; the matrix A and the vector b are the coefficients of the linear inequality constraints; the matrix A_{eq} and the vector b_{eq} are the coefficients of the equality constraints; lb and ub are the vectors of the lower and upper bounds on x, respectively; *options* sets the parameters described in `optimset`; and $p1, p2, \ldots$ are the additional arguments that are passed to **UserFunction** and **NonLinConstr**. The quantity **NonLinConstr** is a function that defines the nonlinear constraints in the order prescribed in the Help file for `fmincon`. The arguments $p1, p2, \ldots$ of **UserFunction** and **NonLinConstr** *must be identical* even if only one of the functions uses these values. If lb, ub, and *options* are not specified, use []; similarly for A, b, A_{eq}, and b_{eq}.

We now demonstrate the use of `fmincon`.

Example 13.12   Two-bar truss

Consider the two-bar truss shown in Figure 13.6. The objective is to minimize the volume of the two bars AC and BC. There are three variables in the problem: x_1 and x_2, which are the cross-sectional areas of the two bars AC and BC, respectively; and y, which is the vertical position of joint C. There are also several constraints. The tensile stresses on the two bars are limited by a permissible stress $\sigma = 10^5$ kPa. The variable y

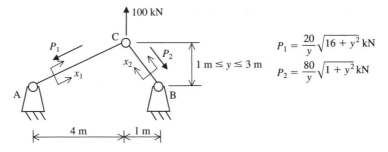

Figure 13.6   Two-bar truss: x_1 and x_2 are cross-sectional areas.

is to remain between 1 and 3 m. Finally, x_1 and x_2 are nonnegative. The optimization problem is formulated as[7]

$$\text{minimize } f_{\text{volume}} = x_1\sqrt{16 + y^2} + x_2\sqrt{1 + y^2}$$

subject to:

$$g_1: \left(20\sqrt{16 + y^2}\right)/(yx_1) - \sigma \leq 0$$

$$g_2: \left(80\sqrt{1 + y^2}\right)/(yx_2) - \sigma \leq 0 \tag{13.26}$$

$$1 \leq y \leq 3$$

$$(x_1, x_2) \geq 0$$

Therefore, $A = b = A_{\text{eq}} = b_{\text{eq}} = C_{\text{eq}} = 0$, $lb = [1, 0, 0]$, and $ub = [3, \infty, \infty]$.
    The script is

```
function TwoBarTruss
x0 = [1, 1, 1]; sigma = 10^5;
lb = [1 0 0]; ub = [3, inf, inf];
options = optimset('LargeScale', 'off');
[x, f] = fmincon(@TrussNonLinF, x0, [], [], [], [], lb, ub, ...
                 @TrussNonLinCon, options, sigma)

function f = TrussNonLinF(x, sigma)
y = x(1); x1 = x(2); x2 = x(3);
f = x1*sqrt(16+y^2)+x2*sqrt(1+y^2);

function [C,Ceq] = TrussNonLinCon(x, sigma)
y = x(1); x1 = x(2); x2 = x(3);
C(1) = 20*sqrt(16+y^2)-sigma*y*x1;
C(2) = 80*sqrt(1+y^2)-sigma*y*x2;
Ceq = [];
```

which upon execution gives $x(1) = y = 1.9519$, $x(2) = x_1 = 0.0005$, $x(3) = x_2 = 0.0009$, and $f = 0.004$. In this example, we have turned off the default selection of the large-scale algorithm; therefore, the medium scale optimization algorithm is used (recall Example 13.4).

---

[7]U. Kirsch, *Optimal Structural Design*, McGraw-Hill, New York, NY, 1981.

Example 13.13   Helical compression spring

Helical compression springs can be found in numerous mechanical devices. They are used to exert force, to provide flexibility, and to either store or absorb energy. To design a helical compression spring, design criteria such as fatigue, yielding, surging, and buckling may have to be taken into consideration. To obtain a solution that meets the various mechanical requirements, an optimization study is performed. The problem as formulated below has one design objective, two design variables, seven constraints, and upper and lower bounds on the variables.

The design objective is to minimize the inverse of the safety factor, which is equivalent to maximizing the safety factor. Referring to Figure 13.7, the two design variables are c and d, where $c = D/d$ is the spring index, D is the mean coil diameter, and d is the wire diameter. The design objective is to minimize the inverse of the safety factor for fatigue or yielding, whichever is critical. For fatigue, the inverse of the safety factor SF_f is obtained from

$$\frac{1}{SF_f} = \frac{\tau_a}{S_{ns}} + \frac{\tau_m}{S_{us}} \tag{13.27}$$

where τ_a and τ_m are, respectively, the alternating and mean components of the shear stress; S_{ns} is the spring's material fatigue strength; and S_{us} is the ultimate strength. For yielding, the inverse of the safety factor SF_y is obtained from

$$\frac{1}{SF_y} = \frac{\tau_a + \tau_m}{S_{ys}} \tag{13.28}$$

where S_{ys} is the shear yield strength. If the condition

$$\frac{\tau_a}{\tau_m} \geq \frac{S_{ns}(S_{ys} - S_{us})}{S_{us}(S_{ns} - S_{ys})} \tag{13.29}$$

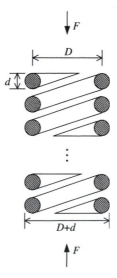

Figure 13.7   Helical compression spring.

is satisfied, then the inverse of the safety factor for fatigue, Eq. 13.27, will be the objective function; otherwise, the inverse of the safety factor for yielding, Eq. 13.28, will be the objective function. The alternating and mean components of the shear stress are, respectively,

$$\tau_a = \frac{8F_a c K_w}{\pi d^2}$$

$$\tau_m = \frac{8F_m c K_w}{\pi d^2} \tag{13.30}$$

where

$$K_w = \frac{4c - 1}{4c + 4} + \frac{0.615}{c}$$

$$F_a = (F_U - F_L)/2 \tag{13.31}$$

$$F_m = (F_U + F_L)/2$$

and F_U and F_L are, respectively, the maximum and minimum applied compressive forces along the spring's axis; F_a and τ_a are, respectively, the alternating force and shear stress; F_m and τ_m are, respectively, the mean force and shear stress; and K_w is the Wahl correction factor for the curvature and direct shear effects on the spring.

The overall design optimization formulation for the helical compression spring is as follows: The design objective is to

$$\text{minimize} \quad \frac{1}{SF_f} = \frac{\tau_a}{S_{ns}} + \frac{\tau_m}{S_{us}} \tag{13.32}$$

for fatigue or to

$$\text{minimize} \quad \frac{1}{SF_y} = \frac{\tau_a + \tau_m}{S_{ys}} \tag{13.33}$$

for yielding, depending on whether Eq. 13.29 is satisfied. The objective function is subjected to the following constraints:

$$
\begin{array}{lll}
g_1: K_1 d^2 - c \leq 0 & \quad & \text{Surging} \\
g_2: K_2 - c^5 \leq 0 & \quad & \text{Buckling} \\
g_3: K_3 c^3 - d \leq 0 & \quad & \text{Minimum number of coils} \\
g_4: K_4 d^2 c^{-3} + K_8 d - 1 \leq 0 & \quad & \text{Pocket length} \\
g_5: K_5(cd + d) - 1 \leq 0 & \quad & \text{Maximum coil diameter} \\
g_6: c^{-1} + K_6 d^{-1} c^{-1} - 1 \leq 0 & \quad & \text{Minimum coil diameter} \\
g_7: K_7 c^3 - d^2 \leq 0 & \quad & \text{Clash allowance}
\end{array}
\tag{13.34}
$$

where

$$
K_1 = \frac{G f_r \Delta}{112800(F_U - F_L)} \qquad K_2 = \frac{G F_U(1 + A)}{22.3 k^2} \qquad K_3 = \frac{8 k N_{\min}}{G}
$$

$$
K_4 = \frac{G(1 + A)}{8 k L_m} \qquad K_5 = \frac{1}{OD} \qquad K_6 = ID
$$

$$
K_7 = \frac{0.8(F_U - F_L)}{AG} \qquad K_8 = \frac{Q}{L_m} \qquad k = \frac{F_U - F_L}{\Delta} \tag{13.35}
$$

$$
S_{ns} = C_1 d^{d_1} \overline{NC}^{B_1} \qquad S_{us} = C_2 d^{A_1} \qquad S_{ys} = C_3 d^{A_1}
$$

The above quantities, along with their assumed values for this problem, are identified as follows:

$A = 0.4$ Dimensionless clearance constant
$f_r = 500$ Hz   Minimum allowable natural frequency
$G = 11.5 \times 10^6$ psi   shear modulus for steel
$ID = 0.75$ in.   Minimum allowable inside diameter of the spring
$OD = 1.5$ in.   Maximum allowable outside diameter of the spring
$N_{min} = 3$ Minimum allowable number of coils
$L_m = 1.25$ in.   Maximum spring length under maximum load
$Q = 2$ Number of inactive coils
$\overline{NC} = 10^6$ cycles   Number of cycles to failure
$\Delta = 0.25$ in   Spring deflection

The spring material is piano wire for which $A_1 = 0.14$, $B_1 = -0.2137$, $C_1 = 630{,}500$, $C_2 = 160{,}000$, and $C_3 = 86{,}550$. The lower and upper bounds on the spring index c and wire diameter d are

$$4 \le c \le 20$$

and

$$0.004 \le d \le 0.25$$

respectively.

The script given below uses three sub functions: **SpringParameters**, which computes the various spring constants required by the subsequent two sub functions; **SpringNLConstr**, which computes the nonlinear constraints; and **SpringObjFunc**, which computes the objective function.

```
function HelicalSpring
A = 0.4;  FL = 15;  FU = 30;  G = 11.5*10^6;
fr = 500;  ID = 0.75;  OD = 1.5;  Lm = 1.25;
NC = 10^6;  Nmin = 3;  Q = 2;  Delta = 0.25;
A1 = -0.14;  B1 = -0.2137;
C1 = 630500;  C2 = 160000;  C3 = 86550;
[K, Fa, Fm] = SpringParameters(A, FL, FU, G, fr, ID, OD, Lm, Nmin, Q, Delta);
x0 = [10,10];  lb = [4, 0.004];  ub = [20, 0.25];
options = optimset('LargeScale', 'off');
[x, f] = fmincon(@SpringObjFunc, x0, [], [], [], [], lb, ub, ...
      @SpringNLConstr, options, K, Fa, Fm, NC, A1, B1, C1, C2, C3)
SafetyFactor = 1/f

function [K, Fa, Fm] = SpringParameters(A, FL, FU, G, fr, ID, OD, Lm, Nmin,
                                               Q, Delta)
Fa = (FU-FL)/2;
Fm = (FU+FL)/2;
k = (FU-FL)/Delta;
K(1) = G*fr*Delta/(112800*(FU-FL));
K(2) = G*FU*(1+A)/(22.3*k^2);
K(3) = 8*k*Nmin/G;
K(4) = G*(1+A)/(8*k*Lm);
K(5) = 1/OD;
K(6) = ID;
K(7) = 0.8*(FU-FL)/(A*G);
K(8) = Q/Lm;
```

```
function [C, Ceq] = SpringNLConstr(x, K, Fa, Fm, NC, A1, B1, C1, C2, C3)
c = x(1); d = x(2);
C(1) = K(1)*d^2–c;
C(2) = K(2)-c^5;
C(3) = K(3)*c^3–d;
C(4) = K(4)*d^2/c^3+K(8)*d-1;
C(5) = K(5)*(c*d+d)-1;
C(6) = 1/c+K(6)/c/d-1;
C(7) = K(7)*c^3-d^2;
Ceq = [];
```

```
function f = SpringObjFunc(x, K, Fa, Fm, NC, A1, B1, C1, C2, C3)
c = x(1);  d = x(2);
Sns = C1*d^A1*NC^B1;
Sus = C2*d^A1;
Sys = C3*d^A1;
Kw = (4*c-1)/(4*c+4)+0.615/c;
Temp = 8*c*Kw/(pi*d^2);
TauA = Fa*Temp;
TauM = Fm*Temp;
Ratio = TauA/TauM;
SS = Sns*(Sys-Sus)/(Sus*(Sns-Sys));
if (Ratio−SS)>=0
   f = TauA/Sns+TauM/Sus;
else
   f = (TauA+TauM)/Sys;
end
```

Upon execution, we obtain $x(1) = c = 8.4987$, $x(2) = d = 0.100$, and safety factor $= 1.8408$. In this example, we have turned off the default selection of the large-scale algorithm; therefore, the medium scale algorithm is used.

Example 13.14   Gear reducer

Consider the design of the gear train with two gears, a gear and a pinion, shown in Figure 13.8. We shall minimize the volume of these two gears and their corresponding shafts. There are seven design variables as follows:

x_1 = gear face width
x_2 = module

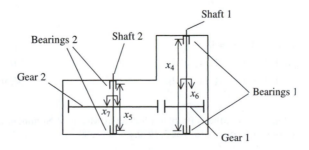

Figure 13.8   Gear reducer.

x_3 = number of teeth of the pinion
x_4 = distance between bearing set 1
x_5 = distance between bearing set 2
x_6 = diameter of shaft 1
x_7 = diameter of shaft 2

The application is such that the lower and upper limits on these variables are

$$2.6 \leq x_1 \leq 3.6$$
$$0.7 \leq x_2 \leq 0.8$$
$$17 \leq x_3 \leq 28$$
$$7.3 \leq x_4 \leq 8.3 \tag{13.36}$$
$$7.3 \leq x_5 \leq 8.3$$
$$2.9 \leq x_6 \leq 3.9$$
$$5.0 \leq x_7 \leq 5.5$$

The design objective is to minimize the overall volume of the shafts, which is given by

$$\text{minimize } f = 0.7854x_1x_2^2(3.3333x_3^2 + 14.933x_3 - 43.0934) - 1.508x_1(x_6^2 + x_7^2) +$$
$$7.477(x_6^3 + x_7^3) + 0.7854(x_4x_6^2 + x_5x_7^2) \tag{13.37}$$

where all the dimensions are in centimeters. The gears are subject to the following constraints[8]

g_1: $\dfrac{1}{(x_1x_2^2x_3)} - \dfrac{1}{27} \leq 0$	Bending stress of gear tooth
g_2: $\dfrac{1}{(x_1x_2^2x_3^2)} - \dfrac{1}{397.5} \leq 0$	Contact stress of gear tooth
g_3: $\dfrac{x_4^3}{(x_2x_3x_6^4)} - \dfrac{1}{1.93} \leq 0$	Shaft 1 deflection
g_4: $\dfrac{x_5^3}{(x_2x_3x_7^4)} - \dfrac{1}{1.93} \leq 0$	Shaft 2 deflection
g_5: $\dfrac{1}{0.1x_6^3}\sqrt{\left(\dfrac{745x_4}{x_2x_3}\right)^2 + 16.9 \times 10^6} - 1100 \leq 0$	Shaft 1 stress
g_6: $\dfrac{1}{0.1x_7^3}\sqrt{\left(\dfrac{745x_5}{x_2x_3}\right)^2 + 157.5 \times 10^6} - 850 \leq 0$	Shaft 2 stress
g_7: $x_2x_3 - 40 \leq 0$	Space restriction
g_8: $5x_2 - x_1 \leq 0$	Space restriction
g_9: $x_1 - 12x_2 \leq 0$	Space restriction
g_{10}: $1.9 - x_4 + 1.5x_6 \leq 0$	Shaft requirement
g_{11}: $1.9 - x_5 + 1.1x_7 \leq 0$	Shaft requirement

[8]J. Golinski, "Optimum Synthesis Problems Solved by Means of Nonlinear Programming and Random Methods," *Journal of Mechanisms*, Vol. 5, 1970, pp. 287–309.

Thus, g_1 through g_7 form the nonlinear inequality constraints, and g_8 through g_{11} form the linear inequality constraints. From the linear inequality constraints, we see that

$$A = \begin{bmatrix} -1 & 5 & 0 & 0 & 0 & 0 & 0 \\ 1 & -12 & 0 & 0 & 0 & 0 & 0 \\ 0 & 0 & 0 & -1 & 0 & 1.5 & 0 \\ 0 & 0 & 0 & 0 & -1 & 0 & 1.1 \end{bmatrix}$$

$$b = [0 \quad 0 \quad -1.9 \quad -1.9]'$$

and $A_{eq} = b_{eq} = C_{eq} = 0$. From Eq. 13.29, we find that $L_{bound} = [2.6, 0.7, 17, 7.3, 7.3, 2.9, 5]$ and $U_{bound} = [3.6, 0.8, 28, 8.3, 8.3, 3.9, 5.5]$.

The script and its two sub functions are

```
function Gears
x0 = [2.6, 0.7,17, 7.3, 7.3, 2.9, 5];
lb = [2.6, 0.7, 17, 7.3, 7.3, 2.9, 5];
ub = [3.6, 0.8, 28, 8.3, 8.3, 3.9, 5.5];
A = zeros(4, 7);
A(1,1) = -1; A(1,2 )= 5;
A(2,1) = 1; A(2,2) = -12;
A(3,4) = -1; A(3,6) = 1.5;
A(4,5) = -1; A(4,7) = 1.1;
b = [0 0 -1.9 -1.9];
options = optimset('LargeScale', 'off');
[x, f] = fmincon(@GearObjFunc, x0, A, b , [], [], lb, ub, @GearNonLinConstr, ..
            options)

function f = GearObjFunc(x)
f =  0.7854*x(1)*x(2)^2*(3.3333*x(3)^2+14.9334*x(3)-43.0934) ...
            -1.508*x(1)*(x(6)^2+x(7)^2)+7.477*(x(6)^3+x(7)^3) ...
            +0.7854*(x(4)*x(6)^2+x(5)*x(7)^2);

function [C, Ceq] = GearNonLinConstr(x)
C(1) = 1/(x(1)*x(2)^2*x(3))-1/27;
C(2) = 1/(x(1)*x(2)^2*x(3)^2)-1/397.5;
C(3) = x(4)^3/(x(2)*x(3)*x(6)^4)-1/1.93;
C(4) = x(5)^3/(x(2)*x(3)*x(7)^4)-1/1.93;
C(5) = sqrt((745*x(4)/(x(2)*x(3)))^2+16.9*10^6)/(0.1*x(6)^3)-1100;
C(6) = sqrt((745*x(5)/(x(2)*x(3)))^2+157.5*10^6)/(0.1*x(7)^3)-850;
C(7) = x(2)*x(3)-40;
Ceq = [];
```

Upon execution, we obtain that $[x_1, x_2, x_3, x_4, x_5, x_6, x_7] = [3.500, 0.700, 17.000, 7.300, 7.7153, 3.3502, 5.2867]$ and $f = 2994.3$.

13.4.3 Quadratic Programming

Quadratic programming refers to a special class of constrained optimization problems in which the objective function is quadratic and the constraints are linear—that is,

$$\underset{x}{\text{minimize}} \quad f = 0.5x^T H x + c^T x$$

$$\text{subject to:} \quad Ax \le b$$
$$A_{eq}x = b_{eq}$$
$$lb \le x \le ub \qquad\qquad (13.38)$$

where H, A, and A_{eq} are matrices and b, b_{eq}, c, x, lb, and ub are column vectors. The function used to obtain a solution to this class of problems is

[xopt, fopt] = quadprog(H, c, A, b, Aeq, beq, lb, ub, x0, options, p1, p2, ...)

where $xopt = x_{opt}$ is the optimum value of x, $fopt = f(x_{opt})$; the symmetric matrix H and the vector c are the set of coefficients of the quadratic objective function f; the matrix A and the vector b are the coefficients of the linear inequality constraints; the matrix A_{eq} and the vector b_{eq} are the coefficients of the linear equality constraints; the vectors lb and ub specify the lower and upper bounds, respectively, on the design variables x; the vector $x0$ sets the starting point; and *options* sets the parameters described in optimset.

We now demonstrate the use of quadprog.

Example 13.15   Production planning revisited

The production-planning scenario discussed in Example 13.2 is slightly revised. It is now assumed that the profits of product A and B are functions of the number of units of each product. For product A, the dollar profit per unit varies according to

$$4 + 2x_1 + 3x_2$$

and that for product B according to

$$5 + 5x_1 + 4x_2$$

The remaining aspects of the problem are the same as those given in Example 13.2. Accordingly, the objective function to be minimized is

$$f = -(4 + 2x_1 + 3x_2)x_1 - (5 + 5x_1 + 4x_2)x_2$$
$$= -(4 + 2x_1)x_1 - (5 + 4x_2)x_2 - 8x_1x_2$$

or

$$f = \frac{1}{2}[x_1 \ \ x_2]\begin{bmatrix} -4 & -8 \\ -8 & -8 \end{bmatrix}\begin{bmatrix} x_1 \\ x_2 \end{bmatrix} + [-4 \ \ -5]\begin{bmatrix} x_1 \\ x_2 \end{bmatrix} \qquad (13.39)$$

The script is

H = [-4, -8; -8, -8];
c = [-4; -5];
A = [1, 1; 1.25, 0.75; 0, 1];

```
b = [200; 200; 150];
lb = zeros(2, 1);
options = optimset('LargeScale', 'off');
[xopt, fopt] = quadprog(H, c, A, b, [], [], lb, [], [], options)
```

Upon execution, we obtain $xopt(1) = x_1 = 50, xopt(2) = x_2 = 150$, and $-fopt = -f(x_{opt}) = 155,950$.

13.4.4 Semi-Infinitely Constrained Method

The semi-infinitely constrained method finds the solution of optimization problems formulated as

$$\begin{aligned}
\underset{x}{\text{minimize}} \quad & f(x) \\
\text{subject to:} \quad & Ax \leq b \\
& A_{eq}x = b_{eq} \\
& C(x) \leq 0 \\
& C_{eq}(x) = 0 \\
& K_1(x, w_1) \leq 0 \\
& K_2(x, w_2) \leq 0 \\
& \quad \vdots \\
& K_n(x, x_n) \leq 0 \\
& \forall(w_1, \ldots, w_n)
\end{aligned} \tag{13.40}$$

where x is the design variable vector, f is the scalar objective function, A is the matrix representing the linear inequality constraints, b is the vector of linear inequality constraints, A_{eq} is the matrix representing the linear equality constraints, b_{eq} is the vector of linear equality constraints, C is the vector representing the non-linear inequality constraints, and C_{eq} is the vector of nonlinear equality constraints. The quantity $K_n(x, w_n)$ is the vector (or the matrix) of semi-infinite functions, a function of vectors x and w_n, with the free variable w_n representing a range of values over which the solution for the design variable x is sought, and $\forall(w_1, \ldots, w_n)$, with $\forall$ representing "for all," indicating that the problem is considered for all values of the free variables $w_1, \ldots, w_n$ within their corresponding ranges. For example, w_n may represent a temperature range in a heat-transfer problem or a frequency range in a vibration problem over which the K_n-constraint has to be satisfied for all temperature or frequency values in the range. The variables $w_1, \ldots, w_n$ are vectors of, at most, length 2.

The function is

$$[xopt, fxopt] = \texttt{fseminf}(@\textbf{UserFunction}, x0, n, @\textbf{SemiConstr}, \ldots$$
$$A, b, Aeq, Beq, lb, ub, options, p1, p2, \ldots)$$

where $xopt = x_{opt}$ is the optimum value of x, $fopt = f(x_{opt})$, and **UserFunction** is the name of the function that computes the scalar function f. The quantity $x0$ sets the starting point; n is the number of semi-infinite constraints in Eq. 13.33; the matrix A and the vector b are the coefficients of the linear inequality constraints; the matrix A_{eq} and the vector b_{eq} are the coefficients of the linear equality constraints; lb and ub specify the lower and upper bounds, respectively, on the design variables x; *options* sets the parameters described in `optimset`; and $p1, p2, \ldots$ are the additional arguments that are passed to **UserFunction** and **SemiConstr**. The arguments $p1, p2, \ldots$ of **UserFunction** and **SemiConstr** must be identical, even if only one of the functions uses these values. If lb, ub, and *options* are not specified, then use []; similarly for A, b, A_{eq}, and b_{eq}. The quantity **SemiConstr** is a function that defines the nonlinear constraints as follows:

```
function [C, Ceq, K1, K2, ..., Kn, s] = SemiConstr(x, s, p1, p2, ...)
% Initial sampling interval

If isnan(s(1, 1)),
     s = ...  % s has n rows and 2 columns
end
w1  = ... % computes sample set
...
wn  = ... % computes sample set
K1  = ... % 1st semi-infinite constraint at x and w
...
Kn  = ...  % nth semi-infinite constraint at x and w
C   = ...  % computes nonlinear inequalities
Ceq = ...  % computes nonlinear equalities
```

where $K1, \ldots, Kn$ are the semi-infinite constraints evaluated for a range of sampled values of the free variables $w_1, \ldots, w_n$, respectively. The rows of the two-column matrix s have the sampling interval for the corresponding values of $\omega_1, \ldots, \omega_n$, which are used to calculate $K1, \ldots, Kn$—that is, the ith row of s contains the sampling interval for evaluating K_i. When K_i is a vector, use only $s(i, 1)$ (the second column can all be zeros). When K_i is a matrix, $s(i, 2)$ is used for sampling of the rows in K_i, $s(i, 1)$ is used for sampling of the columns in K_i. In the first iteration, s is set to NaN so that some initial sampling interval is determined. If C and/or C_{eq} do not exist, then set them to [].

We now demonstrate the use of `fseminf`.

Example 13.16　Planar two-link manipulator

Consider the planar two-link manipulator shown in Figure 13.9. This manipulator is capable of positioning to a point in its plane. The design objective is to maximize the workspace area covered by the manipulator. There are two design variables, a and b, which represent the lengths of the two links. The constraints are the lower (G_1) and upper (G_2) bounds on the ratio a/b, the upper bound (K_1) is a measure of dexterity, and the lower and upper bounds on the two design variables a and b. The dexterity refers to the ease with which the manipulator can either move or exert force or torque along

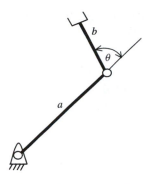

Figure 13.9   Planar two-link manipulator.

arbitrary directions within its workspace. The condition number κ of the Jacobian matrix for the manipulator is used as a metric for dexterity.[9] It is desired that this condition number be as close to unity as possible. The problem formulation is

$$\text{minimize } f(a, b) = -\pi[(a + b)^2 - (a - b)^2]$$

subject to:

$$
\begin{aligned}
&G_1: a/b \geq 1.1 \\
&G_2: a/b \leq 2 \\
&K_1: \kappa \leq 1.26 \\
&0.1 \leq a \leq 2 \\
&0.1 \leq b \leq 2 \\
&\forall \theta \in [100°, 150°]
\end{aligned}
\qquad (13.41)
$$

where the condition number κ is given by

$$\kappa = (a^2 + 2b^2 + 2ab \cos \theta)/2ab \cos \theta \qquad (13.42)$$

and the semi-infinite constraints are to be satisfied for the entire range of $\theta \in [100°, 150°]$ with a sampling interval of 5°.

The script and its sub functions are

```
function PlanarManipulator
x0 = [1, 1];
LBnd = [0.1, 0.1];  UBnd = [2, 2];
[x, fopt] = fseminf(@TwoLinkObjFunc, x0, 1, @TwoLinkConstr, [], [], [], [], ...
                    LBnd, UBnd, [])
text(120, 1.17, 'Initial')
text(113, 1.05, 'Optimum')
ylabel('Condition number \kappa')
xlabel('\theta (degrees)')
```

---

[9]C. Gosselin and J. Angeles, "A Global Performance Index for the Kinetic Optimization of Robotic Manipulators," *ASME Journal of Mechanical Design*, Vol. 113, Sept. 1991, p. 222.

```
function [C, Ceq, K1, s] = TwoLinkConstr(x, s)
a = x(1);  b = x(2);
if isnan(s(1,1))
   s = [5, 0];
end
theta = (100:s(1,1):150)*pi/180;
K1 = (a^2+2*b^2+2*(a*b)*cos(theta))./(2*(a*b)*sin(theta))-1.26;
C(1) = -a/b+1.1;
C(2) = a/b-2;
Ceq = [];
plot(theta*180/pi, K1+1.26, 'k')
hold on

function f = TwoLinkObjFunc(x)
a = x(1);  b = x(2);
f = -pi*((a+b)^2-(a-b)^2);
```

Upon execution, we obtain Figure 13.10 and that $x(1) = a = 2.0$ and $x(2) = b = 1.4433$, with the corresponding workspace area of $-f = 36.2732$. In Figure 13.10, we have plotted the condition number κ as a function of θ for each iteration to show the improvement in the condition number from its initial range to its optimum range. In this optimum range of the condition number, when $\theta = 136°$, we see that the condition number is almost unity. This angle is the most desirable configuration for the manipulator in terms of its dexterity.

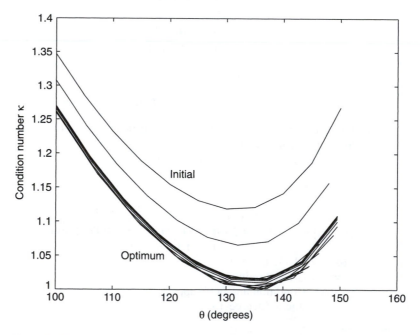

Figure 13.10   The condition number of the planar two-link manipulator as a function of θ as the `fseminf` constraint K_1 progresses from the initial values of a and b to their optimum.

13.5 MULTIOBJECTIVE OPTIMIZATION

Multiobjective optimization refers to the solution of problems with more than one design objective. The objectives in such problems are at least partly in conflict with each other. The conflict arises because of the inherent properties of the problem. For example, consider a structural member in tension with the two design objectives of minimizing weight and stress. These two objectives conflict with each other—that is, as the weight of the member is reduced, the stress is increased, and vice versa. During the optimization process for such a problem then, one reaches a point where it may not be possible to simultaneously improve all such objectives. Hence, in a multiobjective problem, the term "optimize" generally refers to a solution point for which there is no way of further improving any objective without worsening at least one other objective. Such a solution point is referred to as a Pareto point or a noninferior point. Many such Pareto solutions may exist in a multiobjective optimization problem, and these solutions collectively form a Pareto frontier. Figure 13.11 shows, for a two-variable, two-objective problem, the feasible domains in the variable space and the objective space and the Pareto frontier when both f_1 and f_2 are minimized. As shown in the figure, the feasible domain in the objective space is obtained as a result of a mapping from the variable space, and the Pareto frontier solution set corresponds to the "best" that can be achieved. Trade-offs exist between the solutions in the Pareto set; that is, as one objective is improved in the set, the other is worsened. The final preferred solution to a multiobjective problem is selected from the Pareto set according to the decision maker's preference. MATLAB has two functions to solve multiobjective problems: `fminimax`, and `fgoalattain`. The `fminimax` method solves the problem

$$\min_{x} \max_{f} \{f_1, f_2, \ldots, f_m\}$$

$$\text{subject to:} \quad \begin{aligned} Ax &\leq b \quad &\text{(Linear inequality constraints)} \\ A_{eq}x &= b_{eq} \quad &\text{(Linear equality constraints)} \\ C(x) &\leq 0 \quad &\text{(Nonlinear inequality constraints)} \\ C_{eq}(x) &= 0 \quad &\text{(Nonlinear equality constraints)} \\ lb &\leq x \leq ub \end{aligned}$$

(13.43)

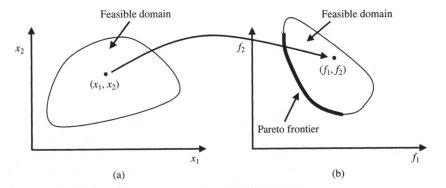

Figure 13.11 Feasible domains in (a) the variable space and (b) the objective space with its Pareto frontier.

where x is the design variable vector; $f_1, f_2, \ldots, f_m$, are the objective functions; the matrix A and the vector b are the coefficients of the linear inequality constraints; the matrix A_{eq} and the vector b_{eq} are the coefficients of the linear equality constraints; C contains the nonlinear inequality constraints; C_{eq} contains the nonlinear equality constraints; and lb and ub specify the lower and upper bounds, respectively, on the design variables x. The `fminimax` method iteratively minimizes the worst-case value of the objective functions subject to the constraints.

The function is

$$[\text{xopt, fxopt}] = \texttt{fminimax}(@\textbf{UserFunction}, \text{x0}, \text{A}, \text{b}, \text{Aeq}, \text{beq}, \text{lb}, \text{ub}, \ldots$$
$$@\textbf{NonLinConstr}, \text{options}, \text{p1}, \text{p2}, \ldots)$$

where $xopt = x_{opt}$ is the optimum value of x, $fxopt = f_i(x_{opt})$, and **UserFunction** is the name of the function that computes the objective function. The quantity $x0$ is the vector of starting values; the matrix A and the vector b are the coefficients of the linear inequality constraints; the matrix A_{eq} and the vector b_{eq} are the coefficients of the equality constraints; lb and ub are the vectors of the lower and upper bounds on x, respectively; *options* sets the parameters described in `optimset`; and $p1, p2, \ldots$ are the additional arguments that are passed to **UserFunction** and **NonLinConstr**. The quantity **NonLinConstr** is a function that defines the nonlinear inequality and equality constraints in a prescribed order as follows:

$$\texttt{function } [\text{C, Ceq}] = \text{NonLinConstr}(\text{x}, \text{p1}, \text{p2}, \ldots)$$

The arguments $p1, p2, \ldots$ of **UserFunction** and **NonLinConstr** *must be identical* even if only one of the functions uses these values or one of the functions uses only some of the quantities. If $lb, ub,$ and *options* are not specified, then use []; similarly for A, b, A_{eq}, and b_{eq}.

The function `fgoalattain` solves the following multiobjective problem:

$$\begin{aligned}
&\underset{x,\, y}{\text{maximize}} \; \gamma \\[4pt]
&\text{subject to:} \quad f_i(x) - \omega_i \gamma \le (\text{goal})_i \quad i = 1, \ldots, m \\
&\qquad\qquad Ax \le b \qquad \text{(Linear inequality constraints)} \\
&\qquad\qquad A_{eq}x = b_{eq} \quad \text{(Linear equality constraints)} \\
&\qquad\qquad C(x) \le 0 \qquad \text{(Nonlinear inequality constraints)} \\
&\qquad\qquad C_{eq}(x) = 0 \qquad \text{(Nonlinear equality constraints)} \\
&\qquad\qquad lb \le x \le ub
\end{aligned} \qquad (13.44)$$

where γ is a scalar variable unrestricted in sign, f_i is the ith objective function, and ω_i and $(\text{goal})_i$ are, respectively, the weighting coefficient and target for the ith objective function. The weighting coefficient controls the relative degree of under- or overattainment of the goal. The term $\omega_i \gamma$ provides an element of slackness in the formulation. For instance, setting all the weighting coefficients equal to the initial goals indicates that the same percentage of the under- or overattainment of the goals is desired.

The function is

x = fgoalattain(@**UserFunction**, x0, Goal, Weight, A, b, Aeq, beq, lb, ub, ...
　　　　　　　　@**NonLinConstr**, options, p1, p2, ...)

where the vector *Weight* contain the elements ω_i, the vector *Goal* contains the elements $(\text{goal})_i$, and the remaining quantities are as defined for fminimax.

We now demonstrate the use of fminimax and fgoalattain.

Example 13.17　Vibrating platform

Consider the system shown in Figure 13.12. The motor is mounted on a beam-type platform composed of three layers of materials. It is assumed that the beam is simply supported at both ends. A vibratory disturbance is imparted from the motor to the beam. The design objectives are to minimize the following:

1. The negative of the fundamental natural frequency of the beam, denoted f_1
2. The cost of the material comprising the beam, denoted f_2

The constraints include an upper bound on the mass of the beam g_1, upper bounds on the thickness of layer 2, g_2, and layer 3, g_3, and upper and lower bounds on the design variables. The five design variables are the beam's length L, its thickness b, the distance d_1 to the central axis of the interface of layers 1 and 2, the distance d_2 to the interface of the layers, and the distance to the top of the beam, d_3. The mass density ρ, Young's modulus E, and cost per unit volume c for the material of each of the three layers are given in Table 13.5. The problem formulation is[10]

$$\text{minimize}\quad f_1(d_1, d_2, d_3, b, L) = -(\pi/2L^2)\sqrt{EI/\mu}$$
$$\text{minimize}\ f_2(d_1, d_2, d_3, b) = 2b(c_1 d_1 + c_2(d_2 - d_1) + c_3(d_3 - d_2))$$

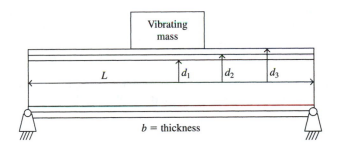

Figure 13.12　Vibrating, multilayered, simply supported platform.

TABLE 13.5　Material Properties and Cost for the Vibrating Platform

Layer i	ρ_i (kg/m^3)	E_i (N/m^2)	c_i ($/volume)
1	100	1.6×10^9	500
2	2770	70×10^9	1500
3	7780	200×10^9	800

---

[10] Revised from A. Messac, "Physical Programming: Effective Optimization fro Computational Design," *AIAA Journal*, 34(1), 1996, pp.149–158.

where:

$$EI = (2b/3)\,(E_1 d_1^3 + E_2(d_2^3 - d_1^3) + E_3(d_3^3 - d_2^3))$$
$$\mu = 2b(\rho_1 d_1 + \rho_2(d_2 - d_1) + \rho_3(d_3 - d_2))$$

subject to:

$$g_1: \mu L - 2800 \quad \leq 0 \qquad \text{Beam mass}$$
$$g_2: d_2 - d_1 - 0.15 \leq 0 \qquad \text{Layer thickness}$$
$$g_3: d_3 - d_2 - 0.01 \leq 0 \qquad \text{Layer thickness}$$
$$0.05 \leq d_1 \leq 0.5$$
$$0.2 \leq d_2 \leq 0.5$$
$$0.2 \leq d_3 \leq 0.6$$
$$0.35 \leq b \leq 0.5$$
$$3 \leq L \leq 6$$

We see that g_1 is a nonlinear inequality constraint and that g_2 and g_3 are linear inequality constraints. Thus,

$$A = \begin{bmatrix} -1 & 1 & 0 & 0 & 0 \\ 0 & -1 & 1 & 0 & 0 \end{bmatrix}$$
$$b = [0.15 \quad 0.01]'$$

and since there are no linear and nonlinear equality constraints, $C_{eq} = A_{eq} = b_{eq} = 0$.

To have the same order of magnitude of the computed functions, the design objectives are scaled according to

$$scaled\_value = \frac{raw - good}{bad - good} \tag{13.45}$$

where the quantity *raw* refers to the actual value (before scaling) of the function, *good* refers to the target (or desired) value of the function, and *bad* refers to the undesirable value of the function. We see from Eq. 13.38 that when *raw* is equal to *good*, *scaled_value* = 0, and when *raw* is equal to *bad*, *scaled_value* = 1.

The following script uses three sub functions: **BeamProperties,** in which $[x_1, x_2, x_3, x_4, x_5] = [d_1, d_2, d_3, b, L]$; **VibPlatNLConstr**, which computes the nonlinear inequality constraint; and **VibPlatformObj**, which computes the objective functions.

```
function VibratingPlatform
x0 = [0.3, 0.35, 0.4, 5, 0.4];
lb = [0.05, 0.2, 0.2, 0.35, 3];
ub = [0.5, 0.5, 0.6, 0.5, 6];
E = [1.6, 70, 200]*10^9;
Rho = [100, 2770, 7780];
c = [500, 1500, 800];
good = [500, 100];
A = [-1, 1, 0, 0, 0; 0, -1, 1, 0, 0];
b = [0.15, 0.01]';
for k = 1:5
   bad = [100+k*10 500-k*50];
   [xopt, fxopt] = fminimax(@VibPlatformObj, x0, A, b, [], [], lb, ub, ...
                    @VibPlatNLConstr, [], E, Rho, c, good, bad);
   for m = 1:2
```

```
      ff(m) = fxopt(m)*(bad(m)-good(m))+good(m);
    end
    f1(k) = ff(1);
    f2(k) = ff(2);
  end
end
[f2sort, indxf2] = sort(f2);
f1sort = f1(indxf2);
plot(-f1sort, f2sort,' ko-');
xlabel('Negative frequency (Hz)');
ylabel('Cost ($)');

function [EI, mu] = BeamProperties(x, E, Rho, c)
EI = (2*x(4)/3)*(E(1)*x(1)^3+E(2)*(x(2)^3-x(1)^3)+E(3)*(x(3)^3-x(2)^3));
mu = 2*x(4)*(Rho(1)*x(1)+Rho(2)*(x(2)-x(1))+Rho(3)*(x(3)-x(2)));

function [C, Ceq] = VibPlatNLConstr(x, E, Rho, c, good, bad)
[EI, mu] = BeamProperties(x, E, Rho, c);
C(1) = mu*x(5)-2800;
Ceq = [];

function f = VibPlatformObj(x, E, Rho, c, good, bad)
[EI, mu] = BeamProperties(x, E, Rho, c);
f1 = pi/(2*x(5)^2)*sqrt(EI/mu);
f(1) = (f1-good(1))/(bad(1)-good(1));
f2 = 2*x(4)*(c(1)*x(1)+c(2)*(x(2)-x(1))+c(3)*(x(3)-x(2)));
f(2) = (f2-good(2))/(bad(2)-good(2));
```

Upon execution, we obtain the Pareto frontier shown in Figure 13.13.

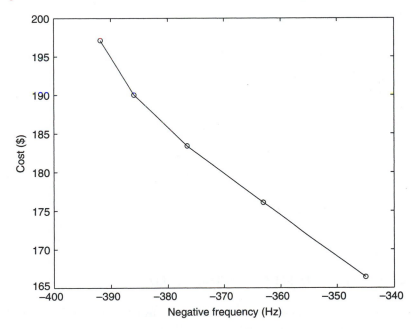

Figure 13.13 Pareto frontier of the vibrating platform.

Example 13.18   Production planning revisited

Consider the production planning problem given in Example 13.2. We now introduce a second design objective, which is to maximize (or minimize the negative of) the production units of product A. Then, the objective function and the constraints are

$$\text{minimize} \quad f_1(x_1, x_2) = -4x_1 - 5x_2$$
$$f_2(x_1) = -x_1$$

subject to:

$$g_1: x_1 + x_2 \le 200$$
$$g_2: 1.25x_1 + 0.75 \quad x_2 \le 200$$
$$g_3: x_2 \le 150$$
$$(x_1, x_2) \ge 0$$

Thus,

$$A = \begin{bmatrix} 1 & 1 \\ 1.25 & 0.75 \\ 0 & 1 \end{bmatrix}$$

$$b = [200 \quad 200 \quad 150]'$$

and $lb = [0, 0]$ and $ub = [\infty, \infty]$. Since there are no equality constraints and no non-linear constraints, $C_{\text{eq}} = A_{\text{eq}} = b_{\text{eq}} = C = 0$.

The script is

```
A = [1 1; 1.25 0.75; 0 1];
b = [200, 200, 150]';
goal = [-950, -50];  x0 = [50, 50];
lb = [0, 0]; ub = [inf, inf];
Weight = abs(goal);
options = optimset('GoalsExactAchieve', 2);
ProdPlanObj = inline('[-4*x(1)-5*x(2), -x(1)]', 'x');
[x, fxopt] = fgoalattain(ProdPlanObj, x0, goal, Weight, A, b, [], [], ...
                         lb, ub, [], options)
```

where we have set the option *GoalsExactAchieve* to 2 (the number of independent variables), which tells the algorithm to try to satisfy the goals exactly, not over- or under-achieve them. If the default value is used, then the solution is a function of $x0$. The execution of the script gives a Pareto solution $[x_1, x_2] = [50, 150]$, with $fxopt = [-950, -50]$.

13.6 SUMMARY OF FUNCTIONS INTRODUCED

A summary of the Optimization Toolbox functions introduced in this chapter and their descriptions are presented in Table 13.6.

TABLE 13.6 MATLAB Functions from Optimization Toolbox Introduced in Chapter 13

MATLAB function	Description
fgoalattain	Multiobjective goal attainment solution
fminbnd	Minimum of a function of one variable on a fixed interval
fmincon	Minimum of a constrained nonlinear multivariable function
fminimax	Minimax solution
fminsearch	Minimum of an unconstrained multiple-variable function
fminunc	Minimum of an unconstrained multiple-variable function
fseminf	Minimum of a semi-infinitely constrained multiple-variable nonlinear function
linprog	Linear programming solution
lsqcurvefit	Nonlinear curve-fitting solution in the least-squares sense
lsqnonlin	Nonlinear least-squares solution
quadprog	Quadratic programming solution

EXERCISES

Sections 13.1.2 and 13.3.1

13.1 Consider the two-pair bar mechanism shown in Figure 13.14 in which links OA and AC have the same length $L_1 = 0.5$ m, and links CB and BD have the same length $L_2 = 0.3$ m. Joint O is a fixed joint, and joints C and D are pin connections on two slides that can move without friction along a horizontal line. The mechanism is subjected to three external forces. They are the vertical forces $P_1 = 3$ kN and $P_2 = 1$ kN at joints A and B, respectively, and a horizontal force $P = 3$ kN at joint D. We assume that before the loads are applied, the bars are lined up (stretched out) along the horizontal line. We also assume that the weight of the mechanism is negligible. The equilibrium of the mechanism under the applied loads is obtained by minimizing its potential energy (PE) function

$$\text{minimize PE} = -P_1L_1 \sin \alpha - P_2L_2 \sin \beta + P[L_1(1 - \cos \alpha) + L_2(1 - \cos \beta)]$$

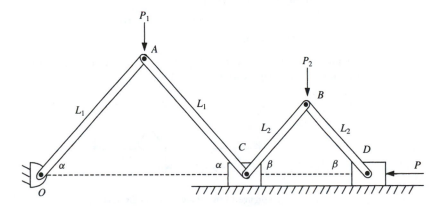

Figure 13.14 Two-pair bar mechanism of Exercise 13.1.

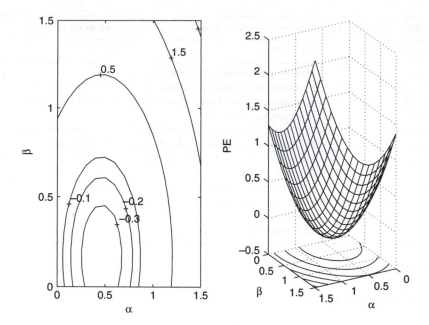

Figure 13.15   Contour and surface plots of Exercise 13.1.

a. Create Figure 13.15.

b. Use fminunc with an initial point $(\alpha, \beta) = (1, 1)$ radians to verify the graphical solution. [Answer: $\alpha = 0.4636$ rad, $\beta = 0.1651$ rad, and PE $= -0.3789$.]

13.2 Consider the water canal[11] shown in Figure 13.16. A water canal with a fixed cross-sectional area is to be designed so that its discharge flow rate is maximized. The design variables are the height h, the width of base c, and the side angle θ. It can be shown that the flow rate is proportional to the inverse of the wetted perimeter p, which is given by

$$p = c + (2h/\sin \theta)$$

The cross-sectional area A is given by

$$A = ch + h^2 \cot \theta$$

If $A = 100$ ft.^{2}, then:

a. Formulate the problem in an unconstrained form to maximize the flow rate $1/p$ as a function of the design variables h and θ.

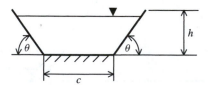

Figure 13.16   Water canal of Exercise 13.2.

---

[11]P. Y. Papalambros and D. J. Wilde, *Principles of Optimal Design: Modeling and Computation*, Cambridge University Press, New York, NY, 1988, p. 151.

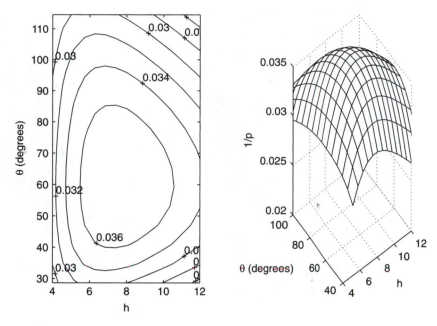

Figure 13.17 Contour and surface plots of Exercise 13.2.

b. Create Figure 13.17.
c. Use fminsearch to validate the graphical solution with an initial point $(h, \theta) = (1, 1 \text{ rad})$. [Answer: $[h, \theta] = [7.5938, 1.0472 \text{ rad}]$.]

13.3 Figure 13.18 shows an unloaded and loaded two-spring system. After the load F is applied at point A, the system is deformed until it is in equilibrium at point B—that is, when the potential energy (PE) of the system is minimum. Find the location (x_1, x_2) of joint B by:

a. Creating the contour and surface plots shown in Figure 13.19.
b. Solving for the optimized displacements x_1 and x_2 using fminsearch, with an initial point $(x_1, x_2) = (1, 1)$. [Answers: PE $= -15.2802$, $x_1 = 4.1289$, $x_2 = 0$.]

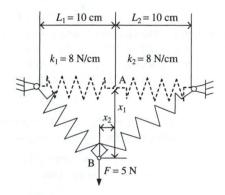

Figure 13.18 Two-spring system of Exercise 13.4.

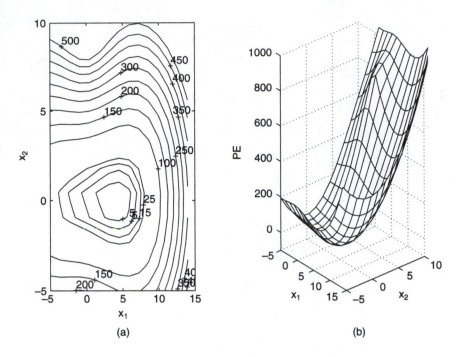

Figure 13.19 (a) Contour and (b) surface plots of the PE function for the two-spring system shown in Figure 13.18.

Sections 13.1.2 and 13.4.2

13.4 The average total production time per work piece for a machining operation is given by[12]:

$$T = t_m + \frac{t_m t_c}{T_l} + t_{aux}$$

where t_m is the cutting time, T_l is the tool life, t_c is the time it takes to change the tool, and t_{aux} is the auxiliary time. Here, $t_c = 7$ and $t_{aux} = 3$ are assumed to be empirical constants. For a turning operation, the cutting time is obtained by

$$t_m = \frac{\pi D L}{1000 V f}$$

where the diameter of the machined surface is $D = 100$ mm, and the length of the work piece to be machined is $L = 500$ mm. Also, V and f are the cutting surface speed and feed rate of the cutting tool, respectively. The influence of the cutting speed, the feed rate, and the depth of cut d on the tool life are estimated from the extended Taylor equation

$$V T_l^n f^a d^b = K_t$$

where $n = 0.17$, $a = 0.77$, $b = 0.37$, and $K_t = 200$ are empirical constants. If V and f are the design variables, then the optimization problem is

$$\text{minimize } T(V, f)$$
$$\text{subject to: } f \leq 2$$

---

[12]D. A. Stephenson and J. S. Agapiou, *Metal Cutting Theory and Practice*, Marcel Dekker, New York, NY, 1997.

If $d = 0.3$, then:

a. Create the contour and surface plots of the problem.

b. Use fmincon with an initial point of $(V, f) = (10, 1)$ to obtain the optimum solutions. [Answers: $T = 3.942$, $V = 100.46$, $f = 2.000$]

13.5 Figure 13.20 shows two frictionless rigid carts, A and B, connected by three linear elastic springs having spring constants $k_1 = 5$ N/m, $k_2 = 10$ N/m, and $k_3 = 8$ N/m.[13] The springs are at their natural positions when the applied force P is zero. Use the following unconstrained optimization problem for the potential energy function

$$\text{minimize } PE = 0.5k_2 x_1^2 + 0.5k_3(x_2 - x_1)^2 + 0.5k_1 x_2^2 - Px_2$$

a. Obtain the contour and surface plots as shown in Figure 13.21.

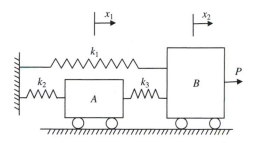

Figure 13.20   Spring-mass system of Exercise 13.5.

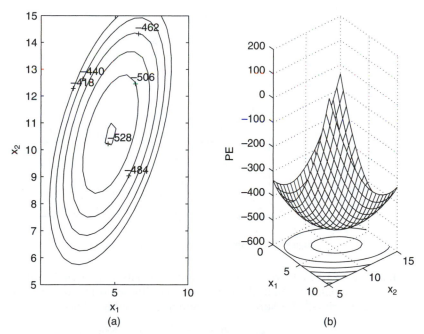

Figure 13.21   (a) Contour and (b) surface plots of the PE function for the two-spring system shown in Figure 13.20.

---

[13]S. S. Rao, *Engineering Optimization, Theory, and Practice*, 3rd ed., John Wiley and Sons, New York, NY, 1996.

b. Obtain the optimized displacements x_1 and x_2 using `fminunc`, with an initial point $(x_1, x_2) = (1, 1)$, and with $P = 100$ N. [Answers: PE = 529.41, $x_1 = 4.759$, $x_2 = 10.5882.$]

Section 13.3.1

13.6 Three carts, interconnected by springs and initially at an unstressed equilibrium state, are subjected to the loads P_1, P_2, and P_3 as shown in Figure 13.22.[14] The displacements of the carts from their original equilibrium position ($x_i = 0$: for all i) are sought by minimizing the potential energy of the system (PE):

$$\text{PE} = 0.5X'KX - X'P$$

where

$$K = \begin{bmatrix} k_1 + k_2 + k_4 & -k_3 & -k_4 \\ -k_3 & k_2 + k_3 + k_5 & -k_5 \\ -k_4 & -k_5 & k_4 + k_5 + k_6 \end{bmatrix}$$

$$P = [P_1 \quad P_2 \quad P_3]'$$

$$X = [x_1 \quad x_2 \quad x_3]'$$

The input data are

$k_1 = 4500$ N/m	$k_4 = 2250$ N/m	$P_1 = 1100$ N
$k_2 = 1650$ N/m	$k_5 = 550$ N/m	$P_2 = 1800$ N
$k_3 = 1100$ N/m	$k_6 = 9300$ N/m	$P_3 = 3300$ N

Find the equilibrium position of the carts using `fminunc` with the initial point $(x_1, x_2, x_3) = (0, 0, 0)$. [Answer: $[x_1, x_2, x_3] = [0.322, 0.714, 0.365]$]

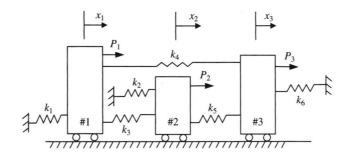

Figure 13.22 Spring-mass system of Exercise 13.6.

13.7 Figure 13.23 shows a spring-weight system in its undeformed position with no supporting weights and in its deformed position with supporting weights at the joints between the springs.[15] The stiffness of the spring i is k_i and is defined by

$$k_i = 450 + 225(N/3 - i)^2 \quad \text{N/m} \quad i = 1, \ldots, 6$$

---

[14] S. S. Rao, *ibid.*, p. 420.
[15] G. N. Vanderplaats, *ibid.*, p. 94.

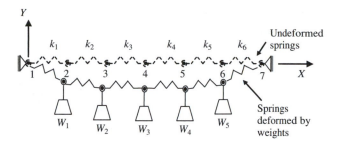

Figure 13.23 Spring-weight system of Exercise 13.6 showing the undeformed position and deformed position.

where $N = 5$ is the number of weights. Weight W_j is defined by

$$W_j = 60j \quad \text{N} \quad j = 1, \ldots, 5$$

The length of each spring before the weights are applied is $L_i = 7.5$ m. The coordinates of the spring joints (points 2–6) are represented by 10 design variables: (X_i, Y_i), $i = 2, \ldots, 6$. To solve for the equilibrium, the following PE function is minimized:

$$\text{PE} = 0.5 \sum_{i=1}^{6} K_i \Delta L_i^2 + \sum_{j=1}^{5} W_j Y_{j+1}$$

where

$$\Delta L_i = \sqrt{(X_{i+1} - X_i)^2 + (Y_{i+1} - Y_i)^2} - L_i$$

Determine the equilibrium positions using `fminunc`—that is, the joint positions for the deformed system shown in Figure 13.23. Use the initial point $(X_2, X_3, X_4, X_5, X_6, Y_2, Y_3, Y_4, Y_5, Y_6) = (7.5, 15, 22.5, 30, 37.5, 0, 0, 0, 0, 0)$. [Answer: $X_2 = 7.9168$, $X_3 = 16.2538$, $X_4 = 24.3557$, $X_5 = 32.223$, $X_6 = 39.303$, $Y_2 = -3.8577$, $Y_3 = -7.1458$, $Y_4 = -8.8364$, $Y_5 = -8.2859$, $Y_6 = -5.1603$.]

Section 13.3.2

13.8 The buckling load F for a tubular column shown in Figure 13.24 may be expressed as the following equation with unknown constants a and b:

$$F = \frac{\pi^a E R^b t^{L_i - b}}{4L^2}$$

where E is the modulus of elasticity, R is the mean radius, t is the thickness, and L is the length of the column. It is assumed that the exact relation for the buckling is unknown, and the constants will be determined through curve fitting of experimental data. To do this, an experiment is conducted wherein columns of different sizes, with $E = 250$ ksi, $L = 5$ in., $t = 1$ in., are loaded until they buckle. The loads at which the buckling occurs for different values of R are recorded in Table 13.7. Determine a and b using `lsqcurvefit` with an initial point $(a, b) = (1, 1)$, and create Figure 13.25 wherein the experimental and fitted curve are shown. Is the fitted curve a good fit? Why, or why not? [Answer: $a = 2.7163$, and $b = 3.1599$.]

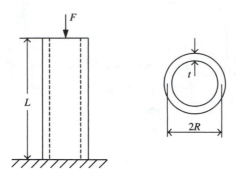

Figure 13.24   Column geometry for Exercise 13.8.

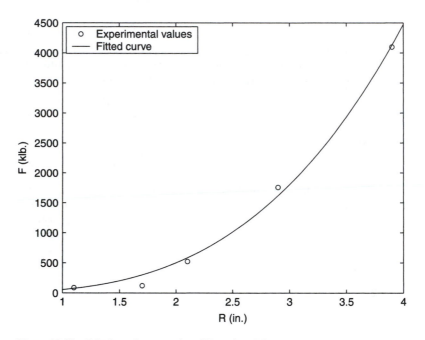

Figure 13.25   Tubular column results of Exercise 13.8.

TABLE 13.7   Radius R and Experimental Load F Data of Exercise 13.8.

Experiments	R (in.)	F (klb.)
1	1.1	86.6
2	1.7	120.5
3	2.1	520.88
4	2.9	1758
5	3.9	4098

TABLE 13.8 Data for Exercise 13.9

Length of time since production (weeks), t	Amount of ingredient, Y	Length of time since production (weeks), t	Amount of ingredient, Y
7	0.488	25	0.405
9	0.473	27	0.403
11	0.448	29	0.391
13	0.435	31	0.403
15	0.431	33	0.398
17	0.453	35	0.393
19	0.421	37	0.398
21	0.405	39	0.388
23	0.405	41	0.388

13.9 Suppose that one of the ingredients in a pharmaceutical drug is to be kept at a certain percentage of the drug volume and that this percentage decreases over time. In the weeks before the drug reaches the market, a decline in the percentage may occur. Since many other uncontrolled factors may also arise, theoretical calculations are not reliable for making an extended prediction of the decrease of this ingredient at later times. To assist the management in making such decisions as to whether the stored drug in a warehouse for an extended period of time should be scrapped or replaced, it is recommended that cartons of the drug be analyzed over a period of time to measure their ingredient content. The results of one such measurement is shown in Table 13.8. It is postulated that a nonlinear model of the form

$$Y = a + (0.51 - a)e^{-b(t-8)}$$

accounts for the variation observed in the data. Estimate the parameters a and b of the nonlinear model using lsqcurvefit with an initial point $(a, b) = (1, 1)$. Is the fitted model a good fit? [Answer: $[a, b] = [0.3918, 0.1394]$.]

Section 13.3.3

13.10 Suppose that you are observing a vehicle at a stop sign. The vehicle stops, and then it rapidly accelerates past five houses whose distances from the stop sign are known. As the vehicle starts from rest, you time the vehicle with your stopwatch as it passes each house. The data collected are shown in Table 13.9. The acceleration as a function of time is of the form

$$a(t) = Ct^2 + Dt + a_0$$

where t is travel time (s), a_0 is initial acceleration (ft./s^2), and C and D are constants. Hence, the position (ft.) of the vehicle as a function of time (s) is given by

$$x(t) = At^4 + Bt^3 + a_0t^2$$

Estimate the equation for the car's velocity $v(t)$ in ft./s as a function of time using the lsqnonlin with an initial point $(A, B) = (0, 0)$. Assume that the initial position, velocity, and acceleration of the vehicle are, respectively, $x_0 = 0$ ft., $v_0 = 0$ ft./s, and $a_0 = 2$ ft./s^2. Calculate the error of the least-square estimation. If this error is high, explain a way to reduce it. [Answer: $v(t) = -0.1084t^3 + 0.8307t^2 + 4t$.]

TABLE 13.9 Position and Time for the Vehicle of Exercise 13.10

Position (ft.)	Time (s)
0	0
9	2.05
20	3.1
60	4.8
90	5.6
120	6.8

Section 13.4.2

13.11 Find the location of the center of a minimum diameter sphere that contains on its boundary and/or inside the following four points: $A = (1, 1, 1), B = (-1, 2, 4), C = (2, 3, 4)$, and $D = (-3, -4, 1)$, which the numbers in the parenthesis are the x-, y-, and z-coordinates of the point. The design variables are the location (x_c, y_c, z_c) coordinates of the center of the sphere and its radius (R). Solve the problem with fmincon with an initial point $(x_c, y_c, z_c, R) = (4, 4, 4, 4)$. [Answer: $[(x, y, z, R] = [-1, -1.5, -1, 3.2016]$.]

13.12 The optimal design of a three-bar truss shown in Figure 13.26 is considered. The vertical deflection of its loaded joint gives the objective function[16]

$$\text{minimize } f = \frac{Ph}{E} \frac{1}{x_1 + \sqrt{2}x_2}$$

where the cross-sectional areas of its members are $A_1 = x_1$ and $A_2 = x_2$; hence, x_1 and x_2 are the design variables. Load P is applied in the direction shown in Figure 13.26.

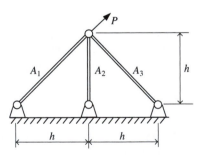

Figure 13.26 Three-bar truss of Exercise 13.12.

The constraints are the applicable stresses on the three members and the lower and upper bounds on the design variables as follows:

$$P\frac{x_2 + \sqrt{2}x_1}{\sqrt{2}x_1^2 + 2x_1x_2} - \sigma^{(u)} \leq 0$$

$$P\frac{1}{x_1 + \sqrt{2}x_2} - \sigma^{(u)} \leq 0$$

$$P\frac{x_2}{\sqrt{2}x_1^2 + 2x_1x_2} + \sigma^{(l)} \leq 0$$

$$x_i^{(l)} \leq x_i \leq x_i^{(u)} \quad i = 1, 2$$

where $\sigma^{(u)}$ is the maximum permissible stress in tension, $\sigma^{(l)}$ is the maximum permissible stress in compression, $x_i^{(l)}$ is the lower bound on x_i, and $x_i^{(u)}$ is the upper bound on x_i. The values for the parameters are $\sigma^{(u)} = 17.5, \sigma^{(l)} = -12, x_i^{(l)} = 0.2, x_i^{(u)} = 6.0 \ (i = 1, 2), P = 25, E = 2$, and $h = 2$. Use fmincon to obtain the optimized values for the cross-sectional areas and the vertical deflection. Assume an initial value of $(x_1, x_2) = (0, 0)$. [Answer: $[x_1, x_2] = [6.00, 6.00]$ and $f = 1.7259$.]

13.13 Consider the bridge network shown in Figure 13.27 consisting of five resistors R_i, each carrying a current I_i, where $i = 1, \ldots, 5$. The voltage drop across each resistor is $V_i = R_i I_i$. Suppose that $V_1 = 3$ V, $V_3 = 1$ V, and $V_5 = 1$ V for R_1, R_3, and R_5, respectively. Also, assume that the current I_i varies between a lower limit of 1 amp and an upper limit of 2 amps for all resistors. Formulate this problem in a constrained optimization form to find R_i for minimum total power dissipation in the network, and then use fmincon to obtain the optimum values for each resistor and total power dissipation. Power dissipation in the resistor R_i is equal to $I_i^2 R_i$. Note that Kirchhoff's first law is that in any branching network of wires, the algebraic sum of the currents in all the wires that meet at a point (point A or B of Figure 13.27) is zero. Kirchhoff's second law is that the sum of the voltage drops around a circuit is equal to the voltage drop for the entire circuit. [Answer: $[R_1, R_2, R_3, R_4, R_5] = [3, 1, 1, 2, 0.5]$ ohms, and total power dissipation = 12 W.]

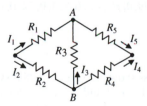

Figure 13.27 Bridge network of Exercise 13.13.

Section 13.4.3

13.14 A company has m manufacturing facilities to produce a product. The product is shipped to n warehouses. The warehouse at the jth location requires at least b_j units of the product to satisfy its demand. The manufacturing facility at the ith location has a capacity to produce a_i units of the product. The cost of shipping x_{ij} units of the product from manufacturing facility i to warehouse j is represented by $c_{ij}x_{ij} + d_{ij}x_{ij}^2$ where c_{ij} and d_{ij} are constants. Thus, the problem can be formulated in a quadratic programming form as

$$\text{minimize} \sum_{i=1}^{m}\sum_{j=1}^{n}(c_{ij}x_{ij} + d_{ij}x_{ij}^2)$$

$$\text{subject to: } \sum_{i=1}^{m}x_{ij} \geq b_j \quad j = 1,\dots,n$$

$$\sum_{j=1}^{n}x_{ij} \leq a_i \quad i = 1,\dots,m$$

$$x_{ij} \geq 0 \quad \text{for all } i, j$$

Assume $m = 6$, $n = 4$, $a = [8, 24, 20, 24, 16, 12]'$, $b = [29, 41, 13, 21]'$,

$$c = \begin{bmatrix} 300 & 270 & 460 & 800 \\ 740 & 600 & 540 & 380 \\ 300 & 490 & 380 & 760 \\ 430 & 250 & 390 & 600 \\ 210 & 830 & 470 & 680 \\ 360 & 290 & 400 & 310 \end{bmatrix}$$

$$d = (-1)\begin{bmatrix} 7 & 4 & 6 & 8 \\ 12 & 9 & 14 & 7 \\ 13 & 12 & 8 & 4 \\ 7 & 9 & 16 & 8 \\ 4 & 10 & 21 & 13 \\ 17 & 9 & 8 & 4 \end{bmatrix}$$

Solve this problem using quadprog to obtain the optimum number of units that should be produced at manufacturing facility i and shipped to warehouse j, x_{ij}. [Answer: $[x_{11}, x_{21}, x_{31}, x_{41}, x_{51}, x_{61}; x_{12}, x_{22}, x_{32}, x_{42}, x_{52}, x_{62}; x_{13}, x_{23}, x_{33}, x_{43}, x_{53}, x_{63}; x_{14}, x_{24}, x_{34}, x_{44}, x_{54}, x_{64}]' = [0, 0, 20, 0, 3, 6, 8, 3, 0, 24, 0, 6, 0, 0, 0, 0, 13, 0, 0, 21, 0, 0, 0, 0]'$.]

Section 13.4.4

13.15 The two-bar truss shown in Figure 13.28 is symmetric about the y-axis. The nondimensional position of links 1 and 2, x/h, and the nondimensional cross-sectional area of the links A/A_{ref}, are treated as the design variables x_1 and x_2, respectively, where A_{ref} is the reference value of the area A and h is the height of the truss. The direction of the applied load P is subject to change within the range $-90° \leq \theta \leq 90°$. The weight of the truss w is to be minimized. Thus,

$$-\sigma_0 \leq \frac{P\sqrt{1 + x_1^2}(x_1 \cos\theta + \sin\theta)}{2x_1x_2A_{ref}} \leq \sigma_0$$

$$-\sigma_0 \leq \frac{P\sqrt{1 + x_1^2}(x_1 \cos\theta - \sin\theta)}{2x_1x_2A_{ref}} \leq \sigma_0$$

$$w = 2\rho h x_2 A_{ref}\sqrt{1 + x_1^2}$$

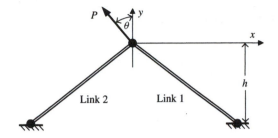

Figure 13.28   Two-bar truss of Exercise 13.15.

where ρ is the weight density. The constraints corresponding to the stresses induced in links 1 and 2 are given in the above equations where P is the applied load. In addition, the following upper and lower bounds are imposed on the design variables x_1 and x_2

$$x_i^{\min} \le x_i \le x_i^{\max} \quad i = 1, 2$$

where the values of the parameters are listed in Table 13.10. Use $\texttt{fseminf}$ to obtain the optimum design variables and create the plot of stresses as a function of θ sampled in 5° intervals as the optimum is approached. The result should look like that shown in Figure 13.29 when an initial design

$$(x_1^0, x_2^0) = (0.1, 0.1)$$

is assumed. [Answer: $[x_1, x_2] = [0.8025, 0.4517]$, and $w = 27.866$.]

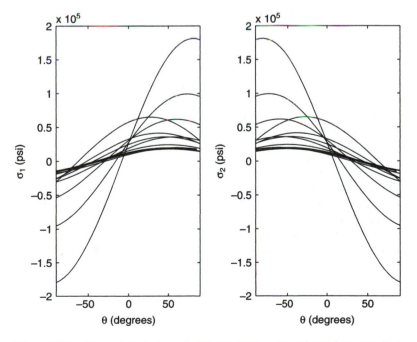

Figure 13.29   Stresses in links 1 and 2 of Figure 13.28 as the optimum is approached.

TABLE 13.10   Input Parameters for Exercise 13.15

ρ (lb./in.^{3})	P (lb.)	σ_0 (psi)	h (in.)	A_{ref} (in.^{2})	$x_1^{\min}$	$x_2^{\min}$	$x_1^{\max}$	$x_2^{\max}$
0.283	8000	18,500	85	1	0.15	0.15	3.0	3.5

BIBLIOGRAPHY

J. S. Arora, *Introduction to Optimum Design*, McGraw-Hill, New York, NY, 1989.

M. Austin and D. Chancogne, *Engineering Programming in C, MATLAB and JAVA*, John Wiley & Sons, New York, NY, 1998.

M. Branch and A. Grace, *MATLAB Optimization Toolbox User's Guide*, The Math Works, Natick, MA, 1996.

V. Changkong and Y. Y. Haimes, *Multiobjective Decision Making: Theory and Methodology*, Elsevier Science Publishing Co., New York, NY, 1983.

N. Draper and H. Smith, *Applied Regression Analysis*, John Wiley & Sons, New York, NY, 1966.

H. Eschenauer, J. Koski, and A. Osyczka, Eds., *Multicriteria Design Optimization*, Springer-Verlag, New York, NY, 1990.

J. Golinski, "Optimum Synthesis Problems Solved by Means of Nonlinear Programming and Random Methods," *Journal of Mechanisms*, Vol. 5, 1970, pp. 287–309.

C. Gosselin and J. Angeles, "A Global Performance Index for the Kinetic Optimization of Robotic Manipulators," *ASME Journal of Mechanical Design*, Vol. 113, September 1991, p. 222.

U. Kirsch, *Optimal Structural Design*, McGraw-Hill, New York, NY, 1981.

A. Messac, "Physical Programming: Effective Optimization for Computational Design," *AIAA Journal* 34, 1996, pp. 149–158.

A. Osyczka, *Multicriterion Optimization in Engineering with Fortran Programs*, Ellis Horwood Limited, West Sussex, England, 1984.

P. Y. Papalambros and D. J. Wilde, *Principles of Optimal Design*, Cambridge University Press, Cambridge, England, 1988.

S. S. Rao, *Engineering Optimization, Theory, and Practice*, 3rd ed., John Wiley & Sons, New York, NY, 1996.

G. V. Reklaitis, A. Ravindran, and K. M. Ragsdell, *Engineering Optimization*, John Wiley & Sons, New York, NY, 1983.

J. Shigley and C. Mischke, *Mechanical Engineering Design*, McGraw-Hill, New York, NY, 1989.

D. A. Stephenson and J. S. Agapiou, *Metal Cutting Theory and Practice*, Marcel Dekker, New York, NY, 1997.

G. N. Vanderplaats, *Numerical Optimization Techniques for Engineering Design*, McGraw-Hill, New York, NY, 1984.

D. A. Van Veldhuizen, and G. B. Lamont, "Multi-Objective Evolutionary Algorithm Research: A History and Analysis," Technical Report TR-98-03, Air Force Institute of Technology, Wright Patterson AFB, OH, 1998.

D. J. Wilde, *Globally Optimal Design*, John Wiley & Sons, New York, NY, 1978.

14

Engineering Statistics

Edward B. Magrab

The solutions to a wide range of engineering statistics applications are illustrated using the Statistics Toolbox.

14.1 DESCRIPTIVE STATISTICAL QUANTITIES

Consider a collection of measured values x_j, where $j = 1, 2, \ldots, n$. The sample mean of these values is

$$\bar{x} = \frac{1}{n}\sum_{j=1}^{n} x_j \tag{14.1}$$

and sample variance is

$$s^2 = \frac{1}{n-1}\left[\sum_{j=1}^{n} x_j^2 - n\bar{x}^2\right] \tag{14.2}$$

where s is the standard deviation. These quantities are the estimates of the true mean μ and the true standard deviation σ. The mean value is determined from

    mean(x)

and the standard deviation from

    std(x)

where x is either a vector or a matrix of values.

   We now create N equal segments over the region that the measured values fall, called bins, and place each x_j into that bin whose lower limit is less than or equal to x_j and whose upper limit is greater than x_j. We denote the center of each bin $b_k, k = 1, 2, \ldots, N$. After all the x_j have been assigned to a bin, the number of x_j falling into each bin is counted. We denote this value n_k, which is the number of data values that fell in the bin whose center is b_k. When the number of values n_k is plotted as a function of the value of the center of each bin, and when each bin is represented by a bar whose width is equal to its upper and lower limits, then the resulting figure is called a histogram. The number of x_j in each bin can be determined from

    [nk, b] = hist(x, N)

where nk is the vector of n_k, b is the vector of bin centers computed by hist, x are the n data samples, and N is the number of bins desired. When N is omitted, MATLAB uses $N = 10$. This same function without the left-hand side plots the histogram—that is,

    hist(x)

One can also use

    bar(b, nk)

to plot the histogram, where hist is frequently used to determine n_k.

   If we define $f_k = n_k/n$, then we have the fraction of the n samples that fall in the bin centered at b_k. If we let

$$c_k = \sum_{j=1}^{k} f_j \quad k = 1, 2, \ldots, N$$

then c_k is called the cumulative distribution function and is obtained from

    ck = cumsum(f)

where $f = [f_1 \, f_2 \, \ldots \, f_k] = [n_1/n \, n_2/n \ldots n_k/n]$. We can also plot c_k versus b_k, which is an approximation to the probability that a measurement has a value less than or equal to b_k.

Now, let us sort x from its lowest value to its highest value. The lowest value can be obtained using min(x), and the highest value from max(x), where $x = [x_1, x_2, \ldots, x_n]$. The range of the values is the difference between the highest and lowest values of the samples and can be determined from either

range(x)

or

max(x)-min(x)

The center of the sorted values is called the median value. If the number of samples n is odd, then the median value is $x_{(n+1)/2}$; if it is even, then the median value is $(x_{n/2} + x_{n/2+1})/2$. The median value is determined from

median(x)

Another statistical metric that is sometimes useful is the geometric mean, which is defined as the nth root of the product of the measurements of n samples—that is

$$\overline{x}_g = \sqrt[n]{\prod_{j=1}^{n} x_j}$$

This quantity can be determined from either

geomean(x)

or from the expression

prod(x)^(1/length(x))

We now illustrate the use of these relations with an example.

Example 14.1   Determination of several statistical quantities

Consider the data given in Table 14.1. We shall find the mean value, median value, standard deviation, geometric mean, range, minimum value, and maximum value and then plot a histogram and the cumulative distribution of these data. We shall place the data

TABLE 14.1   Data Comprising DataSet141

105	97	245	163	207	134	218	199
160	196	221	154	228	131	180	178
157	151	175	201	183	153	174	154
190	76	101	142	149	200	186	174
199	115	193	167	171	163	87	176
121	120	181	160	194	184	165	145
160	150	181	168	158	208	133	135
172	171	237	170	180	167	176	158
156	229	158	148	150	118	143	141
110	133	123	146	169	158	135	149

in nine bins, starting at 80 and ending at 240. We shall color the bars yellow. The data are placed in a function **DataSet141**. Thus,

```
function d = DataSet141
d = [105 97 245 163 207 134 218 199 160 196 221 154 228 131 180 178 ...
     157 151 175 201 183 153 174 154 190 76 101 142 149 200 186 174 ...
     199 115 193 167 171 163 87 176 121 120 181 160 194 184 165 145 ...
     160 150 181 168 158 208 133 135 172 171 237 170 180 167 176 158 ...
     156 229 158 148 150 118 143 141 110 133 123 146 169 158 135 149];
```

The script is

```
data = DataSet141;
n = length(data);
b = 80:20:240;
nn = hist(data, b);
maxn = max(nn);
cs = cumsum(nn*maxn/n);
bar(b, nn, 0.95, 'y')
axis([70, 250, 0, maxn])
box off
hold on
plot(b, c, 'k-s')
title('\leftarrow Histogram        Cumulative distribution \rightarrow')
ylabel('Number of occurrences')
xlabel('Measured values')
text(72, 0.97*maxn, ['Mean = ' num2str(mean(data))])
text(72, 0.92*maxn, ['Median = ' num2str(median(data))])
text(72, 0.87*maxn, ['Geometric mean = ' num2str(geomean(data))])
text(72, 0.82*maxn, ['Standard deviation = ' num2str(std(data))])
text(72, 0.77*maxn, ['No. of samples = ' num2str(ldat)])
text(72,.67*maxn, ['Maximum = ' num2str(max(data))])
text(72,.72*maxn, ['Minimum = ' num2str(min(data))])
text(72,.62*maxn, ['Range = ' num2str(range(data))])
plot([70 250], [maxn maxn], 'k', [250 250], [0 maxn], 'k')
j = 0:.1:1;
lenj = length(j);
text(repmat(251, lenj, 1), maxn*j', num2str(j', 2))
plot([repmat(248.5, 1, lenj); repmat(250, 1, lenj)], [maxn*j; maxn*j], 'k')
```

which upon execution results in Figure 14.1.

Although the centers of the bins are computed by hist, we have chosen to specify them. This permits us to more easily control the presentation of the data. We had to turn off the box function, because this function repeats the tic marks from the horizontal and vertical axes to the top and right-hand vertical axis, respectively. In addition, plotyy cannot be used because two different types of graphs are being plotted. Therefore, we have to consider the labels independently from the tic marks, and we have to draw the top and right-hand figure boundaries separately. Thus, the tic marks appear at

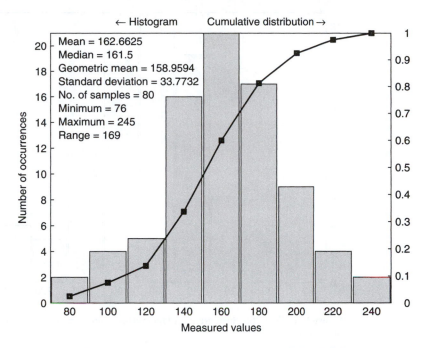

Figure 14.1   Histogram, cumulative distribution, and descriptive statistics for **DataSet141**.

$21j$, where, in this problem, 21 is the maximum value of the y-axis. The maximum value is set with the axis function.

If the bin centers had not been specified, then the resulting histogram would look slightly different because the centers of the bins would be different. This difference may change n_k. Thus, the execution of the statements

```
[nn, b] = hist(DataSet141, 9);
bar(b, nn, 0.95, 'y');
axis([70, 250, 0, max(nn)])
```

results in Figure 14.2.

The differences between the histograms in Figures 14.1 and 14.2 result from the differences in the bin centers. In the first case, the bin centers were defined as

$b = [80, 100, 120, 140, 160, 180, 200, 220, 240]$

whereas in the new script, the bin centers were computed by hist and found to be

$b = [85.38, 104.16, 122.94, 141.72, 160.50, 179.27, 198.05, 216.83, 235.61]$

We see that the number of x_j in several of the bins differs.

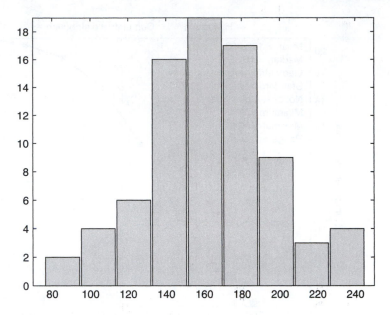

Figure 14.2   Resulting histogram for **DataSet141** when hist computes the bin centers.

Another way of presenting these data is to use a box plot. A box plot of the data in **DataSet141** is shown in Figure 14.3, which is obtained from

boxplot(**DataSet141**, 'Notch', 'on')

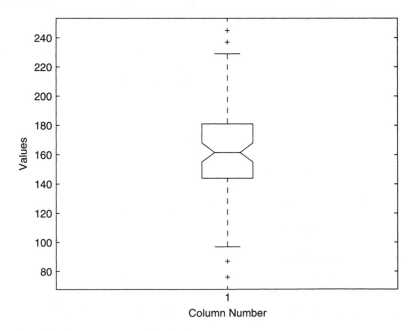

Figure 14.3   Box plot of **DataSet141**.

whereby setting the second argument to 1 produced the notched box. The notch indicates the median of the data. The region within the top and bottom limits of the box represents 50% of the data, with the bottom of the box indicating the end of the first quartile q_1 and its top the end of the third quartile q_3. Note that in general, the box is not symmetrical about the median value. The lines (whiskers) extending from the bottom and top of the box represent the extreme values defined by the regions $q_1 - 1.5(q_3 - q_1)$ and $q_3 + 1.5(q_3 - q_1)$, respectively. Any data points that lie outside these whiskers are called outliers and are denoted in this figure by plus (+) signs. The more general usage of a box plot is to compare several sets of data in this manner (see, for example, Figure 14.14b).

To obtain the values of q_1 and q_3 explicitly, we use, respectively,

q1 = prctile(**DataSet141**, 25)
q3 = prctile(**DataSet141**, 75)

which upon execution gives $q_1 = 144$ and $q_3 = 181$. The second argument in prctile specifies the percentile of interest. When the percentile equals 25%, this is referred to as the first quartile.

To determine whether the data are symmetrically distributed about the mean, we use

s = skewness(**DataSet141**)

which upon execution gives $s = -0.0246$. The negative sign means that the distribution is skewed to the left.

14.2 PROBABILITY DISTRIBUTIONS

14.2.1 Discrete Distributions

The probability $P(X)$ that a discrete random variable $X = x$, where x is from the set of all possible values of X, is defined as

$$f(x) = P(X = x) \tag{14.3}$$

where $f(x) \geq 0$ for all x and

$$\sum_{\text{all } x_i} f(x_i) = 1 \tag{14.4}$$

The quantity $f(x)$ is called the probability mass function for a discrete random variable. If we are interested in the probability that $X \leq x$—that is, $P(X \leq x)$—then

$$P(X \leq x) = \sum_{x_k \leq x} f(x_k) = 1 - \sum_{x_k > x} f(x_k) \tag{14.5}$$

which is called the cumulative distribution function. Conversely, if we are interested in the probability that $X \geq x$—that is $P(X \geq x)$—then

$$P(X \geq x) = \sum_{x_k \geq x} f(x_k) \tag{14.6}$$

Binomial Distribution

If we conduct n repeated trials such that the trials are independent; each trial results in only two possible outcomes, "success" or "failure" and the probability p of a success on each trial remains constant, then the probability mass function is called the binomial distribution given by

$$f_b(x) = P(X = x) = \frac{n!}{x!(n-x)!} p^x(1-p)^{n-x} \quad x = 0, 1, \ldots, n \tag{14.7}$$

where x is the number of trials that meets with success.
    The mean of this distribution is

$$\bar{x} = np \tag{14.8a}$$

and its standard deviation is

$$s = \sqrt{np(1-p)} \tag{14.8b}$$

    The function that computes the probability mass function of the binomial distribution is

    $\mathtt{binopdf(x, n, p)}$

and that which computes its mean and variance (s^2) is

    $[\mathrm{Bmean, Bvariance}] = \mathtt{binostat(n, p)}$

where $x = 0, 1, 2, \ldots, n$.
    Consider a die. The probability of getting any one of its sides to be the top surface is $p = 1/6$. Let the side with three dots be of interest. Then, the probability that with one toss of the die, the side with three dots will appear is

$$P(X = \text{side with three dots}) = \frac{1!}{1!(0!)}(1/6)^1(1-1/6)^{1-1} = \frac{1}{6}$$

which can be determined from the expression

    Pb = binopdf(1, 1, 1/6)

However, the probability that we can get the side with three dots to show up exactly once in two tries is

    Pb = binopdf(1, 2, 1/6)

Upon execution, this expression gives $Pb = 0.2778 < 1/3$.

     Now, consider a coin toss; thus, $p = 0.5$. The probability of getting exactly four "heads" $(x = 4)$ in 10 tosses $(n = 10)$ is determined from

    Pb = binopdf(4, 10, 0.5)

which yields $Pb = 0.2051$.

Example 14.2   Probability of getting airplanes airborne[1]

An Air Force squadron of 16 airplanes should always be ready to become airborne immediately. There is, however, a 20% chance that an aircraft will not start, at which time several minutes must elapse before another start procedure can be attempted. Thus, the probability of an aircraft starting immediately is 0.80.

     We are interested in the probability that exactly 12 airplanes can successfully become airborne. The script is

    Pb = binopdf(12, 16, 0.80)

Upon execution, we obtain $Pb = 0.2001$.

     On the other hand, the probability that at least 14 aircraft can become airborne immediately is determined from (recall Eqs. 14.5 and 14.6)

    Pb = 1-binocdf(13, 16, 0.80)

or

    Pb = sum(binopdf(14:16, 16, 0.80))

The execution of either expression gives $Pb = 0.3518$.

     A graphical representation of this distribution can be obtained from the following script:

```
n = 1:16;
Pb = binopdf(n, 16, 0.80);
plot([n; n], [zeros(1,16); Pb], 'k')
text(8-.7:16-.7, Pb(8:16)+.005, num2str(Pb(8:16)',3))
axis([0, 17, 0, 0.27])
xlabel('Number of aircraft launched on time')
ylabel('Probability')
```

Upon execution, we obtain the results shown in Figure 14.4.

---

[1]A. J. Hayter, *Probability and Statistics for Engineers and Scientists*, PWS Publishing Co., Boston, MA, 1996, p. 167.

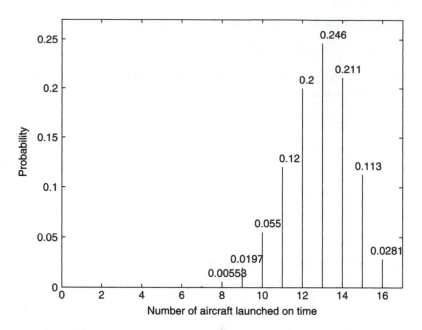

Figure 14.4   Probability mass function of launching 0 to 16 aircraft on time.

Poisson Distribution

Assume that an event occurs randomly throughout an interval and that this interval can be partitioned into smaller subintervals such that the probability of more than one event in the subinterval is zero, the probability of the event is the same for all subintervals and proportional to the length of the subinterval, and the number of events in each subinterval is independent of the other subintervals. Such a series of events is called a Poisson process. If the mean of the number of events in the interval is $\lambda > 0$, then the probability mass distribution

$$f_p(x) = P(X = x) = \frac{e^{-\lambda}\lambda^x}{x!} \quad x = 0, 1, 2, \ldots \tag{14.9}$$

is a Poisson distribution for x events occurring in the interval.

The mean value of the Poisson distribution is

$$\overline{x} = \lambda \tag{14.10a}$$

and its standard deviation is

$$s = \sqrt{\lambda} \tag{14.10b}$$

The probability mass function of the Poisson distribution is obtained from

`poisspdf(x, lambda)`

and that which computes its mean and variance (s^2) is

`[Pmean, Pvariance] = poisstat(lambda)`

Example 14.3   Adequacy of hospital resources

A hospital emergency room receives an average of 46 heart attack cases per week (46/7 per day). The hospital currently is able to handle nine such cases per day. The hospital staff is interested in knowing the probability that their current resources are adequate. Consequently, they want to know the value of $P(X \leq 9)$. Thus,

Pp = poisscdf(9, 46/7)

which upon execution gives $Pp = 0.8712$. Thus, on 13% of the days, additional resources will be required.

14.2.2 Continuous Distributions

The probability $P(X)$ that a continuous random variable X lies in the range $x_1 \leq X \leq x_2$, where x_1 and x_2 are from the set of all possible values of X, is defined as

$$P(x_1 \leq X \leq x_2) = \int_{x_1}^{x_2} f(x)\,dx \tag{14.11a}$$

where $f(x) \geq 0$ for all x, and

$$\int_{-\infty}^{\infty} f(x)\,dx = 1 \tag{14.11b}$$

The quantity $f(x)$ is called the probability density function (pdf) for a continuous random variable.

The cumulative distribution function (cdf) $F(x)$ is

$$F(x) = P(X \leq x) = \int_{-\infty}^{x} f(u)\,du = 1 - \int_{x}^{\infty} f(u)\,du \tag{14.12}$$

and, therefore,

$$P(X \geq x) = 1 - F(x) \tag{14.13}$$

MATLAB has a large family of probability density functions. We shall examine two of them: the normal distribution, and the Weibull distribution. The others are used in a similar manner.

Normal Distribution

The normal probability distribution function is

$$f_n(x) = P(X = x) = \frac{1}{\sigma\sqrt{2\pi}} e^{\frac{(x-u)^2}{2\sigma^2}} \qquad -\infty < x < \infty \tag{14.14}$$

where $-\infty < \mu < \infty$ and $\sigma > 0$ are independent parameters. It can be shown that μ is the mean of the distribution and σ^2 its variance (σ is the standard deviation). If we have a set of data x_j, $j = 1, 2, \ldots, n$, then the normal pdf is obtained from the following script

```
mu = mean(x);
sigma = std(x);
Pn = normpdf(x0, mu, sigma)
```

where $x0$ is the value (or values if $x0$ is a vector) of interest, $mu = \mu$, $sigma = \sigma$, and the size of Pn is equal to the size of $x0$. Estimates for the values of μ and σ can also be obtained from

$$[\text{meanx}, \text{stddev}] = \text{normfit}(\text{x})$$

The cumulative distribution function $\Phi(x)$ is

$$\Phi(x) = P(X \leq x) = \frac{1}{\sigma\sqrt{2\pi}} \int_{-\infty}^{x} e^{-(u-\mu)^2/2\sigma^2} \, du \qquad -\infty < x < \infty$$

$$= \frac{1}{\sqrt{2\pi}} \int_{-\infty}^{(x-\mu)/\sigma} e^{-u^2/2} \, du \qquad -\infty < x < \infty \tag{14.15}$$

or

$$\Phi(z) = P(Z \leq z) = \frac{1}{\sqrt{2\pi}} \int_{-\infty}^{z} e^{-u^2/2} \, du \qquad -\infty < z < \infty \tag{14.16}$$

where

$$z = (x - \mu)/\sigma \tag{14.17}$$

is called the standard normal random variable, for which $\mu_z = 0$ and $\sigma_z = 1$. Thus,

$$P(Z \geq z) = 1 - \Phi(z)$$
$$P(Z \leq -z) = \Phi(-z)$$
$$P(-z \leq Z \leq z) = \Phi(z) - \Phi(-z)$$
$$P(z_L \leq Z \leq z_H) = \Phi(z_H) - \Phi(z_L) \tag{14.18}$$

The regions given by Eq. 14.18 are shown in Figure 14.5.

The normal cdf is obtained from

```
mu = mean(x);
sigma = std(x);
Pn = normcdf(x0, mu, sigma)
```

where $x0$ is the value (or values, if $x0$ is a vector) of interest, $mu = \mu$, $sigma = \sigma$, and the size of Pn is equal to the size of $x0$. If the x are converted to z, then $mu = 0$ and $sigma = 1$. These are the default values; therefore, when $x \to z$, these arguments can be omitted.

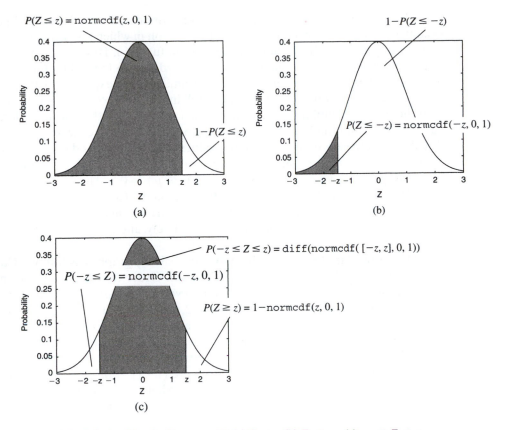

Figure 14.5 Relationship of cdf to normcdf: (a) $Z \leq z$; (b) $Z \leq -z$; (c) $-z \leq Z \leq z$.

Referring to Figure 14.5c and Eqs. 14.18, we see that if we are interested in $P(x_L \leq X \leq x_H)$, then

$Pn = \text{diff}(\text{normcdf}([xL, xH], \text{mean}(x), \text{std}(x)))$

For example, the probability of finding a measured value in **DataSet141** between 120 and 200 is obtained from

$Pn = \text{diff}(\text{normcdf}([120, 200], \text{mean}(\textbf{DataSet141}), \text{std}(\textbf{DataSet141})))$

which upon execution yields $Pn = 0.7623$. The value compares well with the estimated value obtained from Figure 14.1.

In some instances, one would like to determine the inverse of $\Phi(x)$—that is,

$$x = \Phi^{-1}[P(X \leq x)] \qquad (14.19)$$

This is accomplished with the function

$\text{norminv}(p, \text{mean}(x), \text{std}(x))$

where p is the cumulative probability—that is, the shaded area in Figure 14.5a.

To determine whether a set of data can be modeled with the normal pdf, one usually plots the data on a normal probability graph in which the ordinate (y-axis) is scaled using the cumulative normal distribution function. This is analogous to plotting data on which the ordinate has been scaled by the logarithm. On a graph in which the ordinate has been scaled logarithmically, an exponential function will appear as a straight line. Similarly, on a graph in which the ordinate has been scaled with the normal cumulative probability function, a process that has its ordered values distributed normally will appear as a straight line. In other words, for a normal distribution, the cumulative probability values that are one standard deviation σ on either side of the mean μ are $P(X \leq \mu + \sigma) = 0.84$ and $P(X \leq \mu - \sigma) = 0.16$, respectively, while that of the mean is $P(X \leq \mu) = 0.5$. Thus, on a probability-transformed graph, the three sets of coordinates $(\mu - \sigma, 0.16)$, $(\mu, 0.5)$, and $(\mu + \sigma, 0.84)$ specify three points that lie on a straight line. The values of μ and σ are estimated by Eqs. (14.1) and (14.2), respectively, and are computed using `mean` and `std`, respectively.

The procedure for plotting data on a probability graph is as follows: Consider a set of m data values y_i, where $i = 1, 2, \ldots, m$. Order the data from the smallest (most negative) to the largest (most positive) value, and assign the lowest value the number 1, the next-lowest value the number 2, and so on, with the highest value having the number m. Call these ordered data values w_j, where $j = 1, 2, \ldots, m$. Corresponding to each w_j, we assign a cumulative probability of $(j - 0.5)/m$, where $j = 1, 2, \ldots, m$—that is, $P(w \leq w_j)$. The coordinates of each data value that is to be plotted on the probability distribution graph are $(w_j, (j - 0.5)/m)$. When only a linear graph is available, one plots instead (w_j, z_j), where $z_j = $ `norminv`$((j - 0.5)/m)$. The function that performs these computations and does the plotting is

```
normplot(y)
```

where $y = [y_1\ y_2\ \cdots\ y_m]$. The straight line appearing in this plot is determined from the coordinate pairs of the first and third quartiles of y_j and z_j. Recall the determination of q_1 and q_3 in Section 14.1 and the interpretation of Figure 14.3.

Example 14.4   Verification of the normality of data

Let us revisit the data in **DataSet141**. First, we replot its histogram and superimpose on this bar graph the corresponding normal pdf. This is accomplished with the script

```
histfit(DataSet141, 9)
colormap([1, 1, 1,])
```

whose execution results in Figure 14.6. The function `colormap` is used to change the color of the bars to white. Next, we see whether the data are normally distributed. To do these operations, we use

```
normplot(DataSet141)
```

and obtain Figure 14.7. It is seen that a fairly large portion of the data are close to the straight line, leading one to conclude that the normal distribution is a reasonable approximation to these data.

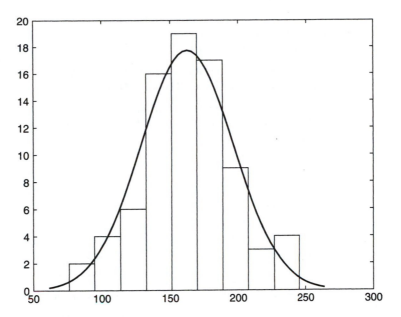

Figure 14.6   Histogram with a superimposed normal pdf.

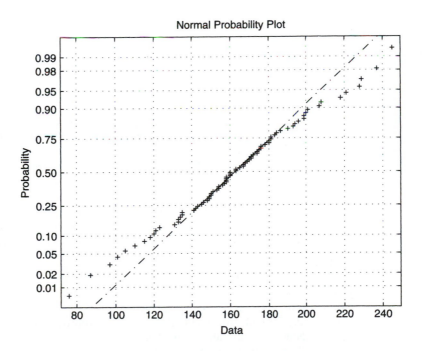

Figure 14.7   Normal cumulative probability plot of **DataSet141**.

If we accept the normal distribution as an adequate representation of these data, then we can determine the values at which, say, 90% of the data lie. Then, referring to Figures 14.5a and 14.5c and Eq. (1.19), we use `norminv` as follows:

```
zh = norminv(.95, mean(DataSet141), std(DataSet141))
zl = norminv(.05, mean(DataSet141), std(DataSet141))
```

Upon execution of this script, we obtain $z_h = 218.2145$ and $z_l = 107.1105$. As a check, we find the difference between the probabilities of these two limits, which are determined from the following script:

```
m = mean(DataSet141);
s = std(DataSet141);
zh = norminv(.95, m, s);
zl = norminv(.05, m, s);
ph = normcdf(zh, m, s)
pl = normcdf(zl, m, s)
```

The execution of this script gives $p_h - p_l = 0.9500 - 0.0500 = 0.90$.

Example 14.5   Normal distribution approximation to Poisson and binomial distribution

The normal distribution is a good approximation to the binomial distribution when $np > 5$ and $n(1 - p) > 5$, and is also a good approximation to the Poisson distribution to obtain $P(X \le x)$ when $\lambda > 5$. For the case of the binomial distribution, the normal standard random variable given by Eq. 4.17 is (recall Eq. 14.8)

$$z_b = \frac{X - np}{\sqrt{np(1 - p)}}$$

and that for the Poisson distribution (recall Eq. 14.10)

$$z_p = \frac{X - \lambda}{\sqrt{\lambda}}$$

To illustrate the normal distribution approximation to the Poisson distribution, we return to Example 14.3, where we determined the probability that a hospital will treat nine or fewer heart attacks a day was 0.8712. We now solve this problem using the normal distribution. Since $\mu = 46/7$ and $\sigma = \sqrt{46/7}$, the script is

```
P = normcdf((9−46/7)/sqrt(46/7), 0, 1)
```

which gives $P = 0.8283$, a result that is within 4.9% of the exact value. To visualize this approximation, we create the following script, which draws the Poisson distribution from Example 14.2 and its approximation given by the above expression:

```
x = 1:16;
y = linspace(00, 16, 50);
yPoisson = poisspdf(x, 46/7);
NormApprox = normpdf(y, 46/7, sqrt(46/7));
plot([x; x], [zeros(1, 16); yPoisson], 'k', y , NormApprox, 'k')
xlabel('Number of aircraft launched on time')
ylabel('Probability density')
```

The results from the execution of this script are shown on Figure 14.8.

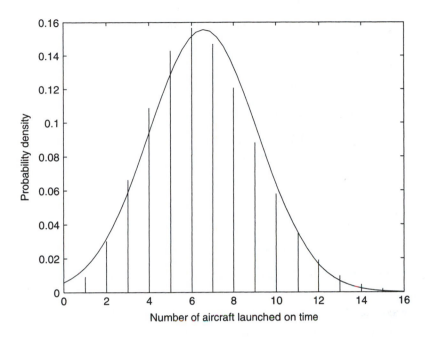

Figure 14.8   Poisson distribution of Example 14.3 and its normal distribution approximation.

Weibull Distribution

The Weibull probability distribution function is

$$f_w(x) = \alpha\beta x^{\beta-1}e^{-\alpha x^\beta} \quad x > 0 \tag{14.20}$$

where $\alpha > 0$ is a scale parameter and $\beta > 0$ is a shape parameter. (Another notation that is commonly used is obtained with the transformation $\alpha = \delta^{-\beta}$.) When $\beta = 1$, Eq. 14.20 reduces to the exponential distribution, and when $\beta = 2$, to the Rayleigh distribution. The mean value of this pdf is

$$\mu_w = \alpha^{-1/\beta}\Gamma\left(1 + \frac{1}{\beta}\right)$$

and its variance is

$$\sigma_w^2 = \alpha^{-2/\beta}\Gamma\left(1 + \frac{2}{\beta}\right) - \alpha^{-2/\beta}\left[\Gamma\left(1 + \frac{1}{\beta}\right)\right]^2$$

where $\Gamma(x)$ is the gamma function. The Weibull pdf is obtained from

    Pw = wblpdf(x, alpha, beta)

where *alpha* $= \alpha$, *beta* $= \beta$, and the size of *Pw* is equal to the size of *x*. The mean and variance are obtained from

    [muW, VarW] = wblstat(alpha, beta)

The cumulative distribution function $F_w(x)$ is

$$F_w(x) = P(X \le x) = 1 - e^{-\alpha x^{\beta}} \quad x > 0 \tag{14.21}$$

and is obtained from

Wcdf = wblcdf(x, alpha, beta)

where the size of *Wcdf* is equal to the size of x.

In some instances, one would like to determine the inverse of $F(x)$—that is, when

$$x = F_w^{-1}[P(X \le x)] \tag{14.22}$$

This is accomplished with the function

wblinv(p, alpha, beta)

where p is the value of the cumulative probability distribution.

Example 14.6   Verification that data can be represented by a Weibull distribution

Consider the sorted data on the longevity of a component given in Table 14.2. We create a function **DataSet142** for these data as follows:

```
function d = DataSet142
d = [72 82 97 103 113 117 126 127 127 139 154 159 199 207]';
```

We now plot these data to determine whether a Weibull distribution can be used to model it. Thus, we use the weibplot function as shown in the script below to obtain Figure 14.9.

wblplot(**DataSet142**)

It is seen that these data are fairly well represented by the Weibull distribution; therefore, we shall adopt it as a model for these data.

To determine the values of α and β, we use

ab = wblfit(x)

TABLE 14.2   Sorted Component Life Data—**DataSet142**

Component life	Component life
72	127
82	127
97	139
103	154
113	159
117	199
126	207

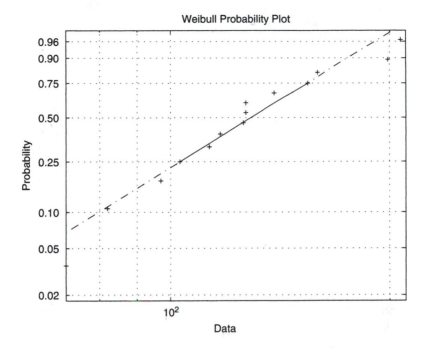

Figure 14.9   Weibull cumulative probability plot of **DataSet142**.

where $ab(1) = \alpha$ and $ab(2) = \beta$. The script to obtain the magnitudes of α and β and the mean value and the standard deviation of the process is

```
ab = wblfit(DataSet142)
[muW, varW] = wblstat(ab(1), ab(2))
sigW = sqrt(varW)
```

The execution of this script gives that $\alpha = 144.27$, $\beta = 3.644$, $\mu_W = 130.09$, and $\sigma_W = 39.70$.

   If a normal distribution had been assumed, then the mean value and the standard deviation are obtained from

```
muN = mean(DataSet142)
sigmaN = std(DataSet142)
```

Upon execution, we find that $\mu_{norm} = 130.14$ and $\sigma_{norm} = 39.39$.

   We now plot the Weibull probability density function for the data in Table 14.2 and, for comparison, the normal probability density function when these data are assumed to be normally distributed. The script is

```
ab = wblfit(DataSet142);
xx = linspace(50, 200, 50);
yW = wblpdf(xx, ab(1), ab(2));
yN = normpdf(xx, mean(DataSet142), std(DataSet142));
plot(xx, yW, 'k-', xx, yN, 'k--')
```

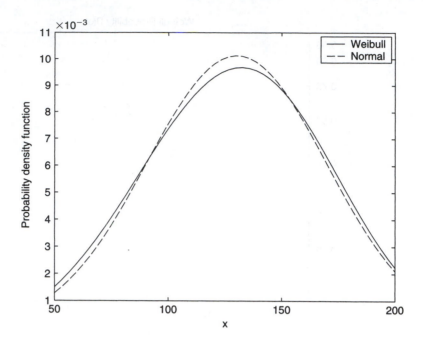

Figure 14.10   Comparison of the Weibull and normal probability density functions for **DataSet142**.

```
legend('Weibull', 'Normal')
xlabel('x')
ylabel('Probability density function')
```

The execution of this script results in Figure 14.10.

Lastly, we determine the probability that a component's life is less than 100 h. The script is

```
ab = wblfit(DataSet142);
p = wblcdf(100, ab(1), ab(2))
```

which upon execution yields $p = 0.2312$, or 23.1%.

14.3 CONFIDENCE INTERVALS

Let θ be a numerical value of a statistic (e.g., the mean, variance, difference in means, etc.) of a collection of n samples. What we are interested in determining is the values of l and u such that the following is true

$$P(l \leq \theta \leq u) = 1 - \alpha$$

where $0 < \alpha < 1$. This means that we will have a probability of $1 - \alpha$ of selecting a collection of n samples that will produce an interval that contains the true value of θ. The interval

$$l \leq \theta \leq u$$

is called the $100(1 - \alpha)\%$ two-sided confidence interval for θ. The quantities l and u are called the upper and lower confidence limits, respectively. Similarly, the $100(1 - \alpha)\%$ one-sided lower confidence interval is

$$l \le \theta$$

and that for the $100(1 - \alpha)\%$ one-sided upper confidence interval is

$$\theta \le u$$

The confidence limits depend on the distribution of the samples and on whether the standard deviation of the population is known. Several commonly used relationships to determine these confidence limits are summarized in Table 14.3. In this table, the following definitions are used:

μ and σ are the true mean and standard deviation, respectively.
$\bar{x}$ and s^2 are determined from Eqs. (14.1) and (14.2), respectively.

TABLE 14.3   Summary of Several Confidence Interval Procedures

		$100(1 - \alpha)\%$ confidence interval $\hat{\theta} - q \le \theta \le \hat{\theta} + q$		
Problem type	$\hat{\theta}$	θ	q	Case
Mean with σ^2 known	$\bar{x}$	μ	$z_{\alpha/2}\sigma/\sqrt{n}$	1
Difference in means with σ_1^2, σ_2^2 known	$\bar{x}_1 - \bar{x}_2$	$\mu_1 - \mu_2$	$z_{\alpha/2}\sqrt{\dfrac{\sigma_1^2}{n_1} + \dfrac{\sigma_2^2}{n_2}}$	2
Mean with σ^2 unknown	$\bar{x}$	μ	$t_{\alpha/2,\, n-1}s/\sqrt{n}$	3
Difference in means with $\sigma_1^2 = \sigma_2^2$ unknown	$\bar{x}_1 - \bar{x}_2$	$\mu_1 - \mu_2$	$t_{\alpha/2,\, n_1+n_2-2}s_p\sqrt{\dfrac{1}{n_1} + \dfrac{1}{n_2}}$	4
Difference in means with $\sigma_1^2 \ne \sigma_2^2$ unknown	$\bar{x}_1 - \bar{x}_2$	$\mu_1 - \mu_2$	$t_{\alpha/2,\, v}\sqrt{\dfrac{s_1^2}{n_1} + \dfrac{s_2^2}{n_2}}$	5

		$100(1 - \alpha)\%$ confidence interval $q_1\hat{\theta} \le \theta \le q_2\hat{\theta}$		
	$\hat{\theta}$	θ	q_1	q_2
Variance	s^2	σ^2	$\dfrac{n-1}{\chi^2_{\alpha/2,\, n-1}}$	$\dfrac{n-1}{\chi^2_{1-\alpha/2,\, n-1}}$	6
Ratio of variances	$\dfrac{s_1^2}{s_2^2}$	$\dfrac{\sigma_1^2}{\sigma_2^2}$	$\dfrac{1}{f_{\alpha/2,\, n_1-1,\, n_2-1}}$	$f_{\alpha/2,\, n_2-1,\, n_1-1}$	7

$t_{\alpha, n-1}$ is the value of the t distribution with $n - 1$ degrees of freedom obtained from `tinv`.

$z_{\alpha/2}$ is the value of the normal distribution obtained from `norminv`.

$\chi^2_{\alpha/2, n-1}$ is the chi-square distribution with $n - 1$ degrees of freedom obtained from `chi2inv`.

$f_{\alpha/2, n-1, m-1}$ is the f distribution with $n - 1$ and $m - 1$ degrees of freedom obtained from `finv`.

Furthermore, for case 4,

$$s_p = \sqrt{\frac{(n_1 - 1)s_1^2 + (n_2 - 1)s_2^2}{n_1 + n_2 - 2}}$$

and for case 5,

$$v = \left(\frac{s_1^2}{n_1} + \frac{s_2^2}{n_2}\right)^2 \left[\frac{(s_1^2/n_1)^2}{n_1 + 1} + \frac{(s_2^2/n_2)^2}{n_2 + 1}\right]^{-1} - 2$$

Confidence Limits for Cases 3 and 7

For case 3, the two-sided confidence limits are

$$\overline{x} - t_{\alpha/2, n-1}s/\sqrt{n} \le \mu \le \overline{x} + t_{\alpha/2, n-1}s/\sqrt{n}$$

and those for case 7 are

$$\frac{s_1^2}{s_2^2}\frac{1}{f_{\alpha/2, n_1-1, n_2-1}} \le \frac{\sigma_1^2}{\sigma_2^2} \le \frac{s_1^2}{s_2^2}f_{\alpha/2, n_2-1, n_1-1}$$

Notice that the degrees of freedom in the subscripts of f are reversed.

We now illustrate the determination of the two-sided confidence limits for cases 3 and 7 of Table 14.3.

Example 14.7   Two-sided confidence limits

Case 3   We again consider the data in Table 14.1, which resides in **DataSet141**. If we set the confidence level to 95%, then the script to determine the confidence interval is

```
meen = mean(DataSet141);
L = length(DataSet141);
q = std(DataSet141)*tinv(0.975, L-1)/sqrt(L);
disp(['Sample mean = ' num2str(meen)])
disp('Confidence interval for sample mean at 95% confidence level –')
disp(['   ' num2str(meen-q) ' <= Sample mean <= ' num2str(meen+q)])
```

Upon execution, the following is displayed to the command window:

```
Sample mean = 162.6625
Confidence interval for sample mean at 95% confidence level –
      155.1466 <= Sample mean <= 170.1784
```

Another way to obtain this confidence interval is with `ttest`, which is illustrated in Section 14.4.

TABLE 14.4   Data for Case 7—**DataFci**

Set 1	Set 2
41.60	39.72
41.48	42.59
42.34	41.88
41.95	42.00
41.86	40.22
42.18	41.07
41.72	41.90
42.26	44.29
41.81	
42.04	

Case 7   We consider the two columns of data in Table 14.4, which are placed in the function **DataFci** shown below.

```
function [set1, set2] = DataFci
set1 = [41.60 41.48 42.34 41.95 41.86 42.18 41.72 42.26 41.81 42.04];
set2 = [39.72 42.59 41.88 42.00 40.22 41.07 41.90 44.29];
```

The script is

```
[data1, data2] = DataFci;
r = var(data1)/var(data2);
L1 = length(data1);
L2 = length(data2);
q2 = r*finv(0.975, L2 -1, L1-1);
q1 = r/finv(0.975, L1-1, L2-1);
disp(['Ratio of sample variances = ' num2str(r)])
disp('Confidence interval for ratio of sample variances at 95% confidence level -')
disp(['   ' num2str(q1) ' <= Ratio of sample variances <= ' num2str(q2)])
```

which upon execution displays to the command window

```
Ratio of sample variances = 0.039874
Confidence interval for ratio of sample variances at 95% confidence level -
   0.0082672 <= Ratio of sample variances <= 0.16736
```

14.4 HYPOTHESIS TESTING

In engineering, there are many situations where one has to either accept or reject a statement (hypothesis) about some parameter. A statistical hypothesis can be thought of as a statement about the parameters of one or more populations. A population is the totality of the observations with which we are concerned. A sample is a subset of a population. Since we use probability distributions to represent populations, a statistical hypothesis can be thought of as a statement about the statistical distribution of the population.

Suppose that we have a parameter θ that has been obtained from n samples of a population, and suppose that we are interested in determining whether this parameter is equal to θ_o. The hypothesis testing procedure requires one to:

1. Postulate a hypothesis, called the null hypothesis, H_0.
2. Form the appropriate test statistic, q_0.
3. Select a confidence level (recall that $100(1 - \alpha)\%$ is the confidence level for θ).
4. Compare the test statistic to a value that corresponds to the magnitude of the test statistic that one can expect to occur naturally, q.

Based on the respective magnitudes of q_0 and q, the null hypothesis is either accepted or rejected. If the null hypothesis is rejected, then we accept an alternative one, which is denoted H_1.

There are three cases to consider:

$$H_0: \theta = \theta_0 \qquad H_0: \theta = \theta_0 \qquad H_0: \theta = \theta_0$$
$$H_1: \theta \neq \theta_0 \qquad H_1: \theta > \theta_0 \qquad H_1: \theta < \theta_0$$

For each case, there are the corresponding test statistics $q_0(n, \alpha)$ and $q(n, \alpha)$. Several hypothesis-testing procedures are summarized in Table 14.5, which parallel the confidence-interval procedures in Table 14.3. The terms appearing in Table 14.5 have been defined in Section 14.3.

Two types of errors that can be made in hypothesis testing:

Type I: Rejecting the null hypothesis H_0 when it is true
Type II: Accepting the null hypothesis H_0 when it is false—that is, when $\theta = \theta_1$.

The probability of making a type I error is α, and that for the type II error is denoted β.

It is becoming more common to replace the confidence parameter α with a quantity called the *p*-value, which is the smallest level of significance that would lead to the rejection of the null hypothesis. That is, the smaller the *p*-value, the less plausible the null hypothesis.

We now illustrate these concepts with three examples from Table 14.5: cases 2, 4, and 7.

Example 14.8   Test for statistical significance of the mean and the variance

Case 2   We again consider the data in **DataSet141**, which appear in Table 14.1. We want to know whether there is any statistically significant difference between the sample mean and a mean value of 168 ($\mu_0 = 168$) at a 95% confidence level. Thus, the hypothesis is

$$H_0: \mu = 168$$
$$H_1: \mu \neq 168$$

We use ttest to determine the validity of this hypothesis. The ttest function is

[h, p, ci] = ttest(Data, muzero, alpha)

TABLE 14.5 Several Hypothesis-Testing Procedures

Null hypothesis H_0	Alternative hypotheses H_1	Criteria for rejection of H_0	Test statistic	MATLAB function	Case
$\mu = \mu_0$	$\mu \neq \mu_0$	$|z_0| > z_{\alpha/2}$	$z_0 = \dfrac{\bar{x} - \mu_0}{\sigma/\sqrt{n}}$	ztest	1
(σ known)	$\mu > \mu_0$	$z_0 > z_\alpha$			
	$\mu < \mu_0$	$z_0 < -z_\alpha$			
$\mu = \mu_0$	$\mu \neq \mu_0$	$|t_0| > t_{\alpha/2,\,n-1}$	$t_0 = \dfrac{\bar{x} - \mu_0}{s/\sqrt{n}}$	ttest	2
(σ unknown)	$\mu > \mu_0$	$t_0 > t_{\alpha,\,n-1}$			
	$\mu < \mu_0$	$t_0 < -t_{\alpha,\,n-1}$			
$\mu_1 = \mu_2$	$\mu_1 \neq \mu_2$	$|z_0| > z_{\alpha/2}$	$z_0 = \dfrac{\bar{x}_1 - \bar{x}_2}{\sqrt{\dfrac{\sigma_1^2}{n_1} + \dfrac{\sigma_2^2}{n_2}}}$		3
(σ_1 and σ_2 known)	$\mu_1 > \mu_2$	$z_0 > z_\alpha$			
	$\mu_1 < \mu_2$	$z_0 < -z_\alpha$			
$\mu_1 = \mu_2$	$\mu_1 \neq \mu_2$	$|t_0| > t_{\alpha/2,\,n_1+n_2-2}$	$t_0 = \dfrac{\bar{x}_1 - \bar{x}_2}{s_p\sqrt{\dfrac{1}{n_1} + \dfrac{1}{n_2}}}$	ttest2	4
($\sigma_1 = \sigma_2$ unknown)	$\mu_1 > \mu_2$	$t_0 > t_{\alpha,\,n_1+n_2-2}$			
	$\mu_1 < \mu_2$	$t_0 < t_{\alpha,\,n_1+n_2-2}$			
$\mu_1 = \mu_2$	$\mu_1 \neq \mu_2$	$|t_0| > t_{\alpha/2,\,v}$	$t_0 = \dfrac{\bar{x}_1 - \bar{x}_2}{\sqrt{\dfrac{s_1^2}{n_1} + \dfrac{s_2^2}{n_2}}}$		5
($\sigma_1 \neq \sigma_2$ unknown)	$\mu_1 > \mu_2$	$t_0 > t_{\alpha,\,v}$			
	$\mu_1 < \mu_2$	$t_0 < -t_{\alpha,\,v}$			
$\sigma^2 = \sigma_0^2$	$\sigma^2 \neq \sigma_0^2$	$\chi_0^2 > \chi_{\alpha/2,\,n-1}^2$	$\chi_0^2 = \dfrac{(n-1)s^2}{\sigma_0^2}$		6
	$\sigma^2 > \sigma_0^2$	$\chi_0^2 > \chi_{\alpha,\,n-1}^2$			
	$\sigma^2 < \sigma_0^2$	$\chi_0^2 < \chi_{1-\alpha,\,n-1}^2$			
$\sigma_1^2 = \sigma_2^2$	$\sigma_1^2 \neq \sigma_2^2$	$f_0 > f_{\alpha/2,\,n_1-1,\,n_2-1}$ or $f_0 < f_{1-\alpha/2,\,n_1-1,\,n_2-1}$	$f_0 = \dfrac{s_1^2}{s_2^2}$		7
	$\sigma_1^2 > \sigma_2^2$	$f_0 > f_{\alpha,\,n_1-1,\,n_2-1}$			

where *Data* are the data, *muzero* = μ_0, *alpha* = α, $h = 0$ if H_0 and $h = 1$ if H_1, p = *p*-value—that is,

    p = 2*(1-tcdf(t0, n-1));

for a two-sided confidence interval, $t0 = t_0$ is defined in the fourth column of the second row of Table 14.5, and $ci(1) = l$ and $ci(2) = u$ are the lower and upper confidence limits, respectively. Thus, for our case,

    [h, p, ci] = ttest(**DataSet141**, 168, 0.05)

Upon execution, we find that $h = 0$—that is, we cannot reject the null hypothesis, $p = 0.1614$, $ci(1) = 155.1466$, and $ci(2) = 170.1784$. Recall case 3 of Section 14.3 where we had determined that $\bar{x} = 162.6625$ and that the confidence interval for this value at the 95% confidence level is $155.1466 \le \bar{x} \le 170.1784$. Since the hypothesized value for the mean, 168, lies within this confidence interval, we should expect that the null hypothesis would not be rejected. In fact, based on its p-value, we see that we are only $100(1 - 0.1614) = 83.9\%$ confident, which is less than our desired confidence level of 95%.

On the other hand, if our null hypothesis is

$$H_0\text{: } \mu = 175$$
$$H_1\text{: } \mu \ne 175$$

then

$$[h, p, ci] = \text{ttest}(\textbf{DataSet141}, 175, 0.05)$$

gives $h = 1$—that is, we reject the null hypothesis and adopt H_1, $p = 0.0016$, $ci(1) = 155.1466$, and $ci(2) = 170.1784$. In other words, we can be $100(1 - 0.0016) = 99.84\%$ confident that the mean of the data in **DataSet141** is different from the mean value of 175.

Case 4   We consider again the data in **DataFci**, which appear in Table 14.4. We want to determine whether there is any statistically significant difference between the means of these samples at a 95% confidence level. Thus, the hypothesis is

$$H_0\text{: } \mu_1 = \mu_2$$
$$H_1\text{: } \mu_1 \ne \mu_2$$

We use ttest2 to determine the validity of this hypothesis. The ttest2 function is

$$[h, p, ci] = \text{ttest2}(x1, x2, \text{alpha})$$

where $x1$ and $x2$ are the data, $alpha = \alpha$, $h = 0$ if H_0 and $h = 1$ if H_1, $p = p$-value— that is,

$$p = 2*(1\text{-}\text{tcdf}(t0, n\text{-}1))$$

for a two-sided confidence interval, $t0 = t_0$ is defined in the fourth column of the fourth row of Table 14.5, and $ci(1) = l$ and $ci(2) = u$ are the lower and upper confidence limits, respectively. Thus, the script is

$$[x1, x2] = \textbf{DataFci};$$
$$[h, p, ci] = \text{ttest2}(x1, x2, 0.05)$$

Executing this script yields $h = 0$—that is, we cannot reject the null hypothesis, $p = 0.6445$, $ci(1) = -0.7550$, and $ci(2) = 1.1855$ are the lower and upper confidence limits, respectively, on the *difference* between the means. Based on the p-value, we see that we are only $100(1 - 0.6445) = 35.55\%$ confident that there is a statistically significant difference between the means, which is substantially less than our desired confidence level of 95%. Therefore, the null hypothesis cannot be rejected.

Case 7   We consider again the data in **DataFci**, which appear in Table 14.4. We want to know whether there is any statistically significant difference between the variances of these samples at a 95% confidence level. Thus, the hypothesis is

$$H_0: \sigma_1^2 = \sigma_2^2$$
$$H_1: \sigma_1^2 \neq \sigma_2^2$$

The test statistic is

$$f_0 = \frac{s_1^2}{s_2^2}$$

and the criteria for rejection of the null hypothesis is either

$$f_0 > f_{\alpha/2, n_1-1, n_2-1} \quad \text{or} \quad f_0 < f_{1-\alpha/2, n_1-1, n_2-1}$$

Execution of the following script

```
[x1, x2] = DataFci;
L1 = length(x1);
L2 = length(x2);
ratio = var(x1)/var(x2);
if  ratio>finv(0.975, L1-1, L2-1)
   disp('Reject null hypothesis')
   disp(['pValue = ' num2str(2*(1-fcdf(ratio, L1-1, L2-1)))])
elseif ratio<finv(0.025, L1-1, L2-1)
   disp('Reject null hypothesis')
   disp(['pValue = ' num2str(2*fcdf(ratio, L1-1, L2-1))])
else
   disp('Null hypothesis cannot be rejected')
end
```

yields

```
Reject null hypothesis
pValue = 6.5379e-005
```

Thus, for these two data sets, there is a statistically significant difference in their variances. It is noted that, in general, the p-value for a two-sided F-test is determined from

```
p = 2*(1-fcdf(r, n1, n2))
```

where $r = s_1^2/s_2^2$ and $n1 = n_1$ and $n2 = n_2$ are the corresponding degrees of freedom.

14.5 LINEAR REGRESSION

14.5.1 Simple Linear Regression

Regression analysis is a statistical technique for modeling and investigating the relationship between two or more variables. A simple linear regression model has only one independent variable. If the input to a process is x and its response y, then a linear model is

$$y = \beta_1 x + \beta_0$$

If there are n values of the independent variable x_i and n corresponding measured responses y_i, where $i = 1, 2, \ldots, n$, then estimates of y are obtained from

$$\hat{y} = \hat{y}(x) = \hat{\beta}_1 x + \hat{\beta}_0 \quad x_{min} \leq x \leq x_{max} \tag{14.23}$$

where x_{min} is the minimum value of x_i, x_{max} is the maximum value of x_i, and $\hat{\beta}_1$ and $\hat{\beta}_0$, are estimates of β_1 and β_0, respectively, and are given by

$$\hat{\beta}_1 = \frac{S_{xy}}{S_{xx}} \tag{14.24}$$

$$\hat{\beta}_0 = \bar{y} - \hat{\beta}_1 \bar{x}$$

and

$$\bar{x} = \frac{1}{n} \sum_{i=1}^{n} x_i \qquad \bar{y} = \frac{1}{n} \sum_{i=1}^{n} y_i \tag{14.25}$$

$$S_{xx} = \sum_{i=1}^{n} x_i^2 - n\bar{x}^2 \quad S_{xy} = \sum_{i=1}^{n} x_i y_i - n\bar{x}\bar{y}$$

The values for $\hat{\beta}_1$ and $\hat{\beta}_0$ are obtained from `polyfit` (recall Section 5.4.2). Thus,

[c, s] = polyfit(x, y, 1)

where $c(1) = \hat{\beta}_1$ and $c(2) = \hat{\beta}_0$, and s is a quantity needed by `polyconf`, which is described below.

The $100(1 - \alpha)\%$ confidence limits on the estimate of $y(x)$, for $x_{min} \leq x \leq x_{max}$, are

$$\hat{y}(x) - w(x) \leq y(x) \leq \hat{y}(x) + w(x) \tag{14.26}$$

where

$$w(x) = t_{\alpha/2,\, n-2} \hat{\sigma} \sqrt{1 + \frac{1}{n} + \frac{(x - \bar{x})^2}{S_{xx}}}$$

$$\hat{\sigma}^2 = \frac{SS_E}{n - 2} \quad SS_E = S_{yy} - \hat{\beta}_1 S_{xy}$$

$$S_{yy} = \sum_{i=1}^{n} y_i^2 - n\bar{y}^2 \tag{14.27}$$

The quantities $w(x)$ and $\hat{y}(x)$ are obtained from `polyconf` as follows:

[c, s] = polyfit(x, y, 1)
[yhat, w] = polyconf(c, x, s, alpha)

where $yhat = \hat{y}(x)$, $w = w(x)$, and alpha $= \alpha$. The vector x determines the values at which $yhat$ and w are evaluated.

One means of determining the adequacy of the model given by Eq. 14.23 is to examine its residuals, which are

$$e_i = y_i - \hat{y}(x_i) \qquad i = 1, 2, \ldots, n \tag{14.28}$$

If e_i are approximately normally distributed, then the model has been correctly applied.

Another indicator of the model's representation of the data is the coefficient of determination R^2, which is given by

$$R^2 = 1 - \frac{SS_E}{S_{yy}} \tag{14.29}$$

The value $100R^2$ is the percentage of the variability of the data that is accounted for by the model. The closer this value is to 100%, the better the model. The quantity R is called the correlation coefficient.

We now illustrate the use of these relationships.

Example 14.9   Regression analysis

Consider the data given in Table 14.6. These data are placed in a function called **DataRegress1**. Notice, however, that these data are not ordered. Since this is inconvenient when it comes time to plot them with straight lines as connections, we sort them in ascending order. Neither polyfit nor polyconf requires the sorting. Thus,

```
function [x, y] = DataRegress1
xx = [2.38 2.44 2.70 2.98 3.32 3.12 2.14 2.86 3.50 3.20 2.78 2.70 2.36 2.42 ...
      2.62 2.80 2.92 3.04 3.26 2.30];
yy = [51.11 50.63 51.82 52.97 54.47 53.33 49.90 51.99 55.81 52.93 52.87 52.36 ...
      51.38 50.87 51.02 51.29 52.73 52.81 53.59 49.77];
[x, index] = sort(xx);
y = yy(index);
```

where *index* gives the original position of each element of x before being sorted. This technique has to be used because the correspondence of the elements in x and y must be preserved. If two sort functions were used, one on x and the other on y, then this correspondence would be lost.

TABLE 14.6   Data for Simple Linear Regression—**DataRegress1**

x	y	x	y
2.38	51.11	2.78	52.87
2.44	50.63	2.70	52.36
2.70	51.82	2.36	51.38
2.98	52.97	2.42	50.87
3.32	54.47	2.62	51.02
3.12	53.33	2.80	51.29
2.14	49.90	2.92	52.73
2.86	51.99	3.04	52.81
3.50	55.81	3.26	53.59
3.20	52.93	2.30	49.77

We now present a script that determines $\hat{\beta}_1$ and $\hat{\beta}_0$, plots $\hat{y}(x)$ and its confidence limits at the 95% level, plots the data and connects their values to $\hat{y}(x)$, and includes the appropriate annotation. In addition, the value for the coefficient of determination will be computed and placed on the graph. The results are shown in Figure 14.11.

```
[x, y] = DataRegress1;
[c, s] = polyfit(x, y, 1);
[yhat, w] = polyconf(c, x, s, 0.05);
syy = sum(y.^2)-length(x)*mean(y)^2;
sse = syy-c(1)*(sum(x.*y)-length(x)*mean(x)*mean(y));
plot(x, yhat, 'k-', x, yhat-w, 'k--', x, yhat+w,'k--', x, y, 'ks', [x; x], [yhat; y], 'k-')
legend('Regression line', '95% confidence interval of y', 'Location', 'SouthEast')
axis([2, 3.6, 48, 57])
xlabel('x (Input)')
ylabel('y (Response)')
text(2.1, 56, ['Coefficient of determination R^2 = ' num2str(1-sse/syy, 3)])
```

We proceed further and investigate the residuals. We first compute the residuals and then plot them using `normplot` (recall Figure 14.7) to determine whether they are normally distributed. The script is

```
[x, y] = DataRegress1;
normplot(y-polyval(polyfit(x, y, 1), x))
```

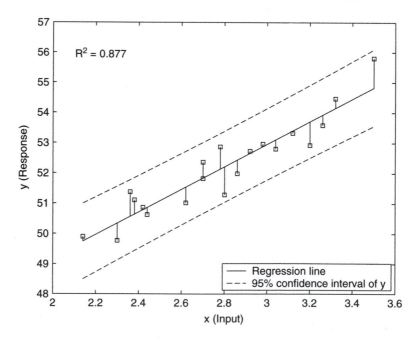

Figure 14.11   Linear regression for the data in Table 14.6 and the confidence limits on y.

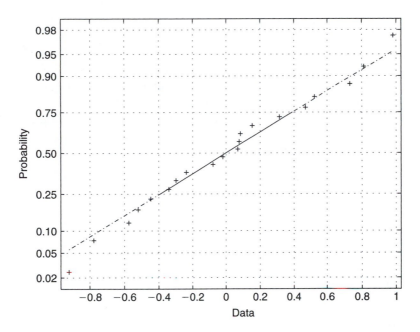

Figure 14.12   Normal cumulative distribution plot of the residuals from the fitted line appearing in Figure 14.11.

which upon execution results in Figure 14.12. Since the residuals are very close to the line representing the normal distribution, we can say that the residuals are very nearly normally distributed and, therefore, that our model is adequate.

14.5.2 Multiple Linear Regression

There are many applications where more than one independent factor (variable) affects the outcome of a process. In this situation, we require a multiple regression model. Consider a process that has one output y and k inputs x_j, where $j = 1, 2, \ldots, k$. This process can be modeled as

$$y = \beta_o + \sum_{j=1}^{k} \beta_j x_j \qquad (14.30)$$

which is called a multiple linear regression model with k independent variables. The parameters β_j, where $j = 0, 1, 2, \ldots, k$ are the regression coefficients. Models that are more complex in appearance often may be analyzed with this multiple linear regression model. For example, suppose that we have a cubic polynomial in *one* independent variable x:

$$y = \beta_o + \beta_1 x + \beta_2 x^2 + \beta_3 x^3$$

If we let $x_1 = x$, $x_2 = x^2$, and $x_3 = x^3$, then we have the linear model shown in Eq. 14.30—that is,

$$y = \beta_o + \beta_1 x_1 + \beta_2 x_2 + \beta_3 x_3$$

However, this class of models is more easily solved with `polyfit`.

Another example is

$$y = \beta_o + \beta_1 x_1 + \beta_2 x_2 + \beta_3 x_1^2 + \beta_4 x_2^2 + \beta_5 x_1 x_2$$

which is of the form of Eq. 14.30 when we set $x_3 = x_1^2$, $x_4 = x_2^2$, and $x_5 = x_1 x_2$.

Thus, we see that any regression model that is linear in the parameters β_j is a linear regression model regardless of the shape of the surface y that it generates.

To estimate the parameters, we run an experiment n times, $n > k + 1$, such that for each set of x_{ij}, where $i = 1, 2, \ldots, n$ and $j = 1, 2, \ldots, k$, we obtain a corresponding set of outputs y_i. In tabular form, this would appear as

y	x_1	x_2	$\ldots$	x_k
y_1	x_{11}	x_{12}	$\ldots$	x_{1k}
y_2	x_{21}	x_{22}	$\ldots$	x_{2k}
$\vdots$	$\vdots$	$\vdots$		$\vdots$
y_n	x_{n1}	x_{n2}	$\ldots$	x_{nk}

Then, Eq. 14.30 becomes

$$y_i = \beta_o + \sum_{j=1}^{k} \beta_j x_{ij} \quad i = 1, 2, \ldots, n \tag{14.31}$$

If these data are arranged in the following matrix form

$$X = \begin{bmatrix} 1 & x_{11} & x_{12} & \cdots & x_{1k} \\ 1 & x_{21} & x_{22} & \cdots & x_{2k} \\ \vdots & \vdots & & & \vdots \\ 1 & x_{n1} & x_{n2} & \cdots & x_{nk} \end{bmatrix} \quad y = \begin{bmatrix} y_1 \\ y_2 \\ \vdots \\ y_n \end{bmatrix} \quad \hat{\beta} = \begin{bmatrix} \hat{\beta}_0 \\ \hat{\beta}_1 \\ \vdots \\ \hat{\beta}_k \end{bmatrix} \tag{14.32}$$

then the solution for the estimates of β_j, denoted $\hat{\beta}_j$, are obtained from the solution of the following matrix equation:

$$\hat{\beta} = (X'X)^{-1}X'y \tag{14.33}$$

The matrix X is, in general, not square. Then,

$$\hat{y}_i = \hat{\beta}_o + \sum_{j=1}^{k} \hat{\beta}_j x_{ij} \quad i = 1, 2, \ldots, n \tag{14.34}$$

where $\hat{y}_i$ is the estimate of y_i.

Once the regression coefficients have been obtained, one indication of the adequacy of the model is to compute the residuals and see whether they are normally distributed. The residuals are defined as

$$e = y - \hat{y}$$

Thus,

$$e_i = y_i - \hat{y}_i = y_i - \hat{\beta}_o - \sum_{j=1}^{k} \hat{\beta}_j x_{ij} \quad i = 1, 2, \ldots, n \tag{14.35}$$

The confidence limits on the regression coefficients β_j are given by

$$\beta_{Lj} \leq \beta_j \leq \beta_{Uj} \quad j = 0, 1, \ldots, k \tag{14.36}$$

where

$$\beta_{Lj} = \hat{\beta}_j - t_{\alpha/2, n-k-1} \hat{\sigma} \sqrt{C_{jj}} \tag{14.37}$$
$$\beta_{Uj} = \hat{\beta}_j + t_{\alpha/2, n-k-1} \hat{\sigma} \sqrt{C_{jj}}$$

and

$$\hat{\sigma}^2 = \frac{y'y - \hat{\beta}'X'y}{n - k - 1}$$

$$C = (X'X)^{-1} = \begin{bmatrix} C_{00} & C_{01} & \cdots & C_{0K} \\ C_{10} & C_{11} & & \\ \vdots & & \ddots & \\ C_{k0} & & & C_{kk} \end{bmatrix} \tag{14.38}$$

In other words,

$$\text{var}(\hat{\beta}_j) = \hat{\sigma}^2 C_{jj} \quad j = 0, 1, \ldots, k$$

is an estimate of the variance of $\hat{\beta}_j$, and

$$\text{covar}(\hat{\beta}_i, \hat{\beta}_j) = \hat{\sigma}^2 C_{ij} \quad i, j = 0, 1, \ldots, k \quad i \neq j$$

is an estimate of the covariance of $\hat{\beta}_i$ and $\hat{\beta}_j$.

The multiple determination coefficient R^2 is given by

$$R^2 = 1 - \frac{y'y - \hat{\beta}'X'y}{y'y - n\bar{y}^2} \tag{14.39}$$

where

$$\bar{y} = \frac{1}{n} \sum_{j=1}^{n} y_j$$

The quantity R is the correlation coefficient.

One can also perform a hypothesis test to determine whether a linear relationship exists between at least one regressor variable (x_i, where $i = 1, 2, \ldots, k$) and the response y. The hypothesis test is

$$H_0: \beta_1 = \beta_2 = \cdots = \beta_k = 0$$
$$H_1: \beta_j \neq 0 \text{ for at least one } j$$

Rejection of H_0 implies that at least one regressor variable makes a statistically significant contribution. The test statistic is

$$F_0 = \frac{(\hat{\beta}'X'y - n\bar{y}^2)/k}{(y'y - \hat{\beta}'X'y)/(n - k - 1)} \quad n > k + 1 \tag{14.40}$$

We reject H_0 if

$$F_0 > f_{\alpha, k, n-k-1}$$

The numerical evaluation of these equations can be obtained from either beta = regress(y, x)

or

[beta, betacl, e, ecl, stats] = regress(y, X, alpha)

where

> $beta = [\hat{\beta}_0 \ \hat{\beta}_1 \dots \hat{\beta}_k]$ as defined by Eq. 14.33
> *betacl* is a $((k + 1) \times 2)$ array of the lower and upper confidence limits β_L and β_U, respectively, as defined by Eq. 14.37 and whose order corresponds to that of *beta*
> $e = [e_1 \ e_2 \ \dots \ e_n]$ are the residuals given by Eq. 14.35;
> *ecl* are the confidence limits on the residuals
> $stats = [R^2 \ F_0 \ p]$, where
> > R^2 is given by Eq. 14.39
> > F_0 is given by Eq. 14.40
> > p is the p-value corresponding to F_0—that is,
> > > p = 1 − fcdf(F0, k, n-k-1)
> $y = [y_1 y_2 \dots y_n]'$ is the column vector of responses
> $X = X$ as defined by Eq. 14.32
> $alpha = \alpha$

We now illustrate the use of these formulas.

Example 14.10   Multiple regression analysis

Consider the data in Table 14.7. We shall fit the following model to these data:

$$y = \beta_0 + \beta_1 x_1 + \beta_2 x_2 + \beta_3 x_3 + \beta_4 x_1 x_2 + \beta_5 x_1 x_3 + \beta_6 x_2 x_3$$
$$+ \beta_7 x_1^2 + \beta_8 x_2^2 + \beta_9 x_3^2$$

First, we create the function **DataMultiRegress1** to create X according to Eq. 14.32:

```
function [y, X] = DataMultiRegress1
y = [0.22200 0.39500 0.42200 0.43700 0.42800 0.46700 0.44400 0.37800 0.49400 ...
     0.45600 0.45200 0.11200 0.43200 0.10100 0.23200 0.30600 0.09230 0.11600 ...
     0.07640 0.43900 0.09440 0.11700 0.07260 0.04120 0.25100 0.00002]';
x1 = [7.3 8.7 8.8 8.1 9.0 8.7 9.3 7.6 10.0 8.4 9.3 7.7 9.8 7.3 8.5 9.5 7.4 7.8 7.7 10.3 ...
      7.8 7.1 7.7 7.4 7.3 7.6]';
x2 = [0.0 0.0 0.7 4.0 0.5 1.5 2.1 5.1 0.0 3.7 3.6 2.8 4.2 2.5 2.0 2.5 2.8 2.8 3.0 1.7 ...
      3.3 3.9 4.3 6.0 2.0 7.8]';
x3 = [0.0 0.3 1.0 0.2 1.0 2.8 1.0 3.4 0.3 4.1 2.0 7.1 2.0 6.8 6.6 5.0 7.8 7.7 8.0 ...
      4.2 8.5 6.6 9.5 10.9 5.2 20.7]';
X = [ones(length(y),1), x1, x2, x3, x1.*x2, x1.*x3, x2.*x3, x1.^2 x2.^2, x3.^2];
```

TABLE 14.7   Data Comprising the Function **DataMultiRegress1**

y	x_1	x_2	x_3	y	x_1	x_2	x_3
0.22200	7.3	0.0	0.0	0.10100	7.3	2.5	6.8
0.39500	8.7	0.0	0.3	0.23200	8.5	2.0	6.6
0.42200	8.8	0.7	1.0	0.30600	9.5	2.5	5.0
0.43700	8.1	4.0	0.2	0.09230	7.4	2.8	7.8
0.42800	9.0	0.5	1.0	0.11600	7.8	2.8	7.7
0.46700	8.7	1.5	2.8	0.07640	7.7	3.0	8.0
0.44400	9.3	2.1	1.0	0.43900	10.3	1.7	4.2
0.37800	7.6	5.1	3.4	0.09440	7.8	3.3	8.5
0.49400	10.0	0.0	0.3	0.11700	7.1	3.9	6.6
0.45600	8.4	3.7	4.1	0.07260	7.7	4.3	9.5
0.45200	9.3	3.6	2.0	0.04120	7.4	6.0	10.9
0.11200	7.7	2.8	7.1	0.25100	7.3	2.0	5.2
0.43200	9.8	4.2	2.0	0.00002	7.6	7.8	20.7

Next, we determine the estimates of the coefficients $\hat{\beta}_j$ and their confidence limits at the 95% confidence level; display the values of R^2, F_0, and its p-value; and plot the residuals to determine whether they are normally distributed. The script is

```
[y, X] = DataMultiRegress1;
[b, bcl, e, ecl, stat] = regress(y, X, 0.05);
lenb = length(b);
disp('Regression coefficients and their confidence limits')
disp([num2str(bcl(:,1)) repmat(' <= beta(', lenb, 1) num2str((0:lenb-1)') ...
    repmat(') = ', lenb, 1) num2str(b) repmat(' <= ', lenb, 1) num2str(bcl(:,2))])
disp(['Coefficient of determination R^2 = ' num2str(stat(1))])
disp(['Test statistic F0 = ' num2str(stat(2)) ' and corresponding p-value = ' ...
        num2str(stat(3))])
normplot(e)
```

Execution of this script displays the following information to the command window and plots the results shown in Figure 14.13. It is seen in this figure that all but five residuals fall close to the line representing the normal distribution. Therefore, the model is adequate.

```
Regression coefficients and their confidence limits
-4.4976        <= beta(0) = -1.7694        <= 0.9589
-0.20282       <= beta(1) = 0.4208         <= 1.0444
-0.054708      <= beta(2) = 0.22245        <= 0.49961
-0.27691       <= beta(3) = -0.128         <= 0.020918
-0.045395      <= beta(4) = -0.019876      <= 0.0056419
-0.0070049     <= beta(5) = 0.0091515      <= 0.025308
-0.012346      <= beta(6) = 0.0025762      <= 0.017499
-0.054932      <= beta(7) = -0.019325      <= 0.016283
-0.032989      <= beta(8) = -0.0074485     <= 0.018092
-0.002231      <= beta(9) = 0.00082397     <= 0.003879
Coefficient of determination R^2 = 0.91695
Test statistic F0 = 19.628 and corresponding p-value = 5.0513e-007
```

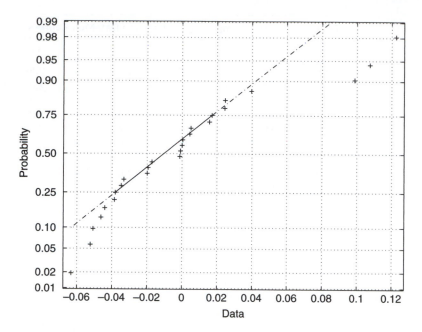

Figure 14.13   Normal cumulative distribution plot of the residuals from the surface modeling the data in Table 14.7.

14.6 DESIGN OF EXPERIMENTS

14.6.1 Single-Factor Experiments: Analysis of Variance

Consider a single-factor experiment with the factor denoted A. We run an experiment varying A at a different levels, A_j, where $j = 1, 2, \ldots, a$, and we repeat the experiment n times—that is, we obtain n replicates. The results are shown symbolically in Table 14.8. The results in the first column of the observations, x_{j1} in Table 14.8, would be obtained by randomly ordering the levels A_j, where $j = 1, 2, \ldots, a$, and then running the experiment in this randomly selected order. Then, the results in the second column of the observations, x_{j2}, where $j = 1, 2, \ldots, a$, would be obtained by generating a new random order for the levels A_j and running the experiment in this new random order. This procedure is repeated until the n replicates have been obtained. Running the experiment in this manner ensures that the values obtained for the x_{jk} have each been independently obtained. Thus, we can define two independent variances using the quantities μ_i and s_i^2 defined in Table 14.8 as follows: The variance of the mean of factor A is

$$s_A^2 = \frac{n}{a-1}\left(\sum_{i=1}^{a}\mu_i^2 - a\bar{x}^2\right) = \frac{SS_A}{a-1}$$

which has $a - 1$ degrees of freedom, and $\bar{x}$ is the grand mean given by

$$\bar{x} = \frac{1}{an}\sum_{i=1}^{a}\sum_{j=1}^{n}x_{ij}$$

TABLE 14.8 Tabulations of the Results of a Single-Factor Experiment with $n > 1$ Replicates

Level	Observations			Average	Variance	Residuals
A_1	x_{11}	x_{12}	$\cdots$ x_{1n}	$\mu_1 = \dfrac{1}{n}\displaystyle\sum_{j=1}^{n} x_{1j}$	$s_1^2 = \dfrac{1}{n-1}\displaystyle\sum_{j=1}^{n}(x_{1j}-\mu_1)^2$	$\varepsilon_{1j} = x_{1j} - \mu_1$
A_2	x_{21}	x_{22}	x_{2n}	$\mu_2 = \dfrac{1}{n}\displaystyle\sum_{j=1}^{n} x_{2j}$	$s_2^2 = \dfrac{1}{n-1}\displaystyle\sum_{j=1}^{n}(x_{2j}-\mu_2)^2$	$\varepsilon_{2j} = x_{2j} - \mu_2$
$\cdots$		$\cdots$ $\cdots$		$\cdots$		
A_a	x_{a1}	x_{a2}	$\cdots$ x_{an}	$\mu_a = \dfrac{1}{n}\displaystyle\sum_{j=1}^{n} x_{aj}$	$s_a^2 = \dfrac{1}{n-1}\displaystyle\sum_{j=1}^{n}(x_{aj}-\mu_a)^2$	$\varepsilon_{aj} = x_{aj} - \mu_a$

The variance of the error is

$$s_{error}^2 = \frac{1}{a}\sum_{i=1}^{a}s_i^2 = \frac{1}{a(n-1)}\left(\sum_{i=1}^{a}\sum_{j=1}^{n}x_{ij}^2 - an\bar{x}^2\right) = \frac{SS_{error}}{a(n-1)}$$

which has $a(n-1)$ degrees of freedom.

The variances s_A^2 and s_{error}^2 are related by the following identity, called the sum-of-squares identity, which has $an - 1$ degrees of freedom.

$$SS_{total} = \sum_{i=1}^{a}\sum_{j=1}^{n}(x_{ij}-\bar{x})^2 = \sum_{i=1}^{a}\sum_{j=1}^{n}[(\mu_i - \bar{x}) + (x_{ij} - \mu_i)]^2$$

$$= n\sum_{i=1}^{a}(\mu_i - \bar{x})^2 + \sum_{i=1}^{a}\sum_{j=1}^{n}(x_{ij} - \mu_i)^2$$

$$= SS_A + SS_{error}$$

$$= (a-1)s_A^2 + a(n-1)s_{error}^2$$

The left-hand side of the equation is called the total sum of squares. The identity has partitioned the total variance into two independent components: that caused by the factor A, and that caused by the variation in the process as expressed by the residuals ε_{ij}.

In the analysis of variance (ANOVA), the convention is to define a quantity called the mean square, denoted MS, which is the sum of squares divided by the number of degrees of freedom. Thus, for the single factor experiment, we have

$$MS_A = \frac{SS_A}{(a-1)} = s_A^2 \qquad (a > 1)$$

$$MS_{error} = \frac{SS_{error}}{a(n-1)} = s_{error}^2 \qquad (n > 1)$$

The objective of the experiment is to determine whether the various levels of A have any statistically significant effect on the output x_{ij}. We now have the ability to determine this by forming the ratio of the mean square of the factor A with the independent mean square of the random error. This tells us whether the variance of A is a statistically significantly large portion of the total variance. Thus, the test statistic is

$$F_0 = \frac{MS_A}{MS_{error}}$$

TABLE 14.9   ANOVA Table for a Single-Factor Experiment with $n > 1$ Replicates

Factor	Sum of squares	Degrees of freedom	Mean square	F_0	p-value
A	SS_A	$a - 1$	MS_A	MS_A/MS_{error}	
Error	SS_{error}	$a(n - 1)$	MS_{error}		
Total	SS_{total}	$an - 1$			

The hypothesis is

$$H_0: \mu_1 = \mu_2 = \ldots = \mu_a$$
$$H_1: \mu_j \neq \mu_i \text{ for at least one } j \neq i$$

Thus, when

$$F_0 > f_{a,\, a-1,\, a(n-1)}$$

the null hypothesis is rejected. The results of this analysis are usually presented in the form shown in Table 14.9.

A single-factor analysis of variance is obtained with

p = anova1(x)

where p is the p-value and x is the *transpose* of data as shown in Table 14.8. There are two additional outputs from this function: One is the ANOVA table shown in Table 14.9, and the other is a box plot of the variations in the medians of each of the a levels.

We now illustrate the analysis of variance of a single-factor experiment.

Example 14.11   Single-factor ANOVA

Consider the data in Table 14.10. We shall write a script to generate the ANOVA table, display the p-value, compute the residuals, and determine whether they are normally distributed. We first create the function **DataAnova1** to convert the data into a form required by anova1.

```
function d = DataAnova1
d = [143 141 150 146; ...
     152 149 137 143; ...
     134 133 132 127; ...
     129 127 132 129; ...
     147 148 144 142]';
```

TABLE 14.10   Data for Example 14.11—**DataAnova1**

Level	Observations			
1	143	141	150	146
2	152	149	137	143
3	134	133	132	127
4	129	127	132	129
5	147	148	144	142

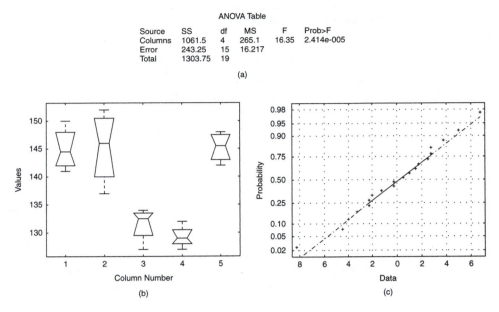

ANOVA Table

Source	SS	df	MS	F	Prob>F
Columns	1061.5	4	265.1	16.35	2.414e-005
Error	243.25	15	16.217		
Total	1303.75	19			

(a)

(b)

(c)

Figure 14.14   Analysis of variance of the data in Table 14.10: (a) ANOVA table; (b) box plot of the five levels; (c) normal distribution plot of the residuals.

The script is

```
vv = DataAnova1;
[r, c] = size(vv);
pp = anova1(vv);
meen = mean(vv);
k = 0;
for n = 1:r
   for m = 1:c
      k = k+1;
      e(k) = vv(n,m)-meen(m);
   end
end
figure
normplot(e)
```

The nested for loop is needed to store the residuals as a vector. The figure function is used to open another figure window, because anova1 opens two windows of its own. If the figure function weren't used, then one of the two figures generated by anova1 would be overwritten. The function anova1 produces the table in Figure 14.14a and the box plot in Figure 14.14b; Figure 14.14c is produced by normplot.

14.6.2 Multiple-Factor Experiments

Factorial Experiments

The results for a single-factor experiment can be extended to experiments with several factors, which are called factorial experiments. This is because the procedure requires that we run all combinations of all the levels of each factor for each replicate of the experiment. We illustrate this for a two-factor experiment, which has the

TABLE 14.11   Data Arrangement for a Two-Factor Factorial Experiment

		Factor B			
		1	2	...	b
	1	$y_{111}, y_{112}, \ldots, y_{11n}$	$y_{121}, y_{122}, \ldots, y_{12n}$		$y_{1b1}, y_{1b2}, \ldots, y_{1bn}$
Factor A	2	$y_{211}, y_{212}, \ldots, y_{21n}$	$y_{221}, y_{222}, \ldots, y_{22n}$		$y_{2b1}, y_{2b2}, \ldots, y_{2bn}$
	$\vdots$				
	a	$y_{a11}, y_{a12}, \ldots, y_{a1n}$	$y_{a21}, y_{a22}, \ldots, y_{a2n}$		$y_{ab1}, y_{ab2}, \ldots, y_{abn}$

factor A at a levels and the factor B at b levels. The number of replicates is $n(>1)$, and the output is x_{ijk}, where $i = 1, 2, \ldots, a$, $j = 1, 2, \ldots, b$; and $k = 1, 2, \ldots, n$. The intervals between each level of each factor do not have to be equal. The tabular form of these data is given in Table 14.11.

The starting point is the sum-of-squares identity. Before proceeding with this identity, however, we introduce the following definitions for several different means:

$$\bar{x}_{ijn} = \frac{1}{n}\sum_{k=1}^{n} x_{ijk}$$

$$\bar{x}_{ibn} = \frac{1}{b}\sum_{j=1}^{b}\bar{x}_{ijn} = \frac{1}{bn}\sum_{j=1}^{b}\sum_{k=1}^{n} x_{ijk}$$

$$\bar{x}_{ajn} = \frac{1}{a}\sum_{i=1}^{a}\bar{x}_{ijn} = \frac{1}{an}\sum_{i=1}^{a}\sum_{k=1}^{n} x_{ijk}$$

and the grand mean

$$\bar{x} = \frac{1}{abn}\sum_{i=1}^{a}\sum_{j=1}^{b}\sum_{k=1}^{n} x_{ijk}$$

The sum-of-squares identity for a two-factor ANOVA, is

$$SS_{total} = \sum_{i=1}^{a}\sum_{j=1}^{b}\sum_{k=1}^{n}(x_{ijk} - \bar{x})^2 = SS_A + SS_B + SS_{AB} + SS_{error}$$

where

$$SS_A = \sum_{i=1}^{a}\sum_{j=1}^{b}\sum_{k=1}^{n}(\bar{x}_{ibn} - \bar{x})^2 = bn\sum_{i=1}^{a}\bar{x}_{ibn}^2 - abn\bar{x}^2$$

$$SS_B = \sum_{i=1}^{a}\sum_{j=1}^{b}\sum_{k=1}^{n}(\bar{x}_{ajn} - \bar{x})^2 = an\sum_{j=1}^{b}\bar{x}_{ajn}^2 - abn\bar{x}^2$$

$$SS_{AB} = n\sum_{i=1}^{a}\sum_{j=1}^{b}(\bar{x}_{ijn} - \bar{x}_{ibn} - \bar{x}_{ajn} + \bar{x})^2$$

TABLE 14.12   ANOVA Table for a Two-Factor Experiment with $n > 1$ Replicates

Factor	Sum of squares	Degrees of freedom	Mean square	F_0	$f_{\alpha, z, ab(n-1)}$	p-value
A	SS_A	$a - 1$	$MS_A = SS_A/(a - 1)$	MS_A/MS_{error}	(f-table, $z = a - 1$)	
B	SS_B	$b - 1$	$MS_B = SS_B/(b - 1)$	MS_B/MS_{error}	(f-table, $z = b - 1$)	
AB	SS_{AB}	$(a - 1)(b - 1)$	$MS_{AB} = SS_{AB}/(a - 1)(b - 1)$	MS_{AB}/MS_{error}	(f-table, $z = (a - 1)(b - 1)$)	
Error	SS_{error}	$ab(n - 1)$	$MS_{error} = SS_{error}/ab(n - 1)$			
Total	SS_{total}	$abn - 1$				

and

$$SS_{error} = \sum_{i=1}^{a}\sum_{j=1}^{b}\sum_{k=1}^{n}(x_{ijk} - \bar{x}_{ijn})^2 = \sum_{i=1}^{a}\sum_{j=1}^{b}\sum_{k=1}^{n}x_{ijk}^2 - n\sum_{i=1}^{a}\sum_{j=1}^{b}\bar{x}_{ijn}^2$$

The quantities SS_A, SS_B, SS_{AB}, SS_{error}, and SS_{total} have $(a - 1)$, $(b - 1)$, $(a - 1)(b - 1)$, $ab(n - 1)$, and $(abn - 1)$ degrees of freedom, respectively. The sum-of-squares term SS_{AB} indicates the interaction of factors A and B. The ANOVA table for a two-factor experiment is given in Table 14.12. The definitions of the mean-square values are also given in this table. It is seen that the analysis of variance isolates the interaction effects of the two factors and provides a means of ascertaining, through the ratio MS_{AB}/MS_{error}, whether the interaction of the factors is statistically significant at a stated confidence level.

The solution to a two-factor factorial experiment is obtained from

anova2(y, n)

where n is the number of replicates. This function produces the Table 14.12. The matrix y follows the form of the data in Table 14.11 as follows:

$$y = \begin{bmatrix} y_{111} & y_{121} & \cdots & y_{1b1} \\ y_{112} & y_{122} & & y_{1b2} \\ \vdots & & & \\ y_{11n} & y_{12n} & & y_{1bn} \\ y_{211} & y_{221} & & y_{2b1} \\ y_{212} & y_{222} & & y_{2b2} \\ \vdots & & & \\ y_{21n} & y_{22n} & & y_{2bn} \\ \vdots & & & \\ y_{a11} & y_{a21} & & y_{ab1} \\ y_{a12} & y_{a22} & & y_{ab2} \\ \vdots & & & \\ y_{a1n} & y_{a2n} & & y_{abn} \end{bmatrix}$$

We shall now illustrate the use of these relationships.

TABLE 14.13   Data for Example 14.12—**DataAnova2**

		Factor B		
		1	2	3
	1	130, 155, 74, 180	34, 40, 80, 75	20, 70, 82, 58
Factor A	2	150, 188, 159, 126	136, 122, 106, 115	25, 70, 58, 45
	3	138, 110, 168, 160	174, 120, 150, 139	96, 104, 82, 60

Example 14.12   Two-factor ANOVA

Consider the data shown in Table 14.13. We create the following function to put these data in the appropriate format:

```
function d = DataAnova2
dc1 = [[130, 155, 74, 180]'; [150, 188, 159, 126]'; [138, 110, 168, 160]'];
dc2 = [[34, 40, 80, 75]'; [136, 122, 106, 115]'; [174, 120, 150, 139]'];
dc3 = [[20, 70, 82, 58]'; [25, 70, 58, 45]'; [96, 104, 82, 60]'];
d = [dc1, dc2, dc3];
```

The script is

```
anova2(DataAnova2, 4);
```

which upon execution displays the following table in a figure window:

```
                     ANOVA Table
   Source       SS            df    MS           F        Prob>F
   Columns      3.912e+004    2     1.956e+004   28.97    0
   Rows         1.068e+004    2     5342         7.911    0.002
   Interaction  9614          4     2403         3.56     0.0186
   Error        1.823e+004    27    675.2
   Total        7.765e+004    35
```

Thus, based on the p-values, we see that factors A and B are statistically significant at the greater-than-99.8% level and that their interaction is significant at the 98% level.

2^k *Factorial Experiments*

If the factorial experiments described above contain k factors and each factor is considered at only two levels, then the experiment is called a 2^k factorial design. It implicitly assumes a linear relationship between the two levels of each factor. This assumption leads to certain simplifications in how the tests are conducted and the results are analyzed.

The convention is to denote the value of the high level of a factor with either "1" or "+" and the value of the low level with either "0" or "−." Then, the 2^k combination of factors that comprise one run, which represents one replicate, is given in Table 14.14 for $k = 2, 3$, and 4. The table is used as follows: For the 2^2 ($k = 2$)

TABLE 14.14   Levels and Run Order of Each Factor for a 2^2, 2^3, and 2^4 Factorial Experiment

Run	Factors and their levels				Data $(y_{m,j})$			Run order number[*]		
m	A	B	C	D	$j = 1$	$j = 2$	$\ldots$	2^2	2^3	2^4
1	$-$	$-$	$-$	$-$	$y_{1,1}$	$y_{1,2}$		3	5	6
2	$+$	$-$	$-$	$-$	$y_{2,1}$	$y_{2,2}$		1	7	11
3	$-$	$+$	$-$	$-$	$y_{3,1}$	$y_{3,2}$		4	8	14
4	$+$	$+$	$-$	$-$	$y_{4,1}$	$y_{4,2}$		2	4	5
5	$-$	$-$	$+$	$-$	$y_{5,1}$	$y_{5,2}$			2	13
6	$+$	$-$	$+$	$-$	$y_{6,1}$	$y_{6,2}$			1	2
7	$-$	$+$	$+$	$-$	$y_{7,1}$	$y_{7,2}$			3	16
8	$+$	$+$	$+$	$-$	$y_{8,1}$	$y_{8,2}$			6	15
9	$-$	$-$	$-$	$+$	$y_{9,1}$	$y_{9,2}$				9
10	$+$	$-$	$-$	$+$	$y_{10,1}$	$y_{10,2}$				7
11	$-$	$+$	$-$	$+$	$y_{11,1}$	$y_{11,2}$				10
12	$+$	$+$	$-$	$+$	$y_{12,1}$	$y_{12,2}$				3
13	$-$	$-$	$+$	$+$	$y_{13,1}$	$y_{13,2}$				8
14	$+$	$-$	$+$	$+$	$y_{14,1}$	$y_{14,2}$				4
15	$-$	$+$	$+$	$+$	$y_{15,1}$	$y_{15,2}$				1
16	$+$	$+$	$+$	$+$	$y_{16,1}$	$y_{16,2}$				12

*One set of randomly ordered runs for $j = 1$ only. For $j = 2$, a new set of a randomly generated run order is used, and so on.

factorial experiment, only the columns labeled A and B and the first four rows ($m = 1, \ldots, 4$) are used. The four combinations of the factors are run in a random order. One such random order is shown in the column labeled 2^2. Thus, the combination in row 2 is run first, with A high (A_{high}) and B low (B_{low}). This yields the output value $y_{2,1}$. Then, the combination shown in the fourth row is run, where both A and B are at their high levels (A_{high} and B_{high}, respectively). This gives the output response $y_{4,1}$. After the remaining combinations have been run, one replicate of the experiment has been completed. A newly obtained random order for the run is obtained, one that is most likely different from the one shown in the column labeled 2^2, and the four combinations are run in the new order to get the output response for the second replicate. For $k = 3$, the factors are A, B, and C, and the first eight rows of the table are used. For $k = 4$, the factors are A, B, C, and D, and all 16 rows of the table are used. One set of a random run order is given for each of these cases in the columns labeled 2^3 and 2^4, respectively.

After the data have been collected, they are analyzed as follows, provided that the number of replicates is greater than one. Consider the tabulations in Table 14.15. The $+$ and $-$ signs in each column represent $+1$ and -1, respectively. The columns for the primary factors A, B, C, and D are the same as those given in Table 14.14, where, again, the $+$ and $-$ signs stand for $+1$ and -1, respectively. The columns representing all the interaction terms are obtained by multiplying the corresponding signs in the columns of the primary factors. Thus, the signs in the columns designating the interaction ABC are obtained by multiplying the signs in the columns

TABLE 14.15 Definitions of Various Terms That Are Used to Calculate the Sum of Squares and Mean-Square Values for a 2^2, 2^3, and 2^4 Factorial Experiment

| Factors and their interactions $(\lambda)^\dagger$ | | | | | | | | | | | | | | | Data‡ | | | | |
A	B	AB	C	AC	BC	ABC	D	AD	BD	ABD	CD	ACD	BCD	ABCD	$j=1$	$\ldots$	$j=n$	S_m #	m
−	−	+	−	+	+	−	−	+	+	−	+	−	−	+	$y_{1,1}$		$y_{1,n}$	S_1	1
+	−	−	−	−	+	+	−	−	+	+	+	+	−	−	$y_{2,1}$		$y_{2,n}$	S_2	2
−	+	−	−	+	−	+	−	+	−	+	+	−	+	−	$y_{3,1}$		$y_{3,n}$	S_3	3
+	+	+	−	−	−	−	−	−	−	−	+	+	+	+	$y_{4,1}$		$y_{4,n}$	S_4	4
−	−	+	+	−	−	+	−	+	+	−	−	+	+	−	$y_{5,1}$		$y_{5,n}$	S_5	5
+	−	−	+	+	−	−	−	−	+	+	−	−	+	+	$y_{6,1}$		$y_{6,n}$	S_6	6
−	+	−	+	−	+	−	−	+	−	+	−	+	−	+	$y_{7,1}$		$y_{7,n}$	S_7	7
+	+	+	+	+	+	+	−	−	−	−	−	−	−	−	$y_{8,1}$		$y_{8,n}$	S_8	8
−	−	+	−	+	+	−	+	−	−	+	−	+	+	−	$y_{9,1}$		$y_{9,n}$	S_9	9
+	−	−	−	−	+	+	+	+	−	−	−	−	+	+	$y_{10,1}$		$y_{10,n}$	S_{10}	10
−	+	−	−	+	−	+	+	−	+	−	−	+	−	+	$y_{11,1}$		$y_{11,n}$	S_{11}	11
+	+	+	−	−	−	−	+	+	+	+	−	−	−	−	$y_{12,1}$		$y_{12,n}$	S_{12}	12
−	−	+	+	−	−	+	+	−	−	+	+	−	−	+	$y_{13,1}$		$y_{13,n}$	S_{13}	13
+	−	−	+	+	−	−	+	+	−	−	+	+	−	−	$y_{14,1}$		$y_{14,n}$	S_{14}	14
−	+	−	+	−	+	−	+	−	+	−	+	−	+	−	$y_{15,1}$		$y_{15,n}$	S_{15}	15
+	+	+	+	+	+	+	+	+	+	+	+	+	+	+	$y_{16,1}$		$y_{16,n}$	S_{16}	16

† The '+' and '−' stand for +1 and −1, respectively, although they also indicate the high and low levels of the factors.

‡ The data are obtained as indicated in Table 14.14.

$S_m = \sum_{j=1}^{n} y_{m,j}$

labeled A, B, and C. For example, in row seven ($m = 7$) $A = -1$, $B = +1$, and $C = +1$; therefore, the sign in the seventh row of the column labeled ABC is $-1[(-1)(+1)(+1)]$. Furthermore, for the 2^2 experiment, the first three columns and the rows $m = 1, \ldots, 4$ are used; for the 2^3 experiment, the first seven columns and the rows $m = 1, \ldots, 8$ are used; and for the 2^4 experiment, all 15 columns and the rows $m = 1, \ldots, 16$ are used.

The sum of squares is obtained for $n > 1$ and for a given value of k as follows:

$$SS_{total} = \sum_{j=1}^{n} \sum_{m=1}^{2^k} y_m^2 - 2^k n \bar{y}^2$$

$$SS_{error} = SS_{total} - \sum_{\lambda} SS_\lambda$$

$$SS_\lambda = \frac{C_\lambda^2}{n2^k} \quad \lambda = A, B, AB, \ldots$$

where

$$C_\lambda = \sum_{m=1}^{2^k} S_m \times (\text{sign in row } m \text{ of column } \lambda) \quad \lambda = A, B, AB, \ldots$$

$$\bar{y} = \frac{1}{n2^k} \sum_{m=1}^{2^k} S_m$$

and S_m is defined in Table 14.15.

The average value of the effect of the primary factors and their interactions is obtained from the relation

$$\text{Effect}_\lambda = \frac{C_\lambda}{n2^{k-1}} \quad \lambda = A, B, AB, \ldots$$

where Effect_λ is called the effect of λ. As seen in Table 14.15, for $k = 2$, there are three λs: A, B, and AB; for $k = 3$, there are seven λs: $A, B, C, AB, AC, BC,$ and ABC; and for $k = 4$; there are 15 λs: $A, B, C, D, AB, AC, BC, AD, BD, CD, ABC, ABD, ACD, BCD,$ and $ABCD$.

The mean-square values for the main effects and their interactions are simply

$$MS_\lambda = SS_\lambda$$

since the number of degrees of freedom for each primary factor and their interactions is one. The mean square for the error is

$$MS_{error} = \frac{SS_{error}}{2^k(n-1)} \quad n > 1$$

The test statistic for each factor and their interactions is

$$F_\lambda = \frac{MS_\lambda}{MS_{error}} = \frac{MS_\lambda}{SS_{error}/[2^k(n-1)]} \quad \lambda = A, B, AB, \ldots \quad n > 1$$

The ANOVA table for the 2^k factorial analysis is given in Table 14.16.

TABLE 14.16 ANOVA Table for a 2^k Factorial Experiment with $n > 1$ Replicates

Factor	Sum of squares	Degrees of freedom	Mean square	F_λ	$f_{\alpha,1,(n-1)2^k}$
A	SS_A	1	MS_A	MS_A/MS_{error}	(value from f-table)
B	SS_B	1	MS_B	MS_B/MS_{error}	(value from f-table)
C	SS_C	1	MS_C	MS_C/MS_{error}	(value from f-table)
$\vdots$					
AB	SS_{AB}	1	MS_{AB}	MS_{AB}/MS_{error}	(value from f-table)
AC	SS_{AC}	1	MS_{AC}	MS_{AC}/MS_{error}	(value from f-table)
BC	SS_{BC}	1	MS_{BC}	MS_{BC}/MS_{error}	(value from f-table)
$\vdots$					
ABC	SS_{ABC}	1	MS_{ABC}	MS_{ABC}/MS_{error}	(value from f-table)
$\vdots$					
Error	SS_{error}	$2^k(n-1)$	MS_{error}		
Total	SS_{total}	$n2^k - 1$			

The results of ANOVA for the 2^k factorial design can be used directly to obtain a multiple-regression model that estimates the output of the process as a function of the statistically significant primary factors and the statistically significant interactions. We first introduce the coded variable x_β

$$x_\beta = \frac{2\beta - \beta_{low} - \beta_{high}}{\beta_{high} - \beta_{low}}$$

where β is a primary variable—that is, $\beta = A, B, C, \ldots$ Thus, if $\beta = A$, then when $\beta = A_{high}$, $x_A = +1$, and when $\beta = A_{low}$, $x_A = -1$. Since $A_{low} \leq A \leq A_{high}$, $-1 \leq x_A \leq +1$.

An estimate of the average output y_{avg} is

$$y_{avg} = \bar{y} + 0.5\left[\sum_\lambda \text{Effect}_\lambda x_\lambda + \sum_\lambda \sum_\beta \text{Effect}_{\lambda\beta} x_\lambda x_\beta \right.$$

$$\left. + \sum_\lambda \sum_\beta \sum_\gamma \text{Effect}_{\lambda\beta\gamma} x_\lambda x_\beta x_\gamma \ldots \right] \tag{14.41}$$

where $\lambda, \beta, \gamma, \ldots$ have the values of $A, B, C, \ldots$ and correspond only to those combinations of subscripts that indicate statistically significant factors and interactions, and the $x_\alpha(-1 \leq x_\alpha \leq +1)$ are the coded values.

We now illustrate the use of these relationships.

Example 14.13   Analysis of a 2^4 factorial experiment

We generate the ANOVA table for the data in Table 14.17, which were obtained from a two-replicate 2^4 factorial experiment. We shall include in the ANOVA table the effects. The run numbers correspond to those of Table 14.14. First, we create a function **FactorialData** for these data:

```
function dat = FactorialData
dat1 = [159 168 158 166 175 179 173 179 164 187 163 185 168 197 170 194]';
dat2 = [163 175 163 168 178 183 168 182 159 189 159 191 174 199 174 198]';
dat = [dat1, dat2];
```

Next, we create a function called **FactorialSigns**, which determines the values ± 1 in Table 14.15 for k factors. Thus,

```
function s = FactorialSigns(k)
s = ones(2^k, 2^k-1);
for r = 1:2:2^k
  s(r,1) = -1;
end
for c = 2:k
  e = 2^(c-1);
  for r = 1:e
```

TABLE 14.17   Data for a Two-Replicate 2^4
Experiment—**FactorialData**

Run*	Data $(y_{m,j})$	
m	$j = 1$	$j = 2$
1	159	163
2	168	175
3	158	163
4	166	168
5	175	178
6	179	183
7	173	168
8	179	182
9	164	159
10	187	189
11	163	159
12	185	191
13	168	174
14	197	199
15	170	174
16	194	198

*Run number corresponds to level combinations given in Table 14.14.

```
    s(r,e) = -1;
  end
  for r = e+1:2^(k)
    s(r,2^(c-2)) = s(r-e,2^(c-2));
  end
end
for m = 2:k
  e = 2^(m-1);
  for j = 1:e-1
    s(:,e+j) = s(:,j).*s(:,e);
  end
end
```

The script to create the ANOVA table is

```
tag = char('A', 'B', 'AB', 'C', 'AC', 'BC', 'ABC', 'D', 'AD', 'BD', 'ABD', ...
           'CD', 'ACD', 'BCD', 'ABCD');
k = 4;  n = 2;
fdata = FactorialData;
s = FactorialSigns(k);
Sm = sum(fdata')';
yBar = sum(Sm)/n/2^k;
SStotal = sum(sum(fdata.^2))-yBar^2*n*2^k;
```

```
for nn = 1:2^k-1
    Clambda = sum(s(:,nn).*Sm);
    SSlambda(nn) = Clambda^2/2^(k+1);
    EffectLambda(nn) = Clambda./2^k;
end
SSerror = SStotal-sum(SSlambda);
MSerror = SSerror/2^k;
f0 = SSlambda/MSerror;
pValue = 1-fcdf(f0, 1, 2^k);
disp('Factor      SS        MS      Effect     f-lambda  p-value')
disp([tag repmat('    ', 15, 1) num2str(SSlambda', 6) repmat('    ', 15, 1) ...
        num2str(SSlambda', 6) repmat('    ', 15, 1) num2str(EffectLambda', 6) ...
        repmat('    ',15,1) num2str(f0', 6) repmat('    ', 15, 1) num2str(pValue', 6)])
disp(['SSerror ' num2str(SSerror, 6) '  ' num2str(MSerror, 6)])
disp(['SStotal ' num2str(SStotal, 6)])
disp(['yBar = ' num2str(yBar, 6)])
```

The execution of this script results in the following information being displayed to the MATLAB window:

Factor	SS	MS	Effect f	lambda	p-value
A	2312	2312	17	241.778	4.45067e-011
B	21.125	21.125	-1.625	2.20915	0.156633
AB	0.125	0.125	-0.125	0.0130719	0.910397
C	946.125	946.125	10.875	98.9412	2.95785e-008
AC	3.125	3.125	-0.625	0.326797	0.575495
BC	0.5	0.5	-0.25	0.0522876	0.822026
ABC	4.5	4.5	0.75	0.470588	0.502537
D	561.125	561.125	8.375	58.6797	9.69219e-007
AD	666.125	666.125	9.125	69.6601	3.18663e-007
BD	12.5	12.5	1.25	1.30719	0.269723
ABD	2	2	-0.5	0.20915	0.653583
CD	12.5	12.5	-1.25	1.30719	0.269723
ACD	0	0	0	0	1
BCD	0.125	0.125	0.125	0.0130719	0.910397
ABCD	21.125	21.125	-1.625	2.20915	0.156633
SSerror	153	9.5625			
SStotal	4716				
yBar =	175.25				

It is seen that at the considerably better-than-95% confidence level, factors A, C, and D and interaction AD are statistically significant and, therefore, influence the outcome of the process. In fact, the sum of the sum of squares of these four quantities is 4485. Thus, the sum-of-squares contribution of the quantities that are not statistically significant is $78 = 4716 - 4485 - 153$, or 1.65% of the total sum of squares.

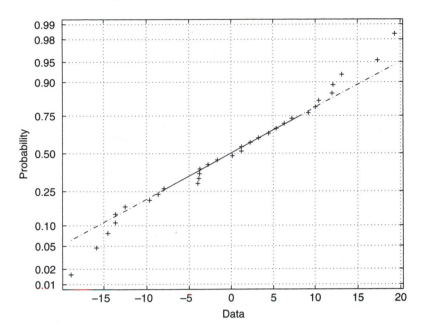

Figure 14.15   Residual plot for the data used in Example 14.13.

We now use Eq. 14.41 and the above results to obtain the following regression equation at the greater-than-95% confidence level.

$$y_{avg} = 175.25 + 8.50x_A + 5.44x_C + 4.10x_D + 4.56x_Ax_D$$

The residuals are the differences between the measured values $y_{m,j}$ and y_{avg} at the 2^4 combinations of coded values of x_γ shown in Table 14.14. We now use the following script to determine the residuals and plot them using normplot.

```
fdata = FactorialData;
s = FactorialSigns(4);
yAvg = 175.25+8.5*s(:,1)+5.44*s(:,3)+4.1*s(:,4)+4.56*s(:,1).*s(:,4);
normplot([fdata(:,1)-yAvg; fdata(:,2)-yAvg])
```

When the script is executed, we obtain Figure 14.15. We see that the residuals are acceptable.

14.7 SUMMARY OF FUNCTIONS INTRODUCED

A summary of the functions introduced in the chapter and their descriptions are presented in Table 14.18.

TABLE 14.18   MATLAB Functions Introduced in Chapter 14

MATLAB function	Description
anova1	One-way ANOVA
anova2	Two-way ANOVA
binocdf	Binomial cumulative distribution function
binopdf	Binomial probability density function
binostat	Mean and variance for the binomial distribution
boxplot	Box plot of statistical data
fcdf	f Cumulative distribution function
finv	Inverse of the f cumulative distribution function
geomean	Geometric mean
hist	Plots a histogram
histfit	Plots a histogram with a superimposed normal distribution function
mean	Mean
median	Median
normcdf	Normal cumulative distribution function
normfit	Estimates parameters and confidence intervals for normal data
norminv	Inverse of the normal cumulative distribution function
normpdf	Normal probability density function
normplot	Normal probability plot
poisscdf	Poisson cumulative distribution function
poisspdf	Poisson probability density function
poisstat	Mean and variance for the Poisson distribution
polyconf	Polynomial evaluation and confidence interval estimation
prctile	Percentiles of a sample
prod	Product of an array of elements
range	Range of data
regress	Multiple linear regression
skewness	Sample skewness
std	Standard deviation
tcdf	t Cumulative distribution function
tinv	Inverse of the t cumulative distribution function
ttest	Hypothesis test for a single sample mean
ttest2	Hypothesis test for the difference in means of two samples
wblcdf	Weibull cumulative distribution function
wblfit	Parameter estimates and confidence intervals for Weibull data
wblinv	Inverse of the Weibull cumulative distribution function
wblpdf	Weibull probability density function
wblplot	Weibull probability plot
wblstat	Mean and variance of the Weibull distribution

EXERCISES

Section 14.2.1

14.1 a. A company's telephone help line receives an average of five calls per minute during its working hours. What is the probability that it could receive:

    i. Eight calls per minute

    ii. Two calls per minute

    [Answers: (i) 0.065278; (ii) 0.084224.]

    b. The telephone system can handle 10 calls per minute; if there is more than this number, the caller gets a busy signal. What is the probability of getting a busy signal? [Answer: 0.013695.]

14.2 The probability that a structural member can withstand a load L_o is 0.7. If 15 of these members are to be used, what is the probability that at least 12 of them can withstand L_o? [Answer: 0.29687.]

14.3 Taguchi defines the average loss factor of a process as being proportional to

$$L_{avg} = s^2 + (\bar{x} - \tau)^2$$

where τ is the target mean. In other words, when comparing two processes, the one whose mean is closest to τ and whose variance is the smallest is the process with the lowest loss factor. For the data in Table 14.19, determine which process has the lowest average loss factor when $\tau = 92.0$. [Answer: $L_1 = 5.5904$, and $L_2 = 2.6936$.]

14.4 A manufacturer found that 20% of one of its products was underweight. There are 24 of these items to a case. If we assume that the weight of each item is independent of the weight of another item, then one can apply the binomial distribution.

    a. What is the expected number of underweight items in a case and its variance?

    b. What is the probability that no more than two items in a case are underweight?

    c. What is the probability that none of the items in the case is underweight?

    d. Plot on the same figure the probability mass function and the cumulative distribution function as a function of the number of underweight items in a case.

    [Answers: (a) expected value = 4.8 and variance = 3.84; (b) 0.11452; (c) 0.0047224.]

TABLE 14.19 Data for Exercise 14.3

Process 1		Process 2	
88.4	89.0	92.6	93.2
93.2	90.5	93.2	91.7
87.4	90.8	89.2	91.5
94.3	93.1	94.8	92.0
93.0	92.8	93.3	90.7
94.3	91.9	94.0	93.8

Section 14.2.2

14.5 The chi-square statistic is used to perform goodness-of-fit tests. Let there be k categories (cells) and in each category the expected value is $\hat{p}_i$, where $i = 1, 2, \ldots, k$. If, in an experiment, the number of observations (occurrences) that fall in each category is x_i, where $i = 1, 2, \ldots, k$, then the chi-square test statistic is

$$\chi^2 = \sum_{i=1}^{k} (x_i - e_i)^2/e_i$$

where $e_i = n = \hat{p}_i$ and

$$n = \sum_{i=1}^{k} x_i = \sum_{i=1}^{k} e_i$$

If, in any category, $e_i < 5$, then the corresponding e_i and x_i must be combined with their respective next adjacent e_i and x_i until $e_i \geq 5$ (see Exercise 4.5).

We use this test statistic to test the hypothesis

$$H_0: p_i = \hat{p}_i \quad i = 1, \ldots, k$$

where $p_i = x_i/n$. If

$$\chi^2 \leq \chi^2_{\alpha, k-1}$$

then H_0 is accepted. In practice, α is not given, and instead, the p-value is determined. The closer the p-value is to 1, the more confident we are that the observed category occurrences x_i are close to the expected number of occurrences e_i.

a. Suppose that a piece of equipment is assumed to have a probability of malfunctioning as follows: from a mechanical malfunction, 0.60 ($\hat{p}_1 = 0.6$); from an electrical malfunction, 0.25 ($\hat{p}_2 = 0.25$); and from an operator-caused malfunction, 0.15 ($\hat{p}_3 = 0.15$). From 55 ($n = 55$) recorded equipment breakdowns, 32 result from mechanical malfunctions ($x_1 = 32$), 14 result from electrical malfunctions ($x_2 = 14$), and 9 result from operator-caused malfunctions ($x_3 = 9$). Using the method described above, determine the plausibility that these $\hat{p}_i$ are representative of this piece of equipment's breakdowns. [Answer: p-value = 0.94979; therefore, very plausible.]

b. The probabilities $\hat{p}_i$ can also be determined from a statistical model. For example, let us assume a Poisson distribution, which is based on a choice (guess) for λ. In this case,

$$e_i = n \frac{e^{-\lambda}\lambda^{i-1}}{(i-1)!} \quad i = 1, 2, \ldots, k+1$$

For $i > k + 1$,

$$e_i = n\left(1 - \sum_{i=1}^{k+1} \frac{e^{-\lambda}\lambda^{i-1}}{(i-1)!}\right) \quad i > k+1$$

If the number of defects found in each product of a sample of 85 products is as shown in Table 14.20, determine whether it is plausible that the number of defects found in the product has a Poisson distribution with $\lambda = 3$. In this case, $k = 8$. Also, some regrouping of e_i and x_i is required. Use the results of Exercise 4.5. [Answer: $x_i = [17\ 20\ 25\ 14\ 6\ 3]$; $e_i = [16.9276\ 19.0436\ 19.0436\ 14.2827\ 8.5696\ 7.1330]$; p-value = 0.40592 and, therefore, somewhat plausible.]

TABLE 14.20 Data for Exercise 14.5

i	Number of defects $(i - 1)$	Number of occurrences, x_i
1	0	3
2	1	14
3	2	20
4	3	25
5	4	14
6	5	6
7	6	2
8	7	0
9	8	1
10	≥ 9	0

14.6 The reliability of a component $R(t)$ is the probability that it operates without failure for a length of time t. If the probability distribution function of the life of the component is $f(t)$, then its cumulative distribution is

$$F(t) = P(T \leq t) = \int_{-\infty}^{t} f(u) \, du = \int_{0}^{t} f(u) \, du$$

which is the probability of the time to failure. Thus,

$$R(t) = 1 - F(t)$$

The hazard rate function $h(t)$ is the chance of a component, which has not yet failed at time t, suddenly failing. It is given as

$$h(t) = \frac{f(t)}{R(t)} = \frac{f(t)}{1 - F(t)}$$

a. Plot the hazard-rate function and the reliability on the same graph when $f(t)$ is the exponential distribution given by

$$f(t) = \frac{1}{\mu} e^{-t/\mu}$$

Assume $\mu = 1$, and use exppdf and expcdf.

b. Plot the hazard-rate function and the reliability when $f(t)$ is the Weibull distribution with $\alpha = 1$ and $\beta = 0.5, 1, 2$, and 4. Use subplot to create a 2 × 2 array of four figures, each with a pair of curves corresponding to a β.

14.7 The cumulative distribution function for the lognormal distribution is given by

$$F(t) = \Phi\left(\frac{\ln(t) - \bar{x}_L}{s_L}\right) \tag{A}$$

where

$$\bar{x}_L = \frac{1}{n} \sum_{i=1}^{n} \ln(t_i) \qquad s_L^2 = \frac{1}{n-1}\left[\sum_{i=1}^{n} (\ln(t_i))^2 - n\bar{x}_L^2\right] \tag{B}$$

TABLE 14.21 Data for Exercise 14.7

1.55	15.70
3.05	16.35
3.65	17.70
5.20	17.95
7.75	19.45
10.45	19.80
10.85	20.05
10.90	32.75
12.65	35.45
15.25	49.35

If we take the inverse of Eq. A, we obtain

$$y = \beta_0 + \beta_1 x$$

where

$$y = \Phi^{-1}(F(t)) \quad x = \ln(t) \quad \beta_0 = -\frac{\bar{x}_L}{s_L} \quad \beta_1 = \frac{1}{s_L}$$

and $\Phi^{-1}(\ldots)$ is obtained from norminv. The mean and variance of t (not $\ln(t)$, which has a normal distribution) are given, respectively, by

$$\bar{x}_t = \exp(\bar{x}_L + s_L^2/2) \quad s_t^2 = (\exp(s_L^2) - 1)\exp(2\bar{x}_L + s_L^2)$$

which can be obtained from lognstat.

a. For the data in Table 14.21, which have already been sorted, determine whether they are distributed log-normally using the technique outlined prior to Example 14.3. In other words, plot $F(t)$ as a function of $\ln(t)$ and the fitted line, and use normplot to display the residuals.

b. Compare the values of x_L and s_L obtained by the graphical method to those obtained from Eq. B. [Answer: From curve fit, $x_L = 2.5072$ and $s_L = 0.88841$; from Eq. A. $x_L = 2.5072$ and $s_L = 0.85441$.]

Section 14.3

14.8 The process capability ratio (PCR) is a measure of the ability of a process to meet specifications that are given in terms of a lower specification limit (LSL) and an upper specification limit (USL). It is defined as

$$PCR = \frac{USL - LSL}{6\hat{\sigma}}$$

for a centered process and as

$$PCR_k = \min\left[\frac{USL - \bar{x}}{3\hat{\sigma}}, \frac{\bar{x} - LSL}{3\hat{\sigma}}\right]$$

for a noncentered process. The quantity $\hat{\sigma}$ is the estimate of the standard deviation of the process, and $\bar{x}$ is an estimate of its mean. When $PCR > 1$, very few defective or

TABLE 14.22 Data for Exercise 14.8

2.5629	2.5630
2.5630	2.5628
2.5628	2.5623
2.5634	2.5631
2.5619	2.5635
2.5613	2.5623

nonconforming units are produced; when $PCR = 1$, then 0.27% (or 2700 parts per million) nonconforming units are produced; and when $PCR < 1$, a large number of nonconforming units are produced. The quantity $100/PCR$ is the percentage of the specification width used by the process. When $PCR = PCR_k$, then the process is centered.

The number of nonconforming parts is Np, where N is the total number of parts produced and

$$p = 1 - \Phi\left(\frac{USL - \bar{x}}{\hat{\sigma}}\right) + \Phi\left(\frac{LSL - \bar{x}}{\hat{\sigma}}\right)$$

where Φ is given by Eq. 14.16. Recall, also, Figure 14.5c and Eq. 14.18.

For the data in Table 14.22 use the function `capable` to determine p, PCR, and PCR_k when $LSL = 2.560$ and $USL = 2.565$. Is the process centered? [Answer: $p = 1.5351e\text{-}004$, $PCR = 1.3103$, and $PCR_k = 1.2099$.]

Section 14.4

14.9 Consider the data shown in Table 14.23. We shall assume two scenarios: All the data in Table 14.23 comprise one set denoted S_0, and the data in each of the five pairs of columns represent five separate sets denoted S_j, where $j = 1, \ldots, 5$.

a. Determine the harmonic mean of data set S_0, and compare it with the mean and the geometric mean. The harmonic mean $\bar{x}_h$ is defined as

$$\frac{1}{\bar{x}_h} = \sum_{i=1}^{n} \frac{1}{x_i}$$

TABLE 14.23 Data for Exercise 14.9

1		2		3		4		5	
1115	1567	1223	1782	1055	798	1016	2100	910	1501
1310	1883	375	1522	1764	1020	1102	1594	1730	1238
1540	1203	2265	1792	1330	865	1605	2023	1102	990
1502	1270	1910	1000	1608	2130	706	1315	1578	1468
1258	1015	1018	1820	1535	1421	2215	1269	758	1512
1315	845	1452	1940	1781	1109	785	1260	1416	1750
1085	1674	1890	1120	1750	1481	885	1888	1560	1642

TABLE 14.24　Data for Exercise 14.10

Group 1		Group 2	
88	81	76	79
79	83	83	85
84	90	78	76
89	87	80	80
81	78	84	82
83	80	86	78
82	87	77	78
79	85	75	77
82	80	81	81
85	88	78	80

b. What are the mean values and standard deviations of the six data sets S_j, where $j = 0, \ldots, 5$.

c. Display a vertical box plot of data sets S_j, where $j = 1, \ldots, 5$.

d. Determine the confidence limits on the differences in the mean values of S_0 and each S_j, where $j = 1, \ldots, 5$, at the 95% confidence level assuming that the standard deviations are unknown but equal (case 4 in Tables 14.3 and 14.5). What are the p-values for each of the data sets? Are any of the mean values of the data sets S_j statistically significantly different from the mean of S_0? Do these conclusions qualitatively agree with the results displayed in part c above?

14.10 To determine whether one should use case 4 or case 5 in Table 14.5, an F-test is first performed on the ratio of the variances as denoted in case 7 of the table. If the variances are statistically significantly different, then case 5 is used; otherwise, case 4 is used. Write a script to determine whether there is a difference between the means of the data given in Table 14.24 and then based on the results, whether the means are different. Also, create a box plot to visualize the data and qualitatively support your conclusions. [Answer: From F-test on the ratio of variances, $p = 0.47092$; therefore, there is no difference in the variances. From a t-test on differences in means, $p = 0.0009342$; therefore, the means are different.]

Section 14.5.2

14.11 a. For the model below, determine β_j for the data in Table 14.25, and show that this model is a good fit to these data:

$$y = \beta_0 + \beta_1 x_1 + \beta_2 x_2 + \beta_3 x_1^2 + \beta_4 x_2^2 + \beta_5 x_1 x_2$$

b. Using the values found for β_j, plot its surface, and use contour to plot the contours of the projection of this surface onto the x_1, x_2-plane.

c. Determine the coordinates of the maximum value of this fitted surface. [Answer: $x_1 = 18.7635$, and $x_2 = 38.0156$.]

TABLE 14.25   Data for Exercise 14.11

y	x_1	x_2
144	18	52
142	24	40
124	12	40
64	30	48
96	30	32
74	26	56
136	26	24
54	22	64
92	22	16
96	14	64
92	10	56
82	10	24
76	6	48
68	6	32

14.12 The correlation coefficient R for a simple linear regression analysis can be obtained from Eq. 14.29. We can test the hypothesis that

$$H_0: R = 0$$
$$H_1: R \neq 0$$

by forming the test statistic

$$t_0 = \frac{R\sqrt{n-2}}{\sqrt{1-R^2}}$$

and comparing it with $t_{\alpha/2,\,n-2}$. If $t_0 > t_{\alpha/2,\,n-2}$, then we reject H_0. In practice, we examine the p-value corresponding to t_0. The confidence limits on the correlation coefficient r, for $n \geq 25$, can be estimated from

$$\tanh\left(\tanh^{-1}(R) - \frac{z_{\alpha/2}}{\sqrt{n-3}}\right) \leq r \leq \tanh\left(\tanh^{-1}(R) + \frac{z_{\alpha/2}}{\sqrt{n-3}}\right)$$

where $z_{\alpha/2} = \mathtt{norminv}(1 - \alpha/2)$ [recall Eq. 14.19].

For the data given in Table 14.26:

a. Determine the regression coefficients when the model is of the form $y = \beta_0 + \beta_1/x$.
b. Plot the fitted line and the data points.
c. Determine if the residuals are normally distributed.
d. Determine whether the correlation coefficient is different than 0 and its confidence limits at the 95% confidence level.

[Answers: (a) $\beta_0 = 8.9366$, $\beta_1 = -41.6073$; (d) $0.976998 \leq 0.98996 \leq 0.99564$.]

TABLE 14.26 Data for Exercise 14.12

x	y	x	y
10.0	4.746	11.6	5.211
12.0	5.466	14.8	6.264
6.8	3.171	7.2	3.411
5.4	1.500	15.7	6.537
20.0	6.708	17.6	6.336
19.4	7.158	14.0	5.400
19.1	6.882	10.9	4.503
6.1	1.674	18.2	6.909
16.3	6.498	20.4	6.930
12.4	5.598	8.2	3.582
5.8	1.959	7.9	3.432
12.7	5.790	4.9	0.369
9.2	4.686		

14.13 In multiple linear regression analysis, one of two types of residuals are frequently examined: the standardized residuals, which are defined as

$$d_i = \frac{e_i}{\hat{\sigma}}$$

where $\hat{\sigma}^2$ is given by Eq. 14.41, and the studentized residuals, which are defined as

$$r_i = \frac{e_i}{\hat{\sigma}\sqrt{1 - h_{ii}}}$$

where h_{ii} is the ith diagonal element of

$$\mathbf{H} = \mathbf{X}(\mathbf{X'X})^{-1}\mathbf{X'}$$

and $\mathbf{X}$ is given by Eq. 14.32.

Using the model in Example 14.10 and the corresponding data in Table 14.7, determine the standardized and studentized residuals. Plot these residuals as a function of the average output $\hat{y}_i$ (i.e., $y_i - e_i$, y_i are the output values given in Table 14.7) on the same graph using two different symbols to differentiate them. Are any of these residuals outliers? In other words do any if them exceed 3? Label the figure and identify the two different sets of residuals with legend.

Section 14.6.2

14.14 The formulas given for the 2^k factorial experiment can be applied when $n = 1$ by modifying the method as follows. The effects Effects$_\lambda$ are computed as described in Section 14.6.2: and then ordered from most positive to most negative. See the column in the tabulated results of Example 14.13 labeled "Effect." During the ordering, one must be keep track of the factors and their corresponding interactions. The ordered effects are then plotted using normplot. The effects that are negligible (not statistically significant) will be normally distributed and will tend to fall on a straight line on this plot, whereas the effects that are statistically significant will lie considerably off this straight line. Consider the data given in Table 14.27, which were obtained from a 2^4 design with a single replicate, and

TABLE 14.27 Data for a 2^4 Factorial Experiment with $n = 1$

Run[†]	y_m	Run[†]	y_m
1	86	9	90
2	200	10	142
3	90	11	96
4	208	12	130
5	150	13	136
6	172	14	120
7	140	15	160
8	192	16	130

[†] Run number corresponds to level combinations given in Table 14.14.

determine which values are statistically significant. This determination is made visually from the results of `normplot` and the listing of the ordered effects and their corresponding factor or interaction. [Answers: $A, C, D, AD,$ and AC, which account for 96.6% of the total sum of squares. The ordered factors and their interactions are, from most positive to most negative: $A, C, B, BCD, BC, ABC, ACD, CD, BD, AB, ABCD, ABD, D, AD,$ and AC. Effect$_A$ = 43.25, Effect$_C$ = 19.75, Effect$_D$ = −29.25, Effect$_{AD}$ = −33.25, and Effect$_{AC}$ = −36.25.]

BIBLIOGRAPHY

T. B. Barker, *Quality by Experimental Design*, Marcel Dekker, New York, NY, 1985.

G. E. P. Box, W. G. Hunter, and J. S. Hunter, *Statistics for Experimenters*, John Wiley & Sons, New York, NY, 1978.

F. W. Breyfogle III, *Statistical Methods for Testing, Development and Manufacturing*, John Wiley & Sons, New York, NY, 1992.

N. Draper and H. Smith, *Applied Regression Analysis*, 2nd ed., John Wiley & Sons, New York, NY, 1981.

E. A. Elsayed, *Reliability Engineering*, Addison Wesley Longman, Inc., Reading, MA, 1996.

N. L. Frigon and D. Mathews, *Practical Guide to Experimental Design*, John Wiley & Sons, New York, NY, 1997.

A. J. Hayter, *Probability and Statistics for Engineers and Scientists*, PWS Publishing Co., Boston, MA, 1996.

L. L. Lapin, *Modern Engineering Statistics*, Duxbury Press, Belmont, CA, 1997.

E. E. Lewis, *Introduction to Reliability Engineering*, 2nd ed., John Wiley & Sons, New York, NY, 1996.

D. C. Montgomery, *Design and Analysis of Experiments*, 3rd ed., John Wiley & Sons, New York, NY, 1991.

D. C. Montgomery and G. C. Runger, *Applied Statistics and Probability for Engineers*, John Wiley & Sons, New York, NY, 1994.

R. H. Myers and D. C. Montgomery, *Response Surface Methodology: Process and Product Optimization Using Designed Experiments*, John Wiley & Sons, New York, NY, 1995.

R. E. Walpole, R. H. Myers, and S. L. Myers, *Probability and Statistics for Engineers and Scientists*, 6th ed., Prentice Hall, Upper Saddle River, NJ, 1998.

Index